29

CHRISTIANITY AND JUDAISM

Two Jews Desecrating the Host with Knives: BL, MS Harley 7026, fol. 13r
(by courtesy of the British Library).

CHRISTIANITY AND JUDAISM

PAPERS READ AT
THE 1991 SUMMER MEETING AND
THE 1992 WINTER MEETING OF
THE ECCLESIASTICAL HISTORY SOCIETY

EDITED BY

DIANA WOOD

PUBLISHED FOR
THE ECCLESIASTICAL HISTORY SOCIETY

BY

BLACKWELL PUBLISHERS

1992

© Ecclesiastical History Society 1992

First published 1992

Blackwell Publishers
108 Cowley Road, Oxford OX4 1JF, UK

238 Main Street, Suite 501
Cambridge, Massachusetts 02142, USA

British Library Cataloguing in Publication Data
A CIP catalogue record for this book is available from the British Library.

Library of Congress Cataloging in Publication Data
Ecclesiastical History Society. Summer Meeting (1991: University of
  Birmingham)
    Christianity and Judaism: papers read at the 1991 Summer Meeting
  and the 1992 Winter Meeting of the Ecclesiastical History Society /
  edited by Diana Wood.
        p.   cm.—(Studies in church history: 29)
    Includes bibliographical references.
    ISBN 0-631-18497-X
    1. Judaism—Relations—Christianity—Congresses. 2. Christianity
  and other religions—Judaism—Congresses. 3. Judaism (Christian
  theology)—History of doctrines—Congresses. 4. Christianity and
  antisemitism—Congresses. I. Wood, Diana. 1940– .
  II. Ecclesiastical History Society. Winter Meeting (1992: King's
  College, London) III. Title. IV. Series.
  BR141.S84 vol. 29
  [.BM535]
  270 s—dc20
  [261-2'6]   92-15569
                                                                          CIP

Typeset in 11 on 12 pt Bembo
by Joshua Associates Limited, Oxford
Printed in Great Britain by T.J. Press (Padstow) Ltd, Padstow, Cornwall.

CONTENTS

v

CONTENTS

CONTENTS

PREFACE

When Professor Barrie Dobson, President of the Ecclesiastical History Society for 1991–2, announced his theme of Christianity and Judaism there were those who predicted few communications and an easy year for the editor. They could not have been more wrong! The number and variety of the contributions in this volume clearly demonstrate the significance and interest of the subject, and editorial decisions on communications proved to be even more difficult than usual. The papers included here represent the main papers delivered at the summer conference of 1991 and the January one of 1992, and a selection of the communications offered in the summer. The Society would like to express its gratitude to the University of Birmingham for its generous hospitality in the summer, and especially to Robert Swanson and to members of the School of History for doing so much to make the conference such a memorable one, and for a series of splendid outings. Our thanks, as so often in the past, are also due to King's College London for its hospitality in January.

The editor would like to add her personal thanks to Barrie Dobson for help with the selection of papers, and to Jan Chamier and Ann McCall of Blackwell Publishers for making the passage of this book through the press such a smooth one.

Diana Wood

LIST OF CONTRIBUTORS

BARRIE DOBSON (*President*)
Professor of Medieval History, University of Cambridge, and Fellow of Christ's College

ANNA SAPIR ABULAFIA
Fellow and College Lecturer in History, Lucy Cavendish College, Cambridge

YAAKOV ARIEL
Lecturer, The Institute of Contemporary Jewry, The Hebrew University of Jerusalem

DAVID BAGCHI
Lecturer in Theology, University of Hull

PETER BILLER
Lecturer in History, University of York

MARGARET F. BREARLEY
Senior Fellow, Centre for the Study of Judaism and Jewish–Christian Relations, Selly Oak Colleges, Birmingham

JOHN EDWARDS
Reader in Spanish History, University of Birmingham

DAVID FELDMAN
Lecturer in the Department of Historical Studies, University of Bristol

KEITH A. FRANCIS
Assistant Professor of History, Pacific Union College, Angwin, California

SEAN GILL
Lecturer in Theology and Religious Studies, University of Bristol

JOAN GREATREX
Former Associate Professor, Carleton University, Ottawa

WALTER HILLSMAN
Member of the Faculty of Music, University of Oxford

ELLIOTT HOROWITZ
Senior Lecturer in Jewish History, Bar-Ilan University

DAVID S. KATZ
Professor of History, Tel-Aviv University

FRANCES KNIGHT
British Academy Post-doctoral Fellow, Selwyn College, Cambridge

TONY KUSHNER
Parkes Lecturer in Jewish Studies, University of Southampton

N. R. M. de LANGE
Lecturer in Rabbinics, University of Cambridge

GAVIN I. LANGMUIR
Professor of History, Stanford University, California

JOHN A. McGUCKIN
Lecturer in Patristics and Byzantine Studies, University of Leeds

R. I. MOORE
Reader in History, University of Sheffield

PETER van ROODEN
Lecturer in Church History, Free University, Amsterdam

EDWARD ROYLE
Reader in History, University of York

MIRI RUBIN
Lecturer in Medieval History, University of Oxford, and Fellow of
Pembroke College

LESLEY SMITH
Post-doctoral Fellow of the British Academy, Linacre College,
Oxford

JONATHAN STEINBERG
Vice-Master, Trinity Hall, Cambridge

KENNETH R. STOW
Professor of Jewish History, University of Haifa

BRIAN TAYLOR
Rector of Guildford St Nicolas'

BRETT USHER

VINCENETTE d'UZER
    Lecturer, University of Lyons, and Member of the Ecumenical
    Commission

NICHOLAS C. VINCENT
    Fellow of Peterhouse, Cambridge

JOHN A. WATT
    Emeritus Professor of Medieval History, University of Newcastle
    upon Tyne

JOSEPH ZIEGLER
    Research Student, Merton College, Oxford

ABBREVIATIONS

Abbreviated titles are adopted within each paper after the first full citation. In addition the following abbreviations are used throughout the volume.

AHDL	*Archives d'histoire doctrinale et littéraire du moyen-âge* (Paris, 1926ff.)
AHR	*American Historical Review* (New York, 1895ff.)
BIHR	*Bulletin of the Institute of Historical Research* (London, 1923–86)
BL	British Library, London
BM	British Museum, London
BN	Bibliothèque nationale, Paris
CChr.SM	*Corpus Christianorum, continuatio medievalis* (Turnhout, 1966ff.)
CChr.SG	*Corpus Christianorum, series Graeca* (Turnhout, 1974ff.)
CCR	*Calendar of Close Rolls preserved in the Public Record Office* (London, 1892ff.)
ClR	*Close Rolls of the Reign of Henry III preserved in the Public Record Office*, 15 vols (London, 1902–75)
CPR	*Calendar of Patent Rolls preserved in the Public Record Office. Henry III*, 6 vols (London, 1902–13)
CUL	Cambridge University Library
CYS	*Canterbury and York Society* (London, 1907ff.)
Decretales	*Decretales Gregorii IX*, ed. A. Friedberg, *Corpus Iuris Canonici*, 2 (Leipzig, 1879), cols 6–928*
Decretum	*Decretum Gratiani*, ed. A. Friedberg, *Corpus Iuris Canonici*, 1 (Leipzig, 1879)*
DNB	*Dictionary of National Biography* (London, 1885ff.)
EHR	*English Historical Review* (London, 1953ff.)
EJ	*Encyclopaedia Judaica*, 16 vols (Jerusalem, 1971)
GCS	*Die griechischen christlichen Schriftsteller der ersten drei Jahrhunderte* (Leipzig, 1897ff.)
Hansard	Hansard, *Parliamentary Debates*
HR	*Historical Research* (London, 1986ff.)
HThR	*Harvard Theological Review* (New York/Cambridge, Mass., 1908ff.)
JBS	*Journal of British Studies* (Hartford, Conn., 1961ff.)
JEH	*Journal of Ecclesiastical History* (Cambridge, 1950ff.)
JHI	*Journal of the History of Ideas* (London, 1940ff.)
JJS	*Journal of Jewish Studies* (London, 1948ff.)
JMedH	*Journal of Medieval History* (Amsterdam, 1975ff.)
JQR	*Jewish Quarterly Review* (London, etc., 1899–1908), ns (1910ff.)
JThS	*Journal of Theological Studies* (London, 1899ff.)
JWCI	*Journal of the Warburg and Courtauld Institutes* (London, 1937ff.)
MGH	*Monumenta Germaniae Historica inde ab a. c.500 usque ad a. 1500*, ed. G. H. Pertz et al. (Hanover, Berlin, etc., 1826ff.)
MGH.Const.	*Constitutiones et acta publica imperatorum et regnum* (1893ff.) – *MGH.L*, sectio 4
MGH.D	*Diplomata*

* References to columns in canon law citations are to those in Friedberg, *Corpus Iuris Canonici*.

ABBREVIATIONS

MGH.DR	Diplomata regum et imperatorum Germaniae (1879ff.) = *MGH.D*
MGH.L	*Leges* (in folio) (1835–89)
MGH.SRG	*Scriptores rerum Germanicarum in usum scholarum* . . . (1826–32), ns (1922ff.)
MGH.SS	*Scriptores* (in folio) (1826–1934)
n.d.	no date
NH	*Northern History* (Leeds, 1965ff.)
n.p.	no place
ns	new series
ODCC	*Oxford Dictionary of the Christian Church*, ed. F. L. Cross (Oxford, 1957), 2nd edn with E. A. Livingstone (1974)
OHS	*Oxford Historical Society*
PaP	*Past and Present. A Journal of Scientific History* (London, 1952ff.)
PG	*Patrologia Graeca*, ed. J. P. Migne, 161 vols (Paris, 1857–66)
PL	*Patrologia Latina*, ed. J. P. Migne, 217 + 4 index vols (Paris, 1841–61)
PRO	Public Record Office, London
PS	*Parker Society* (Cambridge, 1841–55)
RBen	*Revue bénédictine de critique, d'histoire et de littéraire religieuses* (Maredsous, 1884ff.)
REJ	*Revue des études juives* (Paris, 1880ff.), ns (1962ff.)
RS	*Rerum Brittanicarum medii aevi scriptores*, 99 vols (London, 1858–1911) = *Rolls Series*
sc.	scudo
SCH	*Studies in Church History* (London/Oxford, 1964ff.)
SCH.S	*Studies in Church History. Subsidia* (Oxford, 1978ff.)
s.v.	*sub verbo*
TJHSE	*Transactions of the Jewish Historical Society of England* (London, 1893ff.)
TLS	*Times Literary Supplement* (London, 1902ff.)
Traditio	*Traditio. Studies in Ancient and Medieval History, Thought and Religion* (New York, etc., 1943ff.)
VCH	*Victoria County History* (London, 1900ff.)

INTRODUCTION

In one of the more arresting contributions to this not unambitious series of essays, Tony Kushner suggests that it is in the writings of the late James Parkes that we may well find 'a model for multi-cultural Britain'. It is certainly true that if this book could be dedicated to a church historian of the recent past, that historian would have to be the late Reverend James Parkes, not only the author of the pioneering *The Conflict of the Church and the Synagogue* as early as 1934, but also a founding father of the Ecclesiastical History Society and *Studies in Church History* thirty years later. James Parkes, in a long series of influential works, regularly explained the astonishing survival of Judaism through the centuries in terms of its 'encounters' with other religions and other cultures; and he saw it as his mission to encourage Christians to reciprocate by profiting from meetings with Jews past and present. Previous *Studies in Church History* have, of course, often broached the issue of how a dominant Christian Church has regarded its own and other minority religious groups; but, perhaps surprisingly, this is the first volume in a now long series which focuses directly on the theme which James Parkes was the first to place firmly in the centre of whatever church history actually is.

This collection of essays is accordingly most accurately described as a highly varied series of historical encounters between the Christian Church, on the one hand, and the most resilient religious minority in the Western world, on the other. That such relationships were diverse, complex, and often painful emerges from nearly every page of this volume; but so, too, does the existence of those recurrent patterns of hostility, exile, and coexistence exposed by Nicholas de Lange in the Byzantine Empire and still unresolved, according to Yaakov Ariel, as we approach the end of the second millennium. What may strike the reader of this volume as even more interesting, and certainly more unexpected, is how so many of its contributors, like John Watt and Edward Royle, see the relationship between Gentiles and Jews as more fundamental to the past practices and ideals of the Christian Church itself than has usually been allowed. A generation ago Parkes believed that it would be profitable for historians of Christianity to 'encounter' Jews: it seems to transpire from many of the essays in this volume that such meetings may be not only profitable but positively essential to a proper understanding of the structure and development of the Christian Church itself.

Perhaps the poet John Silkin made something of the same point when he once wrote of the massacre of the Jews of York on 16 March 1190 that 'the event has the frigid persistence of a growth in the flesh.' For the historian, as for others, such growths have often proved too painful to ignore, but too complicated to diagnose and too embarrassing to admit. It is for exactly such reasons that until recently the role of the Jews was customarily relegated to a very minor place in the history of the medieval, and indeed modern, Christian Church. However, there are at last signs, fully manifest in this volume, that historians of the Christian Church are restoring Judaism to its rightful place as the religion within whose traditions Christian ideals ought themselves regularly to be reassessed. Nor can there be much doubt that the current transformation of the study of the relationship between Christianity and Judaism is primarily the result of the recent remarkable flood of scholarly activity on virtually every aspect of the Jewish past. As so much of that activity now takes place in the comparatively new State of Israel, it is particularly appropriate that several of the contributors to this volume of *Studies in Church History* should hold distinguished academic posts in Israel's universities. It has often been said that Judaism owes its extraordinary powers of survival and resurgence to its obsession with its own past, an obsession which is perhaps no longer what it was even fifty years ago (despite the labours of the Ecclesiastical History Society) in the case of most denominations of the Christian religion. Certainly no reader of this volume will be left in any doubt at all that the history of Western Christianity can take on a radically different and highly invigorating complexion when seen from the stance of its Jewish minorities and from that of the new generation of Jewish scholars.

It accordingly follows, although not at all by design, that the following *Studies in Church History* tend to provide more insight into the impact of Judaism on Christianity than that of Christianity on Judaism. This generalization applies particularly clearly to the several papers in this volume devoted to hitherto neglected issues in English history between the sixteenth and nineteenth centuries. However, John Edwards's investigation of the Spanish Inquisition and David Katz's study of English philo-Semitism are also alike in explaining (as they have to be explained) these very different phenomena in terms of contemporary Christian attitudes and beliefs. Similarly, and at an even more fundamental level, R. I. Moore and Gavin Langmuir interpret medieval antagonism to the Jews as an outcome of social and religious pressures critical for 'the birth of Europe' itself. One of the more obvious, and most melancholy, conclusions to be drawn from these and many other contributions to this volume is the persistence from century to century not only of such hostility itself, but of the murderously dangerous ideological and emotional patterns which underlay that hostility. Nowhere is this more obvious than in Jonathan Steinberg's account of genocide in Croatia between 1941 and 1945, a study perhaps all the more valuable in reminding us that on occasion Christian can persecute Christian with a ferocity equal to that with which he may persecute Jew. It would, in other words, be unfortunate if the dualism between Christianity and Judaism ever came to be regarded as the only significant dualism in the history of either religion. That said, the following pages can leave no doubt of how strenuously many leaders of the Christian Church attempted, sometimes happily, often less so, to come to terms with a faith which presented them with both their greatest religious challenge and their greatest opportunity. If, which at first sight may seem unlikely, the essays collected in this volume point to any particular morals it must be that Christianity has never been able to ignore Judaism for long; and that its own welfare, past, present, and presumably future, depends upon a determination never to ignore Judaism again.

Barrie Dobson

ORIGEN ON THE JEWS

by JOHN A. McGUCKIN

THIS present study is a note added to what has already become an extensive bibliography concerning Origen's doctrinal relation to Judaism in general, and the extent and significance of his awareness of Jewish exegetical procedures in particular. Among that list[1] of previous studies on the theme, special reference ought to be made to the seminal work *Origen and the Jews*,[2] by Professor Nicholas de Lange, which demonstrated Origen's knowledge of rabbinic traditions in his exegeses. This present study will offer, firstly, a general contextual discussion of the question of Origen's dependence on Jewish tradition, and, secondly, a small test-case analysis of his attitude to the Jewish question from observing his New Testament exegesis of those passages directly concerning the issue. From the latter some interesting biases will emerge that throw some light on his personal attitudes.

The personality and work of Origen of Alexandria (though it may be more to the point to call him Origen of Caesarea Maritima) is a

---

[1] The full bibliographical details for most of the relevant studies can be found chronologically listed in H. Crouzel, *Bibliographie critique d'Origene*, suppl. 1 = *Instrumenta Patristica* VIIIa (Steenbrugis, 1982). Here I will list the relevant works to 1982 with reference to that index, by author and year, with some of the pertinent articles that have appeared since that date: 1898, Ginzberg; 1925, Murawski; 1927, Ginzberg; 1928, Marmorstein; 1929, Ginzberg; 1941, Bieder; 1956, Baer; 1961, Taylor; 1968, Kötting; 1968, Roncaglia; 1968, Simon-Benoit; 1969, Judant; 1970, Philippou; 1970, Roncaglia; 1971, Hruby; 1971, Urbach; 1971, de Lange; 1974, Bietenhard; 1975, Levine; 1975, de Lange; 1976, de Lange; 1976, Sgherri; 1977, Wasserstein; 1979, Judant. There is also a bibliography appended to N. de Lange, *Origen and the Jews* (Cambridge, 1976), pp. 209–15: for other relevant studies listed in that source see entries for Bardy, Daniélou, Daube, Hanson, Krauss, Lachs, Liebermann, Loewe, and Wilde. A short relevant bibliography and discussion of the texts can also be found in E. A. Clarke, *Ascetic Piety and Women's Faith* (New York, 1986), pp. 391–2. Other recent and relevant works mentioned in or relevant to this present study include D. J. Halperin, 'Origen, Ezekiel's Merkabah, and the Ascension of Moses', *Church History*, 50 (1981), pp. 261–75; R. Kimelman, 'Rabbi Yohanan and Origen on the Song of Songs', *HThR*, 73 (1980), pp. 567–95; J. A. McGuckin, 'Origen on the Glory of God', *Studia Patristica*, 21 (Louvain, 1989), pp. 316–24, and 'Caesarea as Origen knew it', in *Origeniana Quinta* (forthcoming, Louvain, 1992); Roger Brooks, 'Straw Dogs and Scholarly Ecumenism: the Appropriate Jewish Background for the Study of Origen', in C. Kannengiesser and W. L. Petersen, eds, *Origen of Alexandria* (Notre Dame, Indiana, 1988), pp. 63–95; Paul Blowers, 'Origen, the Rabbis, and the Bible', in ibid., pp. 96–116; D. Rokeah, *Jews, Pagans, and Christians in Conflict* = *Studia Post-Biblica*, 33 (Jerusalem and Leiden, 1982); S. Krauss, 'The Jews in the works of the Church Fathers', *JQR*, 5 (1983), pp. 139ff. (on Origen).

[2] De Lange, *Origen and the Jews*.

I

particularly fine lens through which to observe a critical period in developing Jewish and Christian self-definitions, when the old apologetics caused by immediate strifes and local frictions in the context of the Diaspora urban communities, throughout the first and second centuries, were giving way to new revisions for a different political and religious climate. The traumatic destruction of central and sacred institutions of Judaism by the Romans, in the latter half of the first century, provided conditions for the rise of a rabbinic Judaism that was much more conscious of its international status as a religious tradition focused on scholarly exegesis of the biblical text, and which was to develop its socio-ethical and theological norms (its Halachah and Haggadah) on that basis.

Alexandria, Rome, Caesarea, Tiberias, and Babylon became important points in the Jewish network of trade and scholarly connections that wrapped the Empire and extended beyond it.[3] In the time (c.230) that Origen took refuge permanently in Caesarea—to escape from the difficulties being caused by his bishop Demetrios in Alexandria—Caesarea, once a notoriously pagan and secular city in all Jewish eyes, was being accepted back into the concept of Eretz Israel, to the extent that a great rabbinical tradition was already beginning to establish itself there, one that would flourish from CE 230 to 260. The most famous name associated with the city in less happy days is the martyred Rabbi Akiba, who lies buried in the unexcavated vaults to the south of the present city ruins, but in Origen's day Rabbi Hoshaya and Rabbi Abbahu are perhaps the most important figures, along with Rabbi Yohanan (later of Tiberias) and Resh Laqish. The 'Rabbis of Caesarea' are mentioned no less than 140 times in the Palestinian Talmud, and there is evidence to suggest that they enjoyed notable legal privileges, to the extent of holding high and important status in the Caesarean judiciary, something for which there is no Christian parallel at this period.[4]

The growing fame of the Jewish academies at Caesarea was possibly one of the main reasons why the scholarly Bishop Alexander of Jerusalem and the Metropolitan, Theoctistus of Caesarea, were so keen to attract Origen to their provincial capital. On his permanent arrival, after a preliminary lecture tour which greatly annoyed his Alexandrian bishop, Origen was ordained as a Caesarean presbyter and given the task of

---

[3] See H. Drijvers, 'Jews and Christians at Edessa', *JJS*, 36 (1985), pp. 88–102; Y. Baer, 'Israel, the Christian Church, and the Roman Empire from the time of Septimius Severus to the Edict of Toleration of A.D. 313', *Scripta Hieroslymita*, 7 (1961), pp. 79–149; H. Bietenhard, *Caesarea, Origenes und die Juden* (Stuttgart, 1974); L. Levine, *Caesarea under Roman Rule* (Leiden, 1975).

[4] Levine, *Caesarea under Roman Rule*, pp. 86–106.

expounding the Scriptures in the two weekday liturgical services. These expositions formed the basis of his extensive published commentaries on the Old Testament books. Bishop Alexander[5] was engaged in establishing the Church's library at Jerusalem, and it seems likely, from Origen's subsequent travels to Athens and around Palestine, from which tours he procured manuscripts, that a similar office was allotted to Origen in Caesarea. The emergence in the next generation of a library that was the glory of the Christian world was a testimony to his success.[6] Knauber[7] has suggested that the establishment of a Christian academy was part of the Caesarean Christian community's conscious attempt to create a missionary outreach among the middle-class civic dignitaries that formed such a large proportion of Caesarea's third-century population. There was also, undoubtedly, a desire to establish an international reputation for the school—something that became a reality even in Origen's lifetime, as we can deduce from the correspondence of Porphyry, and certainly continued into the fourth century, when the footsteps of such luminaries as Gregory Nazianzen, Basil, Didymus, Pamphilus, Eusebius, and Jerome can all be traced in the Caesarean arcades heading for the Christian library.

The valedictory *Thanksgiving Oration*[8] of Theodore (perhaps Gregory Thaumaturgos), one of Origen's pupils at Caesarea, gives an indication of just this type of imperial official's child, entrusted for his philosophical and rhetorical education to Origen and his school; and from that oration we gain an idea of just how wide Origen's curriculum was, covering secular sciences, literature, philosophy, and theology. There is no corresponding indication that the rabbinic schools ever entertained any such desires to extend their curriculum or their clientele so widely, and in terms of the necessity of Jewish birth or conversion, Semitic linguistic constraints, and the strict focus on biblical interpretation and Jewish law, the rabbinic academies surely could not be expected to employ the same strategy as Origen's school. The range and quality of education offered would suggest that Origen's academy was deliberately designed to be

---

[5] Bishop Alexander was a fellow student of Origen at Alexandria, and a personal friend. He died in the Decian persecution, at Caesarea, which also sentenced Origen to suffer torture (cf. Eusebius, *Historia ecclesiastica*, *GCS*, 9: 6.39.2).

[6] For further details see McGuckin, 'Caesarea Maritima as Origen knew it'.

[7] A. Knauber, 'Das Anliegen der Schule des Origenes zu Caesarea', *Munchener Theologische Zeitschrift*, 19 (1968), pp. 182–203. See also H. Crouzel, 'L'École d'Origène à Césarée', *Bulletin de littérature ecclésiastique*, 71 (1970), pp. 15–27.

[8] St Gregory Thaumaturgus, *The Oration and Panegyric Addressed to Origen*, tr. S. D. F. Salmond — *Ante Nicene Christian Library*, 20 (Edinburgh, 1871).

poised between the pagan and Jewish institutions, and, in deliberate contradistinction, attempting to offer the best aspects of both its rivals, while reserving higher Christian studies to a much more restricted circle of hearers—just as had been Origen's earlier practice in Alexandria.

This suggested context of Origen's work is an important factor to keep in mind when discussing the question of his specific dependencies, or his polemical attacks, on Jewish religious traditions. In other words, with Origen, we are not simply dealing with a religious or doctrinally motivated apologetic, but a different cultural and missionary vision is also at work.

Two other aspects of the relation between Origen and the Jews that ought to be kept firmly in mind can be characterized as the local and the universal contexts of how the two respective communities related in third-century Caesarea. In terms of local factors, Origen's homilies give several indications that there was a slight blurring of the line at a popular level between Church and Synagogue practices of worship.[9] Origen complains of Christian women who dress up attractively on Friday evenings. This is not just another patristic tirade against cosmetics, but one of several indications that Christian members of the congregation observed several aspects of the Jewish law, to the great annoyance of the clergy. Origen reminds the women that far from dressing up to celebrate (the Sabbath eve meal), they are expected in terms of their own tradition to be fasting for the Friday commemoration of the Lord's Passion. So, at the local level, we can envisage two ascendant communities who were both cautiously watching their neighbour and rival lest they push ahead, and yet were not averse to pushing ahead themselves if they ever got the chance. Each community was possessed of certain advantages and disadvantages in this matter of the expansion of their intellectual and social fortunes. In terms of the universal context of Jewish–Christian relationships in the third century, we might say that it was a question of the same thing writ larger. Origen is typical of this jostling for position throughout the final century before the Constantinian revolution cast such a decisive lot, but although he is a formidable anti-Jewish polemicist, Judaism and Christianity at that period were not in a position where the one could or did oppress the other, and that made a great difference. Both communities lived energetically by their religious traditions in a world

---

[9] Origen, *Homily on Jeremiah*, 12.13, PG 13, col. 395; see also *Commentariorum in Evangelium secundum Matthaeum* 15, PG 13, col. 1621. For a fuller discussion see Levine, *Caesarea under Roman Rule*, chs 5 and 7.

that was dominated by pagans, who were felt by both to be ultimately untrustworthy, religiously as well as politically.

De Lange's book has admirably set out the extent of Origen's awareness of Jewish exegetical opinions at an important time, when the Mishnah was being laid down. We can observe from the outset that Origen's attitude is not uniform throughout his work. In the *Contra Celsum*, for example, he takes the learned pagan Celsus to task, accusing him of being misinformed in his arguments against Jewish doctrine and practice. It is clear that Origen offsets Celsus's Hellenistic Jewish paradigm with his own knowledge of a rabbinic style of Judaism that was much less universalist in outlook. It is interesting, for example, to see Origen denying that Logos Christology could ever be part of the Jewish religious construct,[10] despite his knowledge of Philo. Where Celsus ridicules the Jewish tradition, however, Origen is not ready to follow him. This is largely because he is defending his own ground on his own terms. Celsus's overall position was that Christianity was a corrupt deviation of a corrupt original system. Origen, in composing his reply to this argument, in a missionary work that has its face set from the outset towards a pagan audience, defends the Jewish tradition as an inspired route of sacred revelation. He has not forgotten Christianity's grounding in the Jewish tradition, but he never follows the line that Christianity 'developed' its religious system from that of Judaism. He uses the argument of the historical relation rather to offset one of Celsus's most sustained attacks on Christian religion—its barbarous novelty. The radical discontinuities, new beginnings, corrections, and patterns of fulfilment that mark Origen's understanding of the theological relationship between Christianity and Judaism do not allow such a historically linear developmental model to stand; and neither does his radically a-historical hermeneutical method.

On the other hand, in his works that were aimed directly at a Christian readership, especially his scriptural commentaries, he engages in a more robust apologetic against Judaism. The range and extent of Origen's knowledge of Jewish exegetical traditions seems to have been mediated to him through a few closely related channels. He speaks of his 'Magister Hebraeus', a shadowy figure, whom opinion largely recognizes as a Christian,[11] and one could be fairly certain that among Origen's several

---

[10] Cf. de Lange, *Origen and the Jews*, pp. 63–73, for a detailed discussion of the relevant passages in the *Contra Celsum*.

[11] Origen, Epistle to Africanus, 6–8, tr. in *Ante-Nicene Christian Library*, 10 (Edinburgh, 1869),

professional assistants and scribes in the Caesarean church he had the services of other Jewish Christians, who occasionally drew his attention to various interesting and relevant points. There is also evidence of direct personal contact in the form of face-to-face disputations with rabbis.[12] The Caesarean halls, not least the well-appointed Odeon near his own school, might also be envisaged as places where more formal lectures and disputations could have taken place. Kimelman[13] has demonstrated a protracted literary exchange between Rabbi Yohanan and Origen on the interpretation of the Song of Songs, but it was an exchange where Origen largely rejected the allegorical interpretations of the rabbis out of hand, bettering them with his own, which he regarded as truly Logos-inspired.

The awareness of Origen's dependence on rabbinic traditions was given an immense boost by the careful analysis of de Lange, and shortly afterwards by Bietenhard,[14] and the number of known parallels greatly increased. Indeed, more instances have since emerged, as in the article by Halperin,[15] which demonstrates Origen's use of an esoteric tradition on the *Merkabah* taken from Caesarean rabbinic homilies on Pentecost.

The initial and very positive assessment of the significance of those rabbinic dependencies for Origen's overall scheme as a biblical theologian was largely provided by de Lange's own conclusion to his study, which suggested: 'Origen's reliance on the living Jewish tradition is one of the most distinctive features and serves to mark him out from all earlier and contemporary Greek fathers. It is no exaggeration to say that there is not a single aspect of his biblical writings that is not touched by it to a greater or lesser degree.'[16] This high claim quickly entered the Origenian canon when Henri Crouzel, without further analysis, adopted it in substance, shifting the limelight in the process from the rabbinic tradition itself back on to Origen: 'The most important influences are clearly Hebraic and Hellenic ... But there are also the rabbinic exegeses which had already influenced the New Testament through Paul, and which were to affect

---

pp. 376–7. Cf. G. Bardy, 'Les Traditions juives dans l'œuvre d'Origene', *RBen*, 34 (1925), pp. 221–3; de Lange, *Origen and the Jews*, pp. 15–37; Levine, *Caesarea under Roman Rule*, p. 205, nn. 209–12.

[12] For references see de Lange, *Origen and the Jews*, pp. 15–47, 1123–31; Levine, *Caesarea under Roman Rule*, pp. 79–80, 205.

[13] R. Kimelman, 'Rabbi Yohanan of Tiberias: aspects of the social and religious history of third century Palestine' (Yale University dissertation, 1977).

[14] See works cited in nn. 2–3, above.

[15] D. J. Halperin, 'Origen, Ezekiel's Merkabah, and the Ascension of Moses', *Church History*, 50 (1981), pp. 261–75.

[16] De Lange, *Origen and the Jews*, p. 134.

Origen too, who shows a very advanced knowledge of them acquired from friends among the rabbis.'[17] Such is the way of our scholarly trade that the subtle and carefully chosen shades of a work such as that by de Lange, when summarized in a few pages of what the author himself describes as initial tentative conclusions, can suddenly re-emerge as great washes of colour when these pages alone travel on in an independent afterlife. The crude, schematized divisions, of Hellenistic, Hebraic, Qumranic, Apocryphal, Rabbinic, and New Testamental, with which Crouzel operates, are not merely non-sustainable as hermeneutic categories for the whole three centuries of nascent Christianity, but in fact they entirely beg the two great questions in hand, which are, firstly, what significance one ought to attribute to any single type of literary borrowing by one of the great polymathic synthesists of the age; and, secondly, how does one begin to separate out a specially distinct kind of 'rabbinic' hermeneutic from the standard use of allegorical analysis common to all the period's interpreters? Moreover, how Origen was transformed into a 'friend of the Rabbis' on available evidence remains a mystery.

Subsequent Origen studies, however, have begun to question the positive nature of that earlier assessment more and more. The elegant monograph by Karen Torjesen[18] demonstrated the great extent to which Origen searched for a systematic literary schema in his commentaries, in a conscious attempt to create a scientific hermeneutic (whatever may be our opinions on the subjectivity of his method). The massive importance Origen gave to the direct inspiration of the Logos led him to set the Logos's own dispensation in the Christ-event as the normative key for the interpretation of all God's salvific revelation, past, present, and future, and to attribute to the Logos's own transfigured saints of the covenant, particularly the Apostles, the God-given power of illuminating the more obscure revelation of the Hebrew Scriptures, which a few chosen saints in the ancient generations, the prophets inspired by the Logos, had sketched out in figures that could only be clarified retrospectively. Such a system is facing in a radically different direction from that of Rabbinism. This is the root of Origen's frequent dismissal of Jewish exegesis in general apologetic terms as 'following only the literal level'. What stands out from his method is its great freedom from any anxiety to follow only linear

---

[17] H. Crouzel, *Origen*, Eng. tr. (Edinburgh, 1989), p. 78.
[18] K. J. Torjesen, *Hermeneutical Procedure and Theological Method in Origen's Exegesis* (Berlin and New York, 1986).

historical process in its unfolding of what he defines as transcendent biblical meaning. Such a systematic orientation is not, *prima facie*, good grounds for allowing us to suppose Origen considered Jewish exegesis of the Hebrew Scriptures to be any more 'normative' or necessarily endowed with any greater historical authenticity than subsequent Christian efforts; in fact, for him, far from it. His presuppositions, therefore, reverse the fundamental belief in linear, historically conditioned, development that characterizes most contemporary scholarly work, and again one ought to be careful to keep this fact in mind when considering the weight and significance of his borrowings. These differences in systematic orientation are precisely the reason Origen himself gives for apparently very negative Christian–Jewish relations in his own experience:

> The Jews are not antagonistic to the gentiles ... but against the Christians they are filled with an insatiable hatred, although we have abandoned idolatry and given ourselves over to God. They are irritated with us; they hate us as though we were a foolish people, and they come saying that they are wise because the first divine oracles were given to them.[19]

Origen's work on the Hexapla suggests that his Hebrew was very limited indeed. He relies heavily on Aquila's version to give him the sense of the Hebrew text, and when he does quote the Hebrew itself it is usually only in the form of a learned allusion, designed to impress his Gentile audience with his general erudition. The very lack of systematic pattern in Origen's use of rabbinic exegeses is indicative.

Four years ago a test study which I conducted on Origen's attitude to the theme of the Shekinah theology, a distinctive and characteristic aspect of the Tannaitic school,[20] demonstrated that his entire awareness of this theme, one that he himself developed considerably, came to him from Paul alone. Other, more recent studies, by Brooks[21] and Blowers,[22] have similarly tended to suggest that although Origen undoubtedly has an awareness of rabbinic traditions, the significance of those dependencies must be questioned.

Brooks's work, analogously to Torjesen's, approaches the question from a desire to establish the overall direction of Origen's systematic

---

[19] *Homily 1 on Psalm 36*, PG 7, col. 1321: cited Bardy, 'Les Traditions juives', p. 227.
[20] Cf. McGuckin, 'Origen on the Glory of God', pp. 316–24.
[21] Brooks, 'Straw Dogs and Scholarly Ecumenism', pp. 63–95.
[22] Blowers, 'Origen, the Rabbis, and the Bible', pp. 96–116.

concern, a systematic, needless to say, which was dominated by the biblical text, just as much as was that of the rabbis. Brooks makes a particular study of passages from Leviticus treated by both Origen and the Mishnah, but finds no points of connection. He therefore concludes negatively:

> The Jewish background and culture available to Origen throughout his life seems to have been remarkably superficial. Certainly Origen had some familiarity with a few scraps of Jewish exegesis . . . yet on the whole Origen simply had no understanding of the rabbinic movement gaining prominence around him.[23]

Blowers, working from a more comprehensive perspective, arrives at a similarly cautious and negative conclusion:

> From most indications, Origen's scholarly and theological interest in Judaism did not betray itself openly in his public disposition towards the Jews. Here Origen's debates with the rabbis over the bible presented less a scholarly exchange of ideas than a platform for mutual disclaimers. Origen's anti-Jewish maneuvers [sic] in his homilies and commentaries reflect just this same inflexibility. There was no question here of negotiation in these 'philosophers'' debates. The rabbis' exegetical arguments had to be dismissed *in toto* because Judaism continued to be a viable threat to the Christian mission, a live option for those seeking to be faithful to the tradition of the bible. In this adamant public posture towards Judaism, Origen remained indeed quite typical of the patterns of Christian–Jewish relations in late antiquity.[24]

This more negative assessment of the significance of the influence of Jewish theology on Origen is borne out by another small piece of evidence which seems hitherto to have received no mention. In trying to ascribe the ⌄ extent of indebtedness, most previous works have attempted to locate the context of Origen in terms of Hellenistic rhetorical practice, the local church–synagogue friction over feast-day observance and the like, or the overarching theological divergences between Christianity and Judaism based on the perennial issues of Christology, Election, Law, and

---

[23] Brooks, 'Straw Dogs and Scholarly Ecumenism', p. 94. He goes on to say (p. 95): 'In an attempt to lay the foundations for modern rapprochement between Jews and Christians, scholars have rendered far too positive an evaluation of Origen's relationship to, and reliance upon, Rabbinism.'

[24] Blowers, 'Origen, the Rabbis and the Bible', p. 116.

Covenant. One picture that formerly emerged from such a synthesis, and still to an extent underlying the image in Blowers's conclusion, though not that of Brooks, was of an Origen who was personally interested in Jewish scholarship, but who presented a more official face, as Christian presbyter in Caesarea, as both a theological and a practical critic of the rival system. The massive extent, however, to which the overall shape of his Jewish apologetic is indebted to Paul might suggest more the image of someone who is more concerned with progressing along in a relatively enclosed system than working by any form of converging dialogue. And it may well be the case that the significance of the points of convergence there are between Origen and the rabbinic interpreters are really provided, by his day, more from the shared Hellenistic hermeneutical method and the partially shared sacred text than from any real ecumenical connection. Such was the conclusion that emerged from an earlier study on Origen's use of the concept of God's Shekinah,[25] and this too is the conclusion suggested by the final exegetical test-case I would like to offer to conclude this paper.

Origen has a phenomenal and encyclopaedic knowledge of the biblical text. He cross-references passages throughout the Scriptures and frequently interprets one text by means of the same or a similar key term that occurs elsewhere. In an age without concordances he demonstrates time and time again how well he knew his sources. In addition, he knew his Pauline literature with the intimate acquaintance of the liturgist and one who had written formal commentaries on most of the Pauline letters. This being so, it is surely indicative, for a revealing indication of how Origen regarded Christianity and Judaism, to look to his overall systematic employment of the primary New Testament materials concerning that theme, and, given Origen's atomistic method, we can best proceed by isolating the textual instances.

This is quite easily accomplished, for there is a very limited number of New Testament texts which engage in a specific apologetic on the relation of Christianity to Judaism, where the two communities start to be more and more understood as different religious entities, moving further away in mutual distinctness. Both sociologically and theologically this systematic separation was not something that happened all over the Hellenistic world at the same time or at a similar pace, but the process is already clearly visible in Acts and the Pauline writings.

There are only eleven texts in Acts that have reference to such an

[25] Cf. McGuckin, 'Origen on the Glory of God'.

explicit Jewish–Christian apologetic;[26] to which we can add five more in Hebrews,[27] and, of course, considerable sections, rather than atomistic texts, in the Pauline writings that focus on the issue, particularly Romans, Galatians, and parts of II Corinthians and Colossians. Many of those texts provide the raw building-materials for centuries of subsequent Christian apologetic against Judaism—themes such as the following of the letter that kills, the stubborn refusal to repent, and so forth. It is not our concern here to look at Origen's employment of those themes, but rather to look at the way he chooses to highlight some texts and relegate others from that relatively small body of primary New Testament materials.[28]

Most of the eleven Acts passages gain only a few mentions in Origen's work, running to approximately three citations throughout the *opera*, but two receive a relatively extraordinary amount of attention, being cited ten times each; and of the eleven there are only two which are entirely neglected. What is of significance, however, is that these two passages which he avoids altogether are the only two texts from the whole Acts apologetic in which the privileges of the Jews and their priority in the story of salvation are freely admitted, indeed, positively emphasized.[29] Moreover, the two texts from the eleven, which he chooses to amplify heavily, are the two most negative from that whole list.[30] Both these negative texts seem to have been highly relevant to Origen's own local context, but the stress he puts on them seems to indicate a sense of failed personal contact more than anything else. It is interesting to see how, by what can only be a highly personal combination of amplification and suppression, he has chosen to sharpen the Jewish polemic significantly.

The evidence from Origen's use of Hebrews needs more careful use, since his surviving commentary on Hebrews is now so fragmentary. Nevertheless, Hebrews offers five texts relevant to the Jewish apologetic.[31] Four of them appear to have little or no interest for Origen,[32] but one of them he applies no less than sixty-nine times—so frequently, in fact, that it is clearly a favourite quotation and an abiding theme for him. This text—'Since the Law has no more than a reflection of these realities, and

---

[26] Acts 2. 29; 2. 34; 2. 23; 2. 38; 3. 25; 7. 35; 7. 42; 7. 51–2; 13. 17; 13. 46; 28. 26–8.

[27] Hebrews 3. 3; 7. 12; 7. 18 (none of these three texts is cited in the extant works of Origen); 10. 1 (69 citations by Origen); 12. 24 (1 citation by Origen).

[28] The Origen citation-instances are listed in *Biblia Patristica*, 3, Centre d'Analyse et de Documentation Patristiques (Paris, 1980).

[29] Acts 3. 26; 13. 17.

[30] Acts 7. 51–2; 13. 46.

[31] See n. 26, above.

[32] Hebrews 3. 3; 7. 12; 7. 18 (entirely neglected); and 12. 24 (only 1 citation).

no finished picture of them, it is quite incapable of bringing worshippers to perfection' (Hebrews 10. 1)—once more demonstrates his favourite conception of a Judaism interpreted through a Platonizing hermeneutic.

Origen's use of the numerous Pauline passages dealing with the stature and place of Judaism demonstrates quite decisively that the policy apparent in the treatment of Acts was not accidental. Ten Pauline texts can be isolated which are of interest for our case. These can be further subdivided into two groups. The first group amounts to a total of six Pauline texts[33] where the Apostle, for all his attacks on the Jewish system, speaks with laudatory affection, as we find also in Acts, emphasizing the privileges of Judaism and its priority in the story of salvation—a priority which he argues has not been forgotten by God, despite a new dispensation. These six texts are quite remarkable in tone and demonstrate a genuine personal feeling on the part of the theologian whom Origen regarded as the great example and leader of all those who had been initiated by God's Logos. Origen, however, though he comments heavily on almost every Pauline verse, quite clearly censors all but one of these laudatory texts, and the one exception he makes[34] is the palest and most non-committal of them all, which refers to the Jews as the people to whom the message was sent. This text receives a high average attention, that is, twenty-three citations restricted to his Commentaries on Romans and Matthew alone. But Paul's doctrine of the priority of Israel has quite clearly and deliberately been overlaid.

This interesting bias of his censorship of the laudatory texts is further borne out by looking at which other Pauline texts, of those specifically dealing with the issue of Judaism, Origen most relies on. The picture that emerges reproduces what we saw in his treatment of Acts. There are four such Pauline passages which Origen uses with a high average level of frequency (some 30 to 40 citations each throughout his *opera*). These are Romans 2. 5, on the refusal of the Jews to repent (26 citations); II Corinthians 3. 13–15, on how the Jewish understanding of Scripture is hindered by a veil over their minds (30 citations); Romans 2. 20, on how real circumcision is a matter of the heart not the flesh (32 citations); and Colossians 2. 16–18, on how the observance of festivals is now outmoded and irrelevant (38 citations). Once again all these apologetic concerns fit exactly the third-century Caesarean context, particularly the last, which also evidences Origen's most abundant use. Origen has clearly been ready

[33] Romans 1. 17; 3. 2; 9. 3; 10. 1; 12. 15; 12. 28.
[34] Romans 3. 2.

to alter the tenor of St Paul himself, his master theologian, to firm up the apologetic at those instances the Apostle might be seen to have given too much away because of his love and respect for Judaism.

The conclusion that seems to arise from this is that Origen's personal attitude, as well as his professional theological approach to Judaism, might not be in reality as positive as has sometimes been suggested; and that his undoubted knowledge and use of rabbinical exegetical traditions may largely have come to him sporadically and without system, implying that the significance of such dependencies must be questioned. Indeed, the personal reshaping by Origen of the Pauline Jewish apologetic suggests someone whose dialogue with the Jewish tradition in Caesarea had been neither successful nor particularly happy. Perhaps, if it really was Origen who was behind Rabbi Yohanan's testy remark,[35] 'A gentile who studies the Torah deserves capital punishment',[36] then the unhappiness might well have been mutual.

University of Leeds

[35] See Blowers, 'Origen, the Rabbis and the Bible', p. 103.
[36] Mishnah, B. Sanhedrin, 58b.

JEWS AND CHRISTIANS IN THE BYZANTINE EMPIRE: PROBLEMS AND PROSPECTS*

by N. R. M. de LANGE

HEARTENING as it is for someone like myself, for whom the study of relations between Christianity and Judaism is a central concern, to see the Ecclesiastical History Society devote its annual conference to this subject, it is proper to recall that it has not been wholly neglected in the past. The very first volume of *Studies in Church History* (1964) contains a contribution by James Parkes under the title of 'Jews and Christians in the Constantinian Empire', which is a short but well-judged summary of the attitudes to Judaism emerging from a reading of the Christian authors, Roman laws, and conciliar canons of the fourth century. I should like to begin now by paying tribute to James Parkes, partly because he was my own mentor, someone who encouraged and influenced my study of our subject, and also because he occupies an important place as a pioneer in the study of Jewish–Christian relations as a whole, and specifically in the part of the subject that concerns me today, the Byzantine phase.

The Conflict of the Church and the Synagogue was written in the early 1930s, as James Parkes's doctoral thesis, and I believe it was the first book to study Christian–Jewish relations from the peculiar standpoint of the history of anti-Semitism. It was written against the background of the rise of Nazism and Parkes's work for the International Student Service, and it marked a turning-point in his own life and thought. As he wrote later, 'I was completely unprepared for the discovery that it was the Christian Church, and the Christian Church alone, which turned a normal xenophobia and normal good and bad relations between two human societies into the unique evil of antisemitism.'[1] So *The Conflict* is a book with a programme, written in a mood of passion; yet it is always reasonably argued and carefully documented, and it is these qualities that have ensured its success: it is still widely read as the most useful introduction to its subject.

The Conflict of the Church and the Synagogue begins with a sketch of the

---

* I am grateful for helpful criticisms to Professor Averil Cameron and Dr William Horbury.
[1] James Parkes, *Voyage of Discoveries* (London, 1969), p. 123.

place of the Jews in the Roman world before the advent of Christianity, and it ends in the eighth century. The story it tells is of an initial fateful rupture between Church and Synagogue, and, after the conversion of Constantine, of what we would now call a progressive alienation and marginalization of the Jews by the official Church and the Christian states. It is a process that relies heavily on the creation of a negative caricature of Judaism based on biblical theology and the needs of Christian apologetics.

Two of Parkes's ten chapters are directly concerned with Byzantium: they are entitled respectively 'Law and History in the Byzantine Empire' and 'The Jews in Byzantine Literature'. There is a clear index of the originality of these two chapters in the short bibliographies which precede each chapter of the book. Whereas for the other chapters the booklists tend to comprise modern monographs and synthetic histories, for Byzantium they consist almost exclusively of primary sources. The only significant exception is Samuel Krauss's *Studien zur byzantinisch-juedischen Geschichte*, which was published in the annual report of the Jewish Theological Seminary of Vienna for 1914. Krauss's work must be saluted as the first attempt to tackle the subject of Byzantine Jewish history, but it has hardly anything to say concerning Christian–Jewish relations.[2] Parkes's work, then, is in a real sense a pioneering effort: it is built not on foundations laid by others, but on a careful study of all the available primary sources. In the first of the two chapters he traces the history of imperial legislation affecting the Jews (mainly in the codes of Theodosius and Justinian), setting the laws as far as possible against their historical background and—a significant feature this—comparing the treatment of the Jews at each point with the treatment of heretical Christians. He also looks at the policy of the Church, as formulated by the various councils. The second chapter draws on both Syriac and Greek Christian sources, to show how a theological image of the Jew was built up, how anti-Jewish polemic became a common preoccupation of Christian writers, and how eventually 'Jewish' came to serve as a term of abuse hurled at rival Christian movements that had nothing to do with Judaism. But Parkes also stresses the good relations between ordinary Christians and Jews attested by these same sources. Eventually these relations broke down under a pressure which, Parkes argues, is essentially religious, stemming from the legislation and the fanaticism of certain monks. Political

---

[2] Krauss had discussed some aspects of Christian–Jewish relations in his earlier work, *Das Leben Jesu nach jüdischen Quellen* (Berlin, 1902).

tensions, associated with the Persian wars of the seventh century and the rise of Islam, are a secondary factor, while economic causes are totally lacking.

Curiously enough, at the same time as Parkes was writing *The Conflict*, another Anglican scholar was at work on a closely related project, albeit from an entirely different point of view. Arthur Lukyn Williams came to his study of the Christian anti-Jewish polemic out of a personal commitment to the conversion of the Jews to Christianity. His book *Adversus Judaeos*, published in 1935, is a very full survey of the literature, from the early years of the Church down to the fifteenth century. Like Parkes, he does not allow his personal motives to get the better of his scholarship, and *Adversus Judaeos*, like *The Conflict*, is still of value today.[3]

Both Parkes and Williams were unusual in making no real distinction between Western and Eastern Christendom. They both treat the history of Christianity, at least in relation to the Jews, as a single tradition, in which the Eastern, Greek- and Aramaic-speaking, Christians have an equal claim to be heard and taken seriously with their Western, Latin counterparts. This attitude stands in stark contrast with that of the generality of Christian—and, it must be said, Jewish—scholarship. Despite these two promising initiatives, relatively little work has been done since the 1930s on Christian–Jewish relations in Byzantium. Even today, most general books about Byzantium or about the Orthodox Church simply ignore the Jewish dimension, just as most histories of Judaism make no mention of Byzantium.[4] As for the handful of books devoted to the history of Byzantine Jewry, they do not address themselves directly to relations between Jews and Christians.[5] It is consequently very

---

[3] It has not been entirely superseded by the more comprehensive and up-to-date if less discursive treatment of Heinz Schreckenberg, *Die christlichen Adversus-Judaeos-Texte und ihr literarisches und historisches Umfeld (1.–11. Jh.)*, 2nd edn (Frankfurt am Main, 1990); *Die christlichen Adversus-Judaeos-Texte (11.–13. Jh.)* (Frankfurt am Main, 1988).

[4] I have discussed this problem elsewhere: N. de Lange, 'Qui a tué les Juifs de Byzance?' in D. Tollet, ed., *Politique et religion dans le judaïsme ancien et médiéval* (Paris, 1989), pp. 327–33. It would be invidious to single out general works which fail to take proper account of the Jewish presence in Byzantium, or the importance of the 'Jewish problem' for the Byzantine Church. On the credit side, it is only fair to mention the sections on the Jews in Louis Bréhier, *La Civilization byzantine* (Paris, 1950), Antoine Bon, *Le Péloponnèse byzantin jusqu'en 1204* (Paris, 1951), and Alain Ducellier, *Byzance et le monde orthodoxe* (Paris, 1986). Among Jewish histories, there is a proper appreciation of the place of Byzantium in the Jewish world in S. M. Dubnow, *Weltgeschichte des jüdischen Volkes* (Berlin, 1925) = *History of the Jews* (New Brunswick, NJ, 1967) and S. W. Baron, *A Social and Religious History of the Jews*, 2nd edn (New York and Philadelphia, 1952–), esp. vol. 17. Cf. Cecil Roth, ed., *The Dark Ages: Jews in Christian Europe, 711–1096* (Tel Aviv, 1966).

[5] See especially Joshua Starr, *The Jews in the Byzantine Empire, 621–1204* (Athens, 1939); Zvi

difficult to approach this important subject, and the remarks that follow must be taken as tentative and provisional. My emphasis throughout will be less on what has been achieved by modern historians (which in all conscience is little enough) than on the nature of the problems in relation to the extant sources.

IMPORTANCE OF THE SUBJECT

There is no doubt, first of all, that this *is* an important subject. The thousand years of the Byzantine state represent one of the major chapters in the history of Christianity. From an external viewpoint, it was a state which included within its frontiers significant Jewish communities, including for a time those situated in what Christians and Jews alike call the Holy Land. From a Western Christian perspective, Byzantium is often categorized (misleadingly) as the East; within the Jewish world of Late Antiquity and the Middle Ages, however, it occupies the centre. This is a simple fact of historical geography, which needs to be emphasized because it is so often forgotten by historians of Judaism. From an internal viewpoint, the Christian faith and the institutions of the Christian Church are of the very essence of the State, which could not be indifferent to the presence within its midst of such a visible non-Christian minority. Moreover, Byzantine Christianity combines a powerful interest in the Bible with a very Greek obsession with definitions and equations; both these concerns have an important bearing on the Church's attitude to the Jews. Lastly, the Byzantine Empire saw itself, not entirely wrongly, as the continuation of the Roman Empire, which had itself, painfully and over a period of several centuries, arrived at its own significant accommodation with Judaism. The ways in which the Byzantine state handled this legacy in the light of its own Christian character are not only instructive in themselves, but, as James Parkes saw clearly, are of great significance for the understanding of the long-term patterns of Christian treatment of Jews down to our own time.

Within the unitary Orthodox Christian state in which all forms of religious heterodoxy were deemed dangerous and were progressively obliterated, the Jews, who survived and maintained their beliefs with

---

Ankori, *Karaites in Byzantium: the Formative Years, 970–1100* (New York and Jerusalem, 1959); Andrew Sharf, *Byzantine Jewry from Justinian to the Fourth Crusade* (London and New York, 1971); Steven B. Bowman, *The Jews of Byzantium 1204–1453* (University, Alabama, 1985).

what a recent writer has justly termed 'stubborn resilience',[6] came to pose a unique problem. Let me offer just one striking example of this.[7] It comes from the Greek lexicon known as the *Suda*, compiled around the year 1000. Most of the 30,000 entries are brief definitions of unusual words, or short articles with illustrative examples from the ancient literature: hardly a propitious source of material for our present investigation. But there is one article that stands out from all the others, both by its subject matter and by its length (it occupies four and a half pages in the standard modern edition): it is the entry 'Jesus our Christ and Lord'. Oddly enough, this long article is entirely devoted to an anecdote concerning a Jew named Theodosios, who is supposed to have been a leading member of the Jewish community during the reign of Justinian, and his Christian friend Philip, who was anxious for his conversion. According to the story, Theodosios revealed to Philip a closely guarded secret: the existence of an authentic Jewish document dating from the time of Jesus, and officially recording that he was the son of the Living God and the Virgin Mary. This intriguing tale, which incidentally testifies to the friendly relations that could exist in Byzantium between individual Christians and Jews, displays simultaneously two facets of Christian–Jewish relations: the Jews must be brought to a recognition of the truth of the Christian message, but at the same time they are potential witnesses to that truth.

BASIC PROBLEMS

Unfortunately the study of Christian–Jewish relations is far from being plain sailing. I shall mention a few of the difficulties under three heads: *attitudes*, *definitions*, and *sources*.

By *attitudes* I have in mind a number of things. First, there is the general neglect of Byzantine history by Western scholars: there is still a tendency for 'medieval Europe' to mean exclusively the West, and in terms of serious historical study and the critical edition of texts Byzantium still remains a Cinderella. Hardly surprising, then, that far less effort had been directed to studying Christian–Jewish relations in Byzantium than in Western Europe.

Secondly, there is the serious neglect of Byzantine Jewish history,

---

[6] J. F. Haldon, *Byzantium in the Seventh Century* (Cambridge, 1990), p. 345.

[7] I am grateful to Dr Pieter van der Horst, of Utrecht, for bringing this text to my notice. A fuller version of the story is preserved in the Arabic *History of the Patriarchs of Alexandria*: cf. James Parkes, *The Conflict of the Church and the Synagogue* (London, 1934; New York, 1969), p. 290. See also Krauss, *Leben Jesu*, pp. 4–5.

which I have already mentioned. The Byzantine Jews do not have many living descendants interested in tracing their own past, as is the case with the central European Jewries (for example); there is not a large presence of Jews in Greece, who might promote the study of the medieval Jewish history of their country, as has happened in England and France; nor have Byzantine historians generally come to see the Jewish element as a vital part of their subject, as (say) Spanish historians do. *Hinc illae lachrymae* ...

Which leads me to a third point. 'Byzantine' in the religious sphere is generally defined, implicitly, as meaning 'Orthodox Christian'. 'Byzantine Judaism' can sound almost like a contradiction in terms. Such an attitude contributes to the marginalization of the Jews of the Empire: they appear at once as less important and somehow less authentic than they really were.

Finally, there has been a tendency, in Byzantine history as elsewhere, to study only or mainly the doings of rulers, of governing elites, of the Church and the army; the discovery that history is (also) about ordinary people was not made yesterday, but it has only slowly had an impact on the object of our study here.

About the problems of *definitions* there is much that might be said, but I shall limit myself to the primary and obvious points. We tend nowadays to think of Christian–Jewish relations as something that exists on two main levels: official attitudes of the Church and the 'Synagogue' on the one hand, and personal relations between individuals or local groups on the other. In the case of Byzantium we can hardly ignore the relationship between the Christian State and its Jewish minority. This, in turn, is something that cannot be studied in isolation from other questions, such as the relationship between the Church and the State, the treatment of other minorities, and the State's external relations, with states professing other religions (including on occasion Judaism), or having influential Jewish populations.[8]

There are other questions, too. When 'Jewish' becomes a term of abuse in Byzantium, which it does quite early, and is applied to Christian groups that have nothing to do with the Jewish community, is that part of

---

[8] Two notable cases of Jewish states were Himyar, in southern Arabia, on the vital sea route to the Persian Gulf and India, and Khazaria, in southern Russia, likewise controlling important trade routes and constituting a potential military menace. The possible implications of relations with these Jewish states for the treatment of the Jewish minorities within the Empire have hardly begun to be explored. The Spanish Jewish courtier Hisdai Ibn Shiprut may perhaps have made the connection: see N. Golb and O. Pritsak, *Khazarian Hebrew Documents of the Tenth Century* (Ithaca, NY, 1982).

Christian–Jewish relations? Is the elaboration of a Christian theology—or demonology—of Judaism a part of Christian–Jewish relations, even if the Jews are not directly involved in the process? On the one hand, there are so many Jewish elements within Christianity that it is impossible to study the latter without the other religion constantly insinuating itself; on the other, the Christian teachings about Judaism, even if they can often be described as internal Christian developments, may be partly influenced by external factors in which Jews may be involved. And they certainly end up by having an effect on the Jews.

And what of the definition of 'Jewish'? There are so many different kinds of Jews in Byzantium: 'Hellenic' and 'Hebraic', native and immigrant, Eastern and Western, Rabbanite and Karaite, not forgetting the Samaritans and other fringe groups. It is rash to lump them all together; and certainly mistaken to imagine that all Jews were, say, Hebrew-reading Rabbanites, living their lives according to the rules of the Talmud. Finally, what of the many Christian groups that practised 'Jewish' observances, including sometimes circumcision and dietary laws, but had no connection with the Jewish community:[9] where do they fit into our enquiry?

Lastly, I must mention briefly the problems concerning *sources*. First, there is a terrible shortage of documentary sources in Byzantium, particularly for the Jewish communities, many of which simply disappear from view for long periods. Secondly, there is a great imbalance between the various types of source: for example, we have incomparably more Christian writing about Judaism than Jewish writing about Christianity. In fact, we have hardly any of the latter at all (a point to which I shall return later). And, thirdly, much of the source material, both Jewish and Christian, is either lost or unpublished.[10]

---

[9] See Gilbert Dagron, 'Judaïser', *Travaux et Mémoires*, 11 (1991), pp. 359–80 [hereafter *TM*].

[10] The problem is more acute on the Jewish side, where very little of the literature actually originating in Byzantium is available in critical editions, and probably the majority has perished for ever. On the Christian side the situation is improving all the time. For some recent contributions see M. Hostens's edition (1986) of a previously unpublished ninth- to tenth-century anonymous *Dissertatio contra Iudaeos* (*CChr.SG* 14); the re-edition with translation of the important seventh-century *Doctrina Jacobi nuper baptizati* by V. Déroche, together with a commentary by the editor and G. Dagron, in *TM*, 11 (1991), pp. 17–273; Déroche, 'La Polémique anti-judaïque au VIe et VIIe siècle. Un mémento inédit, les *Képhalaia*', ibid., pp. 275–311; Dagron, 'Le Traité de Grégoire de Nicée sur le baptême des Juifs', ibid., pp. 313–57; also the exchange of views about the *Apology against the Jews* ascribed to Leontios of Neapolis and its authenticity by Déroche in *Bulletin de Correspondance Hellénique*, 110 (1986), pp. 655–69 and P. Speck in *Poikila Byzantina*, 4 (1984), pp. 242–9, and 6 (1987), pp. 315–22. From a later period, B. Englezakis is preparing an edition of an interesting anti-Jewish tract

Broadly speaking, the sources may be divided into three categories: official texts, quasi-official religious literature, and personal documents. The first category includes laws and edicts, as well as acts of ecclesiastical synods; there is little analogous material on the Jewish side. The second category is the richest on both sides, and includes theological and apocalyptic tracts, biblical commentaries and homilies, and, a source not to be underrated, liturgical texts (including hymns). The personal documents, such as private letters, shed a different and, on the whole, more anecdotal light on the subject.

OFFICIAL TEXTS

The general trend of the imperial legislation and the church councils as regards the Jews is similar: the tone is hostile and the aim is, broadly speaking, to isolate them and deprive them of any opportunity to exercise, collectively or individually, any power or influence over Christians. Of course, there are differences between the two types of text: the imperial laws carry greater authority, in particular with the Jews themselves—the Church can legislate only for Christians. And there is a tendency in the laws to maintain, at least in appearance, a continuity with the legislation of the earlier, pagan, emperors. This earlier legislation had recognized Judaism as a legal religion, and had granted the Jews certain rights and privileges, which were not lightly overturned.[11] From our particular perspective we must recognize that the anti-Jewish trend of the Byzantine legislation is purely and exclusively an echo of the anti-Jewish thrust of the Church: it has no independent source. It is not surprising, therefore, that it is most visible at times of religious crisis, and at times when the power of the Church in the State is particularly high. We see this first in the legislation of the earliest Christian emperors;[12] again in the time of Justinian;[13] in the seventh century, during the crisis of the Persian wars

---

by Neophytos the Recluse of Cyprus (1186) from a Paris MS, and E. Patlagean has studied a *Debate against the Jews* by Nicholas of Otranto (c.1220) preserved in another Paris MS (in M. G. Muzzarelli and G. Todeschini, eds, *La Storia degli Ebrei nell'Italia medievale: tra filologia e metodologia* (Rome, 1990), pp. 19–27).

[11] See Sharf, *Byzantine Jewry*, pp. 20–1; and for a more cynical interpretation A. M. Rabello, 'The Legal Condition of the Jews in the Roman Empire', in H. Temporini and W. Haase, eds, *Aufstieg und Niedergang der römischen Welt*, II.xix (Berlin, 1980), pp. 662–762, esp. pp. 693–4.

[12] Parkes, *Conflict*, pp. 177–82; 'Jews and Christians'.

[13] Sharf, *Byzantine Jewry*, pp. 19–36, and see now the detailed study by A. M. Rabello, *Giustiniano, Ebrei e Samaritani alla luce delle fonti storico-letterarie, ecclesiastiche e giuridiche*, 2 vols (Milan, 1987–8).

and the Arab advance;[14] and so forth. It was during the seventh-century crisis that the emperor, Heraclius (610–41), took the unprecedented step of decreeing that the Jews were to have baptism imposed upon them. The circumstances of this outrageous step are still the subject of debate and confusion;[15] its immediate consequences were mass emigration and no doubt some insincere conversions, and if its aim was to achieve a unified, homogeneous Orthodox state it failed. Judaism survived in the Empire, albeit perhaps on a reduced scale (but then the Empire itself was reduced, and among the provinces lost now and later were some of those with the largest and most important populations). But a precedent had been set, and Heraclius' gesture was repeated in 721–2 by Leo III,[16] in 873–4 by Basil I,[17] by Romanos I Lekapenos in the tenth century,[18] and again in the thirteenth by John Vatatzes.[19]

This was the darkest age of Byzantine Jewry—dark in more senses than one, for we have very little information about Jewish life in the Empire until the end of the tenth century, when a remarkable revival began, with considerable Jewish immigration and a renewal of cultural life.[20] It would be wrong to over-emphasize the negative aspect of the treatment of the Jews by the Byzantine state. There was a positive side as well: the moments of persecution were exceptional, and in general the law offered the Jews, individually and communally, its protection and a certain stability.[21] Indeed, the Jews were generally treated no worse, and often better, than other non-Orthodox subjects. And yet the effect of all the legislation was undoubtedly to give them the status and the consciousness of second-class citizens. Banned from the educational system, from the civil service and the army, from the nobility, from marriage with Christians (is it unfair to call this *apartheid*?), they were compelled increasingly to live in each other's company and off their own spiritual and cultural resources. They were under constant pressure, subtle or crude, to convert to the dominant

14 On this period see Sharf, *Byzantine Jewry*, pp. 42–57, Haldon, *Byzantium in the Seventh Century*, and the various contributions of Dagron and Déroche to *TM* 11.
15 The recent work of Dagron in *TM*, 11 (1991), pp. 17–46, with references to earlier bibliography, marks a significant advance.
16 Sharf, *Byzantine Jewry*, pp. 61–74; Dagron, *TM*, 11 (1991), pp. 43–5.
17 Sharf, *Byzantine Jewry*, pp. 95–102.
18 Ibid., pp. 82–92; Dagron, 'Le Traité', pp. 347–53.
19 Bowman, *Jews*, pp. 16–18.
20 Ibid., pp. 102–27; Ankori, *Karaites*, *passim*.
21 See the positive assessment of P. Yannopoulos, *La Société profane dans l'empire byzantin des VIIe, VIIIe et IXe siècles* (Louvain, 1975), pp. 243–51. He points out (p. 249) that the sister of the Empress Irene married a renegade Jew of Tiberias: there was no racial barrier against Jews.

faith. Our sources preserve a formula for a Jew embracing Christianity to abjure his old faith and practices,[22] just as they give us a formula for converting a synagogue building into a church.[23] They also preserve a special form of oath to be taken by Jews, which is to be administered in a rather bizarre manner:

> He is first to gird himself with the bramble, straddle the wineskin, advance into the sea, and spit upon his circumcision three times, saying thus: by BARASHI BARAA ADONAI ELOI, who led Israel dryshod through the Red Sea and gave them water from a rock, and fed them on manna and quails, albeit they were ungrateful and demanded swine's flesh, etc.[24]

This oath first makes its explicit appearance in the middle of the twelfth century, and it has been interpreted as a symptom of Western influence.[25] It is characteristic of the uncertainty surrounding our subject at every point that it has also been maintained that the origins of the Jewish oath in Byzantium lie in a much earlier period, perhaps as early as the seventh century, and that the oath *more Judaico* in Western Europe actually derived from Byzantium.[26] Be this as it may, it is clear that with the Latin conquest of 1204, Western attitudes to the Jews were introduced into Byzantium by Western Christians, and some of them survived the restoration of a Greek state, co-existing with older Greek attitudes.[27]

RELIGIOUS LITERATURE

This second category of writings is not only the richest, but the hardest to interpret. The Christian religious literature is particularly abundant: it includes a good deal of explicit writing about Judaism, as well as many texts which mention Jews or Judaism in passing. Many of the first type take the form of a dialogue or disputation between a Jew and a Christian, a form which derives from a second-century model, Justin's *Dialogue with Trypho*. Do they recall real encounters, or is the setting a fiction? It has

---

[22] Cf. Parkes, *Conflict*, pp. 397–8; Starr, *Jews*, pp. 173–80.
[23] Parkes, *Conflict*, p. 401.
[24] Full text and discussion in E. Patlagean, 'Contribution juridique à l'histoire des Juifs dans la Méditeranée médiévale: les formules grecques de serment', *REJ*, 124 (1965), pp. 137–56; cf. Starr, *Jews*, pp. 221–2.
[25] Sharf, *Byzantine Jewry*, p. 157.
[26] See Patlagean, 'Contribution'.
[27] See Bowman, *Jews*, pp. 9–40.

been maintained that the dialogues are more or less conventional, repeating well-worn themes and exploiting the same much-thumbed collections of biblical proof-texts. This view is no doubt exaggerated, but no more so than the opposite view, that they always record actual debates.[28] There certainly were debates between Jews and Christians, at different periods; the subjects discussed, and the arguments adduced, were partly constant, partly varied with changing times. On the other hand, allowance must often be made for a certain literary licence, and also for a tendency to use such literary debates as a coded way of discussing issues of internal Christian importance. Much the same is true of the numerous tracts and homilies 'against the Jews' which are not cloaked in dialogue form. Often very conventional in substance, even if prompted by real-life concerns,[29] and clearly addressed, at least in the first instance, to a Christian readership, they serve to display the acuity, eloquence, and orthodoxy of their authors, and to remind us today of the many ways in which 'Jewish' themes continued to exercise the minds of Orthodox Christians long after the decisive rupture between Church and Synagogue as formal institutions. There is, after all, a fundamental dissymmetry between the Jewish and Christian sides. If for the Jews Christianity was a problem only for external reasons, because they found themselves living as a subservient minority under Christian rule, for the Christians Judaism belonged to the very roots of their faith. So long as the Orthodox Church resolutely turned its back on all attempts to sever the Old Testament from the New, to cut the Christ of the Church off from the Jew Jesus, it was inevitable that Judaism would continue to be a living issue for Christian writers, and also perhaps that some Christians would take the more extreme line of observing some biblical practices and clinging to some 'Jewish' beliefs. This phenomenon is to be distinguished from another tendency, also well attested in

---

[28] See M. Waegeman, 'Les Traités *adversus Judaeos*: aspects des relations judéo-chrétiennes dans le monde grec', *Byzantion*, 56 (1986), pp. 295–313, and V. Déroche in *MT*, 11, pp. 282–90. The former view is usually associated with A. von Harnack, the second is attributed, with some exaggeration, to A. L. Williams. Déroche argues cogently that there is a substantial historical basis. J. A Munitiz, 'Catechetical Teaching-aids in Byzantium', in J. Chrysostomides, ed., *ΚΑΘΗΓΗΤΡΙΑ. Essays Presented to Joan Hussey for her Eightieth Birthday* (Camberley, 1988), p. 78, suggests that the anti-Jewish literature served an education purpose.

[29] B. Englezakis has shown (in an unpublished communication) that the anti-Jewish tract of Neophytos of Cyprus is closely related to Jewish eschatological expectations which were current at the time of its composition. Doubtless similar demonstrations could be applied to other works of this type.

the sources, to turn to Jews for certain skills, such as magic and medicine, that were believed to be their special possession.[30]

In surveying this literature as a whole, we need to bear in mind certain considerations which to some extent balance each other out. First of all, the 'anti-Jewish' effort was certainly a major preoccupation of Byzantine intellectuals. Many, if not all, of the best-known Greek Christian writers composed anti-Jewish tracts, or were involved in disputations with Jews, not necessarily from choice.[31] John Moschos describes in his *Spiritual Meadow* how he encountered in Alexandria the learned scholastic Kosmas, a devoted scholar who put his large library at the disposal of all:

> I visited him every day, and I never entered without finding him either reading or writing against the Jews: for he devoted great zeal to bringing the Jews to the truth. That is why he often sent me to debate with certain Hebrews about the scriptures: he himself was unwilling to leave his home.[32]

At the same time it would be misleading to ignore the strong polemical strand that runs through Byzantine literature as a whole. There is a large Christian polemical literature, whose targets include Christian movements as well as alien faiths. Although the anti-Jewish tracts occupy a prominent place within this genre, their existence and the virulence of their language are less shocking than they might be if they stood alone. On the other hand, it is an unbalanced case: we do not hear much from the other side. It is in the nature of our sources that we do not hear a Christian defence of Judaism, only invective against it. At best we sometimes have a grudging respect for the learning of the Jewish disputants. Interestingly, on rare occasions we find a tract quoting a Jewish document such as the Talmud: perhaps in such cases the author was a converted Jew.[33]

The anti-Jewish literature reflects an official theology of Judaism which is essentially negative; at the same time it makes its own contribution to the development and perpetuation of hostile stereotypes, which must surely have had practical consequences for the treatment of Jews.

---

[30] On Judaizing practices and recourse to Jews see now the excellent study by Dagron, 'Judaïser'.

[31] One sometimes senses a reluctance. E.g. Euthymios, in the early eleventh century, unwillingly becomes involved in disputations with two learned Jews; he achieves their conversion by miraculous means. See Starr, *Jews*, pp. 170–1.

[32] Quoted by Déroche in *MT*, 11, p. 285.

[33] E.g. a Christmas homily attributed to Andrew of Crete, Oxford, Bodleian Library, MS Laud. Gr. 81, fol. 164r.

The negative and hostile image of the Jew which pervades the Byzantine Christian literature in general will have crossed the barrier that divided the learned elite from the Christian in the street, particularly through the vehicle of the sermon. At any rate, it is deeply embedded in popular literature and folklore, although we must make some allowance for the development of such stereotypes under Ottoman rule. Interestingly, it seems that anti-Judaism in church was mainly reserved for the sermon: it is not a feature of the prayers, nor, I believe, does it find visual expression in the icons. Only at Eastertide perhaps did the prayers and readings, as well as the hymns, understandably give voice to anti-Jewish sentiments: even then, the prayers speak of the conversion of the Jews rather than their punishment.[34]

When we turn to the Jewish side we find a notably different picture. Considering the pressures on Jews to convert, it is surprising how little apologetic or counter-polemic has survived, although some anti-Christian tracts were composed in Byzantium or imported from elsewhere.[35] The 'anti-gospel' known as the *Toldoth Yeshu*[36] probably circulated widely in Byzantium, even if the numerous surviving manuscripts are mainly either of Western European or oriental provenance. Of the considerable Byzantine Hebrew literature that survives—virtually untouched incidentally by Byzantine historians—only the *Cluster of Henna* (*Eshkol ha-Kofer*) of Judah Hadassi, a Karaite author of the twelfth century, seems to engage seriously with Christianity. The surprising shortage of literature explicitly devoted to the debate with Christianity demands some explanation. It is not necessarily proof of a lack of interest: a prudent self-censorship may have operated. And some writing of this kind has certainly been lost or suppressed. But it is in the synagogue liturgy that the pent-up hatred and resentment of Christian rule bursts through, most notably and specifically in the so-called 'Benediction of the Heretics' (*Birkath ha-Minim*), which is in reality a vehement prayer for the overthrow of Byzantine rule. A version of this prayer, part of the thrice-daily devotions of every Jew, reads as follows:

> For the apostates let there be no hope; speedily uproot, smash and humble the arrogant empire in our days; may the Christians and

---

[34] Cf. Parkes, *Conflict*, pp. 173–4.

[35] See J. E. Rembaum, 'The influence of *Sefer Nestor Hakomer* on medieval Jewish polemics', *Proceedings of the American Academy for Jewish Research*, 45 (1978), pp. 155–85; N. R. M. de Lange, 'A fragment of Byzantine anti-Christian polemic', *JJS*, 41 (1990), pp. 92–100.

[36] See G. Schlichting, *Ein jüdisches Leben Jesu* (Tübingen, 1982) and R. Di Segni, *Il Vangelo del Ghetto* (Rome, 1985).

heretics perish in an instant, and may all the enemies and persecutors of your people be speedily cut off; break the yoke of the gentiles off our necks: Blessed are you, Lord, Destroyer of the wicked and Humiliator of the arrogant.[37]

It is usual to see in this medieval text a form of a prayer originally composed as an anathema of Christianity in the early years of the Church. I personally prefer to read it as a revised form of a prayer directed against the Roman Empire, probably at the time of the Hadrianic persecution in the second century. Whatever its origin, it is a powerful expression of the feelings of Byzantine Jews about the government under which they lived, and about the pressure on Jews to become Christians.

We can follow these same themes in the hymns of the Byzantine Jewish liturgy.[38] For example, one hymn, written to be sung at the feast of Hannukah, the celebration recalling the successful uprising of the Maccabees against the Greek Syrians, includes these lines:

> Remember the nation that trusts in thee
> And rescue them from the viper's clasp,
> Performing wonders at this time.
>
> Spare, O Lord, the myriad folk,
> Consign my tormentors to the flames,
> As thou didst then through the Hasmoneans . . .
>
> Redeemer, hasten our salvation
> That we may delight in thee
> When thou destroyest the evil Greek empire.[39]

It is but a step from this to the apocalyptic visions that are found in both poetic and prose compositions from the Byzantine Empire. Often these seem to be provoked by actual events interpreted as portending imminent redemption, and we hear at different periods of epidemics of Messianic

---

[37] Translated from a Genizah fragment, CUL, T–S 8H10.12 (2). There are many different texts of this prayer. Some add after 'no hope' the words 'unless they return to your Torah'; others begin 'For the Christians let there be no hope . . .' We may contrast the maxim, supposedly going back to pre-Hadrianic times, 'Pray for the welfare of the empire, for were it not for the fear of it, men would swallow each other alive' (*Aboth*, 3.2).

[38] The anthology edited by Leon J. Weinberger, *Rabbanite and Karaite Liturgical Poetry in South-Eastern Europe* (Cincinnati, 1991) [hereafter Weinberger], containing nearly 500 compositions, is a major resource for the study of Byzantine Jewish hymnology.

[39] Abmelech, son of Jeshuah, Weinberger, no. 54, lines 25–30.

fervour that sweep through a Jewish community and sometimes spread far and wide.[40] The Byzantine hymns contain much other material for the study of relations with Christianity: there are frequent reflections on the harsh treatment of the Jews by the Christian Church and State, and occasionally we find polemic of the sort that is mentioned to be refuted in the Christian polemical literature—for example, that the Christians worship man-made idols, and that they subvert God's commandments.[41]

A more sophisticated theology of Christianity may be derived from a study of the abundant midrashic literature, composed under Byzantine rule in Palestine and elsewhere, and generally presented in the form of edited highlights of the sermons of the classical rabbis.[42] The biblical passages concerning the relationship between Jacob and Esau, for example, are read as a paradigm of Jewish–Christian relations, the violence of Esau being contrasted with the mildness and helplessness of Jacob.[43] But there are more positive views of the Empire to be found in the midrashic literature. Most striking, perhaps, is the image of King Solomon represented as the Byzantine emperor.[44]

PERSONAL DOCUMENTS

My third section begins with a work of ambiguous character: the genealogical chronicle of Ahima'as, son of Paltiel of Oria, in southern Italy, written in the year 1054.[45] Its length, its elaborate literary form (it is composed in rhymed Hebrew prose), and its apparent public ambitions may seem to set it with the more formal texts we have just been considering, but in fact it shares some of those characteristics with private letters of its period, and if it was intended for publication (which is uncertain) it does not seem to have achieved its aim, as it survives in one manuscript only. Ahima'as traces the history of his family over several generations, covering some two and a half centuries, and although his concerns are

---

[40] See, for example, Weinberger, English introduction, p. 13; S. Bowman, 'Messianic expectations in the Peloponnesos', *Hebrew Union College Annual*, 52 (1981), pp. 195–202.

[41] See the brief summary in Weinberger, English introduction, pp. 12–13.

[42] I have argued elsewhere that the Midrash is a peculiar Byzantine genre, to be compared with the Greek Christian *catenae*: 'Midrach et Byzance. Une traduction française du "Midrach Rabba"', *Revue d'histoire des religions*, 206 (1989), pp. 171–81.

[43] Ibid., pp. 180–1. For the pre-Christian Empire see N. R. M. de Lange, 'Jewish Attitudes to the Roman Empire', in P. D. A. Garnsey and C. R. Whittaker, eds, *Imperialism in the Ancient World* (Cambridge, 1978), pp. 255–81.

[44] See E. Patlagean, 'Une image de Salomon en basileus byzantin', *REJ*, 121 (1962), pp. 9–33.

[45] Starr, *Jews*, pp. 57–9.

mainly of internal Jewish interest, relations with Christians make an occasional appearance. Among the most interesting examples is the account of Basil I's attempt to secure the mass conversion of the Jews. Ahima'as describes how the Emperor sent a letter to his ancestor Rabbi Shefatiah of Oria, inviting him to take part in a disputation in the capital. So here we have a glimpse of the disputations from the Jewish side, and the implication is that the Jew's arguments carried the day. The subject, we are told, was the rather odd question of which was the more expensive building, the Temple of Solomon or the Church of the Holy Wisdom in Constantinople. The Emperor received the Rabbi well and gave him kosher food to eat; the Empress even took off her own ear-rings and belt and gave them to him as presents for his daughters. Even so, the attempt to convert him is described with disgust, and the city of Constantinople is anathematized in a parenthesis which echoes the *Birkath ha-Minim*: 'May God break down its haughtiness and the whole multitude of its people.'[46] Although he refused to be converted to Christianity, Rabbi Shefatiah was granted one wish: he asked for his city to be exempted from the decree of compulsory baptism, if the Emperor would not agree to cancel the decree altogether.

Ahima'as is writing about the period long past; other Hebrew documents testify to contemporary conditions. Often they afford us a glimpse of a more favourable relationship than that generally depicted in the more official literature. Many private letters mentioning the Byzantine Empire have been preserved in the Cairo Genizah.[47] They date mainly from the eleventh and twelfth centuries, a period when, despite persecution and uncertainty, material conditions were improving, and a weakness in the central power meant that in the provinces[48] it was possible for Jewish communities to prosper undisturbed. The letters make it clear that there was a good deal of immigration of Jews to the Empire from Arab lands, and they seem to be happy there. One, an Egyptian physician who has settled in Seleucia, speaks enthusiastically of the good conditions and urges his relations in Egypt to join him. He has obviously settled in well, since he refers to the Byzantine military leaders as '*our* commanders'.[49]

---

[46] Translated excerpts, ibid., p. 127–31. For a similar curse on Constantinople in a private letter of the mid-eleventh century see ibid., pp. 199–200.

[47] For particulars see Nicholas de Lange, 'Byzantium in the Cairo Genizah', forthcoming in *Byzantine and Modern Greek Studies*.

[48] In Constantinople itself, a Spanish visitor, Benjamin of Tudela, reports (*c.*1165) that 'the Greeks hate the Jews, good and bad alike, and subject them to severe restrictions; they beat them in the streets and force them to hard labour' (Starr, *Jews*, p. 231).

[49] See S. D. Goitein, 'A letter from Seleucia (Cilicia) dated 21 July 1137', *Speculum*, 39 (1964), pp. 298–303.

A different image of Byzantium appears in various fearful or angry references to the activity of the Byzantine navy. It is interesting that in general there is no reference to the Christian religion when Byzantium is mentioned. The Jews living in Byzantium seem to be set firmly within a Jewish community, apparently enjoying, at this date, few contacts with Christians. Yet there are exceptions. Most remarkable are the cases of Jews who take Christian wives, including a prominent figure of the Karaite community of Constantinople, Tobias, son of Moses. In one letter he mentions the hardships suffered by his estranged wife when she decided to abandon Christianity and return to him; in another, written a few years earlier, in 1040, he writes from Jerusalem to his daughter in Constantinople: 'My daughter, I do not know who you are with, whether you are with Jews, who are your father's people, or with your mother's race, the Gentiles.'[50] Such problems of identity may seem rather modern; it is surprising to discover that they could exist in the Middle Ages.

DESIDERATA

I should like to conclude this all-too-rapid survey of a complicated subject with some suggestions about possible future research. I have already hinted at some aspects which require further work. I should like now to single out three areas that would be particularly profitable and promising.

The first is the *image* of the Jew in Christian literature and art. There is ample material available, but so far as I am aware no one has ever tackled the question in a systematic way. It would be interesting to see how the Jew is portrayed at different times, and whether changing circumstances (for example, the moments of persecution, the adoption of Judaism as the state religion by the Khazar kingdom, the influx of Jews from Muslim lands, or the Latin conquests) affected the picture.

The second area is *conversion*, both to and from Judaism: how much of it was there, what were the motives, and the effects?

Thirdly, and finally, the question of possible *influence* of one religion

---

[50] On Tobias see Zvi Ankori, 'The Correspondence of Tobias ben Moses the Karaite of Constantinople', in J. L. Blau *et al.*, eds, *Essays on Jewish Life and Thought Presented in Honor of Salo Wittmayer Baron* (New York, 1959), pp. 1–38. The letters mentioned here are discussed by Moshe Gil, *A History of Palestine, 634–1099* (Cambridge, 1992), pp. 814–18.

on the other. Did Judaism make any real contribution to Byzantine Christianity? And did Byzantine Judaism have any distinctive traits that should be ascribed to Christian influence?

University of Cambridge

ANTI-SEMITISM AND THE BIRTH
OF EUROPE*

by R. I. MOORE

I N August 1976 the remains of a substantial building were uncovered
in the courtyard of the Palais de Justice at Rouen, by the street which
has been called at least since 1116 the rue aux Juifs (see plate 1).[1] That
it was a Jewish building is confirmed by the Hebrew graffiti on its interior
walls. It can be dated firmly to the years around 1100 by its scale, style, and
workmanship, which are strongly reminiscent of the so-called 'Norman
exchequer' in the ducal castle at Caen. The quality of its masonry is as
good as may be found anywhere in northern Europe at this time. The
function of the building is not altogether certain. At 14.14 × 9.46 metres,
with at least one storey above the ground floor, it seems too large for a
private dwelling, and indeed it is bigger than any known synagogue of this
date north of the Alps. Not only the graffiti, but the lions of Judah finely
carved at the base of one column, and the dragon from Psalm 91 on
another, strongly suggest a religious purpose.[2] The synagogue was on this
street, but it is usually thought to have been on the south side, opposite the
Palais de Justice site. This has led Norman Golb, the author of a major
study of the Jewish community at Rouen, to suggest that the building
unveiled in 1976 was a school, which acted as a centre of advanced study,
not only for the Jewry of Rouen, but for a much larger region in which
educational and scholarly activity is attested throughout the twelfth
century by a rich crop of surviving manuscripts and other references,
including many from places like Pont-Audemer, Touques, Falaise,
Evreux, and Coutances, which were by no means major urban centres at
this time.[3]

---

* An earlier paper on this subject was presented to The Parting of the Ways conference at York
in July 1988, and to meetings at Brandeis and Southampton Universities, the University of
Pittsburgh, and the Free University of Amsterdam. I have benefited greatly from all the
comments received on those occasions, and especially from those of Professors Colin Morris
and Bernard Wasserstein.
[1] C. Varoqueaux, 'Découvertes de vestiges médiévaux à Rouen, Rue aux Juifs', in R. Foreville,
ed., *Les Mutations socio-culturelles au tournant des xie.–xiie. siècles* (Paris, 1984), pp. 147–8.
[2] Dominique Halbout-Bertin, 'Le Monument juif d'époque romane du Palais de Justice de
Rouen', *Archéologie médiévale*, 14 (1984), pp. 77–125 (with plates).
[3] Norman Golb, *Les Juifs de Rouen au moyen âge: portrait d'une culture oubliée* (Rouen, 1985),
pp. 77–168.

Plate 1   Jewish Building in the Courtyard of the Palais de Justice at Rouen, excavated in 1976 (photo by courtesy of *Archéologie médiévale*).

Golb's suggestion is not universally accepted,[4] but even to consider it is to be firmly reminded how much higher was the level of Jewish than Christian literary and learned culture in northern Europe at this time. Whatever the building in the rue aux Juifs was used for, it is only one, though perhaps the most spectacular, of a growing list of monuments which attest the prosperity, vigour, and sophistication of the Jewish communities of northern France, the Rhineland, and England in the first half of the twelfth century; Joe Hillaby presented a most interesting account of what has been found in England at the Society's last summer conference.[5]

Few would care nowadays to dismiss so many solid and well-designed dwellings as indicating nothing more than the money-lender's need for physical security. It was widely recognized by their Christian contemporaries that European Jews possessed a higher level of literary culture and sophistication than their own, and by at least some of them that this was the expression not merely of ambition or greed, but of a love of learning for its own and religion's sake. As the pupil of Abelard, whom we know as the *Commentator Cantabrigiensis*, writing before 1153, remarked:

> If Christians educate their sons they do so not for God but for gain, in order that one brother, if he be a clerk, may help his father and mother and his other brothers . . . but the Jews, out of zeal for God and love of the law put as many sons as they have to letters that each may understand God's law—and not only their sons but their daughters.[6]

It is probably no longer necessary to argue at length that the systematic persecution of European Jewry and the anti-Semitic rhetoric which has fuelled and rationalized it are very largely the product of the twelfth and thirteenth centuries.[7] There is little doubt that during the 'Dark Ages' the

---

[4] Blumenkranz thought the building more probably a synagogue, de Boüard a residence: Halbout-Bertin, 'Le Monument', pp. 99–105.

[5] J. G. Hillaby, '*Beth miqdash me'at*: the synagogues of medieval England', *JEH* (forthcoming).

[6] *Commentarius Cantabrigiensis*, quoted by Beryl Smalley, *The Study of the Bible in the Middle Ages*, 1st edn (Oxford, 1941), p. 55. On the author and date, D. E. Luscombe, *The School of Peter Abelard* (Cambridge, 1969), pp. 145–53.

[7] See R. I. Moore, *The Formation of a Persecuting Society: Power and Deviance in Western Europe, 950–1250* (Oxford, 1987), pp. 27–9, 80–5. In general, I would distinguish, with Gavin I. Langmuir, *History, Religion and Antisemitism* (Berkeley, 1990) *passim*, between anti-Semitism, based on irrational and unfounded beliefs about Jews and Judaism, and anti-Judaism, based on essentially correct information, though possibly containing irrational inferences from it. I am not convinced, however, that this justifies a distinction between the various grounds upon which Jews were characterized as the conscious enemies of Christ in the twelfth century, as

Theodosian prohibitions on the holding of office, the ownership of land, the possession of Christian servants, and so on by Jews were not widely enforced, and that with the possible (but not agreed[8]) exception of Visigothic Spain, if there was persecution it was occasional and spasmodic rather than a sustained expression either of royal or ecclesiastical policy or of popular animosity. The tradition that the attacks on Jewish communities in the Rhenish cities and others on the route of the armies of the First Crusade inaugurated the age of persecution has been effectively challenged, at least so far as the regions to the west of the Rhine are concerned.[9] At Rouen, if Guibert of Nogent is to be believed, which is never quite certain, the crusaders 'herded the Jews into a certain place of worship, rounding them up either by force or by guile, and without distinction of age or sex put them to the sword', sparing only those who agreed to be baptized,[10] but we have already seen in the elegant form of the building on the rue aux Juifs that the community was re-established and prospering within a very few years. A crop of sour stories in the Norman chroniclers' accounts of the years 1097 to 1099, to the effect that William Rufus accepted bribes to allow converts from Judaism to return to their former religion, obviously reflects recovery from the forced conversions, and confirms what we would expect in any case, that it was done under royal protection.[11]

The Jewry of Rouen continued to flourish, despite intermittent outrages, until well into the thirteenth century, seemingly unaffected by the fall of Normandy, and able to provide refuge for many of those expelled from England in 1290. It maintained a large and celebrated school through most or all of that time. The thirteenth-century commentator Samuel of Falaise speaks of three great masters of Rouen with whom he had studied, and Golb has shown that the finely illuminated liturgical manuscript known as the Great Mahazor of Amsterdam was the

---

argued ibid., pp. 289–303. In these terms Anselm of Laon's teaching seems to me anti-Semitic rather than anti-Judaic: see pp. 42, 49, below.

[8] Bernard S. Bachrach, *Early Medieval Jewish Policy in Western Europe* (Minneapolis, 1977), pp. 9–26; cf. Roger Collins, *Early Medieval Spain* (London, 1983), pp. 130–45; Pierre Bonnassie, *From Slavery to Feudalism in South-Western Europe* (Cambridge, 1991), pp. 67–8, 96–9.

[9] Robert Chazan, *Medieval Jewry in Northern France* (Baltimore and London, 1973), pp. 24–9; *European Jewry and the First Crusade* (Berkeley, 1988), pp. 85ff.

[10] Guibert of Nogent, *De vita sua*, II.5, ed. E. R. Labande, *Guibert de Nogent: Autobiographie* (Paris, 1981) [hereafter *De vita sua*], pp. 246–8.

[11] Eadmer, *Historia Novorum in Anglia*, ed. M. Rule, RS (1884), pp. 99–101; William of Malmesbury, *Gesta Regum Anglorum*, ed. W. Stubbs, RS (1887–9), II, p. 371.

work of Crespia bar Isaac, who was active in Rouen between 1220 and 1260.[12] In 1306 Philip the Fair's order that their goods should be confiscated inaugurated for the Jews of Rouen, as throughout the realm, the miserable cycle of expulsions, confiscations, and dearly purchased readmissions which Charles VI brought to an end when there was no more to take, with a final expulsion in 1394.

It does not appear, then, that the attack of 1096 inflicted lasting damage. None the less, although we find European Jewry probably more numerous, prosperous, and vigorous in the early twelfth century than it had been at any time in its history, it was already under threat as a result of certain developments of the previous hundred years or so which, though in no way anti-Jewish in intent, or indeed particularly concerned with Jews at all, had potentially fatal consequences for the Jewish community and its position within Christian society. Most obviously, the entire movement for the reinvigoration of the Church, the revival of learning, and the reassertion of royal authority, which goes under the amorphous but universal heading of 'reform', was founded on the conviction that the laws, customs, and standards of antiquity must be restored, both in religious and in secular matters. Without implying special hostility or malice on the part of any group or individual, such a programme was bound to heighten awareness of the patristic account of the position of Jews in Christian society, to be preserved securely but miserably as a reminder to Christians of the death of their Saviour. No less ineluctably it entailed the recollection, and suggested the enforcement, of the long list of social and legal disadvantages and prohibitions imposed on Jews by the *Codex juris civilis*, mainly with the object of ensuring that they should never be in a position to exercise power over Christians either in a public or a domestic capacity. This was precisely the contention of the first and most famous attack on the position of the Jews (not necessarily on the Jews themselves) of the ninth century, delivered to the empty air of the imperial court of Louis the Pious by Agobard of Lyons, but taken up by a growing number of his successors.[13]

Among those prohibitions one in particular would, to whatever extent it was enforced, have weakened Jews still further in a fundamental though almost wholly invisible respect. The greatest losers by the enormous

[12] Golb, *Juifs de Rouen*, pp. 101–416; William Chester Jordan, *The French Monarchy and the Jews* (Philadelphia, 1989), pp. 52–5.

[13] Agobard of Lyons, *De judaeorum superstitionibus*, ed. E. Dümmler, *MGH Epistolae: Epistolae Karolini Aevi*, V, pp. 182–9.

changes which engulfed rural Europe in the eleventh century had been those who possessed land, but not in sufficient quantity or with sufficient patronage to defend it against the castellans and greater lords, who in those years established their seigneuries wherever there was profit to be had from the cultivation of the soil. Among such landowners in several regions were Jews, in numbers certainly not negligible, though incapable of any kind of useful estimation.[14] Their fate can only be guessed at, but the guessing is easy enough. Their choice, if they had a choice, must have lain between staying on their land at the price not only of enserfment but of conversion, and leaving it to find what living they could elsewhere. The story of Mar Reuben ben Isaac of Rouen is all too believable. 'Rich in gold, silver and lands', he lost his only son to armed robbers in 1033 (an inherently suspicious date, it must be acknowledged) and went for justice to Duke Robert. 'You are old', said the Duke, 'and you have no son. All your possessions henceforth will be mine.' So Mar Reuben became an exile, and died a few years later in Jerusalem.[15]

I stress this point about Jewish landholding, despite the unsurprising silence of the sources (which have little more to say about the far larger number of Christians who suffered the same fate), because obvious though its importance may be, it does not always seem to be in mind when the fate of European Jewry in the twelfth century is discussed. For a reminder that the process was still incomplete we need look no further than Philip Augustus's expulsion of Jews from the royal demesne in 1180, when their lands, among much else, were confiscated, or than William C. Jordan's admirably detailed and differentiated account of *The French Monarchy and the Jews* from then until the expulsion of 1306, which discovers Jews still in possession of land in many parts of the expanding kingdom through much of that period.[16] Nevertheless, at least until the subject has received the systematic attention it deserves it is right to suppose that by the early twelfth century a very large proportion of Jews had been enserfed or driven from their land in many regions, that it was pretty generally held that if Jews did have land they shouldn't, and that this in itself would have gone far to rob what land remained to them of

---

[14] Georges Duby, *La Société aux XIe et XIIe siècles dans la région maconnaise* (Paris, 1953), pp. 119–21; Robert Fossier, *Enfance de l'Europe* (Paris, 1982), p. 591.

[15] Golb, *Juifs de Rouen*, pp. 51–63.

[16] See n. 12, above. The estates of twelfth-century Rhenish Jews 'with the exception of houses and an occasional vineyard . . . were composed exclusively of moveable property. Even when Jews did own land they do not seem to have worked it': Kenneth R. Stow, 'The Jewish family in the Rhineland in the High Middle Ages: form and function', *AHR*, 92 (1987), p. 1097.

the greater part of its social, as distinct from its economic, value—that is, of the ability it conferred to hold one's head up in the world, and to give important protection and support in so many ways to one's relations and dependants. The rise of the seigneurie, in other words, not only contributed some uncountable number of rootless and penurious Jews to the tale of wanderers on twelfth-century roads and immigrants to twelfth-century towns, but deprived the Jewish community as such of the general support and protection that would have resulted from having among its number some with an acknowledged stake in the only real source of stability and respectability that an agrarian society knows.

In declaring himself, in effect, the heir of Mar Reuben ben Isaac, Robert of Normandy illustrated another point of occasional short-term advantage but immense long-term vulnerability in the position of the Jews, namely, their special dependence on the king or, as in this case, on those who claimed to exercise royal prerogatives. If fully established, that dependence would no doubt have nullified to a very large extent whatever advantages might otherwise have been associated with landholding. However, modern opinion, on the whole, is that the doctrine that Jews were royal serfs was worked out in its full form only during the twelfth century, and in some regions later.[17] It appears to originate in the special protection accorded by Louis the Pious when, appointing his *magister Judaeorum*, he barred cases concerning Jews from all other courts but his own. Robert's assumption of a prerogative corresponding to the protection which Mar Reuben had sought in vain is echoed by others during the eleventh century. It is not necessary to postulate that he required any special theoretical justification for doing so. We need not view this as anything more subtle than an exercise of the *districtio*, which was the ordinary means by which seignorial powers were established and maintained. None the less, both circumstance and action point clearly towards another dimension of the vulnerability of twelfth-century Jewry to exploitation and spoliation: that absolute dependence for protection on the king or those who claimed to exercise his powers, which, in turn, forced them into an increasingly close and odious identification with some of the most bitterly resented developments of royal government, including notoriously the creation and manipulation of debt.[18]

---

[17] Moore, *Formation of a Persecuting Society*, pp. 39–42.
[18] This familiar aspect of the Jewish predicament has been greatly illuminated in recent years, notably by R. C. Stacy, '1240–60: a watershed in Anglo-Jewish relations', *HR*, 61 (1988), and Jordan, *French Monarchy*.

This long prologue has been necessary for two reasons. First, it underlines the fact that the stereotype of the Jews of Europe in the High Middle Ages and beyond as possessing a particular relationship with commerce, and especially with money-lending, is the result and not the cause of persecution. The process of driving them from the land was critically important in reducing them to poverty and social impotence. It also exemplifies a more general process, in which Jews were gradually excluded from other ways of making a respectable living. For example, in the first half of the twelfth century craft guilds were increasingly successful in restricting entry to many trades and *métiers* to their members, and since many of the guilds were by origin religious associations, this in itself tended to narrow the opportunities open to Jews, though even in this a fatalistic interpretation should not be embraced unthinkingly: there were still Jewish vintners and goldsmiths in London in the reign of Henry I, and a Jew could still be admitted, albeit exceptionally, to a merchant guild.[19] The result is very clearly expressed by the character of the Jew in Peter Abelard's *Dialogue between a Christian, a Philosopher and a Jew*, of about 1125:

> Confined and constricted in this way as if the world had conspired against us alone it is a wonder that we are allowed to live. We are allowed to possess neither fields nor vineyards nor any landed estates because there is no one who can protect us from open or covert attack. Consequently the principal gain that is left for us is that we sustain our hateful lives here by lending money at interest to strangers. But this only makes us more hateful to those who think they are being oppressed by it.[20]

In the light of all this, we find the Jews of Rouen, who may perhaps stand for their brethren through much of northern Europe, in a somewhat contradictory situation at the turn of the eleventh and twelfth centuries. The excavations on the rue aux Juifs bring vividly to light a community far removed from the wretched and degraded creatures of the traditional stereotype of the medieval Jew, and the long history of that community is a firm reminder that the transition from the one to the other was a slow and gradual affair. Most Jews continued not only to live

---

[19] H. G. Richardson, *English Jewry under the Angevin Kings* (London, 1960), p. 27.
[20] Abelard, *Dialogus inter Philosophus, Judaeus et Christianus*, ed. R. Thompson (Stuttgart, 1970), p. 51, tr. P. J. Payer (Toronto, 1970), p. 31. On the date, C. J. Mews, 'On dating the works of Peter Abelard', *AHDL*, 52 (1985), pp. 122–6.

among their Christian neighbours but, in the ordinary course of daily life, to hold their heads high and maintain a vital and broadly based international culture. In this respect Eadmer's account of how William Rufus accepted a bribe from a Jew of Rouen to order his baptized son to return to the faith, only to be frustrated by the steadfastness of the youth in his new faith, is revealing. When the King demanded the promised payment, despite his failure to secure the recantation, he received the reply: 'First carry out what you have undertaken to do and then talk about promises. That was the agreement between us', and was compelled to settle for half the amount.[21] Eadmer had his rhetorical purpose, of course, which doubtless included that of contrasting the haughtiness of the wealthy Jew with the humility which Anselm invariably adopted in the King's presence. Even so, that he could conceive or present a Jew as speaking to William Rufus in such a way suggests a very different image from that which would prevail a hundred years or so later.

That the periodic physical atrocities of the twelfth century were not in themselves at the core of the destruction of European Jewry is suggested by the signs of relatively rapid recovery of the devastated communities after 1096, and even after the massacre at York a hundred years later. Nevertheless, at the moment when the splendid school at Rouen was being built, the builders were already vulnerable to the political and social degradation which eventually reduced them to poverty and humiliation, to daily insult and harassment, and eventually to expulsion from large parts of Christian Europe. Anti-Semitism not only played an obvious if ultimately unquantifiable part in fomenting the violence, but provided an impetus beyond that of mere conscientiousness to enforce, and go beyond enforcing, the disabilities imposed by civil and canon law, and a practically operative justification for ever more relentless royal predation. Above all, by annihilating the true identity of Jews, both individually and collectively, and substituting for it an alternative diametrically opposite in almost every important respect, anti-Semitism effectively destroyed for centuries to come—and substantially diminishes until the present day—whatever appeal there might have been within the Christian community to justice or compassion, and even the will or conviction to demand them within the Jewish one itself.[22] This could not have been

---

[21] Eadmer, *Historia Novorum*, pp. 99–101.

[22] Cf. Gavin I. Langmuir, 'Historiographic Crucifixion', in *Towards a Definition of Antisemitism* (Berkeley, 1991), pp. 282–98. My own interest in this subject was first awakened by the apparent willingness of so distinguished a historian as Léon Poliakov (in *The History of*

achieved by mere anti-Judaism—that is, by a more or less rationally based statement of Christian objections to Judaism and Jewish customs, however extremely or implacably formulated.

The elements of medieval anti-Semitism are too familiar to need extensive recapitulation here. In addition to the consequences of their dependence on money-lending, and to the general reputation which they shared with other stereotyped victims of the age's thirst for persecution—shiftiness and untrustworthiness, personal uncleanliness and proneness to spread disease, preternatural sexual appetite and endowment—Jews were widely asserted by the middle of the thirteenth century to be in the sworn service of the Devil, and hence to nourish a particular vindictiveness towards the person of Christ, and to the Sacrament of the Eucharist, which had become increasingly central to Christian devotion during the previous two hundred years. Consequently, they had not only demanded the Crucifixion, which they regularly re-enacted upon Christian children, but seized every opportunity to desecrate the Eucharist itself, as well as to pollute the vessels with which it was celebrated if they should be entrusted to their care by way of security. The essentials of this account had been established during the preceding century, when knowledge of the real cultural and theological differences between Christians and Jews, which some contemporary scholars had explored with genuine curiosity and at least a measure of objectivity, began to be supplemented, eventually to be superseded, by a new set of legends about Jewish belief and practice. In the 1090s Anselm of Laon became the first important Christian commentator since Bede to argue that the Jews who called for the Crucifixion did so in the full knowledge that Christ was the son of God;[23] Guibert of Nogent, writing in 1115, had contributed, amid a welter of stories representing Jews in the most unfavourable light, the first which showed one summon the Devil and enter his bondage with a libation of sperm;[24] Peter the Venerable worried in the 1140s about the fate of the chalice with which he had secured a loan to his chronically impecunious abbey;[25] Thomas of Monmouth's account, around 1150, of

Anti-semitism, 1 [London, 1974]) to seek the explanation for the persecution of Jews in the Jewish rather than in the Christian community.

[23] Jeremy Cohen, 'The Jews as the killers of Christ in the Latin tradition from Augustine to the friars', *Traditio*, 39 (1983), pp. 1–27.

[24] *De vita sua*, I.26, p. 202; cf. Joshua Trachtenberg, *The Devil and the Jews* (New Haven, 1943), pp. 66, 213.

[25] Letter 130, *The Letters of Peter the Venerable*, ed. Giles Constable (Cambridge, Ma., 1967), 1, p. 329.

the death of William of Norwich created the myth of ritual murder, which provided the basis of about 150 cases we know of in which Jews—often, of course, whole Jewish communities—were accused of murdering Christian children,[26] though it was not until 1235 that cannibalism was added to crucifixion in the catalogue of atrocities, or until the later thirteenth century that Jews were portrayed as physically threatening the Host as the Body of Christ.[27] The association between Jews and money, itself a symbol of various forms of filth and corruption, with distinct diabolic associations, begins to appear in Christian iconography, for instance on the west front of Lincoln Cathedral, around the middle of the twelfth century, though the stereotypical drawing of the Jew himself, with hooked nose and generally sinister features, does not emerge until the thirteenth.[28]

We have seen that the vulnerability of twelfth-century Jewry to these developments was in large part a by-product of the creation of the seigneurie and the movement for ecclesiastical reform, which together had the effect of depriving Jews of independent standing and security, barring them from every acceptable means of subsistence, and throwing them into exclusive dependence on the princes. Vulnerability, however, does not of itself explain misfortune. We have still to account for the swift decline of European Jews from a position of prosperity, general security, and even occasional if grudging respect, to that of downtrodden, increasingly impoverished, and viciously stereotyped outcasts. In doing so, we will avoid a certain amount of prejudgement if before asking 'Why?' we turn to the rather more precise, and even to an extent answerable, question, 'By whom?' The answer, I wish to insist at once and without qualification, is not 'the people'. The intensification and universalization of social stratification which the changes of the eleventh century had brought about gives that term a perfectly clear and precise meaning. The *populus*—or more often the *pauperes*, *rustici*, *plebs*, or *illiterati*—was that great majority of the population which, being effectively subject to the seigneurial ban, enjoyed neither noble nor clerical status, the unfree, and the illiterate. Modern historians have no excuse for blurring a distinction

---

[26] *The Life and Miracles of William of Norwich*, ed. and tr. Augustus Jessopp and M. R. James (Cambridge, 1896); cf. G. I. Langmuir, 'Thomas of Monmouth, detector of ritual murder', *Speculum*, 59 (1984), pp. 820–46, and *Towards a Definition*, pp. 209–36.

[27] Langmuir, *Towards a Definition*, pp. 263–81; Miri Rubin, 'Desecration of the Host; the Birth of an Accusation', pp. 169–85, below. I am grateful to Miri Rubin for a copy of her paper.

[28] Lester K. Little, *Religious Poverty and the Profit Economy* (London, 1978), p. 53; Bernhard Blumenkranz, *Le Juif médiévale au miroir de l'art chrétien* (Paris, 1966), pp. 15–32.

which is quite plain, socially, legally, and conceptually, in their sources, and in particular no excuse for using 'popular' as a synonym for 'lay'. Doubt and dispute about the exact status and obligations of particular individuals and groups there certainly were, but the desperate passion with which they were contested—of which the most famous and resonant example is perhaps the murder of Count Charles the Good of Flanders by the Erlembald clan to prevent him from acting on the revelation of its servile origins—is itself the most eloquent proof of the reality, the recognition, and the importance of the general distinction. If it was not always precisely clear who belonged among 'the people', the knights who led attacks on the Jewries of Speyer, Worms, Mainz, and Cologne in 1096 certainly did not.[29] Neither did the monks who provide so many of the anecdotes which illustrate the evolution of anti-Semitic mythology. To the best of my knowledge no careful examination of any serious attack on Jews in this period has yielded convincing evidence of popular—as distinct from lay—instigation in this sense.

To say this, of course, is not to overlook a good deal of evidence that Jews were habitually subjected to a certain amount of casual hostility and violence, or to underestimate either its seriousness or its extent:

> If the mosaic law is one that ought everywhere to be observed why should you treat those who observe it as though they are dogs, driving them forth and pursuing them everywhere with sticks?[30]

The bitter response of the Jew of Mainz to Gilbert Crispin's remark in the winter of 1092–3, that the canons enjoined observance of the Judaic law by those who were bound to it, is an eloquent testimony from one side; Alexander III's injunction at the Third Lateran Council against pelting Jews with missiles during religious processions and desecrating their cemeteries equally so from the other.[31] This canon may also suggest that we should already take account by 1179 of the equally obvious point, certainly increasingly true from that time onwards, that forms of hostility towards Jews which originated among the privileged, including anti-Judaic teachings and anti-Semitic fantasies, first compounded by the

[29] Jonathan Riley-Smith, 'The First Crusade and the persecution of the Jews', SCH, 21 (1984), pp. 51–72.
[30] B. Blumenkranz, ed., Gisleberti Crispini Disputatio inter Iudei et Christiani (1965): quoted by Richardson, English Jewry, p. 34. On the date, R. W. Southern, St. Anselm and his Biographer (Cambridge, 1963), p. 91n.
[31] J. D. Mansi, Sacrorum conciliorum nova et amplissima collectio (Venice, 1776, repr. Paris and Leipzig, 1903), 22, col. 356.

learned and the powerful, could be and were readily passed down to the populace at large, and received and made current for all the depressingly familiar reasons. Cohen's account of how in the thirteenth century the friars exploited the legend of the Jew as the foe of the Eucharist is an important example of a process more often carried on by less articulate and less visible means.[32] That medieval anti-Semitism *became* popular, doubtless without great difficulty, and that it was at the popular level that its most vicious and insidious forms were frequently peddled in later centuries, nobody could deny. Equally compelling is Jordan's observation that the social isolation of the Jews, the lack of ties and loyalties created over time by marriage, conviviality, and the sharing of worship and ritual, deprived them of the popular sympathy, and even a measure of support against tyranny and extortion, which were sometimes accorded to other victims of persecution from above, such as the Cathars in Lombardy and the Languedoc in the face of the Dominican inquisition.[33]

To acknowledge those unpleasant truths is another matter altogether from accepting or supposing that either anti-Semitism or the systematic persecution of Jews which it fuelled and rationalized was popular in origin, and might be regarded in Humean fashion as contaminating from beneath an essentially rational and humane intelligentsia. For such a view there is no evidence, and what evidence there is tells very firmly against it. Relations between 'Christianity and Judaism' or between 'Church and Synagogue', in effect, what the secular or religious leaders of either faith may have said or thought about the other, is one thing. Relations between Christians and Jews living side by side in any particular community is quite another. Even those who (for reasons which I cannot pretend to understand) are reluctant to concede that the attack of a crusading army on the Rhine cities in 1096 was not an expression of 'popular' sentiment can hardly refuse to acknowledge that the attacks, however characterized, were initiated and carried out by outsiders. At Speyer and Worms they apparently received some support within the cities, but elsewhere, and notably at Mainz, Christian citizens called on the bishops to protect the Jews, and Jews entrusted their children and valuables for safe keeping to their Christian neighbours.[34]

A hundred years after the attack in Rouen the massacre at York, which was the greatest single atrocity perpetrated against Jews in our period, was

---

[32] Jeremy Cohen, *The Friars and the Jews* (Cornell, 1982).
[33] Jordan, *French Monarchy*, pp. 253–5.
[34] Chazan, *European Jewry*, pp. 61–84.

also instigated and led by outsiders, as our President's justly celebrated account of it shows so clearly. It was incited, in his words, by 'a prominent group of local Yorkshire *nobiles*', whose speculation in land and office had left them in classical fashion with debts and grievances which were caused by the times and the King, but blamed on the Jews.[35] The mob which they were able to rouse apparently contained youths, clerks, and working men from the city—it would be astonishing if it had not, in almost any circumstances—as well as a large number of countrymen, but the minster clergy, the members of the religious orders, the wealthier citizens—*nobilitas et cives graviores*, says William of Newburgh—did not take part. In York, as at Rouen, the Jewish community was quickly re-established. To borrow Dobson's words again, its members 'proceeded to play a more prominent role in almost every sphere (except that of scholarship) than their martyred predecessors had done',[36] and continued not only to live in the city, but to build and dwell among its Christians in the 1220s and beyond.

Among those whom we have begun to identify as leaders of assaults on the Jews further distinctions remain to be made. The knights who attacked the Rhine cities and set up the massacre at York had specific needs and problems of their own, which they sought to solve by orchestrating or carrying out attacks on Jews. What they may have thought or felt about the Jews themselves we have no way of knowing. At the least, we must suppose that they were indifferent to their fate and suffering, and willing to welcome any suggestion that to inflict it was good work for a Christian to perform; and we certainly cannot exclude the possibility that beyond that their actions were prompted by personal antipathy to Jews, or by fears and expectations arising from the propagation of anti-Semitic stories and stereotypes. After all, these knights themselves conform to a stereotype. Whether they appear as landless adventurers in search of easy money or as small proprietors struggling to maintain their fortune and rank in inflationary times against falling rents and rising royal importunity, the knighthood, that vast, amorphous body, which in the twelfth century seems always to be struggling for identity, contained a good proportion of the century's 'poor whites'. It is not particularly surprising that they should have been enthusiastic to reinforce their precarious place within the borders of respectable society

---

[35] R. B. Dobson, *The Jews of Medieval York and the Massacre of March 1190* — Borthwick Papers, no. 45 (York, 1974), p. 33.
[36] Ibid., p. 38; see also E. Miller, 'Medieval York', *VCH Yorkshire: City of York* (London, 1961), p. 47.

at the expense of outsiders and newcomers, or that they should have provided the impetus and muscle of any physical assault.

The Black Monks, from whose ranks came so many of the chroniclers who assiduously recorded every suggestion of demonolatry, ritual murder, or desecration of the Host, and, to borrow Dobson's words again, 'wrote of the Jews in a manner which reveals their complete commitment to the classic medieval stereotype of the blaspheming and sacrilegious enemy of Christ',[37] were similarly placed. Their vulnerability to debt, so bitterly and vividly turned against the Jews by a Jocelin of Brakelond or a Matthew Paris, reflected not only the declining value of their rents, but their background as members of a class which, both in the cloister and in the world, daily found its former eminence mocked and its former leadership supplanted. In these respects a still more famous monastery than Bury St Edmunds or St Albans shared their problems, and a far more influential Black Monk than Jocelin or Matthew Paris had anticipated their feelings.

> How much more are the Jews to be execrated and hated who . . . reject, blaspheme and ridicule the virgin birth and all the sacraments of human redemption . . . God wishes them not to be killed or wiped out but to be preserved in a life worse than death, in greater torment and humiliation than the fratricide Cain. . . . Let their lives be spared and their money be taken away.[38]

Peter the Venerable's reputation as one of the more attractive figures among the great men of the twelfth century makes the coldness and brutality of his anti-Semitism all the more shocking—and all the more salutary a reminder of the inappropriateness of applying our own categories and associations to the tangle of terrors and hatreds that we are seeking to make intelligible here.[39] One of Peter's constant preoccupations throughout his abbacy was the indebtedness of Cluny, including substantial obligations to Jewish money-lenders,[40] but one of the many merits of

---

[37] Dobson, *Jews of York*, p. 20.
[38] Peter the Venerable, letter 30, pp. 328–30.
[39] Cf. Langmuir, 'Peter the Venerable: Defense against Doubt', in *Towards a Definition*, pp. 197–208, at p. 202; ibid., p. 383, nn. 14–21, on the difficulties which Peter's anti-Semitism has presented to his scholars.
[40] Georges Duby, 'Le Budget de l'abbaye de Cluny entre 1080 at 1155: économie domaniale et économie monétaire', *Annales ESC*, 7 (2) (1951), pp. 155–71, also in *Hommes et structures du moyen âge* (Paris, 1973), pp. 61–82. Langmuir, 'Peter the Venerable', comments that Peter does not direct his execrations equally at the Christian usurers whose existence he casually confirms.

Gavin Langmuir's analysis, to which we will turn in a moment, is to have uncovered a much deeper and subtler root for Peter's anti-Semitism than simple material anxiety.

Considerations like these have encouraged some of the most sophisticated discussion of recent years once again to associate the roots of twelfth-century anti-Semitism with the capacity of the Jews to take advantage of economic change. Thus, for example, Alexander Murray suggests that 'the reaction against them came not from the ranks of their counterparts and successors but from the usual enemies of the *nouveaux riches*: the old-rich, and the poor.'[41] On the whole, however, the chroniclers, like their cousins who led the mobs, were reflective rather than creative. They welcomed and used the anti-Semitic stereotypes; in a jargon whose usefulness barely excuses its ugliness, they had no hesitation or difficulty in internalizing them; but with one or two important exceptions they did not create them. The exceptions, indeed, might be said to prove the rule, or at any rate to confirm that categories such as 'rising' and 'declining' are neither absolute nor comprehensive. It must be doubtful whether a family like Peter the Venerable's[42] was yet beginning to feel disadvantaged by the streams of commerce in the early twelfth-century Auvergne, and nobody would call Peter himself a marginal or a marginalized figure just because Cluny had financial problems. The other Black Monk who made an important original contribution to the theory of anti-Semitism, Guibert of Nogent, is similarly resistant to pigeon-holing. Although he never achieved more potent office than a very minor abbacy, his temperament and abilities, and his frustrated ambitions, would have fitted him more for a career at court than in the cloister.[43] Neither of them rebuts the suggestion that to find the true begetters, the theorists of anti-Semitism and the initiators of systematic anti-Semitic action, we must look to the world, and not to its backwaters or margins but to the centres of change, to where the Middle Ages were being made, the courts and the schools.

We have already noted the essential contribution which was made to

---

[41] Alexander Murray, *Reason and Society in the Middle Ages* (Oxford, 1978), p. 69, and similarly Little, *Religious Poverty*, pp. 42–57.

[42] Constable, 'The Family of Peter the Venerable', in *Letters*, 2, pp. 233–46: 'A feudal family of secondary or tertiary rank in terms of wealth or political power which was able through the church to exercise influence of the first importance.'

[43] R. I. Moore, 'Guibert of Nogent and his World', in H. Mayr-Harting and R. I. Moore, eds, *Studies in Medieval History Presented to R. H. C. Davis* (London, 1985), pp. 107–17. We have no information about Thomas of Monmouth's social origins or what he did before entering Norwich Cathedral Priory.

the demonization of the Jews by the belief that the Crucifixion arose not through simple ignorance, but from a deliberate rejection of Christ, and hence that Jews must be expected to indulge in wilfully diabolic acts. After showing that the doctrine achieved wide popular currency only during the thirteenth century, as a result of certain theological orientations developed by Franciscan and Dominican preachers, Jeremy Cohen turned his attention to its intellectual history. The patristic view, as expounded by Ambrose and Augustine, was that the killers of Christ did not know that he was the son of God. Among early authorities only Bede disagreed, and his opinion was not generally accepted: the Augustinian teaching was retained in the Carolingian tradition, from Haimo of Auxerre and Sedulius Scotus to Bruno of Cologne and Anselm of Canterbury. The first commentator to return to the Bedan opinion was Anselm of Laon, who held that the leaders (*majores*) of the Jews knew *deum esse vel Dei filium numquam dominum gloriae crucifixissent*, distorting the views of earlier commentators in order 'to attribute greater validity to the tradition of intentionality in the Jews' murder of Christ'.[44]

Cohen finds that Anselm's teaching on this point was not immediately influential among fellow masters and commentators. He had no particular reason, of course, to remark that among Anselm's friends and admirers was Guibert of Nogent—of Nogent-sous-Coucy, that is, a few miles from Laon. Anselm, indeed, is one of the very few among his acquaintance for whom Guibert had a good word to say, and among the words which he put into the mouths of those who decided to launch the massacre at Rouen was the description of the Jews, 'than whom no people is more hostile to Christ—*Judaei, quibus inimicior existat gens nulla Dei*'.[45]

The promulgation of this characterization by Anselm of Laon was soon followed by another change, which Noël Coulet has uncovered.[46] The place of the Jews in the ceremony in which citizens turned out to give a ritual welcome to their king or bishop at his entry to their city has classical antecedents, and is recorded regularly from Gregory of Tours's description of Guntramn's entry to Orléans until the fourteenth century. As it is described by Gregory, and up to the period with which we are concerned, it shows the Jews as a part of the community like any other, and often dispersed among it. In contrast, Suger's description of Innocent II's entry

---

[44] Cohen, 'The Jews as killers of Christ', pp. 9–15.
[45] *De vita sua*, p. 246.
[46] Noël Coulet, 'De l'intégration a l'exclusion: la place des juifs dans les cérémonies d'entrée solonelle au moyen âge', *Annales: Economies, sociétés, civilisations*, 34.4 (1979), pp. 672–83.

to Paris in 1130 describes the 'blind synagogue' of the Jews of Paris holding up a roll inscribed with the law, while Innocent says to them, 'Let God
strip the veil away from your hearts.'[47] The roll, in conjunction with these
words, symbolizes the deliberate blindness of Jews to the law, and is here
associated with a change in the welcoming ritual, whose effect was to
exclude them from the political community. Henceforth they were
segregated, and their exclusion was justified by their deliberate refusal to
see the truth, by which they proclaimed themselves the deliberate enemies
of Christ. In the Capetian kingdom at least the theoretical deterioration in
the position of the Jews represented by Anselm's teaching had been very
promptly translated into political action. What a pity it is, in that light,
that William of Malmesbury does not elaborate his casual reference to the
participation of the Jews in the welcome which Innocent received at
Rouen, on the same journey.[48]

Just as the attacks on Jews and Jewish communities in this period
were initiated, so far as both theory and practice were concerned, by
certain of the socially privileged and not by 'the people', Anselm of
Laon's reference to the *majores* among the Jews as possessing the knowledge that Christ was the son of God implies that his quarrel was with
their leaders—specifically, their intellectual leaders—and not necessarily
with all Jews as such. In other words, we are confronting, in the first
place, not a conflict between communities, but a conflict between elites.
That may seem almost too obvious to be worth stating. It was, after all,
not in the streets but in the courts of kings and princes (much more than
of bishops or popes) that the policies and procedures were devised and
implemented which steadily and systematically reduced European Jewry
from a position of relative security and substantial prosperity to that of
helpless victims of casual predation. Nobody, I suppose, is likely to suggest that the consuming avarice of a Philip Augustus or a John Lackland
was impelled, or even suggested, by pressure from the grass roots. Quite
to the contrary, from their point of view, one of the advantages of the
circulation of anti-Semitic stories was that they were capable of providing a rare instance where royal avarice might be made to seem acceptable.

Once again, so far as the kings and princes themselves are concerned,
there is motive in plenty without requiring us to postulate the superfluous
entity of anti-Semitism, though in the case of Philip Augustus, Rigord

---

[47] Suger, *Vie de Louis VI le Gros*, ed. H. Waquet (Paris, 1964 edn), p. 264.
[48] William of Malmesbury, *Historia Novella*, ed. K. R. Potter (London, 1955), p. 10.

notoriously supplies ample evidence of it.[49] The extent to which anti-
Semitism may have been nourished by the hope of securing their favour is
another matter. In an earlier discussion of this subject I drew attention to a
number of episodes—such as the accusation of witchcraft levelled against
the Jews of Le Mans in 992 by a convert named Sehok ben Esther, and the
destruction of the Jewry of Blois in 1171 after a wholly unsubstantiated
accusation of child-murder was accepted by the Count, who had recently
discarded a Jewish mistress—to suggest that conflict involving the
presence or influence of Jews at courts was an important source of
influential anti-Semitism, and that an obvious motive for it was the
evident superiority of Jews to their Christian counterparts in literacy,
numeracy, and legal sophistication, the very skills upon which the
immense growth in the power and scope of government in our period was
founded.[50] One indication of its persistence is the promptness and
regularity with which kings and kingdoms entering the sphere of papal
influence during the thirteenth century were admonished to rid themselves of Jewish counsellors and officials.[51]

Grateful as I would be for the emergence of more substantial corroboration of that jealousy in the courts of northern Europe, and especially in
the earlier part of our period, which is most pertinent to my argument, I
remain unembarrassed by its scantiness. The desperate and ruthless
competition of twelfth-century courtiers to serve without scruple their
masters' every whim is vividly commemorated in their writings, and has
regularly been described by far better historians than I. In the feverish and
conspiratorial atmosphere of a court dominated by rootless and landless
men, who might be raised from the gutter to the heights in a moment by
the smile of their lord, and hurled back again in another, no tale of
intrigue was too far-fetched to believe or too shocking to relay. The very
presence of those who possessed superior skills and their proximity to the
throne provided a focus for special hostility. There is not much direct

[49] R. H. Bautier, 'La Personnalité de Philippe Auguste', in R. H. Bautier, ed., *La France de Philippe Auguste: le temps des mutations* (Paris, 1982); cf. J.-P. Poly and Eric Bournazel, in ibid., p. 228.

[50] Moore, *Formation of a Persecuting Society*, pp. 140–53; on the episodes mentioned see respect-ively Chazan, *European Jewry*, pp. 32–5; B. Blumenkranz, 'Les Juifs à Blois au moyen âge: à propos de la démographie historique des Juifs', *Etudes de civilisation médiévale (ix–xiis.): mélanges . . . E. R. Labande* (Poitiers, 1975), pp. 33–8.

[51] For example, Shlomo Simonsohn, *The Apostolic See and the Jews: Documents, 492–1404 — Studies and Texts* 94 (Toronto, 1988), pp. 120, 130 (Hungary); 136, 227–8 (Portugal); 225 (Poland); 239 (Languedoc), etc. It should perhaps be added, though it is a familiar point, that the thirteenth-century papacy was no less determined to insist that the canonical disabilities of the Jews should not be exceeded than that they should be enforced.

evidence of Jewish involvement in government, as far as I know, from northern Europe, but since those who valued the skill of Jewish doctors included several kings and a long line of popes, it is not surprising that twelfth-century legend attributed the deaths of Charlemagne, Charles the Bald, and Hugh Capet to their sinister ministrations. Once again we find Guibert of Nogent in the thick of things. In one group of anecdotes the Jew whom Guibert carefully associates with lechery, filth, and pimping is in the (undefined) service of the notoriously brutal and licentious John, Count of Soissons; the protagonist of the story in which he makes the first specific assertion of a special bond between Jews and the Devil is, almost inevitably, a physician; and Alais, Countess of Soissons, had employed the skill of another Jew to poison her brother.[52]

I have already mentioned Sehok ben Esther of Le Mans. Another reminder of the special enthusiasm of the convert is supplied by Petrus Alfonsi, at some time doctor to Henry I of England, who confirmed, in his *Dialogus Petri et Moysi Judaei* of 1110, the opinion that his erstwhile co-religionists had organized the Crucifixion out of malice, not ignorance.[53] In a sense, however, all of these men were converts. The reconstruction of the Catholic faith is an even more familiar achievement of the period with which we are concerned than the reconstruction of lay society. We must not allow its familiarity to obscure the demands which its architects placed upon their own credulity. In the generations around 1100 the central issues were those which related to the dual nature of Christ, the purpose of the Incarnation, and the place and meaning of the Eucharist in Christian life and faith, questions which also raised that of the *modus operandi* of the Devil and his intervention in human affairs. Sir Richard Southern pointed out many years ago, and has recently reiterated, that Jews constituted 'the only learned, the only uncompromising opponents of the whole idea of the Incarnation',[54] not only a body of obstinate and articulate unbelievers deeply versed in the Scriptures, but one whose questions and objections pressed uncomfortably upon the very points which caused the greatest anxiety to Christians. Gavin Langmuir has taken

---

[52] *De vita sua*, pp. 426, 202, 422.

[53] Petrus Alfonsi, *Dialogus Petri et Moysi Judaei*, *PL* 157, cols 537–672—e.g. at cols 573–4, 581. I am grateful to John Toland for directing my attention to this work, of which he is preparing an extensive study.

[54] Southern, *St. Anselm and his Biographer*, p. 88; *Saint Anselm: a Portrait in a Landscape* (Cambridge, 1990), pp. 198–202. I am grateful to Professor D. E. Luscombe for drawing my attention to the latter. Susan Reynolds notes continuing indications of intellectual insecurity in the face of Judaism, even in the thirteenth century: 'Social mentalities and the case of medieval scepticism', *TRHS*, ser 6, 1 (1991), pp. 34–5.

up and extended this insight to show how for Peter the Venerable the Jews became not only scapegoats for the scepticism of the divinity of Christ which some of his monks expressed, but the object upon which he projected his own temptation to doubt.[55] Similarly, for Miri Rubin the depiction of Jews as the enemies of the Eucharist, the very heart of thirteenth-century anti-Semitism, assisted its credibility to withstand the strains of its enormous role in thirteenth-century religious practice.[56]

Until very recently it has been the habit of historians—Jewish ones, I think, almost as much as non-Jewish—to describe the growth of anti-Semitic ideas and actions in twelfth- and thirteenth-century Europe in terms which suggest that so far as the history of that period itself is concerned, it was a somewhat peripheral issue. Whatever moral despair it may have induced, however dreadful the anti-Jewish legends and actions of the Middle Ages in themselves, however terrifying a portent they may have seemed for the future—and for many the agony of the discussion was greatly ameliorated by the illusion which Langmuir, in particular, has finally laid to rest, that anti-Semitism as we have known it in the twentieth century is a product of industrial modernization, for which medieval civilization need bear no responsibility—close examination of Jews in the medieval world has generally been confined to specialist studies. The insignificance of the place which the Jews and their achievements (perhaps even more than their misfortunes) have commanded in our general accounts of the tremendous changes in European society, government, and culture at that time is itself an unresolved and embarrassing historiographical issue.[57] The nearest anti-Semitism usually came to centre stage was the somewhat trite observation that it tended to be stimulated by enthusiasm for crusades, illustrated perhaps by the set piece of the massacres of 1096.

The burden of this argument has been, on the contrary, that the persecution of Jews, and the growth not only of anti-Judaism but of anti-Semitism, were quite central to the developments which taken together I choose to describe, without the faintest tincture of originality, as the birth of Europe. I do not mean to suggest by this that the birth of Europe could not have taken place without them. That is a judgement which I know no way to attempt, though I should like to think that the distinguished scholar who congratulated me on demonstrating in *The Formation of*

---

[55] Langmuir, *Towards a Definition*, pp. 197–208.
[56] Rubin, 'Desecration of the Host'.
[57] Cf. Langmuir, 'Majority History and Post-Biblical Jews', in *Towards a Definition*, pp. 21–41.

a Persecuting Society that, as he put it, one can't make an omelette without breaking eggs, may have been mistaken. But, to extend his unfortunate metaphor, this search has unquestionably led us to the kitchen, and the work we have examined was that of the cooks, in the sense that the arguments which justified the persecution of Jews in the High Middle Ages were propounded, the attitudes which demanded it were moulded, and the actions which constituted it were carried out by *clerici*—a term which rightly embraced both scholars and officials, between whom we should not try to draw too clear a line. They came from the same backgrounds, shared the same formation, and pursued fluid and interacting careers, moving back and forth between the overlapping worlds of the schools and the courts. Above all, they were committed to a common enterprise, the creation of a new spiritual and political order, founded on the most profound social transformation of pre-industrial Europe, and upon the mobilization of wealth and power hitherto undreamt of through the agency of a cultural revolution. Instead of being exercised from horseback by the issuing of direct orders to personal followers and the direct commandeering of booty, rents, and taxes, in the form of goods in kind and personal services, power began to flow through the written instruction and to be stored in the written record, and wealth began to be collected and accumulated in the form of money.

In this context the clerks of western Europe, irrespective of whether they were in the service of 'Church' or 'State', worked out between the beginning of the twelfth and the middle of the thirteenth century both the theory and the practical implementation of what I have called 'the persecuting society'. It enabled them to drive deep the foundations of their own power, to flex its muscles and extend its field of action, turning it at will against any section of society or any part of the world where they wanted to exert it, while at the same time proclaiming and consolidating their own position, not simply as the beneficiaries of political and social change—always a dangerous role—but as the guardians and, indeed, the definers of the beliefs, values, and behaviour which were the foundation of Christian society itself, and its vigilant protectors against the constant and devious plots of the Devil and his allies to subvert it.

The stereotype of the Jew which was established in this process displays very clearly the characteristics which are associated in many cultures with sorcery accusations that reflect the struggle for power in a changing world—the inversion of qualities like youth, beauty, purity, benevolence, and truthfulness, which epitomize the ideals of the society in question. In such struggles the accusations may take much the same form whether made by 'new men' trying to dislodge established holders of influential positions, or by the old ones trying to fend them off.[58] The anti-Semitic stereotype also corresponded closely to that of other excluded and persecuted groups—heretics, lepers, and sodomites in particular—which began to be elaborated and publicized in north-western Europe at the same time.[59] But here there is an instructive difference. In the case of other groups the process of stereotyping—of constructing, that is to say, an object capable and deserving of persecution—began with the creation of a new identity, or at least the sharpening and redefinition of an old one. In that of the Jews it began with the destruction of an identity which was already altogether too well established, possibly even too attractive, for comfort. Scattered, disunited, and on the whole disparate and poorly supported, heretical preachers became the emissaries of an alternative church, with vast numbers of hidden followers, a coherent doctrine with scriptures and organization going back to biblical times, its own schools, its own bishops, even its own pope lurking in the Balkans, and with secret churches in every part of Christendom where it did not already operate brazenly in the open. All this was built up so convincingly, in its final form by the papal inquisitors of the thirteenth century, that there are still historians who believe in it, as virtually everybody did until thirty or forty years ago. Similarly, a spectre of leprosy was elaborated, propagated, and 'proved' by diagnosis well beyond the evidence of any real epidemic. The sin of sodomy was singled out from the opulent variety of sexual mis-demeanours available in the penitentials to bring upon those accused of it increasingly enthusiastic pursuit and savage retaliation as the bearers of a peculiarly contagious and virulent threat to Christian society.[60]

In contrast, the anti-Semitic stereotype which was constructed in the twelfth and thirteenth centuries was designed to magnify the danger which they represented, certainly, but to diminish the Jews themselves. Its

---

[58] Cf. Peter Brown, 'Sorcery, Demons and the rise of Christianity: from Late Antiquity into the Middle Ages', *Witchcraft Confessions and Accusations = Association of Social Anthropologists Monographs*, 9 (1970), pp. 17–45; also in Brown, *Religion and Society in the Age of Saint Augustine* (London, 1972), pp. 119–46.

[59] Moore, *Formation of a Persecuting Society*, pp. 66–99.

[60] Ibid., pp. 91–4, based almost entirely on John Boswell, *Christianity, Social Tolerance and Homosexuality* (Chicago, 1980), esp. pp. 169–302. Even if Boswell's critics (e.g. Southern, *Saint Anselm*, pp. 148–53) had successfully rebutted his contention that male homosexuality was first clearly distinguished and set apart from other forms of non-reproductive sexual activity during our period, it would remain the case that 'sodomites' were singled out for particularly savage persecution at this time, and that the chronology and rhetoric of this development corresponded closely to those of other persecutions.

depiction of them as mean, dirty, poverty-stricken, repulsive, and contemptible compared with their Christian neighbours was the very opposite of the truth. And the truth was much more dangerous than any of the fantasies. Except in the matter of their faith, the Jews were in fact what the clerks represented themselves as being. At least until the end of the twelfth century they were culturally far superior to their Christian counterparts. They had maintained a widespread and coherent educational structure from a much earlier date.[61] They had an authentic claim to that very continuity from antiquity, and since biblical times, upon which Catholic legitimacy and authority so precariously depended. At a more mundane level, the skills of numeracy, literacy, and the manipulation of legal texts were much more widely disseminated among them. Wherever there were Jewish communities, there were schools. We have seen the substance and standing of the one at Rouen at a time when it is unlikely that the bishop's school in that city did more than teach the elements of grammar to half a dozen aspirant clerks. So long as power grew, as it were, out of the hilt of a sword this was of no great consequence. But the bureaucratic revolution, and with it the birth of Europe, was founded on the very skills in which Jews so far outpaced Christian clerks. That is why they were able to make themselves so useful at courts—and why they represented such a danger to the clerks who sought that power for themselves. It is also why the resultant rivalry was most intense here in north-western Europe, where the economic and institutional precocity which signalled the new age was most obvious, while in literacy, education, and general sophistication the Christian community remained relatively backward.

To leave it at that would be as crude a mistake—and one which I may inadvertently have given the appearance of making—as to imagine that Anselm proved the existence of God for the sake of impressing the examiners. It is not my contention that the religion and culture of the High Middle Ages can be reduced to a handful of job skills. Simply from the perspective of the social theorist, the struggle to establish them was also a struggle for identity—for nothing less than the identity of a new civilization. They provided its makers not only with particular capacities—with language, goals, and values—but with the means to order their lives and the possibility of belief in the legitimacy as well as the

---

[61] A. Grabois, 'Écoles et structures sociales des communautés juives d'occident aux ixe.–xiie. siècles', *Gli ebrei nel alto medio evo, Settimani di studio del centro Italiano nel'alto medio evo*, 26 (1978) (Spoleto, 1980), pp. 937–62.

purpose of their actions. In doing so, they endowed European civilization, in the century of its birth, with some of its most piercing insights, its most moving representations, and its noblest aspirations. Nobody could imagine that all this was achieved without toil and pain of body and mind. The tragedy is that the more elevated the view we adopt of those achievements, the more fearful become the consequences of acknowledging the superiority (from every human point of view) of the attainments and culture of the Jews of early medieval Europe. It simply underlines that the reason for their destruction, in the last analysis, was that their Christian counterparts could not bear the comparison.

University of Sheffield

JEWISH CARNALITY IN TWELFTH-CENTURY RENAISSANCE THOUGHT

by ANNA SAPIR ABULAFIA

I

DISAGREEMENT between Jews and Christians about the meaning of the words of the Hebrew Bible is as old as the emergence of a Christian sect in Judea. The perennial debate on hermeneutics was not a simple bandying of words between two competing parties. What was discussed really mattered, for it gave expression to the essence of what separated Jew from Christian.

Jews found in what Christians called the Old Testament an understanding of their past, guidelines for their present situation, and hopes for future redemption. As the nexus of the growing corpus of rabbinic writings, the Torah, together with the Prophets and the Writings, gave shape and meaning to Jewish existence. It was precisely this shape and this meaning that Christians saw as the negation of everything they believed about themselves to be true. Christians interpreted the Old Testament as the portal to the New. Not to read in the words of Moses or the Prophets the message of Jesus Christ was in their eyes not only fallacious; it was tantamount to a denial of the Incarnation and what Christians understood God's scheme of salvation for mankind to be.

Christians accused Jews of reading the Bible 'carnally' or literally on account of the fact that Jews refused to accept the Christological message which Christians believed it to contain. Yet it is important to emphasize that the contrast between the Jewish literal interpretation of the Bible and the Christian spiritual one, which has become such a trademark of the Jewish–Christian debate, is in fact misleading. It implies that Jews never went beyond the letter of their sacred texts, and it suggests that Christians had no eye for the plain meaning of what they read. As we shall see, this is not true. What is true is that Jewish exegetes refused to adhere to the specific form of spiritual interpretation which a Christological understanding of the Bible demanded. It is because Jews could not offer this that their reading of the Bible was dubbed unspiritual or carnal. In the context of the Jewish–Christian debate the actual richness of Jewish exegesis mattered little. Christians attacked what they understood its implication to be. Christians, for their part, were not at all oblivious to the importance

59

of the straightforward meaning of scriptural texts. Different schools of Christian exegetes had their own priorities, but traditionally the literal or historical signification was considered the first step towards the full understanding of a biblical passage, which, in turn, could include allegorical, tropological, and anagogical aspects as well.[1]

The Jewish–Christian debate on the correct reading of the Bible evolved as relationships between Jews and Christians unfolded and as changes took place within the Christian and Jewish milieux themselves. We shall focus our attention on part of the story of what was happening in England and northern France in the Twelfth-century Renaissance. It is in this period that teaching at the famous school of Laon by the brothers Anselm and Ralph centred on the books of the Bible. Questions which arose from the reading of scriptural passages ranged from those concerning the nature of God to those which related to the created world, the problems of good and evil, the role of man in creation, his redemption, and so on. Answers were sought in the first place by comparing and reconciling patristic comments on these complex topics. In other schools more attention was given to the newly discovered classical texts, and rational arguments were marshalled to illuminate questions of faith.[2] But whatever the preference of a particular school or scholar was, the Bible always remained a central point of reference. In monastic houses, but also in the schools, the language of the Latin Bible was part and parcel of human consciousness: the Bible was perused for its own sake, and sections of it were repeatedly used in the daily offices. As intellectual thought grew more sophisticated and scholars became more interested in the semantics of language on account of their growing knowledge of the Trivium, the desire to fathom the words of the Bible could only grow in importance. But because Christians shared the Old Testament with the Jews, turning to the Bible often meant that Christian scholars had to look at the Jewish side of the coin.[3] This is why so much of the theological writing of the

[1] For a full treatment of Christian biblical exegesis see H. de Lubac, *Exégèse médiévale. Les quatres sens de l'Ecriture*, 1.1–2.2 (Paris, 1959–64). Useful, too, is chapter 6, 'The Exposition and exegesis of Scripture', in G. W. H. Lampe, ed., *The Cambridge History of the Bible. 2, The West from the Fathers to the Reformation* (Cambridge, 1969), pp. 155–279.
[2] On the school of Laon see H. Weisweiler, *Das Schrifttum der Schule Anselms von Laon und Wilhelms von Champeaux in deutschen Bibliotheken* = Beiträge zur Geschichte der Philosophie und Theologie des Mittelalters, 33.2 (Münster, 1936); and M. Colish, 'Another look at the School of Laon', *AHDL*, 53 (1986), pp. 7–22; but also V. I. J. Flint, 'The "School of Laon": a reconsideration', *Recherches de théologie ancienne et médiévale*, 43 (1976), pp. 89–110.
[3] It was especially Beryl Smalley who did pioneering research in this area. See her *The Study of the Bible in the Middle Ages*, 3rd edn (Oxford, 1983), pp. 149–72.

period in some way touches on the Jewish–Christian debate. An extremely interesting example of the way in which an exercise in Christian theology could converge with anti-Jewish polemics is the *Ysagoge in theologiam*, and it is to this work that we now turn.

II

The *Ysagoge in theologiam* is a compendium of theology which appears to have been composed in England some time in the 1140s. The only extant manuscript of the full text is Cambridge, Trinity College, MS B.14.33, which dates from the twelfth century. This manuscript was in the possession of the abbey of Cerne, in Dorsetshire, in about 1200. But by the fourteenth century it had been presented to the library of Belvoir Priory, in Lincolnshire. The script points to an English provenance. Moreover, the contents of the *Ysagoge* were abridged and rearranged in two other manuscripts which seem to have been written in England as well: London, BL, Royal 10.A.XII, folios 117v–123r, and Harley 3038, folios 3r–7v.[4]

The text of the prologue to the *Ysagoge* begins on folio 5r of the Trinity manuscript. Folios 3–4r carry a dedication of the work, written by a certain Odo for Gilbert Foliot, who had been a master in the schools, and prior first at Cluny and then at Abbeville before returning to England as abbot of St Peter, in Gloucester, in 1139. Foliot is addressed as *magistro scolarium patri cenobitarum*. The editor of the *Ysagoge*, Arthur Landgraf, has claimed that this dedication does not, in fact, belong to the *Ysagoge*.[5] But David Luscombe has refuted this successfully. Contrary to Landgraf's assertions, the section of the manuscript containing the dedicatory letter and the section containing the text of the *Ysagoge* both carry inscriptions referring to Cerne and Belvoir. Thus it would seem that the dedication and the text were together at these places. Moreover, Luscombe claims that the language of the dedication is not so dissimilar to that of the *Ysagoge*. Moreover, in both the letter of dedication and the text of the *Ysagoge*, Aristotle is referred to as *philosophus*. In the mid-twelfth century this was not yet the common practice it would become in the thirteenth. The gap of time between the hand responsible for the dedication and the hands which wrote the text of the *Ysagoge* is not as wide as Landgraf

---

[4] D. E. Luscombe, 'The authorship of the *Ysagoge in theologiam*', *AHDL*, 43 (1968), pp. 9–16.

[5] A. Landgraf, *Ecrits théologiques de l'école d'Abélard, textes inédits = Spicilegium Sacrum Lovaniense*, 14 (Louvain, 1934) [hereafter Landgraf edn], pp. xliv–xlvi. The letter of dedication is printed as an appendix to the edition on pp. 287–9.

thought. Nor does the collation of the manuscript prove that the dedicatory letter and the text of the *Ysagoge* were originally separate. Finally, Gilbert Foliot, to whom the letter of dedication is addressed, had close links with the abbey of Cerne. It is therefore very likely that the dedication letter does indeed belong to the text. This, in turn, would confirm the English provenance of the work. For in the penultimate sentence Odo writes that he dedicates his work to Gilbert, 'so that what England sends to Gaul will strive for fame on both sides [of the Channel].' The sentence does not, incidentally, mean that Gilbert was in France when Odo wrote these words. Because Odo has earlier addressed Gilbert as abbot, Foliot must have been in Gloucester when the *Ysagoge* was sent to him. Odo evidently hoped that through Foliot, who had enjoyed a great reputation in France before returning to England, his work would come to the attention of the French schools. Finally, it is clear that the *Ysagoge* must pre-date 1148, the year that Foliot became bishop of Hereford. The puzzle that still eludes solution is the identity of this Odo, who does appear to be the author of the *Ysagoge*.[6]

The text is an interesting mix of ideas coming from the schools of Abelard and the Victorines. Whole chunks of the compendium are based on the *Summa Sententiarum*, itself a compilation of many sources, following the tradition of the school of Anselm of Laon and William of Champeaux on such issues as original sin and free will. The *Summa Sententiarum* has in the past been ascribed to Hugh of St Victor. Although this attribution has been proved to be false, the work does represent much of Hugh's critique of Abelard's work. On the other hand, there are instances where the *Summa* agrees with Abelard, whilst disagreeing with Hugh. But taken as a whole, the work can be said to represent the crystallization of anti-Abelardian thought in the school of St Victor. The genesis of the *Summa Sententiarum* is highly intricate, but Luscombe asserts that it was circulating by 1140.[7] Thus the *Ysagoge* must have been written after this date.

Odo's extensive use of the *Summa Sententiarum* points primarily in the direction of the Victorines, as does his more limited usage of Hugh of St Victor's *De sacramentis*. But Odo did also rely on Abelard and his school. His ideas on the Trinity, the Incarnation, and sin have a distinctly

---

[6] Luscombe, 'Authorship', pp. 9–16; *contra* R. W. Southern, *Medieval Humanism and Other Studies* (Oxford, 1970), p. 159, n. 1. I am grateful to the Master and Fellows of Trinity College, Cambridge, for allowing me to examine the MS.

[7] D. E. Luscombe, *The School of Peter Abelard* (Cambridge, 1970), pp. 198–213 and 'Authorship', p. 13.

Abelardian flavour. As we shall see, he incorporated a chunk of Abelard's *Commentaries on Romans* in his discussion of Jewish objections to the Incarnation. And he relied heavily on the *Petri Abelardi epitome theologie Christiane* by Hermann, a pupil of Abelard, which would have been composed by 1139.[8] Richard Southern has pointed to the fact that the arguments in the *Ysagoge* concerning the rationale of the Incarnation are similar to those in Anselm's *Cur Deus homo*.[9] Avrom Saltman has drawn attention to Odo's borrowings of Gilbert Crispin's *Disputatio Iudei et Christiani*, and has hinted at some parallels between the *Ysagoge* and Pseudo-William of Champeaux's *Dialogus inter Christianum et Iudeum* (written between 1123 and 1148).[10] Parallels can probably also be drawn with Pseudo-Anselm's *Dialogus inter Gentilem et Christianum* (written before the second half of the twelfth century).[11] One work which Odo does not seem to have known is Peter Lombard's *Sentences*, which appeared after 1150.[12] This indeed concurs with the evidence we have already mustered that the *Ysagoge* must have been written before 1148.

The *Ysagoge* is divided into three books. The first concerns the creation of man, the branches of knowledge, the virtues, the fall of man, and sin. The second is devoted to the redemption of man, starting with a discussion of the efficacy of the Law of Moses as a remedy for sin, and leading up to the necessity of the Incarnation via the so-called Christological promises of salvation in the Prophets. The book closes with a detailed examination of the sacraments. The third book of the text treats of the angels and the divine nature of the triune God. It is especially in the second, but also in the third, book that Odo comes to consult and to quote the Old Testament in Hebrew. Indeed, it is his use of Hebrew that constitutes Odo's claim to originality.

---

[8] For a list of Odo's sources see the relevant index in Landgraf's edition, pp. 309–12. See also O. Lottin's review of the edition in *Bulletin de théologie ancienne et médiévale*, 2 (1935), pp. 415*–16*. On Hermann, see Luscombe, *The School of Peter Abelard*, pp. 158–64.

[9] R. W. Southern, *Saint Anselm and his Biographer* (Cambridge, 1963), p. 91, n. 2.

[10] A. Saltman, 'Gilbert Crispin as a source of the anti-Jewish polemic of the *Ysagoge in theologiam*', in P. Artzi, ed., *Bar-Ilan Studies in History*, 2: *Confrontation and Coexistence* (Ramat Gan, 1984), pp. 89–99, and 'Odo's *Ysagoge*—a new method of anti-Jewish polemic', *Criticism and Interpretation*, 13–14 (1979), pp. 265–80 (in Hebrew). On Pseudo-William of Champeaux's dialogue see my 'Jewish-Christian disputations and the twelfth-century renaissance', *JMedH*, 15 (1989), pp. 105–25.

[11] On this work see my 'Christians disputing disbelief: St Anselm, Gilbert Crispin and Pseudo-Anselm', in *Conference proceedings of 25 Wolfenbütteler Symposium, 11. bis 15. Juni 1989* (forthcoming).

[12] See Lottin's review, cited in n. 8, above. On the dating of the Sentences see Luscombe, *The School of Peter Abelard*, p. 262.

In the prologue to book ii Odo almost at once points to the vital role that the Hebrew language has to play in Christian–Jewish relations. The builders of the tower of Babel sought to challenge God; the fragmentation of human language was nothing but their just desert. But all these different languages were brought together again in a holy way by those wise architects embarked on building a true tower of celestial ascent. For a common language is what inclines human beings to lead a life together, whilst discordance of tongue is a powerful force that separates them. That is why the Church has always had in its midst those who could teach unbelievers in their own tongue. Thus no one who wished to join the fold was prevented from doing so. In the same way, Christians today must learn Hebrew so that they can reach out to recall the Jews from their erroneous sect. In any case, if Christians spend time discussing the meaning of the divine page, how can they not take on those who are the enemies of the Catholic faith?[13] We see here how Odo immediately draws the link between Jewish understanding of the Hebrew Bible and the inimical separation between Christians and Jews. And it is clear that for him the end of all divisiveness between nations lies in the unity of the Church. Hebrew is seen here as the prerequisite to getting a Jewish audience; the purpose of getting that audience is, of course, a Christian one.

Odo goes on to say that Christians would be more successful in converting Jews if they relied on biblical arguments rather than on rational ones. Odo is no opponent to philosophy—his treatment, for example, of the person of Christ precludes any such suggestion[14]—but he feels that it is in the area of Hebrew studies that Christians still need to establish their superiority over Jews. As far as Hebrew is concerned, the Jew in a religious debate with a Christian is still Goliath. Whenever he wishes, the Jew can say that the Hebrew Bible does not contain what the Christian says it does. This must come to an end. And it can, if, and only if, Christians will concentrate on the Hebrew language with the same fervour with which they have hitherto assimilated philosophy. For the message of Christ was written in Hebrew before it was translated into Greek and Latin. Following Jerome, Odo claims that what was crystal clear in the original was not always plainly conveyed in translation. It was thought too risky to expose pagan Greeks and Romans to the message of a triune God. But it is all there in the original Hebrew to be savoured by

[13] Landgraf edn., pp. 126–7.
[14] Ibid., pp. 162–5.

Christians. To clinch his argument Odo points out that Hebrew is read from right to left and not from left to right as Greek and Latin are. This points to the eclipse of the Jews by the Gentiles who heard and understood the message of Christ.[15]

Odo closes the prologue by unfolding his plan of action. Each time he quotes from the Old Testament he will give not only the Latin text, but also the Hebrew original, together with a Latin transliteration of the Hebrew. And he gives some instruction on the way he proposes to transfer Hebrew sounds into Latin characters. All this will serve those who still need to learn the Hebrew alphabet. In the event, this projected three-tiered system breaks down almost as soon as it is started. Only one Hebrew quotation is transliterated into Latin characters. And only four Hebrew quotations are punctuated. We cannot be absolutely sure whether this is the fault of the scribes involved in the preparation of the Trinity manuscript or whether Odo was loathe to put in all the work his ambitious plan required. It would seem, however, that the manuscript evidence does speak in Odo's favour. For in each case the Hebrew lines are spaced in such a way that there would have been ample room to accommodate the Latin transliteration. Moreover, when, on folio 61r, the Hebrew word for hell is incorporated into the Latin text, it is written first in Hebrew characters and then transliterated.[16] Finally, when, at the very end of the *Ysagoge*, Odo quotes a line in Greek, the words are written in Greek characters, followed by a Latin transliteration and translation. In other words, we do know that Odo was conscious of his three-tiered system throughout the text, and it would seem likely that he did provide the transliterations which have now disappeared.[17]

The immediate question is: where did Odo acquire his knowledge of Hebrew? And because the Trinity manuscript is not Odo's autograph,[18] we can ask the same of the scribe who supplied the Hebrew in the spaces provided for him by the Latin scribe. We know that a separate scribe was responsible for the Hebrew, because on folio 109v spaces left for the

---

[15] Ibid., pp. 127–8.

[16] The Hebrew characters used for the word '*sheol*' on fol. 61r seem different from the Hebrew characters used in the biblical quotation the word comes from. It seems that someone other than the Hebrew scribe wrote the word.

[17] Saltman argues that Odo and not a scribe is responsible for the system breaking down, in 'Odo's *Ysagoge*', pp. 272 and 273, where he discusses Odo's method of transliteration. J. Fischer argued the opposite in 'Die hebräischen Bibelzitate des Scholastikers Odo', *Biblica*, 15 (1934), pp. 52–3. Saltman (p. 266) points to the fact that the two existing fragments of the *Ysagoge* do not contain the Hebrew part of the text.

[18] The MS is written in more than one hand.

Hebrew have remained empty. On folio 46r the Hebrew scribe seems to have added a comment to Odo's Latin translation.[19] On folio 50r the Latin scribe left space for Hebrew where it was not needed. On folio 52r–v and elsewhere, too much space was left for the Hebrew text. The expert in Hebrew palaeography, Malachi Beit-Arié, has studied the Hebrew letters of this scribe, and he is in no doubt that the scribe was a Christian.[20] Indeed, the script is highly artificial, and it cannot be ascribed to a Jew.

Because we know no more about our author than that his name was probably Odo and that he was obviously *au fait* with what was going on in the French schools, we cannot say where and how he managed to learn enough Hebrew to do what he did. All we can say is that he does not stand alone in twelfth-century England in knowing Hebrew. A certain Maurice, writing between 1153 and 1181, claims to be prior of Kirkham and tells us that as a young man he spent three years learning Hebrew. He copied forty Psalms in Hebrew from the Hebrew manuscripts in the possession of Archbishop Gerard of York (1100–8). Unfortunately we know nothing more about this Maurice. As far as Gerard is concerned, we do know he had close links with Rouen, and it is from Rouen that Jews emigrated to England after the Conquest. And Gerard had the reputation of being a great scholar.[21] A far better-known figure is Herbert of Bosham, who served as a secretary to Thomas Becket, and who was a fine Hebraist. But Herbert probably learnt his Hebrew in France, where he resided during Becket's exile from 1164 to 1170.[22] It is quite possible that Odo too learnt his Hebrew there.

There is, of course, no comparison between Odo's knowledge of Hebrew and that of Herbert. Yet it must have been more than minimal. For the Hebrew quotations contained in the *Ysagoge* contain many elements which are inconsistent with the developing consensus amongst Odo's Jewish contemporaries about the correct spelling and vocalization of the Hebrew Bible. This led Fischer, who was responsible for the Hebrew in Landgraf's edition, to suppose that we have in the Hebrew sections of the *Ysagoge* an example of a forerunner of the Tiberian system

[19] Landgraf edn, pp. 142; 282. For Fischer's comments on fol. 109v see Landgraf edn, p. 282n, and his article 'Die hebräischen Bibelzitate', pp. 55, 81.

[20] Saltman, 'Odo's *Ysagoge*', p. 268.

[21] R. B. Dobson, *The Jews of Medieval York and the Massacre of March 1190* (York, 1974), pp. 3–5; R. Loewe, 'The Medieval Christian Hebraists of England: Herbert of Bosham and earlier scholars', *TJHSE*, 17 (1953), pp. 234–5.

[22] Loewe, 'The Medieval Christian Hebraists', pp. 240–5; Smalley, *The Study of the Bible*, pp. 186–95. See also Saltman, 'Odo's *Ysagoge*', pp. 267–9.

of vocalization which was in due course incorporated in the masoretic text.[23] This tantalizing view was, however, almost immediately discredited by Peters. Peters brings us back to earth by showing that Odo's Hebrew is strongly influenced by the Latin not only of the Vulgate, but also of the *Vetus Latina*.[24] Saltman even adds to this the version of Old Testament texts as they are found in the New Testament.[25] All this must mean that our Odo knew enough Hebrew to work from a Latin text back to the Hebrew, and that he was not simply copying the words from a Hebrew Bible. It also confirms what we have already surmised: Hebrew is used here for none other than for Christian purposes.

The second book of the *Ysagoge* starts with a discussion of the Law of Moses. A great deal of the discussion derives from the *Summa Sententiarum*. Mosaic law was intended to repair the damage done to natural law by sin. And it would prepare its recipients for the truth to come with the coming of Christ.[26] It is with the listing of the Ten Commandments that Odo starts using his Hebrew. But what he does seems more geared to a Christian audience than a Jewish one. The only direct allusion to the Jewish–Christian debate is when he records the Jewish challenge to Christians that they are guilty of idolatry. As Gilbert Crispin did before him, Odo refers Jews to Moses' and Solomon's activities in decorating the Tabernacle and Temple. He concludes that the prohibition against idolatry concerns the making of images in order to serve them.[27]

In discussing the fifth commandment prohibiting murder, Odo follows the *Summa Sententiarum* by explaining that homicide is committed in three ways: by hand, by tongue, and by consent. The Jews killed Christ by their mouths.[28] When Odo examines the seventh commandment against theft, he states that theft comprises *sacrilegium et rapina*. And he quotes Jerome and Augustine to prove that usury is a form of robbery. All

---

[23] Fischer, 'Die hebräischen Bibelzitate', pp. 84ff.

[24] C. Peters, 'Aussermasoretische Überlieferung in den Zitaten des Scholastikers Odo?', *Muséon*, 51 (1938), pp. 137–49; see also Loewe, 'The Medieval Christian Hebraists', pp. 245–6.

[25] Saltman, 'Gilbert Crispin', pp. 94–5.

[26] Landgraf edn, p. 132; *Summa Sententiarum* [hereafter *SS*] IV, 2; *PL* 176, col. 120.

[27] Landgraf edn, pp. 134–5; Gilbert Crispin, *Disputatio Iudei et Christiani*, 155–6, ed. A. Sapir Abulafia, in A. Sapir Abulafia and G. R. Evans, eds, *The Works of Gilbert Crispin. Auctores Britannici Medii Aevi*, 8 (London, 1986) [hereafter *Disp. Iud.*], pp. 51–2. Odo and Crispin do not use exactly the same references.

[28] Landgraf edn, p. 136; *SS* IV, 4: *PL* 176, col. 122. In Odo's numbering of the commandments what would be the two initial commandments according to Jewish tradition is counted as commandment one. Commandments nine and ten according to this reckoning are what is the last commandment according to Jewish tradition. Later on Odo refers to the torments Christ would have suffered at the hands of the Jews (Landgraf edn, p. 149).

this comes straight from the *Summa Sententiarum*; no mention is made of Jewish usury. Indeed, the section ends with the statement that the Hebrews did not break this commandment when they despoiled the Egyptians before leaving Egypt. For they simply did what God told them to do.[29] A final point of interest is found in the analysis of the eighth commandment forbidding the giving of false testimony. Again using the *Summa Sententiarum*, Odo discusses what it is to tell a lie. He comes to the conclusion that you can tell a lie even when you speak the truth. His example is a Jew declaring that the Son of God is God and man. According to Odo and the model he used, the Jew is speaking the truth here; none the less he is lying, because he is speaking against what he feels in his soul.[30]

Odo then moves on to the Prophets. For a while the *Summa Sententiarum* is set aside as he launches into a fairly typical array of the Christological texts which were used in the Jewish–Christian debate. Odo uses Hebrew here to prove to Jews and to confirm for Christians that the language of the Hebrew Bible contains the message of Christ. Using many of the words of Gilbert Crispin, he closes this section by asking the Jews what they are waiting for and for how long they plan to wait now that it is clear that all the words of the Prophets about the coming of the Messiah have been fulfilled. The Jews have been trampled underfoot throughout the world; while at the same time all the nations gather to Jerusalem to worship Jesus Christ. The reference here is probably to the Crusades.[31]

By far the most interesting moment in this section of the *Ysagoge* is when Odo comes to the well-known passage in Baruch 3.36–8 which says: 'This is our God; and there shall no other be accounted of in comparison of him. He found out all the way of knowledge and gave it to Jacob his servant, and to Israel his beloved. Afterwards he was seen on earth and conversed with men.' Gilbert Crispin had used the same passage in his disputation. But whereas Gilbert was aghast that his Jewish opponent disclaimed all knowledge of this part of the Old Testament,[32] Odo writes that if a Jew claims he has not read these words he is probably speaking the truth. For neither the Books of Judith, Tobias, and the Maccabees, nor the

---

[29] Landgraf edn, p. 149.

[30] Ibid., p. 138; *SS* IV, 5: *PL* 176, col. 123.

[31] Landgraf edn, pp. 153–4; *Disp. Iud.*, 162, p. 53. Gilbert does not mention the trek to Jerusalem. His work was probably composed a few years prior to the First Crusade. See my comments in *The Works of Gilbert Crispin*, pp. xxvii–xxx.

[32] *Disp. Iud.*, 85, 130, pp. 28–9; 43–4. Saltman was the first to notice this, see 'Odo's *Ysagoge*', pp. 276–80. The translation I give of biblical passages comes from the 1914 official English translation of the Vulgate. Where the Hebrew reference differs from the Vulgate it is given in brackets.

Books of Wisdom and Baruch are in Jewish hands today. All they have are some excerpts in Hebrew taken from the Greek version of Judith, Tobias, and the Maccabees. Odo explains that the books of the Hebrew Bible were destroyed by Nebuchadnezzar. The Hebrews preserved only what Ezra had rewritten from memory and what others received from the Greeks.[33] It is indeed not without reason that Odo does not give a Hebrew text for his quotation from Baruch.

The fact that Odo can go beyond Crispin's brittle cry that every word of the Latin Bible corresponds to the right word in the Septuagint, and beyond that to the correct word in the Hebrew Bible,[34] does not mean that he has any doubts of his own about the canonicity of the Book of Baruch. He remains convinced that Baruch faithfully recorded the words of Jeremiah.[35] Whatever one may think about his ideas about the transmission of the Hebrew Bible, one has to admit that his Hebrew studies did alert him to the discrepancies between the Jewish and Christian canons of the Bible. Saltman sees in Odo's words a further indication of twelfth-century revival in Christian interest in Jerome's textual work and the corresponding decline of support for the Septuagint. Jerome did not think the Book of Baruch belonged to the prophecy of Jeremiah.[36]

Having dealt with what he regards as scriptural proofs for the coming of Christ, Odo is now ready for the rational arguments which the scholars of the Twelfth-century Renaissance were so keen to find for the Incarnation. As he puts it himself, 'Because your disbelief, O Jew, either does not know or pretends not to know the reasons of the mystery of our redemption, let us start with your objections on the subject.'[37] But what follows is nothing else than a recasting of Peter Abelard's commentary on Romans 3. 26.[38] Chapter 23, 'Cur Deus homo' of Hermann's *Epitome* seems to have been used too.[39] In the footsteps of Anselm of Canterbury and Abelard, Odo takes the view that the Devil did not have jurisdiction over man after the Fall. Man was, therefore, not redeemed from the Devil by Jesus' death. Why, then, was the Incarnation necessary; could God in his omnipotence

---

[33] Landgraf edn, p. 143.
[34] *Disp. Iud.*, 122, pp. 40–1.
[35] Landgraf edn, p. 143.
[36] Saltman, 'Odo's *Ysagoge*', pp. 273–80.
[37] Landgraf edn, p. 155.
[38] Abelard, *Commentaria in Epistolam Pauli ad Romanos*, II (iii, 26) ed. E. M. Buytaert, *Petri Abaelardi opera theologica*, I, CChr.CM, 11 (1969) [hereafter *Comm. in Rom*], pp. 113–17: 'Through the forbearance of God, for the shewing of his justice in this time: that he himself may be just and the justifier of him who is of the faith of Jesus Christ.'
[39] *PL* 178, cols 1730–2.

not simply have pardoned mankind for Adam's sin? Why was it necessary for God to undergo spitting, flagellation, and a most shameful death in order to redeem man?[40] The parallels with Anselm's *Cur Deus homo* are obvious.[41]

What is also obvious is that this section, which Odo entitled *Oppositiones Iudeorum*,[42] has merged with internal Christian deliberations about the central doctrine of their faith. Almost immediately we are referred to Christian disagreement about whether or not Jesus saved man from the Devil. Jews are not mentioned at all. At the very end of the section Odo rephrases the relevant phrase in Abelard's commentary to say, 'Because this and similar material, which we have introduced from an opponent under the guise of an unbeliever, impels the important question of our redemption, let us repel him who argues in vain by putting forward the reasons transmitted by the Fathers concerning the Incarnation and death of Christ.'[43] But the person whom Odo addresses in this section as 'you' is hardly an 'unbelieving' Jew. For Odo speaks of 'your John [the Baptist]' and 'your Gospel'.[44] At the most, Odo's opponent is a nominal Christian coming up with a number of sticky questions concerning the rationale of the Incarnation. The fact, of course, is that Odo and others were fully aware that the core of this questioning overlapped with the basic Jewish position that the proposition of God assuming flesh was unthinkable. In Christian terms the question was *Cur Deus Homo*?[45]

It is, therefore, hardly surprising that Odo continues with expounding the necessity of the Incarnation. It is in the midst of a passage asserting that before the Incarnation no man was saved that Odo once again turns to Hebrew. He wants to prove that the Hebrew Bible confirms the Christian

---

[40] Landgraf edn, pp. 155–8.

[41] *Cur Deus homo* I.3 and *passim*, ed. F. S. Schmitt, *S. Anselmi opera omnia*, 2 (Edinburgh, 1946), p. 50 and *passim*. See also Luscombe, *The School of Peter Abelard*, pp. 238–40.

[42] Landgraf edn, p. 155. The title is given in a rubric of the MS (fol. 58v) and in the table of contents (fol. 37r).

[43] Landgraf edn, p. 158: 'Quoniam et hec et his similia, que ex adverso sub persona infidelis induximus, non mediocrem movent de nostra redemptione questionem, incarnationis et mortis Christi rationes a patribus traditas afferendo frustra arguentem refellamus.' The relevant sentence in Abelard is in *Comm. in Rom.* II (III.26), p. 117: 'Haec et similia non mediocrem movere quaestionem nobis videntur, de redemptione scilicet vel iustificatione nostra per mortem Domini nostri Jesu Christi.'

[44] Landgraf edn, p. 157.

[45] On Southern's views on the relationship between the Jews and Anselm's *Cur Deus homo* see his *Saint Anselm. A Portrait in a Landscape* (Cambridge, 1991), pp. 198–202; for my own position see my 'St Anselm and those outside the Church', in D. Loades and K. Walsh, eds, *Faith and Identity: Christian Political Experience* — SCH.S, 6, pp. 11–37.

view that everyone was doomed to go to hell before the coming of Christ. The view is essential if one wants to argue that man needed to be redeemed by God-man. Jews, of course, denied that their holy ancestors, such as the Patriarchs, ever entered hell. Thus Odo declares that the use of the word '*sheol*' in Psalm 48(9). 16 ('God will redeem my soul from the hand of hell when he shall receive me') proves that '*sheol*' does not always mean 'pit', as Jews say it does. Here it clearly means hell. Odo addresses his words directly to Jewish opposition here.[46] This passage bears a marked resemblance to Crispin's *Disputatio Iudei*.[47] Odo carries on with his proof that God had to become man by continuing to make use of Crispin and, especially, St Anselm. He will not use Hebrew again until the very end of the third and final book of the *Ysagoge*.

The rest of book ii concerns what one might call the mechanics of uniting divine and human nature in the person of Christ and a full discussion of that person. Interesting is the Abelardian emphasis that Odo places on Christ's role as an example for man.[48] Odo completes the book with a full discussion of the sacraments of the Church.[49]

Odo ends his third book, which concerns angels and God, by attempting to show that proof-texts from both the Old Testament and Greek philosophy demonstrate what the Church holds to be true concerning the triune God. In a breath-taking adaptation of the Mosaic principle in Deuteronomy 19. 15, that 'in the mouth of two or three witnesses every word shall stand', Odo says: 'Let the unbeliever become still when he hears faithful witnesses assert the same in Hebrew, Chaldean (by which he means Aramaic) and Greek.'[50]

For all his reliance on Gilbert Crispin for his anti-Jewish polemical material, the author of the *Ysagoge* is not taking the abbot of Westminster's lead here. In Gilbert's eyes it was only proper to discuss the

---

[46] Landgraf edn, pp. 160–1.

[47] *Disp. Iud.*, 97–9, p. 33. It is closer to Crispin than to a similar passage in Pseudo-William of Champeaux, *Dialogus inter Christianum et Iudeum* (*PL* 163, cols 1050–1), where an interesting discussion follows on what the actual position of the saints of the Old Testament was in hell.

[48] Landgraf edn, pp. 170, 177.

[49] Ibid., pp. 179–219. Marriage is one of the sacraments Odo lists. He is not particularly positive about it, seeing it more as an indulgence and a remedy for evil than as something good for its own sake. The manner in which an exposé on the sacraments follows an analysis of the Incarnation reminds us of Pseudo-Anselm, *Dialogus inter Gentilem et Christianum*. This twelfth-century dialogue is a recasting of Anselm's *Cur Deus homo* into a debate between a Christian and a pagan. Once the pagan converts to Christianity, the Christian, taking on the role of a master, instructs him in the sacraments of Baptism and the Eucharist. See my 'Christians disputing disbelief' (forthcoming).

[50] Landgraf edn, p. 279.

Trinity amongst believers. He, for one, did not believe that Christians could prove the triunity of God from Old Testament texts.[51] Here Odo seems rather to be following Abelard's ideas concerning God's double or parallel revelation of himself through the Prophets of Israel and the true philosophers of the Gentiles.[52]

Odo proceeds to give the original Hebrew for some of the standard texts Christians tended to use when they discussed the Trinity with Jews: for example, Genesis 1. 26, 'Let *us* make man to *our* image'; Isaiah 6. 3, 'Holy, Holy, Holy the Lord God of hosts, all the earth is full of his glory.' And he quotes Aramaic by citing Daniel 3. 92(25) where Nebuchadnezzar says, '[I see four men loose, walking in the midst of the fire, and there is no hurt in them:] and the form of the fourth is like the Son of God.'[53] He concludes with some mangled Greek, which he ascribes to Plato, and which he translates as 'Father of everything, mind, world soul; one and two, an undivided substance.' This would prove that Plato knew that God is triune and that God the Father and his Wisdom and his Spirit are of the same substance.[54]

Odo, however, does not limit himself to the signification of the Hebrew words he musters for his argument. He delves into the spelling of the Hebrew words in order to prove his point. Thus he informs us that 'Adonai' ('The Lord' in Hebrew) is spelt in three different ways: (1) by using the Tetragrammaton; (2) by the use of three 'yods' ('yod' is the Hebrew letter 'i'); and (3) by writing 'Adonai' in Hebrew characters. The

---

[51] I discuss Gilbert's attitudes towards the Trinity in my 'Christians disputing disbelief'.

[52] See, for example, T. Gregory, 'The Platonic Inheritance', in P. Dronke, ed., *A History of Twelfth-century Western Philosophy* (Cambridge, 1988), pp. 57–60.

[53] Landgraf edn, p. 282. On Odo's alleged knowledge of Aramaic see Fischer's comment, Landgraf edn, pp. 142–3.

[54] Landgraf edn, p. 284. Landgraf says that he was unable to trace the reference. The transliteration given is 'Togatos nois cosmoisiche, apaz chaidis epichena usia' ('nois' seems to have been added by the scribe who wrote the Greek [fol. 111r]); the first three words are also given in painstakingly artificially-drawn Greek characters (fol. 110v): Θωγαθος νωυς κοσμωυκη. M. R. James suggested that 'Togatos nois cosmoisiche' is a corruption of τοῦ παντὸς νοῦς κόσμου ψυχή and 'apaz chaidis epichena usia' a corruption of ἅπαξ καὶ δὶς ἐπικοινὴ οὐσία: *The Western Manuscripts in the Library of Trinity College*, 1 (Cambridge, 1900), pp. 433–4. Because 'cosmoisiche' of the transliteration is closer to κόσμου ψυχή than κοσμωυκη, it would seem that what remains of the Greek is even more corrupt than the transliteration. But the fact that the transliteration itself is such a mess would seem to indicate that Odo had little Greek. His Hebrew was obviously much better. I am very grateful to Dr John Vallance of Gonville and Caius College, Cambridge, for his advice on this passage. He assures me that the words are not Plato's own. I have not yet been able to trace where exactly Odo got the Greek for this Abelardian reading of the *Timaeus*. See n. 52, above, for Abelard's references to Plato's alleged knowledge of the Trinity.

first two spellings indicate that God is ineffable; for the Hebrew letters in themselves do not join up to make the word 'Adonai' or any other word. The letters simply indicate that 'Adonai' is to be read. The second spelling Odo gives is the most fascinating. In his eyes God's name could not be written more appropriately; for what can express better the Trinity than the triple use of the same letter?[55]

Jews have traditionally used a number of combinations of letters to signify the unpronounceable name of God in their writings. Usually when 'yods' are used, two are written. Sometimes the two 'yods' are separated by a diacritical sign; sometimes they are followed by one. The sign, which can be quite similar in shape to a 'yod', serves to indicate that the letters stand for a word they do not actually spell. It is possible that Odo had seen the diacritical sign used and that he mistook it for a 'yod'. It is also possible that he did once see a Hebrew manuscript giving three 'yods' for 'Adonai'.[56] But it is equally possible that he simply amended Hebrew usage to what he thought was more convenient. What matters is Odo's conviction that not only the meaning of Hebrew but even its orthography is Christological. It was not without purpose that Odo had so strongly encouraged his co-religionists to take up the study of Hebrew.[57]

III

Jewish understanding of the Old Testament could arouse many different emotions in twelfth-century Christian scholars, ranging from anger and disgust to stimulating curiosity. Nor should one imagine that only one emotion at a time could be felt by any one scholar. Much depended on the particular setting in which he encountered Jews or Jewish ideas. What might be stimulating in the framework of private biblical studies could become hateful when it entered into the arena of the Jewish–Christian debate. Yet of one thing we can be certain: no Christian theologian coming face to face with the Jewish non-Christological reading of the Scriptures could remain indifferent to it. For that too much was at stake.

The scholars of the Twelfth-century Renaissance set into motion the development of the study of theology as a discipline. Slowly but surely classical philosophy, as it became known to them, was absorbed into their

---

[55] Landgraf edn, pp. 281–2. Odo has indeed used the triple 'yod' for 'God' in the Hebrew quotations he gives prior to this passage, e.g. p. 135 in the edition.
[56] V. Aptowitzer, *Das Schriftwort in der rabbinischen Literatur* (Vienna, 1906–15, repr. New York, 1970), p. 10, indicates that older MSS exist where the triple 'yod' is used.
[57] Landgraf edn, p. 127.

Christian view of God and creation. The same process of Christianization can, I believe, also be detected in Christian attitudes towards the materials which Jews were seen to offer Christianity. The Hebrew Bible, long since regarded as the Old Testament, became more than ever a Christian book. If and when Hebrew was used or at times rabbis were consulted on the Hebrew words of the Bible, this was done in order to learn more about Christian truths. Notwithstanding the fact that in the process good relations might be established between individual Jews and Christians, the purpose of this consultation went in one and only one direction. Christians were not supposed to engage in these activities in order to learn more about Judaism for its own sake. In fact, interest in Hebrew studies could prove to be dangerous. For within the existing paradigm of religious belief where there was room for only one perception of divine truth, too much sympathy for Jews could easily lead to doubts about absolute Christian truth or even the authority of the Church to interpret it. We know, for instance, that Herbert of Bosham at one time in his life did wonder whether Christians were right in their conceptions about Jesus Christ and how God would deal with them in the afterlife if they had got it wrong.[58] It is not without cause that Andrew of St Victor's own colleagues thought he was a Judaizer because he showed such interest in Jewish commentaries in his literal interpretation of the Bible. In the event, they could have worried less. Andrew was quite open about his view that a literal reading of the Bible was only the first step in comprehending the text. Moreover, on several occasions he used pejorative terms to describe the 'Hebreus' he was quoting. None the less, it does remain true that his biblical commentaries were strongly influenced by rabbinical thought. And that in itself could be seen as positing a danger to the authority of the Church.[59] The danger for Jews lay in the fact that Christians could and indeed did use against them what they had found to be useful in Jewish writings or the study of Hebrew. This type of anti-Jewish argument added many new dimensions to the Jewish–Christian debate. In the second half of the thirteenth century it culminated in the use of sections of the Talmud in an attempt to prove to Jews that Jesus Christ was the Messiah they were waiting for.[60]

[58] Smalley, *The Study of the Bible*, p. 192. Herbert speaks about his doubts in his *De vita S. Thomae*, III.3, ed. J. C. Robertson, *Materials for the History of Thomas Becket*, 3, RS (1877), pp. 212–15.

[59] Smalley, *The Study of the Bible*, pp. 149–72, 110–11; Loewe, 'The Medieval Christian Hebraists', pp. 238–40.

[60] On use of the Talmud in the Jewish–Christian debate see A. Funkenstein, 'Basic types of Christian anti-Jewish polemics', *Viator*, 2 (1971), pp. 381–2. Funkenstein makes the

The anti-Jewish polemic of the *Ysagoge* is so enmeshed in Christian theological issues that it is difficult to gauge exactly what success Odo hoped to achieve in converting Jews to his faith. All we can say is that he seems confident that his method of using Hebrew against Jews will work. The words of his prologue to book ii of the *Ysagoge* attest to that, as does his assumption that any unbeliever will fall silent when confronted with his proof-texts concerning the Trinity.[61] We have seen that the study of biblical Hebrew gave Odo a sharper understanding of Jewish attitudes towards the Apocrypha, but that is not to say that Odo underwent any significant changes of opinion on account of his interest in the language of the Jews. On the contrary, one might say that the Hebrew Odo cared about was not really the Hebrew language Jews knew. Odo's Hebrew was what one might call Christological Hebrew, for it was only that kind of Hebrew that could function as a unifying language of the Church.

In other words, the true implications of Odo's study of Hebrew is not flattering to the Jews or even beneficial to them if they wish to remain Jews. The implications of his studies can be none other than that Jews do not really know their own language. If they did, how could they remain insensitive to its inherent Christology? Christians had argued for centuries that Jews were incapable of understanding their own Bible. Odo's more learned approach, which involved going back to the original Hebrew meaning, and, at times, spelling of the words of the Old Testament, would seem to take the argument a step further. Whereas Christians had laid claim to the Hebrew Bible as their book, now Odo was claiming Hebrew as a Christian language rather than a Jewish one. In this sense one might say that Odo had Christianized Hebrew to the extent that Jews would no longer be able to identify themselves with it. It had been transformed into a common possession of Christians. And because Odo's view of the world was a Christian one, with the Church unifying mankind in Christ, continued Jewish refusal to accept the Christological meaning of the Hebrew words of the Old Testament had to be more than just an affront to Christendom. It had become a spoke in the attempt to bring mankind together through the Christianization of the world.

Lucy Cavendish College, Cambridge

---

important point that the increase in Christian knowledge of Judaism served to strengthen their stance against Jews. It did not make them more tolerant of Jews.

[61] The term 'infidelis' as used in this passage (Landgraf edn, p. 279) certainly includes Jews.

THE FAITH OF CHRISTIANS AND
HOSTILITY TO JEWS

by GAVIN I. LANGMUIR

THERE is a fundamental question that any historical analysis of the relations between Christianity and Judaism must face. What is the relation between the hostility that Christians have directed at Jews and their faith as Christians? It is a hard question to answer for both conceptual and evidential reasons. The conceptual problem is that historians may be misled by some of the theological categories which are so deeply embedded in the languages of Western culture. Let me give an example close to home. At the first conference of the Society, C. N. L. Brooke spoke of *the* Christian religion and of *the* Church with a capital 'C'.[1] Similarly, several titles of the volumes of *Studies in Church History* and many of the contributions in them have used 'the Church' as if there was such a thing as the universal Christian Church. Indeed, the style sheet for *Studies in Church History* states that a capital is required for 'the Church' where the universal Church is implied and gives as an example the sentence, 'The Church preaches tolerance'—an assertion that may seem passing strange in the context of this year's conference.

The danger of that usage is that it diminishes human responsibility by attributing agency to a theological *deus ex machina*, for the universal Church has no empirical existence except as a theological concept in some people's minds. When we look over the data available to the historian as historian, we cannot observe a single Christian Church or a single Christian religion. We can only detect a variety of Christian social organizations—sects, denominations, and churches—whose leaders pre-scribed differing beliefs and practices. To put it bluntly, the problem with this kind of discourse is that it admits, even relies on, the use of theological beliefs as premises for historical interpretation.

The problem has not passed unnoticed. In his introduction to the com-munications of the 1985 conference on 'Voluntary Religion', Collinson observed that the hegemony of ecclesiastical history, whether the history of the Church or of particular churches, celebrated 'more or less defensively and apologetically, the perdurance of institutionalized truth

---

[1] C. N. L. Brooke, 'Problems of the Church Historian', *SCH*, 1 (1964), pp. 1–19.

in the teeth of subversive error'.[2] That perdurance has had many effects, but one of the most tragic has been the way theological convictions have impeded historical understanding of Christian attitudes toward Jews. Perhaps that is why the formulation of our subject for this year has avoided the problem. Instead of a title in the hallowed form of 'The Church and Judaism', we have 'Christianity and Judaism'.

Unlike 'the Christian religion' or 'the universal Church', Christianity is an empirical term. It refers to the faith that millions of people through many centuries have had in the divinity of Jesus of Nazareth and to the beliefs, actions, and institutions by which they have expressed their faith in their Christ, and those phenomena are anything but uniform. At present, Christianity consists of an amazing diversity of Christians, Christian beliefs, and Christian religions or churches. And once that is recognized, obvious questions arise: Why is there such diversity? What dynamics are at work? The answer which springs to mind is that the faith of Christians and the ways they express it have varied throughout history and now vary immensely. To speak of faith, however, raises another conceptual problem. Because the term has been central in Christian theology, it also can block historical understanding. That happens whenever people speak as if there was a single entity called *the* Christian faith that historians could observe. But *the* Christian faith, like the universal Church, exists only as a theological concept. All historians can observe is an amazing diversity of faiths.

There is no single Christian faith, because faith is a mental state, an attribute of individual human beings. It cannot, save metaphorically, be attributed to societies, for a society does not have a mind. Churches transmit beliefs, but they do not have faith, only their individual members do. Church authorities may communicate ideas; they may exhort or command people to believe those ideas; and that indoctrination may produce a great similarity in the beliefs of those who listen. But faith is a much more mysterious matter. What each of those individuals makes of the ideas prescribed as beliefs depends on how he or she understands the words used to express them, on the associations they stimulate, and on the emotions they arouse; and that differs somewhat, at times greatly, from individual to individual. Moreover, the manifestly religious beliefs of each of those individuals are linked in complicated ways to personal beliefs about matters far removed from their creeds, and these beliefs will differ even more from individual to individual. Thus belief in the divinity of Jesus of Nazareth may be linked in complicated ways with specific conservative or liberal political convictions.

Faith is not simply an aggregate of beliefs. Even when individuals use identical words or rituals to profess specific religious beliefs, their acts of faith differ from individual to individual in content, quality, strength, occasion, and expression because the faith that informs those beliefs, whether that of the leaders of a church or of their followers, differs in varying degrees from individual to individual. For although beliefs and believing may be inseparable, believing is an ongoing activity very different from its expression in specific affirmations of belief.

Believing is a complex process with many components, many of which are hidden from the believer and from the historian, so that evidence for it is often lacking.[3] Genetic endowments, childhood nurture, social indoctrination, knowledge, psychological traits, specific social relations, and personal experiences all play a role. To these we might add free will. These and other components and their interactions differ in each individual. Consequently, individuals vary not only in their explicit beliefs, but also and more broadly in how and why they maintain the same explicit beliefs. They differ in what might be called their religiosity or the structure of their faith.

From this it follows that though there are Christian beliefs, there is no such thing as *the* Christian faith; there are only the faiths of Christian individuals. It also follows that, whatever we may say about Christian hostility to Jews, we cannot say that it is a result of *the* Christian faith. It can only be an expression of the faiths of individual Christians. And since their faiths have varied, so, too, has their hostility to Jews. Throughout the centuries, individuals who lived at approximately the same time, believed in the divinity of Jesus of Nazareth, and even adhered to the same Christian religion have varied markedly in faith and in their attitudes toward Jews.

Differences in faith and in attitudes to Jews and Judaism are evident in the earliest documents of Christianity. Paul was horrified to hear that some Christians in Corinth did not believe in immortality.[4] He feared that the Corinthians might be led astray from what he considered sincere and pure devotion to Christ, 'For if some one comes and preaches another

---

[3] For a brief and lucid description of some of the complexities involved in believing, see Jonathan Glover, *I: The Philosophy and Psychology of Personal Identity* (London, 1988), pp. 139–63. For a longer discussion see my *History, Religion, and Antisemitism* (Berkeley, 1990), pp. 143–76.

[4] I Cor. 5. 1.

Jesus than the one we have preached, or if you receive a different spirit from the one you received, or if you accept a different gospel from the one you accepted, you submit to it readily enough.'[5]

Particularly revelatory is the dispute between Paul and James that led to the cleavage between Gentile Christians and Judeo-Christians.[6] It demonstrates how much differences in upbringing or culture affected the way in which Christians believed in Jesus. Unfortunately, we can say little about variations in attitudes to non-Christian Jews at that early date, because we only have evidence of Paul's attitudes, and it is even difficult to determine what his attitude was, because his language was so ambivalent and ambiguous that scholars still argue about its meaning.[7] None the less, it seems clear that he was both proud of being a Jew and critical of Judaism,[8] an ambivalence that would be used later to justify both protection of Jews and attacks on them.

When we come to the Gospels, differences in faith and in attitudes to Jews are obvious. The texture of the faith expressed in the basically narrative Gospels of Mark and Luke differs noticeably from that expressed in the theologizing Gospel attributed to John. Thus, whereas Mark cites Hebrew Scripture 70 times and Luke 109 times, the fourth Gospel does so only 27 times.[9] That difference is paralleled by a great difference in their attitudes to non-Christian Jews. The description of Jesus' trial and death in the fourth Gospel is not only much longer than in Mark and Luke, but also makes the Jews collectively responsible for Jesus' death in a way they do not.

Variations in belief and in the texture of faith in the next three centuries are so obvious as to need little comment. The faith in Christ of those involved in the debates about the Trinity and the substance of Christ that led to the Council of Nicaea differed so greatly that they could not even agree on a verbal formulation of the central belief that made them Christians. At the same time, the way Christians believed in Christ was being changed in fundamental, if less conscious, ways as a result of syncretism. The influence of Neoplatonism significantly altered the texture of faith of Christian theologians, deflecting their attention from empirical diversity, and linguistic differences and the division of the

[5] II Cor. 11. 4.
[6] Gal. 2; Acts 15.
[7] See John G. Gager, *The Origins of Anti-Semitism* (New York, 1985).
[8] Rom. 3–11; I Cor. 9. 19.
[9] *The Anchor Bible: The Gospel According to John*, tr. Raymond E. Brown (Garden City, NY, 1966), p. lix.

Roman Empire laid the ground for the emergence of two distinct churches.

By 400 there was great hostility to Jews, but also great variation in attitudes to Jews. On the one hand, there were the attacks on synagogues, Ambrose's support of them, and the intense hostility of John Chrysostom's homilies. On the other hand, the fact that most Christians in Antioch were friendly to Jews was what provoked Chrysostom's anger. The anti-Judaism of ecclesiastical officials such as Chrysostom and Ambrose was counterbalanced by an equally strong philo-Judaism among the people, including some of the clergy.[10] Despite those differences, however, or partly because of them, by 400, individual churchmen had developed the basic elements of the doctrine about Jews and Judaism that would endure almost to the present.[11]

The doctrine was not set forth in an official document. It existed as ideas scattered through the writings of individual theologians and ecclesiastics from Paul to Augustine. Taken together, they asserted that Judaism was superseded, that Jews could not understand the spiritual meaning of their own scriptures, that they had killed Christ, that though they were being divinely punished for it, their continued existence served to demonstrate the truth of Christianity, that they should therefore not be killed but be protected in a degraded condition, and that their remnant at the end of days would be saved. This teaching did not express what all Christians believed either then or later, but it decisively influenced ecclesiastical teaching, preaching, and legislation about Judaism and Jews in the long run because it was elaborated by individuals who came to be considered Fathers of the Church.

Its influence, however, was anything but uniform over time or at any given time. For though the doctrine clearly condemned Judaism and Jews, it did so in a remarkably ambivalent way. On the one hand, it condemned Jews for the greatest of conceivable crimes and demanded that they be degraded and made to serve Christians; on the other, it gave Jews a central role in providential history, protected them in the practice of their religion, prohibited attacks on them, and encouraged their conversion. The doctrine was also ambiguous in its practical implications. Couched for the most part in rather abstract terms, it did not specify with any

---

[10] Marcel Simon, *Verus Israël*, 2nd edn (Paris, 1964), pp. 257–9, 272.

[11] James Parkes, *The Conflict of the Church and the Synagogue* (London, 1934; New York, 1969), pp. 95–107; Simon, *Verus Israël*, pp. 93–117, 166–213; Rosemary Reuther, *Faith and Fratricide* (New York, 1979), pp. 117–81.

precision how Christians should react concretely to the Jews in their midst in various situations. Consequently, individual Christians could and did emphasize some features and neglect others in order to justify almost antithetically different attitudes toward Jews and treatment of them. In the second half of the fifth century, Bishop Hilary of Arles would not even exchange salutations with a Jew. But Bishop Sidonius Apollinarius of Clermont-Ferrand recommended a Jew to Bishop Eleutherius of Blandin with the comment that, though the error of Jews that brought them to perdition did not please him, 'we ought not to declare any of them irremediably damned.'[12]

At times, indeed, the doctrine was neglected almost completely. From the fall of Rome down to the eleventh century, the doctrine had almost no influence on how most Christians thought about or treated Jews, as can be seen from Archbishop Agobard of Lyons's inability to persuade the Carolingian Emperor Louis the Pious to treat Jews more harshly.[13] But after the watershed in medieval history around the year 1000, the character of faith in western Europe changed radically. The new image of Jesus of Nazareth as a suffering human being emerged, a new church organization was created, and new techniques of scholarship were developed. At the same time, there was a sudden increase in hostility to Jews, the first great massacres of them, and a rash of polemics against Judaism.

I shall not try to explain why those changes in Christianity brought a decisive change in attitudes towards Jews.[14] Suffice it to say that they did. What is striking for my present purposes is that, if we look beneath those generalities, we can detect great variations both in people's faith and in their attitudes toward Jews. A glaring example is the contrast between the faith of the Christians who massacred Jews in 1096 during the First Crusade and the faith of the bishops who tried to prohibit such attacks and of the citizens who tried to shelter them. The example is interesting because it indicates something frequently observable, to wit, that people's faith and their attitudes to Jews have tended to vary according to their social status and education. But great variations can also be observed in people of high status, great education, and indisputable devotion to Christ, as the following example demonstrates.

Probably at no time in the Middle Ages and at no time thereafter,

---

[12] Bernhard Blumenkranz, *Les Auteurs chrétiens latins du moyen âge* (Paris, 1963), pp. 43, 67.
[13] See Bernhard Blumenkranz, *Juifs et chrétiens dans le monde occidental, 430–1096* (Paris, 1960).
[14] I have tried to do so in *Toward a Definition of Antisemitism* (Berkeley, 1990), pp. 100–33.

except for the early years of the Reformation, were people so focused on their faith and its implications as in the first half of the twelfth century, roughly from the First to the Second Crusade. Eremetic evangelists were traversing Europe, preaching to lay people and founding new monastic orders. Popes and canon lawyers were establishing a new kind of church organization. Thinkers from Anselm to Peter the Lombard were elaborating a new kind of theology. Bishops, abbots, and architects were changing church architecture from the great Romanesque of the third church at Cluny to the Gothic of Suger's Saint-Denis and the west façade of Chartres. These monumentally impressive developments laid the groundwork for what has been called the synthesis of the thirteenth century. Yet if we look at the lives of three prominent contemporaries, each of whom was well aware of the other two, we cannot help but be struck by the differences in their faith and in their attitudes to Jews.

Peter the Venerable was born in 1092 or 1094, just before the First Crusade, and died in 1156.[15] Vowed in infancy as an oblate, he entered Cluny and was made abbot of the Cluniac Order in 1122. The Order, founded in 909 and famous for its incessant liturgy, was the first and for long the only monastic order. With its wealthy houses stretched across Europe under the central authority of the abbot of Cluny, it provided a model of trans-European ecclesiastical organization before the Investiture Contest and the creation of the papally centralized Church. By 1122, however, Cluny had fallen on hard times, in part, perhaps, because the new papally organized Church provided a more effective bond between widely dispersed Christians.

Peter the Venerable's task was not easy. Cluny's finances were in such bad shape that he had to borrow from Christians and Jews. He also had to face the competition of the new monastic orders, which began to appear in northern Europe in 1084, above all, the competition of the Cistercians. To make matters worse for someone who believed that Christ ruled the world and that Christians should be united in harmony, Peter became anxiously aware that people he deemed heretics, people who believed in Christ but questioned the efficacy of the rituals on which Cluny was based, were multiplying alarmingly in Europe. Alarming also was his realization that the Muslims had not only arisen after Christ but had come to control a vast part of the world. And so, in an effort to defend his faith, Peter devoted most of his intellectual energies to writing treatises against

---

[15] For a more extensive discussion of Peter, see my *Toward a Definition of Antisemitism*, pp. 197–208.

the heretics, against the Muslims, whose Koran he was the first to have translated, and against the Jews. As he said, he could not suffer any or the slightest rejection of the Christian faith.

It is therefore not surprising that Peter hated Jews viciously and libellously. In 1146, on the occasion of the Second Crusade, he wrote to Louis VII of France that the Jews were more to be hated than the Saracens, and that they should not be killed but should be preserved in a life worse than death. He exhorted Louis to take their money, since it was all acquired immorally, and use it to support the crusade. And in 1147 he completed his great treatise against the Jews. It is the most substantial and interesting of the rash of new polemics against Jews that began to appear around 1100.[16] Most of the treatise is devoted to an unusually full development of the traditional arguments about passages in the Old Testament that Christians interpreted so as to prove the divinity of Jesus of Nazareth and the error of the Jews. Toward the end, however, Peter changed his argument dramatically.

It is as if he suddenly remembered that the arguments about the meaning of the Old Testament had never convinced Jews and felt the need for a new kind of argument. It may also have been because of his own obsession with doubts. In any case, he asked himself the fundamental question posed by Jewish disbelief: How do people acquire truth faith? It could not, he argued, be the result of authority, because there must first be faith before there can be acceptance of authority. It could not be reason, because the Greeks had reason but not the true faith. What creates faith is the experience of miracles, purposeful actions which, since they cannot be explained by reason, any reasonable person must recognize to be revelations of God. And taking that as established, Peter then gave his final and peculiarly empirical or, as he said, corporeal and solid argument for the truth of his beliefs. It was a miracle he claimed anyone could observe. Every year, at midnight on Easter Saturday, a miraculous fire would descend from heaven and light the lamps in the Holy Sepulchre to reveal that it was here that Christ rose from the dead to give eternal light to the world.[17]

One suspects that the proof was intended more to fortify Peter and other Christians in their faith than to convince Jews, for Peter knew that

---

[16] Heinz Schreckenberg, *Die christlichen Adversus-Judaeos-Texte* (11.–13 Jh) (Frankfurt am Main, 1988).

[17] Peter the Venerable, *Adversus Judeorum inveteratam duritiem*, ed. Yvonne Friedman, *CChr.CM*, 58 (1985), pp. 122–4.

Jews had no more been convinced by that miracle than they had by arguments about Scripture. But why not? Since Peter could not admit that there was anything wrong with his argument, something more had to be wrong with the Jews than Christians had realized. Starting with Paul, Christians had explained that Jews could not recognize that Christ was foreseen in their Scripture, because God had miraculously blinded them to the spiritual meaning of the Bible so that they could only understand its literal meaning. But why were these literal-minded people not convinced by a visible miracle? Peter angrily answered that they were not only spiritually blinded; even reason was extinct in them, or at least so buried that Jews were more like beasts than human beings.

It was said at the time that Peter was a man whom everyone loved, but it is a relief to turn from him to a more irrascible but much more impressive figure. Bernard of Clairvaux was born in 1091 and died in 1153. He was Peter's almost exact contemporary. Unlike Peter, he did not become a monk until he was twenty, and when he did, in 1111, he chose the new and struggling Cistercian Order, not the Cluniac Order, which he would later criticize severely. In contrast to Cluny, with its wealth and emphasis on liturgy, the Cistercians were severe ascetics who made love or charity the key symbol of their way of life. That concern with love was closely connected with the new image of Jesus, and the Order became a major propagator of the new worship of Mary. Its vision of salvation appealed so widely that recruits and donations poured into the Order.

To a remarkable extent, however, the Order owed its success to Bernard's charismatic appeal. He was made abbot of Clairvaux, the third daughter house of Cîteaux in 1115, and very soon thereafter he was the most influential Christian in Christendom. Whereas Peter the Venerable was rather literal minded, relied heavily on authority, loved ritual, and lived like a prince of the Church, Bernard was a ferocious ascetic. His theology, which he preached with unsurpassed eloquence, was mystical,[18] and there was no room for doubt in his faith. If he sometimes judged people he did not know unjustly, on the basis of other people's report, he was highly introspective, and he analysed what we would call empathy with sensitive insight and prized it highly.[19] However we characterize his faith, it was very different from Peter the Venerable's, as was his attitude

---

[18] Étienne Gilson, *The Mystical Theology of Saint Bernard* (London, 1940).
[19] St Bernard, *Liber de gradibus humilitatibus et superbiae*, *Opere di San Bernardo*, ed. Ferruccio Gastaldelli (Milan, 1984–7), 1, pp. 48–54.

to Jews. He could recognize that Christians as well as Jews lent money at interest, and he protected Jews.

Bernard was, of course, fully aware of the old anti-Judaic doctrine. He took it for granted and could summarize it succinctly. But he interpreted it according to the texture of his own faith, and it meant something very different to him than it did to Peter the Venerable, as the relative mildness of his exposition of it indicates.

> The Jews are for us the living words of Scripture, for they remind us of what our Lord suffered. They are dispersed all over the world so that by expiating their crime they may be everywhere the living witnesses of our redemption. ... Under Christian princes they endure a hard captivity, but 'they only wait for the time of their deliverance.' Finally, we are told by the Apostle that when the time is ripe all Israel shall be saved. But those who die before will remain in death.[20]

Though Bernard was the most influential preacher of the Second Crusade, summoning people to enlist by notably bellicose letters and sermons, he did not incite persecution of the Jews. On the contrary, he insisted that they should not be persecuted, killed, or even put to flight. When Rudolph, a Cistercian monk who was preaching the crusade in the Rhineland, defied the commands of the archbishop of Mainz and incited massacres of Jews, the archbishop appealed to Bernard for help. In response, Bernard not only condemned Rudolph in writing;[21] frail though he was toward the end of his life, he came in person, silenced Rudolph, and did all he could to stop the massacres. Yet if Bernard could love, he could also hate, and one person he hated was Peter Abelard.

Abelard was born in 1079 and died in 1142. Like Peter and Bernard he became a monk, but only when he was about forty, after a far wider experience of life than either Peter or Bernard, and he was impelled more by the force of circumstances than by choice. But once he became a monk, it seems that he carried his decision out as he did everything else—fully and without compromise.[22] Héloise aside, if she ever can be, what marked Abelard was the character of his faith and the form of expression it took. That he fully believed in the divinity of Jesus we have no reason to doubt. Bernard accused him of many things but not that. But the dynamics of

---

[20] *The Letters of St. Bernard of Clairvaux*, ed. Bruno Scott James (London, 1953), pp. 462–3.
[21] Ibid., pp. 465–6.
[22] Étienne Gilson, *Héloise and Abelard* (London, 1931), p. 68.

their faith in the divinity of Christ were very different. What so angered Bernard was Abelard's confidence in reason.

As Bernard saw it, Abelard was discussing the most sacred matters recklessly, opening things closed, changing things according to his pleasure, putting everything quite differently from what people were accustomed to hear, coining perverse dogmas, forging a new gospel, and making void the virtues of the Cross.[23] For Bernard, faith believed, it did not dispute. But for Abelard, as for the Scholastics after him, faith, reason, and disputation were quite compatible. Abelard's faith in his God-given power of reasoning did not conflict with his belief in Christ. Far from voiding the virtues of the Cross, his faith emphasized it.

> It seems to us that this is the way in which we have been justified in the blood of Christ, that [by persevering until death] . . . he bound us more fully to himself by love. . . . And so our redemption is that great love awoken in us by the passion of Christ, which not only frees us from the slavery of sin, but acquires for us the true liberty of the sons of God, that we may fulfil all things more by love of him than by fear.[24]

Since the constituents of Abelard's faith differed so markedly from those of Peter the Venerable or Bernard, we would expect Abelard's attitude to Jews to have differed equally. And so it did. His *Dialogue of a Philosopher with a Jew and a Christian* betrays none of the hostility so obvious in Peter the Venerable's bitter polemic.[25] His *Ethics* or *Scito te ipsum*—which Bernard forcefully condemned—showed an understanding of Jewish attitudes that far exceeded Bernard's qualified toleration.[26]

Abelard argued in the *Ethics* that whether an individual's actions should be judged good or evil depended not on the actions in and of themselves, but on the intentions that informed them.[27] To illustrate the implications of his position he gave examples that indicate his sharp awareness of realities around him. Moreover, being Abelard, he did not shrink from applying his conclusion to the most extreme case, the condemnation of Jews for the death of Christ. Abelard asserted that if those who did not know that Christ was God believed in conscience that

---

[23] *Letters of St. Bernard*, pp. 316–18.
[24] Peter Abelard, *Commentarium super S. Pauli epistolam ad Romanos*, PL 178, col. 836.
[25] *A Dialogue of a Philosopher with a Jew and a Christian*, tr. Peter J. Payer (Toronto, 1979).
[26] *Letters of St. Bernard*, p. 316.
[27] *Peter Abelard's Ethics*, ed. D. E. Luscombe (Oxford, 1971), p. xxxii.

Christ or his disciples ought to be persecuted, then they would have sinned more gravely had they not persecuted them.

Peter, Bernard, and Abelard were contemporaries who lived in northern France, spoke French, wrote in Latin, professed the same creed, were priests of the same Church, and were highly influential in that Church. It would be hard to find another medieval example of equally influential churchmen whose background was so similar. Yet these men differed markedly in faith and in their attitudes toward Jews. And since none of them knew much about real Jews, and all of them were mightily concerned with their faith in Jesus, we may safely conclude that the difference in their attitudes to Jews was primarily the result of the differences in their faiths. In other words, their attitudes toward Jews were a constituent of their faiths and not a reaction to the conduct of contemporary Jews, except for the Jews' disbelief in the person they called 'the hanged one'.

Yet if that is true in their case, it is not true of many other Christians then and thereafter. By the middle of the twelfth century a new cause of hostility was at work, indebtedness to Jewish money-lenders. By the middle of the twelfth century, when the commercial revolution had brought a rising demand for credit, and when the Jews in northern Europe had been excluded from most other occupations, Jews became disproportionately involved in money-lending. And at that time, and for the first time, they were stereotyped as usurers. There were, in fact, many Christians then and thereafter who lent money at interest, but, because of the prevailing religious hostility, the stereotype of usurer was applied above all to Jews.

Money-lenders have never been popular, and once the Jews were stereotyped as usurers, hatred focused on them for something that had nothing to do with their disbelief in Christ. Indeed, we can see that new motive of hatred already at work in Peter the Venerable, though not in Bernard or Abelard. Cluny's financial straits had forced Peter to borrow from both Christians and Jews, but he only blamed the Jews. And though the character of his faith would have made him very hostile to Jews anyway, his indebtedness to them increased it greatly, as we can see from the violence and distortions of his letter to Louis VII.

Indebtedness to Jews accounts for much of the hostility of many Christians from the middle of the twelfth century on. A good example is the massacre of 1190 at York, which Barrie Dobson has so ably described. The massacre was occasioned by the preaching of the Third Crusade, and the attack on the keep where the Jews had taken refuge was egged on by the wild preaching of a Premonstratensian canon, who was inspired, we may assume, purely by his religious convictions. In the attackers, however, hatred of the Jews as money-lenders played a major role. As soon as the massacre was over, the leaders went to York Minster to destroy the Jewish loan contracts kept there. In Dobson's words, 'The massacre was the product not only of misguided religious zeal but also of a calculated conspiracy of local notables intent on liquidating their debts to the Jews by force.'[28]

As we look back at that tragedy of 1190, we are likely to contrast what we might term the religious and secular motives at work. And we can see the same combination of contrasting motives at work in the massacres accompanying later crusades and in the way kings used religious considerations to justify the confiscations and exiles they imposed on Jews. Yet if we ourselves see a sharp contrast, that is because our knowledge of economics, the nature of our faith, and our attitudes to Jews are very different from those of the participants in medieval massacres. At that time most people did not distinguish between Jews as usurers and as Christ-killers. Their belief that Jews were evil usurers was part of their religious faith.

As Innocent III would put it in 1205, the Jews were Christ-killers who sought by their usury and in other ways to get back at Christians because they were Christians. They were attacking Christians 'like a mouse in the pocket, a snake around the loins, a fire in the breast'.[29] The importance of the Jew as a religious symbol was so great for Christianity then that the symbol pulled everything Jews did into its religious orbit. Indeed, it even induced Christians to attribute conduct to Jews that existed only in the imagination of Christians. They came to believe that Jews crucified Christian children, consumed their blood, and poisoned wells to destroy all of Christianity.[30]

These are but a few examples of the ways in which differences in faith affected attitudes to Jews. There many other illustrations—for example, the contrast between the absence of hostility in Francis of Assisi and the remarkably moderate hostility of Thomas Aquinas, on the one hand, and the virulence of later friars, such as Giovanni da Capistrano, Bernardino da Siena, Bernardino da Feltre, and Vincent Ferrer, on the

---

[28] R. B. Dobson, *The Jews of Medieval York and the Massacre of March 1190 = Bothwick Papers*, no. 45 (York, 1974), p. 26.

[29] Solomon Grayzel, *The Church and the Jews in the Thirteenth Century*, 1, 2nd edn (New York, 1966), no. 18; see also nos. 14, 17, and 24.

[30] See my *Toward a Definition of Antisemitism*, chs 8–12.

other. Another highly relevant example would be the peculiar hostility to Jews and Judaism of certain Jews who had converted to Catholicism.

I have concentrated here on medieval Christians because I am a medieval historian. Were I a modernist, I would have used other examples where the differences in faith are easier to demonstrate. After 1521 it becomes possible to examine not only the effect on attitudes to Jews of subtle differences in the faiths of Christians who adhered to the same church, but also the effect of obvious differences in faith made explicit by adherence to the new churches. Just as Luther's and Calvin's prescriptions of belief differed, so also did their attitudes to Jews. A simple example is the contrast between Luther's famous, or rather infamous, pamphlet on *The Jews and Their Lies* and Calvin's relatively calm pamphlet, *A Response to the Questions and Objections of a Certain Jew*.[31] And their attitudes influenced their followers.

Another example worth investigation would be the seventeenth-century debate in England about the readmission of Jews and the diverse reactions at the time to Menasseh ben Israel's treatise, *The Hope of Israel*. Or, to jump to the later nineteenth century, when intense nationalism infused the faith of many Christians, it would be interesting to examine the contrast between Adolf Stöcker and his contemporary Hermann Strack. Stöcker, 'the second Luther' and court preacher at Berlin, hated Jews bitterly. Strack, also a Lutheran and Professor of Theology at Berlin, wrote courageously in their defence. Were we to go on to the twentieth century, we could find further, often painful, material—for example, how Christians before 1945 varied in their reactions to what they knew about Hitler's treatment of Jews, and how their reactions varied after 1945, when they could not avoid knowledge of the horror of the camps.

Many other examples will spring to mind, but I hope the few I have presented are sufficient to demonstrate what I indicated at the outset. If we examine Christianity empirically and not through the lens of theological categories, it is clear that hatred of Jews is not a necessary result of belief in the divinity of Jesus of Nazareth. Neither is it an expression of something that never existed, *the* Christian faith or the universal Church. Christian hostility to Jews has been an expression of the faiths of individual Christians, and because their faiths have varied, so, too, have their attitudes to Jews. Let me give one final striking example.

---

[31] Martin Luther, *Works*, ed. Jaroslav Pelikan and Helmut T. Lehman (St Louis, Missouri, 1955–75), 47, pp. 137–306; John Calvin, 'Ad quaestiones et obiecta Judaei cuiusdam responsio', *Ioannis Calvini Opera*, 9, ed. Wilhelm Baum, Eduard Cunitz, and Eduard Reuss = *Corpus Reformatorum*, 37 (Brunswick, 1870), cols 657–74.

In 1962 James Parkes gave a paper about Jews at the first meeting of this society.[32] It was in 1931, however, thirty-one years earlier, that he first began to study the early relations of Christians and Jews in order to understand the origins of anti-Semitism.[33] The result was that courageous and singularly prescient book, *The Conflict of the Church and the Synagogue*, which was published in 1934 by the Soncino Press after the Oxford University Press had refused it. Parkes not only recognized, long before most people, the moral outrage of the horror that was developing in Germany, he was also the first to write a profound and scholarly work on Christian attitudes to Judaism in the first and formative centuries of Christianity.[34] Since then others, from Hans Libeschütz and Jacques Maritain to Rosemary Reuther and Gilbert Dahan, have followed in the path he blazed.[35] But Parkes was the first, and no one would have been happier than he that the Society's conference this year is devoted to 'Christianity and Judaism'.

Parkes was ordained in the Church of England and wrote theological treatises on the Trinity under the pseudonym John Hadham. By any normal definition he was a deeply committed Christian. In 1931, however, Parkes was not expressing the norms of scholarship of his day or the beliefs prescribed by his church. Objective study of the relations between Christianity and Judaism was still blocked by the hostile attitudes toward Jews that had been sanctified in Christendom and become part of Western culture. Before 1945 non-Jewish historical societies did not devote sessions, to say nothing of whole conferences, to the problem of relations between Christians and Jews. On the contrary, hatred of Jews was rising among non-Jews. A few Christians had indeed begun to think more positively of Judaism as an ally, because they had recognized that both Christianity and Judaism were seriously threatened by Marxism and

---

[32] James Parkes, 'Jews and Christians in the Constantinian Empire', *SCH*, 1 (1964), pp. 69–79.

[33] James Parkes, *Voyage of Discoveries* (London, 1969), p. 120.

[34] See also his *The Jew in the Medieval Community* (London, 1938). It concludes (p. 387) with the judgment that 'It was Christendom which decided that the price of that loyalty [of Jews to Judaism] should be psychological and social degradation.'

[35] E.g. Hans Liebeschütz, *Synagoga und Ecclesia* (Heidelberg, 1983), completed in 1938 but only published forty-five years later; Jacques Maritain, *Les Juifs parmi les nations* (Paris, 1938); Maurice Samuel, *The Great Hatred* (London, 1943); Jules Isaac, *Jésus et Israël* (Paris, 1948) and *Genèse de l'antisémitisme* (Paris, 1956); Marcel Simon, *Verus Israël*, 1st edn (Paris, 1948), 2nd edn (Paris, 1964); Léon Poliakov, *Histoire de l'antisémitisme* (Paris, 1955–77); Bernhard Blumenkranz, *Juifs et Chrétiens dans le monde occidental, 430–1096* (Paris, 1960); Edward H. Flannery, *The Anguish of the Jews*, 1st edn (New York, 1965), 2nd edn (New York, 1985); Reuther, *Faith and Fratricide*; Gilbert Dahan, *Les Intellectuels chrétiens et les juifs au moyen âge* (Paris, 1990).

Nazism. But most Christians were not concerned about the fate of Jews, and Christian hostility to Jews had by no means disappeared. It took Hitler's atrocities to tear the veil that had sanctified hostility toward Jews and blinded Christian and agnostic historians alike to the reality of Jews; and the great price for that liberation was paid by Jews, not Christians.

What moved Parkes in 1931 was not *the* Christian faith, *the* Church, or even the prescriptions of his own church; it was the nature of his unique religiosity. Why it was as it was is as difficult to say as it is for anyone else. As is clear from his autobiography,[36] from boyhood on he was anything but a conformist, and his work as a young man with international student movements had made him acutely aware of how horribly the times were changing. But that is a very superficial explanation. It would take a probing scholarly biography to explain his life, faith, and attitudes to Jews more deeply. Unfortunately we do not have one. It is to be hoped that someone, perhaps a member of this society, will write that biography soon, before all those who knew Parkes have died. Parkes deserves no less.

Stanford University

---

[36] Parkes, *Voyage of Discoveries*.

JEWS AND CHRISTIANS IN
THE GREGORIAN DECRETALS

by JOHN A. WATT

WITH the promulgation of the five books of the *Decretals* by Gregory IX in 1234, that part of the law of the Church which regulated the Christian–Jewish relationship was to all intents and purposes authoritatively finalized. Christendom thenceforward had its norms: for episcopal legislators in the diocesan and provincial councils which carried universal law into the localities; for academics to analyse, expound, and pass on in their teaching and writing to form the outlook of successive generations of ecclesiastical leaders; for lay governments to accept or reject in detailing their policies towards Jews. The papacy had defined its position. Basic principles and their application in practice had been made clear in official tones. The law of the Latin Church had come of age, and with that, medieval ecclesiastical Jewry law had received formulation at the highest level. There had been nothing previously to match the authority of the Gregorian codex.

It was undoubtedly an important matter that the papacy had laid down for the ecclesiastical and civil leadership of Europe, governmental and academic, where it stood on many particularities of the position of Jews in Christian society. But we may well ask, as indeed did the medieval canonists themselves, why Jews should figure in the canon law at all. 'For what have I to do to judge them that are without?' St Paul had asked. 'Do not you judge them that are within? For them that are without, God will judge.' (I Cor. 5. 12–13). The canonists knew the text well. They encountered it three times in the authorities of their discipline: once by way of Augustine in Gratian's *Decretum* (2.q.1, c.18), a second time in the words of Gratian himself (dict. ante 23.q.4, c.17), and a third time in a decretal of Innocent III (*Decretales*, 4.19.8). If St Paul and with him, apparently, patristic and papal opinion ruled that judgement of outsiders should be left to God, why should Jews be subject to canon law? How could the sanctions of the courts Christian—penances, excommunication, interdict, refusal of Christian burial—be brought to bear on those *qui foris sunt*? The canonists distinguished: outsiders could not be under ecclesiastical jurisdiction directly, that is to say, so far as spiritual penalties were concerned. Indirectly, however, was another matter. Jews might be coerced into obeying ecclesiastical rulings by way of pressure on

Christians: on rulers who were held to enforcing them and on Christians in general who might be excommunicated for wrongful conduct towards Jews or commanded, in appropriate circumstances, to withdraw themselves from all social and commercial contact with Jews—to remove themselves *a communione Christianorum* in the medieval phrase; to boycott them in modern language.

Discussion of the Pauline principle under the question, *Quid ad nos de hiis qui foris sunt*? followed by a list of the occasions when the indirect jurisdiction operated became a standard feature of medieval canonistic literature and perhaps its most characteristic mode of summarizing canonical Jewry law.[1]

The modern student is even more needful of the guidance of such summaries than the medieval canonist. For the relevant material is very miscellaneous, and it is scattered, under different subject headings, through the *Decretum* and likewise through the *Decretales*. The number of relevant decretals in the Gregorian *Codex* is not large: some 30 from the total content of 1,971. It would undoubtedly have assisted the modern student if Raymond of Peñafort, the general editor of the *Decretales*, had considered the whole Christian–Jewish relationship under a single heading. But he did not. He chose to place the texts in four of the five books of the *Gregoriana*. At one point, however, in book v, he did put together about half the number of relevant decretals under the title 'Concerning Jews and Saracens and their *servi*'. I leave the word *servi* untranslated deliberately because it has to be understood broadly. A *servus* in the context might be a slave or a serf or a servant. It was as part of their commentary on that title that canonists asked their question about ecclesiastical jurisdiction over outsiders, with its attendant summary of Jewry law. This makes it the obvious place to begin a brief review of the content of that law.

It is with *servus*, meaning slave, that the title begins. The suggestion of anachronism that might be thought to attend such a subject tends to be confirmed by the dates of the selected texts: the first is a decree of the

---

[1] *Glossa ordinaria ad Decretales* (Paris, 1561), 5.6.5, *s.v.* 'permittantur': 'Sed quid ad nos de his qui foris sunt: ut ii. q.i. multi. et xlv. dist. qui syncera? Solutio: de his qui foris sunt non iudicat ecclesia ut poenam spiritualem infligat. In casibus tamen iudicat de eis, quia repellit Iudeos a communione Christianorum (there followed a list of such cases) . . . Hic ergo ecclesia excommunicat tantum illos Christianos qui cum eis habitare praesumunt, quandoque tamen indirecte excommunicat eos, quia excommunicat Christianos ne cum eis aliquod commercium habeant.' For a number of earlier decretist and decretalist texts on this theme, W. Pakter, *Medieval Canon Law and the Jews* (Ebelsbach am Main, 1988), pp. 58–66, 201.

Council of Mâcon of 581; the second is a decretal of Gregory I. But a third decretal to be concerned with slavery was of Gregory IX himself.[2] Slavery, then, was a live issue in thirteenth-century Europe. The registers of Innocent III show that this was the case particularly in Spain. Conversion to Christianity brought freedom to Muslim slaves when their owners were Jewish. But the owners were to be allowed compensation for consequent loss of service. In 1205 Innocent III complained to Alfonso VIII of Castile that to allow Jews to exact a sale price at a rate they themselves had assessed was to break the canonical regulation which had fixed the price. The canon he cited as fixing the price was that of the Council of Mâcon just mentioned.[3] Innocent III intervened in another slavery issue which had arisen in Aragon in 1206. When 'general baptism' was being celebrated in the churches of Barcelona, and many Muslim slaves were obtaining their freedom on becoming Christians, their masters, both Christians and Jews, resenting their loss of property, sought their compensation from the clergy, exacting pledges by force.[4] Not a procedure that recommended itself to Innocent III.

The Mâcon decree ruled that if a slave in Jewish ownership was baptized, or expressed a wish to be baptized, he was not to be retained, 'because it is abominable that one whom Christ has redeemed should be held in servitude to a blasphemer of Christ.' But the Jew was allowed ten solidi as his price. Gregory IX reiterated and updated the regulation (5.6.19). No Jew was allowed to buy or retain as his slave any Christian or anyone wishing to be baptized. If he had bought a slave who was baptized after purchase, he could be sold for twelve solidi. If within three months he had not freed him, the slave was to go free, even if the canonical price had not been obtained.

Raymond of Peñafort did not include any decretal which bore directly on the question as to whether Jews were to be allowed to hold Christian serfs. He did, however, include a text of Gregory I which, while prohibiting Jews from owning Christian slaves, did permit them to employ Christian *coloni* to work their fields. The canonist's attempt to adapt Roman law and the circumstances of sixth-century Sicily to thirteenth-century feudal Europe is not easy to follow. The distinction was attempted between *servi* in a condition of personal unfreedom whom Jews were

<hr/>

[2] *Decretales*, 5.6.1 (col. 771); 5.6.2 (col. 772); 5.6.19 (col. 778).
[3] Shlomo Simonsohn, ed., *The Apostolic See and the Jews. Documents: 492–1404* (Toronto, 1988), no. 81.
[4] Simonsohn, *Documents*, no. 83.

forbidden to retain and *servi* who were the *ascriptivi* of Roman law, bound to the soil and transferred with it from one possessor to another. These last were allowed to Jews as tillers of their estates, though their transfer to other estates was forbidden.[5]

By contrast with this uncertain handling of serfdom, the canon law concerning Jews employing Christians as servants was clarity itself. The Third Lateran Council had ruled that 'neither Jew nor Saracen under pretext of providing for the feeding of their children or for any other reason may have Christian servants in their homes; those Christians who dare to live with Jews are to be excommunicated.' A second text of Alexander III repeated the same regulation. Innocent III reiterated the veto and strengthened the sanction: Jews who did not dismiss their Christian servants were to be subject to boycott by Christians, who were to be excommunicated if they did not enforce it.[6]

The canon law concerning Christian *servi* and their Jewish masters is not perhaps the most important part of ecclesiastical Jewry law. But it derived from an important basic principle of that law. This principle might be posited in quite mild language, such as that used by Alexander III: 'It is contrary to the sacred canons that Christians should be subject to Jews.'[7] It could be put more trenchantly and elaborately, as it was by Innocent III: 'It is too absurd for a blasphemer of Christ to exercise the force of power over Christians.' In a rather tortuous paraphrase of Genesis 21, he argued that it was wholly unacceptable for the children of the bondswoman Hagar (that is, the Jews) to have as servants the children of the freewoman Sara (that is, the Christians). For Christ's death in setting Sara's children free had made *servi* of Hagar's. Jews were the *servi* of Christians; anything suggesting the converse was wrong. For Jews the condition of *servitus* was the appropriate one.[8] Quite how we should translate and interpret that word will need attention later.

---

[5]   *Decretales*, 5.6.2 (col. 771) and *Glossa ordinaria*.

[6]   *Decretales*, 5.6.5 (col. 773); 5.6.8 (cols 773–4); 5.6.13 (cols 775–6).

[7]   Simonsohn, *Documents*, no. 54: 'Prohibentes omnibus Dei fidelibus sub interminatione anathematis, ne quis Judaeis hominia vel fidelitates faciat; quoniam contrarium est sacris canonibus ut Christiani debeant Judaeis adstringi.'

[8]   *Decretales*, 5.6.16 (col. 777) (Lateran IV, c. 69): 'Cum sit nimis absurdum ut blasphemus Christi in Christianos vim potestatis exerceat.' Simonsohn, *Documents*, no. 82; *Decretales*, 5.6.13 (*Etsi Iudeos*): '(. . . ne cervicem perpetue servitutis iugo submissam presumant erigere contra reverentiam fidei Christianae) inhibemus ergo districte ne de cetero nutrices vel servientes habeant Christianos, ne filii liberae filiis famulentur ancillae, sed tanquam servi a Domino reprobati, in cuius mortem nequiter coniurarunt, se saltem per effectum operis recognoscant seruos illorum quos Christi mors liberos, et illos seruos effecit.' That part of the text in brackets is in the original papal letter, as edited by Simonsohn, but was omitted in the *Decretales* version.

Any scrutiny of the *Gregoriana* will reveal how important were two popes, Alexander III and Innocent III, in the fashioning of the medieval canon law, not merely in the quantity of their decretals, but more especially in their significance and influence. This is no less true of Jewry law. This brief review of that law will now proceed by way of an examination of the contribution to it of each of these great papal legislators.

Looked at in perspective, Alexander III (1159–81) is the first pope since Gregory I (590–604) from whose pontificate sufficient evidence has survived for us to be able, with some confidence, to analyse a systematic and consistent papal attitude towards Jews. A distillation of that attitude found its way into the *Gregoriana*. Raymond of Peñafort had selected seven Alexandrine decretals (three of them from the Third Lateran Council of 1179) and a further one, the celebrated *Sicut Iudeis*, which though attributed by Raymond to Clement III, had, in fact, already been promulgated by Alexander III in the first version to have survived. In sum, one suggests that these decretals are about protection; protection in a threefold sense. Jews and the practice of Judaism are to be protected from abuse by Christians; Christians and Christianity are to be protected from abuse by Jews; Jewish converts to Christianity are to be protected from abuse by both Christians and Jews.

Solomon Grayzel, author of the standard analysis of *Sicut Iudeis*, underlined its central importance by noting that it was the papal document 'repeated more frequently than any other papal utterance concerning the Jews, being used by six popes during the twelfth century (including Innocent III), by ten popes in the thirteenth, by four popes during the fourteenth (including an anti-pope) and by three during the fifteenth century.' Its precise origins are unknown, but the text itself makes it clear that it was the result of Jewish petitions, and there can be little doubt that the continuing repromulgations were also the result of Jewish requests. It was to receive significant additions in some of the later versions, most notably in that issued first by Gregory X in 1272, rejecting the blood-libel accusation.[9] But the canonistic version remained unchanged, a somewhat abridged version of the first surviving text. In modern language, it guaranteed basic Jewish rights. Jews were to be protected from forcible baptism, from arbitrary violence, from punishment without legal process, and they were to be allowed the practice of their religion. Toleration of Judaism included the right to have synagogues and to repair them at need,

---

[9] S. Grayzel, 'The Papal Bull *Sicut Judeis*', in Meir ben Horin, *et al.*, eds, *Studies and Essays in Honor of Abraham Neuman* (Philadelphia, 1962), pp. 243–80, at pp. 243–4.

though they were not to be enlarged or made more ornate. Nor was the building of new synagogues to be permitted.[10] Alexander III was here reissuing Justinian, already assimilated into papal teaching by Gregory I.[11]

The Third Lateran Council commanded that on Good Friday the doors and windows of houses inhabited by Jews should remain closed—'because then in contempt of their creator they were most wont to mock Christians', explained the Glossa ordinaria. The Fourth Lateran Council was to extend the restriction: the civil authorities were to compel Jews to remain indoors during Passion Week. The threat of their offering contempt to the Redeemer was the reason given for this confinement. Christianity was then to be protected from insult, and Christians were to be protected from Jewish proselytism, being lured into what was labelled Jewish superstitio and perfidia. Service in Jewish households was forbidden because simple people were 'easily' converted. 'Frequent abode and constant living with a Jewish family' (continua conversatio ac assidua familiaritas) was an unacceptable risk which all bishops were instructed to prevent.[12] Finally, from Alexander III, in the context of protecting Christians, were two decretals relating to the giving of evidence in cases in the lay courts in which both Jews and Christians were involved. Excommunication was to be pronounced on anyone who gave preference to evidence given by Jews, 'since Jews ought to be subject to Christians.'[13]

As to the third category of persons whose protection the Alexandrine legislation sought, convert Jews, it is again to the Third Lateran Council we must look:

> If under divine inspiration, Jews were to be converted to the Christian faith, no one should dispossess them, since it is fitting that converts to the faith should be in a better position than they enjoyed before conversion. If anyone treats them otherwise, we order princes and local authorities under pain of excommunication to ensure full restitution of their inheritance and of their own property.[14]

Originality and novelty is not the hallmark of this Alexandrine legislation. Much of it is no more than an updating by official reception of the

---

[10] Decretales, 5.6.7.

[11] Decretales, 5.6.3.

[12] Decretales, 5.6.5. Decretales, 5.6.8: 'Quoniam Iudeorum mores et nostri in nullo concordant, et ipsi de facili ob continuam conversationem et assiduam familiaritatem ad suam superstitionem et perfidiam simplicium animas inclinarent.'

[13] Decretales, 2.20.21 (col. 322); 2.20.23 (cols 322–3).

[14] Decretales, 5.6.5.

canons of earlier times. Of Innocent III's contribution to Jewry law, it can be said, in the first place, that some of it was a strengthened restatement of Alexander III. But most of it was original. The list of his legislative acts which broke new ground is impressive: two important clarifications of juridico-theological doctrine, the introduction of the boycott sanction against Jews, the first papal legislation concerning Jewish usury, the introduction into the *Corpus Iuris* of a shorthand version of the medieval theology of anti-Judaism, and, of course, the introduction of distinguishing dress for Jews, which Europe evolved into the Jewish badge, 'the badge of shame'.

Baptism by force was the subject of the first doctrinal ruling. The Archbishop of Arles, challenged by heretics about the validity of infant baptism and raising by extension the whole concept of consent to baptism, submitted his uncertainties to Innocent III, who produced what was, in effect, a minor treatise on this concept, destined to become something of a classic statement of the *magisterium*. The Archbishop had made no specific reference to Jews. It was the Pope himself, when considering consent in infant and adult baptism, who raised the matter of the use of force. He reiterated that forced conversions were contrary to the Christian religion. But he adverted to a decree of the Fourth Council of Toledo (633), well known to canonists because it had a place in the *Decretum*, which argued (at least in Gratian's own interpretation) that 'Jews are not to be compelled to the faith, yet even if unwilling, they have accepted it, they are to be compelled to hold fast to it.'[15] Seeking to harmonize this text with the forbidding of forcible conversions, he argued for a distinction between a baptism forced *absolute* which was null, and one forced *conditionaliter*, which was valid. As the distinction was to figure prominently in all future discussions of the subject, it is worth setting out the whole argumentation:

> It is true that it is contrary to the Christian religion to force anyone, always against his will and against his total opposition, into receiving and practising Christianity. Wherefore some, without absurdity, distinguish between unwilling and unwilling and between coerced and coerced: that he, forced violently through fear and punishment, who receives the sacrament of baptism to avoid harm to himself, such a one, just like the one who comes to baptism in bad faith, receives the imprint of the Christian character; and since he gave his consent

---

[15] *Decretum dict. ante* D45 c. 5 (col. 161).

as if conditionally (*tamquam conditionaliter*), though not absolutely (*absolute*), he is to be held to the observance of the Christian faith. It is in this context that the decree of the council of Toledo should be understood, in which it is stated that he who long ago had been forced into Christianity, as happened in the time of the most religious king Sisebut, because it is already undisputed that they had united with the divine sacraments and the grace of baptism, been anointed with chrism and had shown themselves as partakers of the body of the Lord; for it is proper that they should be compelled to hold to the faith which through necessity they had accepted, lest the name of the Lord be blasphemed [cf. Rom. 2. 24] and the faith they had undertaken should be held as vile and contemptible. But one who never consents and is unwilling in the absolute sense received neither the reality nor the character of the sacrament because it is more to dissent strongly than to give minimal consent, just as he who shouts out his dissent incurs no guilt when forced violently to offer incense to idols.[16]

The subject of the second doctrinal ruling also emerged from the context of heresy. The problem was put to Innocent: was a marriage dissolved when one partner lapsed into heresy? 'No', was his reply. But his explanation involved making a distinction between a marriage between baptized persons and marriage *inter infideles*. St Paul, in making the same distinction, in a famous passage, known to modern theologians and canonists as the Pauline privilege, had taught the possibility of dissolving a marriage when one of the partners of a marriage between the unbaptized became a Christian and the other refused cohabitation. (I Cor. 7. 15: 'But if the unbeliever depart, let him depart. For a brother or sister is not under servitude in such cases.') Innocent III interpreted the text to mean that in circumstances where the non-Christian partner refused cohabitation, or if cohabitation was at the cost of blasphemy or serious moral danger to the convert, the marriage could be dissolved and remarriage permitted.[17] Jews are not specifically mentioned by the Pope, but the relevance is obvious.

While on the subject of marriage when one party became Christian, it

---

[16] *Decretales*, 3.42.4 (cols 646–7).

[17] *Decretales*, 4.19.7 (cols 722–3): 'Si enim alter infidelium coniugum ad fidem catholicam conuertatur, altero vel nullo modo, vel non sine blasphemia diuini nominis, vel ut eum pertrahat ad mortale peccatum, ei cohabitare volente, quia relinquitur, ad secunda si voluerit vota transibit, et in hoc casu intelligimus: *Si infidelis discedit, discedat. Frater enim vel soror non est seruituti subiectus in huiusmodi* (1 Cor. 7. 15).'

is appropriate to notice an important decretal of Gregory IX. In 1229 the diocesan council of Strasbourg submitted a problem to the Pope. A convert Jew who wished to have custody of his four-year-old son, so that he might bring him up as a Christian, was opposed by his wife, who had chosen to remain in the Jewish faith. She argued that the boy was still of an age to need a mother's care more than a father's and that the boy ought to be allowed to choose between the two religions when he was of an age to do so. Gregory IX ruled that the boy should go to the father: a son was in the power of the father and was of the legal age to leave his mother's charge. At his age, he ought not to be allowed to remain among those persons of whom it could be suspected that his life and salvation would be at risk. If he remained with his mother, she might mislead him into unbelief. Therefore he should be assigned to the father. The canonists concluded that this decision *in favorem fidei christianae* should apply irrespective of the age of the child.[18]

The introduction into canon law of the boycott as a means of coercing Jews has already been mentioned. If Jews did not dismiss their Christian servants, Innocent had ruled, prelates were to prohibit Christians from all trade and communication with Jews, under pain of excommunication of those Christians who ignored the ban. This type of pressure, by boycott, could, of course, be extended into other contexts; it could be applied wherever it was thought appropriate. And Innocent III thought it appropriate in five other contexts: when a lay authority neglected to punish a Jew who had struck a cleric;[19] to coerce Jews to restitution when they had extorted oppressive and excessive rates of interest;[20] to force Jews to pay the tithe and other dues leviable on properties they owned;[21] to compel them to stop exercising public authority over Christians and under the supervision of the local bishop, and to make restitution for the use of the Christian poor of all they had gained through tenure of the office;[22] to compel them to remit interest charges on the loan debts of crusaders.[23] All save the first of these were canons of the Fourth Lateran Council. Indirect jurisdiction of this sort suffered, however, from a

---

[18] *Decretales*, 3.33.2 (cols 588–9); *Glossa ordinaria*, *s.v.* 'ad infidelitatis errorem': 'Hac de causa etiam si esset minor triennio, vel pater vellet eum perducere ad fidem, cum sit in eius potestate, patri debuit assignari in fauorem fidei christiane.'

[19] *Decretales*, 5.6.14 (col. 776).

[20] *Decretales*, 5.19.18 (col. 816).

[21] Ibid.

[22] *Decretales*, 5.6.16 (col. 777).

[23] Lateran IV, c. 71, *Ad liberandam*. The edited *Decretales* version (5.6.17) omitted the boycott reference.

serious limitation which neither Innocent III nor the canonists ever
mentioned: that to be enforced the boycott needed the acquiescence or
active co-operation of the controlling secular power. This was not
generally to be relied on, if only because the civil authorities stood to lose
by the weakening of the economies of their Jewish communities.

There was yet another context wherein Innocent advocated recourse to
the boycott, another usury text. But it has a more particular interest.
Editorial pruning by decretal collectors brought about a major and
influential distortion of Innocent III's meaning. In 1198 the Pope
instructed lay rulers to force Jews to remit usury to crusaders. When an
abridged version of this decretal passed into *Compilatio tertia*, and then was
accepted by Raymond for the *Gregoriana*, all reference to its specific
application to crusaders had been excised.[24] The result was to credit
Innocent III with demanding a blanket ban on all charging of interest by
Jews. This was not Innocent III's position; his ban, that of the Fourth
Lateran Council, was on the levying of extreme and immoderate usury.
This remained the position adopted in practice by the thirteenth-century
papacy.[25] By contrast, the canonists stood by the truncated text and
demanded a total ban, which, ironically enough, was to gain acceptance
from Louis IX and Edward I.

A last reference to the Fourth Lateran Council may well be fitted in
here. Canon 68 enjoined on all Jews and Saracens of both sexes the
wearing in public of distinctive dress to distinguish them from Christians
'lest in error they unite carnally'. The reason given for the introduction of
this sign of recognition was to prevent inter-marriage and extra-marital
sex of Christians with those of other faiths.[26] Jewish historians have
generally seen this instruction as a deliberate attempt to degrade Jews. The
thirteenth-century canonists, however, always read the text at its face
value.[27] They offer no hint that there was intent to humiliate or degrade,

---

[24] *Decretales*, 5.19.12 (cols 814–15). Simonsohn, *Documents*, no. 67 omits that part of the text
limiting its application to crusaders. The text printed by S. Grayzel, *The Church and the Jews in
the Thirteenth Century* (Philadelphia, 1933), no. 1, does not.

[25] Kenneth R. Stow, 'Papal and royal attitudes toward Jewish lending in the thirteenth century',
Association for Jewish Studies Review, 6 (1981), pp. 161–84, at pp. 162–74.

[26] *Decretales*, 5.6.14. The *Glossa ordinaria* summarized: 'In quibusdam prouinciis Iudei seu
Sarraceni per habitum distinguuntur a Christianis, in quibusdam vero non. Unde contingit
aliquando quod Christiani Iudeis et Iudei Christianis mulieribus per errorem carnaliter com-
miscentur. Ne igitur tam damnatus excessus per talem errorem ulterius committatur, statuit
concilium generale ut Iudei sive Sarraceni utriusque sexus in qualibet prouincia Christianorum per habitum distinguantur a Christianis.'

[27] The argument of Hostiensis was typical: *Summa* (Cologne, 1612), *De Jud. et Sarrac. et eorum
seruis*, n. 6: 'Hec differentia est inter Judeos et Christianos ideo facienda, quia in quibusdam

though it is not difficult to appreciate that it might well appear differently to those compelled to wear distinguishing dress or badge, and that it might come to be imposed in order to humiliate.

There remains one last decretal of Innocent III to be considered. *Etsi Iudeos* was one of particular importance. In it Innocent accepted the truth of an allegation made by two of France's most distinguished prelates, Peter of Corbeil, Archbishop of Sens, and Odo of Sully, Bishop of Paris. They had complained that for three days after Christian wet-nurses had received the Easter Eucharist, their Jewish employers, in deliberate insult of the Christian faith, forced them to express their milk into the latrine before they were allowed to resume their Jewish charges. Innocent's reaction was twofold—one practical, one theoretical.

The practical one—dismissal of Christian domestic staff by their Jewish employers under threat of boycott—has already been noticed. The theoretical one was a statement of the nature of, and reason for, Jewish subjection to Christians. It was through their own fault that Jews submitted themselves to Christians in permanent servitude (*perpetue servituti*) when they crucified the Lord: 'As *servi* rejected by God in whose death they wickedly conspired . . . they must acknowledge themselves the *servi* of those whom the death of Christ made free and made [Jews] *servi*.'[28]

Use of these words *servitus* and *servi* has occasioned much discussion, particularly concerning its relevance and significance in the evolution of the concept of Jewish serfdom. This discussion—I have in mind particularly that of Guido Kisch in his important book on the medieval German Jewry[29]—hinges on the correct understanding of not merely the face value of the word *servitus*, but also of the nuances it carried in the thirteenth-century ecclesiastical vocabulary.

I should not want to confine discussion of *servitus* to the concept of *Kammerknechtschaft* or any other variant of Jewish serfdom. That concept belonged essentially to the legal status of Jews in civil law. Innocent III was concerned with something he thought considerably more important than that. He was looking to the source from which the juridical tradition of

---

partibus tanta confusio inolevit, quod propter ignorantiam contingit ipsos aliquando carnaliter adinvicem commisceri, que commixtio seu coniunctio merito condemnatur, et ne sub hoc velamine velint aliqui errorem suum palliare, ideo est qualitas habitus discernenda . . . et idem de Sarracenis.'

[28] *Decretales*, 5.6.13. For the text, n. 8, above.

[29] Guido Kisch, *The Jews in Medieval Germany. A Study of their Legal and Social Status* (Chicago, 1949), pp. 146–52.

the Church towards the Jews derived. He was looking therefore towards the Bible. He was looking in particular towards St Paul and, beyond him, to the Book of Genesis.

Examination of each of the occasions when Innocent used the term *servitus* in the Jewish context, including *Etsi Iudeos* itself, shows that typically it was contrasted with *libertas*: the liberty of Christians, the servitude of Jews, the liberty of the children of the freewoman with the children of the bondswomen, the sons of Sara contrasted with the sons of Hagar. In looking to Genesis 21 for types for Christians and Jews, Innocent was following St Paul: 'So then brethren, we are not the children of the bondwoman but of the free; by the freedom wherewith Christ has made us free ... Stand fast and be not held again under the yoke of bondage' (Galatians 4. 31–5. 1).[30]

St Paul, however, had been pursuing the argument that Christians were the freeborn sons of Abraham because Christ had set them free from the servitude of the law. Innocent's argument was rather different. He was arguing that Jews 'were the *servi* of those whom the death of Christ has made free'. In what did their service consist? Innocent's answer was classically Augustinian: 'Through them our faith is truly verified ... [the faith] which they, though not understanding it themselves, present in their books to those who do understand it.'[31] This service they cannot perform if they are allowed to assume positions of authority over Christians.

Did Innocent go further and in speaking of Jewish *servitus* intend a reference also to the civil relationship of Jews to lay authorities? He certainly thought that Jews owed service to kings and said so clearly in a letter to Philip Augustus: 'Although it is not displeasing to the Lord, but rather is acceptable to him, that the dispersed Jews should live under Christian kings and princes and serve them ...'.[32] But nowhere does he

---

[30] Simonsohn, *Documents* no. 78: '... cum constet non iam esse filios ancille, sed libere, qui elegerunt ibi in libertate spiritus Domino deservire'; ibid., no. 79: '... nec deterior sit Christianorum libertas quam servitus Iudeorum.'

[31] Ibid., no. 71: 'Licet perfidia Iudeorum sit multipliciter improbanda, quia tamen per eos fides nostra veraciter comprobatur, non sunt a fidelibus graviter opprimendi, dicente propheta: *ne occideris eos ne quando obliviscantur legis tue* (Ps. 58. 12), ac si diceretur appertius, ne deleveris omnino Iudeos, ne forte Christiani legis tue valeant oblivisci, quam ipsi non intelligentes, in libris suis intelligentibus representant.'

[32] Ibid., no. 79: 'Etsi non dispiceat Domino, sed ei potius sit acceptum, ut sub catholicis regibus et principibus christianis vivat et serviat dispersio Iudeorum ...'. Ibid., no. 88: 'Blasphematores enim nominis christiani non debent a christianis principibus in oppressionem servorum Domini confoveri, sed potius comprimi servitute ...'.

spell out precisely in what that service to kings and princes consisted. Nor would one expect him to. Such precisions were for the lay legislator. His concern in the lay area was simply to ensure, as the letter went on to say, that the canon law governing acceptable Jewish behaviour was not violated.

Thus *Etsi Iudeos* brought the notion of Jewish service to Christianity and to Christian kings and princes into canon law. It also brought into canon law the concept of Jewish corporate guilt for the death of Christ. It also conveyed the thought that Jewish hostility to Christianity was a continuing presence in the life of contemporary Christendom. Jewish guilt, its perpetuation down to the present time, and its punishment was thus one dimension of medieval canonical doctrine. But there was another: Judaism was to be tolerated and Jews protected. *Etsi Iudeos* was complemented by *Sicut Iudeis*, the guarantee of that toleration and protection, equally prominent in canon law, and which Innocent III himself had confirmed at the beginning of his pontificate. Perhaps to a modern eye the two documents do not sit well together. But the medieval canonists reconciled them with a formulation, almost paradoxical, perhaps ambivalent, but made classical by its position in the *Glossa ordinaria*: 'Jews indeed are not to be considered as enemies, although they are enemies of our faith.'[33] Or in the somewhat fuller version of the leading thirteenth-century canonist, Hostiensis: 'Although Jews are enemies of our faith, they are our *servi* and are tolerated and defended by us.'[34] Such *dicta* expressed in shorthand form the essential organizing principle of the medieval canonical Jewry law and, with that, of the official medieval Church.

University of Newcastle upon Tyne

---

[33] *Glossa ordinaria ad 5.6.9 (Sicut Iudeis) s.v.* 'cemeterium': 'Iudei vero non reputantur hostes, xxiii. q. viii. dispar (*Decretum* 23.q.8 c. 11), licet sint hostes fidei nostre, infra eo. etsi Iudeos (5.6.13).

[34] Hostiensis, *Apparatus* (Paris, 1511), *ad* 5.6.9, *s.v.* 'cemeterium': 'Etsi sint fidei nostre hostes i. eo. etsi iudeos, serui tamen nostri sunt, et a nobis tolerantur et defenduntur, ut hic patet, et xxiii. q. viii. dispar.'

WILLIAM OF AUVERGNE AND THE JEWS

by LESLEY SMITH

[He] is in the line of the great souls of the Middle Ages who spanned the whole compass of current knowledge. Bishop and doctor, William of Auvergne is one of the noble figures of the thirteenth century (F. Vernet).[1]

William was chaplain to Queen Blanche, King Louis' mother, and in an age of great bigotry he excelled in excessive bigotry (Ch. Merchavia).[2]

IN 1240 William of Auvergne, Bishop of Paris, was present at a form of hearing, trial, disputation, or inquisition between Christians and Jews to determine whether or not the Parisian Jews should have their copies of the Talmud destroyed. The Talmud was condemned. Some two years later the large quantity—probably twenty-four cartloads—of Jewish books which had been confiscated in 1240, and locked since then in the Dominican convent, was publicly burned. The consigning of the books to the flames is reminiscent of the burning of heretics and is one of the circumstances of the whole event which has led some commentators to see the trial as a form of Inquisition.[3]

William was neither the instigator of the trial nor the senior ecclesiastical or secular person present. The meeting was chaired by Blanche of Castile, the Queen Mother; the senior ecclesiastic was the Archbishop of Sens, Walter Cornut. Both are generally considered to have been sympathetic to the Jews.[4] The evidence is not entirely clear (and modern

---

[1] F. Vernet, 'Guillaume d'Auvergne', in A. Vacant and E. Mangenot, eds, *Dictionnaire de Théologie Catholique* (Paris, 1913), 6, p. 1974.

[2] Ch. Merchavia, *The Church versus Talmudic and Midrashic Literature* [500–1248] [Hebrew] (Jerusalem, 1970), p. 351. I am indebted to Joseph Ziegler for help with Hebrew, and for general discussion.

[3] Letter of Odo of Châteauroux to Innocent IV, '... incendio fuerunt tunc cremati': see S. Grayzel, *The Church and the Jews in the XIIIth Century* (Philadelphia, 1933), p. 276 (the letter begins on p. 275, n. 3) or J. Markus, *The Jew in the Medieval World: a Source Book. 315–1791* (Cincinnati, 1938), pp. 146–8; and see Ch. Maccoby, *Judaism on Trial: Jewish–Christian Disputations in the Middle Ages* (London, 1982), p. 23. We should not forget that heretical Christian books had been burned at Paris before this time, e.g. the works of David Dinant in 1210.

[4] See Maccoby, *Judaism on Trial*, p. 22, 'The Jewish sources, which avoid mention of Louis (1214–27; canonized 1297), refer to [Blanche] with some warmth, as one who was fair and

accounts vary), but others present appear to have been Adam of Chambly, Bishop of Senlis, Geoffrey of Belleville, the king's chaplain, Odo of Châteauroux, Chancellor of the University of Paris and papal-legate-to-be, and, possibly, the Dominican Henry of Cologne.

The trial, if we may call it that, is recorded in partial and partisan accounts left by both the Jewish and Christian factions. Neither was written as an eye-witness account. Both claim 'victory', by which one must mean moral superiority over the other side. Feelings run high over the event, now, it would seem, as then. William has not had friends amongst Jewish historians;[5] and yet, amongst historians of exegesis and intellectual and university history, he is rarely spoken of with anything but high respect.[6] I would like to consider William's attitude towards the Jews as revealed in his writings; but it is obviously impossible to do this without the constant remembrance of his attendance at the Talmud trial, and his signature on the subsequent 1248 restatement of the ban on the Talmud engineered by Odo of Châteauroux. (Time allowed for this paper is too short to deal with the events of 1248.[7]) I am acutely aware of the tightrope I walk as I do this, for it may be impossible to reconcile the irrationality—non-rationality—of anti-Judaism with an otherwise consistent character.

A brief biography: William of Auvergne, born about 1180, was canon of Notre-Dame and master of theology at Paris—the premier theology school of its day—in the early 1220s. We know very little of his early life or education, although he probably came from a reasonably good family from around Aurillac, in the Auvergne. In 1227 Bartholomew, Bishop of Paris, died. William and some others were unhappy with the choice of his

---

humane in her dealings with Jews.' A. Temko, 'The burning of the Talmud in Paris', *Commentary*, 17, no. 5 (1954), says that Walter was the only impartial judge at the trial. He also considers Walter responsible for the two-year gap between the condemnation of the Talmud and the actual burning (pp. 453–5).

[5] See the opinions of J. Guttman, 'Guillaume d'Auvergne et la littérature juive', *REJ*, 18 (1889), pp. 243–55, Grayzel, *The Church and the Jews*, and Maccoby, *Judaism on Trial*.

[6] See, e.g., Beryl Smalley, 'William of Auvergne, John of La Rochelle and St. Thomas Aquinas on the Old Law', in *St. Thomas Aquinas, 1274–1974. Commemorative Studies* (Toronto, 1974), 2, pp. 11–71; I. Kramp, 'Des Wilhelm v. Auvergne "Magisterium divinale"', *Gregorianum*, 1 (1920), pp. 538–616.

[7] I hope to deal with the events of 1240–8 more fully in a subsequent paper. In the meantime, however, I would point out that Odo's restatement comes less than a year before William's death, and was signed by many other prominent members of the university world. It seems to have been of importance only to Odo himself; for the others, signing was only consistent with the previous statements, and avoided charges of confusion and capriciousness on the Christian side.

successor, considering the election uncanonical under the rules of the Fourth Lateran Council.[8] William was sent to Rome to put their case to the pope, Gregory IX. He set out a deacon; he came back Bishop of Paris. The letter Gregory sent to announce his choice speaks of William as 'a man of highest learning and spotless virtue',[9] unsurprising, perhaps, as a piece of advertising and explanation; but, indeed, no other Christian source has a bad word to say for him either. William was involved in interesting times. He was bishop at the time of the Great Strike of the University of Paris (1229–31). It was his refusal to overlook or be lenient towards the murder of a townsman by scholars, despite the orders of the Pope, that escalated events. Like his English friend Robert Grosseteste, William was a supporter of the Mendicants; it was he who admitted them to teaching chairs in the University,[10] a move which affected both university theology and the Mendicant Orders.

William wrote a large number of works, which have survived in at least 250 manuscripts.[11] His views are simply orthodox, by which I mean that, even if he occasionally produces opinions slightly out of the ordinary, he would wish to be a straightforward believer in the Catholic faith, as handed down by the Catholic Church. In the pattern of his career, he was a model Christian bishop, trained in higher learning, and yet putting his learning only to the service of the building up of the faithful through the pastoral office.

Throughout his writings William shows an almost dogged sense of purpose. He is always writing with an audience in mind, and with the questions of an audience on the tip of his pen. He is often chatty and personal—I, you, we: 'Let's go back to what we were talking about before'—the questions are straightforward and unfussy, and the audience is very often one of clerics, men about to go out and face the wondering, straightforward, blunt mass of a congregation. There are lots of metaphors and images. He's urban—or he knows his audience is; many of

---

[8] Bartholomew was first to be succeeded by Nicholas the Chanter then, when that choice proved unsatisfactory, by one Philip. See N. Valois, *Guillaume d'Auvergne* (Paris, 1880), pp. 8–13.

[9] Quoted from Valois, *Guillaume d'Auvergne*, p. 11; Gregory's letter of 10 April 1228 reads, 'virum eminentis scientie, vite ac conversationis honeste ac opinionis preclare': *Les Registres de Grégoire IX*, ed. L. Auvray (Paris, 1896), 1, no. 191, cols 109–11.

[10] Roland of Cremona, O.P., was granted his chair in 1229, during the strike; Alexander of Hales was allowed to retain his chair when he entered the Franciscan Order in 1225.

[11] Although incomplete, the most easily accessible printed version of his *opera* is a 1963, Minerva, Frankfurt reprint of the 1674 Paris edition of *Opera omnia*. I shall refer to works in this edition.

the images are of cities and government; he's fond of metallurgical images too—mines, furnaces, heat. Hell is cold; grace warms the soul. 'All men are naturally social'; one gets the sense that he certainly was.

But straightforwardness is deceptive. William is idiosyncratic and original in an age when those characteristics were not much valued. 'Does it matter', he asks, 'what we believe, as long as we believe it sincerely?'[12] This still-perplexing question is wildly out of place in an early thirteenth-century treatise. It may have been brought on by the company he's been keeping, for William is the first Latin theologian, or amongst the first, to use Maimonides, Avicebrol (Ibn Gabirol), Aristotle in the service of theology, Avicenna, and a number of lesser-known Arabic writers.[13]

A number of original opinions, many attributed to Thomas Aquinas thirty or more years later, are, in fact, from William's works. One example (pointed out by Beryl Smalley) is especially interesting because it shows him changing over time. In the treatise *De fide et legibus* ('On faith and the Law'), which contains most of his references to Jews, William questions the use of non-literal senses of Scripture, noting that many people are offended by the twisting and bending of meaning in this way. Surprisingly, William is sympathetic, and thus begins a rethinking of the meaning of the literal sense of Scripture which, classically, is credited to Thomas Aquinas.

Let us then move to William's writings on the Jews. William's published *opera*, in the standard Paris 1674 edition, run to about 1,350 folio-sized pages. I estimate this represents about two-thirds of his known works; the rest still unprinted. William talks about Jews at any length only in *De fide et legibus*. Written before 1236, it runs to about 100 pages, of which fewer than the first fifty pages concern issues raised in Maimonides and keenly concerning Jews. References to Jews in other of his works seem to me to be few. We may compare this to large sections of his *De universo* which deal unfavourably with Plato, Aristotle, and various Christian heretics. Even in *De fide et legibus*, the chapter which introduces questions on the Muslims marks a change in tone. William says he is moving now to 'the destruction of the absurdities and madness of Mahomed which, by an intolerable abuse, usurp the name of "law"'.[14] He *tends* not to go in for throwaway 'nasty' (to our ears) remarks against Jews; he reserves these for heretics, and—sometimes—for Muslims.

---

[12] William of Auvergne, *De fide et legibus*, *Opera omnia*, 1, c. 21, pp. 57a *et seq.*
[13] For a list of his sources so far discovered, see Valois, *Guillaume d'Auvergne*, pp. 198–206.
[14] *De fide et legibus*, c. 18, p. 49bC.

Following its name, *De fide et legibus* divides into two parts. The first section, on faith, is quite short and not terribly exciting. The argument, slight though it is, is directed against philosophers who are interested in religion for the sake of the argument rather than for the building up of charity, as theologians are. He also wants to distinguish the faithful from the merely credulous—those who believe only what is obvious, or what they can prove. Anyone can believe what's provable: there's no virtue in it. The virtue of faith comes from believing the incredible and unprovable when this belief is inspired by the love of God.

The second, much longer, section on the Law, is far more interesting and unusual. Contemporary commentators on the Law, as found in treatises on the Decalogue, divide it into three: moral law (*moralia*), judicial law (*judicialia*), and ceremonial law (*caerimonialia*). Only the moral law remained in the New Covenant and could justify. These commentators recognize many absurdities in the Old Law, but understand them simply as figures or types, with only allegorical meaning in the New Law. William takes a quite different view. To begin with, he divides the Law into seven parts, including the traditional three but adding to them. He admits that his 'extras' are not part of the Law proper, but claims they will help understand the actual observance of the precepts, before the Law was given. This sense of the actual, of observation, of real people, and of the Old Law as a living entity used by living people, is especially William's.

Nothing that God has given in the Law can be absurd or ridiculous; nothing can be ignored. There is a literal meaning and reason for all the laws, and we should try to find it. In need of help, he turns—without credit—to Maimonides' recently translated *Guide of the Perplexed*. For the next several chapters William followed Maimonides, sometimes straight, sometimes with his own emphases and alterations, through interesting and earnest discussions of sacrifices, uncleanness, and circumcision.

As Beryl Smalley has also noted,[15] William makes a real effort to enter into the historical consciousness of the Jews. It may always appear a somewhat negative assessment, but compared with his contemporaries William attempts seriously to understand Old Testament Jews. With his enormous faith in the reasonableness of the Law, he has decided that there must be a point to everything—if only he can find it. He is at least sensible enough to go to the Jews for the answers. Obviously neither the religion of the Jews nor that of the Muslims can be graceful—one could not expect a

---

[15] Smalley, 'William of Auvergne', p. 37.

Christian to say anything else; but whereas Muslims are positively vicious, the Jews are merely children, given the alphabet of the Law, although not ready yet for full sentences. Several times William repeats the simile of Jews to children: they are ignorant and unlearned; they tend towards idolatry; and they need so many laws to cover all eventualities, so that they won't have to make decisions for themselves. But William distinguishes between Old Testament Jews and modern Jews who have been lead astray by philosophers, especially foreign, Saracen philosophers. Few remain untainted by this error, which is responsible for the loss of their land to the Arabs.

William is, indeed, offensive to Jews, but in a different way than he is to Muslims or heretics. He must have known of the debate in Judaism over Maimonides, and the burning of his works in Montpellier in 1232. William treats the 'children of the Hebrews' as silly youngsters who need protection from themselves. Consider his comment on the Jewish interpretation of the Prophets:

> We say this on account of the Jews, who are right about many articles of faith and, persuaded by the witness of the Prophets, agree with the Catholic faith; but where they dissent from the pronouncements of the prophets they err not so much by a false interpretation but by a comical [*ridiculosa*] one.[16]

William's use of 'comical' here, where we might expect a more denigratory term, points to an indulgent view of childish foolishness rather than to hatred.

We should note alongside this William's method of proceeding. Many commentators have noted, with disapproval, that William used Maimonides without citing his source. This seems to have been viewed as an intentional slight, as well as a way for William to use Maimonides as it suited him, sometimes approvingly, sometimes not, without consistency. But this is to misunderstand the usual medieval method of citation of someone who is alive, or recently dead. William is writing sometime before 1236, probably in 1230 or so. Maimonides did not die until 1204, too soon for him to be counted as a named authority. William would do the same for Christian writers who were his near-contemporaries, such as Hugh of St Victor (d. 1141), who is an unnamed source for the *De claustrale animae*.[17] This general practice is emphasized by William's method of

[16] *De fide et legibus*, c. 3, p. 18aE.
[17] Valois, *Guillaume d'Auvergne*, p. 204; Kramp, 'Des Wilhelm v. Auvergne', pp. 580–1; K. Werner, *Wilhelms von Auvergne Verhältniss zu Platonikern des XII. Jahrhunderts* (Vienna, 1873), p. 2.

working. He does not use any of the standard ways of proceeding; in this, as in much else, he is unorthodox and prefers to go his own way. Unlike most medieval commentators and writers, William does *not* like to base his argument on authorities; he likes to think they stand on reason, and on reason alone. In this way, not only the believer, but the non-believer—Christian heretic as well as Jewish and Muslim—can be brought to faith. Although the number and range of his sources is vast, Latin, Greek, Jewish, and Arabic, from Plato and Aristotle to the latest on the market, William does not give catenae of authorities and is even quite sparing in his use of biblical quotations and allusions.

William has been criticized for using Maimonides to mean whatever he wanted. Sometimes he disapproves of Maimonides' opinion and argues against him, sometimes he approves and uses him to support an argument or provide a fact.[18] Once more, this is a completely common medieval method of proceeding, especially with a contemporary source—one who could not be considered 'authoritative'. William does exactly the same with Aristotle: 'Although, as is right and just, Aristotle must be contradicted in many opinions where he speaks contrary to truth, he must also be admired and upheld on all occasions when he is found to be right.'[19] Modern philosophers who wish to turn William into the 'pure' philosopher he was not, and would not have wished to be, complain of this same tendency. But this is precisely William's originality—at once his gift and his curse—that he cannot be easily put into boxes and labelled 'pre-Thomistic' or 'pre-Aristotelian',[20] any more than he can be called 'sub-Maimonidean'. What is true is that he sought out the new Latin translation of Maimonides and thoroughly assimilated it. He saw in Maimonides answers to his questions on the Laws, and in the *De legibus* produced his own guide for the perplexed.

If in his writing he seems questioning and original, seeking new sources and relying on reason, what makes William burn the Talmud? I should like to look briefly at the events of 1239–42. Things were set in motion by a Jewish convert from Paris, Nicholas Donin, who went to Gregory IX with thirty-five quotations for which, he said, the Talmud should be condemned; he succeeded in persuading the Pope to order an

---

[18] Guttman, 'Guillaume d'Auvergne', analyses William's use of Maimonides most closely, and is followed by other writers, especially Merchavia, *The Church versus Talmudic and Midrashic Literature*.

[19] *De anima*, *Opera omnia*, 2, suppl., p. 82b.

[20] This is Switalski's phrase to describe his use of Aristotle: B. Switalski, *William of Auvergne. De Trinitate* (Toronto, 1976), introduction, p. 4.

investigation. It is generally said that Gregory sent letters (dated 9 and 20 June 1239 in the Registers) ordering the Jews' books to be seized, on the first Sunday in Lent (3 March) 1240, given over to the Friars, investigated, and, if found to contain errors, burned. The letters were addressed to the kings of France, England, Portugal, Navarre, Aragon, Leon and Castile; to the archbishops in these kingdoms; and to the bishop (William), Prior of the Dominicans, and Minister-General of the Franciscans in Paris. In fact, the Pope sent a letter to William, by the hand of Nicholas Donin, enclosing, it would seem, all the others, and asking William 'as soon as you deem it expedient after having examined them, to transmit the said letters which we sent about . . . the books of the Jews'[21] to all the persons named above. Gregory did not send the letters himself, he asked William to do it for him. One modern commentator thinks Gregory's strategy clever: the Pope knew that William was a devout Southern Frenchman who hated Jews; but if the scheme failed, William, not Gregory, would take the blame.[22] In fact, only Louis IX, the King of France, obeyed the letter, with Nicholas Donin at his side as he did so.

These actions of Louis serve to focus attention on the kingdom of France. If the other states are mentioned by historians, it is only to say that they ignored the papal letter. But it is here I find the story unconvincing. Graetz uses this inaction as a comment on papal power, and on Louis IX: only if a ruler was particularly bigoted did he bother to obey the papal order.[23] It seems to me unlikely that everyone else should have, in witting or unwitting unison, done nothing. I should like to question whether William sent the letters at all. I cannot prove—and, indeed, the evidence for proof or disproof seems likely to be lost for ever—this suggestion; but I would like to assemble the circumstantial evidence in its favour.

It seems improbable that the five other kings and their archbishops all simultaneously did nothing about a papal letter. At about this time some

[21] Letter of Gregory IX to William of Auvergne, dated 9 June 1239; not registered but quoted in the letter of Odo to Innocent IV: see Grayzel, *The Church and the Jews*, pp. 238–40, no. 96; and H. Denifle and C. Châtelain, eds, *Chartularium Universitatis Parisiensis*, I (Paris, 1889) no. 173, pp. 202–5. It is difficult to ascertain where exactly the letters are registered and where they have simply been inserted into the relevant parts of printed registers from the copies in Odo's letters. For the 'sample letters' to be sent to the kings, archbishops, and friars see Grayzel, *The Church and the Jews*, pp. 240–3, nos 96–8.

[22] Temko, 'The burning of the Talmud', p. 450.

[23] H. Graetz, *Geschichte den Juden* (Leipzig, 1910), p. 95: 'sonst aber, wenn sie nicht besonders bigott waren, gingen sie auch im Mittelalter über päpstliche Dekrete mit Stillschweigen hinweg. In Spanien und England wurden die Befehle Gregors, den Talmud zu knofiszieren, gar nicht beachtet, wenigstens verlautet gar nichts von einem feindseligen Akt gegen denselben in diesen Ländern.'

of these same kings were taking other, independent actions against the Jews. In England, Henry III was busy extorting money from Jews in June 1239; in 1240 a fine was levied on Jews who were said to have seized and circumcised a Christian boy in Norwich in 1235.[24] A *domus conversorum* had been established in London in 1232. In 1242, in Aragon, James I published an edict stipulating that Jews had to listen to sermons specifically arguing for conversion preached by friars, bishops, or the archbishop.[25] This is the time of increase of houses for converts, forced conversion sermons, fines, expulsions, taxes, prohibitions, distinctive dress, and other actions humiliating or disadvantageous to Jews. Even if the other kings were not particularly interested in the Talmud, is it not likely that they might have seen a way of making money out of the Jews by ransoming books seized under papal orders, or of using the books as a means of coercion? Yet they did nothing.

Chaim Merchavia[26] is the only commentator I have come across who in any way considers the fate of the letters, but his notes are cryptic, and his general tone is so antithetical to the Christian actors that it is hard to know whether to give much more credence to his text than to Valois' equally but oppositely biased account. In a footnote, Merchavia mentions a 'late copy' of a letter to the kings of Aragon, Portugal, and Castile and Leon, which is in the Madrid National Archives. Another letter, or copy of a letter, undated, unaddressed, and, if the transcription is correct, only a partial and inaccurate text, is in Toledo.[27] The Madrid letter is apparently dated 18 June 1239, which is not the date on the registered papal letter (20 June 1239); and the papal letter is addressed not only to the kings of Aragon, Portugal, Castile and Leon, but also to those of France and England. Since England retains the best documentary records of the period, it is odd that Merchavia 'did not find traces of letters either in the Public Record Office in London or in Libson'.[28] As yet, I have been unable to examine these copies (or possibly one copy and one letter), and Merchavia's report is unclear enough for me to retain doubts. The issue is not helped by the medieval practice of registering letters one had sent oneself, but rarely

---

[24] *Calendar of Close Rolls of the Reign of Henry III* (London, 1911): 1240, *De Judeis Norwici*, p. 168.

[25] Edict of James I of Aragon, 1242, referred to in a papal letter of 1245: see Robert Chazan, *Daggers of Faith: Thirteenth Century Christian Missionizing and Jewish Response* (Berkeley, 1989), p. 38.

[26] Merchavia, *The Church versus Talmudic and Midrashic Literature*, pp. 239–40, n. 43.

[27] J. Amador de Los Rios, *Historia social, politica y religiosa de los Judios de España y Portugal* (Madrid, 1875), I, p. 363, n. 1. The document is given as Arch. de la Catedral de Toledo, Caj. A, leg.4, num. 11.

[28] Merchavia, *The Church versus Talmudic and Midrashic Literature*, pp. 239–40, n. 43.

retaining or registering replies. I fall back on action as evidence: all commentators are agreed that none of the other supposed recipients acted. It is
this *concerted* non-action that makes me most suspicious of the letters'
reception.

We might consider what was going on in this odd arrangement that the
Pope would send letters to postman William, rather than directly himself.
William was not the senior cleric in the kingdom; this was the Archbishop
of Sens, Walter Cornut, who was also present at the 1240 trial. Walter is
generally considered to have been sympathetic to the Jews; only after he
died were the books finally burned. Perhaps Gregory wanted to by-pass
Walter for someone better disposed to the cause, but more likely that,
since Nicholas Donin was going back home to Paris, and to Louis,
William was closest to hand.

It is difficult to judge relations between Gregory and William. Like
many others, he sometimes carried out commissions for the Pope and had
acted for Honorius III whilst still a deacon. He seems, from the Christian
record, to have been a man of tact, respected for his sense of fairness.
Louis and Blanche used him as a negotiator and arbitrator. He was no
particular friend of the Pope, since he would ignore authority in favour of
his own sense of truth. They had crossed swords over the university strike,
and William had shown himself to be independently minded. Gregory
rebuked the Bishop for his 'lack of initiative',[29] but what he was really
complaining of was his *different* initiative: William did not do nothing; he
simply did not do what the Pope wanted.

This business with the letter is not the usual sort of thing William
was given to do. Generally the Pope employed a local agent exactly
because he needed someone close to the situation, known and respected
by the parties, and physically near at hand. This is not the case here.
Would the papal communication machine not have been equally as
effective as the Bishop of Paris? I find myself even considering that
Gregory sent the letters to William exactly because he was half-hearted
about the affair and did not care to proceed further.[30] But we need not
necessarily impute positive motives to William in not acting, for it was
merely the prudent, simpler thing to do. With Nicholas Donin agitating
all over Paris, he had to send the letter to Louis (who was ready to act, in

---

[29] As Switalski, *William of Auvergne. De Trinitate*, introduction, p. 1 describes it; see Gregory's
letter 23 Nov. 1229: '. . . non tam negligentiam quam malitiam in te . . . curabimus'; and his
letter of 24 April 1231,'in the same vein.

[30] Amador de Los Rios, *Historia*, p. 363, n. 1, notes that the letter was at odds with Gregory's
protection of the Jews from the Crusaders in France in 1236.

any case) and to the friars; but there was no need to go on. Although the books in France might be burned, there were plenty of others to be copied elsewhere.

There is also Gregory's letter to William itself, curiously unspecific and undemanding: 'transmittas cum videris expedire' ('send them when it seems expedient to you'), and placing the date for the seizure of the books almost a year in the future. If Gregory had wanted swift action by someone known to dislike Jews, he needed to look no further than the Chancellor, Odo of Châteauroux, who was, indeed, soon to become papal legate.[31] As bishop in the city of the trial, and as confessor to Blanche of Castile (who comes out of both reports well), William was involved *ex officio*; he could hardly get out of it.

William is not an ecumenist. But I am uncertain that he is the Jew-hater that he has been drawn. He was an ecclesiastical leader with a simple and direct faith; doubt was not an issue he addressed in himself, although a story of Joinville shows him tolerant of doubt in others.[32] He was fiercely pastoral, wanting the best for the Church of Christ, the people of God on earth. In this aim, mistaken insiders—heretics—and even perhaps Muslims, who misused their knowledge of Jesus of Nazareth and who were politically much stronger than the Jews,[33] were much more of a threat to the right ordering of the world. The Jews were part of that established order of things. It is more likely that William's paternalism thought to save the Jews from their own internal heretics, from the philosophy that at that moment seemed to threaten both covenants. William was torn; he was a lover of reason and balanced argument; but he also believed strongly in right and wrong. Having listened to the rabbis reject reasoned argument, he may have felt that there was no choice but to burn the books to save the children from themselves; but as a man who respected the Old Law, gave preference to the literal sense of Scripture, and who acknowledged the Jews as guardians of exegesis and arcane knowledge, it is unlikely that he did so with the Jew-hating zeal of Nicholas Donin.

Linacre College,
Oxford

---

[31] Odo was the re-instigator of the ban on the Talmud in 1248. See Grayzel, *The Church and the Jews*, pp. 275–81; Denifle and Chatelain, *Chartularium*, no. 178, pp. 209–10.

[32] See G. Langmuir, *History, Religion, and Antisemitism* (Berkeley, 1990), pp. 259–60.

[33] William notes the physical expansion of Muslim territories in *De fide et legibus*, c. 18, p. 49bC.

JEWS, POITEVINS, AND THE BISHOP OF WINCHESTER, 1231–1234

by NICHOLAS C. VINCENT

AMONGST the many questions concerning the Jews of thirteenth-century England, by no means the least interesting turn upon the hardening of Christian–Jewish relations, the collapse of the wealth of the Jewish community, and the eventual expulsion of the Jews in 1290. Quite when and why did these processes originate and evolve? By which authority, Church or King, were they most keenly sponsored? Robert Stacey has provided answers to many of these questions, nominating the years 1240 to 1258 as 'a watershed in Anglo-Jewish relations' and showing the diversity of religious and financial pressures underlying Henry III's attack on the Jews.[1] Whilst in no way challenging Stacey's basic approach, the purpose of the present essay is to extend his concept of a watershed back by a decade or so to the regime which governed England between 1232 and 1234. At the same time I shall suggest that the misfortunes of the English Jewry need to be viewed in the wider context of Jewish–Christian relations throughout northern Europe, in particular with an eye to the anti-Jewish legislation of Capetian France.

From the summer of 1232 until May 1234 the court of Henry III was dominated by one great minister, Peter des Roches, Bishop of Winchester, a veteran of the service of King John and for more than thirty years one of the most powerful men in English politics. Des Roches was a Frenchman, and his regime of 1232 to 1234 was packed with his fellow aliens. Traditionally it has been dubbed the regime of the Poitevins, although neither des Roches nor the majority of his satellites were natives of Poitou. Des Roches himself sprang from the Touraine, and it was from the Touraine, Anjou, and Normandy, the Plantagenet heartlands lost in 1204, that most of his supporters came. None the less, to the extent that he and his followers shared a desire for the reconquest of the Plantagenet lands overseas, and that after 1204 hopes for such reconquest focused especially upon Poitou, it is by no means foolish to detect a Poitevin bias to their regime. After 1232 they were to devote much energy to the preservation of alliances with Poitou and Brittany and this, in turn, was to have a considerable impact upon their approach to the Jews.

---

[1] Robert C. Stacey, '1240–60: a watershed in Anglo-Jewish relations?', *HR*, 61 (1988), pp. 135–50.

Des Roches had long been involved with the Jews. His cathedral city of Winchester housed a thriving Jewish community.[2] As a bishop, he was bound to be interested in anti-Jewish legislation sponsored by the Church. As a courtier, especially associated with matters financial, he was necessarily concerned with the King's exploitation of Jewish money-lending and the imposition of Jewish tallages. After 1215 the English Church set about implementing the Lateran decrees concerning the Jews.[3] The severity with which such measures were applied varied widely from diocese to diocese, depending upon the bent of individual bishops. Archbishop Langton of Canterbury incorporated the Lateran decrees into his provincial legislation at the Council of Oxford in 1222, prohibiting the building of new synagogues, forbidding Jews to retain Christian maidservants or to enter Christian churches, and obtaining the execution of a deacon accused of apostacy to Judaism.[4] The Bishop of Worcester, William of Blois, was, if anything, even more ferocious than Langton in his denunciations of the Jews. His diocesan legislation, composed several years before the Oxford decrees, includes many of the same anti-Jewish elements, and in 1219 it was William who appealed to the papacy to persuade Langton to enforce the wearing of the *tabula*, the distinctive badge insisted upon for all Jews.[5]

Compared with such anti-Jewish enthusiasts, des Roches emerges if not as a friend of the Jews, then as someone perfectly prepared to tolerate Jewish activity in the light of the great advantages Jewish money-lending and taxes continued to bring to the hard-pressed royal Exchequer. In 1218 he was responsible for imposing swingeing terms upon seven Yorkshire and Lincolnshire knights, farming their debts to Elias of Lincoln on pain of confiscation should they fail to meet Elias's terms.[6] At the same time he issued orders encouraging free travel to Jews wishing to enter England, and on the same day the Exchequer was notified that since September 1218 des Roches had received one mark a day of the fine of 10,000 marks

---

[2] See D. Keene, *Survey of Medieval Winchester — Winchester Studies*, 2, 2 vols (Oxford, 1985), pp. 384–7.

[3] In general, see J. A. Watt, 'The English Episcopate, the State and the Jews: the evidence of the thirteenth-century conciliar decrees', in P. R. Coss and S. D. Lloyd, eds, *Thirteenth Century England*, II (Woodbridge, 1988), pp. 137–47.

[4] F. M. Powicke and C. R. Cheney, eds, *Councils and Synods with other Documents Relating to the English Church: II AD. 1205–1313*, 2 vols (Oxford, 1964), 1, pp. 100–1, 105–6, 120–1.

[5] Ibid., p. 55; Lambeth Palace Library, MS 1212, fol. 129v, a papal mandate directed to Langton, dated 27 Nov. 1219.

[6] *Patent Rolls, 1216–25* (London, 1901) [hereafter *Pat. R, 1216–25*], pp. 179–80, discussed by C. Holt, *Magna Carta* (Cambridge, 1965), pp. 276–7.

made between King John and Isaac the Jew of Norwich, which sum the bishop passed on to pay for work at Dover Castle.[7] Isaac of Norwich and Elias of Lincoln were amongst the most prominent Jews in England. By sponsoring their activities des Roches hardly courted popular sympathy, resorting to methods all too reminiscent of King John's exploitation of Jewish debt, and doing so in the midst of a crusade, a period traditionally associated with heightened anti-Semitism.[8]

The activities of Isaac of Norwich were the subject of specific criticisms from the papal legate Pandulph, not surprisingly, given that Isaac's business activities centred upon Pandulph's cathedral city of Norwich. The Norwich monks had only recently cleared their debts to Isaac, who owned an imposing stone house in the city centre, built by the same masons who had constructed the nearby cathedral priory, possibly as a *quid pro quo* in return for loans to the monks.[9] In July 1219 Pandulph wrote to des Roches and the Justiciar, complaining of Isaac's usurious relations with the convent of Westminster, conducted, as des Roches was reminded, in direct contravention of the Lateran decrees.[10] As late as December 1221 des Roches supervised the collection of Isaac's fine at the Exchequer, and he was subsequently to authorize the first of several writs by which Isaac's liabilities were reduced from 365 marks a year to 250 marks, 200 marks, and eventually, by 1226, to £100.[11] There is a suggestion that a more personal relation existed between the two men. In 1223 Isaac delivered 58,000 herrings to the Bishop's manor of Southwark, later distributed amongst the religious.[12] In 1218/19 Isaac's close associate,

---

[7] *Pat. R, 1216–25*, pp. 179–81. For the question of free travel see H. G. Richardson, *The English Jews under Angevin Kings* (London, 1960), pp. 178–9. For Isaac's fine for release from prison following the tallage of 1210–11 see ibid., p. 170; V. D. Lipman, *The Jews of Medieval Norwich* (London, 1967), p. 104. For the expenditure at Dover see T. D. Hardy, ed., *Rotuli litterarum clausarum* [hereafter *Rot.l.c.*], 2 vols (London, 1833–4), 1, p. 459; B. E. Harris, ed., *Pipe Roll 4 Henry III = Pipe Roll Society*, ns 47 (1981–3), p. 59, which includes the period of the fine originally paid to des Roches.

[8] Richardson, *English Jews*, p. 182; J. M. Powell, *Anatomy of a Crusade 1213–21* (Philadelphia, 1986), pp. 21, 45.

[9] Lipman, *Jews of Norwich*, pp. 111–12; B. Dodwell, ed., *The Charters of Norwich Cathedral Priory = Pipe Roll Society*, ns 40 (1974), p. 241, no. 381, and see *Rot.l.c.*, 1, p. 323b, where in Sept. 1217 the prior was set to guard Isaac's starrs and chirographs.

[10] W. W. Shirley, ed., *Royal and other Historical Letters Illustrative of the Reign of Henry III*, 2 vols, RS (1862–6), 1, no. 28. Richardson, *English Jews*, pp. 183–4, suggests that Pandulph was lenient in his dealings with the Jews, but the evidence cited is entirely negative and Richardson himself (p. 186) recognizes that the anti-Jewish measures proposed by Hugh of Wells and Langton were vigorously adopted only in the dioceses of Lincoln and Norwich.

[11] London, PRO, MSS E368/4, memb. 3d; C60/17, memb. 7; E368/6, memb. 5; C60/23, memb. 4. In 1234 the fine was further reduced to 60 marks p.a.; C60/33, membs. 8, 9.

[12] Winchester, Hampshire Record Office [hereafter HRO], MS Eccles. II 159278 (Pipe Roll of

Benedict Crispin, Jew of London, was engaged in provisioning the Bishop's manor of Southwark, whilst another prominent Jew, Chere of Winchester, paid a fine of £20 via des Roches, which the Bishop allocated to the Christmas court of 1219.[13]

This is not to suggest that des Roches was a friend of the Jews; the Winchester pipe rolls record his almsgiving over several years to converted Jews at Marwell and Twyford. Yet in 1220/1 he paid for the entertainment of Jews, not specified as converts, at Fareham, and in 1225/6 he received 4s. de ferme Iudei hoc anno at Taunton, implying personal exploitation of the Jews on his own estates.[14] His diocesan statutes contain few of the anti-Jewish restrictions found in other sees, merely enjoining a boycott against Jews who purchased or advanced loans on the security of church lands, books, or plate, to last until the goods were restored.[15] In general, the financial usefulness of the Jews was to ensure that the royal authorities did much after 1215 to soften what might otherwise have proved a crippling onslaught from the Church. As a courtier bishop, des Roches undoubtedly pursued the interests of the King at the expense of what many churchmen regarded as unacceptable contact with the Jews. For most of his career his association with the Jews appears to have been harmonious, even symbiotic. What, then, determined the change in these relations after 1232?

In 1224 des Roches was ousted from court by an alliance headed by the Justiciar, Hubert de Burgh, and Archbishop Langton. Three years later, frustrated in his political ambitions in England, he set out for the crusade. In his absence, and against the wishes of de Burgh, the King became involved in alliances with Brittany and with various of the great magnates of Poitou, directed towards the reconquest of the Plantagenet lands in France. In 1230 Henry III headed an expedition to Brittany and Poitou; an enormously expensive venture, obtaining few if any territorial gains, but

the Bishopric of Winchester, 1223–4), memb. 12. For an earlier connection see Rot.l.c., 1, p. 181b; Norwich Cathedral Charters, 1, p. 25, no. 39.

[13] HRO, MS Eccles.II 159275 (Winchester Pipe Roll, 1218–19), memb. 12d, where Benedict delivered 5 loads of herrings; Rot.l.c., 1, p. 387. For Benedict and Isaac as mutual attorneys see H. Cole, ed., Documents Illustrative of English History in the Thirteenth and Fourteenth Centuries (London, 1844), pp. 311, 312, 314, 325, 326; Curia Regis Rolls of the Reigns of Richard I, John and Henry III [hereafter CRR], 16 vols (London, 1922–79), 9, pp. 153–4.

[14] HRO, MSS Eccles.II 159271 (Winchester Pipe Roll, 1211–12), memb. 1d; 159272 (Winchester Pipe Roll, 1213–14), memb. 3; 159275 (Winchester Pipe Roll, 1218–19), memb. 3d; 159277 (Winchester Pipe Roll, 1220–1), membs 6d, 7d; 159278 (Winchester Pipe Roll, 1223–4), memb. 12; 159279 (Winchester Pipe Roll, 1224–5), memb. 3.

[15] Powicke and Cheney, Councils and Synods II, pt 1, p. 131, no. 32.

leaving the King on the verge of bankruptcy, committed to the payment of enormous pensions to his Breton and Poitevin allies.[16] Combined with an already tense relationship between King, Justicier, and baronage, these financial pressures left England on the verge of civil disorder. Des Roches returned in the summer of 1231 to find a war raging on the Welsh marches, and a substantial group, headed by the King's brother Richard of Cornwall and the claimant to the earldom of Pembroke, Richard Marshal, in open defiance of the court. The process by which des Roches exploited these divisions for his own advantage need not detain us here, save to note that in ousting de Burgh from power des Roches made great play of the financial difficulties into which his rival had allowed the court to sink.[17] In 1231 a truce had been negotiated with France, due to expire in the summer of 1234. In the meantime, if the King's continental policy were to be salvaged, it was imperative that Henry find money to pay the enormous subsidies promised to his allies in Brittany and Poitou, a task of which de Burgh was quite incapable. It is in these circumstances that the regime began looking to the Jews to meet its needs.

The Christmas court of 1231 was held in des Roches' cathedral city of Winchester, the Bishop laying on an especially lavish entertainment, which must have contrasted markedly with the King's own financial predicament.[18] In the course of these celebrations a fine of 5,000 marks was extracted from the sons of Hamo of Hereford to inherit their father's estate, 1,700 marks of it set to be paid in the first year.[19] Like Isaac of Norwich, another of the great Jewish plutocrats, the sons of Hamo were henceforth to be exempt from ordinary tallages and impositions, which, as a result, would fall with ever greater severity upon the rest of the Jewish community, least able to pay. At much the same time there appears to have been an attempt to reform the administration of the Jewish Exchequer. Master Alexander of Dorset, Justice of the Jews since at least 1218, was dismissed, and his lands seized temporarily by the Crown.[20]

In the spring of 1232 the Duke of Brittany crossed to England to discuss the subsidies promised to him for the past several years. De Burgh

---

[16] In general, see F. M. Powicke, *King Henry III and the Lord Edward*, 2 vols (Oxford, 1947), pp. 178–84; S. Painter, *The Scourge of the Clergy: Peter of Dreux, Duke of Brittany* (Baltimore, 1937), pp. 69–78.

[17] In general, see D. A. Carpenter, 'The Fall of Hubert de Burgh', *JBS*, 19 (1980), pp. 1–17.

[18] H. R. Luard, ed., *Annales Monastici*, 5 vols, RS (1864–9), 3 (Dunstable), p. 127.

[19] PRO, MS C60/31, memb. 7. The fine was rescheduled after 1,000 marks had been paid, being reduced to 300 marks p.a. by May 1233; PRO, MSS C60/31, memb. 3; C60/32, memb. 5.

[20] PRO, MSS C60/30, memb. 2; C60/32, memb. 6. Alexander died about March 1233; PRO, MSS E40/1915; E40/2073; *ClR, 1231–4*, pp. 197, 201–2.

requested a general aid from the Church and baronage, but his request was refused, accelerating his decline in royal favour. None the less, on 10 March, the Duke was promised 3,000 marks to be paid in full by the end of April.[21] Meanwhile the King's plate and jewels were pawned, and a loan of 2,420 marks cobbled together from various Italian merchants to make good the shortfall.[22] As security, the King turned to the Jews, who on 2 March were forced to undertake repayment of 2,360 marks of the Italian loan by Michaelmas 1232, in return for a quittance meanwhile from the arrears of earlier tallages.[23] It appears that the terms of this arrangement were met, the Italians recouping their money from the Jews.[24]

Control of Jewish finance figured prominently in the storm which broke at court that summer, with de Burgh ousted from power and des Roches' nephew, Peter de Rivallis, promoted to a host of custodies and offices, including a life appointment as Keeper of the Jews both in England and Ireland.[25] On a day to day basis de Rivallis appears to have deputed administration of the Jews to the Englishman Robert Passelaw and the Anglo-Scotsman Peter Grimbaud. Together all three were to be accused after 1234 of personal profiteering at the expense of the Jewish community.[26]

In the immediate term, de Burgh's fall, the confiscation of his vast estate, the fortuitous vacancy of various important escheats, and, above all, the grant of a fortieth on moveables which greeted the appointment of the new regime enabled des Roches and his colleagues to solve the Crown's financial crisis and to begin paying off the backlog of obligations contracted in Poitou and Brittany during the campaign of 1230. But by

---

[21] *ClR, 1231–4*, p. 128; *Patent Rolls, 1225–32* (London, 1903) [hereafter *Pat.R, 1225–32*], pp. 465–6; *Rogeri de Wendover Chronica sive Flores Historiarum*, ed. H. O. Coxe, 5 vols (London, 1841–4), 4, pp. 233–4.

[22] *Pat.R, 1225–32*, pp. 466, 490, 514–15.

[23] PRO, MS C60/31, memb. 6.

[24] *CRR*, 15, nos 1066, 1181; PRO, MS E159/12, memb. 10, which notes that 670 marks were still owing from the Jews in February 1233, to be paid within a month of Easter on pain of the release of an unidentified charter, presumably a bond detailing financial penalties, to the representative of the Italians.

[25] *Calendar of the Charter Rolls 1226–1257* (London, 1903) [hereafter *Cal.Ch.R*], pp. 163, 167.

[26] *CRR*, 15, nos 1110–24, discussed by Michael Adler, 'The testimony of the London Jewry against the ministers of Henry III', *TJHSE*, 14 (1935–9), pp. 159–85. Adler describes Grimbaud as a Poitevin, but in fact his family were tenants of the honour of Huntingdon; W. Farrer, ed., *Honours and Knights' Fees*, 3 vols (London, 1923–5), 2, pp. 301–7; *Calendar of Liberate Rolls 1226–1240* (London, 1917) [hereafter *Cal.Lib.R*], pp. 309, 312, 315, 317; *ClR, 1234–7*, p. 262; *Liber Feodorum. The Book of Fees commony called Testa de Nevill*, 3 vols (London, 1920–31), p. 1354.

the spring of 1233 these windfalls were running short. Once again it was the Jews who were forced to bail Henry III out of his difficulties. On 2 March 1233 we receive the first indication of a new tallage of 10,000 marks imposed upon the Jews, £1,000 to be paid by Easter 1234, £1,000 by Easter 1235, the remainder at £2,000 a year thereafter.[27] Not only was this the heaviest tax imposed upon the English community for over twenty years, but it fell upon those members least able to pay, the great financiers of Hereford and Norwich being exempt by virtue of their own heavy fines contracted earlier with the Crown. Within a month of the tallage's announcement, the Exchequer disbursed well in excess of 10,000 marks in the arrears of pensions owed to Poitou and Brittany.[28] Exploitation of the Jews provided a mere drop in the ocean compared to such vast sums shipped to the King's allies in France.

The size and severity of the tallage were determined by the King's need for cash to support reconquest abroad. At the same time taxation was only one aspect of what appears to have been a wider, deliberate campaign against the Jews in England. Already in January 1232, with des Roches as witness, the King had founded a house for Jewish converts in London, on the site of a former synagogue. Des Roches' suffragan, Bishop John of Ardfert, consecrated the new foundation, to which the King pledged an income of 700 marks a year, payable at the Exchequer; a lavish endowment at the best of times, and one which in the circumstances of 1232 was positively ridiculous.[29] Needless to say, only a fraction of the money promised was ever forthcoming. It may be that the King hoped to salve his conscience at profiting from usury by putting at least a proportion of those profits towards a Christian mission to the usurers. It is also likely that his actions were prompted by pressure from the Church. The archbishopric of Canterbury stood vacant between 1231 and 1234, the King making several unsuccessful attempts to fill it with courtiers or with an

---

[27] *CPR, 1232–47*, pp. 12–13, which suggests that the tallage itself had been imposed some time earlier. However, I cannot agree with Robert C. Stacey, *Politics, Policy and Finance under Henry III 1216–1245* (Oxford, 1987), p. 144, who attempts to redate the tallage to 1232. The 10,000-mark tallage is unmentioned in the receipt roll of the Jewry for Hilary/Easter terms 1233, which none the less refers to earlier levies of 2,000, 4,000, and 6,000 marks; PRO, MS E401/1565.

[28] PRO, MS E401/10B, memb. 1; *Cal.Lib.R*, pp. 210–12, 239.

[29] William Dugdale, *Monasticon Anglicanum*, ed. J. Caley *et al.*, 6 vols (London, 1946), 6, p. 683; Michael Adler, *Jews of Medieval England* (London, 1939), pp. 279–306. Adler (p. 283) states incorrectly that des Roches left money to the house of converts in his will, based on a misreading of *ClR, 1242–7*, p. 22. For the house's consecration by Bishop John (of Ardfert), see PRO, MS E372/76, memb. 8d.

adherent of des Roches. His failure here was both symptomatic and provocative of a more serious breach with the bishops, who were to prove the bitterest and the most persistent critics of des Roches' regime. Pious gestures such as the foundation of the London house were almost certainly intended to smooth relations between King and clergy. It is in this light that we should view the most striking of Henry's anti-Jewish measures during these years, the statutes of the Jewry issued at Canterbury in April 1233.[30]

The place of their issue and the terms of the statutes themselves both argue an association with the King's intervention in the Canterbury election. In the most comprehensive statement of policy since King John's charter of the Jewry of 1201, it was decreed that interest on Jewish loans should be restricted to two pence in the pound per week, the equivalent of an annual interest rate of 43 per cent.[31] Compound interest was outlawed, with only the initial loan subject to charges. Loans by tally were hence-forth invalid. Instead, such transactions were to be recorded by tripartite chirograph, one part each for lender and borrower and a third to be deposited in the official *archa* for the storage of Jewish bonds. No loan was to be advanced on the security of church plate, or on cloth that was blood-stained, wet, or torn, as if in a fight, restrictions already found in John's charter of 1201, designed to prevent the pawning of clothes taken from murder victims. Finally, any Jew unable to obtain pledges of good conduct by Michaelmas 1233 was to leave the realm on pain of imprisonment.

The Canterbury statutes represent the first attempt by the secular authorities to embody the Lateran decrees into a coherent body of law. The enforcement of a reasonable rate of interest and the prohibition of church goods as pawns are both found in the conciliar legislation of 1215, although, as we shall see, their transmission into English law was the result not so much of papal influence as of the example already set by the kings of France. For the moment, rather than dwell upon these French precedents, we should carry the story of des Roches' regime through to its conclusion in 1234. By the summer of 1233 not only the Church but the secular baronage was in uproar against the court, spurred on by des Roches' inequitable exercise of patronage and by the squandering of vast resources on the King's allies in Brittany and Poitou. Headed by Richard Marshal and his household, a substantial group rebelled against

---

[30] The statutes are printed by H. G. Richardson, 'Glanville continued', *Law Quarterly Review*, 215 (1938), p. 393.
[31] For John's statute see T. D. Hardy, ed., *Rotuli Chartarum* (London, 1837), p. 93.

the King, leading to war on the Welsh marches. Once again the King found himself close to bankruptcy, the windfalls of the past two years dissipated in the cost of pensions to allies overseas, in the patronage of des Roches and his satellites, and in the costs of civil war. It was Henry's misfortune that bankruptcy came on at the precise moment he was most in need of supply. The truce with France, agreed in 1231, was due to expire in July 1234. To salvage anything from the wreckage of his continental policy it was essential that the King continue to buy allegiance in Brittany and Poitou, but by the spring of 1234 he had barely enough money to support domestic expenses.

At the end of February 1234 the King wrote despairingly to the treasury, asking that he be sent £1,000—a paltry sum by comparison with the riches he had disposed of in 1232, but in the circumstances of 1234 all too much for the treasury to raise, especially as it was commanded to reach the King at Northampton in less than a fortnight.[32] To fulfil this commission, the treasurer, Robert Passelaw, turned to the London Jewry, forcing them to advance £500 over and above the tallage of 10,000 marks to which they were already committed. According to later testimony, the money was raised amidst extortion and embezzlement by Passelaw's officers. Passelaw, Peter de Rivallis, and Peter Grimbaud were to be accused of taking bribes from the Jews, of destroying Jewish bonds for their own private gain, and in February 1234 of extorting an extra £200 in private profit over and above the £500 raised towards the King's needs at Northampton.[33] The King obtained his money, but £1,000 was insufficient to rescue either de Roches' regime or the alliances abroad. Des Roches was dismissed in the summer of 1234, having failed to secure a prolongation of the truce with France. Unable to obtain further supply in England, the Duke of Brittany and the magnates of Poitou defected to Louis IX. At court, a group of bishops came forward to replace the disgraced administration. Amongst their first actions was to launch an enquiry into offences by the disgraced ministers, encouraging the London Jewry to express their grievances.[34] At the same time, the new regime saw the imposition of yet further, extraordinary taxation. At Tewkesbury in June 1234 the King accepted an unspecified fine from the Jewry over and above the 10,000-mark tallage. At the same time the 10,000-mark tallage

---

[32] *ClR, 1231–4*, p. 551.

[33] *CRR*, 15, nos 1110–24, esp. no. 1118. For the dispatch of money from the treasury to Northampton see PRO, MS E372/78, memb. 7; *CPR, 1232–47*, p. 40.

[34] *CRR*, 15, p. 257n., and see *ClR, 1231–4*, pp. 585–6 for inquests into the Jewries of Oxford, York, Nottingham, Northampton, and Lincoln.

was rescheduled but in no way reduced. The size of the Tewkesbury tallage is unknown, but that it was heavy can be gauged from a contribution of £100 from a single Jew of Nottingham.[35]

Far from repealing the anti-Jewish measures of the past few years, the new regime tightened restrictions against the Jews. It was his desire to appease the bishops which had encouraged the King's anti-Jewish campaign after 1231. With the bishops themselves in power, and the King keen to demonstrate his piety and contrition, the campaign continued apace. By the end of 1234 new measures had been enforced to prevent the King's sokemen or villeins from using their lands as pledge for Jewish loans and to expel the Jews from various small towns. Expulsions took place at Warwick, High Wycombe, and Newcastle upon Tyne, where the burgesses fined 100 marks for a charter forbidding any Jew to reside there in future.[36] In November 1234 the sheriff of Norfolk and Suffolk was ordered to proclaim a general prohibition against Christian maidservants serving in Jewish households.[37]

Taken altogether, the tallages, forced loans, and extortions, the foundation of the London house of converts, the statutes of April 1233, and the expulsions and restrictions imposed in 1234 constitute a coherent and deliberate campaign against the Jews, the first stage in a prolonged deterioration of Christian–Jewish relations which was to culminate in 1290 with banishment for the entire Jewish community. What was the immediate impact of the campaign of 1231–4? Inevitably increased financial pressures on the Jewry led to heightened tensions with their Christian creditors. As we might expect, the period of des Roches' regime witnessed an outbreak of popular attacks on the Jewry. There were problems, for example, amongst the Jews of des Roches' own cathedral city.

At some time in 1232 a year-old boy, named Stephen, was found strangled near St Swithun's Priory, in Winchester. According to those who found the body, it had been dismembered, castrated, and its eyes and heart plucked out. The boy's mother promptly fled the city, but popular suspicion fixed on Abraham Pinche, a Jew who, it was claimed, had purchased the child from its nurse so as to carry out some sort of crucifixion ritual. The sheriff was forced to imprison the city's entire

---

[35] PRO, MS C60/33, memb. 4.
[36] ClR, 1231–4, pp. 515–16, 592; ClR, 1234–7, p. 20. For Newcastle see PRO, MS C60/33, membs 4, 6; Newcastle upon Tyne, Tyne and Wear Archives, MS 574/95.
[37] ClR, 1234–7, pp. 13–14.

Jewry, probably as much for their own protection as for anything else. In June 1232, following consultations at court, they were released in return for a fine of 20 marks. Officially guilt for Stephen's murder was fixed upon his mother, who later abjured the realm.[38] None the less, Abraham Pinche failed to escape the citizens' retribution. Accused of stealing 2s. from a shop in Winchester as long ago as August 1230, he was tried at the Hampshire eyre of 1236 and hanged as a felon.[39] At least part of his unpopularity derived from his position and that of his father, Chere Pinche, amongst the most active usurers in Hampshire. Between 1231 and 1234 des Roches was to exploit the Pinche family enterprise, persuading their debtors to part with land for religious foundations at Selborne and Titchfield, which he was in the process of founding.[40] In short, whilst presiding over a period of exceptional hardship for the Jews, des Roches was quite prepared to exploit Jewish enterprise for his own private ends. Nor was it only at Winchester that tensions between citizens and Jews reached fever pitch. Accusations of child murder and crucifixion were made against the Norwich Jewry at some time between 1230 and 1234, and a number of the city's leading money-lenders executed or banished for their supposed offences.[41] There may also have been disturbances at Lincoln.[42]

So far we have treated the anti-Jewish measures enforced in England in isolation from any continental precedent. Yet the tightening of the screws against Jewish finance was directed specifically towards providing subsidies for the King's allies in Poitou and Brittany. What is more, the regime of 1232–4 was packed with the alien supporters of des Roches; Frenchmen almost certainly familiar with contemporary measures against the Jews of France. In general, it has become customary to regard Planta-genet exploitation of the Jews as more sophisticated and of far longer standing than anything attempted by the Capetian kings of France. For example, King John's charter of the Jewry of 1201 predates any equivalent

---

[38] *Annales Monastici*, 2 (Winchester), p. 86 dates the murder to 17 Oct., which cannot be correct. For details of the case see *ClR, 1231–4*, p. 80; PRO, MS JUST1/775, memb. 20. In 1225 Abraham had been amongst several of the Winchester Jews implicated in the death of William fitz Richard fitz Gervase. The accusation was laid by William's father, but Abraham was subsequently acquitted; *Rot.l.c.*, 2, pp. 50b, 51b.

[39] PRO, MS JUST1/775, memb. 20d; *Cal.Ch.R*, p. 218; *ClR, 1234–7*, p. 239.

[40] *ClR, 1227–31*, p. 539; *ClR, 1231–4*, p. 103; W. D. Macray, ed., *Charters and Documents relating to Selborne and its Priory*, 2 vols, Hampshire Record Society (1891–4), I, pp. 4, 6, ii, pp. 46, 51; Cole, ed., *Documents*, p. 302; Dugdale, *Monasticon*, 6, pp. 933–4.

[41] *CRR*, 15, no. 1320; Lipman, *Jews of Norwich*, pp. 59–62.

[42] *ClR, 1231–4*, p. 571.

Capetian legislation. Its prohibition on the pawning of bloodstained clothing was adopted five years later in one of several decrees of the Jewry issued by Philip Augustus.[43]

None the less, for all that the Plantagenets appear to have been more successful and more precocious in their exploitation of Jewish finance, there is a correspondence between Jewish policy in England and France unlikely to be the outcome of mere coincidence. In 1210 John and Philip Augustus both ordered the arrest of their respective Jewries, demanding fines and pledges for their release in strikingly similar circumstance.[44] Thereafter, far from the Capetians copying Plantagenet methods in respect to the Jews, it appears that English law followed examples set in France. Of the anti-Jewish measures introduced after 1231, virtually all had French precedent. Thus, of the statutes promulgated at Canterbury in April 1233, the restriction of Jewish usury to two pence in the pound and the prohibition of compound interest are already to be found incorporated in Capetian decrees of 1206 and between 1206 and 1219.[45] The insistence upon tripartite loan agreements with one part entrusted to official custody is already to be found in French ordinances of between 1206 and 1219, and 1228.[46] The London house of converts has its counterpart in the forced reconsecration of French synagogues as Christian churches as long ago as the 1180s.[47] Well in advance of Henry III, Louis IX had initiated a campaign against usury, motivated by a combination of piety and financial self-interest, and culminating in 1235, after a series of decrees attempting to ensure the repayment of all Jewish loans, with a blanket prohibition on usury.[48] The expulsion of Jews from all but the greater cities began in France long before anything similar was attempted in England.[49] A series of proposals put before a provincial synod of the archdiocese of Tours about 1230 explains the desirability of such expulsions; living in small towns and villages the Jews find it easier to

---

[43] *Rotuli Chartarum*, p. 93; H.-François Delaborde, ed., *Recueil des actes de Philippe-Auguste, Roi de France*, 3 vols (Paris, 1916–66), 2, no. 955. In general, for French legislation see Robert Chazan, *Medieval Jewry in Northern France* (Baltimore and London, 1973), pp. 63–153; G. Langmuir, '"Judei Nostri" and the beginning of Capetian legislation', *Traditio*, 16 (1960), pp. 183–244.

[44] Chazan, *Jewry*, pp. 79–80, 95; Lipman, *Jews of Norwich*, p. 104.

[45] Chazan, *Jewry*, pp. 84–5.

[46] Ibid., p. 78; E. Martène and U. Durand, ed., *Veterum scriptorum et monumentorum historicorum*, 9 vols (Paris, 1724–33), 1, cols 1222–3.

[47] John W. Baldwin, *Masters, Princes and Merchants*, 2 vols (Princeton, 1970), pp. 120–1.

[48] Langmuir, '"Judei Nostri"', pp. 215–27; Chazan, *Jewry*, pp. 100–111.

[49] Chazan, *Jewry*, p. 86.

pervert their Christian neighbours into apostasy and to prey upon women who come to them for loans.[50]

As a native of Tours, long involved in diplomacy with France, Peter des Roches was no doubt familiar with such arguments. However, there is no reason to suppose that it was des Roches who was chiefly responsible for the correspondence between Jewish policy in France and England after 1231. The inspiration may have come from any number of sources. The chief sponsor of anti-Jewish legislation in the 1220s, Archbishop Langton, was a product of the schools of Paris, familiar with the debate on Judaism amongst the scholastic circle of Peter the Chanter which did so much to inform the Lateran decrees of 1215.[51] In 1231 the Frenchman Simon de Montfort was permitted to succeed to his family lands in England. Amongst his first actions was to expel the Jews from Leicester, well in advance of the expulsions ordered by the King.[52] Montfort's charter on this occasion is framed as a pious award, for the salvation of his soul and the souls of his ancestors and successors; a telling indication of the approval expected for what was, in effect, an act of unprovoked persecution.[53] The Jews he expelled from Leicester sought refuge within the neighbouring lordship of the Countess of Winchester. It is the diatribe inspired by the Countess's actions from the schoolsman Robert Grosseteste which provides perhaps our keenest insight into contemporary scholastic attitudes to the Jews. According to Grosseteste, the Jews, like Cain, were accursed of God. As the killers of Christ, they merited if not death, then slavery. Rulers who indulged them or profited from their usury became themselves tainted with sin; in St Paul's words: 'Not only those who do these things, but those who consent to them are worthy of death.' Lords who benefit from Jewish usury drink the blood of victims they ought to protect; their hands and garments are steeped in blood, and they themselves become fuel for the eternal fire.[54] With these or similar injunctions ringing in his ears, it is hardly surprising that Henry III should have assumed a violent antipathy towards the Jews.

Nor was it only amongst scholars and Christians that links persisted to

---

[50] Joseph Avril, ed., *Les Conciles de la Province de Tours* (Paris, 1987), pp. 130–1.

[51] Baldwin, *Masters, Princes and Merchants*, chs 14 and 15, esp. pp. 296–311.

[52] H. R. Luard, ed., *Roberti Grosseteste episcopi quondam Lincolniensis Epistolae*, RS (1861), no. 5.

[53] J. Nichols, *The History and Antiquities of the County of Leicester*, 4 vols (London, 1795–1815), 1 pt 1, appendix, p. 38, no. 13, a reference I owe to John Maddicott. See also N. C. Vincent, 'The first quarrel between Simon de Montfort and King Henry III', in P. Coss and S. D. Lloyd, eds, *Thirteenth Century England IV* (Woodbridge, 1992, forthcoming).

[54] *Grosseteste Epistolae*, no. 5, as paraphrased by R. W. Southern, *Robert Grosseteste: the Growth of an English Mind in Medieval Europe* (Oxford, 1986), pp. 244–9.

the anti-Semitism of Louis IX and the schools of Paris. The English Jewry was itself in communication with France; of the Jews accused at Norwich after 1230 at least one was unavailable to stand trial, the note *manet in Francia* being inserted beside his name.[55] Beyond such personal contacts, Jewish or Christian, the piety of Henry III was modelled to a considerable extent upon the example set by Louis IX. Just as in the 1240s Henry's rebuilding of Westminster Abbey was carried out in conscious and competitive imitation of Louis' work at the Saint-Chapelle, so a decade earlier Henry may have set out deliberately to emulate the French King's policy towards the Jews.

The consequences of such imitation are clear. By 1234 the English Jewry was under serious attack; the watershed in Christian–Jewish relations had been reached. New and swingeing taxes were making inroads upon Jewish wealth and souring relations with Christian creditors. Expulsions and restrictions were already being adopted as part of official policy towards the Jews, with the fierce support of the Church and in tandem with a similar onslaught across the Channel. In all of this, Henry III's relations with France, his alien ministers, his need to supply allies in Brittany and Poitou, and his desire to emulate the piety of Louis IX played no small part.

Peterhouse, Cambridge

[55] Lipman, *Jews of Norwich*, p. 62.

MONASTIC CHARITY FOR JEWISH CONVERTS: THE REQUISITION OF CORRODIES BY HENRY III*

by JOAN GREATREX

THE controversy which concerns us now, as it once concerned the thirteenth-century participants, centres upon the king's right to demand corrodies in monastic establishments for his own nominees. Thus it is necessary to begin by defining the term 'corrody' in the present context. In describing a corrody as 'nothing more than an allowance consisting of a share in a common fund', Professor Hamilton Thompson neatly encapsulated the multifarious forms which it could take; he also drew attention to its potentially disastrous effects when he noted that at least one person, who should have known better, believed that corrodies were so called because they were corrosive.[1] The allowances or provisions were specified in a written agreement between the monastic chapter and the prospective recipient and might include board, lodging, items of clothing, and cash payments, or any one of these, or a combination of them; and so they were often entered on monastic officials' expense accounts as annuities, pensions, or liveries (*liberationes*). Acting on their own initiative and often against episcopal injunctions, religious houses in financial straits made such grants to laymen, whose wives were sometimes included, in return for a lump sum or a donation of property. The corrodian who paid cash or bequeathed part of his estate provided an immediate and welcome boost in income for the community which received him, and he and his family gained security and comfort in their declining years. But the financial relief for the monastery which had guaranteed hospitality for life could, and did, turn into a liability when the beneficiaries lived longer than had been anticipated.[2] In addition,

---

* I should like to thank Professor R. C. Stacey for his comments and suggestions with regard to this paper, and for his generosity in lending me the typescript of his article, referred to in nn. 20 and 43, below.

[1] A. Hamilton Thompson, *The English Clergy in the Later Middle Ages* (Oxford, 1947), p. 174. In fact, the word *corrodium* or *corredium*, and sometimes *conredium*, first appears as a medieval Latin term with the meaning given above.

[2] As Barbara Harvey pointed out, with colourful examples from Westminster Abbey, in the Ford Lectures of 1989; these will soon appear in print with the title 'Living and dying in England, 1200–1540: the monastic experience'.

outsiders, by virtue of their rights as founders and benefactors, made certain claims on religious houses, among which was the requisition of corrodies on behalf of relatives or retainers.[3] It was this form of exploitation in which the King himself was the chief offender, and Henry III, in financial straits, would argue that he was in principle the patron of all religious establishments in the country.[4]

Converts from Judaism were recipients of corrodies long before Henry assumed the throne in 1216, as a few known examples make clear. Archbishop Anselm showed his concern for one, whom he sent to Prior Arnulf at Christchurch, Canterbury;[5] another occurs in a papal mandate of 1199 addressed to the canons of St Mary de Pré, Leicester, and requesting maintenance for the bearer, who had been left destitute by the death of his patron.[6] There is also an entry in a list of muniments of Ramsey Abbey; the cartulary itself is lost, but it included an undated papal instrument entitled 'provisio unius conversi ad fidem'.[7]

Both the policy of the Government and the attitude of the Church to the Jewish minority in thirteenth-century England have been examined in depth by historians, and they continue to be the subject of studies that are by no means entirely dispassionate, for living in our midst are survivors of the recent Jewish holocaust, which remains a controversial and emotive issue today. In the context of this paper it is sufficient to bear in mind that the Jewish presence was always considered a potential source of danger to the faith and morals of the Christian community; and it was consistent with this policy to urge segregation or even deportation.[8] As Professor Gavin Langmuir has observed, the doctrinal and canonical position of the Church was consistent and clear, but the treatment applied varied accord-

---

[3] Susan Wood, *English Monasteries and their Patrons in the Thirteenth Century* (Oxford, 1955), esp. ch. 6.

[4] Matthew Paris relates a conversation between the abbot of Buildwas and the King in 1256, when the former tactfully remonstrated with the latter on this point; see his *Chronica Majora*, ed. H. R. Luard, *RS*, 7 vols (1872–83), 5, pp. 553–4.

[5] *S. Anselmi, Cantuariensis Archiepiscopi, Opera Omnia*, ed. F. S. Schmitt, 6 vols (Edinburgh, 1946–61), 5, ep. 380.

[6] C. R. Cheney and M. G. Cheney, eds, *The Letters of Pope Innocent III (1198–1216) Concerning England and Wales* (Oxford, 1967), no. 169.

[7] William Henry Hart and Ponsonby A. Lyons, eds, *Cartularium Monasterii de Rameseia*, *RS*, 3 vols (1884–93), 1, p. 68; it was a request from Innocent IV (1243–54).

[8] Abbot Samson expelled the Jews from Bury St Edmunds in 1190; see Jocelin of Brakelond, *Chronicle of the Abbey of Bury St. Edmunds*, tr. and notes by Diana Greenway and Jane Sayers (Oxford, 1989), pp. 41–2. As Archdeacon of Leicester, Grosseteste approved of Simon de Montfort's action in removing the Jews there; see R. W. Southern, *Robert Grosseteste, the Growth of an English Mind in Medieval Europe* (Oxford, 1986), p. 246.

ing to local conditions and influences.[9] The attitude to conversion and to the converted Jew, though a separate issue, cannot be isolated from the contemporary surroundings, that of the interplay of two communities existing side by side and responding to the inevitably frequent encounters in business negotiations and in the common exchanges which are part of daily life. Did the *conversus* continue to be the focus of suspicion and distrust; had he whole-heartedly embraced the faith and totally rejected his Jewish past? Motives underlying conversion in this period remain hidden, but among the forces at work, and inextricably bound up with any inner convictions which may be attributed to the gift of faith, are the external factors that, without being determinative, could have proved sufficient to tip the scales. These were the increasing economic and financial pressures, in addition to a more flagrant anti-Jewish lobby, especially of the middle decades of the century, which resulted from Henry's inability to live within his means.[10]

What lay behind Henry's establishment of the *Domus Conversorum*, which was designed as a semi-monastic community for converts, in London, in the year 1232? On the one hand, he was engaged in extorting the Jews for all they were worth, and now, on the other hand, he was offering them his personal care and protection in return for their acceptance of the Christian faith. In this he incurred the risk of adding to the Crown's already heavy burden of debt by cutting off one of his main sources of revenue. The Jews, as Jews, were, in effect, the King's property, and as converts they forfeited all their goods to the Crown; but afterwards they remained in his care as a liability at the rate of $10\frac{1}{2}d.$ a week for men and $8d.$ for women and the cost of accommodation in the *Domus*.[11] It should be noted that, although both Church and Crown were on the whole in agreement over Jewish affairs, it was the Crown which manifested itself in two guises, that of relentless financial exploiter and money-grubber and that of pious benefactor and almsgiver. As to Henry's personal interest in the *conversi*, there are other convincing proofs, such as the baptism of Philip of Reading in the King's presence in 1234, and converts whom he permitted to take his own baptismal name.[12] Professor

---

[9] G. I. Langmuir, 'The Jews and the archives of Angevin England: reflections on medieval anti-semitism', *Traditio*, 19 (1963), pp. 235–6.

[10] R. C. Stacey, *Politics, Policy and Finance under Henry III, 1216–1245* (Oxford, 1987), ch. 4, *passim*, and pp. 243–59.

[11] For details of the foundation of the London *Domus* see the appendix of documents in Michael Adler, *The Jews of Medieval England* (London, 1939), pp. 340–1.

[12] *ClR, 1231–4*, p. 415 for Philip. In the 1255 list discussed below Henry was, with Philip, the sixth in order of the most frequently chosen among masculine names.

Watt has stated that it was no doubt royal piety which lay behind Henry's assumption of responsibility for the material welfare of the *conversi*; but what prompted this initiative?[13] Adler suggests a possible source of influence in some of the signatories of the foundation charter of the *Domus*, namely, Bishops Peter des Roches and William Mauclerc, and Hubert de Burgh; but none of these men is known to have sponsored a convert, which is presumably what happened when converts are found bearing the names of Robert Grosseteste, John of Darlington, John Mansell, and John Plessetis.[14]

In 1247, only fifteen years after the opening of the *Domus*, the close rolls provide us with a list of about seventeen *conversi* whom the King had decided to send for maintenance to fourteen religious houses in various parts of the country.[15] There is no possibility of ascertaining if this decision was the result of an overcrowded *Domus* or a shortage of funds for its support, or both. In Henry's straitened circumstances at this time the latter was almost certainly a major factor. However, this was not the first occasion on which Henry had directed religious superiors to extend their monastic charity to Jewish converts, for Adam Page and his wife had been sent to Shaftesbury sometime in or before 1246.[16] There are two other requests which, although later, suggest that the King's tactics with regard to corrodies for both *conversi* and his retainers and clerks may not have been an innovation. Mandates addressed to the abbesses of Barking and Romsey in 1253 state that as long as they provide for the royal nominees, there will be no further demands on their hospitality on behalf of *conversi* or any other persons; and it is a reasonable assumption that the *conversi* to whom Henry refers in this context are not laybrothers.[17]

---

[13] J. A. Watt, 'The English Episcopate, the State and the Jews: the evidence of the thirteenth-century conciliar decrees', in P. R. Cross and S. D. Lloyd, eds, *Thirteenth Century England II, Proceedings of the Newcastle upon Tyne Conference* (1987), p. 143.

[14] John de Darlington, a Dominican, was the King's confessor; John Mansell and John de Plessetis, Earl of Warwick, were both royal counsellors and held various offices of state. Dr Nicholas Vincent has informed me that although Peter des Roches, Bishop of Winchester, did not mention the *Domus* in his will, he did support some converts whose names are to be found on the Winchester pipe rolls during his episcopate.

[15] *ClR, 1247–51*, p. 100.

[16] *ClR, 1242–7*, pp. 418 and 165, where it is made clear that they were also in the *Domus* both before and after this date.

[17] *CPR, 1247–58*, p. 180, and *ClR, 1251–3*, p. 432, respectively. Laybrothers are not known to have been royal nominees and would hardly have been posted to nunneries! It is to be noted (1) that the abbess of Barking had been distrained the year before for failing to pay the 49½ marks due for tallage from her tenants during the recent vacancy, *ClR, 1251–5*, p. 70; and (2) that the royal nominee at Romsey was Matilda, sister of Robert Walerand, seneschal of the

Among the converts in the early 1250s were Mabilia, whom the King sent to the Cluniacs at Bermondsey, directing them to pay her one mark 'pro exhibicione sua in domo predicto' for a two-year period.[18] When four others, who had been accommodated by the abbot of Thorney, moved elsewhere in 1253, Henry wrote a letter of thanks and released the abbot from his obligation.[19]

The year 1255 appears to mark a turning-point in the billeting of *conversi* in monastic establishments. This judgement is based on the fact that the dorse of the fine roll for this year lists about 150 converts assigned to some 125 religious houses, including 37 Benedictine monasteries, 34 Cistercian, 31 Augustinian, 10 Premonstratensian, 7 Cluniac, 3 Gilbertine, and 3 hospitals.[20] In addition, two spaces between these lists are taken up by shorter lists of about 16 or 17 names headed 'De servientibus regis missis per abbatias and prioratus'. The first group of converts' names is preceded by a copy of the writ, addressed to the prior of Walsingham but intended to be used as the model for all, in which Henry explains that the war in Gascony as well as other affairs have prevented him from giving his attention to the welfare of the *conversi*. He therefore requires the abbot or prior to provide food and the other necessities of life for the bearer of the royal letter for two years; or, if the *conversus* preferred maintenance in cash, the superiors could choose to pay at the daily rate of $1\frac{1}{2}d$. This writ was dated at Merton on 20 January, and was soon followed by another from Westminster on 6 February; it, too, has been copied on to the fine roll between the first and second lists of converts, and is a sternly worded reprimand for the lack of response to the royal command. To judge from the confusion apparent in the compilation of these lists there were protracted negotiations with more than a few religious houses over the allocation both of *conversi* and of royal servants; names are repeated or crossed out, and marginal notes and signs added in an attempt to

---

New Forest, who had arranged for the abbess to have 16 oaks 'ad fabricam ecclesie sue' only a few months before the corrody was requested, ibid., p. 375.

[18] *ClR, 1251–3*, p. 509.

[19] Ibid., p. 457.

[20] PRO, C/60/52; three of the Benedictine houses were nunneries. Adler has printed a partial and somewhat inaccurate list in *Jews of Medieval England*, pp. 342–6. R. C. Stacey's reckoning, in 'The conversion of Jews to Christianity in thirteenth-century England', *Speculum* (forthcoming), results in a slightly higher number of converts; but the difference is accounted for by the uncertainties surrounding entries like 'Robert and Hugh, sons of Richard, converts', followed by another entry naming Robert alone, or Hugh. How many of these are references to the same person?

bring order out of the muddle and explain the reasons for the many alterations.[21] Why are these records found on a fine roll instead of on close or patent rolls like the earlier entries already noted? Does it, perhaps, reflect a state of disorganization at the Exchequer upon the King's return from Gascony in late 1254, and also suggest that a number of monasteries not included on the list paid fines for exemption or successfully pleaded poverty? A single memorandum among the allocations of converts states that Chertsey was one house which obtained exemption by means of a fine, and others may have been recorded elsewhere.[22]

There are other possible reasons which may explain the absence of a number of the larger religious communities from the 1255 lists. Bermondsey, for example, had been burdened with William, *conversus*, in 1247, and with Mabilia in 1253.[23] Barking and Romsey had recently received royal nominees, with the royal promise that nothing more would be required. Other houses favoured by exemption were those whose superiors were actively engaged in royal affairs, notably Westminster, Newburgh, and Pershore.[24] For the rest, it is probable that monasteries were not selected or omitted in accordance with any predetermined schedule, and we may not be far from the truth in regarding the entries on the dorse of the fine roll as no more than rough working lists which were never enrolled. It is unlikely that the converts themselves had some influence in the arrangements, as most of them were placed in houses which were at a distance from their home surroundings, that is, if we may rely on toponymics. Christiana of Gloucester and William de Wigorn' (or of Worcester) can be picked out as two exceptions: the prior of St Oswald's, Gloucester, was directed to take Christiana, but not without repeated demands, and she may have had to go to St Guthlac's, Hereford, in the end; and the prior of Worcester received two requests on behalf of William.[25]

---

[21] One marginal comment 'quia non habuerunt' clearly shows the resistance of some of the monasteries to the King's excessive demands; another annotation was 'preter habunt secundum breve'.

[22] None of the fines which are entered on the face of the roll have any connection with this type of fine.

[23] *ClR, 1247–51*, pp. 100 and 509.

[24] The Abbot of Westminster was a friend and adviser of the King and must have been frequently concerned with Henry's building programme at Westminster; in 1249–50 he was also actively involved with the affairs of the *Domus* at Henry's request. *ClR, 1247–51*, pp. 238, 246, 260. John de Skipton, Prior of Newburgh, was chaplain to the King between c.1250 and 1255, and as such occurs *passim* in the close rolls for these years. Between 1252 and 1256 the Abbot of Pershore was an escheator and is found authorizing many letters in *ClR, 1251–3*, e.g., pp. 29–31, 37–8, etc.

[25] Constance of Reading may be another example. The name Constance without further

A large number of the *conversi* must have travelled many weary miles before they found a welcome. For example, the road from Dore Abbey, near Hereford, to Bridlington Priory, on the Yorkshire coast, was traversed by Robert Windour and his wife Ysabella;[26] and although William of Kent was destined for Battle Abbey, according to three entries in the lists, the King tried unsuccessfully to send him to Fécamp in 1260, and then to Cormeilles.[27] The Cistercian house at Croxden, Staffordshire, was repeatedly pressed to accept William of Canterbury after he and his son had been twice rejected by their Cistercian brethren at Stanley, Wiltshire. Lavendon had also been suggested for William, but it was crossed off; and he had been put down for Hailes and St James's, Bristol, as well. Where did the poor man find a haven and what happened to his son? The confusion was compounded by the fact that Nicholas le Waleys, described as the King's *nuncius*, was also proposed for Croxden.[28]

One of the most painful consequences of conversion was the breaking up of family units, William of Canterbury and his son being but two of an unknown number who suffered.[29] Members of the families of John Mansell and Robert Grosseteste furnish other examples of this policy, which can only be judged as heartless even if those responsible saw no other way out of the difficult circumstances of the moment. John Mansell went to Lewes, while his daughter Dionysia found refuge at Michelham; Robert Grosseteste appears to have been more fortunate in being sent to St

---

identification occurs on two of the lists as destined for Reading Abbey, and there is a Constance of Reading at the *Domus* in 1292, T. Rymer, *Foedera. Conventiones, Litterae*, 3 vols in 6 (London, 1816–30), 2, pp. 62–3.

[26] Their names occur together on the first and second lists, and Robert's name alone is repeated lower down on the second list, an indication that the small Cistercian house of Dore may have agreed to accept only one of them. In the end Dore probably received a royal servant instead, according to entries on the two lists of these officials.

[27] *ClR, 1259–61*, p. 262. Henry also attempted to place John of St Albans and his family in the French Abbey of Lire in 1254 (*CPR, 1247–58*, p. 386); but in the following year the fine roll indicates that they were being shunted back and forth, together and separately, between the three Cistercian houses of Cleeve, Kingswood, and Woburn. Dr Emma Mason has suggested to me that Henry was attempting to assert his patronal claims over these Norman abbeys: Fécamp, which was a ducal foundation, and Lire and Cormeilles, which were baronial foundations but had been drawn into the royal orbit by Henry I when he seized the Fitzosbern lands in England and Normandy; see David Bates, *Normandy before 1066* (London, 1982), pp. 68, 115, 121, 165, 193. It should also be noted that Henry did not accept the loss of Normandy until the Treaty of Paris in 1259.

[28] Nicholas is found still engaged in the royal service in 1259–60, *CPR, 1258–66*, pp. 57 and 103.

[29] It should be noted that the 1255 lists do not provide clear evidence of the breaking up of many of the convert families, unless we include the unknown number of families who became divided because only some of their members were converted.

Swithun's, Winchester, for, when his wife, Matilda, and daughter, Joanna, were rejected by Horton Priory, Dorset, the family were almost reunited as the monks at Hyde, Winchester, took Matilda and Joanna.

Statistics are a hazardous game, especially for medievalists. On the basis of the entries on the 1255 fine roll there is relatively little numerical certainty, because the same Christian names recur frequently, many without any distinguishing surname or toponymic.[30] It is also difficult to ascertain how many were actually received by some religious houses, as, for example, three names were proposed for the small Cistercian house of Flaxley, which would hardly have been able to support more than one. If we may be permitted to estimate, with due caution, it seems that about 35 converts, or convert families, were placed as the result of a single writ to the first house addressed, but there are more than 50 instances when two requests were required, and probably about 10 houses were approached three times.[31] In some 16 instances, several of which have been noted above, two or more houses were approached on behalf of the same converts. As to the choice of Christian names, the most frequently used were Richard, John, Thomas, and William (in that order) among males, but among females the range is wider and the preferences less striking: Juliana and Matilda being the most frequent and Joanna close behind.[32] If we assume that a toponymic designation indicates the place of origin, the lists contain 7 converts from London, 5 from Northampton, 4 from Lincoln and Worcester, and 2 from several other main centres where the Jewish population formed a substantial minority. Some of the converts may be traced, both before and after 1255, as members of the community in the London *Domus*,[33] an indication of the transient nature of the arrangements for many of them, probably on account of the two-year requirement stipulated in most of the royal writs.

Although 1255 may have been a peak year for the billeting of *conversi*, there is sufficient evidence to show that the allocation of places for both *conversi* and other royal nominees continued through the remaining years of Henry's reign and beyond; the opposition also continues and probably hardens. The Augustinians at Leeds, Kent, accepted William of London, *conversus*, and his son in 1258; and in 1265, that fateful year, the King— this time obliged to record the approval of his council of magnates—

---

[30] Three are designated as *clerici*. See also n. 20, above.

[31] It would be incorrect to regard each entry as evidence that a writ was sent; it is more likely that the same writ was delivered more than once.

[32] There are 18 female names which appear only once, one of these being Maria.

[33] See nn. 16 and 25, above.

wrote at length to the abbot of St Osyth's, demanding provision for Roger of Westminster, another convert.[34] Earlier, in 1260, the abbot of St John's, Colchester, had written to the King to request him to remove his servant, John Prat, for none of the brethren was willing to have him.[35] Similarly, at a later but unknown date, the Abbot of Ramsey turned down the royal request to accept M. William, *cyrurgicus* as a corrodian.[36]

Finally, it is possible to trace some of the details of the fate of Alice of Worcester, whose reception by the prior and convent at Worcester, her subsequent wanderings, and hoped for return are revealed through the fortunate survival of three letters. She first comes to notice about 1274, when she sent a letter written in French to Edward I, reminding him that his father had put her in the care of the Worcester monks and that he himself, while still in Gascony, had provided her son with a letter continuing the arrangements until his return to England. She now begged him for a further letter of renewal and assured him that this was also the wish of the Worcester chapter.[37] Another letter, written while Robert Burnell was the Bishop of Bath and Wells and also Chancellor (1275–92), in Latin and penned in a neat chancery-style hand, was again delivered by her son. It recounts a dramatic and woeful tale of Alice, *captiva*, and her homeless state: the 'domus' of Coventry (presumably, the Cathedral Priory) to which she had been temporarily directed had refused to accept her, and she had taken refuge at Chester until the Chancellor could make other arrangements. She likened herself first to Hagar, the bondwoman in the Old Testament, who was persecuted and driven into exile, and then to Mary Magdalene, the penitent in the Gospels; and she begged him to follow Christ's example in showing mercy.[38] The third letter cannot be placed in chronological sequence, but it was addressed by Edward I to the Worcester chapter and was copied into the notebook of John Lawerne, Worcester monk and Oxford scholar, in the mid-fifteenth century. The King severely reprimanded the chapter for disobeying his father by their refusal to continue their maintenance of Alice and her son, for he had intended it to extend throughout their lives.[39] It seems unlikely that

---

[34] For William see PRO, SC1/2/79, and for Roger, *ClR, 1264–8*, pp. 109–10.

[35] *ClR, 1259–61*, p. 108.

[36] PRO, SC1/28/92. The Prior of Dunstable turned down a papal request on behalf of a convert in 1275, H. R. Luard, ed., *Annales Monastici*, RS, 5 vols (1864–9), 3, p. 265.

[37] PRO, SC1/16/65, and printed in Adler, *Jews of Medieval England*, p. 347.

[38] PRO, SC1/24/201. I am grateful to Dr Crook at the Public Record Office for his help with regard to this letter. The reference to Hagar is in Gen. 21.

[39] Oxford, Bodleian Library, MS. 692, fol. 89v. Alice may have spent time in the *Domus*, see Adler, *Jews of Medieval England*, p. 352, where he quotes from Rymer, *Foedera*.

Alice's case was unique, and her correspondence, together with the other details discussed above, suggest that before the *conversi* were settled, there must have been an almost visible trail of worn-out boots and shoes; and in the Chancery and Exchequer, in 1255 at least, a large sum spent on ink and on candles for the late-night shift. Alice's persistence in corresponding with the King and Chancellor also suggests that, though destitute and dependent on royal and monastic charity, she and the other *conversi* cannot be dismissed as unlettered and ignorant, although the extent of their formal education is unknown.

There are unifying themes to be found in the reign of Henry III: his persistent adherence to the lofty view of kingship inherited from his ancestors and his building programme at Westminster; and, we might add, his concern for Jewish converts. However, his frequent shifts in foreign policy, which resulted from a series of ambitious and extravagant schemes, reveal his lack of political sense and incompetence; while the succession of minor crises at home during the middle years, which were caused by a recurring state of tension in his relations with the magnates, reflect an absence of tact and discernment.[40] He alienated his supporters, convinced church leaders that their liberties were at stake, and demanded more and larger sums in financial aid from all his subjects, above all from the Jews, who in the 1240s were reduced to bankruptcy by his excessive tallages.

In 1253, when the Jewish community had become so debilitated that they requested leave to emigrate, the King's reply was to close the ports.[41] They were now no longer in a position to support their poorest members, who found themselves with their backs to the wall. Professor Dobson has pointed to the 'corrosive effects of excessive tallages' and the 'increased anti-Jewish propaganda and blood-libel accusations' of these years;[42] and there can be no doubt of the heart-rending impact on the individual Jew. Among those who sought baptism as their only recourse, relief would have been marred by the painful experience of homelessness, and rejection by their Jewish relatives and friends.[43] When they were eventually given monastic hospitality they would have found themselves in daily

[40] Stacey, *Politics*, p. 259.
[41] For a discussion on this point see R. C. Stacey, '1240–60: a watershed in Anglo–Jewish Relations?', *HR*, 61 (1988), p. 140.
[42] R. B. Dobson, 'The decline and expulsion of the medieval Jews of York', *TJHSE*, 26 (1979), p. 36.
[43] Stacey, 'The conversion of Jews to Christianity', gives several examples of continued contact between converts and their former co-religionists.

contact with a Christian community, a setting in which their assimilation would surely have been facilitated more easily than that of the *conversi* in the London *Domus*; for the latter, who remained in the company of their former co-religionists, would have found themselves in a situation which could have fostered the survival of a ghetto mentality.

It is not a lack of monastic charity which accounts for the reluctance of the religious houses to co-operate with the King in his welfare programme for convert Jews. Enforced almsgiving under these conditions was seen as yet another attempt to burden them with the additional expense of more corrodians. By constantly asserting and attempting to extend his claims with regard to corrodies he was, in effect, thereby expropriating places which were needed for their own retainers and associates, and also reducing the amount of their own donations to the poor, who were their neighbours, waiting at their gates.

Symonds Yat

THE ROLE OF JEWISH WOMEN IN
MEDIEVAL ENGLAND
(*PRESIDENTIAL ADDRESS*)

by BARRIE DOBSON

IN devoting its attention to the relationship between Christianity and
Judaism, the Ecclesiastical History Society has self-evidently
addressed a theme as fundamental as it is often distressing to the
practitioners of both religions. For many historians of the English
Church, as for many of this Society's members themselves, that relationship presents the additional irony that it would have been almost
impossible actually to encounter a Jew in this country during those three
centuries which tend to interest them most. As it is, Edward I's expulsion
of all his Jewish subjects from his realm on 18 July 1290 ('without any
hope of ever remaining there')[1] not only aborted a still inconclusive
experiment in religious co-existence, but for centuries relegated the lives
of the Jews and Jewesses of Anglo-Norman and Plantagenet England to
the obscurity of the historically irrelevant. No longer in 1991 does that
seem at all so obvious; and one supposes that nothing would have
surprised Henry III and Edward I more than that their treatment of the
Jewish minority within their realm should now often seem more 'relevant'
to the churches of the modern world than any other feature of their
respective reigns. For that reason, above all, there must be every prospect
that the relationship between Jews and Christians in twelfth- and
thirteenth-century England will soon be subjected to more detailed
analysis than ever before.[2] Nor, for similar reasons, has it ever been quite
so obvious as it is today that the study of medieval Anglo-Jewry is too
important to remain the exclusive preserve of historians who are themselves Jews.

Nowhere are such developments likely to have more of an impact than
upon the obscurities of the role played by Jewish women within their own
communities and within English urban society as a whole during the
century and more before the expulsion of 1290. For there can indeed be

---

[1] *Chronicle of Bury St Edmunds, 1212–1301*, ed. A. Gransden (London, 1964), p. 61.

[2] See, e.g., R. Stacey, 'Recent work on medieval English Jewry', *Jewish History*, 2 (1987), pp. 61–
72; J. Hillaby, 'The Worcester Jewry, 1158–1290: portrait of a lost community', *Transactions of
the Worcestershire Archaeological Society*, ser. 3, 12 (1990), pp. 73–122; R. Mundill, 'Anglo-Jewry
under Edward I: credit agents and their clients', *TJHSE*, 31 (1988–90), pp. 1–21.

no doubt that in practice the female members of medieval Jewish households were of more critical importance to the relations between Christians and Jews than has ever been allowed: in thirteenth-century England at least, the Jewish woman is nearly always revealed at the most personal, painful, and significant interface between the two religions. It is therefore not a little surprising that whereas all sorts and conditions of medieval Christian women have been studied with ever-increasing intensity in recent years, the Jewish wife, widow, and daughter of medieval England still linger in comparative obscurity. Such neglect is no longer likely to persist indefinitely, above all, perhaps, because the Jewish woman seems to offer so interesting a non-Christian alternative 'role model' for the many historians now intent on recapturing the life of the medieval female within and outside her family. For very obvious reasons, French and German rabbinical opinion in the twelfth and thirteenth centuries usually projects a very different, more sensitive, and even more respectful image of the female sex than do the pronouncements of contemporary Christian popes and bishops.[3] Such an image can, of course, itself be deceptive; and this paper will suggest that one of the hazards facing the historian of the medieval Jewess may be the temptation to idealize her just because she is a Jewess. Similarly, it can be dangerously easy to exaggerate the very real contrasts there inevitably were between the material and emotional values espoused by medieval Jewish and Christian women in thirteenth-century England. In both cases their male contemporaries almost always—and altogether predictably—laid greatest public emphasis upon the ideal of female domesticity and the truism that 'the functions of women were in the home.'[4]

However, there can equally be no doubt that highly important as well as extremely complex differences existed between both the real existences and the contemporary stereotypes of medieval Jewish and Gentile women.

[3] I. Abrahams, *Jewish Life in the Middle Ages* (London, 1896), pp. 113–210; L. Rabinowitz, *The Social Life of the Jews of Northern France in the Twelfth to Fourteenth Centuries as reflected in the Rabbinical Literature of the Period* (London, 1938), pp. 137–65; I. A. Agus, *Urban Civilisation in Pre-Crusade Europe: a Study of Organised Town-Life in Northwestern Europe during the Tenth and Eleventh Centuries based on the Responsa Literature*, 2 vols (Leiden, 1965), 2, pp. 554–690.

[4] Rabinowitz, *Social Life*, pp. 164–5. It might still be argued that most Jewish women of the eleventh and twelfth centuries seem to have escaped the so-called 'family revolution' which allegedly did so much to depress the status of prominent Christian women in north-western Europe at this period: see F. and J. Gies, *Marriage and Family in the Middle Ages* (New York, 1989), pp. 121–32; G. Duby, *The Knight, the Lady and the Priest: the Making of Modern Marriage in Medieval France* (New York, 1983); C. N. L. Brooke, *The Medieval Idea of Marriage* (Oxford, 1989); and (for a very different perspective) P. Biller, 'The Common Woman in the Western Church in the thirteenth and early fourteenth centuries', *SCH*, 27 (1990), pp. 127–57.

Among their male partners, it was self-evidently much more true of the latter than the former that 'most of those who wrote explicitly about women did so to denigrate them, and most of those who wrote for other purposes were apt to give them short shrift.'[5] The fact that the activities of thirteenth-century English Jewesses are frequently more fully and more favourably documented than those of their Christian counterparts was, in fact, the most significant revelation of the late Reverend Michael Adler's pioneering paper on 'The Jewish Woman in Medieval England', originally delivered as a Presidential Address to the Jewish Historical Society of England in November 1934. In that lecture, still the only substantial study of the topic, Adler was at pains to point out that 'the lives of English Jewish women are recorded in the archives of the period in fuller detail than in any other country.'[6] Nearly sixty years later, such an opportunity should surely no longer be neglected, even if this lecture can do no more than attempt to provide a few fleeting insights into the role of women in the more substantial Jewish households and financial businesses of thirteenth-century England. Even more fleeting, but all the more precious for that reason, are the occasional glimpses afforded by the governmental records of the reigns of Henry III and Edward I into the Jewish woman's relations with her Christian neighbours, as well as her reactions to the increasing threat of deliberate persecution during the years immediately before the final catastrophe of 1290. Neither of these last two issues was of great concern to Adler, who had indeed no particularly general thesis upon the role of the Jewish woman in medieval England to advance. However, Adler's most important conclusion—the 'unequalled' importance of the Jewish woman 'within and without the community'—can certainly still afford to stand.[7] More important still, perhaps, Adler was the first scholar to reveal that when the full history of the Jewish woman in medieval England comes to be written, it will have to be based in most of its essentials on the tantalizingly incomplete fragments of minor narrative to be extracted from the plea rolls of the Exchequer of the Jews.[8]

It accordingly seems appropriate to approach the experience of at least

---

[5] J. T. Rosenthal, ed., *Medieval Women and the Sources of Medieval History* (Atlanta, Georgia, 1990), p. viii. For a pioneering attempt to expose 'the contradictory ideas about women formulated during the Middle Ages', see E. Power, *Medieval Women* (Cambridge, 1975), pp. 9–34.

[6] M. Adler, 'The Jewish Woman in Medieval England', in *Jews of Medieval England* (London, 1939), p. 39.

[7] Ibid., pp. 17–18.

[8] The long-awaited fifth volume in the series of *Calendars of the Plea Rolls of the Exchequer of the Jews*, inaugurated by J. M. Rigg in 1905 [hereafter *Cal. Jewish Plea Rolls*], appeared too late to be consulted for the purposes of this paper.

some Jewish women in medieval England by means of such a fragmentary narrative, a very painful narrative, in fact, but one which has at least the incidental value of demonstrating that Jewish women were quite as capable of conflict with one another as they were with the wives of Christian townsmen. This is a story, moreover, which has the additional interest of starting at the door of one of those fundamental, if obscure, centres of Jewish life in medieval England, the synagogue in the high street of Warwick, then the site of the most substantial English Jewish community and Jewish *archa* in the Midlands, and, as such, the greatest source of credit available in the region.[9] A little after noon on Monday 19 September 1244 Bessa, wife of Elias, was walking out of the door of that synagogue (*ad janitum scole*) when she encountered, apparently by chance, another Warwick Jew, Leo of Deubelen, who was accompanied by a positive bevy of his womenfolk—his wife Henna, his two daughters, Ancerra and Sigge, and his sister Muriel. According to Bessa's version of what followed, Leo violently kicked her (*percussit eam cum pede*) inside the doorway of the synagogue, so that she fell there in a fit, as if dead. Nevertheless, all four female members of Leo's family then proceeded 'to drag the said Bessa out of the doorway by the hair and beat her and so ill-treated her that when she was brought home she miscarried of her infant; but the child was as yet too young for its sex to be distinguished.' According to testimony later submitted on her behalf by her husband, Elias of Warwick, injury was then added to dire insult when the defenceless Bessa was robbed by Leo and his family of a gold buckle and eight of her gold rings, to the value of ten marks.[10]

This most detailed surviving account of the ill-treatment of a medieval English Jewish woman by other Jewish women was not, however, allowed to go unchallenged. The detailed charges brought by Elias in his subsequent appeal before the justices of the Jews were systematically denied by Leo's family, partly on the grounds that Elias had not been an eyewitness of the alleged assault, and partly because Bessa was still alive and might have sued, but did not do so. More generally, Leo and his relatives accused Bessa of complete falsehood: according to their version of events, the latter had herself begun the affray by assaulting members of Leo's family in the Warwick high street and then by gnawing at the nose

[9] PRO, E. 9/4, memb. 4d; J. M. Rigg, ed., *Select Pleas, Starrs and other Records from the Rolls of the Exchequer of the Jews, 1220–1284* = Selden Society, 15 (London, 1902) [hereafter Rigg, *Select Pleas*], pp. 11–12.
[10] *Cal. Jewish Plea Rolls*, 1, pp. 103–4; Adler, 'Jewish Woman', p. 36.

and ears of his daughter Ancerra. Even the alleged miscarriage (*horribile dictu*) was no miscarriage at all because the blood on Bessa's body and bed had, in fact, been animal blood deliberately placed there to deceive. Whatever the exact circumstances of this unsavoury assault, the justices of the Jews and the jurors at the Warwickshire County Court, to which the case was referred, found it possible to come to a decision at some speed. Bessa disappears from the records for ever, her husband, Elias, was fined for making a false charge of robbery, while Leo and all his womenfolk ('his wife and his two daughters and his sister and his household') were first imprisoned and then forced to 'abjure the town of Warwick, thence to depart with all their chattels and never to return'. So might an inter-necine quarrel between families, and especially between their female members, affect the crucial—and still mysterious—issue of Jewish migration within the English realm.[11]

No doubt so vivid and sanguinary a conflict demands an anthropologist, perhaps even a Lévi-Strauss, rather than a historian for its full elucidation. More prosaically and predictably, the real or alleged assault on Bessa of Warwick serves to illustrate particularly well many of the themes and problems which characterize the place of Jewish women in thirteenth-century English society. In the first place, the Jewish wife and daughter could freely walk the streets of provincial towns; and it would obviously be unwise to assume that they usually lived either the secluded or the gentle life advocated in Hebrew religious literature. In fact, and not too surprisingly, female involvement in acts of violence and occasionally even of murder against fellow Jews was a not uncommon feature of their communities, subjected as the latter were to sustained psychological pressure from the Christian population around them.[12] Moreover, as the case of Bessa of Warwick demonstrates equally well, our knowledge of

---

[11] PRO, E. 9/4, memb. 4d; Rigg, *Select Pleas*, pp. 11–12. No member of the Jewish community at Warwick in 1244 can have been particularly secure: only ten years earlier all their predecessors had been temporarily expelled from the town and county there: see C. Roth, *A History of the Jews in England*, 3rd edn (Oxford, 1978), p. 58.

[12] For several examples of murder-allegations brought against Jewish women in Bristol and Oxford, see Adler, 'Jewish Woman', pp. 34–5. More intriguing is the case of Milo or Meir of York, who accused three Christians of killing his wife, a crime he apparently committed himself because of his affair ('*rem*') with Belina, another Jewess: *Curia Regis Rolls of the Reigns of Richard I, John and Henry III*, 16 vols (London, 1922–79), 5, p. 256; R. B. Dobson, *The Jews of Medieval York and the Massacre of March 1190* = *Borthwick Papers*, no. 45 (York, 1974), p. 39. No doubt much more common (but much less often recorded) is the experience which befell an Exeter Jewess named Henna, who had stones thrown at her in South Street by a boy attending the city school: *Unity and Variety, a History of the Church in Devon and Cornwall*, ed. N. Orme (Exeter, 1991), p. 47.

conflicts between Jews, let alone between Jews and Christians, is utterly dependent on the records compiled and preserved by Christian clerks. In the absence of *responsa* and other forms of Hebraic literary source material available on the other side of the Channel, the historian of the Jewish woman in medieval England has accordingly little alternative but to approach his subject through the clinically dispassionate or even hostile eyes of the Angevin and Plantagenet bureaucracy. To that extent, she was both less and more fortunate than her Christian counterpart: at times, as will be seen, more liberated than the latter, she is most often—in the nature of things—to be observed at times of private and public (especially financial) distress. Within what the late Dr Cecil Roth quite properly categorized as the 'artificial' world of medieval Anglo-Jewry, it may well be that the role of the Jewish woman has a variety of admirable moral qualities to display, but only at the cost of tragic risks to be run.[13]

However, the most important moral to emerge from the assault on Bessa, wife of Elias, is obvious enough. Whatever the precise reasons for the violence at Warwick in 1244, both she and her adversary, Ancerra, were clearly the victims less of a personal than of a family conflict. Moreover, this proved a conflict which could only be properly resolved by the exiling of one of the two families at serious and violent odds with one another from Warwick itself. It needs no urging that the lives of Jewish women in thirteenth-century England were quite as inextricably part of the history of their own households as were those of their Christian neighbours.[14] It is accordingly all the more regrettable that it proves so difficult, even in the best documented provincial Jewries of thirteenth-century England, to estimate the total number of such households in any one Jewish community. As is well known, demographic uncertainty is the single most frustrating problem facing the historian of medieval Anglo-Jewry. Unfortunately, the only surviving national statistics for the size of the English Jewry as a whole derive from the accounts of the annual poll-tax, or chevage, levied on approximately 1,150 Jewish males and females (over the age of twelve) as late as the very early 1280s.[15] Half a century

---

[13] Roth, *History of Jews*, p. 91. If anything, however, the persecution and insecurity undergone by Jewish women in northern France during the late thirteenth century was even more protracted than in England: R. Chazan, *Medieval Jewry in Northern France: a Political and Social History* (Baltimore, 1973), pp. 154–205.

[14] Cf. B. A. Hanawalt, *The Ties that Bound: Peasant Families in Medieval England* (Oxford, 1986), pp. 107–55; C. M. Barron, 'The golden age of women in medieval London', *Reading Medieval Studies*, 15 (1989), pp. 35–58.

[15] PRO, E. 101/249/24, discussed in R. B. Dobson, 'The decline and expulsion of the medieval Jews of York', *TJHSE*, 26 (1979), p. 51, n. 78.

earlier, during the reign of Henry III, the total number of Jews in England was certainly higher, but perhaps only in the order of the 4,000 to 5,000 souls once suggested (admittedly on no very certain evidence) by the late Dr V. D. Lipman.[16] Slightly more valuable is the latter's better informed guess that 'the Jewish population of Norwich is unlikely ever to have been much above 200': such an estimate is not only more persuasive in itself, but seems likely to have been true of more or less all Jewish communities in thirteenth-century England, with the obvious exception of London.[17] It seems more likely than not that all the adult women of a provincial English Jewry could have been gathered together within their one local synagogue.

Admittedly these calculations, if such they can be called, are open to the criticism that many of the poorer Jewish families in English provincial centres may well have escaped documentation altogether, so creating what might be a seriously distorted impression of the size and social structure of medieval Anglo-Jewry as a whole. Nowhere, moreover, is such distortion more likely to confuse than in the case of the Jewish woman. For very familiar reasons, Jewesses identifiable in extant financial and legal records tend to be heavily weighted towards that minority of women (and especially widows) who conducted business by written contract, secondly, towards women whose inheritances caused envy and dispute, and finally, towards women who committed, or were alleged to have committed, felonies and lesser crimes. It follows that most medieval English Jewish wives and mothers—much as can be known about the exceptions—must always be as impossible to identify as they are to count. To take only one example, perhaps the most important document left to posterity by the *archa* of the medieval Cambridge Jewry is a list of the bonds of deposit there in or about 1240 by forty-seven named Jews: of those forty-seven names, only four are those of women, one a widow and three others designated as daughters.[18] Among the almost innumerable surviving lists of loans and tallages owed to and by individual members of the thirteenth-century English Jewry, it is very rare indeed to encounter

---

[16] V. D. Lipman, *The Jews of Medieval Norwich* (London, 1967), pp. 36–8; Roth, *History of Jews*, pp. 91, 93, 276.

[17] Lipman, *Jews of Medieval Norwich*, p. 38. According to Ephraim Bonn, the most reliable authority for the atrocity, approximately 150 Jewish men and women lost their lives at Clifford's Tower during the (not necessarily total) massacre of the York Jews in March 1190 (Dobson, *Jews of Medieval York*, p. 15).

[18] PRO, E. 101, 249/3; printed in H. P. Stokes, *Studies in Anglo-Jewish History* (Edinburgh, 1913), pp. 252–75.

an instance where the names of males do not surpass those of females by at least a ratio of four or five to one. The same ascendancy of male over female names is still absolutely evident to the very end, when in 1290 and 1291 the royal sheriffs were systematically stripping the assets of the last members of the medieval English Jewry.[19]

In a situation of such demographic insecurity, not too unfamiliar, of course, to students of thirteenth-century *Christian* women, it is at least reassuring that a little, if only a little, is beginning to be known about the composition of the Jewish family itself. Some light on male–female sex ratios is about to be afforded by the forthcoming report on the 497 Jewish skeletons examined and studied in the aftermath of the York Archaeological Trust's excavation at Jewbury, York, in 1982–3. Not all these skeletons proved easy to sex; but provisional findings suggest the presence in this cemetery, probably used continuously by the York Jews from about 1180 to about 1290, of the remains of 151 females (31.7 per cent), as compared with 163 males (34.2 per cent) and 141 children (29.6 per cent).[20] However, a fuller reconstitution of some of the better-documented urban Jewish households of medieval England still awaits the systematic analysis of first and second personal Jewish names—no easy matter, but one which seems the most urgent desideratum for our enhanced understanding of the kindred ties that bound medieval Anglo-Jewry together in a hostile environment.[21] Meanwhile, it seems clear enough that at least the most substantial Jewish families of thirteenth-century England were normally small and normally very close-knit. Dr Cecil Roth's discussion of the evidence for the Oxford Jewry, more impressionistic accounts of other provincial Jewries, and, above all, V. D. Lipman's treatment of the incomparable documentation for Norwich, suggests that, in the latter's words, 'a family of more than three or four

---

[19] *Rotulorum originialium abbreviatio* (London, 1805–10), 1, pp. 73–6; B. L. Abrahams, 'The condition of the Jews of England at the time of their Expulsion in 1290', *TJHSE*, 2 (1896), pp. 76–105.

[20] These figures are cited from the draft (June 1991) of the forthcoming report on the Jewbury excavation to be published as York Archaeological Trust AY/12/3. For a preliminary indication of the importance of the site see P. Turnbull, 'Jewbury', *Interim Bulletin of the York Archaeological Trust*, 9 (1983), pp. 5–8.

[21] The reasons why so many English Jewesses bore French rather than Hebraic first names, and why so many of their sons were identified by their mothers' rather than their fathers' names, are only two examples of issues which deserve much further consideration. For a very incomplete list of 'Names of Jewesses in England', see Adler, *Jewish Woman*, p. 21; and cf. the brief account of 'Nomenclature' in R. R. Mundill, 'The Jews in England, 1272–1290' (D.Phil. thesis, St Andrews, 1987), pp. xviii–xix.

children must have been a rarity.'[22] Indeed, in the great majority of documented medieval Jewish families it seems difficult to find in-
controvertible evidence that a Jewish father and mother had more than
two living children; while it is even more noticeable that the copious
records of the Jewish plea rolls are more or less totally devoid of references
to extant grandparents or even to uncles, aunts, and cousins.[23] On the basis
of this very treacherous if extensive evidence, one must hesitate to be too
positive. But it now seems as if the Jewish households of Plantagenet
England may often resemble, not too surprisingly, those late twelfth-
century Jewish family units in the Rhineland recently revealed by
Professor Kenneth Stow as—in his own words—'small, comprising an
average of five souls, and two generational only'.[24] If so, it seems more
likely than not that the great majority of the small, nucleated, urban
Jewish households of medieval England, of which there were perhaps
rarely more than thirty or forty in any provincial Jewry, were no larger,
and conceivably smaller, than those of their Christian neighbours.

Such a possibility, perhaps a little unexpected although not in itself at
all startling, may make some well-known features of the history of the
medieval Anglo-Jewry easier to explain, but leaves others as inexplicable
as ever. How did these groups of tiny, family economic units regulate
between themselves the competitive processes of money-lending, upon
which one assumes they nearly all depended for their survival?[25] How
could large concentrations of financial capital be safely accommodated,
managed, and invested within these often insubstantial nuclear-family
businesses? How did a variety of such small, family concerns co-exist
within the exceptionally inegalitarian financial regime revealed to us by
every royal tallage return of the period, and with the literally colossal
fortunes amassed by such great Jewish entrepreneurs as Aaron of Lincoln,
David of Oxford, and Bonamy of York?[26] To those questions, economic

---

[22] Lipman, *Jews of Medieval Norwich*, p. 47; cf. C. Roth, *The Jews of Medieval Oxford* — OHS, ns, 9 (1951), pp. 16–45; Dobson, 'Decline and Expulsion', p. 43.

[23] See also the particularly informative accounts of receipts from Jews in the Tower of London between 1275 and 1278 (*Cal. Jewish Plea Rolls*, 4, pp. 148–94).

[24] K. R. Stow, 'The Jewish family in the Rhineland in the High Middle Ages: form and function', *AHR*, 42 (1987), pp. 1085–97.

[25] This problem is largely unaffected by the recent argument that after 1275 the English Jewry experienced a fundamental 'change from moneylender to credit agent': R. Mundill, 'Anglo-Jewry under Edward I: credit agents and their clients', *TJHSE*, 31 (1988–90), pp. 1–21.

[26] J. Jacobs, 'Aaron of Lincoln', *TJHSE*, 3 (1899), pp. 157–79; Roth, *Jews of Medieval Oxford*, pp. 40–9, 87–8, 132–3; Dobson, 'Decline and Expulsion', pp. 45–6. The names of the major Jewish contributors to the tallages of 1221, 1223, and 1225 are now conveniently listed in

questions upon which a proper understanding of the social structure of the English medieval Jewry must ultimately depend, there still seem no very easy answers. However, it might well be conceded (the argument has now become almost obligatory in the case of *Christian* women in English towns after the Black Death)[27] that the smaller the household, the more significant, more necessary, indeed, the economic contribution to be made by its female members. Not long ago Dr Judith Bennett claimed that the subordination of the Christian woman in the medieval English countryside was rooted in her household:[28] by contrast, in the case of the Jewish woman her household was the primary agency of some very real, if admittedly limited, liberation.

Ever since 1655, when William Prynne published the second part of his *Short Demurrer to the Jewes Long discontinued Remitter into England*, from what he called 'the rich unknown Magazine of our generally neglected, slighted precious old records', it has been a commonplace that by associating his wife with him in business the medieval English Jew was unlike his Christian neighbour.[29] Not quite unlike; for as the late H. G. Richardson once pointed out, Christian money-lenders did the same. However, Richardson's own explanation for the ubiquity of this marital business association between Jews—that it 'facilitated the transfer of debts to the widow or heir on the death of the head of the household'—clearly goes nowhere near far enough.[30] From the time, at least by the minority of Henry III, that the financial affairs of the English Jewry were firmly integrated into a complex royal governmental machine, it was as axiomatic to the justices as to the officials of the Exchequer of the Jews that a Jewish woman had as much right to resort to that machine as did her husband or her son. Although this 'liberal' practice is readily explicable in terms of the Crown's interest in the recovery of the debts to all of his Jewish subjects, male and female, such complete legal sexual equality remains remarkable—if perhaps slightly less remarkable than the ability of so many Jewish wives to exercise independent business initiatives within

J. Hillaby, 'A magnate among the marchers: Hamo of Hereford, his family and clients, 1218–1253', *THJSE*, 31 (1988–90), pp. 30–1.

[27] P. J. P. Goldberg, 'Female labour, service and marriage in northern towns during the later Middle Ages', *NH*, 22 (1986), pp. 32–5; 'Mortality and economic change in the Diocese of York, 1390–1514', *NH*, 24 (1988), pp. 42–53.

[28] J. Bennett, *Women in the Medieval English Countryside: Gender and Household in Brigstock before the Plague* (Oxford, 1987), pp. 48–64, 198.

[29] W. Prynne, *Short Demurrer* (London, 1655–6), pt ii, p. 136.

[30] Richardson, *English Jewry*, pp. 44–5.

their households themselves. To state the obvious, it is as a business-woman that the English Jewess of the thirteenth century tends to be known to us at all. Naturally enough, a few Jewish women managed to remain comparatively distant from their husband's financial affairs. It was discovered, for example, of Avegaye of London, in 1267, that the wife 'had nothing that is not her husband's'.[31] However, even in such a case, the plea rolls of the Exchequer of the Jews make it abundantly clear that a wife might (and often did) negotiate a loan and prepare a bond on her husband's behalf, most obviously in his absence. Indeed, the frequent absences from home of the Jewish male heads of the household, again thoroughly documented in the plea rolls, gave their wives an opportunity not only to carry on a family business while their husbands were away, but also to lend money without their husband's knowledge (like Godenota of Lincoln in 1220) or even to falsify documents and forge seals (like Belassez of York in 1277).[32]

More significantly still, it may well have been the female members of the Jewish family who handled the lion's share of the (much neglected) pawnbroking activities of her household. In medieval England, as in other places and at other times, the pledging of chattels for small advances of cash was not a form of business likely to lead to much in the way of permanent record; but its prevalence, and its significance for Christian–Jewish relations, certainly deserves more thought than it has usually received.[33] To take only one example, in 1224 a certain Robert Cristfinesse of Chichester borrowed 3s. on the deposit of a bowl of mazer-wood and two silver buckles. However, he then endured the mortification of seeing the coins in question confiscated by the town bailiff on the grounds that they were clipped: only for that reason do we know that the loan had been made by Bona, wife of the Jew Diaia, on this occasion allegedly in her husband's presence and at his command.[34] For many of her closest Christian neighbours, one may fairly safely surmise that the Jewish woman of pre-Expulsion England (like so many of her successors in years to come) was seen less as a subversive threat to belief, even less in her legendary role as a sinister seductress of young Christian clerks, but rather as a useful if hazardous source of credit in times of trial.

---

[31] *Cal. Jewish Plea Rolls*, 1, pp. 145–6; cf. pp. 200–1.

[32] Ibid., 1, pp. 43–4; *CCR, 1272–79*, p. 487.

[33] For the plausible suggestion that pledging of chattels to the Jews was not only very common indeed, but led them into contact with 'all classes of society, from clergy and knights down to thieves', see Richardson, *English Jewry*, pp. 76–8.

[34] Rigg, *Select Pleas*, pp. 8–9. Cf. ibid., p. 11; *Cal. Jewish Plea Rolls*, 1, p. 73, for examples of Jewesses being accused of coin-clipping.

Such themes might be elaborated at length; but it may be more important to summarize a few of the legal rights and obligations customarily
enjoyed by the thirteenth-century Jewess but usually denied, in practice if
not in theory, to her Christian counterpart. As Michael Adler pointed out
sixty years ago, the Jewish woman could hold landed property, including,
of course, town houses and tenements, with no lord intervening between
herself and the king.[35] She could also manage and control both a local and
a national money-lending business, usually, no doubt, in partnership with
her husband or her sons, but on frequent occasions in her own right too.
The Jewish wife or widow was able to prosecute both Jews and Gentiles in
the royal courts, most often before the Justices of the Jews but not
exclusively so.[36] She had the right to find sureties and mainpernors when
impleaded at law herself; and she could similarly act as surety for others,
including an imprisoned husband. She was entitled to lease urban
property for rent, with the incidental result that, according to Cecil Roth,
the Jewesses of medieval Oxford may have been among the very first
student landladies at the new university there.[37] Finally, in this highly
incomplete list, the Jewish woman could lend money, as has been implied,
upon the security of estates, rents, and chattels of all types, not excluding
such considerable collections of grammar and legal manuscripts as those
(including a copy of the *Institutes* valued at 4s. 0d.) still in the possession of
Belaset and Hittecote, Jewesses of Oxford, when they were converted to
Christianity early in the reign of Edward I.[38] No historian who has
wrestled with the admittedly tantalizing evidence in this field has ever
doubted the bewildering variety of such traffic: it would be hard to
exaggerate the extent to which, despite official ecclesiastical prohibition,
Bibles, chalices, church ornaments, and other items central to the practice
of the Christian religion were regularly pledged to the members (often
female) of the English provincial Jewries.[39]

[35] For some unusually explicit examples of the purchase and sale of town houses by several
Jewesses of Canterbury in the early thirteenth century, see Adler, 'The Jews of Medieval
Canterbury', in *Jews of Medieval England*, pp. 68–9, 72.

[36] See Comitissa of Gloucester's explicit declaration before the Justices of the Jews in 1220 that
she would 'prove as Jewess against Jew' the conspiracy whereby her late husband had been
thrown to his death from the walls of Gloucester Castle: *Cal. Jewish Plea Rolls*, 1, p. 45; cf.
Hillaby, *Worcester Jewry*, pp. 91, 100; and for examples of Jewesses' appearances before the
Beth Din, see Adler, 'Jews of Medieval Canterbury', p. 73; M. D. Davis, ed., *Shetaroth: Hebrew
Deeds of English Jews (1180–1290)* (London, 1888) [hereafter *Shetaroth*], pp. 5, 29, 40.

[37] Roth, *Jews of Medieval Oxford*, pp. 136–50.

[38] Rigg, *Select Pleas*, p. 114.

[39] Ibid., p. lv; Roth, *History of Jews*, p. 105; Richardson, *English Jewry*, pp. 76–7, 187–8.

The diversity of economic activity on the part of the medieval Jewish woman was, however, never to be more manifest than when she became—as she so often did—head of her own household. In other words, it was as widows that the more substantial Jewesses of Angevin and Plantagenet England are unquestionably revealed at their most wealthy, most influential, and, at least in some senses of the word, most liberated. Here again there exists an obvious analogy between the feminine elite within both Christian and Jewish society: for it was as a widow that a thirteenth-century Christian heiress like Lady Isabella de Fortibus (to take perhaps the most relevant contemporary example) was at her most formidable too, during her long years of widowhood from 1260 to 1293.[40] Nevertheless, there can be no doubt at all that the legal and public status of the Jewish wife and widow was buttressed by conventions, customs, and practices largely or completely denied to her Christian counterparts. Not all of these advantages derived from radically different legal practices between the two religious persuasions. One of the most important, if prosaic, reasons for the English Crown's readiness to recognize the rights of a bereaved Jewess to her due share of her husband's estate was its disinclination to see the excessive fragmentation of a complex financial business in which it had its own interests. Accordingly, and although it was usual for the royal government to appropriate the third part of a deceased Jew's estate '*ad opus regis*' soon after his death, his widow was emphatically not likely to be deliberately driven into complete penury forthwith.[41] With the solitary exception of Licoricia of Winchester's remarkable payment of no less than 5,000 marks in 1244, itself a tribute to the quite exceptional wealth of her deceased husband, David of Oxford, the fines levied on Jewish widows to secure their husband's chattels were usually considerably less than the financial appetites of the Plantagenet monarchy might lead one to expect.[42]

As the English monarchy, its own profits apart, always expected its Jewish communities to be largely self-regulatory, it was no doubt most important of all that Jewish matrimonial law and custom protected the

---

[40] *Complete Peerage*, 12 vols (London, 1910–59), I, pp. 355–6; N. Denholm-Young, 'The York-shire Estates of Isabella de Fortibus', *Yorkshire Archaeological Journal*, 31 (1934), pp. 389–420; *Seignorial Administration in England* (Oxford, 1937).

[41] *Shetaroth*, p. 60; Adler, 'Jewish Woman', p. 19.

[42] Ibid., pp. 39–40; Roth, *Jews of Medieval Oxford*, pp. 55–6. More characteristic of the fines imposed upon Jewish widows to receive delivery of their husbands' moveables and houses is the 400 marks paid by Floria on the estate of Master Elias of London: Rigg, *Select Pleas*, pp. 131–2; cf. ibid., pp. 35, 42, 61.

interests of Jewish widows, and, indeed, of Jewish wives and daughters too, much more scrupulously than Christian marriage conventions safe-guarded those of their Gentile neighbours. Naturally enough, the realities of Jewish marriage practice in thirteenth-century England can only be observed through a glass very darkly indeed; but, at the least, sufficient scraps of incidental information survive on this side of the Channel to make it clear that the English Jewess was expected to live her life within behavioural codes familiar enough to readers of Rashi and his successors in northern France.[43] In principle, such codes—not, of course, without their own inherent contradictions—naturally rarely envisaged anything but female subordination to the male head of the household; but in practice that subordination was often qualified, most notably by the recognition that 'Our Women transact business these days', and that in extreme situations divorce could be a viable alternative to marital dis-harmony.[44] More specifically, it is well known that Jewish marriage customs placed more practical and rational emphasis upon arrangements for the bride's (and future widow's) well-being than was likely to be encountered by most Christian women at their equivalent rites of passage.

Such differences seem, in fact, to be reflected in the contrast to be observed between the celebration of Christian and Jewish weddings themselves during the thirteenth century. On the basis of admittedly highly impressionistic evidence, medieval Jewish weddings show every sign of having been more spectacular, more lavish, and, above all, better attended affairs than those of Christian townswomen during the period. In the summer of 1255, for example, it was the presence of a so-called 'unusually large concourse' of Jews attending a great wedding in Lincoln which encouraged the fabrication of that most fatally influential of all English blood-libel allegations, the supposed martyrdom of 'little St Hugh'.[45] However, the *locus classicus* in this field is undoubtedly the well-known Jewish wedding allegedly celebrated within the comparatively

---

[43] Rabinowitz, *Jews of Northern France*, pp. 140–57; Agus, *Urban Civilization*, pp. 554–95. For the argument (quite probably applicable to thirteenth-century England) that diametric opposi-tions between the elite culture of Jews and Christians could nevertheless coexist with similar perceptions of marriage, see E. Cohen and E. Horowitz, 'In search of the sacred: Jews, Christians, and rituals of marriage in the later Middle Ages', *Journal of Medieval and Renaissance Studies*, 20 (1990), pp. 225–49.

[44] For 'the most famous divorce of the period', of Muriel of Oxford from her husband David, see Adler, 'Jewish Woman', pp. 28–9; cf. M. D. Davis, 'An Anglo-Jewish Divorce, A.D. 1242', *JQR*, 5 (1893), pp. 158–65; Rabbinowitz, *Jews of Northern France*, p. 163.

[45] Matthew Paris, *Chronica Majora*, 7 vols, RS (1872–83), 5, pp. 516–19; Rigg, *Select Pleas*, pp. xxx–xxxii.

small and obscure Jewry of Hereford in 1286, only four years before the Expulsion. Our knowledge of that event derives exclusively from Bishop Richard Swinfield of Hereford's indignation ('*dicto horrendum est*') that so many Christian acquaintances of the Jewish couple had accepted their invitation to be present at an unprecedentedly magnificent series of festivities, complete with 'displays of silk and cloth of gold, an equestrian procession, stage plays [unspecified, alas], sports and other acts of minstrelsy'.[46] Although this Jewish wedding at Hereford in 1286 may be rather brittle evidence on which to support the case, as is sometimes done, for deep personal harmony between Christians and Jews at the local level during the last years of medieval Anglo-Jewry, it seems to reveal—not a little surprisingly—that a late thirteenth-century English bishop positively expected a Jewish wedding to be highly attractive to Christians.

For the well-connected Jewish bride—whose marriage was in any case quite as likely to be arranged by her father as was that of her Christian counterpart—it was less her wedding than her *Kethubah* or betrothal contract, together with her dowry from her own family, which safe-guarded her long-term future.[47] Fortunately enough, a few such contracts, so crucial to the welfare of the Jewish wife and widow, survive in English archives; and references to several more are probably still to be discovered.[48] Perhaps the most informative English example, preserved among the muniments of Westminster Abbey, records how at Lincoln in 1271, after approval by a duly constituted Beth Din, a Jewess called Belassez promised a dowry of twenty-marks value to the future husband, Aaron, of her daughter Judith. Among Bellasez's other gifts to Aaron the most intriguing is a Hebrew copy of the twenty-four books of the Old Testament: as the manuscript in question is said to have been written on duly punctuated and embellished calf-skin, the interesting implication here may be that the bridal couple would in due course read this Bible together. For his part, the bridegroom, Aaron, undertook to provide his prospective bride, Judith, with her *Kethubah*, or marriage settlement proper, a cash sum totalling £100, as 'is the custom of the Isle'.[49] Not all

---

[46] *Registrum Ricardi de Swinfield episcopi Herefordensis, A.D. 1283–1317*, ed. W. W. Capes, CYS, 6 (1909), pp. 120–2. The local context of this wedding is interestingly discussed in Hillaby, 'Magnate among the Marchers', pp. 74–5.

[47] Abrahams, *Jewish Life*, pp. 186–210; T. and M. Metzger, *Jewish Life in the Middle Ages* (New York, 1985), pp. 227–33, including a photograph of the only illustrated *Kethubah* (from Krems in Austria, dated 1392) known to have survived from the medieval West.

[48] *Shetaroth*, pp. 32, 43–6, 94.

[49] Ibid., pp. 298–302, tr. in Adler, 'Jewish Woman', pp. 43–5.

Jewish brides did in the event secure so valuable a *Kethubah* as the standard £100; but several received an even more generous settlement, certainly comparable with the *maritagium* or dower enjoyed by their Christian equivalents. Usually more valuable still were the gifts of the bride's father to herself and her new husband: it was apparently by no means unusual for the Jewish bride to receive a gift of one or more houses at the time of her marriage.[50] Generous endowments of this type from her father, as well as her husband, probably help to explain the important issue of how several Jewish wives could gain access to sufficient capital to begin credit operations in their own right during the early years of their marriage.

However, the main objective of the *Kethubah*, as of a Christian heiress's dower, was to protect the Jewish wife's position at the time of her husband's death. On all the evidence available, this is certainly what it served to do. Naturally enough, the amount and proper assignment of the *Kethubah* could lead to dispute between Jewish families themselves; but there is abundant evidence among their plea rolls that the Justices of the Jews rapidly came to the aid of widows whose claims to dower were being disregarded or subjected to illegal distraint.[51] Not surprisingly, therefore, several widows of the more substantial members of the English Jewry were eventually in a position to retire from business and household cares, probably not a future available to many Christian townswomen. A particularly well-documented example of this practice is afforded by a certain Gentil of Norwich, who, in 1251, had surrendered her late husband's estate to her three sons in return for a variety of concessions, ranging from a maintenance allowance of five marks a year to the quiet and exclusive possession of a large house in Mancroft Street.[52] Many, and probably most, Jewish widows, however, sought to maintain and even augment their deceased husbands' business concerns, with the inevitable result that they thereby enhanced their attractiveness to an aspiring Jewish male. Here again both Jewish and Christian legal convention protected the Jewish widow a good deal more actively than her Christian counterpart. A particularly instructive example of a common syndrome is provided by the later career of Milla of Royston, who had lost her husband at the hands of Simon de Montfort's adherents in the early 1260s. She was immediately

---

[50] *Cal. Jewish Plea Rolls*, 1, p. 192; *Shetaroth*, p. 136.

[51] For the principle that Jewesses 'ought not to be distrained after the death of their husbands in the dowers they have of tenements, goods and chattels for any fines due from their late husbands', see *CCR, 1279–88*, p. 47; Adler, 'Jewish Woman', p. 30.

[52] Lipman, *Jews of Medieval Norwich*, pp. 137–40, provides an exceptional insight into the marriage relationships which characterized this 'typical Jewish middle–class family'.

thereafter courted by a Master Samuel of Bolum, who later claimed that 'by reason both of contract and commerce between them' she had become his wife. However, Milla appealed to a group of rabbis, who had no hesitation, like many other Jewish authorities in similar circumstances, in pronouncing this alleged second marriage null and void: they accordingly left Milla in full possession of her first husband's property and directed Master Samuel to leave her in peace thereafter.[53] On the limited evidence available, Jewish widows also seem to have been even more successful than Christian ones in petitioning the Crown either not to marry a particular individual or not to marry at all.[54] Fear of disparagement, one might well suppose, was quite as powerful an emotion among well-born Jewesses and their families as it was in aristocratic Christian circles: here is one of several indirect indications that Jewish concepts of status were not unaffected by the principles and practices of contemporary Christian knighthood and inheritance.

However, the main conclusion seems obvious enough: all in all, it was considerably easier for a Jewish woman to resist remarriage than it was for her Christian neighbour to do so. Nor was it for that reason alone that the figure of the Jewish widow seems to move especially prominently into the centre of the scene the closer one approaches Edward I's final solution of 1290. As Jewish husbands, sons, and brothers were subjected to ever more severe and often murderous harassment during the 1270s and 1280s, so their mothers and sisters often become increasingly conspicuous, in taxation and other records, among the last survivors of medieval Anglo-Jewry.[55] Nor is it likely to be a coincidence that the two best-documented and almost certainly most wealthy Jewesses known to medieval England belonged to this last doomed generation. Admittedly neither Henna, widow of Aaron of York, nor Licoricia of Winchester, widow of David of Oxford, lived quite long enough to see the final expulsion of all their co-religionists from the England they had made their homeland.[56] However,

---

[53] *Cal. Jewish Plea Rolls*, 1, pp. 152, 154, 163; Stokes, *Studies in Anglo-Jewish History*, p. 164.

[54] J. Jacobs, *The Jews of Angevin England: Documents and Records* (London, 1893), pp. 28, 44–5, 332; Stokes, *Studies in Anglo-Jewish History*, p. 128.

[55] PRO, E. 101, 249/22; *Cal. Jewish Plea Rolls*, 4, pp. 16–17, 139–94; Hillaby, 'Worcester Jewry', pp. 106–13. Proof that almost 300 Jews were hanged for alleged currency offences in 1278–9 is now provided by Z. E. Rokeah, 'Money and the hangman in late thirteenth-century England: Jews, Christians and coinage offences alleged and real', *TJHSE*, 31 (1988–90), pp. 83–109.

[56] Henna, regularly called widow of Aaron of York throughout the 1270s, seems to have died soon after she received—in 1280—a royal licence (as Henna, daughter of Leo de Eboraco and mother of Elias) to sell one of her houses in Coney Street: *CPR, 1272–81*, p. 380. Licoricia's

the careers of both these women would still repay more attention than they have received: for they provide not only the best commentary upon how wealthy and influential a thirteenth-century Jewess could become, but also illustrate to perfection the fragility of that wealth and influence during the lingering decline of the medieval English Jewry in its melancholy penultimate years.

Henna, daughter of Leo de Eboraco and therefore a member of the most distinguished Jewish family in early thirteenth-century York in her own right, first becomes prominent in surviving records as the wife of Aaron, regarded by Matthew Paris as both the richest and ultimately the most unfortunate Jew of Henry III's England.[57] Although husband and wife were increasingly engaged in property transactions together during the last period of Aaron's life, it was only in the dozen or more years after his death in 1268 that Henna fully demonstrated her own business acumen and stamina. One of the few medieval English Jewesses known for certain to have been able to write in Hebrew, until her death in or about 1280 she pursued a relentless campaign designed to preserve (which in the end it failed to do) the shattered remnants of her husband's once phenomenal business empire.[58] A not dissimilar attempt to preserve the no longer preservable seems to characterize the final stages of the remarkably picaresque life of Licoricia of Winchester. Born in that city about 1220, Licoricia's turbulent career illustrates the special advantages of being widowed not once but twice, especially if one's second husband was a figure as substantial as David of Oxford, whose estate was subjected to an almost unparalleled royal relief of 5,000 marks on his death in 1244.[59] The central figure in the most notorious and controversial Jewish divorce case in thirteenth-century England, the last twenty years of Licoricia's life were most notable for the aggression with which she pursued her Christian debtors, the hostility she aroused among her fellow Jewesses at Winchester, and her remarkable powers of survival. After several periods of imprisonment, sometimes on false accusations of theft, Licoricia was eventually murdered under highly mysterious circumstances in 1277, two years before Benedict, the most successful of her five sons, was hanged

murder was investigated by a specially appointed Winchester jury in 1277: *Cal. Jewish Plea Rolls*, 3, pp. 248, 293.

[57] *Cal. Jewish Plea Rolls*, 1, pp. 181, 186, 210–11; Matthew Paris, *Chronica Majora*, 5, p. 136; Adler, 'Aaron of York', in *Jews of Medieval England*, pp. 127–73.

[58] *Cal. Jewish Plea Rolls*, 1, p. 270; 3, pp. 31, 78, 102, 156, 202, 244, 278; Dobson, *Jews of Medieval York*, pp. 43–4.

[59] Roth, *Jews of Medieval Oxford*, pp. 54–7; see n. 42, above.

in the course of Edwardian England's greatest outburst of collective murder.[60]

Although Licoricia, like her son, was almost certainly killed by Christian hands, her remarkable career may serve to introduce some of the ambiguities inherent in the final theme of this paper, the mysterious relationship between thirteenth-century Jewish women and the Christian society around them. That this relationship was often one of bitter irony is clear enough. There is considerable circumstantial evidence, for example, that until her death Licoricia herself owed much of her economic resilience, exemption from taxation, and indeed sheer ability to survive to the personal protection and at times patronage of no less a person than King Henry III himself.[61] The career of Bonamicus of York, that royal financier who in 1290 left the service of Edward I for that of Philip the Fair, also shows that monarchs and prelates who fulminated against the usurious practices of their Jewish subjects were at times perfectly ready to welcome the most successful Jewish money-lenders into their own entourage.[62] In the very different and much smaller world of the English provincial town, it is not hard to find similar ironies in play. Shortly after the great York massacre of 16 March 1190, the well-informed chronicler William of Newburgh went out of his way to observe that 'the *nobilitas et cives graviores* of the town, fearing the dangers of the king's reaction, had cautiously declined to take part in such madness.'[63] Recent accounts of certain thirteenth-century provincial Jewries, notably perhaps Dr Derek Keene's survey of the Jews of medieval Winchester, have also tended to advance the case, however marginally, for a reasonable degree of harmonious co-operation—if not necessarily of friendship—between Jewish families and the more substantial Christian townsfolk who were literally their neighbours.[64]

In the nature of the evidence, amicable relationships between Jewish

---

[60] H. P. Stokes, 'A Jewish family in Oxford in the thirteenth century', *TJHSE*, 10 (1925), pp. 193–206; Adler, *Jews of Medieval England*, p. 92.

[61] Henry III's personal intervention on Licoricia's behalf in her complex plea against the Charlecote family in 1253 is well documented in Rigg, *Select Pleas*, pp. 19–27. For the 'inexplicable absence' of Licoricia from the tallage of 1239–42 see R. Stacey, *Politics, Policy and Finance under Henry III, 1216–1245* (Oxford, 1987), p. 151.

[62] Dobson, 'Decline and Expulsion', pp. 44–6; cf. Chazan, *Medieval Jewry in Northern France*, pp. 183–4; Roth, *History of Jews*, pp. 56, 274 (for the best-known case of personal patronage of a Jew by a member of the English royal family, Richard of Cornwall).

[63] *Chronicles of the Reigns of Stephen, Henry II and Richard I*, RS, 82 (1884–9), 1, pp. 322–4; cf. the translation by Dr P. P. A. Biller in *Clifford's Tower Commemoration* (York, 1990), p. 38.

[64] D. Keene, *Survey of Medieval Winchester = Winchester Studies*, 2 (Oxford, 1985), pp. 76–9, 385–6, 324–5, 384–7, 1034–5; Hillaby, 'Hamo of Hereford', pp. 74–5.

women and Christian families in thirteenth-century English towns is not, however, likely to be well reflected in surviving plea rolls. According to Henry III's well-known provisions sent to the Justices of the Jews on 31 January 1253, the only purpose of female as well as male Jews, from the hour of their birth onwards, was to 'serve us in some way': no Christian man or woman was 'to serve any Jew or Jewess, or to eat with them or remain in their houses'.[65] Perhaps the most interesting indication that such conditions of complete apartheid did not, in fact, apply, either before or after 1253, are the occasions when Jewish and Christian families are known to have sheltered each other's chattels. During the last three threatening decades of the medieval English Jewry's existence, it was obviously not at all uncommon throughout the country for alarmed Jewish families to deposit their valuables, their linen, and their kitchen equipment for security's sake under the floor, under the straw, or under the beds of their Christian acquaintances. Only when such activities led to mutual recrimination and eventually to litigation is one likely to discover, as in a Surrey case of 1266, that according to a certain Matilda Pepper, Aaron the Jew had come 'to her house and hid certain goods under the straw' while she was at church. More frequent was the situation illustrated by a London plea of 1267, where it was agreed by both parties that Isaac of Warwick and his wife, Ivetta, had deposited for safe keeping with Hugh de Dernestall and his wife not only an expensive vestment, but a casket of jewels, six silver spoons, a bowl of mazer-wood, and other valuables.[66]

In this, yet again ambiguous, display of at least a modicum of trust between some Jewish and some Christian families, women—on both sides of the divide—are often likely to have been more involved in the safe keeping of chattels than their menfolk. The same generalization applies much more obviously to one of the most notorious issues presented by medieval Jewish settlement in western Christendom, the consequences (primarily sexual) which it was feared might follow from the employment within one's household of female servants—and especially wet-nurses—from outside one's own religion. It has often been argued, almost certainly correctly, that the very frequency of English royal and ecclesiastical legislation on the subject is itself an indication of its ineffectiveness: as late as 1273, for example, the presence of a Jewish nurse 'in the house of a

---

[65] Rigg, *Select Pleas*, p. xlix.
[66] Ibid., pp. 33, 38, 108–9. Such cases can sometimes be hard to distinguish from instances of Christian males borrowing from Jews on the security of items of household equipment or of their wife's clothing (see *CCR, 1261–64*, pp. 19–20).

certain Christian, of London' seems to have caused no surprise at all.[67] Rather more surprisingly, at the time of her murder in 1277, Licoricia of Winchester's own handmaid was herself a Christian, who died with her mistress.[68] On the whole, official attitudes were usually much more hostile to the prospects of Christians serving in Jewish households (most probably 'as nurses of children, bakers, brewers, and cooks') than vice versa; and in practice, too, it seems to be the case that there were more Christians working as domestic servants for Jews than Jewish women acting as nurses for Christians.[69] Comparatively few such offences, however, are known to have been brought to trial; and in any case thirteenth-century bishops, like some modern historians, probably exaggerated the importance of these and analogous daily contacts between Christian and Jewish women. On the whole, and with due allowance made for the dangers that such delicate issues might be suppressed from the record, sexual relations between Christians and Jews surface in the plea rolls comparatively rarely; even in the single most apparently circumstantial case, where Isabel of Lockerley charged a Jew from Windsor with assault in the street, followed by rape in his own home, the jury of twelve Christians and twelve Jews found the case to be without substance.[70]

What little documentary evidence survives therefore fails to confirm (although no doubt it does little to disprove) the hypothesis that in thirteenth-century England a stereotyped image of the Jewess as an insidious *femme fatale*, luring young Gentile males into apostasy, had already begun to inform the prejudices of her Christian contemporaries. However, an even more important question to raise within the context of 'Christianity and Judaism' is whether there is the slightest hope of discovering how the Jewish women of thirteenth-century England responded to the Christian Church within whose interstices they lived their always precarious lives. Although that question too is unanswerable, except in the vaguest of terms, the cumulative impression left by the surviving records is undoubtedly one of Jewish female religious resilience rather than of complete demoralization. Here perhaps the most severe test

---

[67] The nurse in question later migrated to Normandy with her ward (Rigg, *Select Pleas*, p. 75).

[68] *Cal. Jewish Plea Rolls*, 3, p. 293.

[69] *CCR, 1234–37*, p. 13; Rigg, *Select Pleas*, pp. xlviii, lv; *The Life and Miracles of St William of Norwich by Thomas of Monmouth*, ed. A. Jessopp and M. R. James (Cambridge, 1896), p. 89. The long-standing canonical denunciation of unduly close propinquity between Christian and Jew reaches its English climax with Edward I's 1275 Statute of Jewry, forbidding Christians to live in Jewish households: see J. A. Watt, 'The Jews, the law, and the Church: the concept of Jewish serfdom in thirteenth-century England', *SCH.S*, 9 (1991), p. 163.

[70] Rigg, *Select Pleas*, p. 104.

was presented by the various campaigns to convert the king's Jews and Jewesses to Christianity, campaigns pursued—as far as we know—only intermittently during the reign of Henry III, but much more intensively during the so-called Edwardian experiment of 1275–90.[71] However, there will never be a serious hope of knowing how large a proportion of the thirteenth-century English Jewesses abandoned their faith as a result either of Dominican sermons, local persecution, or urgent economic considerations; and it is almost as difficult to decide whether Jewish women were marginally more resistant—as they quite conceivably were—to the attractions of conversion than their male relatives. It would be a brave act to make much of the fact that of the ninety-six Jewish converts apparently lodged in the *Domus Conversorum* in Chancery Lane between 1280 and 1308, fifty-two were women and forty-four were men.[72] It seems considerably more revealing that of the once notorious fifteen relapsed Jewish apostates of London, brought to light in 1283 during the course of one of Archbishop Pecham's most persistent witch hunts, no less than thirteen were women.[73]

Much more certainly it is absolutely clear that under the pressure to convert to Christianity Jewish wives and Jewish husbands of thirteenth-century England sometimes, perhaps often, took quite different decisions. Would it be too facile, for instance, to interpret the apostasy of Joiette, wife of Solomon fil' Lumbard of Cricklade, who in 1268 'convertit ad fidem Christianam' without her husband, as a manifestation of the Jewish female independence, however qualified, which has been one of the themes of this lecture?[74] Perhaps not; for in a *cause célèbre* at Canterbury in 1235 the Jewess Chera not only defied legal expectation by refusing to follow her husband into the Christian faith, but continued to claim her house as part of her original marriage settlement.[75] It is yet another tribute to the status of the Jewish woman (and future mother) that her conversion to the Christian faith was, apparently, often more fiercely opposed by her

---

[71] It seems less than clear whether Edward I's famous mandate of 1280 instructing his sheriffs to ensure that Jews should attend the new conversionary sermons to be preached throughout the realm by the Dominican friars were meant to apply to women as well as to men: see *CPR, 1272–81*, p. 356; D'Bloissiers Tovey, *Anglia Judaica* (Oxford, 1738), pp. 215–16.

[72] Adler, *Jews of Medieval England*, pp. 350–2.

[73] F. D. Logan, 'Thirteen London Jews and conversion to Christianity: problems of apostasy in the 1280s', *BIHR*, 45 (1972), pp. 216, 227.

[74] Rigg, *Select Pleas*, pp. 42–3 (confirming that female converts to Christianity forfeited their bonds to the Crown not to their husbands).

[75] Adler, *Jews of Medieval England*, pp. 67–8.

community than that of her husband or son. The most dramatic example of such opposition is provided by the well-known story of Juliana of London, who not long after her conversion to the Christian religion in 1274 was kidnapped by nine Jews (four of them women) from a house in Coleman Street. Before the Jews smuggled Juliana out of the country by means of a ship, which was finally driven back to Sandwich, she was subjected to intense pressure to revert to Judaism: according to Juliana's possibly suspect testimony, a Jewish widow named Antera even went so far as to fasten a cord around Juliana's neck and threaten to hang her 'if she would not abjure the Christian faith and return to their disbelief'.[76]

Jewish women of the 1270s and 1280s could, in other words, react to the possibility of Christian conversion in very different ways, and not necessarily always passive ways. How could it be otherwise? Since the days of William Prynne, Edward I's ejection of his Jews from England in 1290 (in Cecil Roth's words, 'the first general expulsion of the Jews from any country in the medieval period') has been made to serve many different models: is it altogether a coincidence, to take a recent example, that the Jews were expelled *en masse* from England at that very point of time which witnessed (as we are currently being informed by the CNRS) *le genèse de l'état moderne?*[77] Nor would anyone wish to deny that in thirteenth-century England, as in the very different world of the late medieval Mediterranean, it was the profound differences in the economic forces shaping the development of the Jewish and Christian communities which played the primary role in creating such remarkably contrasting roles for the family and the female.[78] However, the experience of the Jewish women of Plantagenet England is nothing if not a demonstration of how the economic and religious influences upon their lives were inextricably intertwined. The reasons for Edward I's banishment of the Jews from England in 1290 will no doubt always be a contentious matter; but there can at least be no doubt, to end with the bitter argument from which thirteenth-century Jewish women could

---

[76] London, PRO, E. 9, 4/17, memb. 12d; *Cal. Jewish Plea Rolls*, 2, pp. 209–10; 3, pp. 18, 41, 111.

[77] Roth, *History of Jews*, p. 90; J. Cohen, *The Friars and the Jews: The Evolution of Medieval Anti-Semitism* (Cornell, 1982), pp. 13–16, 242–64; *L'État moderne: genèse: bilans et perspectives* (Actes du Colloque tenu au CNRS à Paris. 19–20 September 1989), ed. J.-P. Genet (Paris, 1990), pp. 7–13, 261–81.

[78] G. Todeschini, 'Families juives et chrétiennes en Italia à la fin du moyen âge: deux modèles de développement economique', *Annales*, 45 (1990), pp. 787–817; S. D. Goitein, *A Mediterranean Society: The Jewish Communities of the Arab World as portrayed in the Documents of the Cairo Geniza*, III, *The Family* (Berkeley, 1978).

find no escape, that expulsion, like persecution, is likely to be the result of a Christian failure to convince—as well as a more profound failure to understand.

Christ's College,
Cambridge

DESECRATION OF THE HOST:
THE BIRTH OF AN ACCUSATION

by MIRI RUBIN

A NEW tale entered the circle of commonplace narratives about Jews which were known to men and women in the thirteenth century: the tale of Host desecration. This new narrative habitually unfolded (1) an attempt by a Jewish man to procure (buy, steal, exchange) a consecrated Host in order to (2) abuse it (in re-enactment of the Passion, in ridicule of bread claimed to be God), (3) only to be found out through a miraculous manifestation of the abused Host, which leads to (4) punishment (arrest and torture unto death, lynching by a crowd).[1] The tale was a robust morality story about transgression and its punishment, and it always ended with the annihilation of the abusing Jew and often of his family, neighbours, or the whole local Jewish community. It was a bloody story, both in the cruelty inflicted on the Host/God and in the tragic end of the accused abuser and those related to him. This basic narrative was open to myriad interpretations and combinations, elaborations at every stage of its telling. It is a particularly interesting narrative inasmuch as it was often removed from the context of preaching and teaching, of exemplification, into the world of action and choice. The Host-desecration tale was not only a poignant story about Jews, it was also a blueprint for action whenever the circumstances of abuse suggested themselves in the lives of those who were reared on the tale. The story's fictionality was masked from the very beginning of its life: it was always told as a report about a real event, with no irony or explicit elaboration. It was a concrete, new tale, which provided tangible knowledge about Jews, and through the actions of Jews, about the Eucharist.

It is usually claimed that the archetype of the Host-desecration tale is that of Paris at Easter of 1290.[2] A Jew named Jonathan, who lived in the

---

[1] For a general survey of the Host-desecration accusation see P. Browe, 'Die Hostien-schändungen der Juden im Mittelalter', *Römische Quartalschrift*, 34 (1926), pp. 167–97.

[2] For accounts of this event see 'De miraculo hostiae a Judaeo Parisiis anno Domini MCCXC multis ignominiis effectatae', *Recueil des historiens des Gaules et de la France* [hereafter *RHGF*], 22, pp. 32–3; 'Ex brevi chronico Ecclesiae S. Dyonisii ad cyclos paschales', *RHGF*, 23, p. 145; 'Extrait d'une chronique anonyme finissant en MCCCLXXX', *RHGF*, 21, pp. 123–30; 'Extrait d'une chronique anonyme française, finissant en MCCCVIII', *RHGF*, 21, pp. 132–3; 'Chroniques de Saint-Denis depuis 1285 jusqu'en 1328', *RHGF*, 20, pp. 654–724; *Les Grandes chroniques de France*, ed. J. Viard (Paris, 1934), 8, pp. 144–5. On the case see W. C. Jordan, *The*

parish of St Jean-en-Grève, approached a woman who had come to redeem some pawned clothes around Eastertime. He offered to hand over the clothes 'sens rien prendre de son argent' if she would bring to him the Host which she would receive at Easter Communion.[3] The covetous woman was tempted to do so and provided the man with the Host, who then proceeded to abuse 'la digne personne' in it. He threw it into a boiling pot of water, then pierced it with a knife, only to find that the Host was not destroyed and that the water 'devint vermeille comme meslée avecques sang'.[4] An elaborate Latin version of the case imputed to the Jews a desire to ridicule that which Christians claimed to be their God.[5] He pierced it with knives and pins and saw it bleed, threw it into boiling water, only to see it turn into a figure of the crucified Christ hovering over the boiling cauldron.[6] Here the figure of Christ appeared above the boiling cauldron, and the Jew, his wife, son, and daughter looked on. The desecration was revealed when the Jew's son ran into the parish church and called out to the Christians there that they were wrong to think that Christ was on the altar, since he was being killed at his own home, by his own father.[7] A woman of the congregation came forth, and after making the sign of the Cross came to the Jewish house and saw the scene of abuse. She had the parish priest called, and the Host recuperated, after which the Jew was arrested; and in another version the bishop, Simon de Bucy, was alerted, and two sergeants were called to arrest the Jew.[8] It goes on to say that the regent professors of theology were consulted, and together with the judgement of the people this led to a verdict of death by fire, while the Jew's family converted, and his daughter joined the monastery of Filles Dieu.[9] The Jew's house was confiscated, and by 1295 a licence was granted

---

French monarchy and the Jews: from Philip Augustus to the Last Capetians (Philadelphia, Pa., 1989), pp. 192–4.

[3] 'Extrait d'une chronique . . . MCCCVIII', p. 133.

[4] The descriptions in the 'Grandes chroniques', pp. 144–5, the 'Extrait d'une chronique . . . MCCCLXXX', p. 127, and the 'Chroniques de Saint-Denis', p. 658, give very similar versions of the tale. A Latin account claims that a group of Jews had perpetrated desecration: 'Quidam Judaei hostiam sacram a quodam pessimo habuerunt', anno 1289. It also places the piercing with knives before the boiling in water: 'Ex brevi chronico', pp. 145–6.

[5] On the imputation of intentions or beliefs to the Jews in cases of Host-desecration see C. Roth, 'The mediaeval conception of the Jew', in I. Davidson, ed., Essays and Studies in Memory of Linda R. Miller (New York, 1938), pp. 171–90, at pp. 180–2.

[6] 'De miraculo hostiae', p. 32.

[7] Ibid., 'Frustra in ecclesia illa Christianos Deum suum quaerere ait, quem flagellatum injuriis affectum et male tractatum, modo pater suus occidisset.'

[8] 'Extrait d'une chronique . . . MCCCVIII', p. 133.

[9] 'Chroniques de Saint-Denis', p. 658.

by Pope Boniface VIII for the building of a chapel on the site of the Jew's house.[10] A cult soon developed there, around the miraculous Host, as well as in the parish church of St Jean-en-Grève, which held the 'holy knife' with which Jonathan was said to have perpetrated the desecration. It attracted pilgrims and the attentions of a branch of the Carmelite Order, which settled and ran the miracle chapel. The chronicle of Saint-Denis and the court chronicle soon helped spread the story in the monastic milieu of the Île-de-France. By 1294 the chronicler John of Thilrode of St Bavo's abbey, in Ghent, recorded the tale in the early version which placed a maid in the Jewish household as the accomplice.[11] By 1299 a royal ordinance for the south of France relating to Jewish 'perfidy' included among the Jewish offences the desecration of the Host:

> Iudei . . . Christianos sollicitant de heretica pravitate . . . a plerisque receperunt et suis nephandis manibus presumpserunt nequitur pertractare sanctissimum corpus Christi et alia sacramenta nostre fidei blasphemare, simplices plurimos seducendo et circumcidendo seductos.[12]

Yet there are reasons to question the uniqueness of the Parisian attribution. Further to the east, in the Rhineland, Alsace, and Franconia, we encounter already earlier in the century the development of narratives about Jewish abuse which come just short of the fully-flung Host-desecration accusation. There is the case of the young man of Cologne, son of a convert, who received the Host and took it out of his mouth in the churchyard, only to find the Host turn into a tiny infant on the palm of his hand. Mysterious voices threatened him in utterances made up of scriptural verses. When he buried the little creature and hoped to get away he was stopped by the Devil. He finally gave up and called a priest, to whom he confessed, convinced of the truth of Christian faith.[13] This tale

---

[10] *Les Registres de Boniface VIII*, 4 vols (Paris, 1884–93), 1, no. 441. See also 'De miraculo hostiae', p. 32, and S. Simonsohn, ed., *The Apostolic See and the Jews. Documents: 492–1404* (Toronto, 1988), no. 175, pp. 283–4.

[11] 'Iohannis de Thilrode Chronicon', *MGH.SS*, 25, ed. J. Heller (Hanover, 1880); or in *RHGF*, 23, pp. 145–6.

[12] G. Saige, *Les Juifs du Languedoc antérieurement au XIVe siècle* (Paris, 1881), no. 20, pp. 235–6, at p. 236. See S. Menache, 'Faith, myth, and politics—the stereotype of the Jews and the expulsion from England and France', *JQR*, 75 (1984–5), pp. 351–74, p. 364. See also R. Chazan, *Medieval Jewry in Northern France: a Political and Social History* (Baltimore, Md., 1973), pp. 182–3.

[13] Told in the *Viaticum narrationum* of Herman of Bologna, *Beiträge zur lateinische Erzählungsliteratur des Mittelalters: III. Das Viaticum narrationum des Hermannus Bononiensis*, ed. A. Hilka (Berlin, 1935), no. 72, pp. 100–2.

is the product of a reworking of more traditional material, which was common in the early Middle Ages and which had the Jew act as a witness to, and a conduit for, the manifestations of faith which ultimately swayed him and his to join the faith. Here, not a Jew, but a convert's son, and a witnessing of miracles served to strengthen the young man's faith and fortified that of the future audiences of the tale. Some time in the 1280s it was told in St Dié, near Epinal, that a Jew had procured a Host and was apprehended by the parish priest just in time, before the abuse had taken place. Two of the eight glass medallions in the local church describe scenes related to the planned abuse: one shows the Jew in a burgess's house, giving the Christian a box in which to place the Host, and another shows a suspicious priest catching the Jew.[14] Some time in the late 1280s an accusation of Host desecration in Büren (Westphalia) resulted in the killing of Jews and the building of an expiatory chapel.[15]

Within the secular and the religious legal systems an awareness of this category of activity becomes evident in these very decades. The Council of Vienna of 1267 required Jews to stay indoors behind closed windows and doors from the time of the sounding of the bell which announced a procession with the Eucharist to the sick.[16] In 1281 King Rudolf of Austria sat in judgement during a visit to Vienna in the case of a Jew who had thrown stones at a priest carrying the Eucharist to the sick.[17] Godfrey Giffard, Bishop of Worcester, sent a mandate to the archdeacons of Westbury and Bristol to pronounce excommunicate the Jews of the city, following a case of injury inflicted on the Host as it was being taken to a sick person by the priest of St Peter's parish, passing by way of the Jewish quarter.[18]

So a preoccupation with the contact which Jews might have with the Eucharist provided the insight at the heart of the new evolving tale of abuse, and determined the possibilities of punishment and redress inherent in it. The emphasis in the tales will move from witness to transgression and its punishment, from the possibilities of inclusion and absorption of the doubting Jew to the insistent need to purge him and his effects out of the Christian body.

---

[14] The sequence is enshrined in the stained-glass windows of the abbey church of St Dié of *c.*1280, described to me by Professor Meredith Lillich, whom I warmly thank.

[15] See document on foundation of chapel in B. Brilling and H. Richtering, eds, *Westfalia judaica: Urkunden und Regesten zur Geschichte der Juden in Westfalen und Lippe* (Stuttgart, 1967), no. 31, p. 56 (1292).

[16] C.-J. Hefele and H. Leclercq, *Histoire des conciles* (Paris, 1914), 6, 1, p. 138.

[17] 'Heinrici de Heimberg Annales', *MGH.SS*, 17, ed. G. H. Pertz (Hanover, 1861), p. 717.

[18] *Register of Bishop Godfrey Giffard*, ed. J. W. Willis Bund (Oxford, 1902), 1, p. 71.

It is interesting to note that the Jew was always the male Jew, and, in particular, the Jew as father. Already in the early Middle Ages a fascination with the hard-hearted, stubborn Jewish male encapsulated the whole attitude to Jews. Whereas Jewish children in their purity could be made to see the light of Christian truth, and the tender mother might be swayed by her son's insight, the Jewish father stood in the way. The Jewish father stood for the Law in its cruel and unyielding nature; whereas the woman/ mother was assimilated into the image of female gentleness, seen as a person easily influenced, and more readily moved by affective manifestation, the person who might convert through miraculous illumination, together with her children, as in the most important tale of the early medieval repertoire, that of the Jewish Boy. In this tale a Jewish boy, who went to school with Christian boys, saw the child Christ in the consecrated Host while attending and receiving Communion at Christmas with his friends.[19] When the boy returned home and was asked by his father of his whereabouts, he said that he had been in church and had seen a little boy given to each communicant. This incites the Jewish father to anger and moves him to commit the worst sin of all— infanticide—by throwing his son into a furnace (see plate 1). The Jewish mother cries out, and her wailing summons Christian neighbours, who peer into the oven only to find the boy intact. The boy told of a lovely lady in whose lap he had rested secure within the fire, the woman who had appeared painted in the altar-piece he had seen earlier that day. The mother and son and many other Jews were moved to conversion, while the father received the punishment, justly inverted, of being thrown into the same furnace. For him, there was no hope, no redress. It is this type of male, paternal, proprietorial Jew who is the active and evil actor of the new type of tale—the Host-desecration tale. This was a typical early medieval tale which moved in the sixth century from Greek material into Gregory of Tours's hagiographical *De gloria martyrum*, a tale which came to be used in the ninth century as a central miraculous proof in debates about the Eucharist and subsequently was enshrined in the popular genre of Marian tales collected and distinctively codified in the twelfth century.[20]

So the Host-desecration accusation was developing throughout the thirteenth century out of the eucharistic lore and the tales about Jews. The

[19] On the story and its development and dissemination see T. Pelizaeus, *Beiträge zur Geschichte der Legende vom Judenknabe* (Halle, 1914); T. Nissen, 'Zu den ältesten Fassungen der Legende vom Judenknabe', *Zeitschrift für französische Sprache und Literatur*, 62 (1938–9), pp. 393–403.

[20] R. W. Southern, 'The English origins of the "Miracles of the Virgin"', *Mediaeval and Renaissance Studies*, 4 (1958), pp. 176–216.

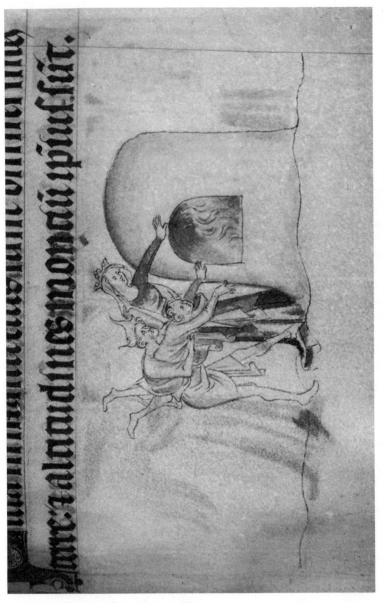

Plate 1   Jewish Boy thrown into the Furnace: Queen Mary Psalter, BL, MS Royal B VII 2, fol. 208r (c.1310) (by courtesy of the British Library).

Eucharist raised so many difficulties and doubts, not only in the minds of theologians, but in the questions of simpler folk and in the context of pastoral practice, and these were often treated through the genre of tale, through miraculous exemplification, through edification by recounting of prodigious proofs of eucharistic truth.[21] The Host-desecration tale also came to live another life: one of action and violence, as it provided a line of action against real Jews, who had allegedly committed the abuse described so carefully in the tale. The powerful eucharistic awareness and the peculiar vulnerability of Jews in late medieval towns, as well as the political and legal settings which constructed their modes of existence, all combined to create the circumstances which made the eucharistic desecration tale a tale of life, applicable, to be enacted and re-enacted. Its immediacy and relevance was universal, just as was the sense of the Eucharist's vulnerability, and of Jewish otherness. This is not to say that such sentiments were entertained by all, or that all accusation against Jews succeeded, but rather to say that to the phobic psyche, and to the poor parish priest, and to poor townsfolk, and to indebted knights, participation in the narrative could be constructed as an act equally pious and advantageous.

How does a new story travel, how does it become established among the commonplaces of a culture, so as to suggest a routine, a truth about the actions of, in this case, Jews? Tracing the tale through its Italian vernacular route is a good example. Out of the many possible transmissions we can trace two: one in the preaching of Giordano da Rivalto, the Florentine preacher whose vernacular sermons in the city squares were popular, much excerpted and copied.[22] In November 1304 he was able to tell of recent massacres of Jews following a Host desecration: a Jew had sent his maid to church to get a Host and rewarded her with payment or some other evil, and when she returned he began to abuse the Host, which turned into a little boy. Though his numbers are exaggerated (he claims the death of 24,000) Jews, and details sparse, he knew that a regional pogrom following the abuse of the Host had touched the Jews in another region (he is probably referring to the Franconian massacres of 1298–1300). Now the Dominican Giordano may well have been privy to

---

[21] M. Rubin, *Corpus Christi: the Eucharist in Late Medieval Culture* (Cambridge, 1991), pp. 109–29.
[22] Giordano da Rivalto, *Prediche del B. Giordano da Rivalto recitate in Firenze*, ed. D. Moreni, 2 vols (Florence, 1831), 2, pp. 227–8; on this report see J. Cohen, *The Friars and the Jews: the Evolution of Medieval Anti-Judaism* (Ithaca, NY, 1982), pp. 239–40. On Giordano see D. R. Lesnick, *Preaching in Medieval Florence: the Social World of Franciscan and Dominican Spirituality* (Athens, Ga., 1989), pp. 103–8, 111–33, 257–8.

the account of a Dominican friar, Rudolf, Prior of Schlettstadt, who produced a series of tales about those events, the *Historiae memorabiles*.[23] He may also have heard it on the grape-vine of an international order such as his, or even from Florentine merchants who had visited the Rhineland. Giordano told it authoritatively, and with interpretation. He linked these events with others concerning his Order, the expulsion of Jews from Sicily, following the intervention of the Dominican Bartholomew of Aquila and his influence on Charles II of Sicily to introduce the inquisition to Apulia, with special attention to Jewish crimes, and to force Jews to convert or to go into exile.[24] He told it not as a miracle tale, but as a relevant and stirring event woven into his homiletic structure in the sermon for St Saviour's Day. Three decades later Giovanni Villani told the story of Paris, and again as part of his historical account under the year 1290, as 'd'uno miracolo ch'avvenne in Parigi', recounting the tale as it had crystallized in Paris, a tale of a usurer who procured and abused a Host through a simple and poor woman.[25] Giovanni had spent years in the service of the Bardi firm in Flanders between around 1304 and 1312 and, as the tale was known there, could he not have learnt it during his stay in the north, only to use the poignant story in his rich and varied history? It was exactly the tale of Villani which provided the narrative on which a *sacra rappresentazione* came to be composed, known to us only from the fifteenth century, and, in turn, to provide the version which animated the mind and the eye of Paolo Uccello when choosing the scenes for the six *predella* scenes commissioned of him by the Confraternity of Corpus Domini of Urbino between 1465 and 1468.[26]

So the Host-desecration accusation moves dynamically between the world of tale, the self-conscious recounting and listening to stories, experienced at leisure, or in the ritualized event of a sermon, and the world of action, as a useful narrative came to be applied and followed in a specific context. By 1294 an accusation was made against Jews in Laa (Austria) for the theft and burial of a consecrated Host in the manure of a

---

[23] Rudolf of Schlettstadt, *Historiae memorabiles*, ed. E. Kleinschmidt (Cologne, 1974); on the author, pp. 9–12.

[24] Giordano da Rivalto, *Prediche*, 2, pp. 231–2. On the introduction of the inquisition into Jewish matters in France see M. Kriegel, 'La Jurisdiction inquisitoriale sur les juifs à l'époque de Philippe le Hardi et Philippe le Bel', in *Les Juifs dans l'histoire de France: premier colloque international*, ed. M. Yardeni (Leiden, 1980), pp. 70–7.

[25] *Croniche di Giovanni, Matteo e Filippo Villani — Bibliotheca classica italiana secolo xiv*, 21 (Trieste, 1857), c. 143, p. 166.

[26] M. A. Lavin, 'The altar of Corpus Christi in Urbino: Paolo Uccello, Joos Van Ghent, Piero della Francesca', *Art Bulletin* (1967), pp. 1–24, at pp. 1–10.

stable, an accusation which destroyed the lives of some members of the Jewish community and banished others from the town.[27] Some of the cases recounted by Ruldolph of Schlettstadt are highly instructive: his account of the regional persecutions in Franconia which have come to be known as the 'Rintfleisch' massacres, and which lasted for the three years 1298 to 1300, which saw the annihilation of some 146 communities and at least 3,000 Jews.[28] Rudolf identified the spark which set off the terrible blaze in a Host desecration perpetrated in Röttingen, on the river Tauber. Here, the sense of misdeed arose when the cries of a child emanated from a Jewish house inhabited by a childless couple. Children at play who had heard the sound alerted their parents, and the parish women approached the house only to find the scene of abuse, in the course of which the Host manifested itself as the Christ-child and wailed in agony. The local priest was called to acknowledge the events and pronounce the miracle, while a man, sometimes called a butcher, but most likely a knight from the vicinity, led a crowd which set out to avenge the wrong in a collective punishment of the Jews by death.[29] The group led by Rintfleisch further- more carried the events over into the countryside, where massacres of Jews in the villages and small towns around Röttingen habitually led to the discovery of abused eucharistic species in nooks and crannies of smouldering Jewish houses.[30] Thus an explanation and justification of the terrible violence is constructed through the presentation of an almost instinctively motivated vengeance. The regional aspect of massacres following Host-desecration accusations was also grounded in the very tropes of eucharistic understanding.[31] The Eucharist was, after all, the species whole and perfect, without limit to its quantity, divisible and yet

---

[27] 'Continuatio Zwetlensis tertia', *MGH.SS*, 9, ed. A. Wattenbach (Hanover, 1851), p. 658.

[28] On the massacres see F. Lotter, 'Hostienfrevelvorwurf und Blutwunderfälschung bei den Judenverfolgungen von 1298 ("Rintfleisch") und 1136–1338 ("Armleder")', in *Fälschungen im Mittelalter* (Hanover, 1988), 5, pp. 533–83, at pp. 548–60; F. Lotter, 'Die Judenverfolgung des "König Rintfleisch" in Franken um 1298. Die endgültige Wende in den christlich-jüdischen Beziehungen im Deutschen Reich des Mittelalters', *Zeitschrift für historische Forschung*, 15 (1988), pp. 385–422. For a map of the massacres see Z. Avneri, ed., *Germania judaica* (Tübingen, 1968), 2, 1, at end. See the Jewish sources in S. Salfeld, ed., *Das Martyrologium des Nürnberger Memorbuches* (Berlin, 1898), pp. 162–200, 231–6.

[29] Rudolf of Schlettstadt, *Historiae memorabiles*, c. 6, pp. 49–51.

[30] Ibid.: '(Iudei) furati sunt plus quam centum hostias consecratas, que postea in domibus eorum in destructione cum nequciia eorum palefacta fuerat, illese hinc inde inventa sunt. Nam in pluribus locis acramentum Christi diversis modis obtinuerint.'

[31] See the report of the chronicle of St Peter's, Erfurt: 'Christiani ... post interfectionem ipsorum ipsa secreciora eorundem purgantes invenerunt corpus Christi plurimis locis confossum': *Chronica S. Petri Erfordiensis*, ed. O. Holder-Egger, *MGH.SRG*, 42 (Hanover, 1899), p. 319.

powerful even in its smallest fraction. The Eucharist was eminently divisible, made to be parcelled and portioned, by the consecrating priest at the altar, but also by the abusing Jew. In Enns (Upper Austria) in 1420 a Host-desecration accusation was made which ultimately led to the great expulsion of Austrian Jewry in 1421. The rich Jew Israel of Enns was said to have procured from the Church of St Lawrence 'multas sacramenti particulas', which he sent to his Jewish associates in the region. The arrests, confiscations, and expulsions under ducal mandate merely followed the route of this alleged dissemination.[32]

So we observe in this story of origin of the event of 1298–1300 an enactment of a narrative of abuse and its punishment, but also the creation of a blueprint for future action. In these dramas certain characters play an important role: the neighbours observing the evidence, the parish priest pronouncing the miracle, the local leader, in Germany most frequently a knight from the lower gentry of the region, the Jew's accomplice in the figure of a Christian woman. Women played an important part in the narrative: they were represented as weak links in the Christian armour, accomplices and procurers of Hosts for Jews. A maid in a Jewish household was the most common provider of the Host for Jewish pleasure, in other cases a poor sexton persuaded by his wife, a female convert, a female debtor. William the Procurator, the Egmont chronicler, describes the woman 'mulier quaedam, filia diaboli' chosen by the Jews of Rymagen about 1323 to bring them the Host after Christmas Communion.[33] Female agency could be very active. In Metz about 1385 a Christian woman and a Jew were burnt. The rich widow had consulted a Jew in pursuit of the lucrative sale of her corn, and he agreed to help her on condition that she bring him Christ's Body ('selle ly voloit livrer le St corps nostre seigneur le sacrament il ly aideoit'). She feigned illness and received Communion, fulfilling her part in the bargain. But having put the Host in a box in her cupboard, her servants later discovered that it turned into a toad, and later into a little child.[34]

[32] Thomas Ebendorfer, *Chronica austria*, *MGH.SS*, ns 13, ed. A. Lhotsky (Hanover, 1967), bk 3, pp. 370–1. Such a pattern also falls in with the economy of the ritual murder, which in the Norwich version imputed to the European Jewry an annual rotating schedule of child-murder by which a community was chosen annually to murder and provide the blood for the Paschal ritual; on this myth see G. I. Langmuir, 'Thomas of Monmouth: detector of ritual murder', in *Towards a Definition of Antisemitism* (Berkeley, 1990), pp. 209–36.

[33] William the Proctor *Chronicon comitum et nobilium Hollandiae ab 1206–1332*, ed. A. Matthaeus (The Hague, 1738), 2, pp. 496–718, at p. 611.

[See opposite page for n. 34]

So the Host-desecration narrative provided voices, roles, and gestures for its actors, but it could also be contested, its very applicability to local circumstances could be brought into question. In Pulkau a bloodied Host was found on the threshold of a Jew's house and was taken to the local church (see plate 2). A massacre of the Jews ensued. But the narrative of Host desecration was contested. Responding to local doubts and pressure from the Duke of Austria, the Bishop of Passau set up an investigation into the affair.[35] He was sufficiently anxious to place a consecrated Host side by side with the 'miraculous' host, to save simple worshippers from the danger of idolatry if the 'hostia inventa' turned out to be false. In 1341 the investigator Frederic, a canon of Bamberg Cathedral and doctor of canon law, handed in his report, a tract which was no less than a tract on the Eucharist in ten points, which wholly endorsed any miraculous manifestation by a Host as an obvious proof of the alleged preceding abuse.[36] He further claimed that any magnate who wished to absolve the Jews from the crime was surely acting for the basest of financial motives, greed which had ensnared them into Jewish debt. So the local cult lived on, and in 1396 the *Blutkapelle* was built even as the very truth of its miraculous endorsement was in doubt.

Now the investigation in Pulkau was made in a very special context, and it is undoubtedly the exception; most accusation of Host desecration and the ensuing massacres passed with little subsequent comment, and usually without punishment, to be noted only by the chronicler as 'in X y Judei cremati sunt', and in the heart-rending verses of Jewish laments. But in Pulkau some very important local knowledge had come to bear on interpretations of the accusation. Some forty years earlier in the same diocese and not very far away, in Korneuburg, near Vienna, a similar Host-desecration accusation resulted in the establishment of a eucharistic cult and in a massacre of Jews in 1305. A Jew, Zerkl, a Jewish school-master, had been caught by a Christian baker and accused of blasphemy and abuse of the Host over a period of three years.[37] The Hosts were recuperated and began working miracles. Yet some doubts had existed as to the nature of the abused Host: had it already been consecrated or was it simply a piece of baked dough? The investigator, a Cistercian scholar,

---

[34] Paris, BN, MS nouv. acq. 4857, fol. Q262. On this case see J. Weill, 'Un Juif brulé à Metz vers 1385 pour profanation d'hostie', *REJ*, 53 (1907), pp. 270–2.

[35] Simonsohn, ed., *The Apostolic See*, pp. 372–4.

[36] Vienna, Austrian National Library, MS 350, fols 1ra–17vb.

[37] *Urkundenbuch des Stiftes Klosterneuburg bis zum Ende des vierzehnten Jahrhunderts*, ed. H. Zeibig, *Fontes rerum austriacarum, Diplomataria et acta*, 28 (Vienna, 1868), pp. 172–5.

Plate 2 Host-desecration at Pulkau: Holy Blood Chapel, Pulkau, altar-piece c.1510.

Ambrose of the Holy Cross, raised some doubts. But the evidence brought to him by witnesses was overwhelming. Miracles took place in front of the eucharistic particle salvaged from the Jews: candles being lit up spontaneously, the lame beginning to walk, and the blind gaining sight.[38] Ambrose's doubts were not shared by the local community, and he passed on the investigation to a higher instance, to a papal investigator. Yet there must have been some further assessment of the case of which we have no remaining evidence, since in his letter of 1338 authorizing the investigation into the Pulkau events, Pope Benedict XII recounted the recent case of Korneuburg ('in opido Newmburch') as a precedent of fraudulent action.[39] Indeed, some of the contemporary local chroniclers telling the story of Pulkau recounted it as a fraud perpetrated by a poor parish priest, like John of Winthertur, who explained the priest's motivation, 'for reason of his indigence'.[40] A Host stained red with blood, found on the threshold of a Jewish house, provided sufficient material for the remaking of the Host-desecration narrative, which ends badly, in death to the perpetrator and to his fellow Jews. And then this, in turn, became a famous case, to be told and retold by preachers and chroniclers.

To say that the Host-desecration accusation was a blueprint for action is not simply to suggest some inexorably self-fulfilling force to it; it is rather to suggest that authoritative narratives in any culture provide patterns within which actions it is to be understood, and its shapes appreciated. Every accusation and every massacre which followed it were products of specific contexts; yet they sought to fulfil the requirements for legitimation suggested by the Host-desecration narrative. The events which prompted the second large regional massacre in south-west Germany, the 'Armleder' movement of 1336–8 is a good example.[41] It was told as the consequence of an offence planned by Jews as they saw the Eucharist carried by a priest pass in the streets. A knight, Arnold of Ussinkeim, whose brother had been murdered by a Jew, and who was in

---

[38] On the case of Korneuburg see K. Lohrmann, *Judenrecht und Judenpolitik im mittelalterlichen Osterreich* (Cologne, 1990), p. 105; see also the case of St Pölten, p. 106; see also with a reproduction of the altar-piece *Die Zeit der frühen Habsburger. Dome und Klöster 1279–1379* (Vienna, 1979), no. 119, p. 364; Lotter, 'Hostienfrevelvorwurf', pp. 559–60.

[39] Simonsohn, ed., *The Apostolic See*, p. 372.

[40] *Die Chronik Johanns von Winterthur*, ed. C. Brun and F. Bathgen, *MGH.SRG*, ns, 3 (Berlin, 1924), pp. 142–3: 'Iudeorum tribulatio orta et propter quendam sacerdotis nimia inopiam oppressum, qui hostiam sangwine aspersoit et a se proiectum iuxta Iudeos ipsos suspectos reddidit et graviter infamavit.'

[41] On which see K. Arnold, 'Die Armledererhebung in Franken 1336', *Mainfränkisches Jahrbuch für Geschichte und Kunst*, 26 (1974), pp. 35–62.

town for a court hearing, appointed himself leader on a *tour* of revenge. A well-known local trouble-maker, Arnold had been banished from the region by the territorial lord, and his gift for arousing armed crowds is manifest in the events of 1338. He led a group of armed townsmen (named after the leather arm-guards which they wore) joined by knights on a rampage which all but annihilated Franconian Jewry. His forces were finally stopped around Kitzingen, and he was arrested, tried, and executed. Yet Arnold's tomb quickly became a site of pilgrimage as his body was reported to work miracles. And another leader took over as the 'Rex Armleder' and led the second and then the third waves throughout Franconia, Alsace, and Bavaria.[42]

So the universal tale, told all over Europe, conveyed in collections of *exempla*, in chronicles, in wall-paintings, in religious drama,[43] and enshrined in the chapels and pilgrimage sites commemorating specific desecrations, spread near and far, even to England, from which Jews were expelled in 1290.[44] The spread of accusations is striking: there were recurrent massacres in the centres of Jewish settlement in the Rhineland, in southern imperial lands and in Austria by the last years of the thirteenth century, in Polish lands from the 1320s, a single case in the Low Countries, in Brussels, in 1370,[45] and a few cases in Spain, in Hueca in 1377 (see plate 3), and in Segovia in 1410.[46] Bohemia, which had been comparatively untouched by the massacres of the Black Death, experienced the accusation in Prague in 1398.[47] By the fifteenth century Host-desecration crises could directly cause the end of settlement with mass killings and deportations from a region; in some cases it simply provided the final spur in towns where the citizenry had been agitating for expulsion over decades, like Regensburg and Nuremberg.[48] By the late

[42] Arnold, 'Die Armledererhebung', pp. 44–53.

[43] In the fifteenth century Alfonso da Spina claimed that the tale decorated many a French chapel, *Fortalitium fidei* (Lyons, 1511), bk 3, *consideratio* 9; L. Muir, 'The mass on the medieval stage', *Comparative drama*, 23 (1989–90), pp. 314–30, at pp. 317–18.

[44] On the English version of the drama of Host-desecration see S. Beckwith, 'Ritual, Church and Theatre: medieval dramas of the sacramental body', in David Aers, ed., *Culture and History, 1350–1660: Essays on English Communities, Identities and Writings* (London, 1992), pp. 65–89.

[45] For a short account and a bibliographical survey see J. Stengers, *Les Juifs dans le Pays-Bas au moyen-âge* (Brussels, 1950), pp. 24–7, 132–47.

[46] J. Miret y Sans, 'El procés de les hosties contra ls Jueus d'Osca en 1377', *Annuari d'Estudis Catalanas*, 4 (1911–12), pp. 59–80; J. Bruyn, *Van Eyck Problemen* (Utrecht, 1957), pp. 143–4.

[47] F. Graus, *Struktur und Geschichte. Drei Volksaufstände im mittelalterlichen Prag* (Sigmaringen, 1971), pp. 50–60.

[48] On the process of expulsion from late fifteenth-century Imperial territories see M. J. Wenninger, *Man bedarf keiner Juden mehr. Ursachen und Hintergründe ihrer Vertreibung aus den deutschen Reichsstädten im 14. Jahrhundert* (Vienna, 1981).

Plate 3   Desecration of the Host in a Boiling Cauldron: late fourteenth-century
altar-frontal, Las Monjas, Barcelona, Catalan Museum of Art.

fifteenth century, when most of western Europe was empty of Jews (most of France, Spain, England, the Low Countries, some Italian towns), the story grew even more fantastic as it came to be superimposed upon the ritual-murder accusation. The most infamous late medieval accusation, that of the ritual murder of the child Simon of Trent, followed by a trial whose copious records have survived, developed into an accusation of Host desecration.[49]

The cases of Rintfleisch, Pulkau, and Armleder show us that the universal narrative was always told and unfolded within the immediate context of power and politics of a town and its region. That this was not the only course of action, and that there may have been dissenting voices and unsuccessful 'tellings' of the narrative is evident from the eloquent testimony of a case like that of Pulkau, where the narrative was *not* believed by all, or in a city like Regensburg, whose town council stopped the Rintfleisch crowds from entering and injuring its Jews.[50] The tale's force derived from the rich world of eucharistic knowledge and myth which was being imparted as the very heart of the religious culture, and it was bolstered by an ongoing tension between the eucharistic claims and the realities or appearances which most people apprehended in and around it. It also derived from the strange vulnerability of Jews: even when legally protected, and their status was very clearly defined in those very imperial lands in which most accusations took place, their lives were always liable to be transposed on to a whole different plane, into the heart of the anti-Jewish discourse which turned them from neighbours, friends, and business partners into polluting, bestial, and life-denying creatures whose very existence depended on a cost or a loss to the non-Jews. The Host-desecration tale was a narrative produced within this discourse, and the unfolding of a Host-desecration accusation was the creation of a *mise-en-scène* for the enactment of gestures and the making of utterances learnt and legitimated within it. Versed in these roles, women, priests, children, dukes, Christian knights, all had compelling parts to play.

---

[49] W. P. Eckert, 'Beatus-Simoninus—aus den Akten des Trienter Judenprozesses', in *Judenhass—Schuld des Christen?!*, ed. W. P. Eckert and E. L. Ehrlich (Essen, 1964), pp. 329–58; W. P. Eckert, 'Aus den Akten des Trienter Judenprozesses', in *Judentum im Mittelalter*, ed. P. Wilpert (Berlin, 1966), pp. 283–336. Professor R. Po-chia Hsia is currently investigating afresh the contents and influence of the Trent affair.

[50] In the words of a local chronicler, 'Cives tamen Ratisponenses suam volentes honorare civitatem ipsos Iudeos absque iudicio occidi et destrui vetuerunt', 'Eberhardi archidiaconi Ratisponensis annales': *MGH.SS*, 17, ed. G. H. Pertz (Hanover, 1861), p. 597.

To concentrate on the birth of a single anti-Jewish narrative is simply to set a single context through which some larger questions can be asked. It points us towards the investigation of the power of narratives within the culture and the element of agency and choice as actors in the past supported or accepted them. It seeks to problematize the complexity of Jewish existence at the heart of the mysteries of Christian culture and in the heart of towns and villages and to suggest some of the terrifying mechanisms which move or facilitate that awful transformation of neighbour into persecutor, of community into murderous crowd, of tolerated other to the object of all phobic energy and destructive desire.

Pembroke College,
Oxford

VIEWS OF JEWS FROM PARIS AROUND
1300: CHRISTIAN OR 'SCIENTIFIC'?[1]

by PETER BILLER

'A TERM in many ways inappropriate to the Middle Ages': so begins a recent medieval encyclopaedia article on 'antisemitism'.[2] It is the first worry of the medievalist. On the one hand, he or she hears the *c'est la même chose* cry of the non-medievalist when the latter looks at examples of medieval hatred of the Jews. On the other hand, he or she is acutely aware both of the modernity of racial thought and the way in which twelfth- or thirteenth-century texts, when discussing Jews, use religious vocabulary, not 'racial'. Painful modern Jewish and Christian concern to examine the Church's guilt pushes in the same direction as the medievalist's anxiety about anachronism. The effect is to underline religion.

The intention here is not to criticize either the caution or the concern, but to suggest that exclusive preoccupation with them leads to a second worry, which is this. One may be led to ignore another side of the vulgar prejudiced views and learned prejudiced views of Jews which were held in north-western European in the thirteenth century. For the former, take as an example the early thirteenth-century collection of *exempla* of Caesarius of Heisterbach, a good source for what was once 'folklore' and is now 'popular culture'. Its tales about Jews have religious themes and vocabulary, such as conversion and responsibility for Christ's Passion. Jean-Claude Schmitt has suggested that such *exempla* are the meeting-point of clerical learned culture and popular oral culture; peel off the former from an *exemplum* and one is left with the latter.[3] If one does this with the stories about Jews, removing the stratum which may be attributed to the 'clerical culture' of the Cistercian monk Caesarius, this is the residue: a physical ailment involving blood;[4] the beauty of a young

---

[1] I owe much to David d'Avray, who corrected errors in the edition given in Appendix B; he is not responsible for those which remain. A debt to Bernard Barr is acknowledged in n. 48, below.

[2] R. Chazan, 'Antisemitism', *Dictionary of the Middle Ages*, 13 vols. (New York, 1982–9), 1, p. 338.

[3] J.-C. Schmitt, '"Jeunes" et danse des chevaux de bois. Le folklore méridional dans la littérature des "exempla" (XIIIe–XIVe siècles)', *Cahiers de Fanjeaux*, 11 (1976), pp. 127–58.

[4] Caesarius of Heisterbach, *Dialogus miraculorum*, ed. J. Strange, 2 vols (Cologne, Bonn, and Brussels, 1851), II.23, 1, p. 92: 'Tunc enim Judaei laborare dicuntur quadam infirmitate, quae fluxus sanguinis dicuntur.'

Jewish girl, 'in the manner of her race', or sex with her;[5] dirty bodies;[6] lavatories;[7] 'Jewish stench'.[8] These are, disturbingly, very like the constituent elements of vulgar racial stereotypes in the modern world.

When one turns to learned prejudiced views, the different weights of texts from different faculties bear heavily—or lightly—on what one sees. So many texts survive from theology or canon law faculties, and they are so much studied, while fewer survive from arts and medical faculties, and these are less studied. Looking through texts from theology and canon law faculties to get at views of Jews may be like looking through scarlet and yellow stained glass in the effort to see medieval green fields. The first part of this paper is an attempt to see how hyperbolic this proposition is. It investigates it by taking one academic form, the quodlibetic question, at one university, Paris, and comparing the views of Jews in quodlibetic material coming from two different faculties, theology and arts. The second part tries to explore the roots and ramifications of the 'scientific' view found in one arts faculty quodlibet.

Two lists of theological quodlibets, which were published by Palémon Glorieux in 1925 and 1935, established modern understanding of the genre, the outlines of which are as follows.[9] In its classic form, a quodlibet was one of a series of questions raised during special sessions during Advent or Lent. It was raised during one session, and responded to at another session, perhaps several days later. It was oral. Like a disputed question it had four parts, a formally raised question, arguments both pro and con, a central, determining response, and finally replies to particular objections. Unlike a 'disputed question' it was quodlibetic, 'what you will'. This meant that it was *de quolibet*, about any theme, and raised *a quolibet*, by anyone in the audience: medieval academics' 'Question-time'. Surviving written versions may preserve any one of various stages: a master's

---

[5] Caesarius of Heisterbach, *Dialogus miraculorum*, II.23, 1, p. 93: 'Judaei cuiusdam filia, et secundum genus suum speciosa. Hanc iuvenis quidem ... concupivit ... eam quotidie ad commixtionem sollicitaret ... nocte eadem ad virginem venit, et usque ad matutinum cum illa dormivit'; II.24, 1, p. 94; 'Judaeus quidam manebat, filiam habens formosam. Hanc iuvenis quidam clericus, in vicino habitans, adamavit, devirginavit et impraegnavit.'

[6] Ibid., X.69, 2, p. 263: 'Judaeos, qui corpore ... omnino inmundi sunt.'

[7] Ibid., II.26, 1, p. 98: 'Ego, inquit Judaea, tribus vicibus te sursum traham per latrinam.'

[8] Ibid., II.25, 1, p. 96: 'foetor judaicus'. This appears in the German vernacular—*ein stinkender Jude*—in the vernacular version of Berthold of Regensburg's sermons, R. Cruel, *Geschichte der deutschen Predigt im Mittelalter* (Detmold, 1879), p. 621.

[9] These are cited in Appendix A. The most recent survey is J. F. Wippel, 'Quodlibetal Questions, Chiefly in Theology Faculties', in B. C. Bazan, G. Fransen, D. Jacquart, and J. W. Wippel, *Les questions disputées et les questions quodlibétiques dans les facultés de théologie, de droit, et de médecine — Typologie des sources du moyen âge occidental*, 44–5 (Turnhout, 1985), pp. 153–222.

preliminary notes, a report (*reportatio*), or an abbreviated report. After emerging in the Paris theology faculty by about 1230, the quodlibet achieved its classic form by the 1250s and 1260s, flourished till the 1320s, and declined sharply about 1330. It spread elsewhere, for example, to the Oxford theology faculty, by about 1280, and it also spread to other faculties, although, as will be seen, less is known about this.

A first impression when reading quodlibets is that they are, as they should be, miscellaneous in subject, and that much in them reflects a Gordon Leff view of medieval thought: abstract, metaphysical. A second look qualifies this, as does also an article by Leonard Boyle which drew attention to the substantial minority of quodlibets which dealt with concrete pastoral themes, and thereby catered for the pastoral interests of the audiences. This meant canon-legally tricky cases about marriage, money-lending, restitution, almsgiving, and whether a doctor should save a foetus or a mother.[10] Elsewhere it has been pointed out that the peculiar interest of these quodlibets lies partly in the fact that they represent the mature rather than early thought of masters,[11] and partly in the fact that the form could accommodate reactions to contemporary political events. Thus in 1291 and 1294, for example, the fall of Acre and Pope Celestine's resignation were events the news of which generated quodlibetic questions.[12] Through their surviving reports sometimes, then, one can dimly discern the transient interests of Paris academic audiences.

A survey of the debates about Jews in quodlibetic questions in the Paris theology faculty shows a series of theology masters which runs from Guéric of St Quentin (probably 1230s, certainly prior to 1245) up to Jacques de Thérines (1306), and possibly John of Naples (1315–17).[13] They are both seculars and religious. Among them are several of the major quodlibetic disputers, Gérard of Abbeville, St Thomas Aquinas, Gervais of Mont-Saint-Éloi, and Henry of Ghent. Some questions are of the Leonard Boyle type, cases of baptism or marriage, raising knotty issues of canon law. For example, the second of Gérard of Abbeville's raises the case of marriage between Jews who are within three degrees of relationship, which is forbidden in Christian law but permitted in Jewish. What is the status of this marriage if both convert? Some reflect contemporary pressures. Thus Gervais of Mont-Saint-Éloi's question is whether parents

---

[10] L. E. Boyle, 'The Quodlibets of St. Thomas and Pastoral Care', *The Thomist*, 38 (1974), pp. 232–56.

[11] Wippel, 'Quodlibetal Questions', p. 221.

[12] Ibid., p. 193.

[13] For the texts discussed in this paragraph, see Appendix A.

have grounds for action against a Jew who kills their child, and then flees to a church, and has himself baptized. The Jews can be raised at the broadest level, as a general problem. Thus Guéric's question is, 'Should Jews be killed by the faithful, or sustained (that is, tolerated)?' And there is the possibility of very direct reaction to a major, public, event. The Cistercian Jacques Thérines raises his question in the Paris of 1306—where August saw the expulsion—and his question is whether Jews expelled from one region should be expelled from another.

Jews in these questions are discussed in terms of theology and canon law. Explicitly or implicitly they are invariably Jews only in terms of their religion, the principal problems are case problems concerning the hostile border between two religions; these problems are dealt with in terms of canon law or theology or both. Theme, thought, and vocabulary are religious. Emphasis here is not on this evident truth, but on the point that this is what one expects from a *theology* faculty, and that it is not immediately evidence for the views of men from other faculties.

The author of the most recent treatment of arts faculty quodlibets, John Wippel, writes, 'I have been unable to uncover solid evidence indicating what the precise structure was for quodlibetic disputations either in Arts or in Medicine' at Paris. Referring to a particular manuscript which contains the main surviving Paris arts quodlibets he adds that 'Unfortunately, we ourselves have not had an opportunity to examine this ms.'[14] This Paris manuscript, Bibliothèque nationale, latin 16089, comes from the Sorbonne, and contains a variety of arts material from just before and just after 1300. A late nineteenth-century survey article by Hauréau[15] and then, in 1943, a sharp analysis of part of the manuscript by Grabmann,[16] provide the foundations of the following comments on it. The manuscript is difficult to read, and prior to editions of its contents and systematic study of their authorship and sources these comments must be provisional.

The manuscript contains several sets of questions from masters in the arts faculty. These are four: Henry the German, Henry of Brussels, John

---

[14] Wippel, 'Quodlibetal Questions', pp. 206 and 204, n. 119.
[15] J. B. Hauréau, 'Notice sur le numéro 16089 des manuscrits latin de la Bibliothèque Nationale', *Notices et extraits des manuscrits de la Bibliothèque Nationale et des autres bibliothèques*, 35.i (1896), pp. 213–19.
[16] M. Grabmann, 'Die Aristoteleskommentare des Heinrich von Brüssel und der Einflüss Alberts des Grosen auf die mittelalterliche Aristoteleserklärung', *Sitzungsberichte der bayerischen Akademie der Wissenschaften, philosophisch-philologisch Klasse*, 1943, 10 (Munich, 1944), pp. 17–28.

Vate, and a certain Guéric. Best known among these is Henry of Brussels, who also left several commentaries on logical works by Aristotle and his *Metaphysica*. He was already a master in the arts faculty in 1289, and is listed as rector of the University in 1316.[17] Quite well know is John Vate or Bate, who was possibly a relation of the arts master Henry Bate of Malines. John Vate was the author of a question on Aristotle's *De genera-tione animalium*, is noted as a witness in an act of 1289, and was rector of the University in August 1290.[18] Little is known about Henry the German, apart from his being a master of arts, and the fact that a document still mentions him in May 1313.[19] Nothing beyond mastership and authorship is known about Guéric.

The questions are contained in three sets, one each to John Vate and Guéric. The third, belonging to both Henrys together, is scrutinized here. The *explicit* makes the nature of the questions clear: here end the quod-libets of Master Henry of Brussels and Master Henry the German. The form and vocabulary are conventional. First a question is raised, *queritur utrum*. Then pro and con are given, *quod non* and *oppositum patet*. Then comes the main response, *ad questionem dicendum*. Finally there are responses to particular objections or arguments, *ad raciones . . . dicendum quod*. The text seems to be a *reportatio* drawn up after the questions were raised and responded to. Thus it begins, 'The first question was', and it has introductions to particular questions, such as, 'Another question was' or 'Following this, it was asked whether . . .'. Further, it groups questions to some degree in relation to a common text, for example, 'These are questions on Aristotle's book of *Problemata*'. Did this follow grouping in the original sessions, or was it an effort at systematization by the reporter? The report gives no hint which Henry was responding to which question, and therefore, unless one supposes that each Henry kept very austerely to areas not touched by the other, the obvious conjecture is that much

---

[17] See J. B. Hauréau, 'Henri de Bruxelles, religieux d'Afflighem', *Histoire littéraire de la France*, 27 (1877), pp. 105–8, and 'Notice sur le numéro 16089', p. 214; Grabmann, 'Heinrich von Brüssel', pp. 29–39, and the summary note in P. Glorieux, *La Faculté des arts et ses maîtres au XIIIe siècle — Études de philosophie médiévale*, 59 (Paris, 1971), p. 182, no. 183.

[18] See J. B. Hauréau, 'Jean Vate, recteur de l'université de Paris', *Histoire littéraire de la France*, 27 (1877), pp. 68–70; M. Grabmann, 'Gentile da Cingoli, ein Italienischer Aristoteleserklärer aus der Zeit Dantes', *Sitzungsberichte der bayerischen Akademie der Wissenschaften, philosophisch-philologisch Klasse*, 1940, 9 (Munich, 1941), pp. 14ff. and 49–50, and 'Heinrich von Brüssel', pp. 46–7; Glorieux, *Faculté des arts*, p. 240, no. 278.

[19] See Hauréau, 'Numéro 16089', p. 214; P. Glorieux, *Répertoire des maîtres en théologie au XIIIe siècle*, 2 vols, *Études de philosophie médiévale*, 17–18 (Paris, 1933–4), 2, p. 317, no. 406, and Glorieux, *Faculté des arts*, p. 179, no. 179; Grabmann, 'Heinrich von Brüssel', pp. 35–6.

rearrangement has occurred. Another very probable conjecture is that the report is an extreme abbreviation. At a time when the report of a theological quodlibetic question would run from perhaps a thousand words—the length of Jacques de Thérines's discussion of expulsion of Jews—to several thousand, the brevity of these arts quodlibetic questions is startling. Typically one will run to two or three hundred words only, and eighty-nine of them appear in twenty-nine columns! If they resembled theological quodlibets in the way they were held, it is difficult to conceive of the original, oral, debates being anywhere near as short as these reports. A possibility is the literary influence of the brevity of individual parts of earlier medical and natural philosophical problem literature which used the question form—this literature is discussed later.

In one of the reports one of these masters, either Henry of Brussels or Henry of Germany, responded to a quodlibetic question about Jews. In translation, the report goes like this:

Following this [the report starts] it was asked whether Jews suffer a flux of blood.

[After the question, a formal argument contra is put]: no, because Christians and some Jews are of the same complexion. [Formal support is then given]: the opposite appears in truth, because for the most part these lechers suffer a flux of blood. [There then follows the main statement, *Ad questionem dicendum*]: Jews have a flux of blood of the haemorrhoids, and the first cause of this, is that doctors say that a flux of blood is caused by gross indigested blood which nature purges. This abounds more in the Jews because for the most part they are melancholics. [Melancholic is here in a technical, medical sense, meaning that of the four humours they abound in black bile, other-wise known as melancholy, and therefore their type, medically, is melancholic]. [They are melancholics] because the melancholic shuns dwelling and assembling with others and likes cut off or solitary places. However, Jews naturally withdraw themselves from society and from being connected with others, as is patent, therefore they are melancholics. Item, they are pallid, therefore they are of melancholic complexion. Item, they are naturally timid, and these three are the contingent properties of melancholics, as Hippocrates says. But he who is melancholic has a lot of melancholic blood, and manifestly must have a flux of blood, but Jews are of this sort. I prove this, because they use roast foods and not boiled or cooked [cooked here means in a way other than roasting or frying], and these are difficult to digest, as is said in the fourth book of the *Meteora*. Item, they have roast fat, such as oil, etc, and these are difficult to digest. Another cause is that digestion with wine ... [here a blank in the manuscript]—therefore those who do not drink wine have many superfluous not digested humours. They are of this sort, therefore, etc. Item, they do not have blood-letting, or very little, therefore they emit blood through outside pores, therefore, etc .

[Finally, there is the briefest of replies to the first contra argument which was stated]. The solution to the arguments is clear: it is to be said that some Christians have a flux of blood, therefore, etc. Item, Christians have some aids whereby they repel a flux of blood.[20]

The following discussion of this text addresses these questions. What were the roots, earlier in the thirteenth century, of this text? What were the contemporary ramifications, around 1300, of the ideas it contained? More speculatively, was it part of a broader growth of this type of thought in the thirteenth century? And what were the later fortunes of the ideas contained in it?

The text unites two earlier traditions, one of learned natural philosophical and medical thought, held and transmitted in the *studia* of mendicant convents and the arts and medical faculties of universities, the other of a myth about the Jews, which was held and transmitted both orally and in texts. Look further at the other quodlibetic questions in the manuscript. The questions themselves are scientific or natural philosophical questions, miscellaneous in nature, though with a strong bias towards medical, biological, and zoological themes. They are an odd ragbag. They include weather prediction, the physical characteristics of nobles and monks, the king of France's curative powers, sexual characteristics, and aspects of the human body, such as hair and skin colour, for example, 'Is crinkliness of hair generated by heat?' Recurring themes are the physical basis for certain psychological or moral characteristics, for example, physical features which explain boldness or timidity. Among the authors and texts cited the most frequent is Aristotle—his *De animalibus*, *De generatione animalium*, *De historiis animalium*, *Parva naturalia* (in particular *De somno et vigilia* and *De longitudine et brevite vitae*), *De caelo et mundo*, *Meteora*, *De anima*, and from the moral works, but rarely, *Ethica* and *Politica*; and among works attributed to him, the *Phisionomia* and

---

[20] A provisional edition is given in Appendix B. Another question in the manuscript, fol. 82vb, not studied here, deserves further attention: 'Utrum ebrei calefacti a sole maxime gaudent'.

Problemata. In Aristotle's case, many references have the precision of book number or, in the case of the *Problemata*, *particula* number, which reinforces one's initial impression that the author may have been using this source directly. There is less precision with the other authors, whose citation usually takes the simple form of 'as the Commentator [Averroes] says', or 'as Albert says', without specification of title or part of work. Second in frequency after Aristotle comes Albert, and other authors include Averroes, Hippocrates, and Galen. The list given here is not exhaustive.

These quodlibetic questions are not isolated exotica. They lie in a tradition of collections of medical or natural problems dealt with in question and answer form, the history of which has been given a preliminary, exploratory chart by Brian Lawn.[21] Earlier landmarks in this history were collections of the so-called 'Salernitan questions', of which one important English example from about 1200 has been edited by Lawn;[22] from about 1230 a Paris text containing comparable questions;[23] from 1258 a long series of questions on Aristotle's *De animalibus*, raised and debated by Albert the Great.[24] Another landmark was the translation into Latin in the mid-thirteenth century and subsequent diffusion of Aristotle's (attributed) *Problemata*.[25] These texts had marked out a particular territory, investigation by question and answer of a wide range of natural philosophical problems, miscellaneous ones, usually medical, biological, and zoological. The questions of the Paris masters continue this tradition, but within the precise boundaries of the quodlibetic form.

The quodlibetic question on the Jews draws upon a precise selection of authors and texts within this tradition. It explicitly cites Hippocrates—his *Aphorisms*, though the title is not given—and what *medici* say. In scholastic texts an opinion attributed to a plurality—*aliqui dicunt*—often turns out in reality to mean one person. Here an obvious probable candidate, because of his and the work's centrality, is Avicenna and his *Canon medicinae*, the

[21] B. Lawn, *The Salernitan Questions. An Introduction to the History of Medieval and Renaissance Problem Literature* (Oxford, 1963). The Italian translation, *I Quesiti Salernitani* (Salerno, 1969), contains additional bibliography.

[22] *The Prose Salernitan Questions*, ed. B. Lawn, *Auctores Britannici medii aevi*, 5 (London, 1979).

[23] Lawn, *Salernitan Questions*, pp. 81–2.

[24] Albert the Great, *Quaestiones super De animalibus*, ed. E. Filthaut, *Opera omnia*, 12 (Cologne, 1955), pp. 77–351.

[25] On this *nova translatio*, see G. Lacombe, A. Birkenmajer, M. Dulong, E. Franceschini, and L. Minio-Paluello, *Aristoteles Latinus. Codices*, 2 vols (Rome, 1939, Cambridge, 1955), 1, pp. 86–7; a specimen text is given pp. 181–2; see 2, p. 1345, for the index entry to MSS of the work.

reading and citation of which had spread by the second quarter of the thirteenth century.[26] Elsewhere in this set of quodlibets one question cites Aristotle's *Problemata* on melancholy.[27] A survey of these known and probable sources shows the following. Avicenna can provide the connections, as other medical authors, between eating things which are not easy to digest, the generation of melancholy, and haemorrhoidal flux.[28] He can supply the melancholic signs, timidity and love of solitude.[29] Hippocrates supplies the properties of timidity and pusillanimity.[30] Aristotle's *Problemata* supply principally melancholy and lechery, alluded to near the beginning of the quodlibet, where the author refers to Jews as 'these lechers'. Pallor is also discussed in the *Problemata* quite extensively, but not in connection with melancholy, and I have not yet traced a plausible medical source for this. Isidore's *Etymologies* either directly or through many intermediaries—a later dictionary which incorporated much of Isidore, such as Balbi's *Catholicon*, would be an obvious example[31]— supply the theme of avoiding human *conversatio*, social intercourse.[32] Apart from pallor, all of these are themes found ubiquitously in medical treatises, medical question literature, and some of Aristotle's natural works. Any more precise disentangling of sources is unlikely to come before a critical edition of the whole set of quodlibetic questions, where

---

[26] On the translation into Latin of Avicenna's *Canon*, see R. Lemay, 'Gerard of Cremona', *Dictionary of Scientific Biography*, 15 (1978), p. 185, no. 63, and on its spread M. McVaugh, 'The "Humidum radiale" in Thirteenth-Century Medicine', *Traditio*, 30 (1974), p. 265.

[27] Paris, BN, lat. 16089, fol. 57rb: 'Consequenter queritur utrum melancholici sint luxuriosi . . . dicit philosophus in *De problematibus*.' Aristotle's statement that melancholics are inclined to sex is in *Problemata* IV.30 (880a30).

[28] I have used Avicenna, *Liber Canonis Medicinae* (Venice, 1527). See liber I, fen 1, doctrina 4, chs 1–2 (fols 5vb–7va) on humours in general, and ch. 1 (fol. 6vb) on melancholy; fen 2, doctrina 2, summa 1, ch. 15 (fol. 29ra), on the kind of diet which generates *sanguis grossus*, and summa 2, ch. 25 (fol. 32vb) on pain brought on by bad humours; doctrina 3, ch. 7 (fol. 35va), on the signs of dominion of melancholy. In liber 3 see fen 1, tractatus 4, chs 18–19 (fols 150ra– 151va) on melancholy and its cure; fen 16, tractatus 2, ch. 5 (fol. 253ra), on cure of the melancholic's flux; fen 17, tractatus 1, chs 1–10 (fols 264rb–265bv), on haemorrhoids. In this general treatment, ch. 2 (fol. 264ra) discusses the generation of haemorrhoids from melancholy and melancholic blood, while ch. 10, on the appropriate diet, advises abstaining from *omne grossum*, and eating only food whose digestion is quick.

[29] Ibid., liber 3, fen 1, tractatus 4, ch. 18 (fol. 150va): 'Signa principii melancholie sunt existimatio mala, et timor sine causa, et velocitas ire, et dilectio solitudinis . . .'; 'nigredo pilorum' is also mentioned.

[30] See Appendix B, n. 3.

[31] J. Balbi, *Catholicon* (Mainz, 1460), *s.v.* 'melancolia'. The *Catholicon* was written in 1286.

[32] Isidore, *Etymologiae*, ed. W. M. Lindsay, 2 vols (Oxford, 1911), liber 10, *s.v.* 'malus': 1, 10.176 'melancholici appellantur homines qui et conversationem humanam refugiunt et amicorum carorum suspecti sunt.'

light thrown on the sources of other questions might throw reflective light on this one.

The second earlier thirteenth-century tradition which is united in this question is a myth about Jews having a flux of blood, which was held both orally and in texts. Some earlier stages in its history have left traces in surviving texts. It appears in Caesarius of Heisterbach's *Dialogus miraculorum*, in a story set in an English city.[33] Here it is seen entering a text, but it is described by Caesarius as a matter transmitted orally: the Jews 'are said' to suffer it. Its brief mention points in two directions: on the one hand, the flux of blood is an *infirmitas*, illness, while, on the other hand, it happens at Easter. The belief, then, already had some oral circulation, predating the period during which this Rhineland Cistercian was compiling his work (1219–23), and it already had its potentially separable, religious and medical components. A Rhineland city which was the largest in Caesarius's mental landscape, Cologne, was the setting for the next stage, in 1258. While lector at the Dominican convent of Heilige Kreuz, Albert the Great held a long series of lectures on Aristotle's *De animalibus*, a *reportatio* of which was made and preserved by a friar called Conrad of Austria. One among these many *quaestiones* was devoted to influences over the flow of menstrual blood, and in the last part of this Albert turned to another flow of blood.

> Haemorrhoids are caused by a superfluity of gross blood, because when such blood abounds in the body, it descends below . . . and then frequently one or two veins are ruptured, and then the blood flows sometimes on account of the opening of these veins. Whence this happens mostly to those who live off gross and salted food, such as the Jews, [and this happens thus] according to nature.[34]

Set in date half-way between the early thirteenth-century belief reported by Caesarius and the Paris quodlibet of around 1300, this represents a

---

[33] Caesarius, *Dialogus*, II.23, ed. Strange, 1, p. 92; see n. 4, above. For other occurrences of the story in which this detail appears, see F. C. Tubach, *Index Exemplorum. A Handbook of Medieval Religious Tales* (Helsinki, 1969), p. 221, no. 2811. See the discussion of early references to flux of blood in J. Trachtenberg, *The Devil and the Jews. The Medieval Conception of the Jew and Its Relation to Modern Antisemitism* (Yale, 1943), p. 148, and the statement that haemorrhoids are found in Thomas of Chantimpré. Thomas, referring to 'sanguis eius super nos', writes, 'ut per hanc importune fluidam proles impia inexpiabiliter crucietur, quosque se ream sanguinis Christi recognoscat poenitens, et sanetur': *Bonum universale de apibus*, II.29, ed. G. Colvenerius (Douai, 1627), p. 305. Blood and the notion of needing to be healed are present, but not explicitly the medical term.

[34] Albert, *Quaestiones super De animalibus*, IX.7, ed. Filthaut, p. 206.

crucial development, the transposition of the myth into the context of natural-philosophical and medical academic learning. This context is supplied both by the general character of Albert's lecture series, and also the particulars of this question. These are, to begin with, the absence of the religious reference or explanation; Albert's positive statement that this Jewish flux is *per naturam*; and, finally, the systematic use of technical medical vocabulary and explanation. 'Flux of blood' is now 'haemorrhoids'. These are caused by 'gross blood' *sanguis grossus*. 'Gross blood' in turn is caused by a specific diet, *nutrimentum*. 'Haemorrhoids', 'gross blood', 'gross' food, and the notion of this being 'according to nature' constitute vocabulary and themes which will reappear in the Paris quodlibet. Two points to note. First, in 1258 Albert—and others?—may not yet be thinking of making the further medical connection with melancholy. Nor is taking the further step of developing melancholy towards ascribing and explaining (alleged) Jewish psychological, moral, and social characteristics. 'May not': Albert may not have thought these themes appropriate to his lecture, and the present article may be ignoring some texts which would alter the picture. Secondly, since most of the medical vocabulary of Albert's lecture reappears in the Paris quodlibet, and the other quodlibets in the Paris manuscript often cite Albert, Albert's lecture is worth considering as a source of the Paris quodlibet. Notable, however, is the fact that the latter does not preserve the wording of Albert's reference to salty food.

This Paris quodlibet seems to represent a third stage. As in Albert's lecture, the religious interpretation is missing, as also the religious cause. What is at issue is an explanation according to nature. This explanation takes in the effect of diet, which brings about the predominance of one of the humours, black bile or melancholy, in Jews. The argument goes in two directions, in that diet proceeds towards melancholy, which proceeds toward flux of blood, while at the same time Jews' possession of the psychological and social and physical characteristics of those whose predominant humour is melancholy shows that this is what they are medically. These characteristics are keeping away from society, assembling or being connected with others, being timid, and having pale faces. All these things Jews are *naturaliter*, according to nature, as the quodlibet says twice, and this is the principal significance of the quodlibet from the arts faculty. Just as a quodlibet from the theology faculty discusses things in terms of theology and canon law, a quodlibet from the arts faculty does so in terms of nature. This is what Jews are, by nature, in the view of one man, an arts master from Brussels or Germany, when debating Jews in the centre of higher learning in north-western Europe, Paris University, around 1300.

Not only one arts master: by this time the belief was circulating widely. The medical faculty of the University of Montpellier was the setting, between 1303 and 1305, of Bernard of Gordon's writing of his *Lilium medicinae*.

> Note [he wrote in this] that Jews for the most part suffer a flux of haemorrhoids for three reasons. Generally they are in [a state of] idleness, and for this reason superfluities of melancholy are gathered. Secondly, they are generally in [a state of] fear and anxiety, and for this reason melancholic blood is multiplied, according to this [dictum] of Hippocrates: 'Fear and timidity, if they have had a lot of time [to work], bring about melancholic humour.' Thirdly, this [occurs] because of divine punishment.[35]

While there is considerable overlap with the Paris quodlibet, this version is briefer in that it omits diet and some of the characteristics ascribed by the quodlibet, while adding idleness and anxiety. It is markedly simpler in positing only a one-way causal relationship, namely, from psychological and moral characteristics to physical make-up, but not vice versa. Unlike Albert and the Parisian master, Bernard includes among his three causes one which is theological.

A more substantial treatment appears in a text about which, unfortunately, less is known precisely. The anonymous collection of natural-philosophical and medical questions which was ascribed to Aristotle but is now known by its *incipit*, *Omnes homines*, has been conjecturally ascribed by Lawn to Germany, because its manuscripts were strongly diffused there, and the first vernacular into which it was translated was German. Although the earliest manuscript so far found is from 1408, the latest among the many authorities quoted in it is from before 1280. The likelihood, then, is a date of composition roughly contemporary with the Paris quodlibet, and there is a possibility that it is

---

[35] Bernard of Gordon, *Lilium medicinae*, V.21.9 (Lyons, 1559), p. 519: 'Sexto, advertendum, quod Iudei ut plurimum patiuntur fluxum haemorrhoid. propter tria, et quia communiter sunt in ocio, et ideo congregantur superfluitates melancholicae. Secundo, quod communiter sunt in timore et anxietate, ideo multiplicatur sang. melancholicus, iuxta illud Hipp. Timor et pusilanimitas si multum tempus habuerint, melancholicum faciunt hum. Tertio quia hoc ex ultione divina, iuxta illud. Et percussit eos in posteriora dorsi, opprobrium sempiternum dedit illis.' On date and place of composition, see L. E. Demaitre, *Doctor Bernard de Gordon: Professor and Practitioner = Pontifical Institute of Medieval Studies, Studies and Texts*, 51 (Toronto, 1980), p. 50.

the earlier of the two texts.[36] After discussing the flux of haemorrhoids which is suffered by melancholic men, the author of *Omnes homines* proceeds to ask:

> Why do Jews indiscriminately [*indifferenter*] suffer this flux? One should reply first of all theologically, because at the time of Christ's passion they cried out, 'Let his blood . . .'. . . . One should reply in another way, and more according to nature, that the Jews eat phlegmatic and cold foods, for many good meats are forbidden to them in their law; [and] from these meats melancholic blood is generated, which is purged through the flux of haemorrhoids. The second natural reason is that Aristotle says in the book *De caelo et mundo* that motion makes heat, and motion is the cause of health, and heat causes digestion, as is evident through Aristotle in the fourth [book] of the *Meteora* and the second book of the *De anima*. But because the Jews are not in work or motion nor in converse with men, and also because they are in great fear because we avenge the passion of Christ our redeemer—all these things produce coldness and impede digestion. For this reason much melancholic blood is generated in them, which is expelled or purged in them at the menstrual time.[37]

'Jews' here are 'Judei', that is, Jews in general, not Jewish women, and in a (probably later) text, a commentary on Sacrobosco's *De sphaera*, which was written shortly before 1324, the Italian astrologer Cecco d'Ascoli was to spell out this proposition with complete clarity: 'After the death of Christ all Jewish men, like women, suffer menstruation.'[38]

---

[36] Lawn, *Salernitan Questions*, pp. 101–2.

[37] A convenient modern edition is *Problemata Varia Anatomica: MS 1165 The University of Bologna*, ed. L. R. Lind, *University of Kansas Publications, Humanistic Studies*, 38 (Lawrence, Kansas, 1968), pp. 38–9; see also the annotations, p. 92, nn. 157–60. For the reference to *Meteora*, see Appendix B, n. 4, below; the other references are *De caeol.*, II.7 (289a20–30) and *De anima*, II.4 (416a10). I have compared this with the passage in *Omnes homines* in Erfurt Amplon, MS. F.334 fol. 200ra. Apart from omitting 'et motus est causa sanitatis' and the reference to 'secundo de anima', this passage in the Erfurt MS shows only negligible divergence from the Bologna MS edited here.

[38] Cecco d'Ascoli, *In spheram mundi ennaratio iv*, in *The Sphere of Sacrobosco and Its Commentators*, ed. L. Thorndike (Chicago, 1949), p. 409. On Cecco, see G. Sarton, *Introduction to the History of Science*, 3 vols in 5 parts (Baltimore, 1927–48), 3, pt 1, pp. 643–5. The statement that Jews emit blood *per virgam* every month is found in two MSS of the *Liber introductorius* of Michael Scot (d. *c.*1235), L. Thorndike, *Michael Scot* (London, 1965), p. 80. Thorndike's reference implies that this comes from Scot, but the passage is not discussed in the present article because these MSS contain later, interpolated, material, at least up to 1320 (ibid., p. 7), and there is a clear possibility that the statement about Jewish flux is also a later addition.

Like Bernard of Gordon, the author of *Omnes homines* is simpler in seeing a one-way causal relationship, like him, he includes idleness, and, like him, he uses a distinctive distortion of a line in the Psalms which suggests the two share a common source.[39] Converse with men may be derived from a source such as the quodlibet, or, with perfect ease from Isidore's *Etymologiae*. There is more remarkable overlap in the use by both of the fourth book of Aristotle's *Meteora*. There is a need for further editorial and critical work on these two texts, and their juxtaposition with other passages on Jewish flux which may be found in scientific and medical texts—which are in such abundance from this period, and so little read by modern scholars. Though the precise interrelationship of these texts may remain unclear, one aspect of their authors' views is clear: sharp awareness of seeing Jews 'according to nature'. While the Parisian master does this by excluding theology and insisting on explanations 'according to nature', the author of *Omnes homines* proceeds differently, including theology, but stating that one must answer both, and separately, 'theologically' and 'according to nature'.

Two questions of more general import arise from the examination of this cluster of texts, one pointing to the decades before 1300, the other to a later period. The first is suggested by the other questions in the Paris quodlibet. Jewish flux was not the only theme where these masters attempted to look at groups of people in terms of their physical or psychological or social characteristics, based on arguments from nature. Others of their questions made distinctions according to colour or climatic region. 'Are white men bold?' is one quetion. Another is, 'Do white women or black women have stronger sexual desire?'[40]

Robert Bartlett has brilliantly described the development of 'ethnographic' thought in twelfth-century Latin Christendom.[41] Very speculatively, I would like to raise a question about the later progress of this genre of thought, in particular under the impact of the new Greek and Arabic natural philosophy and medicine, in north-western Europe in the decades preceding the Paris quodlibet. Take Vincent of Beauvais's *Speculum naturale*, the scientific section of his vast encyclopaedia, and turn to the section on the generation of man in book 31. Here one finds in four

---

[39] 'Percussit eos in posteriora dorsi', *Problemata Varia*, p. 39; compare n. 35, above. This is a conflation of Ps. 77. 66 and 67. 14.

[40] BN, MS lat. 16089, fols. 57vb, 'Consequenter queritur utrum homines albi sint audaces'; fol. 63ra, 'Alia questio fuit utrum mulier alba magis appetit virum quam nigra'; fol. 74va, 'Utrum albe mulieres magis appetant coire quam nigre'.

[41] R. Bartlett, *Gerald of Wales, 1146–1223* (Oxford, 1982), pt 3.

chapters the medical material on humours which could supply much of the quodlibet.[42] They come immediately after material on complexions. These complexions have signs, colour, hair, appearance, actions, and these vary according to various factors, including region. Thus crinkly hair, black skin, and lack of spiritedness are found in men in Ethiopia and Egypt, while in northern cold regions one has blonde men with boldness and strength.[43] Now, none of the constituent elements of this material is in itself remarkable. It comes from well-known sources, Greek texts, the Latin encyclopaedic tradition, and Arabic authors, such as Avicenna, and can be replicated elsewhere. My question arises from the very ease of its juxtaposition with humours in a section in Vincent which ends with an account of monstrous races of men,[44] and in an encyclopaedia, another part of which goes very far in the description of the distinctive facial appearance of one race of men, the Mongols.[45] Is there a significant acceleration in the transmission and diffusion of such proto-racial material during the thirteenth century, and of interest in it? Further, can one see the higher learning of Latin Christendom at this period displaying both universality and regionalism on this theme? Thus the theme studied here seems to have been developed mainly, but not entirely, in north-western Europe: in the Rhineland (Caesarius), and Cologne, in particular (Albert), in Germany (*Omnes homines*), and in Paris by a master from Germany or Brussels.

The second question concerns what in 1300 was the future. I know of no direct evidence of the later dissemination or influence of the quodlibet. Some of its thought, however, was in Bernard's *Lilium medicinae*, which is known in over fifty later medieval Latin manuscripts, leaving aside those of the French, German, Spanish, and Irish translations, and had six printed editions. It was a prescribed text in medical faculties—at the University of Montpellier after 1400, at the University of Vienna in 1520.[46] More of its thought was in the *Omnes homines* collection. This had a more modest Latin manuscript circulation—over twenty manuscripts

---

[42] I have used the Venice, 1591, edition. Vincent of Beauvais, *Speculum naturale*, XXXI.69–72, pp. 401–2. See also the ch. *De coloribus corporum*, XXXI.111, pp. 407–8.

[43] Ibid., XXXI.67–8, p. 401.

[44] Ibid., XXXI.126–32, pp. 409–11. Much of the monstrous race material is repeated in Vincent, *Speculum historiale*, I.76–95, pp. 12–13, following the world geography of chs 63–75 (pp. 9–12), which incorporates material on colours of *gentes*, their fertility, climatic influences on their physical differences, and variety of diet and mores. Jewish avarice (*avaritia Judaeorum*) is alluded to ibid., X.24, p. 125.

[45] Vincent of Beauvais, *Speculum historiale*, XXIX.71, p. 420.

[46] Demaitre, *Bernard de Gordon*, pp. 51–2 and 185–8.

are known—but a quite extraordinary circulation in the early modern period: fifty-six Latin editions before 1668, at least thirty-one German ones before 1668. This has continued in modern times, for example, with at least twenty-five English editions between 1684 and 1930.[47] As science itself progressed, what was learned 'science' in 1300 became pseudo-science of early modern and modern times. The *Omnes homines* treatment of the myth about the Jews continued its existence, jostling with curious medical, particularly sexual and gynaecological, material, in the verna-cular translations—in English, that little book known as *Aristotle's Master-piece*, which still litters second-hand bookshops, and was still being marketed actively in the early 1960s.[48] No study is put forward here, only a suggestion. This is that a footnote to the history of modern anti-Semitism may be supplied by investigation of the massive diffusion of this tacky little book among the ignorant of modern Europe. This footnote itself might qualify the statement which opens and introduces this article.

University of York

Appendix A
A Chronological List of Theological Quodlibets Concerning Jews

The fundamental guide is P. Glorieux, *La littérature quodlibétique de 1260 à 1320*, 2 vols, Bibliothèque Thomiste, 5 and 21 (Kain, 1925, Paris, 1935) [hereafter Glorieux, 1, and Glorieux, 2]. The indices, otherwise very full, do not contain an entry for Jews or Judaism.

(1) Paris. Guéric of Saint-Quentin, O.P. Taught at St Jacques, 1233–42, where he was the fourth master of theology of the Dominicans, and d. 1245. See on him T. Kaeppeli, *Scriptores Ordinis Praedicatorum medii aevi* (Rome, 1970ff.), 2, pp. 61–2.

---

[47] Lawn, *Salternitan Questions*, pp. 99–102.
[48] An example is *Aristotle's Works Illustrated, containing the Masterpiece, Directions for Midwives, Counsel and Advice to Child-bearing Women with Various Useful Remedies* (Halifax, c.1880–90), p. 233: 'Why are the Jews much subject to this disease?' I am indebted to the librarian of York Minster, Bernard Barr, for the information that there were many undated printings from the late Victorian period onwards, and that copies were still being disseminated in the 1960s to what had been, in his description, 'a vast underground market'.

i.3: 'Utrum iudaei deberent occidi a fidelibus et non sustineri sicut nec pagani'; Glorieux, 2, p. 107, and Kaeppeli, *Scriptores*, 2, pp. 69–70, no. 1395.

(2) Anonymous, in a Florentine MS; pertaining to Franciscan school, and in Glorieux's opinion, 'entre 1255 et 1275'.
Anon, xiv.4: 'Si Judaeus convertatur iterum ad judaismum prius factus christianus, vel etiam haereticus, utrum filii ejus debeant privari rebus paternis'; Glorieux, 2, p. 291, and n. 1 on MS.

(3) Paris, Easter 1266. Gérard of Abbeville. See on him Glorieux, 1, p. 111.
vi. 6: 'Utrum ille qui in iudaismo contraxit cum uxore fratris sui ut fratri praemortuo semen suscitaret, post suam conversionem ad fidem posset stare cum illa.'

(4) As no. 3.
vi.7: 'Utrum ille qui in infidelitate, sicut accidit in ritu iudaico, contraxit cum aliqua in gradu prohibito ab Ecclesia, sicut in iudaismo solent contrahere in tertio gradu, si ambo convertantur ad fidem, possit stare cum illa post conversionem.'

(5) As no. 3.
vi.8: 'Utrum alter coniugum iudaeorum transiens ad fidem, teneatur habitare cum alio volente cohabitare sine contumelia Salvatoris'; Glorieux, 1, p. 117; MSS ibid., p. 116, n. 2, and Glorieux, 2, p. 290.

(6) Paris, Christmas 1269. St Thomas Aquinas, O.P. On chronology, dating, and editions, see the summary in J. A. Weisheipl, *Friar Thomas d'Aquino: His Life, Thought and Works* (Oxford, 1975), pp. 367–8.
ii.7: 'Utrum pueri Iudaeorum sint baptizandi invitis parentibus'; Glorieux, 1, p. 278. The numbering is different—ii.4, art. 7—in the convenient edition, St Thomas Aquinas, *Quaestiones quodlibetales*, ed. R. Spiazzi (Turin and Rome, 1949), p. 28.

(7) Paris, Easter 1272. St Thomas Aquinas.
vi.5: 'Utrum possit esse matrimonium inter christianum et Iudaeam baptizatam ab eo, quam carnaliter cognovit post fidem de contrahendo datam'; Glorieux, 1, p. 282; vi.3, art. 2, in *Quaestiones quodlibetales*, ed. Spiazzi, p. 121.

(8) Paris, between 1282, when the author was regent in theology, and his election as abbot in 1291. Gervais of Mont Saint-Éloi, canon regular; see on him Glorieux, 1, p. 133.

29: 'utrum parentes habeant actionem contra Iudaeum qui interficiens filium eorum fugit ad ecclesiam et ibi fecit se baptizari'; Glorieux, 1, p. 136, and p. 134, n. 1 on the MS.

(9) Bologna or Rome, 1284–5. Matthew of Aquasparta, O.F.M.; see Glorieux, 2, p. 194.
vi.9: 'Utrum iudaei et alii infideles sint de foro ecclesiae'; Glorieux, 2, p. 198, and n. 1 on the MSS.

(10) Paris, 1289. Henry of Ghent; on him and his quodlibets, see Henry of Ghent, *Opera omnia* (Louvain and Leiden, 1979ff.), 5, *Quodlibet 1*, ed. R. Macken, pp. vi–xxiv.
xiii.16: 'Utrum curatus possit aliquid accipere a Iudaeis pro iure parochiae in qua manent'; *Opera omnia*, 17, *Quodlibet XIII*, ed. J. Decorte, p. 203–4.

(11) Paris, 1290. Henry of Ghent.
xiv.15: 'Utrum iudaeus pungens hostiam consecratam, si viso sanguine convertatur et baptizetur, debeat puniri pro crimine illo a iustitia'; Glorieux, 1, p. 198, based on the edition of Paris, 1518.

(12) Florence, 1296. O.F.M.; Peter de Trabibus? See Glorieux, 2, p. 229.
ii.4: 'Utrum Christus possit probari Judaeis jam venisse'; Glorieux, 2, p. 231, and n. 1 on MS.

(13) Paris, Christmas 1306. Jacques de Thérines, Cistercian. On him and his quodlibets, see Jacques de Thérines, *Quodlibets I et II*, and Jean Lesage, *Quodlibet I*, ed. P. Glorieux, *Textes philosophiques du moyen âge*, 7 (Paris, 1958) pp. 7–23.
i.14: 'Utrum iudaei expulsi de una regione debeant expelli de alia'; ed. Jacques de Thérines, *Quodlibets*, pp. 157–9.

(14) Paris, c.1307? Glorieux, 1, p. 303, n. 1, points out that this accompanies Hervé Nedellec's quodlibets in the MS, and has some similarities in style; Nedellec's quodlibets were held in Paris in 1307.
Anon. vii.20: 'Utrum parvuli iudaeorum invitis parentibus sint baptizandi'; Glorieux, 1, p. 303, and n. 1 on the MS.

(15) Paris, 1309. Nicholas of Lyre, O.F.M.
I.1: 'Utrum Judaei cognoverunt Jesum Nazarenum esse Christum sibi promissum'; Glorieux, 2, p. 201.

(16) As no. 15.
I.2: 'Utrum ex scripturis receptis a Judaeis possit efficaciter probari Salvatorem nostrum fuisse Deum et hominem'; Glorieux, 2, p. 201.

J. Cohen, *The Friars and the Jews. The Evolution of Medieval Antisemitism* (Ithaca and London, 1982), devotes ch. 7 to a text by Nicholas of Lyre which he calls a quodlibet; P. Glorieux, *Répertoire des maîtres en théologie de Paris au XIIIe siècle*, 2 vols, *Études de philosophie médiévale*, 17–18 (Paris, 1933–4), 2, p. 216, no. 345, treats it as a disputed question, not a quodlibet.

(17) Paris, 1315–17, or Naples, from 1317. John of Naples, O.P.; last mentioned 1336. See Kaeppeli, *Scriptores*, 2, pp. 495–6.
ix.26: 'Utrum Iudaeus dicens publice extra synagogam Christum fuisse hominem quendam deceptorem et Eucharistiam esse solum panem, sit puniendus ut hereticus aut blasphemus'; Glorieux, 2, p. 168, and Kaeppeli, *Scriptores*, 2, pp. 496–7, no. 2528.

(18) As no. 15.
x.27: 'Utrum talis sit puniendus per iudicem ecclesiasticum aut per iudicem saecularem'; Glorieux, 2, p. 168.

(19) Oxford, 1332–4. Robert Holcot, O.P. See Kaeppeli, *Scriptores*, 3, pp. 313–14, and R. E. Gillespie, 'Robert Holcot's Quodlibeta', *Traditio*, 27 (1971), pp. 480–90.
ii.11: 'Utrum observantia legis mosaice fuit Judaeis meritoria vitae aeternae'; Glorieux, 2, p. 259, Kaeppeli, *Scriptores*, 3, p. 318, no. 3500, and Gillespie, 'Holcot's Quodlibeta', p. 489, where it is no. 72.

Appendix B
Arts Faculty Quodlibetic Question on Jews: Provisional Edition of Paris, Bibliothèque nationale, MS Lat. 16089, fol. 57ra

Consequenter queritur utrum iudei paciuntur fluxum.

Arguitur quod non, quia xpistiani et aliqui iudei sunt eiusdem complexionis, ergo etc.

Oppositum patet ex veritate quia illi leccatores paciuntur fluxum ut in pluribus.

Ad questionem dicendum quod iudei habent fluxum sanguinis hemoreidarum. Et causa est prima quia dicunt medici quod fluxus sanguinis causatur ex sanguine grosso indigesto quem [que *MS*] natura purgat.[1] Sed iste [istis *MS*] magis habundat in iudeis quia ipsi sunt melancolici ut in pluribus. Quia melancolicus fugit cohabitacionem et congregacionem[2] et diligit loca secretaria vel solitaria; sed iudei naturaliter retrahunt se a societate et coniuncti [possibly recte coniungi] cum aliis ut patet, ergo sunt melancolici.

Item, pallidi sunt, ergo sunt melancolice complexionis.

Item, timidi sunt naturaliter et hec tria sunt [supra ? *MS*] accidencia propria melancolicorum, ut dicit Ipocras.[3]

Sed ille qui multum est melancolicus multum habet de sanguine melancolico, et inde debet habere fluxum sanguinis, sed iudei sunt huiusmodi.

Probo quia utuntur alimentis assatis et non elixatis non coctis, et hec sunt difficile digestibilia, ut dicitur 4to Me[teorum *or* -teologicorum].[4]

Item, utuntur assarem [*recte* assatam] pinguedinem scilicet in oleo etc. et hec sunt difficile indigestibilia [*recte* digestibilia], ut patet manifestum sens[i; manifestum sensui *perhaps recte* ubi supra], ideo etc.

Alia causa huius est quia digestio per vinum [per vinum *with erasure line in MS*] quod   [*blank in MS*], ergo illi qui non habent bibere vinum habent multos f [*sic*] superfluos humores indigestos; ipsi sunt huiusmodi, ergo etc.

---

[1] See n. 28.

[2] See nn. 29 and 32.

[3] Hippocrates, *Aphorisms* 6.23. The Latin translation is conveniently available in the edition of a text of the 1360s, *Les commentaires de Martin de Saint-Gille sur les Amphorismes Ypocras*, ed. G. Lafeuille, *Travaux d'Humanisme et Renaissance*, 66 (Geneva, 1964), p. 172: 'Si timor et pusillanimitas multum tempus perficiunt, hujus modi melencholici.' The *Aphorisms* were part of the *Articella*, a compilation of medical texts put together in the twelfth century and henceforth a basic text in medical education.

[4] Coction is discussed in Aristotle's *Meteora*, book 4, 379b–81b. See the text in Thomas Aquinas, *In Aristotelis libros de caelo et mundo*, *De generatione et corruptione*, *Meteorologicorum expositio*, ed. R. M. Spiazzi (Turin and Rome, 1952), p. 656: 'assatum fit et non elixatum (381a26)'. On the Latin translations of the *Meteora* [*Meteorologica*] see G. Lacombe, A. Birkenmajer, M. Dulong, E. Franceschini, and L. Minio-Paluelo, *Aristoteles Latinus. Codices*, 2 vols (Rome, 1939, and Cambridge, 1955), 1, pp. 56–7, nos 23–5, and 2, p. 788, no. 25. On William of Moerbeke's translation—new in the case of book 4—see L. Minio-Paluello, *Opuscula: the Latin Aristotle* (Amsterdam, 1972), pp. 83–6, and various discussions in *Guillaume de Moerbeke. Recueil d'études à l'occasion du 700e anniversaire de sa mort (1286)*, ed. J. Brams and W. Vanhamel, *Ancient and Medieval Philosophy, De Wulf-Mansion Centre*, ser. 1, 7 (Louvain, 1989), pp. 25–7, 136, 147, 291, no. 10; bibliography, pp. 327–8, no. 2.8.

Item, ipsi non minuunt, vel valde parum, ideo ipsi emittunt sanguinem per poros extrinsecos, ideo etc.

Ad raciones patet solucio, dicendum quod aliqui xpistiani habent fluxum sanguinis, ideo etc.

Item, xpistiani habent aliqua iuvamenta per que repellunt fluxum sanguinis.

REFLECTIONS ON THE JEWRY OATH IN THE MIDDLE AGES*

by JOSEPH ZIEGLER

THE Jewry Oath[1] (*juramentum Judaeorum, Judeneid*) was the judicial oath demanded from Jews involved in legal litigation when summoned to appear in a Christian court both as plaintiffs and defendants. The special formulae which were created for the Jews, who could not use the Christian formulae, usually included two parts: a ceremony and a verbal part. The ceremony could be long and elaborate, but was usually short and simple. The swearing Jew was asked to lay his right hand on a scroll of the Torah, the Pentateuch, or from the later thirteenth century, though more rarely, even on the Talmud. Sometimes more specific instructions were given, and the hand had to be laid on the page of the Ten Commandments, or even specifically on the commandment prohibiting the taking of the name of the Lord in vain (Exodus 20. 7). The verbal part included an invocation of God, a judicial declaration regarding the nature of the obligation corroborated by the oath, and a list of maledictions which would be inflicted in the case of perjury. The oath itself could be taken in a synagogue or at its gate, but usually it was conducted in the court itself on a Jewish holy book kept there specially for that purpose.

The traditional explanation of these oaths allegedly exacted from Jews appearing in Christian courts has hitherto been overshadowed by some verbal and ceremonial items contained in the formulae, which seem absurd to the modern spectator. Very often the *Schwabenspiegel* version of the oath, which demanded, among other things, that the swearing Jew stand on a sow's skin and make reference to the Jews as Christ's killers, is quoted as a representative example for that judicial phenomenon.[2] It is

---

* This paper is based on research done for an M.A. thesis which was submitted to the Faculty of Humanities in the Hebrew University of Jerusalem in 1988 under the supervision of Professor A. Linder.

[1] See G. Kisch, *The Jews in Medieval Germany* (Chicago, 1949), pp. 275–89: on the various circumstances under which Jews appeared in Christian courts see pp. 173–4.

[2] V. Zimmermann, *Die Entwicklung des Judeneides; Untersuchungen und Texte zur rechtlichen und sozialen Stellung der Juden im Mittelalter* (Frankfurt, 1973), p. 81. This is the most detailed compilation of the Oath's formulae, and it should be used cautiously, for the texts are not always edited accurately and the explanations are sometimes dubious. See the criticism of W. Roell, 'Zu den Judeneiden an der Schwelle zur Neuzeit', in A. Haverkamp, ed., *Zur Geschichte der*

asserted that though not all formulae were as detailed or as harsh, all meant to frighten the Jewish deponent and to demonstrate visibly his inferior status. The ludicrous and fantastic elements in the ceremony and the verbal parts of the oath are seen as having been invented mainly to convey a message of humiliation, degradation, and rejection.[3] Thus the Jewry Oath is used as another favourite example of the negative facets of the Christian–Jewish encounter in the Middle Ages.

It is my intention to suggest another reading of this judicial phenomenon. I will not try to vindicate the ceremonial parts which demanded that the Jew stand on a sow's skin or the hide of an animal that had given birth during the preceding fortnight, and whose skin was cut open along the back and spread out displaying the teats.[4] It is hardly possible to give this motif an explanation other than that the judicial process was used to convey publicly a set of anti-Jewish attitudes. However, explaining a historical phenomenon relies on the contextualization of the texts which reveal the phenomenon. I will try to show that by looking not at a single text but at the broad phenomenon against the background of the judicial and social reality, one may have to reconsider the role of the Oath in the Middle Ages. If my reading is correct, then the Jewry Oath, as a judicial procedure, is to be regarded more as a necessary, practical tool which was intended to further the integration of the Jews into daily commercial life than as a humiliating ritual.

Even though some of the older formulae are dated to the later Carolingian period,[5] the vast majority of known texts of the Oath is from the later twelfth century onwards. While the earlier texts were in Latin, as we approach the thirteenth century most of the formulae are in the vernacular. Most of the texts are part of collections of urban statutes or widely-used collections of territorial laws. In the rare cases which reveal the type of judicial litigation which made such an oath necessary, only commercial issues arise. Most of the texts from the twelfth century

---

Juden in Deutschland des spaeten Mittelalters und der fruehen Neuzeit = Monographien zur Geschichte des Mittelalters, 24 (Stuttgart, 1981) [hereafter Roell], pp. 163–4.

[3] Isaac Levitas, in *EJ*, 12, pp. 1302–3; B. Blumenkranz, *Histoire des Juifs en France* (Toulouse, 1972), p. 50; G. Kische, *Forschungen zur Rechtsgeschichte der Juden in Deutschland waehrend des Mittelalters* (Sigmaringen, 1978), p. 164, where he rejects Baer's argument that one could not force on the Jews the formula of an oath which they would regard as absurd. Arguing for the Spanish region, Baer claimed that the anachronistic perspective of the Enlightenment distorted the interpretation of the phenomenon: I. Baer, *Die Juden im Christlichen Spanien; Urkunden*, 1.1 (Berlin, 1929), pp. 1029–35, 1031, n. 3.

[4] Zimmermann, *Die Entwicklung*, pp. 100, 120–1, 129–30, 186–7.

[5] A. Boretius, ed., *Capitularia Regum Francorum*, *MGH, Leges*, 2 (Hanover, 1882), pp. 258–9.

onwards come from the territories of the Empire.[6] This chronological, geographical, and thematic layout of the various formulae is interrelated with the social and legal developments of that period, and can contribute to our understanding of the whole phenomenon.

From the second half of the twelfth century the traditional methods of producing judicial evidence were gradually moving from the divine, supernatural premises to more 'rational' ones. Investigation of witnesses, taking of tangible evidence, judicial enquiry, and written documents were more and more used. This most complex process, which was related to the changing patterns of literacy, to the development of central bureaucratic government, and to the growing influence of the Roman Law, evolved gradually and at varying rates from place to place. In a more mobile society, in a society experiencing vigorous demographic expansion, and where commercial turnover was larger and faster, it was no longer possible to defend the existing legal order on the basis of the traditional judicial methods of producing evidence, such as the ordeal, the duel, or the oath. These methods, which had been quite efficient in a small, close society where everyone knew everyone else, turned, under these new circumstances, into methods encouraging lies and evasions. The process of transformation of the modes of producing evidence, which involved the rejection of traditional ones, was the fastest in England.[7] This is probably the reason why we do not have English examples for formulae of the Jewry Oath, and why a few formulae from both France and Italy survived. In Germany the oath continued to be the main tool for producing evidence well into the fifteenth century, and this accounts for the large number of surviving formulae from that region.

Yet the Jewry Oath was connected not only to the changing judicial reality, but also to the changes in the judicial administration of the towns, especially in Germany. From the end of the twelfth century, legal juris-diction was gradually transferred from the lord of the town to local burgesses. The outcome of this evolving process was the formation of new, autonomous town courts, presided over by elected burgesses. These courts gradually annexed the authority to decide on cases in which Jews

---

[6] The Spanish towns also included in their law books versions of the Jewry Oath. See J. Amador de los Rios, *Historia social, politica y religiosa de los judios de Espagna y Portugal* (Madrid, 1960), pp. 897–912.

[7] Thus canon 18 of the Fourth Lateran Council, which eliminated the sacral basis for the ordeal by prohibiting clerics to participate in it, was not a call for a revolutionary change, but a legal institutionalization of an existing reality. See C. M. Radding, 'Superstition to science: nature,

were involved—cases which were hitherto under the sole jurisdiction of the lord, the Jews' protector.[8] In the situation of a growing mobility of merchants in general, and of Jewish merchants in particular, and without a special department to deal with the Jews, it seems that the urban judicial system offered a mechanism which could produce evidence swiftly and efficiently. From the twelfth century onwards, the Jewry Oath was basically an essential instrument enabling the integration of the Jews into the legal system and, through it, into economic life.

In most of the texts, from the very earliest Latin formulae, the Jew did not undertake simply to speak the truth, but to declare his innocence of a crime which he had allegedly committed. The Jewry Oaths were thus mainly oaths of purgation, and this leads us to a further perspective on the phenomenon. Until the twelfth century, oaths played an important role in the judicial procedures of the Latin West. The judicial oath was a dramatic, public, and sacred ritual, which very often took place in the church or at her porch. The oath-taker performed it by touching a holy object and invoking God to be his witness and to validate his claim.[9] Oaths were used not only to corroborate a testimony or to strengthen a promise, but also as an important tool that produced evidence and which could decide the outcome of the trial.[10] It was usually the defendant who was regarded 'nearer to prove innocence by purgation' (meaning that he could virtually end the process by purging himself through a judiciary oath).

---

fortune and the passing of the medieval ordeal', *AHR*, 84 (1979), pp. 945–69; R. Bartlett, *Trial by Fire and Water* (Oxford, 1986), ch. 5.

[8] H. Fischer, *Die Verfassungsrechtliche Stellung der Juden in den Deutschen Staedten* (Aalen, 1968), pp. 123–40; E. Isenmann, *Die Deutsche Stadt im Spaetemittelalter 1250–1500* (Stuttgart, 1988), pp. 84–8, 101.

[9] D. M. Stenton, *English Justice between the Norman Conquest and the Great Charter, 1066–1215* (Philadelphia, 1964), p. 120.

[10] On the Oath in the Middle Ages, see Bartlett, *Trial*, pp. 30–3; A. Erler, ed., *Handwoerterbuch zur Deutschen Rechtsgeschichte*, 1 (Berlin, 1971), pp. 861–71; R. Lasch, *Der Eid* (Stuttgart, 1908); H. C. Lea, *Superstition and Force* (Philadelphia, 1892); P. Hofmeister, *Die Christlichen Eidesformeln* (Munich, 1957); *Lexikon des Mittelalters*, 3 (Zurich, 1986), pp. 1671–92. On the Oath as a major tool for producing evidence during the Middle Ages, see the various articles in the special issue entitled *La Preuve = Recueils de la Société Jean Bodin*, 17 (1965), especially pp. 9–70, 99–165, 519–46, 691–753; H. Levy-Bruhl, *La Preuve judiciaire* (Paris, 1964), pp. 85–107; H. Nottarp, *Gottesurteilstudien* (Munich, 1965). On the question of the rationality of the medieval system of divine justice and its social function see Bartlett, *Trial*, chs 4–5; P. Brown, 'Society and the supernatural: a medieval change', *Daedalus*, 104 (1975), pp. 133–51; R. V. Colman, 'Reason and unreason in early medieval law', *Journal of Interdisciplinary History*, 4 (1974), pp. 571–91; P. R. Hyams, 'Trial by Ordeal: the key to proof in the early common law', in M. S. Arnold *et al.*, eds, *On the Laws and Customs of England. Essays in Honour of Samuel E. Thorne* (Chapel Hill, 1981), pp. 90–126; C. Morris, '*Judicium Dei*: the social and political significance of the ordeal in the eleventh century', *SCH*, 12 (1975), pp. 95–111.

The judiciary oath of purgation was regarded as a special type of divine judgement precisely like the duel and the other ordeals. In an oral culture, these demonstrative ways of producing evidence were not only useful and efficient, they were essential. God's will decided whether the accused was just and justified (*justus, justificatus*) or guilty (*culpabilis*). However, custom determined that the oath of purgation could be taken only by free men. For it was believed that only such people would be reliable enough to refrain from perjury. All the rest, including freemen who could not find oath-helpers for compurgation, strangers, and those reputed to be dishonest, had to exonerate themselves through other judicial trials. The Jews, despite being not simply aliens but also non-believers who adhered to their disreputable faith, were allowed to purge themselves by taking the oath, like all freemen. Thus the Jewry Oath seems to be rather a privilege which the Jews enjoyed, being exempt from undergoing trials by ordeal.[11]

The Christian punishment for perjury was excommunication, but here the authorities were confronted with a double problem in the case of Jews. On the one hand, they had to invent a formula which would not entail ceremonial or verbal parts incompatible with the Jewish faith, and which would be binding upon the Jews according to their laws. On the other hand, the oath had to neutralize the fear of Christians, who were giving the right of justification by oath to an outsider who was not a member of the Christian community, who belonged to a group long reputed for its perfidy, and who could not be threatened by the punishment of excommunication. It was this dilemma which determined the basic structure of the Oath. It has been suggested that the various parts of the formulae are essentially Jewish, thus laying the emphasis on the first part of the dilemma.[12] I would like to elaborate on its second part.

Three ways were used to overcome this second part of the dilemma. The first was to insert Christian motifs into the texts, which in order to make them binding for the Jews were saturated with biblical elements. Thus, for example, in the Oath of Barcelona the Jew was asked to swear not only by the saints of the Jews, but also by the Prophets who had

[11] The Jews were exempt from providing proof by ordeal from the time of Louis the Pious. See K. Zeumer, ed., *Formulae Merowingici et Karolini aevi*, *MGH.L*, sectio iv (Hanover, 1886), p. 310. The exemption was renewed by the Emperor Henry IV in 1090; *MGH.DR*, 6.2, *Henrici IV*, ed. D. von Gladiss (Weimar, 1972), p. 547, and by Frederick I in 1157: *MGH.DR*, 10.1, *Friderici I*, ed. H. Appelt (Hanover, 1975), p. 286. See also Bartlett, *Trial*, pp. 53–4; S. Eidelberg, 'Trial by ordeal in medieval Jewish history: laws, customs and attitudes', *American Academy for Jewish Research*, 46–7 (1979–80), pp. 105–20.

[12] Kisch, *The Jews*, p. 276.

prophesied the coming of the Son of God. God was called here Alpha and Omega. The Oath of Navarre was even more explicit; there the Jew was asked to swear on the Messiah who is Jesus Christ and on the Day of Redemption.[13] Other oaths included among their maledictions a variety of threats regarding the fate of the perjurer at the end of time. The threat that the perjurer's soul would not be carried by the angels into Abraham's bosom (Luke 16. 22) was most frequent.[14]

The second way was to turn the ceremonial parts of the oath into ordeal-like ritual. The ordeals were often performed when the person under trial was partly or fully naked, shaven, and barefooted. These demands were not necessarily regarded as humiliating, but were grasped as necessary precautions against the possible interference of demonic powers. One can speculate that demands for the Jew to take the oath while standing barefoot, wearing special clothes, or with his body partly naked could hint at letting in elements of the ordeal through the back door. The formula demanding that the Jew take the oath while standing in a ditch may be parallel to the ordeal of the earth.[15] The frequent use of water in the Byzantine versions is most similar to various water ordeals and to rituals of purification,[16] and even the bushy wreath that the oath-taker was sometimes asked to put on can be interpreted as a shield against demonic powers. In such a manner one can find pagan precedents for many of the ceremonial parts of the oaths. The importance of this speculation lies not in the dubious proof that there really was a direct influence of pagan rites on the Jewry Oath, but rather in dimming the alleged absurdity of this or that medieval ceremony. What seems to modern eyes offensive did not necessarily do so to the medieval people. There is no trace in the Jewish sources of that period of complaints regarding the procedures of taking an oath, and though this is not a decisive proof, it does strengthen our argument that the oaths were not seen by the medieval Jew as offensive.[17] The late medieval court, which

---

[13] Amador de los Rios, *Historia*, pp. 902–6, 910–12.

[14] Zimmermann, *Die Entwicklung*, pp. 63, 81, 136.

[15] Nottarp, *Gottesurteilenstudien*, p. 31; Lasch, *Der Eid*, pp. 34, 36; Zimmermann, *Die Entwicklung*, p. 38.

[16] E. Patlagean, 'Contribution juridique à l'histoire des Juifs dans la Méditeranée medievale: les formules Greques de serment', *REJ*, 4 (1965), pp. 138–43, 149–50.

[17] Rabbi Israel Ben Petachia Isserlein was confronted with a question from the Jews of Breslau who asked how should they accept the new oath which compelled them to swear by the Tetragrammaton, publicly and bareheaded. He responded that the intention of the authorities should be checked. If it is not their intention to force conversion on the Jews, but they exact these demands only because they believe that thus the oath will be made more binding

has recently been called the 'Theatre of Terror',[18] did try to frighten the Jew, but it did it in a much more moderate manner than that for the ordinary Christian litigant, who had to undergo a trial by ordeal or to wait for the implementation of a violent sentence.

But however plausible these speculations may be, they remain speculations. We need more tangible evidence, and primarily from texts. Here I arrive at the third manner in which the oath was rendered acceptable to Christians as well. The characteristic part of the Jewry Oath was the list of maledictions at the end of the formula. The maledictions were to be realized if the oath-taker was lying. In most of the known formulae the list was short and included three to five curses, although it could be much longer and include over twenty maledictions, all taken from biblical references. But short or long, bearing in mind that the Christian oath did not include such a punishment clause in the case of perjury, the very existence of this clause in the Jewry Oath demands an explanation. Long lists of maledictions were an integral part of the sanction clauses in formulae of Christian excommunication and anathema as early as the ninth century. A comparison between them and the maledictions in the Jewry Oath reveals remarkable similarities, which suggest a direct influence of the Christian excommunication or anathema maledictions on those included in the Jewry Oath. One of the most frequent maledictions, which inflicted upon the sinner the fate of Dathan and Abiram, appeared as a standard curse in many of the formulae of the Jewry Oath.[19] It was also used as a common ecclesiastical curse. For example, it was inflicted in the first canon of the Third Lateran Council of 1179 on the supporters of a pope who had been illegally elected. The frequently-used curse in the Jewry Oath, inflicting on the perjurer all the maledictions of the Torah, is preceded by a similar liturgical Christian malediction, which inflicts on the sinner all the maledictions of the Old and New Testaments; the Devil and his aids as agents of punishment, denial of enjoying the fruits of the Second Coming of the Messiah, the leprosy of Gehazi and Naaman—all are maledictions which appear equally in both types of sources. Like the ecclesiastical maledictions, many of the maledictions of the Jewry Oath were based on

for the Jews, then one can perform it as demanded, and no blasphemy is caused: *Terumat ha-Deshen le-Rabbi Isserlein* (Jerusalem, 1959), pt 2, p. 203.

[18] R. van Duelmen, *Theater des Schreckens: Gerichtspraxis und Strafrituale in der fruehen Neuzeit* (Munich, 1985).

[19] L. K. Little, 'La Morphologie des maledictions monastiques', *Annales*, 34 (1979), pp. 43–60; 'Formules monastiques de malediction aux IXe et Xe siècles', *Revue Mabillon*, 58 (1975), pp. 386–99.

direct quotations from Deuteronomy 27–8 and Psalms 68. 23–8 and 82. 11–19. The oath in a twelfth-century Latin manuscript from Germany includes among its maledictions the term 'Anathema Maranatha'. These words, which appear in I Corinthians 16. 22, were an integral part of the sanction clause of the excommunication rite.[20] Many of the ecclesiastical maledictions ended with the proclamation *Fiat, Fiat. Amen, Amen*. This ending appears identically in the Arles formula of the Jewry Oath, which is regarded as the most important twelfth-century version because it played a major role in the transmission of a group of fifteenth-century texts.[21] These similarities suggest that at least this part of the oath (which was the longest part in most versions), was intended to inflict on the Jewish perjurer all the punishments of a Christian excommunicate, without calling it literally excommunication. If above we speculated that ordeal may have been let in through the back door, it seems that excommunication was definitely let in. As the severity of biblical maledictions had been perceived since the time of Pope Gregory I as a punishment as harsh as excommunication,[22] it seems that the problem of finding a deterrent sanction for the oath-taking Jew was satisfactorily resolved. It should be stressed, however, that the Church, through its lawyers, was not involved directly in creating an oath for the Jews.[23]

Yet it seems that the need to ensure that the oath-taking Jew did not commit perjury was not due simply to his belonging to a competing religious group. Deep and growing suspicion toward the Jew characterizes the formulae. Unlike the Christian oath of purgation, which was strengthened by oath-helpers in order to make it more valid whenever there was any doubt regarding the oath-taker's honesty, in the case of the Jewry Oath the texts themselves were altered too. In general, the oath's formulae grew longer as time passed. The malediction clauses became denser, and various precautions were taken to make the Oath more

---

[20] Little, *La Morphologie*, pp. 50–2. Zimmermann, *Die Entwicklung*, p. 38.

[21] J. Ramackers, ed., *Papsturkunden in Frankreich*, 5 (Gottingen, 1956), pp. 344–5. Compare the ending of the Arles version of the Jewry Oath—one of the fundamental twelfth-century oaths—with the ending of the Christian Anathema rites: Roell, p. 178. Little, *La Morphologie*, pp. 48–9.

[22] Gregory of Tours, *Libri Historiarum X*, ed. B. Krusch and W. Levison, *MGH. Scriptores rerum Merowingicarum*, 1, 1 (Hanover, 1951), p. 223.

[23] See W. J. Pakter, 'Did the canonists prescribe a Jewish Oath?' *Bulletin of Medieval Canon Law*, 6 (1976), pp. 81–7. The canon *Movet te*, *Decretum*, c.22, q.1, c.16 (cols 865–6) recognized the fact that Jews swear on the True God (*per Deum verum*), and thus made it theoretically possible to accept a simple Jewish oath.

binding.[24] The texts insisted repeatedly that the Oath be taken without any alteration of text or ceremony. This can be explained by the traditional belief that a sacred ritual in which magic and supernatural powers were involved had to be performed accurately to achieve the desired effects.[25] But it is also a sign of a real fear that the Jew might neutralize these effects by altering the ceremony or refraining from saying the words explicitly. Touching the holy book no longer sufficed for the oaths of the later thirteenth century, and the Jew was asked to put his whole hand on the book or scroll as far as the wrist. Sometimes a preliminary oath was exacted in which the 'bishop of the Jews' (*pontifex* or *episcopus Judaeorum*) was asked to verify on oath that the book on which the Jews swore was indeed the book on which they would take oath according to the Jewish law.[26] It seems that there was real fear that Jews might evade the truth whenever they were involved in litigation with a Christian. Explicit prohibitions of mumbling, stuttering, or expression of outward signs of hesitation appear in the formula of Dortmund in the later thirteenth century.[27] In Magdeburg, at the beginning of the fifteenth century, the Jew was asked to perform the Oath while standing on a stool facing eastward towards the sun, as if in prayer. He was allowed to stutter only three times, but had to start the whole ritual from the beginning after each slip. If he stuttered for a fourth time he was fined and might forfeit the case.[28]

Only two of the formulae hint at the motives of their creators. The introduction to the 1364 version of the Nuremberg formula tries to give an air of antiquity to the text and says, 'Since Jews happily cheat Christians (*gern betrigen*), this formula was composed in the reign of King Charles.'[29] In the introduction to the 1285 Augsburg formula, Achilles Pirminius Glasser, the sixteenth-century annalist, added that the Senate of the city ordered the creation of such a formla, 'since in public trials, sojourning

---

[24] See the Augsburg versions in Zimmermann, *Die Entwicklung*, pp. 191–2, 194. The earlier version from 1285 demanded that the Oath be taken in the synagogue, that the Jew lay his right hand on the Pentateuch, and that he swear in the name of the God and the Torah which had been given on Sinai. At the end of the fourteenth century a new formula was given, and it added the demands that the Pentateuch be open where the Ten Commandments are written, and that the hand be laid on the book as far as the wrist. Towards the middle of the fifteenth century the city adopted a formula which included a long list of maledictions and was influenced by the *Schwabenspiegel* formula. See a similar development in Nuremberg, in Roell, pp. 190–5.

[25] Radding, 'Superstition', pp. 955–7.

[26] Zimmermann, *Die Entwicklung*, pp. 63, 82–3.

[27] Ibid., pp. 104–5, 111.

[28] Ibid., pp. 136, 139–40.

[29] M. Stern, *Die Israelitische Bevoelkerung der Deutschen Staedte*, 3 (Kiel, 1894–6), pp. 236–7.

Jews must deliver oaths, and since even our own Jews are to be suspected that they do not accept anything as holy, and do not show anything truly, because of their perfidy, and especially because they lack a form of words which will bind them religiously, the senate decreed . . .'.[30] Even though this introduction may have been inserted by the annalist and thus was not part of the 1285 formula, it is still quite a useful indication for the tension which enveloped the whole issue of receiving oaths from Jews.

Was this fear of being deceived by the Jews justified, or was it the outcome of an unfounded stereotype? In other words, were medieval Jews more lax about perjury when the Oath was directed at a Christian? The information I drew from the Jewish *responsa* literature is too scattered to make any decisive conclusion. There is no systematic discussion of the question of how an oath towards a non-Jew should be regarded. Yet from specific, individual questions one may reconstruct the reality. It can be said that both among the Spanish rabbinic authorities and the German, one can find two different approaches. Most rejected in principle any kind of perjury, but there were those who did not preclude lying to Christian courts, especially when there was a difference between the Jewish and the Christian laws regarding the same offence. The questions reveal various tactics used by Jewish litigants to avoid telling the truth in non-Jewish courts, and I will mention only a few examples from both regions. In a very long and complex dispute between two Jews, R. Yom Tov Ben Abraham Ishbili (1250–c.1330), one of the most important Spanish authorities of his time, describes an incident in which a Jew tried to deceive the Christian court by swearing falsely on the book of the *Haftarot* (the weekly readings from the Bible attached to the regular weekly reading from the Torah), rather than on the Torah. This may account for the sensitivity with which the Christian authorities regarded the issue of verifying the validity of the book on which the Jews swore. The Rabbi determined that swearing on the book of the *Haftarot* is as binding as swearing on the Torah, and rejected in principle any lying to non-Jews. For if lies are revealed, blasphemy would ensue.[31] R. Meir Ben Baruch of

[30] R. Schmidt, 'Judeneide in Augsburg und Regensburg', *Zeitschrift der Savigny Stiftung für Rechtsgeschichte: Germanistische Abt.*, 93 (1976), p. 332. A similar image of the Jew as a liar who cannot be trusted is conveyed by John Bromyard in an article 'on the Oath' in his *Summa Praedicantium* (Nuremberg, 1518), p. CLXXVIv. The Jews are depicted as arch-liars from the time of Jesus. Their blasphemy towards God is compared with the blasphemy of the perjurer, who like them uses God as a false witness. In practice, Bromyard tells us, the Jews do not swear frequently, but when they do it the oath is taken according to their law.

[31] Y. Kafich, ed., *Sheelot u. Teshuvot ha-Ritbah* (Jerusalem, 1959), ch. 186, pp. 223–4. See also

Rothenburg (*c*.1215–1293) rejected the behaviour of a group of Jews who were compelled to take an oath which would oblige them to cease their criminal activity of clipping coins. The Jews, claiming it to be an oath under compulsion, took the oath but annulled it in their hearts (thus performing what is called *reservatio mentalis*) and continued clipping.[32] And R. Yissrael ben Petachiah Isserlein (1390–1460), one of the most important authorities in Austria in the fifteenth century, determined that one of the four types of blasphemers who desecrate the name of the Lord is 'he who lies to the gentile, and whose lie is revealed'. And he adds that 'even if the lie is not revealed it is still a lie', and therefore a sinful act.[33]

But there was the opposing approach, which has been revealed by the incidents mentioned before and which found legal support in some of the authorities. Israel Ben Hayyim Bruna (1400–80), one of the major rabbinic authorities of fifteenth-century Germany, was asked about the custom of perpetrating perjury in Christian courts by performing *reservatio mentalis*. He determined that this custom was permissible according to the Jewish law under three conditions: (1) that according to the Jewish law the accused committed no crime; (2) that the case was a civil one; and (3) that the lie would not produce blasphemy, namely, that the Gentiles would not be aware of it.[34] In the circumstance of great difference between the judgements of Jewish and Christian courts, this determination of Bruna theoretically legitimized perjury to non-Jewish courts in a wide variety of cases of civil law. It is impossible to determine how widely this approach was accepted among Jews in practice. One may also explain this ambivalent attitude of Jews towards Christian courts by the growing feeling among them that the deprived Jews could receive no justice there. But the fact that some Jews could be inclined to deceive the Christian courts, and that their attitude was backed by some of the more important rabbinic authorities, was doubtless known to Christians and increased their suspicion. It is also against this background that the formulae of the Jewry Oath are to be read.

The Jewish sources are practically silent about the Jewry Oath. There is no further evidence to prove whether the long and elaborate texts were used in practice. Scattered information that we have from glosses to

---

Baer, *Die Juden*, p. 210, where a Jew is accused of having cheated a Christian court by swearing on a different book from that containing the Ten Commandments.

[32] *Sheelot u-Teshuvot Maharam Ben Baruch me-Rotenburg* (Levov Printing) (Jerusalem, 1986), 2, p. 246.

[33] Y. Freimann, ed., *Leket Yosher* (Berlin, 1903), pp. 136–7.

[34] M. Hershler, ed., *Sheelot u-Teshuvot Mahari Bruna* (Jerusalem, 1960), ch. 83, p. 120.

German law books,[35] from manuals of courts,[36] from the Jewish *responsa* literature, and from official documents,[37] reveal that in practice simpler and shorter formulae were used. All this casts doubt on the implementation of the long formulae which, had they been used, would have created a tremendous burden on the time and logistics of the judicial process.[38] But whether the longer oaths were used locally or not, one should not use that judicial procedure as an example of a prevailing will to injure the Jews. It reveals, indeed, a growing suspicion of the Jew, but it was formed and used to integrate him into daily life, and was well interwoven into judicial, social, and economic reality. This judicial procedure invented specially for the Jews did eventually acquire a distinct anti-Jewish character. Only from later periods, and most certainly in the eighteenth and nineteenth centuries, when this mechanism of a unique oath for the Jews survived, despite the changes in values and judicial conventions, do we have clear evidence that the Oath became a segregating and humiliating tool that seemed to the Jews to be a burden which must be abolished. When exactly this process took place, and how, are only two of the questions which remain to be answered.

Merton College,
Oxford

---

[35] Zimmermann, *Die Entwicklung*, pp. 147–8; G. Kisch, *Jewry Law in Medieval Germany. Laws and Court Decisions Concerning Jews* (New York, 1949), pp. 49–50, 70ff., 120–1, 131, 134, no. 17.

[36] Kisch, *Jewry Law*, pp. 159, 179, 199, 253; Kisch, *The Jews*, pp. 190–1; Zimmermann, *Die Entwicklung*, pp. 136, 139–40.

[37] See, for example, the charter in *MGH.DR*, 6.1, *Henrici IV*, ed. D. von Gladiss (Hanover, 1952), p. 527, no. 471; *MGH. Constitutiones*, 1, *Friderici I*, ed. L. Weiland (Hanover, 1893), p. 227; R. Chazan, *Church, State and Jews in the Middle Ages* (1980), pp. 85–7, 89–93; T. Rymer, ed., *Foedera*, 1.1 (London, 1816), p. 51. In all of them the Jews are asked to swear simply according to their law or on it (*secundum or per legem suam*). Kisch, *Forschungen*, pp. 123–8, argued unconvincingly that the expression *sua lex* denoted not the Jewish Law but the special Jewry Oath formula.

[38] The evidence comes from various places: see, for example, Baer, *Die Juden*, 1.1, p. 110, 1.2, pp. 300–1; B. Leroy, *The Jews of Navarre in the Middle Ages* (Jerusalem, 1985), p. 31; Y. Assis, *The Jews of Santa Coloma de Queralt* (Jerusalem, 1988), pp. 123–4, 130–1; A. Steinberg, *Studien zur Geschichte der Juden in der Schweiz waehrend des Mittelalters* (Zurich, 1903), pp. 29–31.

WHY THE SPANISH INQUISITION?

by JOHN EDWARDS

IT seems quite extraordinary that an important European country should apparently have wished to go down in history as the originator of calculated cruelty and violence against members of its civil population. Yet the writers of the famous sketches in *Monty Python's Flying Circus* were far from being the first to introduce 'the Spanish Inquisition' as a cliché to represent arbitrary and yet calculated tyranny. By the late sixteenth century, Christian Europe, both Catholic and Protestant, had already formed the image of Spain which has become known as the 'Black Legend'. Just as many Spaniards distrusted Italy, because Jews lived freely there, and France because Protestants were in a similar condition in that country, so Italian opposition to the forces of Ferdinand the Catholic and his successors, together with the ultimately successful Dutch rebels, created, with the help of growing knowledge of Spain's atrocities against the inhabitants of the New World, a counter-myth, in which the Spaniards themselves appeared as heartless oppressors, but also, ironically, as crypto-Jews (*marranos*).[1] Erasmus wrote that France was 'the most spotless and most flourishing part of Christendom', since it was 'not infected with heretics, with Bohemian schismatics, with Jews, with half-Jewish *marranos*', the last term clearly referring to Spain.[2] Not surprisingly, there is also a Jewish story of what happened in Spain before, during, and after 1492, which may best be summed up, in general outline, in the words, written in 1877, of Frederic David Mocatta's study of Iberian Jews and the Inquisition.

> It is . . . hardly likely that a population of little less than a million Jews would ever have been allowed to dwell in peace in a land ruled by monarchs as bigoted as Philip II and his successors, and which almost till our own times permitted a court as arbitrary and as cruel as the Inquisition to hold an undisputed sway. The installation of this tribunal under Ferdinand and Isabella forms an epoch in the history of Spain, and weighing as an incubus on all freedom of thought and

---

[1] Henry Kamen, *Spain, 1469–1714. A Society of Conflict*, 2nd edn (London, 1991), p. 194; J. H. Elliott, 'Spain and its Empire in the Sixteenth and Seventeenth Centuries', in *Spain and its World, 1500–1700* (New Haven and London, 1989), p. 11.

[2] John Edwards, *The Jews in Christian Europe, 1400–1700* (London, 1988), pp. 54–5.

action, was one of the main causes of the decadence of that great country, the effects of which are now so sadly visible.[3]

However, in this Jewish story, the fate of Spain's Jews in 1492 is still commonly blamed on excessive assimilation. For example, in Litvinoff's words, 'The tragedy of Spain, like the tragedy of Germany in 1933, had its roots in the thoroughness of the Jews' accommodation to their environment. . . . Orthodox Jews hungered after the relaxed delights of Christianity.'[4] The last seems a strange phrase with which to describe the fate of the converts, since 'relaxed' (*relajado*) was the word used by the Inquisition to describe the handing over to the 'secular arm' of a relapsed heretic for burning. Perhaps this is a piece of black humour to match the Black Legend, in which case it would not be unjustified.

The 'pre-history' of the refounded Inquisition, though, begins effectively with the attacks on the main urban communities of Spanish Jewry, from Seville in the south-west to Barcelona in the north-east, which took place in the spring and early summer of 1391. After these events, Jews converted with increasing speed to Christianity, subjected as they were to legal, political, and social pressures, including the preaching missions of the Catalan Dominican friar Vincent Ferrer between 1412 and 1415. At Tortosa, in 1413–14, the anti-pope Benedict XIII sponsored a formal theological disputation, in which the Jewish participants appeared to many to be defeated. This, too, seems to have led to conversions. None the less, it took a generation or two for the new success of the more able among the tens of thousands of *conversos* to become conspicuous, both to their 'Old Christian' rivals and to others influenced by the latter's resentment. The areas affected were the Church and secular government, both central and local. The debate which eventually led to Ferdinand and Isabella's decision to seek a papal bull for a new foundation of the Inquisition in Castile, for the first time, and in Aragon to replace an institution which originated in the thirteenth-century battle against the Cathars and Waldensians, became public with the rebellion in Toledo in 1449 against the government of John II. This began as a political revolt and a rebellion against royal taxation, but it produced the first document which singled out converts from Judaism as a group which so threatened Christian society that they should be excluded from public office.[5] It is clear, then,

---

[3] Frederic David Mocatta, *The Jews of Spain and Portugal and the Inquisition* (New York, 1973), p. vi.

[4] Barnett Litvinoff, *The Burning Bush. Antisemitism and World History* (Glasgow, 1989), p. 84.

[5] J. N. Hillgarth, *The Spanish Kingdoms, 1250–1516, 2, 1410–1516. Castilian Hegemony* (Oxford,

that one 'cause' of the Spanish Inquisition was the perception, for whatever reason, that such converts constituted a 'problem' which would have to be 'solved'. None the less, it was only with the victory of Isabella, with her husband Ferdinand, in her wars to secure her succession to the Castilian throne, that the Spanish Inquisition's career began.

Once papal approval, however reluctant, had been secured, in 1478, a network of inquisitorial tribunals gradually spread throughout Castilian and Aragonese lands, often, and especially in Aragon, Catalonia, and Valencia, in the face of strong opposition, much of it constitutionally motivated.[6] The first royal appointments of inquisitors were made in September 1480, and, in the following month, operations commenced in Seville. Further tribunals were set up in Córdoba in 1482, in Jaén and Ciudad Real in 1483 (the latter moving to Toledo in 1485), and, between then and 1492, in the Castilian towns of Avila, Medina del Campo, Segovia, Sigüenza, and Valladolid. In 1484 the onslaught began in the Crown of Aragon, with new foundations in Teruel, Zaragoza, Barcelona, and Valencia. The result of their endeavours, up to about 1520, was the interrogation of thousands of people, most of them converts from Judaism. No more recent study has improved on Henry C. Lea's magisterial work as a source of overall statistics for those tried and punished, a small minority being burnt for 'relapsing' into the 'heresy' of their previous faith, having previously been convicted and punished for the same offence, but although in the areas of some tribunals, such as Guadalupe (Extremadura) in 1485, and Avila in 1490–1500, over 40 per cent of those tried were burnt, while in Valencia the figure was 38 per cent, it none the less seems that most *conversos* survived the Inquisition's early years.[7] Whinnom exaggerated, though, when he suggested that, in the period 1492 to 1505, 'as many as ninety-nine out of every hundred *conversos* lived unmolested by the Inquisition', but it is right to discount wilder modern estimates of the casualties.[8]

1978), p. 149; Eloy Benito Ruano, *Toledo en el Siglo XV. Vida Política* (Madrid, 1961), pp. 34–81, and 'La "Sentencia-Estatuto" de Pero Sarmiento', *Revista de la Universidad de Madrid*, 6 (1951), pp. 207–306, reprinted in *Los Orígenes del Problema Converso* (Barcelona, 1976), pp. 41–92.

[6] John Edwards, 'Religion, Constitutionalism and the Inquisition in Teruel, 1484–5', in Derek W. Lomax and David Mackenzie, eds, *God and Man in Medieval Spain. Essays in Honour of J. R. L. Highfield* (Warminster, 1989), pp. 129–47; William Monter, *Frontiers of Heresy. The Spanish Inquisition from the Basque Lands to Sicily* (Cambridge, 1990), pp. 3–28.

[7] Henry Kamen, *Inquisition and Society in Spain in the Sixteenth and Seventeenth Centuries* (London, 1985), pp. 30–43.

[8] Ibid., pp. 41–2; Keith Whinnom, 'Interpreting *La Celestina*: the motives and the personality of Fernando de Rojas', in F. W. Hodcroft, D. G. Pattison, R. D. F. Pring-Mill, and R. W.

As the years went by, other groups became targets of the new tribunals. The first was converts from the other monotheistic faith 'of the Book', ex-Muslims known as *moriscos*. However, despite the fact that the policy of expelling those who refused to be baptized was extended to Castile's Muslims in 1502, those in the neighbouring Crown of Aragon, and particularly the large Muslim population in the kingdom of Valencia, which had remained since the thirteenth-century conquest, were left largely undisturbed. Indeed, Ferdinand the Catholic made strenuous efforts to protect the Muslims in his own domains, in total contradiction of the policy being pursued at the very same time, by his wife and himself, in Castile.[9] The Inquisition was not introduced to the kingdom of Granada until 1526, and then worked only slowly, while serious efforts to root out Islamic belief and practice in Aragon, Catalonia, and Valencia did not begin until the mid-sixteenth century, culminating in the highly controversial *morisco* expulsions of the early seventeenth.[10]

Somewhat belatedly the Spanish Inquisition turned to dissidence and heresy within the Christian Church, which had, after all, been the original target and purpose of the medieval foundation. Some such movements, showing characteristics similar to those of the *Devotio Moderna* in northern Europe, were lumped together as 'illuminists': they were feared for their tendency to bypass the sacraments, and many of the clergy, of the Church.[11] Others were influenced by outside figures. Although Erasmus had considerable influence, even in royal and high ecclesiastical circles, in the 1520s and for a while afterwards, his ideas and followers were eventually to be condemned, during Philip II's reign,[12] while Luther's name provided the generic inquisitorial term for a Protestant (*luterano*) in the latter half of the sixteenth century. It applied not only to the German booksellers who imported genuine Lutheran works to Spain, in a trade

---

Truman, eds, *Medieval and Renaissance Studies on Spain and Portugal in Honour of P. E. Russell* (Oxford, 1981), p. 59n.

[9] Kamen, *Inquisition and Society*, pp. 101–13; John Edwards, 'Mission and Inquisition among *conversos* and *moriscos* in Spain', *SCH*, 21 (1984), pp. 139–51, and 'Christian mission in the kingdom of Granada, 1492–1568', *Christianity and Islam, Renaissance and Modern Studies*, 31 (1987), pp. 20–33; Mark D. Meyerson, *The Muslims of Valencia in the Age of Fernando and Isabel: between Coexistence and Crusade* (Berkeley, Los Angeles, and Oxford, 1991).

[10] Monter, *Frontiers of Heresy*, pp. 189–92; Stephen Haliczer, *Inquisition and Society in the Kingdom of Valencia, 1478–1834* (Berkeley, Los Angeles, and Oxford, 1990), pp. 244–72.

[11] Kamen, *Inquisition and Society*, pp. 66–70; Alvaro Huerga, *Historia de los Alumbrados*, 2 vols (Madrid, 1978); Haliczer, *Inquisition and Society*, pp. 273–80.

[12] Kamen, *Inquisition and Society*, pp. 70–1; Marcel Bataillon, *Erasmo y España*, 2nd edn (Madrid, 1979); Haliczer, *Inquisition and Society*, pp. 280–5.

which notoriously received the attention of the Holy Office in Iberia and the Netherlands under Philip II, but also indiscriminately to native Spaniards. Some of these were genuinely influenced by Protestant ideas, whether Lutheran or Calvinist, but most had little notion of any kind of religious doctrine, such as the farmers in the Andalusian province of Jaén, who told the Córdoba inquisitors in the 1560s and 1570s that they thought 'Lutheranism' included such things as vegetarianism and free love.[13] Such beliefs, of course, were associated with heresy from at least the eleventh century onwards, but at the popular level they also indicate the extent to which the Spanish tribunals became both police courts for morals and didactic institutions in post-Tridentine conditions. By the late sixteenth century, *judeoconversos* and *moriscos*, and even Protestants, though French and English 'Lutherans' were still being interrogated, had to a large extent been replaced in the inquisitorial gaols by bigamists, sodomites, blasphemers, sorcerers and witches, and the plain ignorant. None the less, despite these important changes of target group over the years, together with constant local and regional variations, there can be no doubt that the answer to the question, 'Why the Spanish Inquisition?' must be sought primarily in the relationship between Christianity and Judaism, and in the late medieval phenomenon of large-scale conversion from the latter to the former in Spain.

The new tribunals believed that their establishment was justified by the religious beliefs and practices that they found when they began work in the 1480s. Despite large-scale losses, especially during the period of French occupation after 1808, ample documentation has survived to illustrate, at least in appearance, the nature of the religion of the *conversos*. On the surface inquisitorial documentation, which has been thoroughly studied, first by Lea around 1900, and in the last twenty-five years or so by a distinguished battery of Spanish, French, Danish, British, American, and Israeli scholars, produces results of such uniformity that they may be readily described in summary.[14] Firstly, inquisition evidence, including

[13] Kamen, *Inquisition and Society*, pp. 71–100; Haliczer, *Inquisition and Society*, pp. 285–90; Monter, *Frontiers of Heresy*, pp. 231–52; Rafael Gracia Boix, *Autos de Fe y Causas de la Inquisición de Córdoba* (Córdoba, 1983), pp. 81, 88; L. de Alberti and A. B. Wallis, eds, *English Merchants and the Spanish Inquisition in the Canaries* (London, 1912).

[14] Henry Charles Lea, *A History of the Inquisition in Spain*, 4 vols (New York, 1906–7). Notable examples of modern work are Jaime Contreras, *El Santo Officio de la Inquisición de Galicia, 1560–1700* (Madrid, 1982); Ricardo García Cárcel, *Orígenes de la Inquisición Española* (Barcelona, 1976), and *Herejía y Sociedad en el Siglo XVI* (Barcelona, 1980); Jean-Pierre Dedieu, *L'Administration de la foi. L'Inquisition de Tolède (XVIe–XVIIIe siècle)* (Madrid, 1989); Gustav Henningsen, *The Witches' Advocate: Basque Witchcraft and the Spanish Inquisition* (Reno, 1980);

pre-trial statements by witnesses, the trials themselves, and the summaries of cases (*relaciones de causas*) sent by local tribunals to the Supreme Council of the Inquisition in Madrid, all show widespread and continuing adherence to Judaism, in both faith and practice, in the period from about 1450 to 1492. Jewish converts continued after baptism, in places as far apart as Andalusia, Old Castile, Aragon, and Catalonia, to make gifts to Jewish charities, to rent seats and pay for lights in synagogues, to attend Hebrew and Talmudic classes and have Hebrew taught to their children, to visit regularly, in person or through servants, Jewish butchers, as well as celebrating in the booths on the Feast of Tabernacles (Succoth), to buy unleavened bread at Passover, to make peace with their enemies on the Day of Atonement (Yom Kippur), to wear prayer-shawls, in the case of men, at home or in other secret places, and to keep the Sabbath and dietary laws at home. Before the expulsion in 1492, local rabbis might be called in to testify that such practices were, in inquisitorial jargon, 'ceremonies of the Jewish law'.[15] There were remarkably few questions about Jewish doctrine, as opposed to practice, in the inquisitorial charge-sheets, so that in these sources the Jewish religion appears somewhat 'untheological'. Whether this is an accurate portrayal may be questioned, but the tribunals' evidence also reveals, on many occasions, hostility to Christian faith and practice. *Conversos* seem often to have rejected basic doctrines of Christianity, such as the Incarnation, the Virgin Birth, the Resurrection, and the Trinity, as well as the sacraments of the Church, such as the Mass in general and the doctrine of transubstantiation in particular. They rejected religious statues and pictures as idols and ridiculed clergy, confraternities, and, sometimes, the feared Inquisition itself.[16]

There are also many statements, however, which seem to fall into the category neither of Christian nor of Jewish orthodoxy. To return to the sacred canon of *Monty Python*, many *conversos* in Spain in this period seem to have been almost out of earshot of the preacher in both synagogue and church, like Brian at the 'sermon on the mount'. It would be quite wrong, though, to ridicule the views of those who found themselves on the

---

Kamen, *Inquisition and Society*; Haliczer, *Inquisition and Society*; Haim Beinart, *Conversos on Trial: the Inquisition of Ciudad Real* (Jerusalem, 1981).

[15] For examples of Jewish belief and practice, see the above works and also John Edwards, 'Religious faith and doubt in late medieval Spain: Soria *circa* 1450–1500', *PaP*, 120 (1988), pp. 6–9. For the Inquisition's use of Jewish testimony, see John Edwards, 'Jewish testimony to the Spanish Inquisition: Teruel, 1484–7', *REJ*, 143 (1984), pp. 333–50.

[16] Edwards, 'Religious faith and doubt', pp. 9–11.

receiving end of rabbinical or priestly instruction, and especially to disparage those who, as so many fifteenth-century Spaniards did, found themselves having to listen to both in a single lifetime. In such circumstances, it is not only unsurprising that many appear to have clung to Judaism and been suspicious of Christianity, but also that so many expressed their frustration against the symbols of, as later inquisitors were similarly to describe the Anglican faith, 'la *nueva religión* (the new religion)'. Such views had been commonly expressed, if the surviving sources are to be believed, in various Western countries throughout the lifetime of the papal Inquisition.[17] However, before addressing such issues, it is inevitable that the validity of the inquisitorial evidence itself should be brought into question. There are two points to be raised here: 'Can inquisitorial evidence in any way be trusted by the historian?' and, secondly, 'Can any religious believer's testimony be trusted by a historian, whether it is to be found in primary or secondary sources?'

On the first point, there is a well-established historical controversy. Ever since the original period of the Black Legend it has been hard to find an assessor of the Spanish Inquisition's work who regarded objectivity as a desirable, let alone an attainable, objective. It is interesting to note that so-called 'rational' and 'secular' scholars of the nineteenth and twentieth centuries have adopted precisely the same Manichaean, or dualist, attitude to Spain and its tribunal as did the Catholics and Protestants of the Reformation and Counter-Reformation period and of more recent years. But, then, terminology may change whereas mental attitudes generally do not, or, as John Elliott put it some years ago, in the context of Europeans discussing and analysing Latin America: 'For the sixteenth-century European, the great line of division lay between the Christian and the pagan. For his twentieth-century successor, the product of a scientific civilization, it lies between the "irrational" and the "rational".'[18] *Plus ça change. . . .* At least the inquisitors had the merit, unlike most modern scholars, of proclaiming their convictions honestly. In the controversy over the reliability or otherwise of inquisitorial evidence, many murky prejudices are to be found hidden in the analysis of current historical practitioners. Thus Ellis Rivkin seems to reverse the traditional Christian convention and cliché about the Jews and assume, not without reason, that inquisitorial evidence is automatically

[17] Ibid., pp. 11–25.
[18] J. H. Elliott, 'The Discovery of America and the Discovery of Man', in *Spain and its World*, p. 46.

invalid because a Christian tribunal was interrogating former Jews.[19] From a simple Marxist perspective, which in the Europe of today may seem somewhat antiquated, the Portuguese historian Saraiva similarly discounted inquisitorial documentation on the grounds that the sole purpose of the tribunals was to rob rich *conversos*.[20] They undoubtedly did so, as the sufferers were in the best possible position to know and report; but such a monocausal explanation can only be based on what might be called the 'irrational', or as Langmuir would say 'non-rational', assumption that the whole of 'religion' is, as a humble Castilian said in Peroniel (Soria) in 1494 concerning official teaching on Heaven and Hell, 'nothing more than a way of frightening us, like people saying to children, "Avati coco" ["the bogeyman will get you"]'.[21]

Is it possible, none the less, in the thousands of pages so meticulously copied by the Inquisition's notaries, yet in such stressed circumstances, including isolation and other sensory deprivation, to hear voices which tell of authentic personal experience, whether 'religious' or not? Despite the strictures of some commentators, the answer must be 'yes'. Those who have immersed themselves in the lengthy and elaborate machinations of the inquisitors, their officials, and other people who were caught in their net, have generally come to the conclusion that more personal, if not spontaneous, testimony can be found in such material than in most other sources in the period, such as local and central government records, or the archives of churches and cathedrals. It says much for the resilience of the human spirit that such an amount of vernacular speech and unorthodox thought is to be found in the pages of records produced under such adverse circumstances. In stark contrast to the destruction of morality and religious values experienced by the victims of so many twentieth-century tyrannies, and in particular the Nazi regime, the prisoners of the Inquisition were able to speak, and transmit their experience to future readers.[22] Thus, despite the proper strictures of Peter Burke, who warns that the inquisitors might very easily put ideas into suspects' heads, it is still true that such records have the potential to be, in Brian Pullan's words, 'the key

---

[19] Ellis Rivkin, 'The utilisation of non-Jewish sources for the reconstruction of Jewish history', *JQR*, 48 (1957–8), p. 193, and 'How Jewish were the New Christians?' in Josep M. Solà, Samuel G. Armistead, and Joseph H. Silverman, eds, *Hispania Judaica: Studies on the History, Language and Literature of the Jews in the Hispanic World*, 1, *History* (Barcelona, 1980), pp. 105–15.

[20] A. J. Saraiva, *Inquisição e Cristãos Novos*, 2nd edn (Oporto, 1969).

[21] Edwards, 'Religious faith and doubt', pp. 24–5; Gavin I. Langmuir, *History, Religion and Anti-semitism* (Berkeley, Los Angeles, and Oxford, 1990), pp. 143–57.

[22] Lawrence L. Langer, *Holocaust Testimonials. The Ruins of Memory* (New Haven and London, 1991).

which unlocks the mind of the people, rather than merely revealing their public acts and their private transactions'.[23]

Given that the evidence accumulated by the Spanish Inquisition in its early years may be regarded as reliable to a significant extent, it still remains to be asked why it mattered so much to churchmen, monarchs, nobles, and other governors that tens of thousands of their subjects or fellow citizens tried to 'have it both ways' in the matter of religion. The answer to this question owes much to the tortured relations between Christianity and its elder brother, Judaism. As a heretical sect of Judaism which set itself up as a new religion, Christianity was still left, even after it achieved almost total religious, political, social, and economic dominance over Judaism, with agonizing self-doubts.[24] These doubts were, paradoxically, exposed, and spread to the more committed members of the Western European laity, by the increasingly professionalized clergy and academics of the eleventh and twelfth centuries.[25] It was out of the desire of these groups to achieve identity and status that many of the conflicts and tensions of the later medieval Church arose. Thus, in a true sense, 'heresy' (the 'wrong' choice) was a product of the increasingly organized, bureaucratic, and self-interested insistence on 'orthodoxy' (the 'right' choice) in the ordering of the Church and of society, which were not, of course, finely distinguished in this period. The result was an increasingly violent and wide-ranging assault on those, in many categories, who were perceived to be 'dissidents', such as Christian heretics, Jews, homosexuals, and lepers.[26] The first violent manifestation of the laity's ability to sense changes in official direction was the massacre of Jews in the Rhineland by the 'crusaders' led by Emicho of Leiningen in 1096.[27] After that, irrational beliefs about Jews' potency as enemies of all Christians developed luxuriant growths. In England, France, and Germany, Jews were accused of kidnapping Christian boys (rarely girls) in order to inflict on them the

[23] Peter Burke, *Popular Culture in Early Modern Europe* (London, 1978), pp. 74–5; Brian Pullan, *The Jews of Europe and the Inquisition of Venice* (Oxford, 1983), p. 117.

[24] Jacob Neusner, *Jews and Christians. The Myth of a Common Tradition* (London, 1991); Gavin I. Langmuir, 'Anti-Judaism as the Necessary Preparation for Antisemitism', and 'Doubt in Christendom', in *Toward a Definition of Antisemitism* (Berkeley, Los Angeles, and Oxford, 1990), pp. 57–62, 100–33.

[25] Langmuir, 'Doubt in Christendom', pp. 114–16; R. I. Moore, *The Origins of European Dissent* (Oxford, 1977).

[26] R. I. Moore, *The Formation of a Persecuting Society* (Oxford, 1987).

[27] Langmuir, 'The Transformation of Anti-Judaism', in *Toward a Definition*, pp. 63–99; Jonathan Riley-Smith, 'The First Crusade and the persecution of the Jews', *SCH*, 21, pp. 51–72; Robert Chazan, *European Jewry and the First Crusade* (Berkeley, Los Angeles, and London, 1987).

wounds that the Jewish authorities were increasingly believed to have inflicted on Jesus, without the mediation of the Romans and with the approval of the crowds which, according to Matthew's Gospel, took his blood upon themselves and upon their children. This accusation began in Norwich in 1150 and spread through France, Germany, and Italy in the succeeding three centuries.[28] From the mid-thirteenth century onwards, Jews were also accused of seizing eucharistic Hosts and torturing and dismembering them—a belief which depended on the paradoxical notion that Jews, too, subscribed to the doctrine of transubstantiation.[29] In northern Europe, Jews were also accused of poisoning wells and thus causing the Black Death of 1348–51, and were increasingly portrayed not only as the crucifiers of Christ, but also as specifically diabolical figures, with horns and tails and other such accoutrements.[30]

In the light of these developments further north, the situation of Spanish Jews seemed remarkably safe, not to say buoyant. The Black Death had a relatively small, though not inconsiderable, effect on the Iberian peninsula, outside Catalonia, and while Jews were attacked, for example, in Toledo, by the rebel forces during the civil war between Pedro and his illegitimate half-brother, Henry of Trastámara, who started a new dynasty by murdering the Castilian king in 1369, the new regime did little to alter the status of Jews in the succeeding years.[31] It is for this reason that the attacks of 1391 seem to have come as such a shock to the members of the leading communities, and to have induced a growing belief that God had abandoned the Jews and given his blessing to the Christian Church.[32] The Church, on the other hand, seems to have begun by defending the traditional theology of baptism, which adhered to the Pauline principle of total conversion, once the sacrament had been validly administered. A typical expression of this view is to be found in the bull issued by Nicholas V, in September 1449, entitled *Humani generis inimicus*,

---

[28] Langmuir, 'Thomas of Monmouth: Detector of Ritual Murder', in *Toward a Definition*, pp. 209–36; Thomas of Monmouth, *The Life and Miracles of St William of Norwich*, ed. Augustus Jessopp and M. R. James (Cambridge, 1896). For the Jewish crowd see Matthew 27. 25. See also Chazan, 'The Blois incident of 1171', *Proceedings of the American Academy of Jewish Research*, 36 (1968), pp. 13–31; Langmuir, 'The Knight's Tale of Young Hugh of Lincoln', in *Toward a Definition*, pp. 237–62.

[29] Langmuir, 'Ritual Cannibalism', in *Toward a Definition*, pp. 263–81, and *History, Religion and Antisemitism*, pp. 301–3.

[30] Robert Bonfil, 'The Devil and the Jews in the Christian Consciousness of the Middle Ages', in Shmuel Almog, ed., *Antisemitism Through the Ages* (Oxford, 1988), pp. 91–8.

[31] Hillgarth, *The Spanish Kingdoms*, 1, pp. 375–87.

[32] Stephen Sharot, 'Jewish millenarianism: a comparison of medieval communities', *Comparative Studies in Society and History*, 22 (1980), pp. 394–415.

which condemned the Toledan rebel statute, excluding *conversos* from public office, whether ecclesiastical or secular, stating that 'Between those newly converted to the faith, particularly from the Israelite people, and Old Christians, there shall be no distinction in honours, dignities and offices.' The *converso* bishop Alonso de Cartagena used Paul's text in Galatians 3. 27–9, to argue for the same point of view: 'As many of you as were baptised into Christ have put on Christ. There is neither Jew nor Greek, there is neither slave nor free, there is neither male nor female; for you are all one in Christ Jesus.'[33]

In the latter half of the fifteenth century, however, this theological position came under increasing pressure. In 1466 the precentor of Córdoba, Fernand Ruiz de Aguayo, excluded *conversos* from serving at the altar in his newly-founded chantry, 'notwithstanding that in this generation of *conversos* there are many virtuous and good persons, and of good conscience and life.'[34] The precentor's example was followed, in a piecemeal fashion, throughout the reigns of Ferdinand and Isabella, and became a major ingredient in the development of the Black Legend as, paradoxically, it created the view abroad that Spain was a nation of false Christians, or 'Judaizing' Marranos. Eventually the 'purity of blood' (*limpieza de sangre*) statutes became just as much a mechanism of assimilation as of exclusion, in the sense that genealogies could be won or lost on the whim, or in the interest, of neighbours, but in the 1460s and 1470s the notion that baptism could not 'purge' Jewish origin, despite what the Scriptures and the Church might teach, played a major part in persuading Ferdinand and Isabella to seek a new Inquisition, given their already insecure position in Castile.[35] The notion that the converts were a 'threat' to Spanish society of course depended on a 'totalitarian' view of religion which could not allow for the rather chaotic personal arrangements which constituted the 'religiosity', to use Langmuir's expression, of those who attempted to make the change from Judaism to Christianity. It may well be argued that the cast of mind which led to the proposal, and

[33] Benito Ruano, *Orígenes del Problema Converso*, pp. 51–2; Alonso de Cartagena, *Defensorium Unitatis Christianae*, ed. Manuel Alonso (Madrid, 1943), p. 94.
[34] Manuel Nieto Cumplido, 'La revuelta contra los conversos de Córdoba en 1473', in *Homenaje a Antón de Montoro en el V Centenario de su Muerte* (Montoro, 1977), pp. 35–6.
[35] A. A. Sicroff, *Los Estatutos de Limpieza de Sangre. Controversias entre los Siglos XV y XVII* (Madrid, 1985); Pere Molas Ribalta, 'El exclusivismo en los gremios de la Corona de Aragón', in *Les Sociétés fermées dans le monde ibérique (XVIe–XVIIIe siècles). Définitions et problématique (Actes de la Table ronde des 8 et 9 février, 1985)* (Paris, 1986), pp. 69–70, 78; Claude Chauchadis, 'Les Modalités de la fermeture dans les confréries religieuses espagnoles (XVIe–XVIIIe siècle)', in *Les Sociétés fermées*, pp. 83–105.

eventually the acceptance, of the Inquisition as a 'solution' to the perceived 'problem' of 'false' conversion itself betokens deep insecurity among the official leaders of Christianity in Spain, both secular and ecclesiastical. The inquisitors might pursue ordinary members of the population for their doubts and scepticism about Christianity in particular, and often organized religion in general, but the similar doubts of the leaders themselves were not to be questioned. At least in the early years of the new Inquisition, 'show trials' of prominent intellectuals, for example, were not in fashion. Diego Rodríguez Lucero was thus allowed to burn dozens of *conversos*, as Inquisitor of Córdoba in the early 1500s, but lost his job when he started a process for 'Judaizing' against the saintly Hieronymite friar and archbishop of Granada, Hernando de Talavera, who had formerly been Queen Isabella's confessor.[36]

However, the trials carried out in Córdoba by Lucero serve to illustrate not only the tyranny of an inquisitor, but also the important economic role of the *conversos*. This phenomenon not only helped to create the envy and fear which, in large part, led to the setting up of the tribunal in the first place, but also helped to bring about the expulsion of those Jews who refused to convert. The existing *conversos* played a large, indeed essential, part in the commercial and industrial life of Spain's major towns. As Kamen has correctly stated, it was the flight of the *conversos* and their capital from the threat of the Inquisition in the decade after 1480 which in reality seriously threatened the national economy.[37] This was certainly the case in Barcelona and Seville, for example, as well as Córdoba. There, although zeal for capital accumulation seems to have been less strong than in developing ports, and particularly Seville, the contracts for the reletting of cathedral properties vacated by *conversos* after the 1473 riots reveal artisans of various kinds, silk-merchants, a draper, a tavern-keeper, and a surgeon, among the former tenants. Lucero's trials between 1500 and 1508 provide what seems to be a fair cross-section of the city's *converso* community, which lived and worked around the Calle de la Feria, where the two annual trade fairs were held. Lucero's victims included two drapers, various merchants and traders, five money-changers, four silversmiths, a candlemaker, and the female relatives of textile workers,

[36] Edwards, 'Religious faith and doubt', pp. 13–25; 'Debate: religious faith, doubt and atheism, a reply to C. John Sommerville', *PaP*, 128 (1990), pp. 155–61; and 'Trial of an inquisitor: the dismissal of Diego Rodríguez Lucero, inquisitor of Córdoba, in 1508', *JEH*, 37 (1986), pp. 240–57.

[37] Henry Kamen, 'The Mediterranean and the expulsion of Spanish Jews in 1492', *PaP*, 119 (1988), p. 50.

chairmakers, other craftsmen, and a tailor.[38] A similar picture emerges from inquisitorial records in other cities, but it is also necessary to add that certain *conversos*, as well as achieving cathedral and other ecclesiastical benefices, also acquired a high political profile, which, as in Córdoba in 1473, often worked to their disadvantage. Typically, support for, or opposition to, *conversos* became the respective political stances, at least on the surface, of the pairs of noble-led factions which fought each other for control of the major cities of central and southern Spain in the mid-fifteenth century, and which Isabella and Ferdinand sought, in the late 1470s, to curb, not least by the introduction of the Inquisition.[39]

The Holy Office, then, was not simply a religious instrument, but also an important manifestation of royal control. None the less, when it comes to the expulsion edict of 1492, it is hard to deny that the notions of religion held by the rulers and their advisers played the crucial role, and among these advisers the most important were the inquisitors. The edict of 31 March 1492, which gave Jews in all Ferdinand and Isabella's kingdoms four months either to be baptized or to dispose of their immovable property and leave, has often been seen, since the sixteenth century, as a catastrophic blow to Spain's economy as well as its social diversity. None the less, writers who witnessed the departure of Jews, such as the Andalusian priest-chronicler Andrés Bernáldez, were convinced that the refugees were a drain on society. He asserted that 'all their wish was a job in the town, and to earn their living without much labour, sitting on their bottoms.'[40] However, by the year 1600 the 'decline' of Spain was being blamed by many on the decision to expel what was now seen as a large and industrious community. Such views have been repeated in modern general works, such as those of Vicens Vives and Lynch.[41] In reality, though, far fewer Jews left than has traditionally been supposed—perhaps as few as 70,000, rather than 100–200,000, out of an estimated peninsular

[38] Kamen, *Inquisition and Society*, pp. 31, 35–6; John Edwards, '"Development" and "underdevelopment" in the western Mediterranean: the case of Córdoba and its region in the late fifteenth and early sixteenth centuries', *Mediterranean Historical Review*, 2 (1987), p. 36, and 'Trial of an inquisitor', p. 249.

[39] Angus MacKay, 'Popular movements and pogroms in fifteenth-century Castile', *PaP*, 55 (1972), pp. 35–67; John Edwards, *Christian Córdoba. The City and its Region in the Late Middle Ages* (Cambridge, 1982), pp. 131–63, 183–4.

[40] Luis Suárez Fernández, ed., *Documentos acerca de la Expulsión de los Judíos* (Valladolid, 1964), pp. 392–3; Andrés Bernáldez, *Memorias del Reinado de los Reyes Católicos*, ed. M. Gómez-Moreno and Juan de Mata Carriazo (Madrid, 1963), p. 54.

[41] Kamen, 'The Mediterranean', p. 54; Jaume Vicens Vives, *Aproximación a la Historia de España* (Barcelona, 1976), p. 103; John Lynch, *Spain under the Habsburgs*, 2 vols (Oxford, 1964–9), 1, p. 15.

population of at least eight million—and those who left were of restricted economic importance. This is in no way to underestimate the personal tragedies and difficulties of those who departed, or the importance of the Sephardic diaspora for the future of world Jewry, but it is simply to suggest that the economic factor is of relatively little importance in assessing the motives and the consequences of the expulsion.[42] It is quite clear that, on the contrary, the purpose of the edict was conversion not expulsion. The publication of the document was accompanied by preaching campaigns directed at Jews, and the text itself included the provision that those who left, were baptized abroad, or else returned to border towns in Castile itself for baptism might be allowed to return and repossess their old property. Many took advantage of this offer and received royal assistance in rebuilding their old lives, but now as Christians.[43] The hand of the Inquisition may be detected in the expulsion edict itself, given that its text is almost identical to that of a draft prepared previously by the inquisitors. Also, local tribunals had earlier asked publicly for, and secured at least in part, smaller-scale expulsions in the dioceses of Seville and Cádiz in 1483, in the Aragonese diocese of Albarracín in 1486, and in the conquered parts of the kingdom of Granada in 1491.[44] Even if these measures were not entirely successful, they clearly reveal inquisitorial policy, and it is virtually certain that the Inquisition deliberately staged, in 1491, the chaotic trial of the Jewish and *converso* group which was accused both of Host desecration and of the ritual murder by crucifixion of the 'Holy Child' of La Guardia, in New Castile. Not only was this Spain's only ritual murder trial, but it purported to demonstrate to all onlookers, with perfect timing, the validity of the conclusion to which the Inquisition had come during its first ten years of existence, that the survival of fully Jewish life in Spain would permanently prevent the assimilation of the converts to Christian society. Typically, there was actually no lost child and no body, but the story

---

[42] Miguel Angel Ladero Quesada, 'Le Nombre des juifs dans la Castille du XVe siècle', in *Proceedings of the Sixth World Congress of Jewish Studies (Jerusalem, 1973)* (Jerusalem, 1975), 2, p. 47; Edwards, *The Jews*, p. 34; Kamen, *Spain, 1469–1714*, p. 42 (in both 1983 and 1991 edns); *Inquisition and Society*, p. 16; and 'The Mediterranean', p. 44.

[43] Suárez Fernández, ed., *Documentos*, pp. 392–3; John Edwards, 'Jews and *conversos* in the region of Soria and Almazán: departures and returns', *Pe'amim* (Jerusalem), forthcoming (in Hebrew).

[44] Haim Beinart, 'La Inquisición española y la expulsión de los judíos de Andalucía', in *Andalucía y sus Judíos* (Córdoba, 1986), pp. 51–81; Kamen, 'The Mediterranean', p. 52; L. P. Harvey, *Islamic Spain, 1250 to 1500* (Chicago and London, 1990), p. 321.

served its purpose, and the government acceded to the Inquisition's demand.[45]

Why, then, the Spanish Inquisition, and what kind of Spain did it create? The answer to the first question has already effectively emerged from the preceding discussion. The political, social, and economic difficulties of the kingdoms that Isabella and Ferdinand inherited were plain for all to see at the time, and have been extensively analysed since. However, the threats to the cohesion of fifteenth-century Spanish society—which might be seen by a modern scholar in terms, for example, of faction-fighting among the upper nobility, with, as spoils, royal patronage at Court and in the country as a whole, or of climatic and other material difficulties—were perceived at the time, by Jews and Christians alike, as symptoms of a moral decay which could only be cured by more whole-hearted adherence to religious orthodoxy, whether by using the Torah to recreate, in a sense, the world as it should be, or by bringing the whole world into the spiritual, and physical, Body of Christ.[46] Political power, and not least the Inquisition itself, apparently gave the victory to the Christian self-perception, but without adopting an impertinent (and false) sense of superiority over the follies of past ages, which would be quite inappropriate, given the 'achievements' of our own century, from the Somme through Auschwitz to the Gulf, it is impossible to avoid the conclusion from this distance that the orthodox religious mindset, of whatever kind, simply did not correspond to empirical and pragmatic reality. However, in order to indicate the practical limitations on the effectiveness of the Inquisition and even of 'purity of blood' statutes in early modern Spain, let the following illustration serve. It emerges from those individual family histories which ultimately compose the histories of grander entities, such as churches, synagogues, and universities, and illustrates the pitfalls involved in trying to exclude from office or privilege those descended from Jews, Muslims, or Christian heretics.

The archives of the Toledo Inquisition record, in 1575, a description of

---

[45] Maurice Kriegel, 'La Prise d'une décision: l'expulsion des juifs d'Espagne en 1492', *Revue Historique*, 260 (1978), pp. 83–5; Fidel Fita, 'La verdad sobre el martirio del Santo Niño de La Guardia, o sea el proceso y quema (16 noviembre 1491) del judío Juçe Franco en Avila', *Boletín de la Real Academia de la Historia*, 11 (1887), pp. 7–134.

[46] Lionel Kochan, *Jews, Idols and Messiahs. The Challenge from History* (Oxford, 1990), pp. 5–7.

the coat of arms of a lesser noble family (*hidalgos*) in the small New Castilian town of Daimiel. Their shield contained:

> A portico with four pillars, and on the portico a cross, a wolf, an eagle
> and four ermines. The four columns are the columns of the faith, on
> a blue field, symbol of the zeal they had for it [the Catholic faith]; the
> cross, the banner under which they came out from obscurity; the
> eagle flying over the wolf, the guardian of the Christian faith [the
> eagle being the emblem of St John the Evangelist]; the wolf, the
> pagan sect [Islam] which had been destroyed; the ermines, symbols of
> the purity [*limpieza*] that they had possessed for all time, and retained
> when they reconquered Spain from the Moorish horde, for the
> ermine dies rather than surrender, and the Oviedo [family] have put
> nothing before their faith and liberty. These arms were given to them
> when the *infante* Don Pelayo reconquered Spain.[47]

On the face of it, then, the Oviedo family went back to the very origin of
the Christian myth of the medieval Reconquest of Spain. However, closer
investigation reveals that the Oviedo were, in fact, *judeoconversos*, whose
origins were so notorious that when the Inquisition came to their town in
the 1540s they did not dare affirm their *limpieza* in the presence of an
inquisitor. However, in the period from 1538 to 1545 they had cheerfully
helped the Holy Office to investigate and undermine a *morisco* community in Daimiel. The four Oviedo brothers, represented by the four pillars
in their shield, had obtained their status by means of a process of *hidalguía*
against the local council, but their arms say more about deceit, and the
willingness of sixteenth-century Spanish authorities, including the
Inquisition itself, to condone it, than about the Asturian kingdom and its
eighth-century ruler Don Pelayo. But then, as the writer V. S. Pritchett
said a few years ago:

> People are always larger than they appear to be. There's more to be
> said about them than one thinks. You have to find out what that is.
> People don't react, as it were, conventionally. They mystify each
> other, and themselves, and this is important to record.[48]

University of Birmingham

[47] Dedieu, *L'Administration de la foi*, p. 337.
[48] V. S. Pritchett, interview in *The Sunday Times*, 10 July 1988.

THE GOOD OF THE CHURCH,
THE GOOD OF THE STATE:
THE POPES AND JEWISH MONEY

by KENNETH R. STOW

I N the early thirteenth century the papal cardinal legate in France, Robert of Courson, painted the business of lending in wholly Utopian colours. Should the pope decree, he said, that lending must cease and all men must earn their sustenance by the sweat of their brow, 'Thus would be removed all usurers, all factious men and all robbers; thus would charity flourish and the fabric of the churches again be builded; and thus would all be brought back again to its pristine state.'[1] The prospect that acting to eliminate lending would so smoothly result in social perfection, one might expect, should have propelled the Catholic Church, led by the popes, to have made a frontal assault on lending, especially that carried on by Jews. It did not. Only more than four centuries later, in 1682, did the papacy decide to end a policy of actually condoning Jewish lending, and only then did it irrevocably close down the Jewish loan banks in the Papal State.

Why the popes refrained from such decisive action until this late date is the question I would now like to investigate. The answer, I believe, will be at once surprising, but also revealing—revealing about the popes and their relationship to the Jews, about the nature of the Papal State itself, and also about the transition of the Jews from a medieval to an early modern reality. Properly to appreciate these issues, nevertheless, we must begin our enquiry in the thirteenth not, as yet, the seventeenth century.

Returning to Robert of Courson, the fact is that in his own day his views were considered to be extreme, and for holding them he was cautioned by the Pope.[2] With reference to lending by Jews, the formal Church was not receptive to his argument. Nor did it act on the plea of Cardinal Odo of Sully, who insisted that all Jewish Christian commercial interchange be forthwith halted, since this was the only way ultimately to

---

[1] Cited in John Mundy, *Europe in the High Middle Ages* (New York, 1973), p. 175.
[2] See K. R. Stow, 'Papal and royal attitudes toward Jewish lending in the thirteenth century', *Association for Jewish Studies Review*, 6 (1981), pp. 161–84, esp. p. 176.

stop lending and 'usury', that is, interest.[3] The thirteenth-century Church rather tolerated modest interest rates charged by Jews. Those contemporaries who were most attentive to preachers like Odo and Robert were not churchmen, but the kings of England of France, who had been troubled about Jewish capital since the time of Louis VII, nearly a century before. By capital, of course—since this is the Middle Ages—I mean the money that Jews lent; we are not yet talking about moneys invested in the development of industry, or even deposit banking.

On the eve of the Second Crusade, in 1146, Louis VII readily accepted, and even went beyond, the challenge of Bernard of Clairvaux,[4] that papal legislation concerning interest be applied to Jewish as well as to Christian lenders, and forced the Jews to return the interest paid them by crusaders. The pope, Eugenius III, had himself not thought of suggesting even a moratorium. It did not yet occur to him that he might try to regulate Jewish loans. Bernard, too, did not consider that the Church might directly intervene. Nobody took seriously the suggestion of Abbot Peter the Venerable of Cluny that Jewish money was the product of theft and hence could arbitrarily be distrained. In fact, it was only in 1198, fifty years later, that the first ecclesiastical regulation of Jewish lending was made. In the meantime, Philip Augustus confiscated Jewish loans in 1182, and Louis VIII restricted Jewish financial activity in the early thirteenth century. No king acted with such fervour against Jewish lending as did Louis IX, St Louis. Jewish usury, he said, was his problem, a personal problem. As a crusading king, his task was to purify his land. But more than that, Louis clearly—as a most recent study has re-emphasized on every other page—linked his policy of lending to one of conversion.[5] Simply put, by applying severe pressure on the Jews, one broke their will. Louis also made Jews listen to the conversionary sermons of the recent convert Paul Christian, whose words, one Jewish commentator wrote, were 'like stones thrown at us'.[6] Louis proposed, furthermore, inserting Jews into commercial occupations, artisanry, and farming. Theirs was to be a complete rehabilitation. Of course, the proposal was not a realistic one, and the study just mentioned has also suggested that Louis wanted

---

[3] Stow, 'Papal and royal attitudes', p. 176.
[4] K. R. Stow, *The Church and Neutral History* [Hebrew] *Iyyunim be-historiografiah* (Jerusalem, 1988), pp. 101–13.
[5] Wm. Ch. Jordan, *The French Monarchy and the Jews: from Philip Augustus to the Last Capetians* (Philadelphia, 1989), esp. ch. 9.
[6] Cited in Robert Chazan, *Church, State, and Jew in the Middle Ages* (New York, 1980), p. 263.

these occupations to be limited solely to commerce carried on between Jews—as though Louis were taking Odo of Sully literally.

But there was also residual ambivalence. The Jews did not stop lending, since Louis did not possess the administrative mechanisms needed to enforce his policies. Therefore, he compromised, repeatedly seizing and inventorying the Jews' credits (a *captio*), cancelling the interest, and collecting the principal for himself. This device brought Philip IV, Louis' grandson, a handsome windfall in 1306, when he expelled the Jews.[7] Nevertheless, the expulsion's purpose was not to collect these moneys, which were, after all, enormously less than what Philip could have collected from resuming, regulating, and taxing lending. Rather, the Jews were expelled because the programme of conversion had failed, and because lending could not be halted. This was a very medieval solution to a very medieval problem. One purified the *corpus mysticum*, as French kings liked to call their kingdom, by cutting off the impure limb, that is, the Jews. This action also made political sense, since many French counts were still willing to put up with Jewish lending—at obvious royal expense. It was thus preferable to ensure that nobody drank from the well by literally drying the well up. Eventually this meant by resorting to expulsion.

Similar motives and actions may be ascribed to Edward I of England, for whom lending caused inordinate problems, mostly because royal favourites were buying up unredeemed Jewish bonds at discounts. And the result—without going into laborious detail—was that land was being transferred and concentrated in the wrong hands. Senior barons were furious at losing choice estates; lesser ones were up in arms because they were losing the little they had. The King was further embarrassed, since the unwanted purchasers were often his mother, his wife, and large monasteries.[8] The figure 'up in arms' is no loose one either. Jewish loans had generated violence at York in 1190,[9] in the civil war ending in the Magna Carta in 1215—the text is quite explicit—and once again during the baronial revolt against Henry III in 1264. If Edward eventually claimed that he was expelling the Jews because their lending was upsetting the right order and the *communis utilitas*, he must be taken at his word. This was no excuse, nor metaphor, but an accurate analysis of reality, or at

---

[7] Jordan, *French Monarchy*, pp. 200–13.

[8] See, e.g., R. C. Stacey, '1240–1260: a watershed in Anglo-Jewish relations?' *HR*, 61 (1988), pp. 144–6.

[9] R. B. Dobson, *The Jews of Medieval York and the Massacre of March 1190 — Borthwick Papers*, no. 45 (York, 1974), p. 37.

least in the way in which, with faulty medieval economic understanding, that reality was being perceived. 'Purity' and Utopias, Edward understood, might be worldly as well as apocalyptic goals, in this case the Utopia of a stable kingdom. For it was clear to him that the effects and perceptions of Jewish lending were enormously disruptive of governmental functions.

Yet, like Louis IX, Edward also predicated his actions on attaining spiritual ends. For one thing, the Franciscan Archbishop of Canterbury, John Peckham, had in 1285 petitioned the King, wanting to know when Edward was going, at long last, to ensure that lending ceased. Edward sincerely answered that he was doing the best he could.[10] Edward, like Louis IX, also tried to move Jews into alternative professions. But he, too, failed, probably aware that this was no more realistic a goal than was seeking the Jews' conversion, which Edward tried to do, ordering sermons, and even founding a house for converts. Yet more than one convert reverted to Judaism. Indeed, the fear of such so-called apostasy has been named a possible ingredient in the recipe for expulsion.[11] It combined with complaints about Jewish lending and about manipulations of the King's judicial monopolies, including that over the Jews' justice, to make of expulsion what all English contemporaries deemed to be a salutary act.

* * *

The issues here have been considerably syncopated, but a number of points should be clear. First, that Jewish money was perceived in both real and mythical terms: the real ones were that through borrowing people sometimes lost their wealth, and that these losses might raise the spectre of political havoc; the mythical ones were that the source of these losses was considered not to be bad management, climactic conditions, or simply misfortune, but interest itself, especially that charged by the Jews. The way to deal with the myth was a radical one, namely, to halt not only Jewish lending, but also to make the Jews (and, hence, Judaism itself) disappear, preferably through their conversion—or at least their commercial rehabilitation—but, if not, through their expulsion.

As for the myth's dimensions, we note the following: in 1290 a charge that Parisian Jews had desecrated a Host was predicated on the story of a

---

[10] In F. M. Powicke and C. R. Cheney, *Councils and Synods, with Other Documents Relating to the English Church II A.D. 1205–1313*, 2 vols (Oxford, 1964), 2, pp. 955, 959, 961–2, 963.

[11] P. R. Hyams, 'The Jewish Minority in Medieval England', *JJS*, 25 (1974), pp. 276–7; citing F. D. Logan, 'Thirteen London Jews and conversion: problems of apostasy in the 1280s', *BIHR*, 45 (1973), pp. 214–29.

Jewish lender who persuaded a Christian woman client to steal a Host for him to mutilate. This tale widely circulated and was immortalized in a six-part painting by Paolo Uccello in the fifteenth century.[12] More subtly, Jews were accused of ritual murder. A German depiction of one of the most famous of such accusations, that about Simon of Trent, in Northern Italy, in 1475, portrays Simon as being tied down and bled to death, much in the way that Christians sometimes slaughter pigs.[13] Other depictions show Simon being crucified like Jesus, with the Jews once again collecting his blood (as was, in fact, a standard iconographical image in portrayals of the Crucifixion). Two generations earlier, the Franciscan Bernardino da Siena, one of the most active friars in the campaign to establish sources of free credit (in distinction to allegedly dear credit extended by Jews), had compared money to the 'warmth of the town', that is, to its blood, which flows to the heart and keeps it alive. The Jews, however, took ('sucked') this money and carried it away from the heart to a 'gangrenous' limb, that is, to themselves.[14] The link is an obvious one between this image and those used to depict Simon of Trent's purported agonies. Indeed, eight centuries earlier, Bishop Ildefonse of Toledo had called the Jews rebels and criminals, a 'bad limb' that ought to be amputated.[15]

Jewish lending thus was repeatedly and internationally identified with Jewish acts of homicide against Christian society. Yet even though the originators of these 'life and death' images—in contexts that had nothing to do with lending—seem to have been principally ecclesiastics,[16] the truth is that in the height of the Middle Ages, those most ready to accept their validity were the Jews' secular rulers. The words of Ephraim of Bonn, condemning Louis VII, and those of Meir ben Simeon of Narbonne, condemning Louis IX, make this abundantly clear.[17] Indeed, their writings either by hint, or directly, exculpate ecclesiastical

---

[12] On Uccello, see Pierre Francastel, 'Un mystère parisien illustré par Uccello: Le Miracle de l'hostie d'Urbino', *Revue Archéologique*, (1952), pp. 180–91. And see the comments in Solomon Grayzel, *The Church and the Jews in the Thirteenth Century. II 1254–1314* (New York and Detroit, 1990), pp. 197–9.

[13] Joshua Trachtenberg, *The Devil and the Jews* (New Haven, 1943), p. 8; S. W. Baron, *A Social and Religious History of the Jews*, 2nd edn rev. (New York, 1952ff.), 2, p. 137.

[14] Cited in Leon Poliakov, *Jewish Bankers and the Holy See, from the Thirteenth to the Seventeenth Century*, tr. M. Kochan (London, 1977), p. 142.

[15] Bernhard Blumenkranz, *Les Auteurs Chretiens latins du moyen âge sur les Juifs et le Judaisme* (Paris, 1963), p. 120.

[16] See W. A. Meeks and R. L. Wilkens, *Jews and Christians in Antioch in the First Four Centuries of the Common Era* (Missoula, 1978).

[17] See n. 4, above, and K. R. Stow, *The '1007 Anonymous' and Papal Sovereignty: Jewish Perceptions of the Papacy and Papal Policy in the High Middle Ages* (Cincinnati, 1984), pp. 24–6.

authorities. Ephraim made a point of praising Bernard of Clairvaux, whom he ought to have cited, and Meir ben Simeon queried the Archbishop of Narbonne: why did he not adopt the Pope, rather than the King, as the arbiter of his actions *vis-à-vis* Jewish money?

*   *   *

Ephraim and Meir were also objectively correct. As has been said, the Church's role is a surprising one. Indeed, when the popes closed Jewish banks in 1682, they were, at least partially, following a precedent set four hundred years earlier by French and English kings—and Spanish ones, too, for that matter. One seventeenth-century advocate of closing the banks explicitly called upon the popes to emulate this royal example.[18]

In the thirteenth century the popes were quite hesitant on the subject of lending. The Jews, they conceded, had certain rights, guaranteed by tradition and canon law. Did not, then, the acceptance of the Jews and the freedom allowed them to practise Judaism also entitle them to lend money at interest? This is no idle speculation. In the seventeenth century, if not earlier, lawyers hired by Roman Jews to argue their case were saying this in just so many words.[19] Practice, too, backs up the claim. We know that in the thirteenth century, ecclesiastical courts were firmly allowing Jews to collect a rate of about 20 per cent. One bishop, of Minden, in Germany, said in 1270 that this was indeed the licitly-charged rate. The popes seem to have been theoretically allowing interest, too. They never did so openly, which was and remained always against the law. Making money from money itself was believed to be permitted only as an act of war. Yet, in the papal letters issued regulating interest in general—not only, nor specifically, that of the Jews—what the popes did was to prohibit usury entirely to Christian lenders, but effectively to allow Jews to collect what was described as *non immoderatasve usuras* (not immoderate usury).[20]

Canon lawyers had their reservations. 'Immoderate interest', they said, meant any interest whatsoever. There were to be no chinks in the prohibitional fabric. But statutes debated in the law schools are not necessarily those applied in practice. The papal doctrine also received theological support. Thomas Aquinas, not only in his practical advice to the Duchess

[18] Jewish Theological Seminary, New York [hereafter J.T.S.] mic. 9486, fol. 6.
[19] Ibid., fol. 9.
[20] Stow, 'Papal and royal attitudes', p. 165.

of Brabant, which is well known, but also in his *Summa Theologiae*, in discussing usury in general—again, not specifically that collected by Jews—seems to have conceded the papal point.[21]

Beginning with the fourteenth century, and into the fifteenth, the popes pressed their permissive doctrine to the limit, frequently with the help of legal support given by experts hired by towns or by the Jews themselves. The result was a system of papal licensing, which enabled Jews to move out of their old haunts in central and southern Italy—or to descend from France and Germany—to become not major lenders in major centres but the providers of small capital and public financial liquidity in mid-size cities: for example, Siena, when Christian lenders left for more fertile fields.[22] Very few Jewish bankers in fact became, like the Volterra or da Pisa, extremely wealthy. As for the precise origins of the papal licensing system, they are unknown. But what the licences did was to skirt the problem of actually permitting lending at interest by absolving local rulers or communal bodies from any guilt for allowing this sin to occur. For Italian Jewish lenders were violating not only the principle of taking no interest, but the canon of the 1311 Council of Vienne, which prohibited settlement in a place exclusively to lend.

This system thrived even in the popes' own territories. One historian has exuberantly ventured that the popes were to some extent the Jews' silent partners.[23] They certainly did recognize the necessity of lending. For one thing, lending provided liquidity, especially to governments, which often put a clause about the loans the Jews would make the community into the *condotta* contract they made with entering Jewish bankers. It was explicitly to secure such public loans that the community of Siena, for example, asked the pope to license lending within its realms.[24] The positive response this request received was most likely stimulated by a papal realization that towns in the papal realms had similar needs, if not the papal Curia itself. In papal towns, no less than in others, Jewish lending provided small loans of various kinds. Jews were not financing industrial-type ventures, but they were involved in what may fairly be

---

[21] Poliakov, *Bankers*, pp. 25–7.

[22] See, e.g., Sofia Boesch, 'Il comune di Siena e il prestito ebraico nei secoli xiv e xv', in *Aspetti e problemi della presenza ebraica nell'Italia centro-settentrionale* (Rome, 1983), pp. 175–221.

[23] Ariel Toaff, 'Jewish banking in central Italy, thirteenth through fifteenth centuries', in H. Beinart, ed., (Hebrew) *Jews in Italy* (Jerusalem, 1988), p. 118; 'Gli Ebrei Romani e il Commercio del Denaro nei Comuni dell'Italia Centrale alla Fine del Duecento', *Italia Judaica*, 1 (Rome, 1983), p. 191; but the response of Robert Bonfil, 'Jewish lenders in Italy during the Renaissance: an economic force?' *Pa'amim*, 41 (1990), pp. 58–64.

[24] Boesch, 'Il comune', pp. 206–8.

called deposit banking, in that Christians often gave Jews money to lend out, for which the Christians received a return.[25] Jews also borrowed money, at interest, from Christians. This was not, however, a system invented by Jews. We know precisely the rates paid by Christian bankers in Florence for such deposits from the fourteenth century onward.[26]

The actual story of Jewish lending activity in Italy, of the banks that opened, and where, is too well known to need repeating.[27] The same applies to a recounting of the violent attack mounted on that lending by the Franciscan Friars. These friars, it bears adding, were good economists, at least for their day. They knew well that loans were essential. But interest they could not tolerate, and in reaction they began to preach a system of 'Monte di Pietà' Christian loan funds, which would replace the Jewish banks by giving very small, interest-free loans to the poor. Recently, fashion among some Italian historians has been to isolate this attempt to provide interest-free loans from the mythical rhetoric accompanying it.[28] Yet, it was not merely interest that the Franciscans attacked. What especially bothered them was interest taken by Jews. For the Franciscans, what the Jews were doing was subverting Christian society, sucking the blood (their phrase) from the Christian polity, and destroying salvation. The Utopian terms of a Robert of Courson about usury's corrupting effects had been resurrected. The Franciscan cure was to eliminate all usury, following the royal example, by getting rid of the Jews themselves.

*　　*　　*

It is from this vantage point that we must question what happened in the Papal State from about the middle of the fifteenth century. On the one hand, in papal Umbria, the Franciscan centre, pressure generated by the friars' preaching may have indirectly 'coerced' large numbers of the Jews to convert.[29] The popes themselves did not change streams. Nor did they do so in 1555, the year the Roman ghetto was ordered to be constructed by

[25] Brian Pullan, *Rich and Poor in Renaissance Venice* (Cambridge, Mass., 1971), pp. 533–4; Poliakov, *Bankers*, pp. 63–4.
[26] Sidney Homer, *A History of Interest Rates, 2000 B.C. to the Present* (New Brunswick, 1963), pp. 99–132.
[27] See the works listed in Bonfil, 'Jewish Lenders'.
[28] See, e.g., Vittorino Meneghin, *Bernardino da Feltre e i monti di pietà* (Vicenza, 1974), and M. G. Muzzarelli, *Ebrei e cittá d'Italià in etá di transizione: Il Caso di Cesena dal XIV al XVI secolo* (Bologna, 1983); but see the rebuttal of R. Segre 'Bernardino da Feltre, i Monti die Pietà e i banchi ebraici', *Rivista Storica Italiana*, 90 (1978), pp. 818–33.
[29] See Ariel Toaf, *Il vino e la carne* (Bologna, 1988), p. 185.

Paul IV,[30] and even though it has recently been documented that the policies of Paul IV were influenced by Franciscan thinking, especially as it had penetrated the papal inquisition.[31] In fact, however much the popes sought to discipline and control the Jews, they did no more than lower the established interest rate from 24 to 18 per cent.

Other papal actions seemed to expand Jewish lending possibilities. In Rome itself, the number of Jewish bankers grew markedly in the sixteenth century, rising from twenty to seventy. From 1585, Sixtus V started giving hundreds of licences to open, or reopen, banks in dozens of localities in Lazio and elsewhere.[32] There was a Monte di Pietà in Rome from 1539, but it began tentatively, giving only the smallest loans.[33] The age of the worldly Renaissance papacy had passed, yet the 'monastic', rigoristic popes of the Counter-Reformation knew they had to strengthen their secular domain, which is indeed what the Papal State had by this time become.[34] This meant allowing Jewish banks to operate, if only to service the poor; or so the popes formally justified their consent.

Why, then, were the banks closed in 1682? From about 1668, a debate grew in Roman ecclesiastical circles about the future of Jewish banking. This debate continued on and off until 1682.[35] The participants included figures as illustrious as Cardinal G. B. de Luca, the foremost legist of his day, and a favourite of Pope Innocent XI, the reforming pope who actually ordered the banks to be closed. De Luca's participation was perhaps at Jewish instance. His arguments were traditional in the extreme. Lending, he said, was illegal. Popes could only use ruses to permit it. But lending was also like a dangerous medicine administered to save a person gravely ill. It was as such alone that it might continue.[36]

De Luca was answered in equally traditional terms. Those in favour of closing the banks said that Christians were to be considered 'brothers' of Jews, to whom even Jewish law prohibited lending. The notion that the Church, because it tolerated Jewish rites, was obligated to tolerate Jewish lending was also rebuffed by citing the gloss on the canon *Post*

---

[30] See on these events, K. R. Stow, *Catholic Thought and Papal Jewry Policy, 1555–1593* (New York, 1977).

[31] See Paolo Simoncelli, 'Inquisizione Romana e Riforma in Italia', *Rivista Storica Italiana*, 100 (1988), pp. 5–125.

[32] See here E. Loevinson, 'La Concession de banques de prêtes aux Juifs par les papes', *REJ*, 92 (1932), pp. 1–30; 93 (1933), pp. 27–52, 157–78; 94 (1934), pp. 57–72, 167–83; 95 (1935), pp. 23–43.

[33] Jean Delumeau, *Vie economique et sociale de Rome* (Paris, 1957–9), p. 493.

[34] See Paolo Prodi, *Il Sovrano Pontefice* (Roma, 1982).

[35] J.T.S., mic. 9486, *passim*.

[36] Ibid., fol. 62.

miserabilem—one of the original texts governing usury—to the effect that only those Jewish rites which 'offend God' are tolerated, not those against one's 'neighbour'.[37]

Most interesting about this interchange was de Luca's avoidance of that which he normally emphasized, namely, the necessary harmony in the Papal State between spiritual and secular goals. In the event, by invoking only traditional themes and remaining silent about the benefit of lending to the State, de Luca was being prudent. In his day, he knew, Jewish lending was being viewed not as a positive economic factor, but rather as a hindrance to both the political state, as well as to the papacy's spiritual goals.

Responses by an anonymous author and by Bernardino Iacobelli, both doctors of law attached to the papal Curia, explain why this was so.

> It is said [wrote the anonymous] that it would be true Christian piety, were the Jews in no way indulged; indeed, the Jews should be prevented from growing wealthy as much as possible, rigorously in fact, not that they should be coerced to the Faith, but so that an obstacle to their conversion be removed. As [the canonist] Gratian [long ago] put it: If the sons of the Free woman [Christians] may be provoked to doing good through *flagella* of tribulation, how much more should *servi* and the sons of the handmaiden [Jews, on both counts] be incited to converting by withdrawing from them the *amplissimo atque otiosissimo* impediment of usury.[38]

The author goes on to stress the need to convert the Jews, citing at once traditional theology, but also the 1555 bull of Paul IV, *Cum nimis absurdum*.

It was *Cum nimis absurdum* which mandated that the ghetto be built, and it was this bull which also initiated a new era in papal policy toward the Jews. As our anonymous author indicates, conversion was at the centre of that policy, one of whose cornerstones was its tactics. Jews were not to be wooed sweetly to Christianity, as Augustine had argued—and so too had the popes as late as the early sixteenth century; rather, they were to be brought to the baptismal font through what two Camuldulese monks in 1513 called 'pious lashes'. It was this doctrine to which the anonymous was

---

[37] J.T.S., mic. 9486, fol. 9: *Decretales*, 5.19.12 (cols 814–15).
[38] Ibid., fol. 95: 'Quod si filii liberae . . . per flagella tribulationum sunt provocandi ad bonum, quanto magis servi et filii ancillae per laboriosam inopiam, incitandi sunt ad conversionem, subtracto praecipuo ad eam impedimento usurarum . . .'.

referring when he spoke of the *flagella tribulationum*, as well as to the teachings, in 1553, of the Jesuit Francisco de Torres, that Jews would return to the fold more easily should they be made to 'suck at husks' for sustenance.[39]

Yet why were these arguments applied to usury in 1670, not 1555? Most probably the reason was pragmatic. In 1555 poor Christians were still dependent on Jews for loans; the Roman Monte di Pietà was as yet no real alternative. Jewish lending was needed, and so it was allowed to continue, albeit at a reduced and much less profitable rate, and even though at times it served the middle class more than it did the poor. However, only twenty-five years after the policy of ghettos began, there is evidence that Jewish banking was being transformed. Many Jews, including bankers, had become poor and were converting.[40] Those who continued to lend were losing money. A defender of Jewish lending in the 1660s argued that the rate of 18 per cent, once expenses were discounted, often left the Jews with no profit whatsoever.[41]

By the later seventeenth century, Jewish banking had truly deteriorated. On the other hand, the Monte had grown enormously to become the richest institution in the Papal State.[42] By the time the Jews' banks were closed, its cycle of loans was 85 per cent of all those made at Rome, including those made to the poor. Original restrictions, limiting loans to very small amounts, had also been lifted. Loans made by the Monte were big enough (this time Iacobelli tells us) to allow nobles and prelates to frequent the institution and receive up to 2,000 sc. in credits. Additional credit problems were eliminated by the establishment of the Banco di Santo Spirito, a modern (or quasi-modern) banking institution, which secured its deposits by investing in the equivalent of government bonds. Needless to say, these institutions charged interest. But somehow this interest was explained away by the theory of *lucrum cessans* (that is, payment for loss of profit; a theory which in the case of a true investment bank holds some weight).[43]

An additional element reducing the need for Jewish lending was the rise of a new class of wealthy nobility in Rome, originally from commercial stock. As these people became wealthy, they bought land, emulating

---

[39] Cited in Stow, *Catholic Thought*, pp. 217–20.
[40] See K. R. Stow, *Taxation, Community and State* (Stuttgart, 1982), p. 70.
[41] J.T.S., mic. 9486, fol. 96.
[42] M. Petrocchi, *Roma nel Seicento* — *Storia di Rome*, 14 (Bologna, 1970), pp. 82–3.
[43] See John Gilchrist, *The Church and Economic Activity in the Middle Ages* (London, 1969), pp. 62–9.

older nobles, but also reducing their need for constant credit. With respect to surplus funds, it was safer to invest in *rentes*, called in the Papal State *luoghi di monti*—roughly equivalent to modern government bonds—which also paid reasonably high rates of interest, sometimes in perpetuity.[44]

In a word, by 1682, Jewish banking establishments, whether large or small, had become economically superfluous. None, in fact, had ever really been large. By now, only four of them still carried any weight, with capitalizations of 40,000 sc., 35,000, then, 15,000, and 12,000.[45] By way of comparison, a firm of would-be Roman Christian bankers, the Martelli—which was forced to set up shop in Amsterdam—had a capitalization varying from one-and-a-half to two-and-a-half times that of the largest Jewish bank.[46] As for the forty-six additional Jewish banks operating at Rome, their capital varied from 7,500 sc. to a mere 70 sc., with the average being about 3,700 sc. Even the once mighty Toscano family had been reduced to a modest 7,500 sc. The total of 150,000 sc. the Jewish banks were said to be lending annually was also only 15 per cent of the volume of approximately 850,000 sc. being lent by the Monte di Pietà. To the extent that Jews had ever supplied large credits—and that is moot[47]—or served as investment and deposit bankers (more than simply servicing the poor or acting as small-time intermediaries for Christian lenders) they were clearly 'incapable' of doing so any longer. Roman Jews, it should be added, did not leave records of having lent to the state; instead, they paid taxes, at a high yet not ferocious rate (at least not until the time of Paul IV).[48]

Yet, of themselves, these cogent practical reasons, even linked as they were to traditional, or novel, theological justifications, may not alone have led to the end of Jewish lending. Critical, rather, was the correspondence between reality and theories concerning both the State and the Jews that were maturing in the later seventeenth century. For those familiar with events at Venice in the sixteenth century, I note that I am not referring to that which Pullan has described as the pitting of traditionalist negative arguments about the evils of usury against the equally traditional Italian arguments of lending's necessity. Rather, the theoretical issues

---

[44] Petrocchi, *Roma*, p. 83.
[45] J.T.S., mic. 9486, fols 42–3.
[46] J. G. da Silva, *Banque et credit en Italie au XVIIe siècle* (Paris, 1969), pp. 102–3.
[47] See, again, Bonfil, 'Jewish lenders'.
[48] See Stow, *Taxation*, ch. 1.

involved were those of *raison d'état* and mercantilism, as the words of the curialists make clear.[49]

The curialist argument opens by referring explicitly to *ratio status*, which it defines as what promotes the *principis finem* and the *publicum civium . . . bonum*. It then continues:

> Let nobody think that what [has been] said is correct only according to the *Politicam Christianam*, which the pseudo-politicians call trivial, crass, obvious, and common. Rather, it is correct even according to what they call the noble, subtle, and the penetrating . . . Among the pseudo-politicos the art of ruling or the *ratio status* weighs nothing honestly, but what is useful for pursuing, protecting, and augmenting princely power is alone [considered] good, just, licit, and honest.[50]

Consequently, one must ask whether Jewish money benefits the State, on the grounds that according to *raison d'état*, princes derive their strength from persons and goods. In fact, the Jews' money is inconsequential. They bring in taxes worth only 2,600 sc. a year (other payments they make go to individuals alone), which is a drop in the bucket. These taxes are also composed of moneys the Jews effectively stole from poor Christians. Jewish taxes, too, weigh on these people. Indeed, if it is said that the end to lending will lead to 5,000 Jews (a figure too high by at leat 1,000) to desert the city—to the city's loss—let it be said that what will occur rather is the exit of 5,000 thieves.

But what about the Jews' *personas*? Here, too, they 'detract', rather than 'add'. For Jews were *quondam* paupers. And they worked in *fodinis, agris, mechanicis*. But

> now, made rich by leaving behind honest physical labour in favour of the basest luxury, the result has been that the Jews as persons are as useless and unproductive to the State as they are to the Prince; for neither in the halls of learning, the magistracy, the militia and commerce, nor in the workshops or in the fields does this people

---

[49] See Pullan, *Rich and Poor*, pp. 510–38, 576–8.

[50] J.T.S., mic. 9486, fol. 98: 'Ne quis autem existimet dicta duntaxat recte procedere secundum Politicam Christianam, quam Pseudo politici vocant politicam de trivio, crassam, communem, omnibus obviam, ideo examinanda sunt etiam secundum Politicam illam, quam ipsi vocant politicam de penetrali, subtilem, nobilem. . . . Apud pseudopoliticos scientia regnandi seu ratio status nihil honestate metitur; sed quicquid ad consequendam, tuendam, augendamque potentiam principis utile est, illud unum duntaxat est bonum, iustum, licitum atque honestum.'

contribute anything to the arts and the crafts . . . hence . . . the pope should force the Jews to labour with their hands.[51]

These were new arguments. They were not a refurbished version of the medieval call to set Jews to physical labour, nor were they a renewal of the often-made charge that Jewish taxes were indirectly paid by Christians. The thinking rests squarely on the mercantilist conception that all commerce and finance in the State was to serve the Prince. Jewish financial activities did not do so; therefore they were unproductive. (Neither Thomas Aquinas nor St Louis, in their discussions of Jewish economics, said anything of the kind.)

One could, however, argue, independently of the curialist discourse, that Jewish lending was halted in the 1680s for genuinely mercantilist reasons. Like the Martelli firm, which was forced to migrate to Amsterdam to ply its trade, Jewish lenders were no doubt perceived as competitors, interfering with the near-monopoly of the popes on all other financial institutions in the Papal State. And were not state monopolies a common mercantilist goal? It was no coincidence that after 1682, the Roman Monte di Pietà increased its volume of loans by the same amount previously lent by the Jews. To be sure, mercantilism normally favoured Jews, encouraging especially their role in international trade.[52] This encouragement was a prime reason for the settlement of Levantine (Portuguese) Jews in Livorno and even in Ancona, in the Papal State. But it must be remembered that a number of mercantilist theorists construed Jewish trade negatively. Simone Luzzatto's (1638) *Discorso* on Venetian Jews eloquently testifies to this fact.[53]

The curialist arguments against Jewish lending thus were timely and practical. Of equal importance, these arguments were identical with those being made contemporaneously by such as the French Abbé Claude

---

[51] J.T.S., mic. 9486, fol. 98. Once Jews worked 'in fodinis, in agris, in mechanicis . . . [but] at hoc tempore divites facti ob transitum ab honesto corporis labore ad otium turpissimi questus, eo evaserunt, ut Hebraeorum gens quoad personas, sit statui non minus quam principi prorsus inutilis et infructuosa mane neque in aula, neque in magistratu, neque in militia, neque in mercatura, neque in mechanicis, neque in agricultura auget civile corpus huiusmodi artium et officiorum . . . unde . . . papa iudaeos ad laborandum manibus cogat.'

[52] On this issue, see the articles by Benjamin Arbel, J. P. Filippini, Benjamin Ravid, and Renzo Toaff, in Simon Schwarzfuchs and Ariel Toaff, eds., *The Mediterranean and the Jews: Banking, Finance, and International Trade, Sixteenth to Seventeenth Centuries* (Ramat-Gan, 1988); and esp. Jonathan Israel, *European Jewry in the Age of Mercantilism, 1550–1750* (Oxford, 1985), chs 2 and 3.

[53] See Benjamin Ravid, *Economics and Toleration in Seventeenth Century Venice* (Jerusalem, 1978), pp. 39–93.

Fleury.[54] Fleury's theories allow us to understand the vague curialist claim that the Jews 'once' were poor agriculturalists. The *quondam*, as Fleury explained, was the biblical period, after which the Jews were corrupted by money. Now the time for their regeneration had arrived. Similar theories about Jewish 'improvement' and regeneration, including by changing their occupations, were going to be made throughout the Enlightenment period.

Yet the curialists intended their mercantilist argument to be seen as wholly compatible, complementary, and, more, interchangeable with traditional doctrines about usury, as well as with the hope of conversion, to which Iacobelli in particular addressed himself (saying that as long as Jewish lending was allowed, there were Jews who would refrain from converting because of their certain financial loss, and others, who, once converted, would apostatize. He even brought a concrete example of this happening).[55] Indeed, the progression (described by both the curialists and Fleury) of productive Jews, destructive, 'blood sucking', usurious ones, and, finally, regenerated Jews, in which the period of productivity was the biblical one, is an obvious derivative of the traditional Christian division of Jewish history: the positive, believing Jews of the Bible, the faithless deicides of the post-Christian period, and, finally, the reborn ones, through conversion, at the End of Days. Is it any wonder, then, that Iacobelli went on to say that the

> downfall of the Jews from the state of opulence in which they now exist (and its possible effects) . . . cannot be weighed against the evil that Christian borrowers in the Republic suffer; no uncertain, improbable, and unpredictable evil should ever outweigh in consideration a certain, probable, and wholly forseeable one, indeed an evil that now demonstrably exists . . . For the suffering of borrowers is rooted in the very nature of usury, just as the day is rooted in the Sun.[56]

Even in 1682, therefore, the end to Jewish lending could be idealized and perceived in terms of black and white, good and evil, that is, in terms

---

[54] See Arthur Hertzberg, *The French Enlightenment and the Jews* (New York, 1968), pp. 41–3; Israel, *European Jewry*, pp. 218, 232.

[55] J.T.S., mic., 9486, fol. 102.

[56] Ibid., fol. 96. 'Praecipitium Hebraeorum á Stato opulento, in quo nunc sunt . . . haudquaquam . . . praeponderare debeat malo, quod eadem Resp. patitur in Mutuatariis Christianis: quia malo certo, probabili, et absolute futuro, imo iam in sua causa adaequata existenti de facto, praeponderare non potest malum incertum, improbabile, futurum . . . Damnum enim mutuatariorum radicatur in ipsa natura usurae, tanquam dies in Sole.'

differing little from those Utopian ones used four hundred years earlier by Robert of Courson. When, in 1682, the Monte di Pietà of Rome was placed under the control of the Apostolic Treasurer General,[57] an event that most likely provided the spark for finally closing the Jewish banks, the popes—in whose name people like Iacobelli were speaking—were indeed emulating the medieval kings. The end to Jewish lending seemed to offer Utopian prospects. Conversion would be hastened and mercantilist goals achieved. And the Papal State itself would benefit, because for once its secular and spiritual goals were apparently being simultaneously achieved, something whose virtues theoreticians like Cardinal de Luca were forever touting, but whose realization had proved constantly to be elusive. As the historian of the early modern Papal State, Paolo Prodi, has commented, normally, the more that one of these goals was achieved, the more that the other was shunted aside.[58]

There is one final point. If by applying mercantilist logic a Iacobelli could so easily add a secularized dimension to Utopian fantasies about the end of Jewish lending, then so, too, in the future, could others. We must therefore close by wondering—although insistently leaving for others to debate—if we may not, via the Iacobellis, draw a straight line from Robert of Courson, in the thirteenth century, to those in the nineteenth century, like Karl Marx, who—in his well-known, perhaps, one should say, his notorious essay 'On the Jewish Question'—said, 'The Jew's foundation in our world' is 'material necessity, private advantage'? Whence, 'Emancipation from usury and money, that is, from practical, real Judaism, would constitute the emancipation of our time.'[59] This, too, is an unabashedly Utopian statement.

University of Haifa

---

[57] Donato Tamilia, *Il sacro Monte di Pietà di Roma* (Rome, 1900), p. 85.
[58] Prodi, *Il Sovrano*, pp. 136–47, esp. p. 140.
[59] Karl Marx, 'Sur Judenfrage', ed. Stefan Grossmann (Berlin, 1919), p. 42.

CATHOLIC ANTI-JUDAISM IN
REFORMATION GERMANY:
THE CASE OF JOHANN ECK

by DAVID BAGCHI

I N any inquiry into Christian attitudes to Judaism in sixteenth-century Germany, exhibit A would undoubtedly be the later writings of Martin Luther against the Jews.[1] The choice for exhibit B presents more of a problem, but a strong case can be made out for an almost contemporary anti-Jewish treatise from the pen of Luther's staunchest Catholic opponent, Johann Eck. His *Refutation of a Jew Pamphlet*[2] tends to attract superlatives—'the most abusive to have been written against the Jews',[3] 'the most massive and systematic formulation of the blood libel . . . the *summa* of learned discourse on ritual murder',[4] 'the absolute nadir of anti-Jewish polemic in the early-modern period'[5]—and something of its unpleasantness can be gauged from the fact that Trachtenberg cited it so

---

[1] Luther's three treatises of 1543 were *Von den Juden und ihren Lügen*, in J. C. F. Knaake, ed., *D. Martin Luthers Werke. Kritische Gesamtausgabe* (Weimar, 1883–1983) [*Weimarer Ausgabe*—hereafter *WA*] 53, pp. 417–552: English tr. *On the Jews and Their Lies*, in J. Pelikan and H. T. Lehmann, eds, *Luther's Works* (Philadelphia and St Louis, 1955–86) [hereafter *LW*], 47, pp. 137–306; *Vom Schem Hamphoras*, *WA* 53, pp. 579–648; and *Von den letzten Worten Davids*, *WA* 54, pp. 28–100. For a succinct account and analysis of these works in their context, see Mark U. Edwards, Jr., *Luther's Last Battles: Politics and Polemics, 1531–46* (Leiden, 1983), pp. 115–42.
There is, of course, a considerable body of literature on the theme of Luther and the Jews, much of which is reviewed in Johannes Brosseder, *Luthers Stellung zu den Juden im Spiegel seiner Interpreten: Interpretation und Rezeption von Luthers Schriften und Äusserungen zum Judentum im 19. und 20. Jahrhundert vor allem in deutschsprächigen Raum* (Munich, 1972). Reinhold Lewin, *Luthers Stellung zu den Juden. Ein Beitrag zur Geschichte der Juden in Deutschland während des Reformations-zeitalters = Neue Studien zur Geschichte der Theologie und der Kirche*, 10 (Berlin, 1911), is widely regarded as the classic treatment. A recent major contribution to the theme is B. Klappert, H. Kremers, and L. Siegele-Wenschkewitz, eds, *Die Juden und Martin Luther, Martin Luther und die Juden: Geschichte, Wirkungsgeschichte, Herausforderung* (Neukirchen-Vluyn, 1985).
[2] *Ains Juden büechlins verlegung: darin ain Christ gantzer Christenhait zü schmach / will es geschehe den Juden unrecht in bezichtigung der Christen kinder mordt* (Ingolstadt: Alexander Weissenhorn, 1541).
[3] Selma Stern, *Josel von Rosheim. Befehlshaber der Judenschaft im Heiligen Römischen Reich Deutscher Nation* (Stuttgart, 1959), p. 183. I was unfortunately unable to consult the English translation by G. Hirschler, *Josel of Rosheim: Commander of Jewry in the Holy Roman Empire of the German Nation* (Philadelphia, 1965).
[4] R. Po-chia Hsia, *The Myth of Ritual Murder: Jews and Magic in Reformation Germany* (New Haven and London, 1988), p. 126.
[5] Steven W. Rowan, 'Luther, Bucer, and Eck on the Jews', *Sixteenth-Century Journal*, 16 (1985), pp. 79–90, at p. 87.

often in his disturbing book, *The Devil and the Jews*.[6] The year in which our Society has chosen to take for its theme 'Christianity and Judaism' is also the 450th anniversary of the publication of Eck's remarkable treatise. It is perhaps an appropriate occasion on which to explore, in rather more detail than has been done before, the context and nature of Eck's anti-Jewish polemic.[7]

Throughout the second quarter of the sixteenth century, Eck was undoubtedly the most famous Catholic theologian in Germany.[8] His fame was based on his reputation as a polymath, as the victor of the debate with Luther at Leipzig, and as the author of many books against the Reformation, notably the *Handbook of Commonplaces* (first published in 1525), which was destined to serve generations of Catholic priests as an arsenal of knock-down arguments. Why did he decide, in 1541, to turn his attention to the Jews? The immediate occasion was the publication in 1540 of a treatise which cast doubt on the notorious accusation that Jews murdered Christian children and put their blood to ritual use. This charge was unlikely to be true, the author argued, because Jews were forbidden to commit such vile crimes by divine as well as by natural law, because confessions had only ever been extracted under torture, and because an

---

[6] See Joshua Trachtenberg, *The Devil and the Jews. The Medieval Conception of the Jew and its Relation to Modern Antisemitism*, 3rd edn (New Haven, 1945).

[7] The proximity of this work in tone, in subject-matter, and in date to Luther's anti-Jewish treatises makes it natural to compare them, and this is the line most commentators have taken. The majority have used Eck to show that Protestants had no monopoly of offensive anti-Judaic sentiment in the mid-sixteenth century. See Heinrich Graetz, *Geschichte der Juden von den ältesten Zeiten bis auf die Gegenwart*, 9 (Leipzig, 1866), pp. 331–3; I. Elbogen, *Geschichte der Juden in Deutschland* (Leipzig and Berlin, 1920), 2nd edn, pp. 108f.; Karl Grunsky, *Luthers Bekenntnisse zur Judenfrage* (Stuttgart, 1933), pp. 5f.; Brosseder, *Luthers Stellung*, p. 91. See also H. A. Oberman, *The Roots of Antisemitism: In the Age of the Renaissance and Reformation* (Philadelphia, 1983), pp. 36f., and Rowan, 'Luther, Bucer, and Eck', pp. 79–90, for analogous but less tendentious conclusions. Others have gone further. Selma Stern saw the *Refutation of a Jew Pamphlet* as worse than any of Luther's tracts (*Josel von Rosheim*, p. 146), while Hsia regards Eck as more firmly rooted in a magical world-view than the Wittenberger (*Ritual Murder*, pp. 133–5). Bäumer and Ziegelbauer, on the other hand, portray Eck's as a more moderate form of anti-Judaism than Luther's: whereas Eck believed that Jews should be tolerated while they obeyed the law and did not blaspheme against Christianity, Luther urged their outright persecution: Remigius Bäumer, 'Die Juden im Urteil von Johannes Eck und Martin Luther', *Münchener Theologische Zeitschrift*, 34 (1983), pp. 253–78; Max Ziegelbauer, *Johannes Eck: Mann der Kirche im Zeitalter der Glaubensspaltung* (St Ottilien, 1986), pp. 190–3.

[8] The standard biography of Eck is still Theodore Wiedemann, *Dr Johann Eck, Professor der Theologie an der Universität Ingolstadt—eine Monographie* (Regensburg, 1865), now supplemented by Erwin Iserloh, *Johannes Eck 1486–1543: Scholastiker, Humanist, Kontroverstheologe* = *Katholisches Leben und Kirchenreform*, 41 (Münster, 1981), and *Johannes Eck (1486–1543) im Streit der Jahrhunderte* = *Reformationsgeschichtliche Studien und Texte*, 127 (Münster, 1988); and Ziegelbauer, *Eck*.

already despised minority had everything to lose from incurring yet
greater wrath against it. Many Christians, on the other hand, stood to gain
from blaming Jews for the accidental deaths of children: negligent or
violent parents, hit-and-run drivers, friars anxious to establish lucrative
pilgrimage sites, businessmen deep in debt to Jewish money-lenders. The
treatise was anonymous, but Eck suspected the Nuremberg reformer
Andreas Osiander as the author, and since Moritz Stern's edition of the
work this identification has been generally accepted.[9]

Eck's *Refutation of a Jew Pamphlet* is a complex work, lacking the
coherence of Osiander's original, but its major themes show through
clearly enough. Osiander's appeal to divine and natural law was ill
conceived, Eck believed, because the Old Testament and the entire
history of the Jews demonstrate not only their innate belligerence,[10] but
also their belief that in spilling Gentile blood they are doing God's will.[11]
Their special hatred, which they 'drink in with their mothers' milk',[12] is
reserved for Christians, whom they take every opportunity to destroy.[13]
Eck concedes that they may well have no need of blood for ritual
purposes, but if a chance to kill a Christian child arose they would gladly
take it; the same hatred leads them to what Eck calls *landmordt* (an atrocity
ranking somewhere between a massacre and genocide) by poisoning
medicines and water supplies.[14] To suggest, therefore, that the real
perpetrators of child-murder are Christians is to diminish the majesty of
those authorities which have duly convicted and executed Jews,[15] and to
fly in the face both of evidence accumulated over centuries and of natural
reason: what could be more natural than that the descendants of Christ's
killers should wish to honour their fathers by shedding the blood of
innocent Christians?[16] Eck concludes his refutation with a number of
'modest proposals' for the conditions under which Jews should be
tolerated in the Holy Roman Empire, concentrating on the restrictions

---

[9] Stern republished the treatise as *Andreas Osianders Schrift über die Blutbeschuldigung* (Kiel, 1893; repr. Berlin, 1903). For recent summaries see G. P. Wolf, 'Osiander und die Juden im Kontext seiner Theologie', *Zeitschrift für bayerische Kirchengeschichte*, 53 (1984), pp. 49–77, and Hsia, *Ritual Murder*, pp. 136–43.

[10] *Refutation of a Jew Pamphlet*, Ci^{r}f., Ciii^v, Eii^{v}f.

[11] Ibid., Di^{r}f., Ei^v–iii^v.

[12] Ibid., Di^v: 'Dann von ihr mütter brüst her saugent sie den neid gegen der Christenhait'.

[13] Ibid., Ei^v–Fi^v.

[14] Ibid., Fii^r–Gi^r.

[15] Ibid., Aiii^r, Aiv^r, Bi^{r}f.

[16] Ibid., Kiii^v.

necessary if further occasions of ritual murder and desecrations of the eucharistic Host were to be avoided.[17]

This lengthy and painstakingly documented work was written between late 1540 (when Eck received Osiander's pamphlet) and September 1541 (the date of the dedication). It was a busy, indeed a difficult, time for Eck, coinciding with bouts of severe illness and with the colloquies at Worms and Regensburg with which he was heavily involved. Here he had to defend Catholicism not only against Lutherans, but also, as he saw it, against his fellow delegates on the Catholic side, who seemed only too ready to make important concessions in matters of faith.[18] It is not immediately obvious why the professor of theology at Ingolstadt should have bothered to compose such a detailed reply to an anonymous treatise on ritual murder at all—in another context he prided himself on writing only what was absolutely necessary to the theological controversy[19]—still less at this particular time. Hsia thinks that he may have had a literary score to settle with Osiander, or that he was motivated by his emotional recollection of a dead child, an alleged victim of Jewish ritual abuse, whose body he had seen and whose stab wounds he had touched as a teenager.[20] But this is more suggestive than conclusive. One reason, of course, was Eck's extreme hostility towards Jews, which makes the *Refutation of a Jew Pamphlet* such a nasty piece of work. But what provoked Eck into action at this time was that a Lutheran had undertaken to defend the Jews,[21] and it was something typically Lutheran to defend the Church's enemies while undermining the authority of all Christian 'judges, kings, princes, lords, and citizens': this was what was achieved by seeking to acquit Jews of crimes for which they had been condemned by the due process of law.[22]

---

[17] *Refutation of a Jew Pamphlet*, Xiii^v–Zii^r. For recent summaries of this, see Hsia, *Ritual Murder*, pp. 127–31, and Bäumer, 'Eck und Luther', pp. 267–75.

[18] On Eck's attitude to 'semi-Lutheran' Catholics, see his revealing correspondence with the cardinals Contarini and Morone from these months in W. Friedensburg, 'Beiträge zum Briefwechsel der katholischen Gelehrten Deutschlands im Reformationszeitalter (Aus italienischen Archiven und Bibliotheken)', *Zeitschrift für Kirchengeschichte*, 19 (1899), pp. 243–64.

[19] See Eck's letter to Morone of 28 Feb. 1541 (Friedensburg, 'Beiträge zum Briefwechsel', p. 263).

[20] Hsia, *Ritual Murder*, pp. 126, 128f.

[21] One wonders whether Eck knew of the anti-Judaism of Martin Bucer's *Judenratschlag* of 1538, or of even Luther's *Against the Sabbatarians* of the same year, which was already showing a hardening of heart towards Jews. Eck demonstrates no knowledge of these works in the *Refutation of a Jew Pamphlet*, and regards Osiander's philo-Judaism as typical of Lutheranism.

[22] *Refutation of a Jew Pamphlet*, Aiv^r, Bi^{r}f, Ji^r. On the early Catholic polemicists' preoccupation with authority see David V. N. Bagchi, *Luther's Earliest Opponents: Catholic Controversialists, 1518–1525* (Minneapolis, 1991).

The *Refutation of a Jew Pamphlet* therefore fits well into the context of Eck's anti-Protestant campaign. The association of the religious innovators with the Jews was a commonplace of early Catholic polemic against the Reformation. In 1530, the Emperor's theologians at the Diet of Augsburg accused evangelicals of borrowing their teachings from contemporary Jews.[23] Six years earlier, the Franciscan controversialist Augustin von Alveld had claimed to find in the Sadducees' acceptance of the Pentateuch as alone authoritative the origin of Luther's *sola scriptura* principle.[24] Eck's primary target in the *Refutation of a Jew Pamphlet* was not Jewry as such but a leading Lutheran reformer, and he took the opportunity to attack Protestants for being in some respects worse than Jews, for instance, in their rejection of the necessity of good works for salvation.[25]

These doctrinal comparisons of Protestantism and Judaism were by now routine. But there was a more fundamental parallel between the two, which I believe was much more important to Eck's strategy and, for good reason, uppermost in his mind in 1541: both were inimical to the Catholic Church, but both were permitted to continue unmolested. Early in the treatise he laments the fact that Jews are tolerated within Christendom when they are rightly hated by all other peoples on earth.

> It is the greatest fault among us Christians [he wrote] that we allow the Jews freedom, grant them many privileges, and accord them considerable protection. Pope Innocent said that we thereby foster a mouse in our scrip, nurse a viper in our bosom, and carry fire in our clothes. In spite of this, Jews are given more freedom by those of St Paul's faith than are Muscovites in Lithuania.[26]

At the end of the treatise, after his long catalogue of alleged Jewish atrocities, he returned to this point.

> It is greatly to be wondered at that the Church treats Jews so mildly when they are so very hostile towards us, when they murder our children, kill our adults, corrupt the commonwealth as much in town as in countryside, blaspheme Christ, his mother, and all the saints, and so on.[27]

[23] Stern, *Josel von Rosheim*, p. 83.
[24] See Käthe Buschgens, ed., *Augustin von Alveld O.F.M.: Wyder den Wittenbergischen Abgot Martin Luther (1524)* = *Corpus Catholicorum*, 11 (Münster, 1926), p. 33.
[25] *Refutation of a Jew Pamphlet*, Gii^v.
[26] Ibid., Dii^v. See also Pope Innocent III's letter *Etsi Iudaeos*, *Decretales*, 5.6.13 (cols 775–6).
[27] *Refutation of a Jew Pamphlet*, Xi^r.

The problem Eck addressed was, of course, an ancient one, which had exercised a great number of patristic and medieval writers: 'Why had God permitted the continued existence of the Jewish religion?' Surely its Law had now served its purpose as a schoolmaster unto Christ, the words of its prophets had been fulfilled in the coming of the Messiah, and its dispensation was at an end? This sense of redundancy was all too easily transferred from the Jewish religion to the Jewish people. They lived in Christian lands under sufferance, but why were they tolerated at all, who were held to be heretics and deicides?[28]

The parallel with the position of sixteenth-century Christian heterodoxy could not have escaped Johann Eck. Luther's heresy had been condemned by the papal bulls of 1520, and the reformer himself outlawed, with his followers, by the Edict of Worms. And yet, by the time Eck wrote his *Refutation of a Jew Pamphlet* in 1541, Lutheranism existed alongside Catholicism in an uneasy peace which was both *de facto* and, thanks to the Nuremberg Interim of 1532, *de jure*. Charles V's continuing need to appease the Protestants of the Empire until he was strong enough to oppose them resulted in the religious colloquies of the late thirties and early forties. They culminated in April and May 1541 with the Regensburg colloquy, at which consensus was reached on many divisive issues, including the doctrine of justification.

That Regensburg eventually failed was due in no small part to the wrecking tactics of Eck himself. He was present as one of the delegates, but subsequently published a refutation of the agreed statement he himself had helped to formulate.[29] Eck saw that agreement at Regensburg would bring about the unthinkable, the legalization of heresy not only by the State, as a politically necessary evil, but also by the Church. His almost obsessive concern that his fellow Catholic delegates were too tolerant of Lutheranism parallels his concern that Lutherans such as Osiander were

---

[28] Four answers to this question were generally offered: first, Jews constituted, as it were, a walking history lesson, a proof of the historical reliability of the Bible; second, their present humiliation was evidence that Christians, and no longer they, were the chosen people of God; third, the Diaspora itself, and the consequent lack of privileges which Jews suffered in foreign lands, was a punishment for deicide; fourth, the eschatological conversion of the Jews was predicted by St Paul. See Amos Funkenstein, 'Basic types of Christian anti-Jewish polemic in the Middle Ages', *Viator*, 2 (1971), pp. 373–82, at pp. 374f. It is interesting that Eck appeals to these arguments, although he disputes Osiander's belief in the ultimate conversion of all Jews: only a remnant, a very small number, will convert, Eck argues, and he entertains no notion that the Church's salvation depends in any way on their conversion: see *Refutation of a Jew Pamphlet*, Xiᵛ–iiᵛ, Ziiʳ; Xiᵛ; Riiiᵛ).
[29] On Eck's *Adnotationes* to the Book of Regensburg, see Iserloh, *Eck*, p. 78.

too tolerant of Jews. I think it was no coincidence that Eck's *Refutation of a Jew Pamphlet* was published in the same year as Regensburg, nor surprising that Eck found it necessary, at a time when his health was failing and his energies more than usually focused on matters of high ecclesiastical politics, to refute in such detail a single, anonymous treatise on the blood-libel. The problems of Jewish–Christian and of Protestant–Catholic co-existence were two sides of the same coin.[30]

The argument of Eck's treatise supports this view. There was no doubt in his mind that Jews were heretics—not Christian heretics, of course, but deviants from the faith of their forefather Abraham. St Jerome, Peter of Burgos, and William of Paris all agreed that post-Exilic Judaism had been so infected by Eastern philosophy as to have become a different religion. The proof of this was the Talmud, which contained a number of blasphemous and heretical passages, and which was therefore rightly to be burnt.[31] Moreover, Jews frequently insulted and blasphemed the Christian faith itself, and on such occasions they were, in Eck's view, to be treated as Christian heretics and punished accordingly. (For Host-desecration and child-murder, both seen as crimes against Christ, the punishment was the traditional one for heresy, burning at the stake.) And it is significant that Eck was far more favourable to Muslims than to Jews, precisely because he considered them infidels rather than heretics.[32]

---

[30] A strange historical echo is that Regensburg had been host to another religious colloquy in 1474. It was between a Dominican and a Jew, and was on the subject of the true Messiah. The friar, Peter Schwarz or Nigrius, published his side of the disputation as the *Tractatus contra perfidos Iudaeos de conditionibus veri Messiae* (Esslingen: Conrad Fyner, 1475), which was in turn used by Eck in preparing the *Refutation of a Jew Pamphlet*. This theological show trial was the more poignant because it was staged to coincide with the judicial show trial, for ritual murder, of the Rabbi of Regensburg, Israel of Brünn. For details, see Hsia, *Ritual Murder*, pp. 71ff.

The other medieval (and later) anti-Jewish sources used by Eck in addition to Schwarz were Victor of Carben, *De vita et moribus Iudeorum libellus* (Cologne, 1509); Anton Margaritha, *Der Gantz Judisch Glaub* (possibly in Heinrich Steiner's Augsburg edition of 1531); Paul of Burgos, *Scrutinium Scripturarum* (Strasbourg, 1474; Mainz, 1478); Nicholas of Lyra, *Pulcherrimae quaestiones Iudaicam perfidam in catholicam fide improbantes* (Paris, 1500); Salvagus Porchetus, *Viktoria Porcheti adversus impios Hebraeos* (Paris, 1520); Peter Galatinus, *Opus de arcanis catholicae veritatis* (possibly in the Ortona edition of 1518, though he evidently cited the last two from memory: in *Refutation of a Jew Pamphlet*, Hi[v], he wrote: 'Porchetum et Galatinum non habeo ad manus'); Raymund Martin, *Pugio fidei* (Ortona, 1518); Johann Stamler, *Dialogus de diversarum gentium sectis et mundi religionibus* (Augsburg, 1508) (for evidence of the blood-libels); and Alphonse of Castile (a Spina), *Fortalitium fidei* (Strasbourg, 1475; Nuremberg, 1485, 1494).

[31] *Refutation of a Jew Pamphlet*, Oiv[v]–Piv[v].

[32] See ibid., Oi[r], for Eck's view of Islam as *Unglaub*, not *Ketzerei*. For the liability of Muslims only to natural, not to divine, law, see ibid., Eiii[v]. For their inveterate hatred for Jews, which

In spite of their heresy, Jews were still to be tolerated after a fashion and allowed to go about their lawful business unmolested. But Eck himself was clearly unhappy with the degree of freedom Jews in Germany were allowed. He believed that they should be forcibly reminded of their slave status, and made no secret of his preference for total expulsion. He reminded his readers that since the expulsion of Jews from Spain, the Spanish kings had grown great 'in lands and peoples, in honour and in wealth'.[33] The parallel with the contemporary status of Protestantism, while not explicit, is one that can fairly be drawn.

Before turning from the context to the nature of Eck's anti-Jewish polemic, I feel it is important to comment on what has been said so far. In suggesting that Eck's *Refutation of a Jew Pamphlet* is to be seen in the context of his anti-Protestantism, I do not mean to mitigate in any way the full horror of his anti-Judaism: even after 450 years it is still a remarkably unpleasant book to read—indeed, in the light of the Holocaust it is a more unpleasant experience now than ever before. Rather, this approach helps us to take his anti-Judaism more seriously, not as something incidental to his life's work, but as something absolutely central to it; not as some saloon-bar aberration, but as the sober and considered opinion of the leading German Catholic intellectual of his day.

The anti-Protestant aspect of the *Refutation of a Jew Pamphlet* suggests that in it Eck was consciously putting forward what he considered was the Catholic position on the question of the Jews. This explains his dependence on canon law, and especially on Innocent III's bull *Etsi Iudaeos* (1205), which is cited throughout the treatise.[34] The twenty-third chapter of the *Refutation of a Jew Pamphlet* is little more than a catena of canons on the subject of Jews, or more specifically on the restrictions under which Jews are supposed to live in Christian society. Apart from never insulting Christ, his Mother, or the saints, Jews are to remain in their houses and keep their windows shuttered on Good Friday, and should at all times wear a distinguishing badge. They must neither bear public office, nor employ Christian servants or wet-nurses, nor engage in any trade which would put them in a superior position to Christians. Uppermost in Eck's

---

he considers a good example for Christendom, see ibid., Dii^r, Nii^v, Zii^r. For the greater hostility of 'Jews and heretics' than of the heathen towards Christians, see ibid., Hi^r. For God's favour towards Islam, shown by its inexorable rise and spread, compared with the God-forsakenness of Jewish history since the destruction of the Temple, see ibid., Oi^r.

[33] *Refutation of a Jew Pamphlet*, Miii^r.

[34] Ibid., Dii^v, Hi^r, Xii^{v}f (a mistake for *Licet perfidia Iudaeorum*?), Yi^r.

mind is that these obligations all limit the opportunities Jews might other-wise have for criminal activity.[35]

In the twenty-fourth chapter, Eck insists that canonical laws against Jewish involvement in usury should be rigorously enforced. His reasons were fairly predictable: usury puts all Christians, both high and low, in the power of Jews. By ruining the nobles, the Jews hope to gain political influence. (Eck complains that Jews are more welcome in princely courts than are most Christians.[36]) By ruining the poor, they hope to be able to buy Hosts and children from them.[37] Instead of earning their living by 'idle' (*werckloss*),[38] capitalist means, by which they become our masters and we their slaves, Jews must eat bread in the sweat of their brow, doing hard manual labour, such as clearing forests or working in mines.[39] Eck demands the exclusion of Jews from all professions and trades which put Christians in their power: medicine, pharmacy, surgery, catering, retail-ing, commerce, tailoring.[40] The Jews must be made aware at all times that they are the slaves of Christians. Only so might they have cause to reflect on their new exile, their 'Roman captivity', and at last acknowledge the true Messiah.[41]

---

[35] Ibid., Xiii^v–Yii^v.

[36] Ibid., Eiii^v.

[37] Ibid., Yiv^r.

[38] Ibid., 2Aii^r.

[39] Ibid., 2Aii^{r}f; Zii^r. The idea that Jewish money-lending subverts the social order, by making Jews the masters and Christians their slaves, was a common feature of contemporary anti-Jewish polemic. It occurs in Bucer's *Judenratschlag* (see Rowan, 'Luther, Bucer, and Eck', p. 83), in Luther's *On the Jews and Their Lies* (e.g. *WA* 53, p. 529, lines 15f. – *LW* 47, p. 276), and in the papal bull *Cum nimis absurdum*—see G. Tomassetti and M. Marocco, eds, *Bullarium, diplomatum et privilegiorum sanctorum Romanorum pontificum Taurinensis editio*, 25 vols (Turin and Naples, 1857–88), 6, p. 498. Bäumer quite rightly points out that one of Luther's demands was that the Jews should eat their bread in the sweat of their brow ('Eck und Luther', p. 276), but overlooks the same demand made by Eck in identical words.

[40] *Refutation of a Jew Pamphlet*, Zii. *Cum nimis absurdum* would similarly restrict Jews from enter-ing any trade or profession 'necessary for human sustenance', and would allow them to undertake trading only in second-hand clothes: *Bullarium Romanorum Pontificum*, p. 499.

[41] *Refutation of a Jew Pamphlet*, Zii^r. The canons explicitly cited by Eck were drawn mainly from the titulum *De Iudaeis* in the fifth book of the *Decretals* of Gregory IX (many of which were also constitutions of Lateran IV), namely, ch. 4 *Quia super his*, on restricting Jews to their homes during certain Christian festivals (*Decretales*, 5.6.4, col. 772); ch. 8 *Ad haec praesentium*, against Jews keeping Christian servants (*Decretales*, 5.6.8, cols 773–4); ch. 13 *Etsi Iudaeos*, on a similar theme but with an elaborate anti-Jewish *proemium* cited by Eck several times in the course of his treatise (*Decretales*, 5.6.13, cols 775–6); ch. 15 *In nonnullis*, on the wearing of distinguishing clothes or emblems (*Decretales*, 5.6.15, cols 776–7); ch. 18 *Ex speciali*, on the bearing of public office (*Decretales*, 5.6.18, col. 778); and ch. 19 *Nulli Iudaeo*, on enslaving Christians (*Decretales*, 5.6.18, col. 778). It is significant, in the light of this catalogue of restrictions, that Eck nowhere cites the one piece of legislation from *De Iudaeis* to lay down basic minimum rights for Jews, ch. 9 *Sicut Iudaei* (*Decretales*, 5.6.9, col. 774).

Eck's dependence on canon law is, I think, central to understanding the nature of his anti-Jewish polemic. This dependence ultimately distinguishes Eck's anti-Judaism from Luther's, preventing the Bavarian professor from going as far as recommending outright persecution to the point of expulsion (though he sympathized with this policy in the case of Spain), and from abandoning all hope of the Jews' eventual conversion.[42] It also explains the tension Eck felt between the need for and the danger of co-existence, because the same tension is reflected in canon law. The Church's canons, in particular the series of bulls entitled *Sicut Iudaeis*, guaranteed certain basic minimum rights to Jews who lived within Christendom, and Eck was right in thinking that any orthodox Catholic discourse on Jewish–Christian relations, even one as offensive as his own, was bound by them. But by demanding the full implementation of these same canons, Eck was nevertheless able to propose almost complete segregation of the two communities, involving social, professional, and economic restrictions of such rigour that one might imagine expulsion a preferable option to its victims.

There is an interesting postscript to this story. An approach very similar to Eck's was adopted by Pope Paul IV when he established the infamous ghetto in Rome and the other Papal States. His bull of enactment, *Cum nimis absurdum* (1555), has rightly been described as representing a turning-point in Jewish–Christian relations, from which European Jewry never really recovered. But this new bull contains not the slightest hint of novelty. Even the wording is closely modelled on the *proemium* of *Etsi Iudaeos*, the bull upon which Eck relied so heavily, and there are several parallels between the detailed provisions of *Cum nimis* and the recommendations contained in the *Refutation of a Jew Pamphlet*.[43] Paul IV was able to justify the ghetto on the basis of the idea of strict segregation, which was always present in canon law, alongside its apparent liberality, and which Eck had brought out so starkly fourteen years earlier. Ghettoization was no more than the logical result of an approach which rejected

---

[42] In his important work, *Catholic Thought and Papal Jewry Policy, 1555–1593* (New York, 1977), Kenneth R. Stow identifies conversionary expectation as the factor common to papal policy throughout the Middle Ages and into the sixteenth century. He argues convincingly that this distinguishes Catholic from Protestant attitudes to the Jews (pp. 233–42). Less convincing, in the light of the evidence provided by Eck, is Stow's statement that Luther, by writing within the context of the impossibility of conversion, makes Jewish crimes central to his polemic, unlike Catholic writers (p. 238). The criminality of Jews seems rather to be far less telling for Luther than their stubbornness, while the opposite judgement applies to Eck.

[43] For a succinct and recent account of Paul IV's policy towards Jews, see John Edwards, *The Jews in Christian Europe, 1400–1700* (London and New York, 1988), pp. 66–74.

expulsion as uncharitable and co-existence as impractical, and it was a solution that would have appealed to Eck as surely as it did to the late sixteenth-century popes.[44]

It is tempting to suppose some connection between Eck's pamphlet of 1541 and the shift in papal policy in 1555. I know of none. But the fact that two such similar strategies were adopted within a few years of each other is not coincidental, and is testimony to the immense strains under which Catholic (no less than Protestant) attitudes to Judaism were labouring in the sixteenth century. Both Luther's and Eck's anti-Jewish treatises were worst-sellers in their day (which says much for the good taste of the reading public!), and the point is often made that Luther's call for synagogues and Jewish homes to be destroyed was not implemented until *Reichskristallnacht*, on the 455th anniversary of his birth. But Eck's solution to 'the Jewish question' met with more immediate success. A programme very similar to his own was put into practice only a few years later in papal Rome, a programme that would shape official Catholic policy until 1870, the year in which the Roman ghetto was finally abolished.

University of Hull

---

[44] It is clear, however, that not all late sixteenth-century popes can fairly be accused of such charity: Pius V in 1569 and Clement VIII in 1593 expelled Jews outright from all Papal States except Rome, Ancona, and Avignon. Their actions lead Oberman to suggest that the policy of the ghetto was closer to expulsion than it was to integration, and that there is therefore no great difference between the spirit of Luther's recommendations in *On the Jews and their Lies* and that of Paul IV's in *Cum nimis absurdum*: see H. A. Oberman, 'The stubborn Jews—timing the escalation of antisemitism in late medieval Europe', introduction to the *Yearbook of the Leo Baeck Institute*, 34 (London, 1989), pp. xi–xxv, at p. xviii. Eck's admiration for the expulsion of Jews from Spain (*Refutation of a Jew Pamphlet*, Miii^r) reveals his own inner preference and lends weight to Oberman's thesis.

THE JEWS IN THE SIXTEENTH-CENTURY HOMILIES

by VINCENETTE d'UZER

INTRODUCTION

GREAT travellers, great traders, the Jews had spread out all over Europe long before the Roman occupation of their territory or Titus' destruction of Jerusalem. On the whole, they prospered and mixed well with the local people. When these people were converted to Christianity no change seemed to appear at first towards the Jews. As centuries went by, however, animosity towards them, held responsible for Christ's Crucifixion and death, grew to the point of their being expelled successively from England, France, Spain, and various parts of Germany.

The Roman Catholic liturgy, in Latin throughout these countries, as well as in most of the rest of Europe, bears testimony to the growing ill feeling towards the Jews. A turning-point came with the Reformation. In England, the sixteenth-century homilists' teaching on sin and salvation pointed out that sin, and consequently the sinner himself, was alone responsible for Christ's sufferings and death. The Jews were but the instrument of it.

It is on that particular teaching of Cranmer and the homilists that I want to speak today, on its consequences for the Anglican liturgy, and the changing attitude of sixteenth- and seventeenth-century England towards the Jews.

I THE 'HOMILIES'

Let us first briefly recall what the 'Homilies' are. The so-called 'Anglican Homilies' consist of two collections. The first, made up of twelve homilies, was published in London on 31 July 1547 by command of King Edward VI. It went through innumerable editions. The second, published for the first time in July 1563 by command of Queen Elizabeth I, included twenty homilies. A twenty-first, entitled 'Against Disobedience and Wilful Rebellion', was added to the collection in 1570, after the Rebellion of the Northern Provinces. From then on the two groups of homilies were published in one volume, and according to the royal proclamations that accompanied each new edition until 1622, they were to be read from the pulpit on Sundays. The title alone is significant enough: *Certain Sermons or Homilies appointed to be read in Churches in the Time of Queen Elizabeth of Famous Memory*.

It may be useful to recall briefly the historical background to the Homilies. From 1529, King Henry VIII had associated Parliament with the successive reforms he imposed on the Church, and it was Parliament that voted for the Dissolution of the Monasteries and the successive laws by which the sovereign ultimately became the Supreme Head of the Church in England.[1] His successors, Edward VI, Elizabeth I, and James I, acted in the same way. The Tudor sovereigns endeavoured to make this religious reform a joint movement with their people, not an act of their own authority.

It was partly in order to obtain the assent of the people to the reform that the first series of Anglican Homilies was composed under Edward VI.[2] Archbishop Thomas Cranmer took very much to heart the editing and publishing of these Homilies,[3] and succeeded in obtaining the collaboration of several of his brother bishops. He himself wrote five of them: 'A Fruitful Exhortation to the Reading of Holy Scripture', 'Of Salvation', 'Of the True, Lively and Christian Faith', 'Of Good Works', and 'Against the Fear of Death'. Bishop Bonner and Archdeacon John Harpsfield were among the authors, as also was Hugh Latimer, Bishop of Worcester.[4] The reasons for the choice of subjects were, according to Bishop Ridley, 'in commendation of the principal virtues which are commended in Scripture and others against the most pernicious and capital vices that useth, (alas!) to reign in this realm of England'.[5]

Some titles chosen in support of the choice of subjects apply equally to the first collection of 1547 and to the second of 1563. Among those Homilies appropriate for a liturgical season are 'Of the Nativity' and 'For Good Friday concerning the Passion'. Some of the Homilies designed to praise the virtues extolled in Holy Scripture are entitled 'Of Prayer', 'Of Almsdeeds', and 'Of Repentance and True Reconciliation'. Then there are the Homilies designed to rail against 'the most pernicious and capital vices reigning in the realm of England', for example, 'Against Gluttony and Drunkenness' and 'Against Idleness'.

[1] Henry Gee and W. J. Hardy, eds, *Documents Illustrative of the English Church* (London, 1896).
[2] Maurice Powicke, *The Reformation in England* (London, 1941), pp. 34ff.
[3] J. Ridley, *Thomas Cranmer* (Oxford, 1962), p. 265.
[4] J. T. Tomlinson, *The Prayer Book, Articles, and Homilies* (London, 1897), p. 230.
[5] *The Works of Nicholas Ridley*, ed. H. Christmas, PS (1841), p. 400.

The longest and most intense are generally those written by Cranmer himself, or by John Jewel, Bishop of Salisbury (1522–71), author of the celebrated treatise *Apology for the Anglican Church*, which appeared in 1562. Nine of the twenty-one homilies of the second book are attributed to him.

The *Second Book of Homilies* was ready in January 1563, at the time of the signing of the Thirty-Nine Articles by the bishops. The order was also given to all the churchwardens of every parish in the kingdom to obtain copies as quickly as possible at the parish's expense.

The royal proclamations both of Edward VI and Elizabeth I are equally insistent that these Homilies should be read in turn every Sunday in the parishes (and there were many) where the celebrant was not licensed to preach his own sermon.[6] One of the rubrics of the Book of Common Prayer stipulated that one of the homilies should be recited, or rather, read, during the Communion Service on Sundays.[7] Assistance at the Sunday service was, in fact, obligatory by decree, under pain of punishment that was often severe, unless there were sound reasons for abstention.[8] A number of parish registers, including that of Stratford-upon-Avon, are very interesting on this subject. In conformity with yet other royal decrees, pupils of the famous grammar schools, founded in the reign of Edward VI, were bound to assist at the Sunday services and had to repeat the Homily to their teacher on the Monday. An inattentive pupil was punished.[9]

It would be tedious to list all the royal decrees concerning the Homilies, as there are so many. The last royal document to mention them is a letter written by James I to Archbishop Abbot on 4 August 1622, of which a copy was later sent to all the bishops. In it he forbade anyone who was not a bishop or canon to preach anything other than the Homilies, and he again exhorted all the members of the clergy to an attentive

---

[6] W. H. Frere and W. M. P. Kennedy, *Visitation Articles and Injunctions of the Period of the Reformation*, 3 (London, 1910), p. 22.

[7] E. C. Dargan, *A History of Preaching* (New York, 1968), 1, pp. 476–9.

[8] A. T. Lacey, *The Reformation and the People* (London, 1929), p. 21.

[9] N. Wood, *The Reformation and English Education* (London, 1931), p. 167: 'As often as there shall be a sermon, the masters shall send or themselves conduct the boys to church that from their tender years up they be bred to piety and not be negligent hearers. On their return to school the master shall call them out one at a time for examination upon what they have learned from the sermon, and that their childish mind be more stimulated to virtue and industry, the master shall blame the lethargic and slothful, but praise the diligent and attentive' (Canon of 1571).

reading of the two volumes. In 1623 he ordered that the two should be reprinted in a single volume.[10]

II THE POLITICAL SITUATION OF THE JEWS IN CATHOLIC COUNTRIES UP TO THE SIXTEENTH CENTURY

Let us begin with Spain. It was most probably as early as 586 BC that the first Jews, trying to escape persecution by Nebuchadnezzar, settled in the Spanish peninsula ('Sefarad'). The first troubles began in the fourth century, when Christianity became the official religion throughout the Roman Empire. They were condemned by several councils. Then came the Arab invasion of Spain in the eighth century. Things gradually settled down, and there was peace for the Jews between the tenth and the fourteenth centuries. Both in the Christian-ruled north of Spain and in the Muslim-ruled south-east, the Spanish Jews could live freely both as Jews and Spaniards. As bankers they lent money to the rulers, as physicians they were called from one state to another. They even participated in government as diplomats or councillors. They translated Arab texts into Spanish for the sake of the Christians.

In 1492, following an epidemic of the Black Death, Spanish reunification, and the overthrow of the Arabs in southern Spain, a fierce persecution arose, and the Spanish Jews took refuge in France, where Francis I and Henry II welcomed them to Bordeaux. Some went to England, others to Italy, Venice, Ferrara, and as far as Salonica and Istanbul in the Ottoman Empire.[11] Their numbers were never very large.

Nobody knows exactly when they first came to France, but certainly the first colonies were there before the Roman conquest.[12] Though the country became Christian, the Jews seemed to have had no special problems and were even appreciated as money-lenders. The trouble started with the first crusades, the Black Death, and the arrival of Lombards and Caorsins, who also acted as money-lenders. In 1306, King Philip the Fair sent them all away; Louis X recalled them in 1315, but six years later they were again obliged to leave France. After a short respite, Charles VI ordered them all to leave the country once more in 1394. They first took refuge in Provence, then in the county of Avignon, which

[10] E. Cardwell, ed., *Documentary Annals of the Reformed Church of England*, 2 vols (Oxford, 1839), 1, p. 187.

[11] Léon Poliakov, *The History of Anti-Semitism*, 4 vols (London, 1974), 2, pp. 16–17, 91, 95, 106, 119, 130. See also Béatrice Leroy, *L'Aventure séfarade* (Paris, 1986).

[12] Poliakov, *History of Anti-Semitism*, 1, pp. 26, 115–17, and p. 310, n. 31.

belonged to the Pope, who allowed them to remain there. Incidentally, the synagogue in Carpentras is still the largest in France.

As we have mentioned above, Spanish Jews found refuge in France in the sixteenth century under Francis I, but it was only in the eighteenth century that King Louis XV gave them the freedom of the whole kingdom. Even so

> ... the Jews represented less than one per cent of the total population ... though, according to a recent estimate, the Jewish population of the entire kingdom was about 100,000 souls, which amounts to saying that large communities were rare. ...
>
> Even in Italy, which was the only European country to have had a continuous Jewish presence since Roman times, the numbers remained small. There were two hundred Jewish families in Rome in the twelfth century. The Jewish community in Naples numbered 500 souls, that in Salerno, 600, and these were the largest Italian communities.[13]

Italy is the only country where literature speaks well of the Jews up to the fourteenth century, according to Poliakov,[14] and Beugnot adds, 'They were in fact happy in Rome and in Italy.'[15] However, it should be noted that the word 'ghetto' comes from the part of Rome where Pope Paul IV obliged them to live in 1555.

What we now call Germany would require a special study, which is beyond the scope of this communication.

III   THE SITUATION IN ENGLAND

It was at the time of the Norman Conquest that the Jews first settled in England, where they acted as money-lenders, as everywhere else in Europe. Considered as foreigners, they were ordered out of the kingdom by Edward I in 1290; however, Danièle Prudhomme writes:

> There is proof that between the end of the thirteenth and the beginning of the seventeenth centuries, the 'Jews' House' continued to shelter converted Jews in their need. But it is above all in the last years of the fifteenth century, following on the massive expulsion of

---

[13] Simon Schwartzfuchs, *Kahal la communauté juive de l'Europe médiévale* (Paris, 1986), pp. 25–6.
[14] Poliakov, *History of Anti-Semitism*, 1, p. 126.
[15] A. A. Beugnot, *Les Juifs d'occident, ou recherches sur l'état civil, le commerce et la littérature des Juifs ... pendant la duré du moyen âge* (Paris, 1824), repr. *Ressources* (Paris, 1979), pp. 131, 162–3, 170.

the Jews from Spain in 1492, that a small colony of Spanish Jews was established in London, though without being converted. ... The growth of international commerce under Elizabeth brought about an increase in the number of foreign merchants, particularly Jews, resident in London. There were some three thousand foreigners in the capital at the beginning of her reign, whereas at the end there were more than ten thousand. By mid-century there existed a translation of the *Sepherjosippon* into English, this having been done by an anonymous author in 1558. The mass of English Christians could read the post-biblical history of the Jewish people for the first time in a different version to that given by the Church in medieval works. The English would henceforward be able to become truly conscious of the Jewishness of Christ.[16]

The Roman Catholic liturgy of Good Friday reflects the feelings of the different peoples towards the Jews and is an indication of some of their changing attitudes. On that day two different kinds of prayer were used, and they still are, though with altered wording. The first is a sort of long litany sung during the Adoration of the Cross, called the *improperia* or 'Reproaches'. It appears in the *Pontificale* of Prudentius (846–61) and gradually came into use throughout Europe in the eleventh and twelfth centuries, though it only appears in the Roman *Ordo* in the fourteenth century. It certainly had a great influence on the attitude towards Jews in the Middle Ages. In people's minds, they gradually became responsible for Christ's sufferings and death. Hence the hatred which, when added to the historical and social situation, caused their expulsion from different countries.

The other kind of prayer used on Good Friday is also a sort of litany, this time of intercessions, where the Church asks the faithful to pray successively for various categories: catechumens, the afflicted, heretics, schismatics, and Jews, and here we find some interesting details. 'As early as 840', Louis Canet writes, 'in the *Rethel Sacramentary*, whereas you kneel down when praying either for infidels or idolaters . . . you no longer do so when it comes to praying for the Jews.'[17] Paul de Clerck has made an extensive study of these texts from the fifth to the fifteenth centuries,[18]

---

[16] Danièle Prudhomme, 'Les Juifs dans la tradition anglaise du moyen âge et de la Renaissance' (Doctoral Thesis, Paris, 1983), 3 vols, I, pp. 195ff., *passim*.

[17] Louis Canet, 'La prière "Pro Judæis" dans la liturgie catholique Romaine', *REJ*, 61 (1906), p. 213.

[18] Paul de Clerck, *La Prière universelle dans les liturgies latines anciennes* (Münster, 1977), pp. 89–91.

and he asserts that in Latin, then the only liturgical language in the West, they underwent no changes. To prove his point he quotes two of these texts: 'Let us pray for the Jews so that once the veil is lifted from their hearts, the light of truth may appear' and 'Let us pray for the Jews, for whom the light of the Gospel does not shine on account of their blindness.' In the fifteenth century the adjective *perfidis* was added to qualify 'Jews'. Of course, in Latin the word just means 'who lacks faith', but in English, as in French for that matter, it has a derogatory meaning.

It is with reference to these formulas used in the Roman Catholic liturgy in the fifteenth and sixteenth centuries that we want to look at the texts of the Book of Common Prayer and the Homilies, but a word about the special English background is needed first.

IV THE JEWS AND THE PREACHING OF THE HOMILISTS

As the years went by and Jews, expelled from France and England, were slowly trickling back, other important events concerning them had happened. The first, though it may not immediately appear relevant, was the first translation of the Bible into English by Wyclif and his disciples Nicholas of Hereford and John Purvey (1380–92).[19] It opened up new vistas for those able to read it and spurred on the sixteenth-century Reformers to make their own translations and publish them: Luther in 1522; Tyndale, in England, in 1525; Olivetan, in France, in 1536. In 1537, at the demand of Cranmer,[20] Thomas Cromwell obtained from Henry VIII the approbation of the so-called *Matthew's Bible*, and in 1538, a royal proclamation ordered a Bible in English to be placed in every Church in England, the famous 'chained Bibles'. The Renaissance movement had also led scholars to study it in either Greek or Hebrew. Another important translation had been that of the *Sepherjosippon* in 1558, mentioned above. It was thus possible for Englishmen to realize fully that Christ was a Jew and that the Jewish people were the 'people of God'. This idea will be expanded in the Homilies, but it is already reflected in the Collect for Good Friday from the First Prayer Book, where the change is marked from the old Roman liturgy:

> Mercyfull God, who hast made all men, and hatest nothyng that thou hast made, nor wouldest the deathe of a synner, but rather that he

---

[19] *ODCC*, p. 1503.
[20] Ridley, *Thomas Cranmer*, p. 128.

should be conuerted and liue; haue mercy upon all Jewes, Turkes, Infidels, and heretikes, and take from them all ignoraunce, hardnes of heart, and contempt of thy word: and so fetche them home, blessed Lorde, to thy flocke, that they maye bee saued among the remnant of the true Israelites, and be made one folde under one shepeherde, Jesus Christ our Lord; who lyueth and reigneth, &c.[21]

As for the 'Reproaches', they were at once suppressed by Cranmer and disappeared altogether from the Anglican liturgy until 1984, when a new text was produced and authorized, but not in a form castigating the Jews for the Crucifixion.

Now for the Homilies. The Jews are mentioned forty-three times in the thirty-three Homilies, though rarely in passing, and always with a definite purpose. They are chosen as examples of either good or bad behaviour, such as swearing, for instance, or being attentive listeners. The mere fact of that choice by the homilists points to the importance they attach to the Jews as a people, and to the way they behaved. Two negative attitudes towards them can be found, first, in Thomas Becon's 'Homily against Swearing and Perjury', where he calls them 'wicked'[22] and 'malicious', on account of their swearing unduly, which, in itself, is wrong.

In the same way, the unknown author of the 'Homily against Disobedience and Wilful Rebellion' tells his audience that whoever rebels against his sovereign is 'worse than the stubborn Jews'.[23]

On the other hand, John Jewel, in his 'Homily of the Right Use of the Church', gives them as a model to follow in the keeping of the Temple of God: 'If we could compare our negligence in resorting to the house of the Lord ... to the diligence of the Jews ... we may justly ... condemn our slothfulness.' 'Yet', he goes on, coming to a very important point, 'we abhor the very name of the Jews, when we hear it, as of the most wicked and ungodly people.'[24] Obviously he does not approve of criticism against them, as shown by many of his other homilies, but he states the fact that they are generally 'abhorred'. Why is this so?

The answer is in the Homilies themselves. The homilists do not deal

[21] *The First and Second Prayer Books of Edward VI* (London, 1938), p. 102.
[22] *Certain Sermons or Homilies appointed to be read in Churches in the Time of Queen Elizabeth of Famous Memory* (London, 1890), p. 77.
[23] Ibid., pp. 607–8.
[24] Ibid., p. 169.

with any of the historical or social reasons for this abhorrence, but with the theological one. This is plainly expressed in the 'Homily of the Nativity'.[25] The unknown author writes: 'Here is a great controversy between us and the Jews, whether the same Jesus which was born of the Virgin Mary be the true Messias.' 'They', the homilist goes on, quoting Acts 7. 51–2, 'as they are, and have been always, proud and stiffnecked, would never acknowledge him.' This is the explanation of the anti-Jewish feeling among Christians, all the more so as the Jews were made responsible for Christ's death on the Cross. Again, this is where the Homilies with their new and clear teaching on salvation and sin are a turning-point.

In his 'Homily for Good Friday', also called the 'First Sermon of the Passion', the homilist states:

> If we, my friends, consider this, that for our sins this most Innocent Lamb was driven to death, we shall have much more cause to bewail ourselves that we were the cause of his death, than to cry out of malice and cruelty of the Jews, which pursued him to his death. We did the deeds wherefore he was thus stricken and wounded: they were only the ministers of our wickedness.[26]

Not only are thus plainly condemned all negative attitudes towards the Jews, but several Homilists, including two of the most famous, Thomas Cranmer and John Jewel, as we have seen, do not hesitate in proclaiming them our teachers as well. What do they teach us then?

—To obey our sovereign, which is repeated in the two Homilies 'An Exhortation to Obedience' and 'Against Disobedience and Wilful Rebellion'.[27]

—To pray,[28] as Jewel, in the 'Homily of Common Prayer and Sacraments' tells his 'brethren'; and he insists that the English people should consider in what great reverence and veneration the Jews in the Old Law held their Temple, and imitate them.[29] 'I would we were not as far too short from the due reverence of the Lord's house, as they overshot themselves therein.'

—To keep the house of the Lord tidy, such as the Jews did for their

[25] Ibid., p. 429.
[26] Ibid., p. 439.
[27] Ibid., pp. 109, 607.
[28] Ibid., p. 386.
[29] Ibid., p. 173.

Temple. Jewel instructs in 'A Homily for Repairing and Keeping Clean of Churches':

> ... keep your churches comely and clean: suffer them not to be defiled with rain and weather, with dung of doves and owls, stares and choughs, and other filthiness, as it is foul and lamentable to behold in many places of this country. It is the house of prayer, not the house of talking, of walking, of brawling, of minstrelsy, of hawks, of dogs.[30]

For centuries the naves of churches and adjoining cemeteries had been used for entirely secular purposes. Grindal, when Archbishop of York, forbade the giving of dinners in churches and balls in cemeteries. In 1587, in his work *Declaration*, Harrison complained that cathedral naves were 'rather markets and shops for merchandize, than solemn places of praier'.[31] This situation is reflected in Ben Johnson's play *Every Man out of his Humour* (1600),[32] where the scene for the third act is placed in 'the middle aisle of St Paul's'.[33]

In this respect, these Homilies multiply examples from the Old Testament and Jewish practices, while at the same time giving practical details for the present time: 'See whether they take heed to their feet (as they be here warned) which never cease from uncomely walking and jetting up and down and overthwart the church.'[34] There was apparently little progress in the behaviour of the faithful between the proclamation of 1561 and the Homilies of 1563, since the two texts are identical. It was necessary to wait until the end of the reign and the influence of the Puritans for changes to become apparent. In article 36 of the proclamation of 1559 it is laid down 'that no man shall willingly let or disturb the preacher in the time of his sermon, or let or discourage any curate or minister to sing or say the divine service now set forth.'[35] In 1561, Queen Elizabeth published another decree with the significant title: 'For the safeguarding of quiet in churches and cemeteries'. These repeated proclama-

---

[30] *Certain Sermons or Homilies*, pp. 289–90.

[31] D. M. Palliser, *The Age of Elizabeth: England under the Late Tudors 1547–1603* (London, 1983), p. 334.

[32] Ben Jonson, *Every Man out of his Humour*, ed. C. H. Herford and Percy Simpson (Oxford, 1927), 3, p. 496, n. G.

[33] Vincenette d'Uzer, 'Politique et religion sous les Tudors à travers les Homélies' (Doctoral thesis, Paris-Sorbonne, 1988), pp. 155–7.

[34] *Certain Sermons or Homilies*, p. 174.

[35] Proclamation 460, Elizabeth I (1559), art. 36, in P. L. Hughes and J. F. Larkin, C.S.V., eds, *Tudor Royal Proclamations* (New Haven and London, 1969), 2, p. 126.

tions are sufficiently revealing of the difficulties in obtaining silence in church, so the insistence of Jewel is not surprising. He reminds his audience 'with what quietness, silence and reverence those that resort to the house of the Lord ought there to use and behave themselves',[36] citing here again the example of the reverence and behaviour of the Jews in the Temple.

Finally, the Jews also teach us:
—To suppress all idols, and here we refer to Jewel's very long 'Homily Against Peril of Idolatry', in which he keeps repeating that all images should be destroyed. The Jews did so, and whenever they worshipped idols they were severely punished.[37]

Now he goes further. The Jews showed us the way because in this, he wrote, 'They have the true sense and meaning of God's law so peculiarly given unto them.'[38] They are the 'people of God', his chosen ones, and this is repeated again and again throughout the texts.

One of the ways God gave them his law 'so peculiarly' as the homilist says, is the one in which he gave them their government and ruled them. The government of England should also be God's own, and is so, in fact, say the homilists. As early as 1547, in the 'Homily of Good Works' from the *First Book of Homilies*, Thomas Cranmer wrote:

> Honour be to God who did put light in the heart of his faithful and true minister of most famous memory King Henry VIII and gave him the knowledge of his word and an earnest affection to seek his glory . . . as he gave the like spirit unto the most noble and famous princes, Josaphat, Josias and Ezechias.[39]

The unknown author of the 'Exhortation concerning Good Order and Obedience to Rulers and Magistrates' likewise praised the Queen as a gift of God: 'God hath sent us his high gift, our most dear Sovereign Lady Queen Elizabeth.'[40]

Similarly, as he punished the Jews by the death of their good king Josias, God punished England by that of the young King Edward, so goes the argument in 'An Homily against Disobedience and Wilful Rebellion'.[41] Matthew Parker, Archbishop of Canterbury, followed the same

---

[36] *Certain Sermons or Homilies*, p. 171.
[37] Ibid., p. 203.
[38] Ibid., p. 232.
[39] Ibid., p. 59.
[40] Ibid., p. 110.
[41] Ibid., p. 595.

line in his 'Homily for the Days of Rogation Week'. In a moving, lyrical text he adjured England to answer God's special call to her at this time of Reformation:

> O England, which canst not nor will not ponder the time of God's merciful visitation, shewed thee from day to day, and yet wilt not regard it, neither wilt thou with his punishment be driven to thy duty, nor with his benefits be provoked to thanks, if thou knewest what may fall upon thee for thine unthankfulness thou wouldest provide for thy peace.[42]

This insistence on the Jews being the 'people of God', as we said before, shows an entirely new approach on the part of the Church. With the Reformation and the wide use of the Bible by every Christian able to read it, with long readings in church, and a preaching based on the texts themselves, a whole new vista was opened. In the Roman Catholic Church, Bible reading was mainly reserved to the 'learned' until the Second Vatican Council, and liturgical changes concerning Holy Week appeared only in the twentieth century.

The homilists put the problem of the guilt of the Jews in its proper place, while admitting their blindness in refusing to recognize Jesus as the long-awaited Messiah. Hence their use of the adjectives 'stubborn', 'stiffnecked' and 'wicked'.[43] As we mentioned earlier, they said they were not responsible for Christ's death. We Christians, we sinners, who should have known better, did the deed, while the homilists repeated again and again, 'The Jews were only ministers of our wickedness.'

CONCLUSION

The Tudor world is very rich and complex, one of its characteristics is the strong involvement between Church and State with the social changes it brought about. Deep in biblical studies, the first Anglican theologians Cranmer, Jewel, Parker, and their fellow bishops wanted to give their people, through the Homilies, a clear view of what salvation meant. They probably never dreamt that it would also slowly change a whole mentality as far as the Jews were concerned. It did, in fact,[44] since Oliver Cromwell

---

[42] *Certain Sermons or Homilies*, p. 525.
[43] Ibid., p. 429.
[44] Robert Ashton, *Reformation and Revolution 1558–60* (London, 1984), p. 406.

in 1656 was able to reopen England to them at a time when religious tolerance was not the rule.[45]

What those preachers did was to tell their parishioners that the Jews were the 'people of God', and if they, in England, wanted to be chosen too and consider themselves as such, they ought to avoid what the Jews did wrongly, and imitate them in their worship of the Word of God. Cranmer led the way in his liturgical reform to stop the Jews from being held responsible for Christ's death by removing the 'Reproaches' from the Good Friday liturgy and changing the Collect on that day. The Homilists preached that man, as a sinner, was the one responsible for Christ's Crucifixion. The Jews, they said, had only been the instrument of it. For many it must have been an entirely new way of looking at things, but it was in the true line of Bible teaching.

Catholic University of Lyons

[45] Leo Trepp, *A History of the Jewish Experience* (New York, 1973), pp. 243–4.

THE JEW THAT SHAKESPEARE DREW

by BRETT USHER

How far is it legitimate for a director to *correct Shakespeare's antisemitism* in *The Merchant of Venice*?[1]

S O, begging a question or two, wrote the theatre critic Benedict Nightingale in a review of a recent London production of the play in which the Christians were portrayed as rabid Nazis. Almost fifty years after the Holocaust, it appears, it is still difficult for directors and critics alike to approach *The Merchant* without a feeling of unease. Current wisdom—or lingering guilt—insists that the play is, in a real and unacceptable sense, racist.

But is it? Did Shakespeare set out to write a 'comedy' that would minister to the expectations of a London audience which, in the wake of the trial for treason and subsequent execution of Dr Ruy Lopez, the Queen's physician, was—it is asserted—in anti-Semitic mood?

The short answer is 'no'. My reasons for saying so are internal—that is, deduced entirely from the text itself—but they were first coaxed into shape some years ago by the revolutionary, and still too little known, analysis of Christopher Marlowe's *The Jew of Malta* by Dr Wilbur Sanders.[2] Later I was struck by the apparent anomaly that whereas many Elizabethan Calvinists were vigorous in denouncing usury (that sin, above all sins, which was popularly supposed to differentiate the Jew from the Gentile), there was an equally vigorous radical tradition at work behind the scenes for the promotion of Hebraic studies as an aid to a Godly ministry and as a *sine qua non* of a Godly education. And within the very recent past, old accepted truths about the status of Jews in Tudor England have been largely abandoned.

But to begin with the text. *The Merchant of Venice* seems to have presented no particular problems for our grandfathers. The wisest of theatrical writers, Harley Granville Barker, called the play a fairy-tale, acknowledging 'a little Jew-baiting' but no overriding anti-Semitism.[3] And yet it has always, within the canon of Shakespeare's early comedies, been a play apart. Certainly others contain formidable villains, but in no

---

[1] *The Times*, 8 Feb. 1991, p. 18. [My italics.]
[2] Wilbur Sanders, *The Dramatist and the Received Idea* (Cambridge, 1968), ch. 3.
[3] Harley Granville Barker, *Prefaces to Shakespeare, Second Series* (London, 1935), p. 83.

other[4] do we find a villain who achieves Shylock's stature or overshadows the central love-theme to the same degree. And, of course, this 'comedic' villain who almost achieves tragic status is a Jew.

Much ink has been spilt over Shylock, and many hours of preparation by leading actors for twenty-odd generations. To compare the scholars' with the actors' Shylock, and to examine Shakespeare's achievement in forcing us to see him both as villain and victim almost within the same couplet, would justify a weighty monograph and demand a great deal of sociological insight into the bargain. What follows is merely an attempt to chart the guide-lines which Shakespeare clearly marks out for his contemporaries in the oblique waters of Anglo-Jewish relations at the end of the reign of Elizabeth I.

'Sociological': the word should not be shirked, for Shakespeare was hardly the Romantic Bard of legend, carelessly dropping manuscripts upon an adoring populace from the pinnacle of his Ivory Tower. Rather, his efforts were brought up, wine-stained, from the basement: a heady mixture of poetic drama and instantaneous social (though seldom political, and never religious[5]) comment. This particular aspect of his curiously hybrid genius as a writer has been too little emphasized, and whilst the 'otherness' of his proposed 'playworld'—Roman, early British, Ruritanian, medieval English, and so on—always comes first in his scheme, it is inextricably bound up with the sights, sounds, and mores of Elizabethan London.

That said, let us be clear about the dangers of attempting to use a work of art as historical raw material. Dr Wilbur Sanders has much to say on the subject. The historian, he observes, seeks for evidence among mountains of raw material and attempts to draw generalized conclusions from what he finds. The literary critic, by contrast, cannot submit his text to any categories outside the work itself: he refuses to use the work as *evidence* at all, approaching it as 'a complete structure of meaning which will dictate its own categories'.[6] The critic must *respect* his text: 'He must recognize, indeed welcome, the unassimilable, the unpalatable, the indigestible. He must realise that the past, insofar as it diverges from the present, constitutes a challenge to the present—"Justify yourself!"'[7] What can we

---

[4] I am not discussing here the later 'dark comedies', *All's Well that Ends Well*, *Measure for Measure*, and *Troilus and Cressida*.

[5] That is, in the sense that he can ever be found taking sides in an Anglican/Puritan/Roman Catholic debate.

[6] Sanders, *Received Idea*, p. 14.

[7] Ibid., p. 12.

do, then, about a methodological conflict 'which seems so often to make historians bad critics, and critics bad historians'?[8] Dr Sanders concludes with wary optimism; it is open to us

> to strain our faculties to encompass both views of the Elizabethan world, to try to keep a foot in both camps, remaining ready at all times to translate cultural *tradition* into historical *process*, and back again into cultural tradition . . . recognizing the major thinkers and artists as in some sense the products of an age, yet also as the makers of an age and the perennial possession of mankind thereafter.[9]

Wary optimism it has to be, then. And in the words of another fine, though now forgotten, commentator,

> Neither [Shakespeare's] religion nor his morality lies on the surface; and it is idle to look for a definite moral or a definite message in any of his plays; or for a motive, other than an artistic motive, as furnishing a key to any underlying purpose. . . . This further is to be noted: there is never in Shakespeare any conflict between the aesthetic and the moral judgment.[10]

*   *   *

What, next, of attitudes towards the Jews and to usury—the two issues are almost inevitably intermeshed—which clamoured for attention in late Elizabethan England? In his invaluable survey of recent scholarship, Jonathan I. Israel argues that that much-scrutinized year 1570 may be taken to mark the beginning of a transformation in the social and economic standing of Jews in much of the Continent west of Poland. The Jew-myth was gradually replaced by a hard-headed reappraisal of their usefulness as financiers, whilst the Catholic–Protestant deadlock generated a new generation of political thinkers—Montaigne, Bodin, Lipsius, Bacon—for whom religious scruples took second place to *raison d'état*.[11]

By neat coincidence, the long-waged battle for realistic recognition of contemporary business practices—that interest of up to 10 per cent on

---

[8] Ibid., p. 15.
[9] Ibid., pp. 15–16.
[10] Sir Mark Hunter, 'Spiritual Values in Shakespeare', in F. C. Burkitt, ed., *Speculum Religionis* (Oxford, 1929), pp. 116, 118.
[11] Jonathan I. Israel, *European Jewry in the Age of Mercantilism, 1550–1750* (Oxford, 1985), pp. 1–2.

monetary loans was allowable and lawful—was finally won in the English Parliament in 1571. In vain did Thomas Wilson advance the arguments which reached a wider public in his *Discourse upon Usury* the following year. In vain did other members shirk the issue by proclaiming that 'we have no true definition' of usury, or that—and this is no lesser personage than Thomas Norton speaking—'since it is doubtful what is good . . . no allowance should be of it.' Sound monetarist arguments prevailed over anguished reiterations of Aristotle and the Bible. 'Usury and true interest', wrote a certain Mr Tavernor, 'be things as contrary as falsehood is to truth. For usury containeth in itself inequality and unnatural dealing, and true interest observeth equity and natural dealing.'[12]

Somewhere beneath the surface of this debate pulse the birth-pangs of that much-discussed phenomenon, the Protestant business ethic. Calvin's socio-economic teachings have recently been written off as 'ambivalent and inconsistent',[13] but at least he took care to modify traditional Christian thinking on usury, dissociated himself from the virulent anti-Semitism of Luther's later writings, and indeed chose to 'mitigate rather than inflame' the whole Christian–Jewish debate.[14] Thus, whilst the English acceptance of a just system of money-lending was hardly a victory for Calvinism (essentially the Act of 1571 revived that of 1545, suppressed by Northumberland in 1552),[15] the aims of the House of Commons harmonized well enough with certain aspects of Calvin's teaching at the very moment when it was in the process of dominating most areas of English politico-religious thinking.

Not, of course, that the Act of 1571 was the end of the matter. Many Protestant apologists continued to agonize. Some twenty years later, 'silver-tongued' Henry Smith had to pluck up a considerable amount of courage to address his London congregation on the subject of usury:

> Many times have I thought to speak of this theme, but the arguments which are alleged for it have made me doubtful what to say in it, because it hath gone as it were *under protection* . . . for it is said that

---

[12] R. H. Tawney and Eileen Power, eds, *Tudor Economic Documents*, 3 vols (London, 1924), 1, pp. 154–63; 2, p. 364.

[13] William J. Bouwsma, *John Calvin* (Oxford, 1988), p. 198.

[14] Israel, *European Jewry*, p. 13; Gillian Lewis, 'Geneva 1541–1608', in Menna Prestwich, ed., *International Calvinism 1541–1715* (Oxford, 1985), pp. 54–5; Herbert Luthy, 'Variations on a Theme by Max Weber', in ibid., pp. 384–90.

[15] Peter Ramsey, *Tudor Economic Problems* (London, 1965), p. 153.

there be more of this profession in this City than there be in all the land beside.[16]

Nor was unease confined to urban congregations.[17]

It is clear that the 'Hebraic Factor'[18] points to a deep schizophrenia at the heart of the Calvinist Reformation. How, for example, does it come about that Calvin's most loyal follower in Germany, the Elector Palatine Frederick III—'the Pious'—who welcomed anti-Catholic refugees from all over the known world, remained adamantly inhospitable towards wandering Jews? And that a competent modern historian of the Palatinate could therefore not unreasonably conclude that Calvinistic Protestantism was 'far more antisemitic than the old church'?[19]

Such questions, in fact, arise naturally out of Calvin's enforced role as pilot in the stormy waters of religious politics in mid-century Europe. On the one side was the Scylla of academic humanism, speculative, free-ranging and unfettered, the Kabbalah and occultism never very far below its Neoplatonist, if ostensibly Christian, surface; on the other, the Charybdis of harsh political realities involving the survival or extinction of nation states. Many diverse traditions of philosophy, politics, and religious observance jostled for Calvin's attention, and it is not surprising that he was hard pressed to accommodate them all within a satisfactory synthesis.

One particularly unstable element in this already volatile world was that of Old Testament scholarship, for whilst humanism had embraced Hebraic studies, it had not thereby proved itself pro-Jewish. Erasmus, indeed, feared that Christian Hebraism 'would in some way lead to a Jewish revival'.[20] The issues raised by a renewed sympathy with non-Christian traditions, by encroaching mercantilism, and (therefore) of legalized money-lending, bequeathed a perplexing legacy to Calvin's followers.

It used to be assumed that in England the debate could only be

---

[16] Henry Smith, *The Examination of Usury. The First Sermon* (London, 1591; *Complete Sermons*, 1599), pp. 93–4. [My italics.]

[17] P. Collinson, 'Godly Preachers and Zealous Magistrates in East Anglia: the Roots of Dissent,' in *Religious Dissent in East Anglia* (Cambridge, 1991), p. 24.

[18] The phrase was coined by Harold Fisch, *Jerusalem and Albion: the Hebraic Factor in Seventeenth-Century Literature* (London, 1964).

[19] Claus-Peter Clasen, *The Palatinate in European History, 1555–1618*, rev. edn (Oxford, 1966), p. 42.

[20] Israel, *European Jewry*, p. 14.

conducted at a theoretical level, since English society had had no official contact with Jewry since the days of Edward I. There are now solid grounds for inferring that the Crown had been encouraging readmission since about 1540, when Henry VIII began to import whole families of Jewish musicians from Venice—including the Bassanos—to enhance the prestige of his court: 'The new evidence suggests that Jews were not strange or unusual figures to the citizens of Elizabethan London; in certain areas, and in the Court itself, they were encountered every day.'[21] (If Emilia Bassano was indeed Shakespeare's Dark Lady,[22] and if that, in turn, accounts for the name 'Bassanio' in *The Merchant*, then Shakespeare's blending of Jewish and musical themes in the play is explicable in an entirely new way).

It is, moreover, striking that whilst many Calvinist preachers like Silver-tongued Smith felt compelled to speak out against usury *itself*, the English Hebraic tradition was from the first very much the preserve of the most radical Reformers of their succeeding generations, and that they were much more sympathetic to Jewish mores than many of their European counterparts. Elizabethan radicals appear *either* to have over-looked Calvin's hard-headed reappraisals of economic realities *or* to have pursued the ideals of Christian Hebraism largely unhampered by Erasmian reservations. To read the standard work on the subject[23] is to encounter a roll-call of the guardians of the Reformed tradition: the 'Hebraic Factor', germinated in early Tudor Oxbridge, was handed down by the earliest translators of the English Bible, via the English careers of Fagius, Tremellius, and Bucer, to Marian exiles like Whittingham, Sampson, and Humphrey; thence to Elizabethan radicals like Broughton, Fulke, Whitaker, and Udall; and so to the translators of the Authorised Version.[24] By that time, 'there was no country in which the Hebraic spirit was so deeply rooted or so universally spread.'[25]

---

[21] Roger Prior, 'A second Jewish community in Tudor London', *TJHSE*, 31 (1990), pp. 137–52.

[22] A. L. Rowse, *Shakespeare the Man* (London, 1973); and *The Poems of Shakespeare's Dark Lady* (London, 1978).

[23] G. Lloyd Jones, *The Discovery of Hebrew in Tudor England: a Third Language* (Manchester, 1983).

[24] Even so, Lloyd Jones makes no mention of John Foxe and lays no stress on John Jewel's Hebraicism as disseminated through the English Homilies: Vincenette d'Uzer, 'The Jews in the Sixteenth-century Homilies', pp. 265–77, above. He also ignores the claim of Theodore K. Rabb: 'The stirrings of the 1590s and the return of the Jews to England', *TJHSE*, 26 (1979), p. 26, that Richard Hooker be accorded a place of honour because, as a member of the Establishment, 'he did more to alter the consciousness of the people who ruled the land than had a dozen Professors of Hebrew or minor theologians.' In the light of Lloyd Jones's own researches, and the wider Jewish community unearthed by Roger Prior, perhaps the claim was overstated.

[25] Cecil Roth, *A History of the Jews in England* (Oxford, 1941), p. 148; and see also Fisch, *Jerusalem and Albion*.

*   *   *

From about 1540 onwards, then, the English Court appears to have encouraged a pro-Jewish tradition. It can hardly be coincidence that regius professorships of Hebrew were established at Oxbridge precisely at the moment when Henry VIII was persuading both Portuguese Marranos and Venetian musicians to settle in London.[26] By 1590 the agonizings of the likes of Henry Smith will have fallen on royal ears deafened by years of experiencing the necessity of usury in order to survive, and, in any case, Elizabeth herself seems to have been fascinated by Jews.[27]

In London there was no overt hostility to the Marrano community, and Jewish worship in private was probably winked at.[28] At the head of the Marrano community stood Hector Nunez, who enjoyed the confidence of Burghley and Walsingham, whilst Ruy Lopez rose to become physician first to Leicester and, in 1586, to the Queen.[29] Lopez catapults us to the heart of the matter, the clash between contemporary reality and ancient myth, between the respectable Marrano and the scheming Jew who was the deadly enemy of Christendom. Lopez's story has often been told: suffice it to say that in January 1594 he fell victim to the power struggle which had developed between Essex and the Cecils. Convicted of plotting Elizabeth's death by poison, he was executed at Tyburn in June, amid ostensibly spontaneous demonstrations of popular outrage and Essex's Machiavellian posturings as the saviour of his monarch.[30] But the traditional assumption that the Lopez affair gave rise to a wave of violent anti-Semitism[31] is impossible to substantiate. It looks much more like a well-orchestrated attempt, on proto-Nazi lines, to bolster the Essex party over and against the Cecils.[32] The Queen certainly demonstrated her

---

[26] Prior, 'A second Jewish community', p. 149.

[27] Albert M. Hyamson, *The Sephardim of England* (London, 1952), p. 8.

[28] Roth, *Jews in England*, pp. 139–44; C. J. Sisson, 'A Colony of Jews in Shakespeare's London', in S. C. Roberts, ed., *Essays and Studies by Members of the English Association* (Oxford, 1938), pp. 38–51; Edgar Samuel, 'Passover in Shakespeare's London', *TJHSE*, 26 (1979), pp. 117–18.

[29] Roth, *Jews in England*, pp. 140–1.

[30] For the details, see John Gwyer, 'The Case of Dr Lopez', *TJHSE*, 16 (1952), pp. 181–4; Robert Lacey, *Robert Earl of Essex: an Elizabethan Icarus* (London, 1970), pp. 115–20. But in a private conversation with the present writer at this year's conference, Professor David Katz revealed that in his forthcoming book on the Jews in England he will argue that Lopez *was* guilty of treason and that his Jewishness was not a factor in his destruction.

[31] Rabb, 'The Stirrings of the 1590s', p. 26: '. . . perhaps the most strident antisemitism England had seen since the days of the expulsion under Edward I'.

[32] D. C. Collins, *A Handlist of News Pamphlets 1590–1610* (London [Thurrock], 1943), p. 30: there was only one news pamphlet on the subject, *A True Report of Sundry Horrible Conspiracies . . .*, printed by Charles Yetsweirt Esq. in November 1594. Yetsweirt, otherwise unknown as a

disgust at the whole affair by her exceptionally generous treatment of Lopez's widow.

It was a double irony that one of Essex's weapons in his anti-Semitic, anti-Spanish, and anti-Cecil campaign should have been the successful revival on the London stage of Marlowe's *The Jew of Malta*, of 1589. Ironic, in the first place, that a *mythical* Machiavel speaks Marlowe's prologue in order to introduce a *mythical* Jew, with the emotive name Barabas. Ironic, in the second place, that Marlowe's Jew is not actually the uncomplicated stereotype that Essex could have wished. True, stretches of the play apparently pander to an uninformed public taste and therefore *seem* to be presenting the mythical Jew of popular legend, but Marlowe's iconoclasm and his deep suspicion—perhaps even downright rejection—of official religion ensure that it is as much a satire on Christian attitudes as a tract against Jewish enormities. It is over seventy years since T. S. Eliot first suggested that the play only makes sense as a farce,[33] but I know of only one important study of it which takes its cue from Eliot, that of Dr Sanders.[34] As he argues:

> The strongest tendency in the play is to assail the facile and hearty complacency of Christian antisemitism with persistent inversions and permutations of the Jew–Christian antithesis. ... There are moments ... which seem to sum up the whole tortured history of anti-semitism: as when Barabas, with a furious self-loathing, assumes the role the Christians have cast for him:
>
>> We Jews can fawn like spaniels when we please,
>> And when we grin we bite; yet are our looks
>> As innocent and harmless as a lamb's.
>> I learn'd in Florence how to kiss my hand,
>> Heave up my shoulders when they call me dog,
>> And duck as low as any barefoot friar ...
>>   (II.iii.20–5)[35]

---

printer, was by profession a Clerk of the Signet, and was thus in a position to receive and disseminate special information. The pamphlet was therefore perhaps a 'government puff' rather than a response to popular interest.

[33] *The Sacred Wood* (London, 1920; 4th edn, 1934), p. 92.

[34] The prevailing tendency is still to regard the play as unremittingly anti-Semitic. This seems to me untenable, and thus the argument of Frances A. Yates, *The Occult Philosophy in the Elizabethan Age* (London, 1979), pp. 115–25, 203–4, that Marlowe was an intellectual reactionary assailing the tendencies of Renaissance magic and Christian Hebraism in general, and the Earl of Leicester's circle in particular, is here omitted from the discussion.

[35] Sanders, *Received Idea*, pp. 41, 43–4.

That passage—both its phraseology and its very tone—Shakespeare imported wholesale into *The Merchant of Venice*.[36] Elsewhere Marlowe fails to marry his iconoclasm to imaginative identification with his anti-hero and presents instead a kind of flippantly satirical, undergraduate version of the Jew-myth, as when Barabas first explains himself to his henchman Ithamore:

> As for myself, I walk abroad a-nights,
> And kill sick people groaning under walls;
> Sometimes I go about and poison wells . . .
> Being young, I studied physic, and began
> To practise first upon the Italian;
> There I enrich'd the priests with burials . . .
> And after that, was I an engineer
> And in the wars 'twixt France and Germany,
> Under pretence of helping Charles the Fifth,
> Slew friend and enemy with my stratagems.
> Then after that was I an usurer,
> And with extorting, cozening, forfeiting,
> And tricks belonging unto brokery,
> I fill'd the gaols with bankrouts in a year . . .
> And now and then one hang himself for grief,
> Pinning upon his breast a long great scroll
> How I with interest tormented him . . .
> But tell me now, how hast thou spent thy time?
>   (II.iii.176–200)

What is this but a devastatingly sly and comprehensive survey of the Jew-myth, with the clear implication: can an intelligent person actually *believe* any of that? With Barabas we reach a watershed in English attitudes to international Jewry, as adumbrated in *The Croxton Play of the Sacrament* and Robert Wilson's *Three Ladies of London*.[37] It was still possible for a dramatist to call into play all the old phobias inherited from medieval Christian paranoia, where 'Jew' equalled 'Judas', but—Marlowe seems to be asking—if any of it were even remotely true, how could a Jew ever hope to gain a position of trust in a Christian society, as so many Jews

---

[36] See below, p. 291. And for the notion of a Jew-usurer *biting*, see Henry Smith, *Examination of Usury*, p. 96.

[37] *The Merchant of Venice*, ed. M. M. Mahood, New Cambridge Shakespeare (Cambridge, 1987), pp. 21–2 [hereafter Mahood].

actually did? How—and at this point one hopes that Essex was becoming a little hot under his ruff—was it possible that a Dr Lopez could become physician to Leicester, Walsingham, and the Queen of England?

Into this scenario walked Shakespeare, very probably in the latter months of 1596.[38] He was evidently intrigued by the dramatic vistas which Marlowe's unstable, fitful muse had opened up to him, and magisterially picked up where Marlowe had forcibly-feebly left off.[39]

He approached the subject, it must be reiterated, strictly within the framework of romantic comedy,[40] and with a correspondingly romantic view of mercantile Venice and her just laws.[41] And as we are dealing with theatrical conventions here, let us be clear that Shakespeare's people have no existence outside the dramatic structure he creates for them; they are not psychological studies in the novelist's sense of those words. As another wise theatrical director observed:

> The apparent difficulty of accepting the naive simplicity of [the] story has led some producers and players to find new meanings behind the motivation of the characters; to suggest that Antonio is degenerate or that Bassanio is only out to win a fortune, to twist the sympathy of the play on to Shylock, to show Jessica and Lorenzo as a couple of unscrupulous thieves . . . Such attempts to impose psychological motivation on the characters and to create dramatic situations which the play does not possess make nonsense of the love-story, destroy the poetry and render the last scene—perhaps one of the most lyrical in the English language—a mockery of itself.[42]

Psychoanalysis, it appears, must take its place alongside the Holocaust in distorting the outlines of the Jew that Shakespeare drew.

With all these considerations in mind, let us examine the play by means of a sympathetic attempt at an imaginative identification with Shakespeare's original audience.

---

[38] Mahood, p. 1.

[39] Mahood, p. 8, suggests that Marlowe presented Shakespeare with 'a challenge rather than a source', and speaks of a 'fruitful and creative resistance to Marlowe's play'.

[40] Mahood, p. 9, prefers this description to 'fairy tale', which term can induce 'a dangerous condescension in the reader and a dangerous whimsy in the director'.

[41] See 'The Myth of Venice' in Mahood, pp. 12–15.

[42] Hugh Hunt, *Old Vic Prefaces* (London, 1954), p. 150.

We are introduced to Shakespeare's Venice not with talk of wealth and power, but by means of Antonio's inexplicable melancholy.[43] There are certainly references to argosies and merchandise in the opening scene, but its principal function is to conjure up a vision of Belmont and to set Bassanio's quest of its eminently marriageable occupant, Portia, in motion.

When we meet the lady in the second scene, she and her 'waiting-gentlewoman', Nerissa, playfully demolish the claims of all her recent wooers on the 'Englishman, Irishman, and Scotsman' principle. In each case, Shakespeare presents a national stereotype: the Neopolitan who is overfond of his horse; the 'County Palatine' who lacks humour; the Frenchman who is boastful and all things to all men; the Englishman who is unskilled in languages and badly dressed; the Scotsman who is quarrelsome; and the German who is drunk.[44] In the next scene we are to meet another national stereotype: the money-lending Jew, and as the play moves forward we would do well to remember that here we laughed gently with Portia and Nerissa. *They* are not 'racists', are they, just because they poke fun at an extravagant Frenchman or an ill-kempt Englishman? Nor, of course, are we.

Enter SHYLOCK THE JEW, *with* BASSANIO:

—— Three thousand ducats, well.
—— Ay, sir, for three months.
—— For three months, well.
—— For the which, as I told you, Antonio shall be bound.
—— Antonio shall become bound, well.

(I.iii.1–5)

Those repeated 'wells' have 'the same effect as the 'Ha! Ha!' of the pantomime demon-king.'[45] Our villain is launched, and soon he is speaking in Marlovian tones, fulfilling the audience's easy expectations of him:

I hate him [Antonio] for he is a Christian;
But more for that in low simplicity
He lends out money gratis, and brings down
The rate of usance here with us in Venice.

[43] Antonio, and not Shylock, is the 'Merchant' of the title.
[44] I.ii.33–74.
[45] Hunt, *Old Vic Prefaces*, p. 152.

If I can catch him once upon the hip,
I will feed fat the ancient grudge I bear him.

(I.iii.34–9)

Yet within that uncomplicatedly 'villainous' statement of intent, with its echoes of *Richard III*, lies a hint of the subtler portrait that Shakespeare will gradually unfold. Barabas would have used 'usury', the obvious word. Shylock prefers 'usance', which is, in Sir Thomas Wilson's phrase 'a more cleanly name.'[46] It exemplifies Shakespeare's innate ability to *identify*, to give a character his own inner dignity, even in villainy. As if to prove the point, Shylock at once modulates into 'personal' rather than 'theatrical', statement:

> He hates our sacred nation, and he rails
> Even there where merchants most do congregate
> On me, my bargains and my well-won thrift
> Which he calls interest.[47] Cursed be my tribe
> If I forgive him!

(I.iii.40–4)

The oath itself may ring false to Jewish ears,[48] but the passage as a whole rings true: it is the cry of the outcast and articulates an understandable sense of personal injury. Moments later Antonio demonstrates just how understandable it is, addressing Bassanio, with patrician ruthlessness, as if Shylock were not present.[49] Out of this comes Shylock's curiously broken-backed attempt to justify usury by reference to Laban's sheep.[50]

---

[46] Quoted in Mahood, p. 72n., and in *The Merchant of Venice*, ed. John Russell Brown, New Arden Edition (London, 1955), p. 24n. [hereafter Russell Brown].

[47] The commentators have shirked the task of asking why Shylock finds the word 'interest' so repugnant. If Mr Tavernor (p. 282 above) could differentiate between interest as good and usury as evil, why does Shakespeare make Shylock balk at the word? The answer is that 'interest' had quite recently changed its meaning. In medieval Latin usage, 'interest' differed from 'usury' in that the latter was avowedly a charge for the use of money (forbidden by *canon* law); whereas 'interest' referred to compensation which, under *Roman* law, was due from a debtor who had defaulted (*OED*: 'interest', sb. 10.a). Shylock does not recognize canon law; regarding his 'thrift' and 'usances' as quite legitimate, he takes exception to Antonio's equating them with the much more unpalatable business of exacting a penalty from a defaulter. With this subtle semantic point, Shakespeare introduces the central issue of the Shylock–Antonio story: Shylock objects to the suggestion that his business practices smack of revenge; in the event he pursues his revenge mercilessly.

[48] Mahood, p. 73n.

[49] I.iii.56–7.

[50] The commentators have been largely confused by Shylock's arguments and by Antonio's contemptuous dismissal of them (I.iii.86–90). The latter passage in fact accords with general theological opinion on the subject, but is too eliptical, perhaps, to serve as a cogent dramatic

And out of Antonio's lofty disdain comes the first of Shakespeare's piercing shafts of understanding, where Shylock links hands with the Barabas who could speak of learning to fawn and heave up his shoulders when they called him 'dog':

> Signor Antonio, many a time and oft
> In the Rialto you have rated me
> About my monies and my *usances*—

that self-justifying, self-ennobling word again. The speech rises in a crescendo of controlled rage to a climax in which Marlowe's savage sarcasm is replaced by cool Shakespearean irony:

> What should I say to you? Should I not say
> 'Hath a dog money? Is it possible
> A cur can lend three thousand ducats?' Or
> Shall I bend low, and in a bondman's key,
> With bated breath and whisp'ring humbleness
> Say this:
> 'Fair sir, you spat on me on Wednesday last,
> You spurned me such a day, another time
> You called me dog: and for these courtesies
> I'll lend you thus much monies.'
>
> (I.iii.98–121)

Antonio is not in the least moved by such withering scorn, nor by the baleful pun on 'cur' and 'courtesies'; he 'storms' that he would do it all over again.[51] Here we reach one of those 'unpalatable' gobbets of 'otherness' in the play, which Dr Sanders advises us to account for rather than reject. Professor Mahood, the play's most recent and thorough editor, sums up a dominant modern mood when she tries to locate this 'otherness' in a failure of vision on Shakespeare's part:

> If Shakespeare can be accused of antisemitism this can be found not so much in his depiction of Shylock as in an involvement with Antonio that results in his letting the merchant's contempt for the Jew go unchallenged. In Shakespeare's imaginative prospect, Antonio perhaps stands too close to his creator to be in perfect focus.[52]

---

argument. For discussion of Laban in contemporary treatises, see Arnold Williams, *The Common Expositor* (Chapel Hill, NC, 1948), pp. 170–3.

[51] I.iii.122–30.

[52] Mahood, p. 24.

I find that unconvincing. A 'sympathetic' Antonio has shuffled uncomfortably through the opening scene of the play. But now we see him suddenly revealed as a man of *deep moral conviction on the question of usury*, a follower perhaps of Henry Smith:

> For a man cannot love and be a Usurer, because Usury is a kind of cruelty, and a kind of extortion, and a kind of persecution, and therefore the *want of love* doth make Usurers.[53]

Shakespeare will make deft use of this motif of lovelessness later in the play. In the meantime we should be clear that many will have *warmed* to Antonio here for his defence of friendship and resistance to the latent oppression which, it was believed, was the *inevitable* consequence of usury. Shylock claims to have been treated as a 'stranger cur' (I.iii.113). This seems to put Antonio in mind of Deuteronomy's 'Of a stranger thou mayest take usury', and perhaps also of Henry Smith's gloss on the passage:

> Here *stranger* doth signify the Jews' enemies . . . God doth not license the Jews to take usury of any but their enemies, whom they might kill.[54]

Thus Antonio counters with:

> If thou wilt lend this money, lend it not
> As to thy *friends*, for when did friendship
> Take a breed of barren metal of his friend?
> But lend it rather to thine *enemy* . . .
>
> (I.iii.124–7)

For Shakespeare's truly religious contemporaries, the moral issues were literally issues of life and death, and in this play they will be symbolized as such in the trial scene. We do Shakespeare less than justice, and underrate the challenge he throws out to his audience, if we merely conclude that Antonio's implacability upsets our own liberal notions of social intercourse. As always, Shakespeare makes his audience think hard about its own attitudes to a moral dilemma.

It is asked to go on thinking hard. The short, colourful scene which begins Act II pitches us once again into the 'racist' issue with the Prince of Morocco's opening gambit:

[53] Henry Smith, *The Examination of Usury*, p. 95. [My italics.]
[54] Ibid., p. 104.

Mislike me not for my complexion . . . (II.i.1).

There follows the scene in which we meet Lancelot Gobbo, Shylock's clownish (and Christian) servant. Its main import is that the Jew is a devil and that the Devil must have been a Jew. Shakespeare here offers us the worm's-eye view of the Jew-myth, which will have vastly amused the groundlings and simultaneously curled many a lip amongst the ranks of their 'betters'. But we are at last weaned from the slapstick by the quiet dignity of Bassanio's acceptance of Lancelot as his servant:

> if it be preferment
> To leave a rich Jew's service to become
> The follower of so poor a gentleman.
> (II.ii.121–3)

No anti-Semitism there: merely rueful acceptance of the ways of the world.

At the same time Lancelot sketches in a view of Shylock which is new to us: he is parsimonious, a bad master. Lancelot is 'famished in his service' (II.ii.86–7). Here Shakespeare introduces the symbolic theme of the lovelessness which pervades Shylock's household. It is implicitly continued in the third and fourth scenes of Act II, in which the elopement of Jessica, Shylock's daughter, and the Christian Lorenzo gets under way. No anti-Semitism here, either: marriage between Jew and Gentile is perfectly acceptable (provided, of course, that the Jew becomes a Christian). But finally Shakespeare inserts a passage which gives us pause:

> If e'er the Jew her father come to heaven
> It will be for his gentle daughter's sake;
> And never dare misfortune cross her foot,
> Unless she do it under this excuse
> That she is daughter to a faithless Jew.
> (II.iv.33–7)

As Professor Mahood observes, Lorenzo's use of 'faithless' here—'un-Christian', certainly, but also 'untrustworthy'—'the audience may feel comes a little oddly from Lorenzo in the circumstances.'[55] It is a small but telling criticism to set against the fact that Shakespeare is working here within an old theatrical convention: that of miserly fathers 'who are only fit to be the dupes of their children'.[56]

---

[55] Mahood, p. 92n.
[56] Russell Brown, p. xli.

In the following scene we find Shylock—for the only time in his five scenes—in his own home. Shakespeare immediately sets any moral reservations we may have about the elopement in dramatic context: Shylock proves indeed a hard master to Lancelot and a cold, unfeeling father to Jessica. The Usurer is loveless, unloved, and fit to be duped. We thus begin to see that this is a more composite portrait of stage villainy than that which could be encompassed by harping only upon his Jewishness. His parsimony is insisted upon (II, v, 1–5), and then, in a little-noted passage, while he debates the wisdom of dining with Antonio, he remarks:

> But yet I'll go in hate, to feed upon
> The prodigal Christian . . .
>
> (II.v.14–15)

John Earle would surely have recognized in this utterance a 'sordid rich man',

> a beggar of fair estate. . . . He is a man whom men hate in his own behalf, for using himself thus . . . His body had been long since desperate, but for the reparation of other mens' tables, where he hoards meat in his belly for a month, to maintain him in hunger for so long. His clothes were never young in our memory. . . . He never pays anything, but with strictness of law, for fear of which only he steals not. . . . He never sees friend but in a journey, to save the charges of an Inn . . . and his friends never see him, but to abuse him. He is a fellow indeed of a kind of frantic thrift, and one of the strangest things that wealth can work.[57]

This neat pen-portrait projects both backwards and forwards into the fabric of the play. We are apprised of Shylock's 'frantic thrift' at home and his willingness to dine at the expense of others; we are also given a clue about his 'Jewish gabardine' and—most significantly for the trial scene—warned of his insistence upon the letter of the law.

He is also both Puritan and Jesuit. When he discovers that there are to be masques in the street during his absence, he bids Jessica

> Lock up my doors, and when you hear the drum
> And the vile squealing of the wry-necked fife,
> Clamber not you up to the casements then
> Nor thrust your head into the public street

---

[57] John Earle, *Micro-cosmographie*, 5th edn (London, 1629), ed. Edward Arber (London, 1869), pp. 99–100.

> To gaze on Christian fools with varnished faces;
> But stop my house's ears—I mean my casements—
> Let not the sound of shallow foppery
> Enter my sober house.
>
> (II.v.28–35)

That sounds less like a Venetian Jew than an English country parson whose last sermon had failed to prevent the usual May Day revels in the village.

The play sweeps to its mid-crisis in the opening scene of Act III, when Salerio and Salarino (merchant friends of Antonio) are propelled on stage to inform us that one of Antonio's argosies is reported lost. Almost at once Shylock appears, seething at the discovery of Jessica's treachery. The two Christians indulge themselves in a little heartless Jew-baiting.

> —— How now, Shylock, what news among the merchants?
> —— You knew, none so well, none so well as you, of my daughter's flight.
> —— That's certain; I for my part knew the tailor that made the wings she flew withal.
>
> (III.i.19–23)

And so on. This is not pleasant; nor is it meant to be. The dramatic point to be noted is that the scene is left in the hands of two minor characters, whom Shakespeare henceforth virtually discards. Despise them if you like.

They depart in disgust at the approach of Tubal, a Jewish colleague of Shylock's: what follows is black farce. Everything that Tubal has discovered about Jessica's flight-cum-spending-spree causes Shylock to writhe in an agony of 'frantic thrift':

> Thou stick'st a dagger in me; I shall never see my gold again. Four score ducats at a sitting. Four score ducats!
>
> (III.i.87–8)

Out of this emerges one of the greatest *coups de theatre* in the whole of Shakespearean drama. Tubal mentions a ring which Jessica has exchanged for a monkey:

> Out upon her! Thou torturest me, Tubal: it was my turquoise. I had it of Leah, when I was a bachelor. I would not have given it for a wilderness of monkeys.
>
> (III.i.95–7)

In thirty-two words, Shakespeare distils a tragedy: such is the incredible technical skill which he has at his command. That is all ye know of Shylock's marriage, and all ye need to know.[58]

There is no time to follow Shylock into III.iii or IV.i (the trial scene), but all the elements of his villainousness are fully established and are not further elaborated upon, except to insist upon his mercilessness in claiming the bond. In any case, the trial is a farrago of improbabilities, upon which many able legal minds have expended their ingenuity to little effect.

*   *   *

If unleavened lumps of the Jew-myth appear to peep through the fabric of *The Merchant of Venice*, it is not that the play is anti-Semitic in intention; nor should such lumps be used as brickbats with which to lambast a supreme writer. Much twaddle has been talked about Shakespeare's 'universality', the notion that you do not have to be a critic or a historian in order to appreciate his greatness or the general thrust of his arguments. He is a foolish 'universalist', however, who refuses to admit that in certain Shakespearean circumstances a modicum of historical understanding is desirable—for example, before passing judgement on Antonio as smug, Lorenzo as callous, and Jessica as lacking *pietas*.[59] Shakespeare's characters are not to be explained away in terms of proto-Freudian analysis of them, or of a failure of vision in him.

I have reserved one of the play's most famous speeches until now, because it seems to me to hold in perfect equilibrium Shakespeare's dramatic demands on Shylock as villain/revenger and his own humanitarianism. It perfectly demonstrates Sir Mark Hunter's contention that in Shakespeare there is never any conflict between the aesthetic and the moral judgement, and fleshes out Marlowe's perception that a complacent Christian society has only itself to blame for the *social* behaviour of its alien members. Shakespeare shames the Church which bred him—

---

[58] Russell Brown, p. xlii, following E. E. Stoll, finds in 'wilderness of monkeys' a 'kind of comic climax by repetition'. This strikes me as grotesquely wide of the mark; it is surely a *tragic* climax by (typically Shakespearean) exaggeration.

[59] Lack of *pietas* in daughters is one of Shakespeare's abiding themes: Juliet, Desdemona, Celia, and Hermia spring readily to mind. In Shakespearean terms, Jessica is strong and admirable, not weak and contemptible. Strong-minded women fascinated Shakespeare, and strong-minded women who exhibit *pietas* without 'denying' themselves—Rosalind, Viola, Cordelia, and both Portias—are amongst his crowning achievements.

and let us have no more nonsense about Shakespeare 'dying a papist'—
with an unqualified leap into the future of human sensibility. In Act III,
scene i, the Jew—a bear baited after Jessica's flight—faces the jeering of
Salerio and Salarino for more than a dozen exchanges before he turns on
them with a kind of savage humanity. Jessica's treachery notwithstanding,
Antonio remains the real focus of his hatred:

> He hath disgraced me, and hindered me half a million, laughed at my
> losses, mocked at my gains, scorned my nation, thwarted my
> bargains, cooled my friends, heated mine enemies—and what's his
> reason? I am a Jew. Hath not a Jew eyes? Hath not a Jew hands, organs,
> dimensions, senses, affections, passions? . . . If you prick us, do we not
> bleed? If you tickle us, do we not laugh? If you poison us, do we not
> die? And if you wrong us, shall we not revenge? If we are like you in
> the rest, we will resemble you in that. If a Jew wrong a Christian,
> what is his humility? Revenge. If a Christian wrong a Jew, what
> should his suffrance be by Christian example? Why, revenge! The
> villainy you teach me I will execute, and it shall go hard but I will
> better the instruction.
>
> (III.i.43–57)

That is no plea for tolerance; it is the *cri de cœur* of a villain mercilessly
justifying revenge.[60] But so powerful is the thrust of its anti-racist epi-
centre that it challenges, jeopardizes—perhaps (as do so many of Shakespeare's greatest utterances) even wrecks—the dramatic context for which
it was framed. Shylock, a money-lending outcast in a mercantilist-
Christian society, confronts, assaults, and exposes the assumed moral
superiority of the Christians who presume to legislate for his life of
enforced 'humbleness'. If Christians ostensibly profess the New Testament whilst covertly practising the Old, Jews ostensibly 'Christianized'
need little prompting to kick the New Testament into the gutter and spell
out the Old in capital letters.

But inevitably this brings Christian retribution in its wake: Shylock
loses half his fortune and is forced to become a Christian himself
(IV.i.364–93). Musing upon the curious, compromising life which his
Jewish contemporaries in England were forced to lead, Shakespeare
reached beyond simple issues of race-hatred and prejudice towards a more
complex moral: to be tolerated by, and reap the benefits of, a dominant
society by day, but to deny its mores by night, and insist on other values

---

[60] Russell Brown, p. xl.

which are in headlong collision with them, is ultimately an impossible position to hold. The full force of that dominant society can be called into play against such values—as it is here against Shylock's mercilessness in claiming the bond. Shylock, that is to say, is not presented as merciless because he is a Jew, but in order to symbolize Shakespeare's uncomfortable perception that where social tolerance is not accompanied by true *moral* tolerance, on both sides, the prospects of achieving a harmonious multi-racial society are slim. We have to look no further than the recent affair of Salman Rushdie's *The Satanic Verses* to recognize that he was right.

CONCEPTIONS OF JUDAISM AS A RELIGION IN THE SEVENTEENTH-CENTURY DUTCH REPUBLIC

by PETER van ROODEN

O NCE upon a time, probably in the first half of the seventeenth century, David Curiel, a prominent member of the Amsterdam Sephardi community, was attacked by a German robber. Although seriously wounded, Curiel managed to overcome his attacker with the help of his Christian neighbours. The robber was tried and sentenced. After his execution, the States of Holland sent Curiel a letter expressing their regret at the incident and inviting him to witness the medical lesson on the corpse of the robber in the anatomical theatre of Leiden University. This legend has been handed down in at least five different manuscripts, preserved in Jewish libraries. It was probably read at the feast of Purim, which, of course, commemorates an earlier attack on the Jews and the spectacular destruction of their enemy.[1]

The story, whether it is true or not, symbolizes the amazement of the Amsterdam Jewish community at the tolerance they enjoyed in the Dutch Republic. In fact, the Jews were remarkably free in some of the Dutch cities. In Amsterdam they were allowed to exercise their religion publicly. They enjoyed civil rights almost equal to those of Christians and could bring suit in the civil courts. Publications in Hebrew or Spanish were, in fact, free from censorship. Jews were not allowed to become members of the guilds, and could not claim common poor relief, but as they were economically highly specialized and successful, in the seventeenth century this was hardly a discomfort or burden. The Sephardim enjoyed virtually a monopoly in the trade with Portugal and its colonies. Later in the seventeenth century a large Jewish artisan class would be engaged in industries based on colonial products, such as sugar, diamonds, tobacco, silk, and perfumes.[2] Within the highly decentralized political structure of the Republic, the formulation of an internal policy towards the Jews was left to the municipal authorities. However, from 1619 onward the Dutch

[1] L. Fuks and R. Fuks-Mansfeld, 'Jewish Historiography in the Netherlands in the Seventeenth and Eighteenth Centuries', in S. Lieberman and A. Hyman, eds, *Salo Wittmayer Baron Jubilee Volume* (Jerusalem, 1974), pp. 436–8.

[2] J. I. Israel, 'The economic contribution of Dutch Sephardi Jewry to Holland's Golden Age, 1595–1713', *Tijdschrift voor Geschiedenis*, 96 (1983), pp. 505–35.

Republic pursued a consistent Jewish foreign policy. The States General tried to obtain the same foreign-trade rights and protection for their Jewish subjects as the other merchants of the Republic enjoyed.[3]

Thus members of the Jewish community could experience a great contrast between their former life and their position in the Dutch Republic. The growth of the Sephardi community stemmed from the immigration of New Christians, the descendants of forcibly converted Iberian Jews. In Spain and Portugal they had been harassed and persecuted by the Inquisition, which doubted the sincerity of their Roman Catholicism. The traditional conception that the Inquisition was right and that all or most New Christians professed Judaism in their hearts while outwardly conforming to Christianity has recently been challenged.[4] I do not want to go into this debate, but it is clear that many of the converts to Judaism who made up the Amsterdam Sephardi community had had virtually no Jewish religious instruction or experience of Jewish religious practices in their youth. They had lived as baptized Christians in a Christian country.

This aspect of the tolerance towards the Jews in the Dutch Republic has seldom been noted. The Reformed Church regarded a Catholic baptism as valid. The Jews of Amsterdam were officially forbidden to convert Christians to Judaism. Yet Portuguese and Spanish Christians were allowed to let themselves be circumcised. In fact, some Dutchmen and Dutchwomen also converted to Judaism without getting into trouble.[5]

The history and character of the Jewish community were profoundly influenced by the fact that a sizeable portion of its members had not been formed from youth by the religious tradition they observed as adults. It is, I think, useful to describe the history of the Sephardi community as the creation of a new religious community, rather than as the reconstruction of a suppressed religious identity, more or less in the same way as the Dutch Reformed, Mennonites, and Catholics built up new churches in the first century of the Dutch Republic.[6] Strong arguments for such a view can be derived from the great conflicts which divided the Sephardi community in the first half of the seventeenth century. Differences occurred between important laymen and the religious leadership of the

---

[3] J. I. Israel, 'Spain and the Dutch Sephardim, 1609–1660', *Studia Rosenthaliana* [hereafter *SR*], 12 (1978), pp. 1–61.

[4] H. P. Salomon, *Portrait of a New Christian: Fernao Alvares Melo (1569–1632)* (Paris, 1982), p. 41, n. 1, surveys the literature on this question.

[5] I. H. van Eeghen, 'De kinderen van Hansken Hangebroeck', *SR*, 11 (1977), pp. 33–9.

[6] Joke Spaans, *Haarlem na de Reformatie. Stedelijke cultuur en kerkelijk leven 1577–1620* (The Hague, 1989); R. G. Fuks-Mansfeld, *De Sefardim in Amsterdam tot 1795* (Hilversum, 1989), pp. 85–119.

rabbinate, probably on the extent to which the immigrants wanted to conform to halachic norms. The rabbis themselves were divided between a more philosophical conception of Judaism and mystical and kabbalistic interpretations. An undercurrent of radical religious scepticism is only partly known to us, as a result of the conflicts of the community with Uriel da Costa, Juan de Prado, and Spinoza.

*   *   *

Various aspects of the scholarly and theological reactions to the emergence of a Jewish community in the Republic have been studied. I want to restrict myself here to one question, which, due to its generality and indefiniteness, has not yet been posed. What kind of religion was Judaism, according to seventeenth-century Dutch theologians and Hebraists?

The earliest reaction to the presence of Jews and their religion was written in the vernacular. In 1608 Abraham Costerus published his *Historie der Joden*, intending to obstruct the request for a synagogue made by some Jews.[7] Costerus was a fierce Calvinist preacher, who served congregations south of the great rivers, in the front line of the Revolt, where the Spanish troops were never far away. His predecessor in the parish of Hoge en Lage Zwaluwe was a former monk, who used to say Mass in the morning on the royal side of the border, while preaching 'op z'n geus' in the afternoon on the States' side. When Costerus became minister in the newly-conquered village of Ossendrecht, some twelve miles north of Antwerp, his staunchly Catholic flock did not suffer his presence amongst them and forced him to live in the nearby garrison town of Bergen op Zoom. It is hardly surprising that Costerus was not a tolerant man.

His *Historie der Joden* has a simple structure. The first part, making up about half of the book, deals with the faith of the Jews. Starting with Maimonides' thirteen principles of the faith of Judaism, it relates the Jewish conceptions concerning God, salvation, and the Messiah. The second and third parts of the book describe the Jewish religious ceremonies on holy days, and their customs and rituals for eating, going to bed, marrying, divorcing, and so on. Costerus's work cannot be considered a great scholarly achievement. It is part excerpt, part translation of Antonius Margarita's *Der gantz Jüdisch glaub* (Augsburg, 1530) and Johan

---

[7] G. J. Jaspers, 'Schets van Abraham Costerus' leven en werken', *Nederlands Archief voor Kerk-geschiedenis* [hereafter *NAK*], 57 (1976–7), pp. 31–61.

Buxtorf's *Synagoga Judaica, das ist teutsche Judenschul* (Basle, 1603). Costerus derived the structure of his argument from this last work. Buxtorf's *Synagoga* opens with a chapter explicating the Jewish articles of faith on the basis of Maimonides' formulation. The following chapters—about six-sevenths of the book—describe Jewish ceremonies and rituals. I suppose that this structure, which derives religious ceremonies, customs, and rituals from articles of faith, ultimately goes back to the first Protestant confession, the *Confessio Augustana*.

In any case, Costerus considered Judaism to be first and foremost a doctrine, a system of propositions concerning God and his relation to the world. The ceremonies and rituals are but consequences of these propositions. Such a conception of Judaism was shared by all seventeenth-century Dutch theologians and Hebraists, irrespective of their actual knowledge of Jewish literature, acquaintance with Jews, or theological convictions. I will illustrate this thesis with some examples.

The orthodox theologian Gijsbertus Voetius, professor at Utrecht, devoted a long disputation to Judaism in 1637.[8] Voetius combined Protestant scholasticism with a Puritan-inspired programme to discipline Dutch society. His disputation on Judaism is, as was his wont, systematic and thorough. After an exhaustive survey of the existing literature, Voetius places Judaism in the series of deviations from true religion, somewhere between atheism and Roman Catholicism. He announces that he will describe the religious and social condition of the Jews in their reprobated state. The description of the Jewish religion is divided between a sketch of their opinions about God and his cult, and an evaluation of their conduct and piety. In his review of the Jewish faith Voetius follows the traditional ordering of Protestant dogmatics, describing successively the—in his eyes absurd and ridiculous—Jewish opinions concerning revelation, Scripture, God, and salvation and redemption. The manners and ceremonies of the Jews share in this condemnation, as they logically follow from these conceptions. Voetius even accepts uncritically the blood-libel, because he believes ritual infanticide accords very well with a rejection of the doctrine of justification by faith.

Johan Hoornbeek, pupil and colleague of Voetius, likewise deplored the freedom conceded the Jews in the Dutch Republic. His *Eight Books to Convince and Convert the Jews*[9] are devoted to a refutation of the various

---

[8] G. Voetius, *Selectae disputationes*, 5 vols (Utrecht, 1648–69), 2, pp. 77–102; F. F. Blok, 'Caspar Barlaeus en de Joden. De geschiedenis van een epigram', *NAK*, 57 (1976–7), pp. 179–209; 58 (1977–8), pp. 85–108.

[9] J. Hoornbeek, *Pro convincendis et convertendis judaeis libri octo* (Leiden, 1655).

works published by Menasseh ben Israel—publications which, in Hoornbeek's eyes, should not have been allowed in the first place. Hoornbeek starts off with the 'principle' of the Jewish religion, that is to say, its conceptions concerning revelation expressed in its views on the Bible, Talmud, and Kabbalah. Before he proceeds to describe the various dogmas, he cites Maimonides' summary of Jewish belief. According to Hoornbeek, every religion consists of three elements: doctrine, commandments, and promises, but it is clear that he too derives the last two from the first.[10] In his *Summa of Religious Controversies* Hoornbeek carefully explained the logical and temporal priority of beliefs before actions. True religion was original. Division followed from error concerning the truth, which led to controversies and disputes.[11]

Johan Coccejus was a much more original theologian than either Voetius or Hoornbeek. He was, moreover, a competent Hebraist who in his youth had published a rather good translation and commentary of two tractates of the Mishna. Jews for him were not, as they were for Hoornbeek and Voetius, a symbol of all those heretics in the Dutch Republic whose religious exercises unfortunately were not suppressed by the government. Rather, he saw them, following Augustine, as a symbol of God's sovereign wrath and mercy. The fate of the Jews, once God's chosen people but now rejected, must be a warning to all Christians. His inaugural lecture in Leiden dealt with the causes why the Jews had not believed in Christ.[12] His main argument has a sociological ring to it. Coccejus underlined the trust of the Jewish people in their spiritual leaders. To make this point, he referred his audience to their experience with contemporary Jews.[13] Thus in New Testament times the people followed their leaders. The leaders rejected Christ because they presumed they possessed the full truth already in the form of their ancient traditions, orally handed down together with Scripture. Explicating this allusion, Coccejus patiently explained to his hearers that even in their own days a great part of Christianity—Roman Catholicism—had succumbed to the anti-Christ for exactly the same reasons. Coccejus thus also considered Judaism a heresy, the result of a wrong conception of the way in which God reveals his truth.

Like Coccejus, Antonius Hulsius, Minister at Breda and later Professor

[10] Ibid., p. 261.
[11] J. Hoornbeek, *Summa controversiarum religionis* (Utrecht, 1658), pp. 6–7.
[12] The oration was published as an appendix to J. Coccejus, *Judaicarum responsionum et quaestionum consideratio* (Leiden, 1655).
[13] Ibid., p. 15.

at the Leiden theological faculty,[14] explicitly equated Judaism and Christian heresy. But where Cocceius used this comparison to warn the Christians, Hulsius considered the Jews to be the archetype and origin of all heresies and superstitions. 'Nothing strange to the Christian truth has been introduced in the Church, which does not smell of this corrupted Judaism.' The further one recedes from Christian truth, the closer one gets to the false Jewish belief.[15]

It is more difficult to ascertain the conceptions of Judaism of the professors of Hebrew at the Dutch universities, as they usually restricted themselves in their works to linguistic and historical topics. Yet asides, introductions, or historical conceptions make clear that they shared in the theologians' intellectualistic conception of Judaism. The theologian Constantijn L'Empereur was Professor of Hebrew at Leiden from 1627 to 1648, translating and commenting on several rabbinic works. He considered Judaism as only one of many deviant doctrines, which must be attacked and refuted, and against which the truth of Orthodox doctrine must be vindicated.[16] Johannes Leusden, Professor of Hebrew at Utrecht from 1650 to 1699, was, unlike L'Empereur, not a professional theologian. His *Philologus Hebraeo-mixtus* contains several disputations on the history and literature of Judaism. His description of the Talmud starts off with the questions whether this work contains a divine revelation and can legitimately be used by the present-day Jews as a foundation for their theology.[17] Another disputation explains that in the period of the first Temple, when the Prophets were still active, no disputes about religious truth could emerge, and Judaism did not divide into sects. Deviant groups mentioned in the Bible, like the Rechabites, distinguished themselves from the rest of the people not by their opinions, but by their way of life.[18] After the cessation of prophecy, sects emerged. Rabbinic Judaism is the continuation of one of these sects.

Scholars and theologians of dissenting Protestant groups shared the view on Judaism expressed by the Orthodox theologians and Hebraists. G. H. Vorstius was an Arminian preacher with strong Socinian sympathies.

---

[14] P. T. van Rooden and J. W. Wesselius, 'Two early cases of publication by subscription in Holland and Germany: Jacob Abendana's *Mikhlal Yophi* (1661) and David Cohen de Lara's *Keter Kehunna* (1668)', *Quarendo*, 16 (1986), pp. 110–30.

[15] A. Hulsius, *Theologiae judaicae pars prima: de messia* (Breda, 1653), praefatio.

[16] P. T. van Rooden, *Theology, Biblical Scholarship and Rabbinical Studies in the Seventeenth Century. Constantijn L'Empereur (1591–1648) Professor of Hebrew and Theology at Leiden* (Leiden, 1989), pp. 165–7.

[17] J. Leusden, *Philologus Hebraeo-mixtus*, 3rd edn (Utrecht, 1699), p. 100.

[18] Ibid., p. 138.

He was the son of the Conrad Vorstius whose appointment as successor to Arminius in 1610 had given the contra-remonstrants the opportunity to involve the English King in the theological troubles of the Republic and its Church. Vorstius did not repudiate his father. In his *Constitutiones de fundamentis legis*, published in 1638, he called himself 'C. filius' on the title-page. The *Constitutiones* consist of an edition and translation of, and a commentary on, the first chapter of the Mishneh Torah, which offers a version of Maimonides' summary of Jewish belief, together with a translation of Isaac Abravanel's *Rosh Amanah*, a book totally devoted to the principles of Judaism. In the preface to his work Vorstius stated that every religion possesses principles. These principles should concur with revelation, and ought not to be combined with purely human opinions. Vorstius's edition of these works concerning the principles of Judaism was meant to show that the Jews differ among themselves even on these fundamental points. They thus condemn the truth of their own religion.

Daniel van Breen, though just as heterodox as Vorstius, was much friendlier towards the Jews. Van Breen, secretary to the Arminian defendants at the Synod of Dordt, became a millenarian and worse. At the end of the 1640s he was one of the founders of the Amsterdam Collegiants. Until his death in 1664 he took care of the arrangement and correction of the works in the great Socinian publishing venture, the *Bibliotheca fratrum polonorum*. In 1644 van Breen published, anonymously, a translation of a curious work of Saul Levi Mortera, Chief Rabbi of the Amsterdam Sephardi community. In 1631 the latter had received a letter from a Spanish priest in Rouen, asking him twenty-three questions about Judaism and the New Christians. Mortera answered the questions, and in 1640 added forty-six polemical counter-questions, attacking the reliability of the New Testament and the reasonableness of Christianity in general. Van Breen translated this work into Latin and provided some of Mortera's questions and answers with his own refutations.[19] This edition was meant to propagate van Breen's own views. Mortera's attacks on the Trinity, the Two Natures of Christ, and the Orthodox conception of original sin van Breen left unanswered. On the other hand, he did defend dogmas dear to him, unfolding, for instance, a detailed Socinian concept of Jesus' mission in his answer to Mortera's interpretation of Isaiah 53.

---

[19] [D. van Breen] *Amica disputatio adversus Iudaeos continens Examen scripti iudaici a lusitanico in Latinum versi* (Amsterdam, 1644). Cf. H. P. Salomon, *Saul Levi Mortera en zijn 'Traktaat betreffende de waarheid van de wet van Mozes'* (Braga, 1988), pp. lxvi–lxxi.

Thus van Breen could use a Jewish apologetic and polemical work to express his own religious truth.

Philippus van Limborch, Professor at the Arminian seminary in Amsterdam, was an enlightened theologian, a close friend of John Locke, and colleague of Jean le Clerc. In 1687 he published a work with the title *Amica collatio*, containing a discussion between himself and Orobio de Castro, a prominent Sephardi intellectual, who had arrived in Amsterdam in 1662 having been persecuted in Spain. Van Limborch's argumentation in this debate is highly original.[20] He did not want to discuss the interpretations of the Old Testament, but the relative reliability of the revelations contained in the Old and New Testaments. Essentially, he argued that all reasons the Jews adduce to prove the divine provenance of the law of Moses, are equally, and even more, valid for the teachings of Christ. Part of his argument is a devaluation of the Old Testament. This, according to van Limborch, is historically unreliable, contains a defective and particular revelation, is unclear in essential matters, and promises a salvation which concerns only the earthly life. Judaism is, for van Limborch, a superstitious religion, by which he meant that it rests on a faulty intellectual judgement.

*   *   *

I would like to recapitulate briefly. In the seventeenth century, a theologically diverse and culturally viable Jewish community prospered in the Dutch Republic. Dutch Christian theologians and scholars, whether Orthodox or dissenting, generally described Judaism as a kind of mirror-image of Christianity. They considered it to be a creed–orientated religion, attempting to found its principles on revelation. The ethical and legal rules, rituals, and ceremonies, the core of normative Judaism, were judged to be secondary.

I do think this interpretation calls for an explanation. Of course, it is a common tendency to interpret the unknown in terms of the known, and the Protestant scholastics and humanists of the seventeenth century in particular were used to perceiving their world through a haze of book-lore. The prominent Arminian theologian Episcopius and one of Voetius's

---

[20] P. van Limborch, *De veritate religionis christianae amica collatio cum erudito judaeo* (Gouda, 1687). Cf. P. T. van Rooden and J. W. Wesselius, 'The Early Enlightenment and Judaism: the "civil dispute" between Philippus van Limborch and Isaac Orobio de Castro (1687)', *SR*, 21 (1987), pp. 140–53.

theological henchmen, Vedelius, in a dispute about the legitimacy of Arminianism stumbled upon the old law that Christian apostasy to Judaism should be punished with death. Their difference of opinion about the continuing validity of such a law is meaningful only within their sophisticated discussion about the relationship between public authority and religion. Neither of them refers to Christians abjuring their baptism in Amsterdam.[21] Their reference to Judaism was symbolic and did not touch upon the real world.

Although similar mechanisms are to be found in some of the works mentioned above, such an explanation is not completely satisfactory. After all, Dutch Hebraists and theologians had frequent contacts with Jews. The factual knowledge of Judaism and rabbinical literature grew rapidly during the seventeenth century. Voetius, for instance, possessed a manuscript of Leon de Modena's description of the customs of the Jews, even before this excellent work was printed.[22] Hoornbeek had studied with a Jewish teacher, as had all scholars who tried to understand rabbinical literature. L'Empereur and Isaac Aboab de Fonseca were close enough for the Rabbi to call upon the Christian Professor uninvited when passing through Leiden.[23] Leusden was involved in Athias's publication of a Hebrew Bible for scholarly purposes.[24] Vorstius translated one or more of Menasseh ben Israel's works.[25] The Chief Rabbi Mortera probably trusted van Breen well enough to hand over a furiously anti-Christian polemic by his teacher Montalto, which van Breen translated and adopted to propagate his Socinian views.[26] Orobio de Castro, in his discussion with van Limborch, rather impressively defended the loyalty of the Jews to their law. He stated that obedience to commands which are not a consequence of natural law is a positive good, representing a higher value than the common ethical life.[27]

I would like to suggest that a special characteristic of the Amsterdam Sephardi community played a role in the perseverance in the Dutch Republic of the interpretation of Judaism as a creed-orientated religion.

---

[21] Cf. [S. Episcopius] *Vedelius rhapsodus* (Harderwijk, 1633), pp. 179–81; N. Vedelius, *Arcani Arminianismi*, 4 vols (Leiden, 1634), 2, p. 85; 4, pp. 242–3.

[22] Voetius, *Disputationes*, 2, p. 80.

[23] Van Rooden, *L'Empereur*, p. 165.

[24] L. Fuks and R. G. Fuks-Mansfeld, *Hebrew Typography in the Northern Netherlands 1585–1815: Historical Evaluation and Descriptive Bibliography*, 2 vols (Leiden 1984–7), 2, pp. 288, 292, 305.

[25] Van Rooden, *L'Empereur*, p. 192.

[26] P. T. van Rooden, 'A Dutch adaptation of Elias Montalto's *Tractado sobre o principio do capitulo 53 de Jesaias*. Text, introduction and commentary', *Lias*, 16 (1989), pp. 189–238.

[27] Van Limborch, *Amica collatio*, pp. 60–6, 88–9, 118–20.

Creed formulation is a rare occurrence in the history of Jewish thought. Maimonides was the first Jewish thinker to engage in this activity. He laid down thirteen principles of faith which he wanted to be understood as dogmas in the strict sense of the term, that is to say, as necessary and sufficient conditions for attaining salvation. Maimonides found, till the fifteenth century, few followers in this endeavour. Then, under pressure of the Christian attacks which were to lead to the great expulsion of Spanish Jewry, almost all important Jewish thinkers devoted attention to the principles of Judaism. According to Kellner, who studied these works, this tradition of Jewish dogmatics withered shortly after the Expulsion. Isaac Abravanel's *Rosh Amanah*, written in 1494, is the last important work he analyses.[28]

In the first half of the seventeenth century the Sephardi community of Amsterdam had to assimilate many New Christian converts who had had no, or very little, Jewish religious education. The new arrivals tended to think about religion in a 'Christian' way, that is to say, they shared the notion of religion as a complex of dogmas and rules based on revelation. In the instruction they received, this same notion played an important role. Anti-Christian polemics, circulating in manuscript within the community, were used to prove the truth of Judaism. These works, like Montalto's 'Tractate on the Principle of Isaiah 53' or Morteira's 'Tractate on the Truth of the Law of Moses', can best be characterized as lay theologies based on scholastic presuppositions.[29] Most of Menasseh ben Israel's works too were, I think, meant to ease the intellectual problems new converts had with their new faith. Within the Amsterdam Sephardi community existed interpretations of Judaism which agreed with the view, sketched above, shared by Dutch scholars and theologians.

Free University,
Amsterdam

---

[28] M. Kellner, *Dogma in Medieval Jewish Thought: from Maimonides to Abravanel* (Oxford, 1986).
[29] Cf. Fuks-Mansfeld, *De Sefardim*, p. 94; Salomon, *Mortera*; van Rooden, 'Adaptation'.

'A DIFFERENT MODE OF CIVILITY': LANCELOT ADDISON ON THE JEWS OF BARBARY*

by ELLIOTT HOROWITZ

IN 1675 there appeared in London a rather interesting, if somewhat neglected, work entitled *The Present State of the Jews: (More particularly relating to those in Barbary.) Wherein is contained an exact Account of their Customs, Secular and Religious.* One of its more enigmatic features (to which we shall return) was its frontispiece, which featured an illustration not of a Barbary Jew, but of a muscular American Indian holding a spear, to which was attached a banner proclaiming the book's short title. Its author, Lancelot Addison, was described on the title-page as 'one of his Majesties Chaplains in Ordinary', having received that designation in 1671, shortly after returning from eight years in the western part of what was then called Barbary, as chaplain to the British garrison in Tangier. It was largely, although, as we shall see, not exclusively, on the basis of his experiences there between 1662 and 1670 that Addison later wrote his book on *The Present State of the Jews*, with which we will here be primarily concerned.

Lancelot Addison was born in 1632 and entered Queens College, Oxford, at mid-century, receiving his B.A. in 1655 and his M.A. two years later. As his later work attests he did not become much of a Hebraist there (Cambridge was then considerably stronger in that category), but he was known at Oxford as a staunch Anglican and Royalist, whose views brought him into conflict with the reigning Puritan establishment. It was after the Restoration (in 1660) that Charles II appointed him chaplain to the British garrison at Dunkirk, and from there, in 1662, that Addison (at the age of thirty) moved on to his position in Tangier, which had recently been acquired by England. Upon returning home in 1670 he married the former Jane Gulston (sister of the Revd William Gulston, who in 1679 became the Bishop of Bristol), and in 1672 his son Joseph was born. The

* This essay is dedicated to the memory of Jamie Lehmann (1950–82). An earlier version, which he had read, was written as a seminar paper under the guidance of Professor Ismar Schorsch, who first encouraged its publication. Further research on Lancelot Addison and his contemporaries was pursued as a visiting fellow of Trinity College, Cambridge, during the summer of 1987. I wish to thank the College for its generosity, and especially Dr Jeremy Maule, Fellow in English, for many acts of kindness.

latter, as is well known, was to achieve even greater literary distinction than his father as founder and editor (with Richard Steele) of the *Spectator* and the *Tatler*.[1]

Lancelot's literary reputation, however, does not rest exclusively, or even primarily, upon his *Present State of the Jews*. In 1671, almost immediately upon his return from Tangier, he published the first of the seven books he was to produce during his lifetime, an impressive work of reportage entitled *West Barbary*, which was praised as 'a very accurate account both of the country and the inhabitants', containing also 'a multitude of curious particulars'.[2] The author was himself much concerned with the problem, central to travel writing, of maintaining accuracy while at the same time seeking to entertain his readers with 'curious particulars'. He explained in the preface to *West Barbary* that his observations were 'not scrapped up from casual discourses, but the result of some years inspection in the people of whom I write'. And he stated explicitly that he had, in the interests of accuracy, 'rejected several passages' which could not be confirmed to his satisfaction: 'It being not my intent to be known for writing things Strange and Romantick, but to be very civil to the world, in putting nothing upon them but what is firm and solid.'[3]

Addison's concern with civility extended beyond his respect for his audience, reflecting itself in his attitude toward his subjects themselves—the Moors and, in *West Barbary* to a lesser extent, the Jews of North Africa. In the above-mentioned preface he expressed also the desire 'to make known . . . the justice and religiousness of a people esteemed barbarous, rude, and savage', and to demonstrate that this 'uncultivated people agree with the wisest of nations' in their concern for the practice of religion and the administration of justice. He criticized those who, like the ancient

---

[1] For further biographical information on Lancelot Addison see A. à Wood, *Athenae Oxonienses*, ed. P. Bliss, 4 (London, 1820), pp. 517–19; Watt, in *Biographica Britannica . . .*, 1 (London, 1747), pp. 28–30; F. Espinasse in *DNB* 1, pp. 131–3, and the sources cited there. Note also the useful entries on both Joseph and Lancelot Addison by M. J. Kohler in the *Jewish Encyclopedia* [hereafter *JE*] (New York, 1901–6), 1, pp. 188–9. Although the later German *Encyclopaedia Judaica* (Berlin, 1928), 1, p. 813, included a brief entry on Lancelot Addison, there is regrettably none to be found on either father or son in the recent 16-volume English work of that title [*EJ*]. Moreover, the single reference there to Lancelot, in the comprehensive list of Christian Hebraists (ibid., 8, pp. 21–2), is, as we shall see below, rather inappropriate.

[2] Watt, *Biographica Britannica*, p. 29. The full title of the work was *West Barbary, or a short narrative on the revolutions of the kingdoms of Fez and Morocco, with an account of their present customs, sacred, civil, and domestick*. It was dedicated to Addison's patron Joseph Williamson, to whom *The Present State of the Jews* [hereafter *PSJ*] would be dedicated five years later.

[3] L. Addison, *West Barbary* (Oxford, 1671), preface (spelling partially modernized).

Greeks, tended 'to repute all barbarous but themselves', and, in a rather remarkable (and for him repercussive) statement, argued that men must come to the realization that 'what is commonly call'd Barbarous is but a different Mode of Civility.'[4]

Addison's discussion of barbarism in his preface was undoubtedly occasioned in part by the title of the work itself (*West Barbary*), but it also took its place in a wider discourse on the subject which had been developing in European thought and literature since the discovery of the New World.[5] Montaigne, in his famous essay 'On Cannibals', describing the customs of the Indians of Brazil, had advanced the view that 'we all call barbarous anything that is contrary to our own habits', following a line of thought that had earlier been developed by the Spaniard Bartolomé de Las Casas.[6] In the 1580s Addison's own countryman Arthur Barlowe had noted, in his report to Sir Walter Ralegh from Virginia, that the natives he had encountered there were not barbarous, as he had been led to expect, but rather, 'in their behavior as mannerly, and civill, as any of Europe'. Somewhat closer to Addison's own time, John Dryden, in his play *The Indian Emperor*, written in 1665, essentially echoed Montaigne in elegant verse, putting into the mouth of Hernando Cortes the couplet: 'Wild and untaught are terms which we alone / Invent, for fashions differing from our own.'[7] And three years later (as well as three years before the

---

[4] Ibid. The significance of this passage was recently noted by Alasdair Hamilton in his review of Ann Thomson's *Barbary and Enlightenment: European Attitudes towards the Maghreb in the Eighteenth Century* (Leiden, 1987), in which Addison himself is not discussed. See *TLS*, 23–9 Oct. 1987, p. 1161.

[5] See, for example, J. H. Elliott, *The Old World and the New 1492–1650* (Cambridge, 1972), pp. 44–53, esp. p. 47: 'In changing and refining Europe's conception of barbarism and civility . . . the discovery of America was important, less because it gave birth to totally new ideas, than because it forced Europeans to come to face with ideas and problems which were already to be found within their own cultural traditions.' See on this topic now the essays collected in the special issue of *Representations*, 33 (1991), on the *The New World*, which appeared too late to be utilized here in any depth.

[6] 'Chacun appelle barbarie ce qui n'est pas son usage.' See Michel Montaigne, *Essays*, tr. J. M. Cohen (New York, 1984), pp. 108–9; P. Burke, *Montaigne* (Oxford, 1981), ch. 7, and esp. p. 48. Las Casas had observed (in the 1550s) concerning the language of the American Indians that 'We are just as barbarous to them as they to us': see Elliott, *The Old World and the New*, p. 49. His general project, as Anthony Pagden has recently observed, 'was to establish the Amerindians as peoples who could be made fully familiar to the European gaze. If not yet entirely civil . . . they were no more "barbarous" than some of the remote cultural ancestors . . . of the modern Europeans had been . . .': see *Ius et Factum*: text and experience in the writings of Bartolomé de Las Casas', *Representations*, 33 (1991), p. 157.

[7] On Barlowe see Louis Montrose, 'The Work of Gender in the Discourse of Discovery', *Representations*, 33 (1991), p. 7. His report, as Montrose there notes, was first published in the 1589 edition of Hakluyt's *Principall navigations*. . . . On Dryden see Anthony Pagden, 'The

publication of Addison's *West Barbary*) Paul Rycaut, in the dedication to his travel account of *The Present State of the Ottoman Empire*, acknowledged that the Turks 'may be termed barbarous, as all things are which are differenced from us by diversity of Manners and Custom', but asserted that they were, in fact, considerably less savage and rude than was generally supposed.[8]

Yet the relativistic view of barbarism and savagery, which had been formulated primarily with regard to the distant cultures of exotic peoples, especially those of the New World, had barely penetrated the mind of Europe with regard to the somewhat more familiar figure of the Jew, who was still held largely in contempt, and whose culture was still generally identified with barbarism.[9] John Greenhaigh, after visiting the London synagogue in 1662, wrote of his initial reaction to a friend: 'I went in and sate me down amongst them; but Lord ... what a strange, uncouth, foreign, and to me barbarous sight was there ... for I saw no living soul, but all covered, hooded, guized, veiled Jews' in their prayer-shawls. Although he acknowledged in his account that their ritual garb, which had to him at first 'made altogether a strange and barbarous show' came to possess in his eyes 'a face and aspect of venerable antiquity', he continued to rely upon the vocabulary of barbarism in describing other aspects of what he there saw. Thus the synagogue's 'Ruler', referred to by Greenhaigh as 'a big, black, fierce, and stern man', is described as calling out intermittently to his fellow contingents 'with a *barbarous* thundering voice', the congregation itself sings 'with a great and *barbarous* noise', and 'the priest' reads the scroll of the Law 'in a thundering *barbarous* tone, as fast as his tongue could run, for a form only' [emphases added].[10]

---

savage critic: some European images of the primitive', *Yearbook of English Studies*, 13 (1983), p. 135. On the re-evaluation of savagery and barbarism see also Pagden, *The Fall of Natural Man: the American Indian and the Origins of Comparative Ethnology*, rev. edn (Cambridge, 1986) and M. T. Hogden's classic study, *Early Anthropology in the Sixteenth and Seventeenth Centuries* (Philadelphia, 1964).

[8] Quoted by R. W. Frantz, *The English Traveller and the Movement of Ideas 1660–1732* (1934, repr. New York, 1968), pp. 34, 37. Frantz cites Addison's *West Barbary* (but not *PSJ*) on several occasions (pp. 8, 80, 82–3), but makes no connection between his views on barbarism and those of Addison.

[9] On the 'overlapping stereotypes of savages and contemporary Jews in the European imagination' of the sixteenth and seventeenth centuries, and the similar uses to which such stereotypes were put, see the brief but perceptive comments of Howard Eilberg-Schwartz, *The Savage in Judaism: an Anthropology of Israelite Religion and Ancient Judaism* (Bloomington and Indianapolis, 1990), pp. 37–9.

[10] Henry Ellis, *Original Letters Illustrative of English History*, 11 vols (1827, repr. London, 1969), ser. 2, 4, pp. 10–12, 14, 17. Greenhalgh's letter was reprinted, with notes, by W. S. Samuel,

Isaac Barrow, who was appointed Master of Trinity College, Cambridge, in 1673, devoted one of his sermons to what he called the 'Imperfection of the Jewish Religion', but actually chose to speak at great length about the imperfections of the Jews themselves: 'Through all course of times their manners have not procured . . . from any men any good-will or respect, but indeed the common dislike, contempt, and hatred of men.' Moreover, he continued:

> They have always been reputed a sort of people not only above all men vain and superstitious, addicted to fond conceits and fabulous stories, but extremely proud and arrogant, churlish and soure, ill-natured and falsehearted toward all men, not good or kind, yea not so much as just or true toward any but themselves.[11]

Although Barrow had travelled widely in Europe and the eastern Mediterranean, he had found no reason to revise the stereotypical image of the Jew received from such classical authors as Juvenal and Tacitus, upon whom he preferred to rely in evaluating the moral and social proclivities of that nation. By contrast, Lancelot Addison, who in a manner reminiscent of Rycaut called his work *The Present State of the Jews*, attempted to ground his observations in first-hand experience, culled both from his visits to the Jews and their frequent visits to him.[12] He describes, for example, the moral behaviour of the Jews he has encountered as 'very regular and agreeable to the Laws of a well-civilized conduct', and finds their domestic habits 'commendable . . . for their Sobriety and Temperance', adding that 'They cannot be charged with any of those Debauches which are grown into reputation with whole Nations of Christians. Fornication, Adultry, Drunkenness, Gluttony, Pride of Apparel, etc. are so far from being in request with them that they are scandalized at their frequent practice in Christians.'[13]

'The First London Synagogue of the Resettlement', *TJHSE*, 10 (1924), pp. 49–57. For the relevant passages see there pp. 51–5. Much of the letter is also quoted by A. M. Hyamson, *The Sephardim of England: a History of the Spanish and Portuguese Community, 1492–1951* (London, 1951), pp. 15–20. See also Eilberg-Schwartz, *The Savage in Judaism*, p. 38.

[11] Isaac Barrow, *The Works*, 2 (London, 1683), sermon no. 15. The sermon is quoted by D. A. Pailin, *Attitudes to Other Religions: Comparative Religion in Seventeenth and Eighteenth-Century Britain* (Manchester, 1984), p. 184.

[12] These angered at least one of his Muslim acquaintances. See Addison, *West Barbary*, p. 178. Yet, as Macaulay later remarked, Addison 'enjoyed an excellent opportunity, as chaplain of Tangier, of studying the history and manners of Jews and Mohammedans, and of his opportunity he appears to have made excellent use.' See M. F. Modder, *The Jew in the Literature of England* (Philadelphia, 1939), p. 371.

[13] Addison, *PSJ*, p. 13. [All references, unless otherwise noted, are to the 1675 first edition of

It is evidently no accident, then, that the illustration chosen for the frontispiece of Addison's *Present State of the Jews*, whether by him or by his publisher, was that of an imposing though somewhat scantily-clad American Indian, equipped with feathered head-dress and spear (see plate 1). Early in our century Israel Abrahams rightly recognized that 'the almost naked figure is not meant to represent a child of Israel', but he thought for some reason that it was 'less Addison's than his illustrator's idea of a *typical Moor*'. By contrast, James Parkes later found Addison's book 'chiefly remarkable for the extraordinary frontispiece, depicting a well developed and muscular *Barbary Jew* [emphases added]'.[14] The latter felt, moreover, that 'It would be amusing to know whence Addison, or his engraver, drew the inspiration for such a portrait.' The inspiration, if it was the engraver's, may have been linked with the common identification then of the Amerindians with the Ten Lost Tribes of Israel.[15] But Addison had remained silent about this controversial topic in his *Present State*, and therefore it is more probable that the inspiration, especially if it was his own, was rooted in the implicit suggestion of his book that the Jews, like the Indians of the New World, were essentially noble savages, whose ostensibly exotic (and perhaps threatening) barbarism was but a different mode of civility.[16]

---

the work.] This passage, as might be expected, found favour with a number of Jewish scholars and was widely quoted. See, for example, Israel Abrahams, *Jewish Life in the Middle Ages* (Philadelphia, 1896), p. 112, n. 2; 'Lancelot Addison on the Barbary Jews' in Abraham, *By-Paths in Hebraic Bookland* (Philadelphia, 1920), p. 156; Kohler, *JE*, 1, p. 189; Isidore Epstein, *The Responsa of Rabbi Simon Duran as a Source of the History of the Jews in North Africa* (London, 1930), p. 90. The latter used the passage in order to buttress his claim that 'On the whole the morals of the Jews in Northern Africa [in the fourteenth and fifteenth centuries!] were of a high level.' Addison also applauded the conscientious approach of the Barbary Jews to the religious upbringing of their children, remarking that 'There is no youth under heaven can at thirteen years old give so exact an account of the rites of their religion as the Jewish' (ibid., p. 86). Addison's observations on Jewish education were later quoted extensively (in Hebrew translation) by Simha Assaf, *Mekorot le-Toledot ha-Hinnukh be-Yisrael*, 4 vols (Tel Aviv and Jerusalem, 1925–42), 3, pp. 63–6.

[14] Abrahams, 'Lancelot Addison on the Barbary Jews', p. 154; James Parkes, 'Jewish–Christian relations in England', in V. D. Lipman, ed., *Three Centuries of Anglo-Jewish History* (London, 1961), pp. 162–3. Abrahams had commented that he had seen the frontispiece only on a copy of the second (1676) edition of *PSJ*. Although the frontispiece here reproduced is, for technical reasons, from the second edition, I have examined at least one first edition with the Indian picture.

[15] See, among recent studies, D. S. Katz, *Philo-Semitism and the Readmission of the Jews to England* (Oxford, 1982), ch. 4; R. H. Popkin, 'The Rise and Fall of the Jewish Indian Theory', in Y. Kaplan, H. Méchoulan, and R. H. Popkin, eds, *Menasseh ben Israel and His World* (Leiden, 1989), pp. 63–82.

[16] On the later implications of the noble savage tradition for the perception of Jews and Judaism see Eilberg-Schwartz, *The Savage in Judaism*, pp. 68–75.

Plate 1 Title-page of Lancelot Addison, *The Present State of the Jews* (London, 1676) (by courtesy of the Library of the Jewish Theological Seminary of America, New York).

It should be noted, however, that Addison's comments about the Jews he encountered in Barbary are not uniformly what we might call 'philo-Semitic'. He notes their 'Frugality of living', for example, but links this to their desire to maximize the profits from their trading activities 'wherein they are notoriously dextrous and thriving.'[17] In fact, one finds throughout the work that his praise of the Jews is frequently tempered by criticism, and vice versa, as if a policy of even-handedness were almost consciously being pursued. Thus his praise for the sobriety and temperance of Jewish domestic life is immediately followed by the observation that, by contrast, in matters of religion 'wherein they thought to be chiefly Orthodox, they are the most erroneous.'[18] He points, similarly, to the 'stoical patience' of the Jews, remarking that, 'In the midst of the greatest abuses you shall never see a Jew with an angry countenance, or appear concern'd.' Yet Addison is quick to point out that this mode of behaviour 'cannot be imputed to any Heroick Temper in this People, but rather, to their customary suffering, being born and Educated in this kind of slavery.'[19]

The author of the entry on Lancelot Addison in the *Dictionary of National Biography* correctly noted that *The Present State of The Jews* 'contains much curious information' (of which more below), but he may have been somewhat unjust in his assertion that 'Justice is done in it to the private virtues of the Jews of Barbary.' Israel Abrahams, one of the first Jewish scholars to make use of Addison's book, was similarly impressed with the 'many curious and mostly accurate details on rites and superstitions' it contained, but also noted the presence in it of some 'severe remarks on the Jewish character'. These, however, did not prevent him from generously praising Addison's *Present State* as 'a credit to his power of

---

[17] Addison, *PSJ*, p. 9. Cf. George Philips, *The Present State of Tangier* . . . (London, 1676), pp. 88–9, and especially (for purposes of contrast) the later comments of Joseph Addison in the *Spectator* quoted by Kohler, 'Addison, Joseph', *JE*, 1, pp. 188–9.

[18] Addison, *PSJ*, p. 14. Note also with regard to the Jews' Sabbath, to which he devotes nearly three chapters, he remarks that 'Their Offices for the Sabbath contain excellent things according to their way of worship', but adds in the same breath that 'They have therein many things apparently trivial and ridiculous', criticizing, in the traditional Christian manner, their overly carnal and ceremonious observance of the Seventh Day.

[19] Addison, *PSJ*, p. 8. On the Jews' lack of heroism, note also Addison's assertion that they would not be able to conquer Palestine from the Turks since they were 'enclined to a great averseness to everything that is Military; being as destitute of true Courage as of good Nature'. On this basis, Addison has recently been described as a racist by N. I. Matar, 'The idea of the restoration of the Jews in English Protestant thought: from 1661–1701', *HThR*, 78 (1985), p. 138.

observation and his goodness of heart'.[20] Charles Singer, some years afterward, joined the chorus of praise in characterizing Addison's work as 'a very able and knowledgeable account of the Jews from first hand observation', but added the less commonly found assertion that it was 'the first of its kind to appear in English'.[21]

Was this indeed the case? At first glance it would appear that this honour belongs rather to Edmund Chilmead's *The History of the Rites, Customes, and Manner of Life of the Present Jews, Throughout the World* (London, 1650). This work, however, was, as its title-page indicated, but a translation of the *Historia de' riti hebraici*, published by the Venetian rabbi Leone Modena twelve years earlier. What, however, of the work entitled *A View of the Jewish Religion*, which appeared in London in 1656, almost two decades before the publication of Addison's *Present State of the Jews*? Its author, who modestly gave only his initials (A. R.), was almost certainly Alexander Ross, who three years previously had published a larger work entitled *Pansebia, or a View of all the Religions of the World* (London, 1653). Yet a more careful examination of the 1656 *View* than can be carried out here reveals that it, too, was a translation, albeit a pirated and unacknowledged one, of an earlier work dealing with the rites and customs of the Jews. This was the enormously erudite *Synagoga Judaica* of the Swiss Hebraist Johannes Buxtorf, which was first published in 1603, and appeared in subsequent editions in both the German original and Latin translations throughout the seventeenth century. Suffice it to say here that both *Synagoga Judaica* and *A View of the Jewish Religion* contain thirty-six chapters, the titles of which are nearly identical. Both works refer frequently to a variety of Hebrew sources, but whereas Buxtorf was an accomplished Hebraist, who even wrote a grammar of the language,[22]

---

[20] Abrahams, 'Lancelot Addison on the Barbary Jews', pp. 155, 159. Closer to the mark would appear to be the evaluation offered by Kohler, *JE*, 1, pp. 188–9, at the beginning of our century: 'While Addison naturally manifests a strong bias in his view of a different creed, it must be conceded that his work exhibited a liberality of view and keenness of perception *not often encountered at that time*.' See also E. Calisch, *The Jew in the Literature of England* (Richmond, 1909), p. 96.

[21] Charles Singer, 'The Jewish Factor in Medieval Thought', in E. R. Bevan and C. Singer, eds, *The Legacy of Israel* (Oxford, 1928), p. 245. For the view that Addison's *Present State* is 'the best account of the Moroccan Jews at that time', see A. Rubens, *A History of Jewish Costume* (New York, 1967), p. 76.

[22] *Praeceptiones Grammaticae Hebraicae* (1605). The work ran into sixteen editions, and, ironically, appeared in English translation in 1656, the same year in which Ross's 'translation' of Buxtorf's *Synagoga Judaica* appeared: see Z. Avneri, 'Buxtorf, Johannes (I)', *EJ*, 4, p. 1543.

there is no evidence that Ross, who was more of what we would today call a 'comparativist', knew any Hebrew at all.[23]

It was in order to offset the heavily superstitious and generally unappealing view of Judaism presented in Buxtorf's work that Rabbi Modena of Venice composed his *Riti*, the first book about Judaism written by a Jew for the benefit of a non-Jewish audience.[24] And it was possibly as an antidote to Modena's 'Jewish' book, available to English readers since 1650 (in Chilmead's translation), that Ross sought to present an English translation of the Protestant Buxtorf's *Synagoga Judaica*.[25] There was, however, a more obvious reason for making the book available to English readers in 1656. The Jews, who had been expelled from England in 1290, were on their way back. As a result of the efforts of such figures as Menasseh ben Israel, a conference of notables met at Whitehall in December of 1655, to formally consider the readmission of the Jews to England, which actually took place, under Cromwell, in 1657.[26] It is hardly surprising, therefore, that Ross, in his preface to *A View of the Jewish Religion* (probably the only part of the work he actually wrote) made

[23] There are also instances in which Ross translates passages written by Buxtorf in the first person which are clearly inappropriate to a work written in England, e.g. p. 57, concerning a Hebrew edition of *Ben-Sira*: 'And truly my copy of it was printed at Constantinople and is the same which Sebastian Münster mentions at the end of his Latine *Cosmography* . . . and this I bought from a Jew my neighbor who had it from the Library of Munster, who was Professor of the Hebrew Language at Basel. . . .' On Münster, who himself was quite a scholarly plagiarist 'at a time when plagiarism was respectable', see M. T. Hodgen, 'Sebastian Muenster (1489–1552): a sixteenth century ethnographer', *Osiris*, 2 (1954), pp. 504–29, and *Early Anthropology*, ch. 7.

[24] See M. R. Cohen, 'Leon Modena's *Riti*: a seventeenth-century plea for social toleration of Jews', *Jewish Social Studies*, 34 (1972), pp. 287–321.

[25] Although Buxtorf's name did not appear on the title-page of *A View of the Jewish Religion*, neither was credit given to any other author. Rather, it was presented as 'faithfully collected by A. R.' Ross's *View* has recently been discussed in Matar, 'The idea of the restoration', pp. 121–2, where it is described, somewhat unjustly to my mind, as 'one of the most devastating attacks on the Jews', which treats the Jewish way of life as 'highly ritualized and foreign' in an attempt to prove that 'contemporary Jewish practices had strayed from the Mosaic code and followed rabbinical teachings.' The latter was indeed Buxtorf's intention in the work upon which Ross's *View* was based, but that is hardly the same as a 'devastating attack on the Jews'. Matar was on the right track, however, in noting that it was evident that most of Ross's treatise was derived, not from personal experience, but 'from his library'. My claim is that it was based almost exclusively upon a *single* book in his library, and it is that book's critique of contemporary Jewish practice, not Ross's own, which is expressed in *A View of the Jewish Religion*.

[26] On the readmission and some of the literature which it engendered see Cecil Roth, *History of the Jews in England* (Oxford, 1941), ch. 7; M. Wilensky, 'The literary controversy in 1656 concerning the return of the Jews to England', *Proceedings of the American Academy of Jewish Research*, 20 (1951), pp. 357–93.

reference to the imminent return of the Jews, 'Wherefore I conceive it must yield some satisfaction to thee to know with what kind of people we shall have to do. This is the motive,' he continued, 'by which I am induced to present unto thee this present work.'

Ross was not the only person in England to link knowledge about the Jews with their return to that country. In 1657, the very year of the readmission, there appeared in London a work entitled *The Jewish Synagogue: Or an Historical Narration of the State of the Jewes, At this day dispersed over the face of the whole Earth* [the sub-title continues] *In which their Religion, Education, Manners, Sects, Death and Buriall, are fully deliverd, and that out of their own Writers.* In contast, however, to Ross's translation, this one gave full credit on the title-page to the author of the original: 'Translated out of the Learned BUXTORFIUS, Professor of the Hebrew in Basel'. The authors of this translation evidently felt, like Ross, that the return of the Jews to England would create an increasing demand for knowledge about them, but, unlike him, they provided no preface to their work in which this explanation was set forth. In fact, they did not provide even their own names, being so modest that they signed only as 'A.' and 'B.'. The information was provided, however, that Mr A. was of Queen's College, Oxford. It is curious to note that Lancelot Addison had studied at Queen's College in the early 1650s and received his M.A. from that institution in July of 1657—the year in which the translation was published. Whether or not Addison was the Mr A. involved in translating the work (and I think he was not), it can be shown that he was intimately familiar with Buxtorf's *Synagoga Judaica*. In fact, it served him as a major source in writing *The Present State of the Jews*.

*   *   *

Just how major is a question of some delicacy, for Addison's book was purportedly about the customs of the Jews of Barbary, based on first-hand observation, and Buxtorf had written in far away Basle, some three-quarters of a century earlier. Addison's book was about Sephardic Jews, some of them former Marranos, who lived in the predominantly Muslim Maghreb, whereas Buxtorf's was about Ashkenazic Jews, who lived in Christian Europe. It has been recognized that unlike his earlier, more journalistic work, *West Barbary*, which had been written entirely on location, Addison's *Present State of the Jews* had been revised during the years after his return to England, where he had numerous learned works available to him.[27] What has not been fully realized, however, is the extent of his reliance upon some of these works, especially Buxtorf's *Synagoga Judaica*, a work which he cites on occasion, but less frequently than good ethics (or scholarship) might require.

Thus, among the customs of Rosh Hashanah, the Jewish New Year, Addison discusses that of *Tashlikh*, the riverside penitential ritual first practised by the Jews of medieval Germany and hardly known outside of Europe. Addison informs us that 'the Jews have had a Custome on this day to run into the Rivers, and there to shake off their Sins. . . . If at this Lustration they have the good fortune to see a Fish, they shake themselves lustily, on purpose, to load it with their Sins . . . and be as the Scapegoat of old.'[28] This passage was cited approvingly by the scholar Jacob Lauterbach as an independent corroboration from North Africa of the association between *Tashlikh* and the Azzazel goat suggested by Buxtorf (a suggestion with which Lauterbach himself had some sympathy).[29] But he did not realize that the passage in Addison's account was simply lifted from Buxtorf himself, who wrote concerning this New Year custom: 'If they spy any fish, they take it for auspicious, and straight leap for joy shaking their clothes, so that their sins may fall from them upon the fishes . . . as the rain [?] in the Old Testament did bear upon him the iniquities of the people.'[30] Similarly, in his widely-cited chapter (25) on Jewish alms and charity, Addison is more heavily dependent on Buxtorf's parallel chapter in *Synagoga Judaica* (32) than many have realized.[31]

---

[27] Note Watt, *Biog. Britannica*, 1, pp. 29–30, who observed that 'without question he revised it in England, since the disposition of it is perfectly regular, the stile natural and easy, and the whole interspersed with many learned remarks, and moral reflections.' See also Wood, *Athenae*, 4, p. 518.

[28] Addison, *PSJ*, p. 192.

[29] In his view: 'It is evident from the reports of Buxtorf and Addison that in the popular belief the ceremony of Tashlikh served the same purpose which the ceremony of the goal to Azazel served in Temple times.' See J. Z. Lauterbach, 'Tashlikh: A Study in Jewish ceremonies', *Hebrew Union College Annual*, 11 (1936), pp. 305–71 [*Rabbinic Essays* (Cincinnati, 1951), pp. 399–400].

[30] I follow here the 'translation' in Ross's *View*, p. 305. The German original is quoted by Lauterbach, 'Tashlikh', pp. 304–5 [= *Rabbinic Essays*, p. 398].

[31] Thus, for example, Ephraim Frisch, in his *Historical Survey of Jewish Philanthropy* (New York, 1924), p. 129 cites the testimony of Addison, based, he believed, 'on personal observation' that the Jews of Barbary 'have their Kibbuz, or Letters of Collection, by which the Indigent has liberty to go from Synagogue to Synagogue', and by which means also 'the necessitous Father raiseth Portions for his Daughters' without realizing that the testimony was lifted from Buxtorf. (In the *Jewish Synagogue* translation of 1657 the Hebrew word *Kibbuz* appears as *Ribbuz* [!].) For other scholars who have, sometimes uncritically, utilized Addison's testimonies regarding poverty and philanthropy see Abrahams, *Jewish Life*, pp. 307, 318; Abraham Cronbach, 'Jewish Philanthropic Institutions in the Middle Ages', in Cronbach,

Yet Addison did not always blindly copy the learned Buxtorf, and for this reason his book, if read carefully, can provide valuable information concerning North African Jewry in the seventeenth century, sometimes by its silences alone, and sometimes in more explicit ways. In his chapter on the synagogue (11), for example, he contrasts Buxtorf's report that the Jews wrote 'devout and cautionary sentences' on the entrances of their synagogues with his own experience in Barbary, where he found the custom 'wholly out of fashion with the Jews here discoursed of'.[32] In discussing Jewish marriage (ch. 5), Addison found the Jewish 'manner of taking a wife . . . sufficiently orderly and decent', whereas Buxtorf had a somewhat different view. The latter had described with some derision the custom of leading the bride 'upon the day before the marriage . . . to the Bath, and likewise back again, by an attendance of gagling women, making a certain confused noise as they go and return: to the end that every one may see and know that she is a Bride.'[33] Addison, by contrast, notes that 'In some places, as I have been told [!] the Bride goes to the Bath through the streets, accompanied with several women, who dance and sing as they pass.' Such behaviour, in his opinion, 'would be very scandalous', however, to the Jews of Barbary, especially on account of 'the modesty to which from their infancy the women here are inured'.[34] He, of course, had not been 'told' of the custom elsewhere of festively accompanying the bride to the ritual bath—he had read about it in Buxtorf's *Synagoga Judaica*, but he was sufficiently honest in this instance to report that it was not practised among the more modest Jewish women of Barbary.

A similar difference emerges with regard to the week of festivity after the wedding. Buxtorf had written that for eight days neither bride nor groom set foot out of doors and that the latter was continually visited by young men who 'eat, drink, and sport with him'.[35] Addison, too, mentioned the custom of the couple remaining indoors for an identical period of time, but described the visitors as coming to pray with the groom rather than to carouse with him. More importantly, he refers to an aspect of ritual separation of the bride and groom after the consummation of their marriage

---

Religion and its Social Setting (Cincinnati, 1933), pp. 135–6, 142, 148, 151; S. W. Baron, *The Jewish Community*, 3 vols (Philadelphia, 1942), 2, p. 347.

[32] Addison, *PSJ*, p. 90. Note his explanation linking this difference to 'the uncertain tenure of the Houses which they hire for Synagogues'.

[33] Ross, *View*, p. 289.

[34] Addison, *PSJ*, pp. 47–8.

[35] See Ross, *View*, p. 389.

which is not mentioned by Buxtorf, and which is known from few, if any, other sources—the groom spends no time in the company of his new wife other than at meals (apparently on account of her post-coital impurity during the week after the wedding!). Here, too, it is likely that Addison is providing us with authentic information about the customs of North African Jewry, but we know this only after comparing him with his learned Swiss predecessor, and when possible, with other first-hand accounts as well.[36]

Addison's *Present State of the Jews*, then, sometimes reflects what he *saw* in Barbary and sometimes reflects what he *read* upon his return to England. It can only be used selectively, then, as an ethnographic source about North Africa, although beyond ethnography it tells us also about the participant-observer himself, about the impact upon him of his encounter with foreign cultures in a foreign land, and also, inadvertently, about the difficulties for such a foreigner in acquiring information from native informants. I should like to conclude with two more examples from the Jewish life-cycle which suggest some of the complexity of his work. In his chapters on birth and its rituals (6 and 7) Addison praises the Jewish women of Barbary for their 'orderly deportment' during childbirth. Buxtorf, by contrast, had described the Jewish woman's pregnancy and childbirth, with its many superstitious practices, as 'a matter for us of laughter'.[37] Concerning the circumcision ceremony Addison notes, like Buxtorf, that it may take place in the home or in the synagogue, but, unlike the latter, he adds that 'The wealthier Jews seldom neglect to carry their children to the synagogue—for the greater parade.' This last point would seem to qualify, therefore, as authentic testimony, if not necessarily complimentary, about the Jews of Barbary.[38]

Buxtorf, in his *Synagoga Judaica*, had mentioned the distinction between rich and poor with regard to another aspect of circumcision—the choice of a circumcisor. The wealthy Jews, he claimed, could afford to hire one with experience, 'but such Learners (beginners) commonly

---

[36] Addison, *PSJ*, p. 51. Note the use of this section by Issachar Ben-Ami, 'Le mariage traditionnel chez les Juifs marocains', in I. Ben-Ami and D. Noy, eds, *Studies in Marriage Customs: Folklore Research Studies, IV* (Jerusalem, 1974), pp. 65–6, 69–70. For other citations of Addison there see pp. 14, 21, 30, 50.

[37] Ibid., p. 55; Ross, *View*, ch. 2, pp. 54–5.

[38] Addison, *PSJ*, p. 60. Note also ibid., p. 59, his valuable testimony concerning the vigil on the night before the circumcision, at which 'the Women visit their Gossip, with whom they usually pass the whole night in mirth and freedom', discussed in Elliott Horowitz, 'The Eve of the Circumcision: a chapter in the history of Jewish nightlife', *Journal of Social History*, 23 (1989), p. 57.

smooth up some poor Jew with proffer of money to suffer them to make an experiment on their son.' Addison makes a similar observation with regard to the choice of ritual circumcisor ('The rich admit none to perform this office upon their children, who have not . . . long made it their profession', whereas those in the learning stages 'deal with the indigent Jews to circumcise their sons, giving their fathers money for so doing'[39]); but here I would be less confident in the ethnographic accuracy of his information, since he may well have lifted it from Buxtorf. The Venetian rabbi Leone Modena, it might be added, did feel it necessary to neutralize Buxtorf's comments on this matter, for he made a point of stating in his *Riti* that the circumcisor is always 'an expert skilfull man at the businesse'.[40]

Buxtorf had concluded his account of the circumcision ceremony with a description of the *mezizah*, the sucking and spitting out of the residual blood from the glans, which, he claimed, was performed by the circumcisor three times. Although the custom of sucking and spitting *three* times does not appear in R. Joseph Karo's *Shulkhan Arukh* (the standard code of Jewish law), it is mentioned in at least two other sixteenth-century sources of a very different nature—the travel diary of Michel de Montaigne, who witnessed a circumcision in Rome, and that of Thomas Platter of Basle, who recorded his impressions of such a ceremony in Avignon in 1599, shortly, that is, before Buxtorf (also of Basle) wrote his *Synagoga Judaica*.[41] This appears to be the kind of instance in which the kind of descriptive knowledge provided by outsiders is more useful to the historian than the prescriptive information provided by insiders.

Yet travellers and ethographers, too, are sometimes misled when they naïvely rely on native informants, and this is what happened to our stranger in a strange land, Lancelot Addison, on at least one occasion. Unlike Buxtorf and Montaigne, he omits any reference to the sucking and spitting of blood in his discussion of Jewish circumcision, but it would be wrong to infer from his silence that this practice was not observed among the Jews of Barbary—the *Shulkhan Arukh*, after all, had required that the procedure be performed at least once. His silence may be explained, rather, by his acknowledged reliance in matters of circumcision upon 'an

---

[39] Ross, *View*, p. 61; Addison, *PSJ*, p. 61.

[40] Edmund Chilmead, tr., *The History of the Rites* . . . (London, 1650), p. 203.

[41] Ross, *View*, p. 66; *Shulkhan Arukh*, Yoreh De'ah 264: 3; D. M. Frame, tr. *The Complete Works of Montaigne* . . . (Stanford, 1967), pp. 945–6; S. Kahn, 'Thomas Platter et les juifs d'Avignon', *REJ*, 25 (1892), p. 85. Whereas Montaigne mentions the practice as taking place 'up to three times' Platter refers to its performance 'at least three times'.

old *Mohel* [from Fez] who assured me that the whole Ritual ... was summarily contain'd in what is now set down'.[42] That crafty old circumcisor evidently chose not to tell this Christian clergyman about the *mezizah* performed on the child's penis after the circumcision was over, possibly sensing that it might seem barbarous to a civilized man from Europe. It is possible, furthermore, that the old *mohel* had some knowledge of the blood-libel against the Jews, which had enjoyed some popularity in Europe (it had appeared in Spain, from which most of the Jewish families in Barbary originally came, before the expulsion), and which drew visually upon the image of an old, bearded Jew drawing blood from a child.[43]

Addison was apparently emboldened, after the success of the first edition of his book, which was published in 1675, to change its title somewhat for the second edition, which came out a year later.[44] Whereas the first had read *The Present State of the Jews: (More Particularly relating to those in Barbary)*, the parenthetic qualification was removed in the second edition. Its author evidently realized that with the return of the Jews to England during the previous two decades it was the Present State of the Jews in general, rather than those in distant Barbary, that people wanted to read about. He may have felt fairly well justified in his shift to a broader title, since a considerable amount of his material was taken, albeit without acknowledgement, from a Swiss scholar expert in Hebrew and Aramaic who was familiar with the customs of Ashkenazic Jewry in Europe.

Addison, then, was hardly in a position to complain when in 1676, the year in which the second edition of his *Present State of the Jews* was published, there appeared in Nuremberg a collection of accounts, in German, of Asia and Africa, one of which ran to 150 pages and bore the title, *Den gegenwartiger Beschaffenheit des Judenthums: Absonderlich in Africa und der so gennanten Barbaren*.[45] Lancelot Addison's name was nowhere mentioned, but this sort of practice, as we have seen, was fairly common

---

[42] Addison, *PSJ*, pp. 61, 64.

[43] On this topic see the recent work of R. Po-chia Hsia, *The Myth of Ritual Murder: Jews and Magic in Reformation Germany* (New Haven, 1988), and my review in the *Journal of Social History*, 23 (1990), pp. 600–4.

[44] A third edition appeared in London in 1682. See Donald Wing, *Short-title Catalogue of Books printed in England, Scotland, Ireland, Wales, and British America . . . 1641–1700*, 2nd edn, 1 (New York, 1972), p. 17, no. 528. The 1684 edition listed there (no. 529) on the basis of a copy supposedly in the library of Emmanuel College, Cambridge, is based on an error, as I was able to determine by examining the (1682) copy there.

[45] *Asiatischen und Africanischen Denckwurdigkeiten dieser Zeiten* (Nuremberg, 1676), pp. 577–728. See also J. C. Wolf, *Bibliotheca Hebrea*, 4 vols (Hamburg, 1715–33), 2, p. 1074.

in the seventeenth century. If he was a sporting fellow, he might even have been moved to quote the words of King Adoni-Bezek from the King James translation of the Bible he knew so well: 'As I have done, so God hath requited me (Judges 1. 7).'

Bar-Ilan University

THE PHENOMENON OF PHILO-SEMITISM

by DAVID S. KATZ

NO ONE would accuse Martin Luther of being philo-Semitic. Even his first, so-called pro-Jewish pamphlet to the Jews is tentative in the extreme and conditional on their accepting Christianity in its purer Protestant form. But even he could not disguise his admiration for the Jews in two areas. The first was sheer survival.

> The Jews are the poorest people among all nations on earth [he said], they are plagued every where, scattered to and fro in all Countries, they have no certain place, they sit like as on a wheel-barrow, have no Countrie, people nor Government, yet they attend with great desire, they cheer up themselves and saie, It will bee soon better with us.

The second reason for grudging respect was their mastery of the Hebrew language. 'If I were young,' Luther mused, 'so would I contrive a waie and means for the perfect learning of the Hebrew tongue, which is both glorious and profitable, and without which the Holie Scriptures cannot rightly bee understood.' But Luther was anxious to avoid misunderstanding: his attraction to the Jews ended there. 'The Jews [said Luther] do hope, that wee intend to joine with them in their opinions, in regard wee go in hand, teach and learn the Hebrew language, but their hope is meerly vain, they must bee constrained to accept of our Religion and of the crucified Christ.'[1] Luther, as in so much else, points us here in the direction to be taken by many Christians in the early modern period and after: devotion to Scripture often rubbed off on the descendants of the biblical heroes described therein, even to the extent of producing a certain esteem for the Jews and their culture, with or without the desire to see their ultimate conversion to Christianity.

At least from the era of the Renaissance and the Reformation, philo-Semitism was an important phenomenon among intellectuals, and in many cases a popular attitude as well. Two clarifying points need to be made at the outset, however. Firstly, philo-Semitism, like its opposite number, is admittedly an ambiguous term, but it will be used here in the simplest sense, to describe an attitude which finds Jews and Jewish culture

---

[1] Martin Luther, *Colloquia Mensalia: or, Dr Martin Luther's Divine Discourses At his Table*, tr. Capt. Henrie Bell (London, 1652), pp. 502, 512, 515–16.

admirable, desirable, or even in demand. Undeniably the motives for such a turn of mind may be ulterior: conversion of these Jews to Christianity often lurks not very far below the surface and even above it. This is an inevitable consequence before the modern period of any caring Christian applying himself to the Jewish problem. As John Wesley put it in another context, if a man can be brought to Christianity it may be contrary to his inclinations now, but 'his soul shall live, and he will probably bless you to all eternity.'[2] So, too, did Gibbon note that among the early Christians there 'were many who felt a sincere compassion for the danger of their friends and countrymen, and who exerted the most benevolent zeal to save them from the impending destruction.'[3] The desire to convert Jews to Christianity and thereby save their souls has been one of the most powerful motivating forces behind philo-Semitism, and does not automatically exclude a positive attitude towards them. Secondly, looking over the history of Jewish–Christian relations since the Renaissance, it is almost embarrassing to take note of some of the subjects on which the two faiths found common ground. Many of the issues involved seem like classic dead ends of intellectual and religious history, but nevertheless their application has had enormous practical and even political consequences, and we shall need to take these subjects seriously if we can ever begin to understand how a people so often reviled could have become popular and positively portrayed in particular circumstances.

I

The Renaissance emphasis on textual analysis, on reintegrating the classical text with the original classical meaning, was bound to have consequent religious implications. No longer was Greek and Roman literature to be used as a vehicle for demonstrating Christian values and ethics; now it came to be seen again as texts written within a specific temporal and cultural context. Beginning with Erasmus, if not before, these methods were applied to Holy Scripture, although at first with the New Testament alone, which was always conceived to be more the work of man than of God, and therefore a legitimate proving-ground for philological tinkering. Every jot and tittle of the Old Testament might still be

---

[2] R. Southey, *Life of Wesley and Rise and Progress of Methodism* (London, 1890), p. 203: quoted in E. P. Thompson, *The Making of the English Working Class* (New York, 1963), p. 375.
[3] Edward Gibbon, *The Decline and Fall of the Roman Empire*, ed. D. A. Saunders (New York, 1952), p. 279.

seen as divinely inspired, written with the finger of God on Mount Sinai, but it was inevitable that one day the Renaissance would come to the Pentateuch as well.

That revolution in biblical studies was long delayed, for not until the seventeenth century, even in Roman Catholic circles, was the Old Testament considered to be fair game. Nevertheless, the initial interest of Renaissance scholars in the Old Testament was not narrowly textual, but included many occult applications of the biblical message. It was Pico della Mirandola (1463–94) who was the first to introduce the Jewish mystical tradition, the Kabbalah, as a Christian tool for biblical analysis. Pico began to study the Kabbalah in 1486, the year of his famous 900 Theses, of which forty-seven came directly from kabbalistic sources and a further seventy-two were his own conclusions based on kabbalistic research. One of his theses proclaimed that 'no science can better convince us of the divinity of Jesus Christ than magic and the Kabbalah.'[4] Indeed, the kabbalistic techniques of *gematria* (whereby each letter stands for a significant numerical value) and *notarikon* (whereby words are seen as abbreviations) efficiently served Christian needs. The first three letters of the Hebrew Bible, for example, א - ר - ב , could easily be an abbreviation for אב - רוח - בן , Son–Spirit–Father. The placing of the Hebrew letter ש in the median position of the Tetragrammaton produced an approximation of the name 'Jesus'. As the unspeakable word becomes pronounceable, so, too, is the ineffable made tangible, the spirit made flesh. Even the vertical arrangement of the four letters of the Hebrew Tetragrammaton seemed to create the stick figure of a man.[5]

Pico's determination to use the Kabbalah in the context of Christian theological discussion promoted the first genuine scholarly interest in this important Jewish tradition, and at exactly the same time that the Jews were being expelled from Spain. Iberian Jews were instrumental in raising the study of the Kabbalah to new heights in Italy, for one of the intellectual effects of the expulsion from Spain was to turn the entire mystical tradition around from being focused on the origins of the world to its

---

[4] On Pico generally, with reference to the Kabbalah, see, e.g., Ernst Cassirer, 'Giovanni Pico della Mirandola: a study in the history of Renaissance ideas', *JHI*, 3 (1942), pp. 123–44, 319–46.

[5] On Kabbalah generally, see Gershom Scholem, *Major Trends in Jewish Mysticism* (Jerusalem, 1941), and *Kabbalah* (Jerusalem, 1974). On Christian Kabbalah, see J. L. Blau, *The Christian Interpretation of the Cabala in the Renaissance* (New York, 1944); F. Secret, *Les Kabbalistes Chrétiens de la Renaissance* (Paris, 1964); W. J. Bousma, 'Postel and the significance of Renaissance Cabalism', *JWCI*, 17 (1954), pp. 318–32; Frances A. Yates, *The Occult Philosophy in the Elizabethan Age* (London, 1979).

eventual apocalyptic destruction. The flight from Spain was the birth-pangs of the Messiah, and the Kabbalah was reinterpreted during the sixteenth century to reflect these new pessimistic orientations in an era of holocaust. Pico and his spiritual descendants, then, were latching on to a Jewish philosophy in the process of rapid development, as a contemporary Jewish intellectual movement came to influence Christian theology. Furthermore, since Kabbalah was fundamentally biblical, it was not a *prisca theologia*, and thereby was spared the suspicious scepticism that might be connected with the parallel hermetic interest in the Egyptian tradition. Through Pico's influence, Johannes Reuchlin (1455–1522) was led to kabbalistic and Hebraic wisdom, which he studied in Italy under Jacob ben Jehiel Loans, the Jewish court physician of Frederick III. Reuchlin produced in 1506 the first Hebrew grammar in Latin, and published the first full treatises on Kabbalah written by a Gentile.[6]

Certainly, to some extent, the fascination which Pico and Reuchlin had for Hebrew and Kabbalah was part of Renaissance eclecticism, the notion that the truth could be found scattered in a wide variety of sources. Yet, more importantly, there was also the belief that the Kabbalah was part of the original divine message given by God on Mount Sinai, and that it had remained pure, untainted by the intervention of the rabbis and their obfuscating Talmud. Those drawn to Jewish sources were soon in dire need of guidance, such as could only be had from living Jews. Many Jewish rabbis and even medical doctors found themselves sought after by their intellectual Christian neighbours as purveyors of whatever Hebrew knowledge they might have had, no matter how haphazardly it had been acquired. Eventually their monopoly would be weakened, both by the printing of kabbalistical works and the rise of Lurianic Kabbalah, the new variety of the mystical tradition which was being developed at Safed, in Palestine, but for nearly a century Jewish teachers were much in demand.

Rabbi Elijah Menahem Halfan described the new-found popularity of Jewish scholars as somewhat exasperating. 'In the last twenty years,' he wrote,

> knowledge has increased, and people have been seeking everywhere for instruction in Hebrew. Especially after the rise of the sect of Luther, many of the nobles and scholars of the land sought to have thorough knowledge of this glorious science (Kabbalah). They have

---

[6] Johannes Reuchlin, *De rudimentis Hebraicis* (Pforzheim, 1506); *De verbo mirifico* (Basle, 1494); *De arte Cabalistica* (Haguenau, 1517). For an interesting discussion of the Egyptian tradition, see Martin Bernal, *Black Athena* (London, 1987).

exhausted themselves in this search, because among our people there are but a small number of men learned in this wisdom, for after the great number of troubles and expulsions, but a few remain. So seven learned men grasp a Jewish man by the hem of his garment and say: 'Be our master in this science!'[7]

Pico had his Rabbi Yohanan Isaac Allemanno, whom he met in Florence in 1488 and engaged as his teacher. We know little about Allemano, but it appears that he was acquainted with Lorenzo de Medici as well. Allemanno's son Isaac taught Pico's nephew Giovanni Francesco.[8] Flavius Mithradates, that mysterious Sicilian Jew who converted to Christianity, translated kabbalistic texts for Pico, and taught Hebrew, Aramaic, and Arabic, not only in Italy, but in France and Germany as well. He also translated the Koran into Latin for the Duke of Urbino, and preached a sermon before the Pope on the suffering of Jesus.[9]

Indeed, the point has been made that the entire direction of translation was altered. Before the Renaissance many philosophical treatises were translated into Hebrew by Jews for the use of other Jews. From the beginning of the fifteenth century, on the other hand, Jews and converts from Judaism were translating Hebrew works into Latin or Italian and themselves writing in these languages.[10] It has recently been argued that (apart from a Judaized Plato) contemporary Jews were little interested in the Renaissance notion of two sources for ancient theology, pagan and Christian, preferring the single path that led from Mount Sinai.[11] Yet the example of Abraham Yagel (1553–1623), physician and tutor to moneyed Jewish families in northern Italy, shows that many Jews were drawn to classical authors, as he compared them with Jewish sources and concluded that his own tradition was superior to that of Greece and Rome.[12] A great

---

[7] Quoted from a manuscript source in Moshe Idel, 'The Magical and Neoplatonic Interpretations of the Kabbalah in the Renaissance', in B. Cooperman, ed., *Jewish Thought in the Sixteenth Century* (Cambridge, 1987), pp. 186–242, esp. pp. 186–7. See also Idel, 'Hermeticism and Judaism', in I. Merkel and A. Debus, eds, *Hermeticism and the Renaissance* (Washington, 1988), pp. 59–76.

[8] Idel, 'Magical', p. 212.

[9] H. Wirszubski, *A Christian Kabbalist Reads the Torah* [Hebrew] (Jerusalem, 1977).

[10] Idel, 'Magical', p. 187.

[11] Moshe Idel, 'Kabbalah and Ancient Theology in R. Isaac and Judah Abrabanel' [Hebrew], in M. Dorman and Z. Levy, eds, *The Philosophy of Love of Leone Ebreo* (Haifa, 1985), pp. 73–112. Cf. Idel, 'Kabbalah, Platonism and Prisca Theologia: the Case of R. Menasseh ben Israel', in Y. Kaplan, M. Mechoulan, and R. H. Popkin, eds, *Menasseh ben Israel and His World* (Leiden, 1989), pp. 207–19.

[12] David B. Ruderman, *Kabbalah, Magic, and Science: the Cultural Universe of a Sixteenth-Century Jewish Physician* (Cambridge, USA, 1988).

scholar like Azariah de' Rossi (c.1511–c.1578), whose masterpiece *Me'or Einayim* [Enlightenment of the Eyes] was written in the mid-1570s, demonstrated that Jews might participate fully in the intellectual ferment of the Renaissance.

The Reformation strengthened this interest and respect for Jewish learning, not so much in the kabbalistic vein, but more directly for the Jews as the guardians of the Old Testament, which came to be seen as their most important historical function.[13] The Word of God was his legacy to mankind, and his Word was in Hebrew. The principle of *sola scriptura* demanded a mastery of the Hebrew language. Yet even in rationalistic Protestantism, Hebrew soon acquired mystical signification and kabbalistic intonations. Hebrew was the vernacular of Adam and Eve in the Garden of Eden, when Adam gave names to the animals, and there was no poetic ambiguity between words and the things to which they referred. The Bible tells us that God created the universe by speaking, and the language he spoke was almost certainly Hebrew. There was always the hope that one day mankind might recreate this entire technology by a study of the intricacies of the Hebrew language, and thereby take part in the divine process.[14]

During the first half of the sixteenth century, then, both Protestants and Roman Catholics alike were united in the belief that in order to reach full *Christian* understanding it was necessary to study the Old Testament, the Hebrew language, and even the Jewish mystical tradition, the Kabbalah. The Jews of Europe, and especially in Italy, were therefore given positive associations, and a number of Jewish intellectuals found themselves popular and in demand as representatives of an entire people.

This almost idyllic situation came to a swift official end in the middle of the sixteenth century. Throughout the periods of the Renaissance and the early Reformation there had always been an undercurrent of suspicion towards the possible contribution the unbelieving Jews might make to Christianity. Luther, of course, changed his view of 1523, *Das Jesus Christus ein geborner Jude sei* to his final perspective exactly twenty years later, *Von den Juden und iren Luegen*. Erasmus agreed with his old adversary Luther at least on this point, worrying that interest in Hebrew and

---

[13] See also H. H. Ben-Sasson, 'The Reformation in contemporary Jewish opinion', *Proc. Israel Academy of Sciences and Humanities*, 4 (1970), pp. 239–326.

[14] D. S. Katz, 'The Language of Adam in Seventeenth-Century England', in Hugh Lloyd-Jones, Valerie Pearl, and Blair Worden, eds, *History and Imagination: Essays in Honour of H. R. Trevor-Roper* (London, 1981), pp. 132–45.

Kabbalah might overflow into unacceptable theological positions.[15] This ideological anti-Jewish attitude, somewhat dormant at the end of the fifteenth century and the beginning of the sixteenth, mushroomed in the codification of the Catholic faith made during the Counter-Reformation. Pope Paul IV condemned the Talmud in August 1553, the first step in a concerted attack against the Jews and their culture that culminated in his bull *Cum nimis absurdum* of 1555, by which the Jews of the Papal State were confined to ghettos. The burning alive of twenty-five Marranos at Ancona in the same year was clearly part of the same policy.[16]

Abhorrent as his actions were, Pope Paul IV had made dramatically the quite valid point that Christian interest in Hebrew, Kabbalah, and Jewish culture had gotten out of hand. No longer were these subjects mere tools to Christian knowledge, but they were being studied as ends in themselves. Catholic Hebrew scholarship became severely atrophied, contacts with living Jews were reduced, and Catholic philo-Semitism was dealt a mortal blow from which it never recovered. The attraction of the Hebrew Old Testament for Protestants, on the other hand, continued to be dominant, and therefore interest in contemporary living Jews survived. Indeed, to the initial biblical and kabbalistic associations was added an entirely new sphere of pro-Jewish activity, millenarianism, the belief that the Second Coming is imminent, and that certain preparations must be made for the thousand-year rule of Christ and his saints in this world before the final apocalypse. The Jews had a role to play in this great drama, and there was growing interest in the late sixteenth to middle seventeenth century in converting them and possibly restoring them to the Holy Land as part of the required provision. As Luther himself suggested, one of the reasons for the refusal of world Jewry to accept Christianity was that most Jews were acquainted with the Roman Catholic Church alone and therefore were quite naturally repulsed by the mountain of absurdities which the believer was called upon to accept. Contacts with Jews needed to be increased, not only for what they could teach Christian biblical scholars, but, more importantly, in order to reveal the Christian message in its Protestant purity and thereby facilitate the conversion of the Jews and the Second Coming of Christ.

---

[15] W. L. Gundersheimer, 'Erasmus, Humanism, and the Christian Cabala', *JWCI*, 26 (1963), pp. 38–52.

[16] K. R. Stow, *Catholic Thought and Papal Jewish Policy, 1555–1593* (New York, 1977); J. I. Israel, *European Jewry in the Age of Mercantilism, 1550–1750* (Oxford, 1985), pp. 18–19.

II

By the end of the sixteenth century, then, there was a well-defined stratum of intellectual philo-Semitism, at least in the Protestant world. What is most exciting is that at times intellectual philo-Semitism found a political expression, especially in the middle of the seventeenth century. The two most prominent examples of this phenomenon can be found in Sweden and in England. Queen Christina's hope of turning Sweden into the intellectual lion of the North was apparent not only in her systematic acquisition of books, manuscripts, paintings, and sculpture, but also in her importation of European intellectuals who were willing to submit to her service. Descartes was the most prominent of these, dying in Sweden not long after his arrival, having failed to survive early morning icy tutorials in the Queen's library or in the carriage between Stockholm and Uppsala. But so, too, did Christina treat with Rabbi Menasseh ben Israel of Amsterdam, purchasing Hebrew books and manuscripts and simultaneously holding out the hope that he might find employment in Sweden as the Jewish Descartes.[17] The English case is even more dramatic, as Oliver Cromwell and his party took the extraordinary political risk of holding an open conference on the subject of Jewish readmission, thereby acting practically on their intellectual philo-Semitism.[18]

Certain common characteristics can be found among the most clear-cut demonstrations of political philo-Semitism, not only in Sweden and in England, but elsewhere in Europe as well. Firstly, in most of these places there was no established Jewish community. Jews were pure and pious literary biblical characters alone, not a presence to be explained and reviled. Secondly, the Jews under discussion tended to be aristocratic and elegant Sephardim rather than the typical caricatures of Ashkenazi Jews. Thirdly, a political leader was in power whose intellectual views were those of the educated elite. Finally, certain issues were present which enabled people to connect the biblical Jew with his modern counterpart, since in most minds the two figures were as separate and unrelated as ancient and modern Egyptians are to people today.

These characteristics were quite clearly present in England during the middle of the seventeenth century. That Jews were readmitted to that country in that period is not entirely surprising in itself, given the

[17] D. S. Katz, 'Menasseh ben Israel's Mission to Queen Christina of Sweden', *Jewish Social Studies*, 45 (1983–4), pp. 57–72; S. Åkerman, *Queen Christina of Sweden and her Circle* (Leiden, 1991), pp. 178–95.

[18] Generally, see D. S. Katz, *Philo-Semitism and the Readmission of the Jews to England, 1603–1655* (Oxford, 1982).

contemporary phenomenon of intellectual and even religious philo-Semitism. What is startling is that this was done openly and in full public view, an extreme example of political philo-Semitism. This was very different from the procedure followed in other parts of Europe, where (apart from Holland) such improvements as there were in the Jewish condition were done quietly. Although the Jews were officially expelled from Bohemia and Moravia in 1542, for example, a list of 1546 shows that nearly a thousand Jews lived in Prague. Ferdinand I also looked for a balance between those who wanted the Jews to be expelled, such as the Viennese burghers, for example, and those who hoped the Jews would be allowed to stay. Since the Jews were completely dependent on the Emperor's pleasure, in a sense they were his most loyal subjects in Germany. Ferdinand's solution was to discourage Jewish settlement at the same time that he acted to admit them on the sly. Maximilian II, his successor, also followed a policy of shifts and oscillations. Connivance was clearly the most accepted early modern method for dealing with the local Jewish community.[19]

Oliver Cromwell's strategy of admitting Jews to England by means of a public conference was therefore eccentric in the extreme, a bizarre event in an era that did not recognize the desirability of religious plurality or confessional toleration. Since the readmission of the Jews to England provides us with a most exceptional case of political philo-Semitism overlapping with the passive intellectual variety, and since the central themes there will be repeated again and again later, it is worth looking at it carefully. Why was the Whitehall Conference called in 1655 to discuss the readmission of the Jews to England? Where did the idea originate? Why were the Cromwellians willing to take the political risk of readmission? How was the solid economic opposition of the merchant community neutralized? And finally, from where did the support for Jewish resettlement come? Before answering these burning questions, it should also be understood at the outset that this was a Puritan issue of the Cromwellian period, since after the Conference failed, England reverted to the European pattern of informal Jewish toleration, until royal permission was indirectly granted in 1664.

Clearly there were a number of important problems to be overcome before political philo-Semitism could take effect. The most significant of these related to the uniqueness of the Jewish case, which was

---

[19] For an overview, see S. W. Baron, *A Social and Religious History of the Jews*, 2nd edn, vol. 14 (New York, 1969), pp. 147–223, esp. pp. 149–66.

fundamentally different from the situation of other non-Anglicans, even Roman Catholics, who were also persecuted in seventeenth-century England. For Catholics were Englishmen who had made the wrong religious choice. They might even be considered political traitors since they owed allegiance to the pope who had freed Englishmen from their loyalty to a heretical Protestant king. Nevertheless, an Anglican conversion would wholly purify them and put them on exactly the same footing as everyone else. Not so with the Jews, who were not necessarily regarded as completely human, let alone English. Demonic associations, horns, a particular smell, and other distinctive features made the Jews a race apart. The stories of the ritual murders of William of Norwich (1144) and Little St Hugh of Lincoln (1255), kept alive in Chaucer's *Canterbury Tales*, gave eternal life to dormant fear and prejudice. These were obstacles to be overcome if intellectual philo-Semitism were to be translated into political action.

Certainly the high place of Hebrew in the Renaissance and the emphasis on the Old Testament in Protestantism helped to break down some of this antagonism and to place the Jews in a favourable light. But without a doubt it was Rabbi Menasseh ben Israel (1604–57) who caused a latent English philo-Semitism to crystallize as he turned it into a political movement capable of bringing about the readmission of the Jews to this country. That English intellectuals and theologians should have been interested in the living posterity of biblical heroes is a problem in itself, as we shall see, but it is equally curious that this Dutch rabbi should have looked towards London. We now know that during the five years before his arrival in England in 1655, Menasseh's chief goal was to obtain a position at the court of Queen Christina of Sweden as her Jewish librarian, bibliographer, and tutor. In the early 1650s Menasseh's situation verged on the desperate. Despite his fame among prominent Gentiles during the seventeenth century and after, Menasseh, in fact, had never succeeded in establishing himself as a respected and financially secure scholar in the Jewish community at Amsterdam, and was forced to turn to publishing in order to supplement his meagre income, which he received as a teacher in the primary school of the newly-united synagogues of Amsterdam after 1639. At one stage Menasseh even considered emigration to the New World, and it was only his appointment as director of the community school and lecturer at the *yeshivah* that changed his mind. This was followed in 1644 by his appointment as principal of the newly-established talmudic academy founded by Abraham and Isaac Pereira. In spite of these rather minor and poorly paid posts, however, Menasseh was never considered to be a great mind by the Jews of Amsterdam, a fact which encouraged him to seek his honours elsewhere.[20]

Paradoxically, Menasseh's fame had grown in the Christian world during the 1630s and 1640s chiefly through the publication of books on Jewish topics in Spanish and Latin, which made him more well known among Gentiles than finer rabbinical scholars writing in Hebrew. Great men like Vossius, father and son, and Grotius were his admirers, and he was widely regarded as the Jewish ambassador to the Gentile community. Such admiration which he found outside of Jewish society did not help him pay the bills, and financially his situation went from bad to worse. In 1648 his son Joseph died in Lublin, losing the large consignment of books and cash that had been in his possession. Pernambuco, in Brazil, had been under siege since 1645, and by the time his son died, Menasseh had lost his investments in the New World as well. When he published his famous book on *The Hope of Israel* in 1650, dedicated to the English Parliament, he had reached rock bottom, both financially and in terms of any hopes he might still have entertained for a formal position in the Jewish hierarchy in Amsterdam. Queen Christina's abdication in 1654 meant not only a financial loss due to books sent and not yet paid for, but spelled the end of his dream of making a career for himself on the circuit of international intellectuals.[21]

But the seeds he had planted in that important book came immediately to fruition, and now he had the leisure and the will to turn to England, where his works were widely known and respected in the circle of John Dury, one of Cromwell's closest spiritual companions, and his unofficial emissary to the Protestant churches of Europe. For the theme of *The Hope of Israel* was concerned with one of the central questions which occupied English and continental theologians since the Reformation, when they contemplated God's plan, the Second Coming, and the perceived necessary previous conversion of the Jews: that is, the mystery of the Lost Ten Tribes, who would have to receive the Protestant message in order to complete the circle. The debate over the Lost Ten Tribes brought about the rehabilitation of Menasseh ben Israel, and through him the readmission of the Jews to England. More importantly, the issue of these vanished Israelites and the millenarian part all Jews would play in the Second Coming would serve to be one of the themes which would make

---

[20] See generally Kaplan, Mechoulan, and Popkin, eds, *Menasseh ben Israel*. See also Cecil Roth, *A Life of Menasseh ben Israel: Rabbi, Printer, and Diplomat* (Philadelphia, 1934).

[21] Katz, 'Christina'.

philo-Semitism almost an inevitable component until our own day of Protestant denominations that stayed close to the original idea of *sola scriptura*.

III

Ever since Columbus, the presence of the American Indians in a part of the world apparently so distant from the scene of biblical events had been a problem for theologians. Columbus himself had no difficulty with their discovery. He died in the belief that he had landed on the east coast of Asia: the Indians were Asiatics, and their presence was interesting but unremarkable. Columbus reported in his journal that when he sent a reconnaissance party into the interior, he included one Luis de Torres, a converted Marrano who 'understood Hebrew and Chaldee and even some Arabic'. Torres was meant to be the interpreter of the expedition in case they encountered any Hebrew-speaking Indians.[22] It was entirely possible, he reasoned, that these strange people might be the barbarized descendants of the Ten Tribes of Israel whose fate was described in the biblical canon itself:

> In the ninth year of Hoshea the king of Assyria took Samaria, and carried Israel away into Assyria, and placed them in Halah and in Habor *by* the river of Gozan, and in the cities of the Medes . . . So was Israel carried away out of their own land to Assyria unto this day.[23]

The Apocrypha continued the story and revealed further that after the conquest the ten tribes

> took this counsel among themselves, that they would leave the multitude of the heathen, and go forth into a further country, where never mankind dwelt, That they might there keep their statutes, which they never kept in their own land . . . Then dwelt they there until the latter time; and now when they shall begin to come, The Highest shall stay the springs of the stream again, that they may go through.[24]

Although some proto-anthropologists, such as Isaac la Peyrère, suggested that the American Indians might be entirely outside the Scripture story,

---

[22] *The Journal of Christopher Columbus*, ed. C. Jane and L. A. Vigneras (London, 1960), pp. 51, 206. Cf. A. B. Gould y Quincy, 'Nueva Lista Documentada de los Tripulantes de Colon en 1492', *Bol. de la Real Acad. de la Hist.*, 75 (1924), pp. 34–49.

[23] II Kgs 17. 6, 23.

[24] II Esdr. 13. 41–2, 46–7.

338

virtually all men who wrote about the origin of the American Indians agreed that they must in some way be descended from Adam and Eve, if not from Noah as well: the chief difficulty was to describe the route of migration, and to fit the chronology with the accepted timetable of Genesis.[25] The identification of the Indians with the Lost Ten Tribes was one convenient and popular solution, and one which found supporters not only in the Spanish-speaking world, but also in England and France.[26]

These speculations took on a renewed urgency in 1644, when a Marrano named Antonio de Montezinos, recently returned from Quito Province, in Ecuador, testified under oath before Rabbi Menasseh ben Israel that he had met Israelites of the tribe of Reuben there, living secretly, deep in the interior of the territory. Montezinos recounted his arrival at the secret kingdom, where the inhabitants repeated the Jewish credo, the *Shema*, along with nine vague remarks and prophecies, but refused to allow him to cross the river Sambatyon which bordered their country. Montezinos estimated that he spoke with nearly three hundred Israelite Indians during his three days there, but they would see him only in small groups, and declined to elaborate on their nine cryptic statements. Montezinos's Indian guide explained afterwards that these were Israelites who had come to the New World and defeated the Indians in the area. Since then no outsider had been allowed to cross the river and enter the kingdom itself. These Israelites of the Lost Ten Tribes believed that the arrival of the Spanish in the New World, the coming of ships to the South Seas, and the visit of Montezinos fulfilled certain prophecies. Montezinos testified that following his visit he returned to the coast and met other Indians who had visited the Lost Ten Tribes as well.[27]

This startling first-hand account of the current whereabouts and activities of the Lost Ten Tribes was first revealed to the Gentile world in 1649 by Edward Winslow the American missionary, who wrote excitedly to Parliament and the Council of State begging to

> acquaint your Honors, that a godly Minister of this City writing to Rabbi-ben-Israel, a great Dr. of the Jewes, now living at Amsterdam, to know whether after all their labor, travells, and most diligent

---

[25] See now Richard H. Popkin, *Isaac La Peyrère (1596–1676): His Life, Work and Influence* (Leiden, 1987).

[26] See generally, Katz, *Philo-Semitism*, ch. 4.

[27] 'The Relation of Master Antonie Monterinos', in *Ievves in America*, ed. T. Thorowgood (London, 1650). Cf. Menasseh ben Israel, *The Hope of Israel*, ed. Henry Mechoulan and Gerard Nahon (Oxford, 1987), pp. 105–11.

enquiry, they did yet know what was become of the ten Tribes of Israel? His answer was to this effect, if not in these words, That they were certainly transported into America, and that they had infallible tokens of their being there.[28]

It was no secret that this 'godly Minister' of London was John Dury, international crusader for Christian unity. Menasseh had sent Dury a French translation of the testimony, and Dury had it rendered into English and published in Thomas Thorowgood's book *Ievves in America*, which appeared in 1650. John Dury, the man who introduced Montezinos and Menasseh ben Israel to the English public, contributed an 'Epistolicall Discouse' to Thorowgood's collection as well. Although 'at first blush', he confessed, 'the thing which you offer to be believed, will seeme to most men incredible, and extravigent; yet when all things are laid rationally and without prejudice together, there will be nothing of improbability found therein.'[29] Menasseh himself published the full account in his book, *The Hope of Israel*, which appeared at Amsterdam in Latin and Spanish in 1650, and at London the same year in an English edition, translated by Milton's friend Moses Wall; a second English edition is dated 1652.[30] We now know that it was John Dury who decided that the English versions be dedicated to Parliament.[31]

Menasseh's little book reinvigorated the issue of the Lost Ten Tribes and gave the debate a text over which it could centre. More importantly, as we have already seen, Menasseh himself now saw England as a possible fall-back arena of activity should Queen Christina disappoint him, which she would do in 1654 by abdicating and leaving her bills unpaid. Menasseh, in turn, was instantly famous, not only in the circle of philo-Semitic intellectuals, such as Dury and his colleague Samuel Hartlib, but among a much wider group of enthralled readers. Menasseh and Dury worked in concert, although their aims were quite different. John Dury and his group believed that the conversion of the Lost Ten Tribes was a harbinger of the conversion of the European Jews, which, in turn, was a prelude to

---

[28] Edward Winslow, *The Glorious Progress* (London, 1649), repr. *Coll. Mass. Hist. Soc.*, ser. 3, 4 (1834), p. 73.

[29] John Dury, 'An Epistolicall Discourse', in Thorowgood, *Ievves*, sigs D–E2, dated 27 Jan. 1649–50. Dury promises to send Thorowgood a copy of Menasseh's book as soon as it is published.

[30] For the publishing history of *The Hope of Israel*, see the edition of Mechoulan and Nahon, pp. ix–xi.

[31] Ernestine van der Wall, 'Three Letters by Menasseh ben Israel to John Durie: Philo-Judaism and the "Spes Israelis"', *Nederlands Archief voor Kerkgeschiedenis*, 65 (1985), pp. 46–63.

the Second Coming and the millennium, when Christ would rule on earth for a thousand years with his saints. Menasseh, on the other hand, had no intention of converting to Christianity, but relied on the Book of Isaiah, which prophesied that the Lord would 'assemble the outcasts of Israel, and gather together the dispersed of Judah from the four corners of the earth' before the coming of the Messiah. Russia and Palestine might be two corners; South America a newly-discovered third. England was probably the fourth, in part because its designation in medieval Hebrew literature was often קצה הארץ ('the end of the earth'), a Franbreu translation of 'Angleterre'.[32]

It was the issue of the Lost Ten Tribes, then, which caused the rise of Menasseh ben Israel, following neatly upon his fall, as it connected an unemployed and underpaid Dutch rabbi with circles in London who hoped simultaneously to bring the Jews to England, to convert them to true and pure English Protestant Christianity, and through that act to bring closer the Second Coming of Christ. There was an identity of purpose between Christian and Jew in seventeenth-century England, which was already sensitized to philo-Semitism on the basis of the values of the Renaissance and the Reformation common to Northern European culture.

IV

The readmission of the Jews to England was one of the chief practical results of the increased seventeenth-century interest in the Lost Ten Tribes and the imminent Second Coming of Christ. The Jews now being sought were not only the ones wholly in evidence, but their lost brethren as well. This in itself was a variant of the concept of *sola scriptura*, which made belief in the literal text of the Bible almost axiomatic. In Pico's day, Jews were needed for their role as guardians and teachers of sacred information; in Menasseh's, they formed a crucial piece of the divine puzzle. In the following period, biblical and millenarian themes connected to do battle for the authenticity of Scripture, the corner-stone of Protestant theology.

The notion that a long-isolated corner of Jewry could provide a more accurate text of the Bible was much more than the millenarian dream of an imaginative traveller from Ecuador. The European attempt to obtain a

---

[32] Isa. 11. 12; Deut. 28. 64; Cecil Roth, 'New Light on the Resettlement', *TJHSE*, 11 (1928), pp. 113–14.

copy of the biblical manuscripts used by the Chinese Jews of Kaifeng, a struggle which spanned from the late sixteenth until the middle of the nineteenth century, has already been documented.[33] Yet there were other, more immediate, examples of hidden Jewry slightly closer to home, whose location might complete the biblical instruction begun by men like Pico's Jewish teachers. At least from the fourteenth century, European Christians were aware of the existence of a community of Samaritans in Palestine.[34] While prevailing opinion did not place the Samaritans among the Lost Ten Tribes, their very presence and their possession of an ancient text of the Pentateuch made Europeans aware of the possibility that similar and even more important manuscripts might be obtained from the treasures of the Israelites in distant places. It was the Italian traveller Pietro della Valle who first obtained copies of the Samaritan Pentateuch. In 1616 Pietro visited Palestine and Damascus, and in the latter city purchased two manuscripts from a Samaritan there. One of these he gave to the French ambassador in Constantinople; the second he kept for himself, and thereby provided the first Samaritan Pentateuch to arrive in Europe.[35]

The effects of this scholarly infusion were enormous. Richard Simon, the great French pioneer of higher criticism of the Bible, noted at the end of the century that credit for being the first biblical scholar actually to have utilized the Samaritan Pentateuch should go to Father J. Morinus, who was said to have favoured that text over the Masoretic Hebrew version venerated by Jews. In a sense, then, Morinus's use of the Samaritan Pentateuch was the beginning of biblical criticism. He used both of the copies Valle brought back to Europe when compiling his polyglot Bible, and thereby adding a further text to be exploited in conjunction with the Hebrew, Aramaic, Greek, Syriac, Latin, and Arabic versions which were already being submitted to scholarly scrutiny. Simon, summing up his own view, stated that 'the *Hebrew Samaritan Pentateuch* seems to me to be no less authentick, than the Hebrew copy of the same *Pentateuch*, us'd by

---

[33] David S. Katz, 'The Chinese Jews and the problem of biblical authority in eighteenth- and nineteenth-century England', *EHR*, 105 (1990), pp. 893–919.

[34] The Samaritan community was mentioned in earlier non-Christian sources, especially in the twelfth-century travels of Benjamin of Tudela, in his *Itinerary*, ed. M. N. Adler (London, 1907), pp. 33, 37, 38, 44, 46. For a list of such accounts, see N. Shor, 'Reports of Samaritans in the writings of Western Christian travellers from the fourteenth until the end of the eighteenth centuries' [Hebrew], *Cathedra*, 13 (1979), pp. 177–93.

[35] Pietro della Valle, *Viaggi* (Bologna, 1672), I, pp. 406–8, 424: selections in R. Rohricht, *Bibliotheca Geographica palaestinae* (Jerusalem, 1963), p. 947.

the *Jews*, since they are Copies from the same Original, which differ only in Characters, excepting in some various Readings.'[36]

We now know a good deal more about the Samaritan Pentateuch than did Valle or even Richard Simon. The text itself is a version made by the Samaritans of one of the three scriptural traditions in use during the Hasmonaean period (second century BC). This tradition has come to be called 'proto-Samaritan', and along with those known as 'proto-Septuagint' and 'proto-Masoretic', comprise the various strands which existed before the rabbis rejected all others but the third. Simon in his discussion favoured the notion of an *Urtext* from which all others were degenerated, similar to the view which would be promoted by J. G. Eichhorn and other pioneers of *die hohere Kritik* in the late eighteenth century. It seems more likely that the Samaritan Pentateuch derived from an old Palestinian textual tradition which survived there, written in the palaeo-Hebrew script used in the area. The Masoretic text used by Jews and Christians everywhere today derived from the Babylonian tradition introduced into Palestine in the late Hasmonaean period with the influx of Jews from the Diaspora, who also brought with them the modern square form of the Hebrew script. In the late first century AD the rabbis selected the proto-Masoretic text as official and rejected all other traditions. The Samaritans, a Jewish sect established in the early Greek period, defended their text and script against the official ruling, and indeed continue to do so to this day. In brief, then, the Samaritan Pentateuch is not an independent version, but a particular form of the Hebrew text written in a different script. Although the Samaritan Pentateuch differs from the Masoretic text in as many as 6,000 places, most of these are unimportant, and the others are pleonastic, apart from a number of alterations designed to further the interests of the sect itself.[37]

The introduction of the Samaritan Pentateuch into the European biblical arena was bound to create a good deal of controversy. Scholars had long disputed over the relative value of the Masoretic text and the Septuagint, the translation produced by Greek-speaking Egyptian Jews for their

---

[36] Richard Simon, *A Critical History of the Old Testament* (London, 1682), 1, p. 77 [second numbering]; 3, p. 178; J. Morinus, *Exercitationes Biblicae de Hebraei Graecique-textus* (Paris, 1633); G. M. le Jay, J. Morinus, *et al.*, eds, *Biblia* (Paris, 1645). For more on Simon and the Samaritan Pentateuch, see William McKane, *Selected Christian Hebraists* (Cambridge, 1989), ch. 4.

[37] Generally, see J. D. Purvis, *The Samaritan Pentateuch and the Origins of the Samaritan Sect* (Cambridge, Mass., 1968); O. Eissfeldt, *The Old Testament: an Introduction* (London, 1965), pp. 694–5, 782.

own use between the third and first centuries BC. Roman Catholic scholars defended the use of the Septuagint, as well as Jerome's Latin Vulgate (*c.*AD 400): they were not tied to the biblical word alone. Protestants were unable to cast any doubt whatsoever on the Masoretic text of the Old Testament without risking the breakdown of *sola fide* along with *sola scriptura*. The fact that the Samaritan Pentateuch agreed with the Septuagint in about one-third of the variant readings led it to be aligned with that Greek text in early modern biblical discussion. Catholic biblical authorities, such as Morinus and J. H. Hottinger, defended the use of the Samaritan Pentateuch in supplying alternative readings. Protestants, despite the inclusion of a Samaritan text in Brian Walton's polyglot Bible, rejected the Samaritan Pentateuch outright, and it was not until Benjamin Kennicott wrote in its defence in eighteenth-century Oxford that Protestants began to see that the comparison of biblical manuscripts was not necessarily an act of gross atheism.[38]

From our point of view, what is important here is that it was during the seventeenth century that Europeans received for the first time an ancient text of the Scriptures from an isolated Hebrew corner. The Samaritans were no mythical tribe, inhabiting a world beyond the river Sambatyon, that ceased to flow on the Sabbath and rested with God's chosen people. The Samaritans lived in Nablus, in Ottoman Palestine, and came to Aleppo, where Europeans had numerous trade contacts. Pietro della Valle proved that it was possible to confirm the truth of the Bible and broaden our understanding of the text by seeking out Hebrews far away from the mainstream of European life. It was only a matter of time before the millenarian search for the Lost Ten Tribes of Israel would become meshed with the wish of scholars to find documentary evidence for the Divine Word.

Julius Scaliger, the celebrated Dutch orientalist, was the first Westerner to have persuaded the Samaritans to answer his queries. He sent them letters from Cairo and Nablus in 1589, which were translated into Latin by Morinus.[39] Robert Huntington, minister of the church of the English factory at Aleppo, established more intimate contact in the next century, by encouraging the Samaritans to believe that the Jews newly readmitted into England were their lost Samaritan brethren. With

---

[38] Generally, see Purvis, *Samaritan Pentateuch*, pp. 74–5; H. Wheeler Robinson, ed., *The Bible in its Ancient and English Versions* (Oxford, 1940), chs 2 and 4.

[39] Shor, 'Reports', p. 185n.; H. Adams, *The History of the Jews* (London, 1818), pp. 499–500. Scaliger received an answer in 1590 in Hebrew, tr. into Latin in Silvestre de Sacy, *Memoire sur l'état actuel des Samaritains* (Paris, 1812), pp. 16–23.

the help of the German orientalist Job Ludolph, Huntington was able to make his approach to the Samaritans, visiting them at Nablus. In 1672 the Samaritans sent Huntington at Jerusalem a Pentateuch for the Jews of England, with a covering letter to them written from Nablus by Merchib-Ben-Jacob, one of their elders. Huntington sent it all to Thomas Marshal of Oxford, who kept up the correspondence with the Samaritans until his death in 1685.[40] By the time Benjamin Kennicott wrote his controversial defence of the Samaritan Pentateuch in 1753, then, a good deal was already known about their religion and customs, and sixteen Samaritan manuscripts had been removed to England, including seven copies of their Pentateuch deposited at Oxford, Cambridge, and the British Museum.[41]

With the championing of their sacred text by the Protestant Kennicott, it was now acknowledged by the most important European biblical authorities that we might improve our understanding of Scripture by searching for distant outposts of world Jewry. The stakes, in a sense, had been raised. In Pico's time it was enough to find a Jewish teacher of Hebrew and possibly Kabbalah. By the seventeenth and early eighteenth centuries, European Jews had somewhat less to offer, but their brethren in dark corners of the globe were still thought to have important keys to the biblical puzzle as guardians of a text closer to that which their ancestors had heard on the foot of Mount Sinai generations ago. The Jews of Europe, meanwhile, might continue to bask in the reflected glory of their Israelite cousins.

V

Apart from the Chinese Jews and the Samaritans, a third community of 'Lost Israelites' had been located by the end of the seventeenth century, and in whose possession was known to be ancient manuscripts—the Jews of India on the Malabar coast. By their own account, in a Hebrew letter sent in about 1787 to the Portuguese Jews of New York, in 'the course of their wanderings in exile after the destruction of the Second Temple ...

---

[40] Shor, 'Reports', p. 186; Adams, *History*, pp. 500–3, from material in l'abbé Grégoire, *Histoire des sectes religieuses* (Paris, 1810). Ludolph's answers from the Samaritans are repr. in J. Morinus, *Antiquitates Ecclesiae Orientalis* (London, 1682). Their last letter was dated 1689, and reached him two years later.

[41] Benjamin Kennicott, *The State of the Printed Hebrew Text of the Old Testament Considered* (Oxford, 1753–9), 1, pp. 337–9; 2, *passim*; *Proposals for Collating the Hebrew Manuscripts* (Oxford, 1761), [p. 21]; [*Proposals*] (Oxford, 1762), [p. 2].

many Jews, both men and women, came to the land of Malabar and settled in four places, namely Kangnur, Paklur, Modi, and Pa-luta.'[42] Passing reference to India is made in the Book of Esther and in the Talmud, which cites a certain 'Rabbi Judah the Indian'.[43] But the first hard evidence for the settlement of Jews in India is inscribed on copper plates still in Cochin, recording privileges granted by the Hindu ruler of Malabar to Joseph Rabban, leader of the community at Cranganore, sometime at the end of the tenth century or the beginning of the next.[44] Both Benjamin of Tudela (*c.*1167) and Marco Polo (*c.*1293) confirm the presence of Jews there.[45] Contact with Europeans began at least with the capture and forced baptism of an Indian Jew by Vasco da Gama in 1498, who brought his prize back to Portugal and gave him his own name.[46] By that time, the most important Jewish settlement on the Malabar coast was at Cochin.[47]

That some of the Lost Ten Tribes settled in India and still lived there as Hebrews, venerating the Old Testament and its God, received confirmation in Menasseh ben Israel's study of the problem, *The Hope of Israel*. Menasseh did not neglect Christian sources: according to Claude Duret, he writes that 'there are an almost infinite number of Jews in Asia, especially in India, and that the king of Cochin is their great favourer.' Furthermore, Jan Huygen van 'Linschoten says (where he treats of Cochin) that they have synagogues there, and that some of them are of the king's council. So not only was the presence of Jews in India confirmed, but they were apparently prospering as well. This, of course,

---

[42] Jews of Malabar to the Portuguese Jews of New York: repr. Hebrew and English in I. J. Benjamin II, *Three Years in America, 1859–1862* (Philadelphia, 1956), 1, pp. 57–62. Benjamin, a Rumanian Jew, travelled through Asia, Africa, and America between 1845 and 1862 in search of the Lost Ten Tribes, and published accounts of his journeys in the above book and in *Eight Years in Asia and Africa* (Hanover, 1863), a later version of the French (1856), German (1858), and Hebrew (1859) edns. He saw himself as a latter-day Benjamin of Tudela, and was known as Benjamin II.

[43] Esther 1. 1, 8. 9; Kid. 22b; Bab. Bat. 74b.

[44] W. J. Fischel, *The Jews in India: their Contribution to the Economic and Political Life* [Hebrew] (Jerusalem, 1960), pp. 10–11: this book is the best general account of the subject.

[45] *Itinerary of Benjamin of Tudela*, ed. Adler; Marco Polo, *Travels* (Everyman edn, London, 1908), p. 377.

[46] Fischel, *Jews in India*, pp. 15–30, where he notes that the parents of Gaspar da Gama had fled from Poland in the second half of the fifteenth century.

[47] Another important Indian Jewish community, the Bene Israel of the Konkan region, were unknown to Europeans until the eighteenth century, when some of them moved to Bombay and began to enlist in British regiments. The Bene Israel ('Children of Israel') claim to be the descendants of the Lost Ten Tribes: see H. S. Kehimkar, *The History of the Bene Israel of India* (Tel-Aviv, 1937); S. Strizower, *The Children of Israel: the Bene Israel of Bombay* (Oxford, 1971).

was fully in accordance with their Messianic role, as revealed in Isaiah 11. 11, where it was promised that the Lord would 'recover the remnant of his people' from, among other places, 'Hamath', by which, Menasseh noted, 'all the Israelites who are in Greater Asia, India and China may be understood.' Menasseh's authoritative investigation of the whereabouts of the Lost Ten Tribes, then, positively identified them among the Jews of India, and described a community that possessed a thriving religious life, and, it was hoped in the Christian world, ancient manuscripts which might clear up certain textual problems in the Bible.[48]

Menasseh recognized that the Old Testament was often murky. He himself contributed to eliminating such difficulties by producing a large study resolving apparent contradictions in the Bible.[49] But, like all Jews, he would not be prepared to admit that the Masoretic text was anything but an exact representation of the Word of God as spoken on Mount Sinai. Nevertheless, Menasseh's celebrated work had the effect of disseminating information about the Indian and Chinese Jews, and in awakening interest in these distant communities among both Jews and Christians.

According to the eighteenth-century account of the Jews of Malabar, the arrival of the Dutch in 1663 made their lives easier. Eventually,

> In the year 1686 (common era) four men came to Cochin from Amsterdam: Moses Ferrara, Isaac Irgas, Abraham Burata, and Isaac Muchata. They were Portuguese Jews, merchants, who visited all the places where Jews lived. They rejoiced and reported everything to Amsterdam, above all, that there was a great lack of books. When that was learned in Amsterdam, that community sent, as a gift to the community of Cochin, *Humashim* (copies of the Pentateuch), *mahzorim* (holiday prayer-books), copies of the *Shulhan Arukh*, and other books, to the joy of the whole community.[50]

Kennicott, who had been so active in trying to exploit the scriptural potential of the Chinese Jews and the Samaritans, was worried that he would be left out of the Indian spoils. He had an admirer with a son in Bombay, who was asked by his father 'to endeavour to procure me a MS Bible, the older I tell him the better, from among the Jews at Cochin'. But by then the task was almost impossible: 'I fear these poor Jews have been gutted of their MSS Bibles before this', Kennicott was informed. 'If not,

---

[48] Menasseh ben Israel, *Hope*, ed. Mechoulan and Nahon, pp. 141, 154.
[49] Menasseh ben Israel, *The Conciliator*, ed. E. H. Lindo (London, 1842).
[50] Jews of Malabar to the Portuguese Jews of New York: see n. 42, above.

347

I have commissioned my son, to advance a sum sufficient I believe to procure me a MS Bible, or at least some part of one.'[51] It is not known if Dutch chaplains at Malabar managed to bring back to Europe any Indian Jewish texts, but by that time the contact between Holland and Cochin was already regularized.[52]

Moses Edrehi, a colourful Moroccan Jew who passed through France and England in the first decades of the nineteenth century, noted that the discovery of the Indian Jews was critical: 'Before that time, there had been no account of the Ten Tribes', he recorded. So even in the nineteenth century, the Indian Jews were remembered as one of the first of the Lost Ten Tribes found. 'Here we have a certain testimony of a high authority, as a witness', affirmed Edrehi, 'who declares the existence of the Ten Tribes, and also asserts the truth concerning the river Sambatyon; and no one can deny the truth of it, nor doubt it after so many explanations as have been noted in this work.' Edrehi was also careful to insist that

> some Hebrew manuscripts were found also among the Jews, who are established in Cosen in the city of Malabar, and they are supposed to have been handed down from the time of King Hosea, son of Ella, who reigned in the year 824 A.M. after the Jews came out of Egypt . . . and when these Jews were taken captives by Salmaneser, they took with them some Hebrew books.

These, according to Edrehi, consisted of most of the Hebrew Bible, divided into three parts, 'and each part was put separately into a leaden box, and committed to the care of Prince Simeon, of the tribe of Ephraim.' Edrehi was generally fairly careful about his sources, so it is likely that he is reporting here views that were widespread in the seventeenth century, when contact with the Indian Jews was first made.[53]

The Jews of India, then, like the Jews of China, did not fulfil the hopes that had been kindled by the discovery of the Samaritan Pentateuch. Whatever ancient manuscripts they had in their possession were plundered by the Dutch and never became the property of the scholarly

[51] James Bate to Kennicott, 22 Jan. 1761: Oxford, Bodleian Library, MS Kennicott c 12, fols 9ʳ–10ʳ.
[52] See Fischel, *Jews in India*, pp. 125–98; G. Yogev, *Diamonds and Coral: Anglo-Dutch Jews and Eighteenth-Century Trade* (Leicester, 1978).
[53] Moses Edrehi, *An Historical Account of the Ten Tribes. Settled Beyond the River Sambatyon in the East* (London, 1836), pp. 156–81. This is a greatly expanded version of his *Sefer Ma'aseh Nissim* [Hebrew and Yiddish (!)] (Amsterdam, 1818). See also Moses Pereira de Paiva, *Notisias dos Judeos de Cochim*, ed. M. B. Amzalak (Lisbon, 1923).

world. The Indian Jews, for their part, became wary of Christians snooping around their synagogues. When English missionary Claudius Buchanan became interested in the problem and went especially to Cochin in the winter of 1806–7, he barely escaped with his life when the word went out that Christians had come once again to rob the Jews of their old books and manuscripts. Buchanan explained that

> a copy of the Scriptures belonging to the Jews of the East, who might be supposed to have had no communication with Jews in the West, has been long considered a desideratum in Europe; for Western Jews have been accused by some learned men of altering or omitting certain words in the Hebrew text, to invalidate the arguments of Christians. But Jews in the East, remote from the controversy, would have no motive for such corruptions. One or two of the MSS, which I have just procured, will probably be of some service in this respect.[54]

Menasseh ben Israel's curiosity about the Jews of India is an important clue, from the man whose activity sparked the clearest demonstration of political philo-Semitism in early modern Europe. Just as in the days of Pico, contact with living Jews, or now even better, with found Israelites, was essential for Christian theological interests, and placed the Jews in a positive light, so different from the suspicious and hostile treatment to which they were often subjected. Once again, it is the biblical thread on which hangs the phenomenon of philo-Semitism, and which would continue until the modern era.

VI

'Among all those who busied themselves with Hebrew in the fifteenth century,' postulated Burckhardt, 'no one was of more importance than Pico della Mirandola.' Indeed, he mused, 'Looking at Pico, we can guess the lofty flight which Italian philosophy would have taken had not the Counter-Reformation annihilated the spiritual life of the people.'[55] As we have seen, Catholic Hebrew studies certainly did receive a mortal blow in the Counter-Reformation, but even in the Protestant world, so too did the exclusively Hebraic and Jewish areas of intellectual interest shrink in both size and importance, leaving the field of philo-Semitism to those

---

[54] Claudius Buchanan, *Christian Researches in Asia*, 2nd edn (London, 1811), pp. 200–10.

[55] Jacob Burckhardt, *The Civilization of the Renaissance in Italy*, tr. S. G. C. Middlemore (New York, 1958), I, pp. 208, 210.

who were, so to speak, left behind. Indeed, one might say that the question is not why the normative condition of anti-Semitism came to dominate European thinking, but rather why the normative condition of philo-Semitism weakened.

First among the causes of change must be the new attitudes to the Hebrew language of the biblical text which emerged during the eighteenth century, especially the development of modern linguistics, which demonstrated that Hebrew was not, after all, the first language, and that its claim to supernatural inspiration was highly dubious. At a stroke, the discovery of Sanskrit eliminated the Jews as a necessary component in the history of mankind, and reduced them to primitive remnants, freaks who could be persecuted and expelled. Linguistics and anti-Semitism make unlikely bed-fellows, but undoubtedly the normalization of the Hebrew language was a serious blow to Jewish claims to superior knowledge.[56] Another factor was the development of Christian Hebrew scholarship, especially in Germany. Jews were no longer necessarily required for the study of the Bible at a high level, especially when so much of Jewish studies was talmudically based and of little interest to the bibliocentric theologians in the Protestant world.[57]

But philo-Semitism remained and survives as a powerful force, especially among those groups which stress the inerrancy of the Bible and refuse to accept the new biblical criticism, and even more so among those denominations which give the Jews, with or without the Lost Ten Tribes (and sometimes the Israelite Indians), a critical role to play at the End of Days. The first of these religious groups was the Mormons, whose truths were revealed to Joseph Smith on 21 September 1823 by the angel Moroni, son of Mormon. These were written on gold plates, in the Reformed Egyptian language, which could be deciphered with the aid of an accompanying pair of eye-glasses made from two transparent stones, the Urim and Thummim described in the Old Testament. Only four years later was Smith allowed to take possession of the plates and to begin the process of translation. The result was the Book of Mormon, a 275,000-word chronicle about the inhabitants of pre-Columbian America. The

---

[56] See generally, S. N. Mukherjee, *Sir William Jones: a Study in Eighteenth-Century British Attitudes to India* (Cambridge, 1968); R. Gombrich, *On Being Sanskritic* (Oxford, 1978); Maurice Olender, *Les Langues du Paradis* (Paris, 1990). Cf. Frank E. Manuel, 'Israel in the Christian Enlightenment', in his *The Changing of the Gods* (Hanover and London, 1983), pp. 105–34.

[57] John Rogerson, *Old Testament Criticism in the Nineteenth Century: England and Germany* (London, 1984); S. L.Greenslade, ed., *The Cambridge History of the Bible*, 3 (Cambridge, 1963), ch. 7.

story begins in 600 BC in Palestine, when a group of Israelites is inspired to leave Jerusalem immediately before the Babylonian invasion. They flee by caravan to the Indian Ocean, and then by boat to the Promised Land on the west coast of North America. There they divide into two disagreeing groups, the Nephites and the Lamanites, and spend centuries building a civilization and fighting with one another. Following his Crucifixion and Resurrection, Christ appears to them in America, announcing that he will also visit other remnants of the Lost Ten Tribes of Israel. 'I go unto the Father,' he told them as he prepared to leave, 'and also to show myself unto the lost tribes of Israel, for they are not lost unto the Father, for he knoweth whither he hath taken them.' The Nephites and the Lamanites live in harmony after the divine visitation for about two centuries, then begin warring again, and finally, in about AD 421, the Nephites are totally vanquished and destroyed. The victorious Lamanites, however, gradually sink into barbarism, lose their fair skins, and become the ancestors of the American Indians. Moroni, the last prophet of the exterminated Nephites, buries the history of the American Israelites in the hill Cumorah, where they remain until revealed to Joseph Smith in 1823. As is fitting for the first genuine indigenous American variety of Christianity, America is given a starring role: it had been the scene of Christ's work on earth as much as Palestine, and would be once again, as the true American Church would arise against the apostate churches of ungodly Europe.[58]

The Articles of Faith of the Church of Jesus Christ of Latter-day Saints made quite clear the part which the Jews and the Lost Ten Tribes were expected to play. The tenth of thirteen articles affirms that

> We believe in the literal gathering of Israel and in the restoration of the Ten Tribes; that Zion will be built upon this [the American] continent; that Christ will reign personally upon the earth; and, that the earth will be renewed and receive its paradisiacal glory.[59]

This Zion was revealed to be Jackson County, Missouri, confirmed by revelations received by Joseph Smith. This had been promised by Jesus

---

[58] Most of this narrative comes from the First Book of Nephi, in *The Book of Mormon* (Palmyra, 1830), and the introductory material therein, which is part of the canon. See also Whitney R. Cross, *The Burned-Over District* (Ithaca, NY, 1950); Fawn M. Brodie, *No Man Knows My History: the Life of Joseph Smith, the Mormon Prophet* (New York, 1946); Leonard J. Arrington and Davis Bitton, *The Mormon Experience: a History of the Latter-day Saints* (London, 1979). For analogous evidence, see David Philipson, 'Are there traces of the Ten Lost Tribes in Ohio?', *Pubs Amer. Jew. Hist. Soc.*, 13 (1905), pp. 37–46; Lee M. Friedman, 'The Phylacteries Found at Pittsfield, Mass.', *Publications of the American Jewish Historical Society*, 25 (1917), pp. 81–5.

[59] The articles of faith are signed by Joseph Smith, and are often printed in the *Book of Mormon*.

Christ himself during his manifestation before the American Israelites after his Resurrection, foretelling the redemption of

> as many of the house of Israel as shall come, that they may build a city, which shall be called the New Jerusalem. And then shall they assist my people that they may be gathered in, who are scattered upon all the face of the land, in unto the New Jerusalem. And then shall the power of heaven come down among them; and I also will be in the midst . . . at that day shall the work of the Father commence among all the dispersed of my people, yea, even the tribes which have been lost, which the Father hath led away out of Jerusalem.[60]

The Jews themselves, however, as opposed to the Lost Tribes, would be redeemed in a different location, as prophesied in the Book of Isaiah:

> I would gather them together in mine own due time, that I would give unto them again the land of their fathers for their inheritance, which is the land of Jerusalem, which is the promised land unto them forever, saith the Father. And it shall come to pass that the time cometh, when the fulness of my gospel shall be preached unto them; And they shall believe in me, that I am Jesus Christ, the Son of God, and shall pray unto the Father in my name. Then shall their watchmen lift up their voice, and with the voice together shall they sing; for they shall see eye to eye. Then will the Father gather them together again, and give unto them Jerusalem for the land of the inheritance.[61]

The conversion of the Jews to Christianity, then, will precede the Second Coming, the return of the Jews to the Holy Land of Palestine, and the establishment of a New Jerusalem in Missouri, populated by Mormons and found Israelites.

The Mormon attitude to the Bible was somewhat less straightforward. As Joseph Smith explained it in 1842, 'We believe the Bible to be the word of God as far as it is translated correctly.'[62] Believing the Bible to have been incorrectly translated, Smith began the work afresh as early as 1830, producing a text which is not a genuine translation, but the Authorized Version amended, with certain passages corrected and others expanded. Since Smith had no knowledge whatsoever of either Hebrew or Greek, he

[60] *The Book of Mormon*, III Nephi 21.23–6.
[61] Ibid., 20.29–33.
[62] Quoted in Arrington and Bitton, *Mormon Experience*, p. 30.

was forced to rely on inspiration. This claim was problematic, to which one might only reply, 'Judge not, that ye be not judged', or as Smith elegantly put it, 'Judge not unrighteously, that ye be not judged; but judge righteous judgment.'[63]

For the Mormons, then, the Jews form an essential element of their theology, and the fate of the Lost Ten Tribes is one of the pillars of their version of history. The Mormons remain steadfastly philo-Semitic and supportive of Jewish temporal interests, especially the welfare of the modern state of Israel, which most Protestant groups have come to see as part of the divine plan rather than as a human attempt to jump the gun. A beautiful Mormon college sits on Mount Scopus, in Jerusalem, built only recently, and with full support from Israel's right-wing nationalist government.

The Mormons are in some respects an eccentric religious denomination, and there are undoubtedly many who would dispute their essential Christianity.[64] Among more mainstream religious groups who give the Jews and the Lost Ten Tribes a role to play at the End of Days, based on their reading of the inerrant Bible, are those various denominations usually described as fundamentalist or orthodox evangelical.[65] Fundamentalists are almost invariably dispensationalist in theology. Like other pre-millennialists, they argued that Christ's kingdom is entirely future

---

[63] Joseph Smith's new translation is published by the Church of Jesus Christ of Latter Day Saints. See R. J. Matthews, *'A Plainer Translation': Joseph Smith's Translation of the Bible* (Provo, Utah, 1975).

[64] See A. Shupe and J. Heinerman, 'Mormonism and the New Christian Right: an emerging coalition?' *Review of Religious Research*, 27 (1985), pp. 146–57.

[65] The distinction between fundamentalism and evangelicalism has been the matter of some dispute. George M. Marsden, 'Defining American Fundamentalism', in Norman J. Cohen, ed., *The Fundamentalist Phenomenon* (Grand Rapids, 1990), pp. 22–3, postulates that 'a fundamentalist is an evangelical Protestant who is militantly opposed to modern liberal theologies and to some aspects of secularism in modern culture.' Evangelicals are those Christians who accept at least three points, 'derived largely from the Reformation': (1) the authority of the Bible; (2) eternal salvation only through the atoning work of Jesus Christ; (3) the importance of spreading the Gospel. The question of the extent of permitted political involvement in this doomed world has been the cause of further fragmentation. Seymour Martin Lipset and Earl Raab, 'Evangelicals and the Elections', *Commentary*, 71 (1981), pp. 25–31, cite (p. 25) the distinction sometimes made between 'orthodox evangelicals' and 'conversionist evangelicals'. The 'orthodox evangelicals' are the fundamentalists and believe in (1) the literal word of the Bible and (2) that Jesus is divine and the only hope for salvation. Lipset and Raab cite a Gallup poll made in 1978 which showed that 40 per cent of the adult American population falls into this group. The 'conservative evangelicals' differ from the others in having had an explicit religious experience in which they asked Jesus to be their personal saviour. These are 'born-again' Christians and need not be fundamentalists. Lipset and Raab include over a third of American adults in this group. Both types of evangelicals are committed to converting others

and supernatural, and that the divine plan can be worked out by paying careful attention to Daniel 9. 24–7, in which a seventy-week programme is described. 'Know therefore and understand, *that* from the going forth of the commandment to restore and to build Jerusalem unto the Messiah the Prince, *shall be* seven weeks, and threescore and two weeks', it is revealed. These first sixty-nine weeks, on the basis of a day standing for a year, were understood as referring to a 483–year period between the rebuilding of Jerusalem during the days of Ezra and Nehemiah to the time of Jesus. The last and seventieth week, however, was thought to signify the final seven-year period before the Second Coming, so that the entire history of Christianity was seen to take place in a suspended era between the sixty-ninth week and the last. The events of this last week will include the appearance of anti-Christ, a false prophet who will lead the apostate churches, and his cohort the Beast, a political leader who will rule the ten nations which grew out of the Roman Empire, as predicted in the image of the ten toes in Nebuchadnezzar's vision. This last period will also include the return of the Jews to Palestine, the conversion of some of them to Christianity, the persecution of the Jews, and the return of Christ to defeat the anti-Christ, the Beast, and the renewed Roman Empire in a great battle to take place at Armageddon (Megiddo) in the Holy Land. At this point, the thousand-year rule of Christ on earth will begin. According to many dispensationalists, the saints of the Church will be spared the tribulations of the last days by being taken out of the world in the 'rapture'. The term 'dispensation' itself refers to the distinct eras of history, of which the tribulation is the final and seventh one, the others being edenic, antediluvian, post-diluvian, patriarchal (Abraham to Exodus), legal (Exodus to Christ), and ecclesiastical (Christ until the final days).[66]

and spreading the Gospel. Perhaps Marsden's shorthand definitions are the clearest: a fundamentalist is 'an evangelical who is angry about something', while 'the simplest definition of an evangelical is someone who agrees with Billy Graham' (pp. 22, 34).

[66] A good summary of the dispensationalist scheme can be found in George M. Marsden, *Fundamentalism and American Culture* (Oxford, 1980), pp. 51–4, 64–5. Other useful studies of fundamentalism are E. R. Sandeen, *The Roots of Fundamentalism: British and American Millenarianism, 1800–1930* (Chicago, 1970); S. G. Cole, *The History of Fundamentalism* (New York, 1931); L. Gasper, *The Fundamentalist Movement* (The Hague, 1963); James Barr, *Fundamentalism* (London, 1977). For earlier connections, see David S. Katz, *Sabbath and Sectarianism in Seventeenth-Century England* (Leiden, 1988), 'Epilogue'. The term 'fundamentalist' comes from a series of pamphlets published by a group of American Protestant laymen at the beginning of this century: *The Fundamentals: a Testimony of the Truth* (Chicago, 1910–15): 12 parts, produced by the Testimony Publishing Company.

Not all dispensationalists are fundamentalist, but undeniably this general scheme has been very popular with them, not the least because of the influence of C. I. Scofield (1843–1921), the great systematizer of the theory, whose reference Bible (published by Oxford University Press) has been essential in disseminating this interpretation of history.[67] As we have seen, the return of the unbelieving Jews to Palestine is an important part of the preparation for the End of Days as they understand the inerrant biblical passages in Daniel and Revelation. It has sometimes been argued that fundamentalists are inherently hostile to Jews, in part because of the notion of 'triumphalism' or 'supercessionism', that is, that they themselves are the New Israel which has replaced the covenant of old. While it is true that much evidence can be found for this negative attitude even in the 1950s, certainly within recent years the movement has overwhelmingly turned wholeheartedly to the Jews, and especially to the state of Israel, and has become an increasingly important political force, both in the United States and in Israel itself.[68] The Moral Majority, Jerry Falwell's organization, set as one of its goals 'to make the Jewish community aware that we are not an anti-Semitic group and that we probably are the strongest supporter of Israel in this country.'[69] Not all Jews are comfortable with support from that quarter, but as Professor Irving Kristol of New York University put it, 'It is their theology, but it is our Israel.'[70]

---

[67] *The New Scofield Reference Bible* (New York, 1967). See esp. the commentary on Dan. 9, p. 923. Cf. C. I. Scofield's introductions to the 1909 and 1917 edns (pp. viii–xi).

[68] The politicization of fundamentalism is a comparatively recent phenomenon, as can be seen from the famous remark made by the evangelist pillar Dwight L. Moody (1837–99), 'I look upon this world as a wrecked vessel. God has given me a lifeboat and said to me, "Moody, save all you can"' (Marsden, *Fundamentalism*, p. 38). For earlier fundamentalist views about Jews and Zionism, see David A. Rausch, *Zionism Within Early American Fundamentalism, 1878–1918* (New York, 1978); 'Protofundamentalism's Attitudes Towards Zionism, 1878–1918', *Jewish Social Studies*, 43 (1981), pp. 137–52; Y. Ariel, 'An American Initiative for a Jewish State: William Blackstone and the Petition of 1891', *Studies in Zionism*, 10 (1989), pp. 125–37; Yona Malachy, *American Fundamentalism and Israel* (Jerusalem, 1978). An important proto-fundamentalist group which was violently anti-Semitic was the eighteenth- and nineteenth-century Hutchinsonians, who were enormously influential within the Anglican Church in Oxford and in Scotland. They argued that the inerrancy of the Old Testament text applied to the consonants alone, the vowels being Jewish forgeries designed to mislead Christians: see D. S. Katz, 'The Hutchinsonians and Hebraic Fundamentalism in Eighteenth-Century England', in D. S. Katz and J. I. Israel, eds, *Sceptics, Millenarians and Jews* (Leiden, 1990), pp. 237–55.

[69] Quoted in Lipset and Raab, 'Evangelicals', p. 28.

[70] Quoted in Richard John Neuhaus, 'What the Fundamentalists want', *Commentary*, 79 (1985), pp. 41–6, esp. p. 45. Cf. Irving Kristol, 'The political dilemma of American Jews', *Commentary*, 78 (1984), pp. 23–9. For other Jewish views regarding political support from fundamentalists, see David Danzig, 'The Radical Right and the rise of the Fundamentalist minority', *Commentary*, 33 (1962), pp. 291–8; and Lipset and Raab, 'Evangelicals'.

Philo-Semitic fundamentalism is demonstrated quite clearly, for example, in the writings of Hal Lindsey, whose best-selling book *The Late Great Planet Earth* gives specific and particular details on how the dispensationalist scheme will come to fruition. The role of the Jews is more than prominent; it is essential. Referring to the final dispensation, Lindsey writes: 'The general time of this seven-year period couldn't begin until the Jewish people re-established their nation in their ancient home-land of Palestine.' The final great war at Armageddon, he reveals, 'is to be triggered by an invasion of the new state of Israel', at which time each of the four spheres of political power 'will be judged and destroyed for invading the new state of Israel, by the personal return of the Jewish Messiah, Jesus Christ.' These four spheres will be Russia, the Arab coalition led by Egypt, the Eastern alliance led by China, and the Common Market, representing the revived Roman Empire. The capture of the Old City of Jerusalem in 1967 was a crucial part of the divine plan revealed in Zechariah 12–14, and Lindsey confides that there 'remains but one more event to completely set the stage for Israel's part in the last great act of her historical drama. This is to rebuild the ancient Temple of worship upon its old site.' Lindsey admits that the contemporary presence on the Temple Mount of the Dome of the Rock, the second holiest Islamic shrine, is a worry, but 'Obstacle or no obstacle it is certain that the Temple will be rebuilt. Prophecy demands it.' Precise details, including maps of the future and final war, are provided in Lindsey's book, with advice on current signs. 'Keep your eyes on the Middle East', he warns.[71]

Lindsey is a good example of a staunch fundamentalist supporter of Israel who consistently demonstrates admiration and respect for the Jews. Unlike many other philo-Semitic commentators, Lindsey has no plan for Jews to convert to Christianity before the End of Days, although the 'residents of Israel who believe in Jesus will flee to the mountains and canyons of Petra for divine protection, as promised (Matthew 24. 16; Revelation 12. 6, 14)', just before the conflagration. Hal Lindsey has led numerous groups of followers to Israel and the Holy Land, and indeed presented the Hebrew translation of his book to General Ariel Sharon with advice to make plans for the evacuation to Petra, now in Jordanian territory.[72]

---

[71] Hal Lindsey, *The Late Great Planet Earth* (Grand Rapids, 1970), *passim*, but esp. pp. 42–3, 55–6, 184. These themes are expanded in Lindsey's other books, *Satan is Alive and Well on Planet Earth* (Grand Rapids, 1972); and *The Liberation of Planet Earth* (Grand Rapids, 1974).

[72] Lindsey, *Late Great*, p. 153. The story of the presentation to Sharon was told to me by one of Lindsey's co-workers in Jerusalem, June 1991.

Lindsey's views, outlandish as they seem, reflect in many respects a mainstream American Protestant view, and one which is echoed by numerous other fundamentalist groups in the United States. 'God has blessed America because America has blessed the Jew', affirmed Jerry Falwell, the leader of the politically influential Moral Majority.[73] Pat Robertson, who unsuccessfully ran for president in 1988, bought the Star of Hope television station in southern Lebanon in April 1982, and since then has broadcast a beguiling mixture of American programmes and fundamentalist sermons, cartoons, and entertainments to central and northern coastal Israel. 'God's Holy Spirit is about to be poured out on the Holy Land!' he enthused. 'Miracles are about to abound. God's chosen ones are about to see more and more of the direct revelation of Jesus Christ! And when they see Him, they're going to believe.'[74]

Jimmy Carter, the man who brought about the Camp David agreement, believed that the 'establishment of the modern state of Israel is the fulfilment of biblical prophecy'. In his view, he 'considered this homeland for the Jews to be compatible with the teachings of the Bible, hence ordained by God'.[75] So, too, did Ronald Reagan have dangerous musings about the End of Days, telling an American Jewish lobbyist that

> You know, I turn back to your ancient prophets in the Old Testament and the signs foretelling Armageddon, and I find myself wondering if—if we're the generation that's going to see that come about. I don't know if you've noted any of these prophecies lately, but believe me, they certainly describe the times we're going through.[76]

---

[73] Falwell, however, has argued that a nuclear holocaust cannot occur for at least 1,007 years, since the final destruction of the world must be preceded by the seven-year Tribulation and the thousand-year reign of Christ on earth: Marsden, 'Fundamentalism', pp. 22–37, esp. p. 36, quoting from a Falwell promotional tape, c.1983. For more on Falwell, see also E. H. Buell and L. Sigelman, 'An Army that meets every Sunday? Popular support for the moral majority in 1980', *Social Science Quarterly*, 66 (1985), pp. 426–34.

[74] Lawrence J. Epstein, *Zion's Call: Christian Contributions to the Origins and Development of Israel* (Lanham, MD, 1984), pp. 132–4. Cf. Pat Robertson, *Answers to 200 of Life's Most Pressing Questions* (New York, 1987). Pat Robertson, who has claimed to perform healing miracles and control the weather, may be the answer to Gibbon's question, 'In the long series of ecclesiastical history, does there exist a single instance of a saint asserting that he himself possessed the gift of miracles?': Gibbon, *Decline and Fall*, p. 282n. For more on Robertson, see also: P. B. McGuigan, 'The Religious and Political Values of Dr Pat Robertson', *Conservative Digest*, Dec. 1986, pp. 31–8; H. Phillips, 'Pat Robertson', *Conservative Digest*, Jan. 1986, pp. 84–6.

[75] Jimmy Carter, *Keeping Faith: Memoirs of a President* (New York, 1982). p. 274; Ronald R. Stockton, 'Christian Zionism: prophecy and public opinion', *Middle East Journal*, 41 (1987), pp. 234–53, esp. pp. 240–1.

[76] Ronnie Dugger, 'Reagan's Apocalypse Now', *Guardian Weekly*, 6 May 1984, p. 17; Stockton,

Vice-President Dan Quayle's wife and both his and her parents are veteran followers of Colonel Robert B. Thieme of Houston, Texas, whose ministry is based on the notion of imminent Armageddon triggered by inevitable nuclear conflict.[77] In the light of a recent study which shows a statistical correlation between 'Armageddon Theology' and the willingness to risk nuclear war, we might have cause to reflect on the possible permutations of religion and politics.[78]

Already parts of the Doomsday Scenario championed by premillennialist dispensationalists have become somewhat obsolete. Egypt hardly seems likely to lead the Arab coalition after having signed the Camp David agreement, and Russia is in no position to launch a major war against Israel, with or without Arab support. Indeed, it would not be an exaggeration to say that *détente* was a disaster for fundamentalism, demolishing a central pillar of its theology. 'I'm at a loss to explain it in Scriptural terms', confessed one of their leaders recently. Since the 1920s, evolution had been replaced by communism as the bugbear of fundamentalism, an international evil aimed at undermining Christianity, with Russia serving as the worldly headquarters of Satan himself. Recent fundamentalist theorizing has suggested that the apparent softening of the Russian position is merely a temporary stance, designed at fulfilling the prophecy of Ezekiel 38. 8, that 'in the latter years' the Jews shall 'come into the land *that is* brought back from the sword', being 'gathered out of many people', in this case, from St Petersburg and Moscow to Tel-Aviv.[79]

So, too, has the Gulf War been integrated into the divine plan. Billy Graham, perhaps the most mainstream of the evangelical preachers, affirmed recently that these 'events are happening in that part of the world where history began, and, the Bible says, where history as we know it will some day end.'[80] Graham affirmed even twenty years ago that we were living at the End of Days, and has become more cautious about

---

'Christian Zionism', p. 241. See also C. Goldstein, 'What Ronald Reagan needs to know about Armageddon', *Liberty*, 80 (1985), pp. 2–6.

[77] According to E. J. Brecher and B. L. Hines, 'Some See Armageddon Looming in Mideast Crisis', *Lexington [Kentucky] Herald-Leader*, 25 Aug. 1990, p. B3. I am grateful to Professor James E. Force for a copy of this article.

[78] Stephen Kierulff, 'Belief in "Armageddon Theology" and willingness to risk nuclear war', *Journal for the Scientific Study of Religion*, 30 (1991), pp. 81–93. Cf. Andrew J. Weigert, 'Christian eschatological identities and the nuclear context', 27 (1988), pp. 175–91.

[79] The Revd Gordon Matheny, district superintendent, Peninsular Florida District Assemblies of God: quoted in Brecher and Hines, 'Armageddon'.

[80] Press release quoted in ibid.

precise chronology.[81] According to the Revd Timothy Weber, who teaches at a Baptist seminary in Colorado, many pre-millennialists 'have been amazingly silent because of what happened in Eastern Europe … That hacked a major plank out of their plans. Iraq has been a vitamin B-12 shot to the movement.'[82] Even Israelis from their 'sealed rooms' quoted the prophecy of Isaiah 26. 20, advising people to enter 'into thy chambers, and shut thy doors about thee: hide thyself as it were for a little moment, until the indignation be overpast.' Others noted that '16.1.91', the day the Gulf War began, reads the same upside down.[83] A recent survey has revealed that white Protestant evangelicals comprise 20 per cent of the entire American population, a figure which does not include the extensive support for fundamentalism among black congregations.[84] In the most recent American presidential elections, 80 per cent of these white evangelicals supported George Bush, the highest degree of social group unity among white voters.[85] The details of dispensationalist theology have more than religious significance alone.[86]

VII

'Don't make plans for 1985 until you read and see *The Late Great Planet Earth*!' warns the dust-jacket of a recent edition. Former tug-boat captain Hal Lindsey seems very far away from Pico della Mirandola: millenarianism has long been a socially-acceptable scholarly subject for religious historians of the early modern period, and awaits being taken seriously by

---

[81] *New York Times*, 25 May 1970, p. 7.

[82] Quoted in Brecher and Hines, 'Armageddon'. Cf. Timothy P.Weber, *Living in the Shadow of the Second Coming: American Premillenialism, 1875–1925* (New York, 1979).

[83] See, e.g., R. Kampeas, 'All in the Cards', *Jerusalem Post Magazine*, 22 Feb. 1991, pp. 10–12.

[84] Gallup Organization, *Religion in America* (Princeton, 1982), pp. 31–2; Gallup Organization, *Religion in America, 50 Years: 1935–1985* (Princeton, 1985); James Davidson Hunter, *American Evangelicalism: Conservative Religion and the Quandary of Modernity* (Princeton, 1983), pp. 139–41; A. James Reichley, 'Pietist Politics', in Cohen, ed., *Fundamentalist Phenomenon*, p. 79. Lipset and Raab, 'Evangelicals', give even larger figures.

[85] *New York Times*, 8 and 10 Nov. 1988; Reichley, 'Politics', p. 74.

[86] Generally, see Steve Bruce, *The Rise and Fall of the New Christian Right: Conservative Protestant Politics in America, 1978–1988* (Oxford, 1988); S. D. Johnson and J. B. Tamney, 'The Christian Right and the 1980 Presidential Election', *Journal for the Scientific Study of Religion*, 21 (1982), pp. 123–31; 'The Christian Right and the 1984 Presidential Election', *Review of Religious Research*, 27 (1985), pp. 124–33; R. V. Pierard, 'Religion and the 1984 Election Campaign', ibid., pp. 98–113; M. Lienesch, 'Right-Wing Religion: Christian Conservatism as a Political Movement', *Political Science Quarterly*, 97 (1982), 403–25; K. Patel, D. Pilant, and G. Rose, 'Born-again Christians in the Bible Belt: a study in religion, politics, and ideology', *American Political Quarterly*, 10 (1982), pp. 255–72; A. J. Reichley, 'Religion and the future of American politics', *Political Science Quarterly*, 101 (1986), pp. 23–47.

their more contemporary colleagues, who too often write religious history on the investigatory principle of 'round up the usual suspects'. But what unites all of the individuals and groups which I have classified as philo-Semitic is that they see the Jews as essential to Christian interests, and, in some cases, to the destiny of mankind. Initial attraction to the Jews for their own sakes was primarily based on the biblical text and the Hebrew language, when Jews (and possibly Israelites) held the monopoly on that crucial branch of learning so necessary for a full and accurate understanding of the Scriptures, as well as for cracking the code of creation through the use of a language actually designed by God. The fictional Miss Dorothea Brooke thought that 'Perhaps even Hebrew might be necessary—at least the alphabet and a few roots—in order to arrive at the core of things, and judge soundly on the social duties of the Christian.'[87] But she was already old-fashioned: the elimination among scholars of Hebrew's mystical significance after the discovery of Sanskrit left the Jews dangerously exposed, only to be rescued by the continuing vitality of the principle of *sola scriptura* and of millenarianism, appearing in its nineteenth- and twentieth-century form as pre-millenialist dispensationalism. In some ways, modern philo-Semitism is even less threatening, in that actual conversion to Christianity is not necessarily a desirable goal, as it was even in Cromwell's time. The extent to which such activity is purely philo-Semitic may be debated theoretically, but the intense and even excessive devotion which Israeli governments have shown to fundamentalist missions demonstrates that at the political level their support is perceived to be a good thing.

A writer in the *Spectator* at the beginning of the eighteenth century, musing on the economic role of the Jews, wrote that they are so ubiquitous

> that they are become the Instruments by which the most distant Nations converse with one another and by which mankind are knit together in a general correspondence. They are like the pegs and nails in a great building, which though they are but little valued in themselves, are absolutely necessary to keep the whole frame together.[88]

This evaluation probably applies to religion even more than to trade, and as I have said, it may be that we need to think again about whether philo-

---

[87] George Eliot, *Middlemarch* (Penguin edn, Harmondsworth, 1985), p. 88: first pub. 1871–2.
[88] *Spectator*, 495 (27 Sept. 1712): quoted in Werner Sombart, *The Jews and Modern Capitalism* (New York, 1962), p. 171: first pub. 1911.

Semitism rather than anti-Semitism is the normative condition which has degenerated over time. Certainly anti-Semitism is a serious problem: its most recent historian has referred to 'the revival of anti-Semitism as a popular prejudice, as a semi-respectable sentiment and as a political weapon'.[89] But, like most weapons, anti-Semitism can also be used for defence, and when it becomes a catch-all explanation which renders sinister all forms of international opposition to state policy of the most dubious kind, then we need to be on our guard.

Menasseh ben Israel, for his part, was convinced that as long as the Old Testament was venerated by Christians, there would always be a place of honour for the Jews. 'Pico della Mirandola (who used to say that he had but small understanding, who only looked after his own things, and not after other men's) and others had Hebrew teachers', he noted proudly,

> So at this day we see many desirous to learn the Hebrew tongue of our men. Hence may be seen that God has not left us; for if one persecutes us, another receives us civilly and courteously; and if this prince treats us ill, another treats us well; if one banishes us out of his country, another invites us by a thousand privileges.[90]

That this should have been so, from Pico to Hal Lindsey, from Martin Luther to Martin Luther King, was always based on the agreement of those Christians with the Talmudic dictum that 'Moses received the Torah on Sinai, and handed it down to Joshua; Joshua to the elders; the elders to the prophets; and the prophets handed it down to the men of the Great Synagogue.'[91] Anyone who accepts this view will almost inevitably find himself part of the phenomenon of philo-Semitism.

Tel-Aviv University

---

[89] Professor Robert Wistrich, replying to a review by Paul Johnson of his book, *Anti-Semitism: the Longest Hatred* (London, 1990), in the *TLS*, 4598 (17 May 1991), p. 13.
[90] Menasseh ben Israel, *Hope*, ed. Mechoulan, p. 155.
[91] 'Ethics of the Fathers', i. 1.

ALEXANDER'S APOSTASY:
FIRST STEPS TO JERUSALEM

by BRIAN TAYLOR

THE synagogue in Bevis Marks in the city of London, 1700–1, is the oldest in this country. The second is in Plymouth, in Catherine Street. It was built in 1762, and is the oldest Ashkenazi synagogue in the English-speaking world. It is noteworthy for its original furnishings, which are mainly austere—the deal benches, and plain turned balusters for the enclosures, with the eight brass candle-sticks, now electrified, round the *bimah*. The exception is the ornately carved wooden ark, towering almost to the ceiling, with large urns on the entablature, which is supported by Corinthian columns.[1] It is mortifying to the Hebrew congregation that its existence is mostly known not for its historic and architectural importance, but in connection with the defection of one of its ministers, Michael Solomon Alexander, in 1825. A little more than sixteen years later, Alexander was consecrated for the newly constituted Jerusalem bishopric, on 7 December 1841, in Lambeth Palace Chapel. Archbishop Howley was joined in the laying on of hands by Blomfield of London, Murray of Rochester, and Selwyn of New Zealand, who had been consecrated in the same chapel three weeks before.

The Jerusalem bishopric scheme is mainly remembered for the stir it caused among Tractarian churchmen. In the official account of the scheme, published when it was all over, we read of Bunsen's visit to England in 1841. 'The mild and conciliatory Archbishop of Canterbury, Dr. Howley, the noble Archbishop of York, Dr. Vernon Harcourt, and the learned and energetic Bishop of London, Dr. Blomfield, warmly encouraged the plan, and Lord Ashley, now the venerable Earl of Shaftesbury, brought it the support of numerous friends.'[2] Looking back from 1864, however, Newman described it as one of 'three blows which broke me',[3] leading to his departure from the Church of England. The bishopric did not have much significance in the Holy Land, nor did it have any

---

[1] The synagogue is described in B. Susser's leaflet, *Plymouth's Historic Synagogue built in 1762* (1982), and more briefly in Bridget Cherry and Nikolaus Pevsner, *Devon = The Buildings of England*, 2nd edn (London, 1989), p. 648.

[2] William H. Hechler, ed., *The Jerusalem Bishopric, Documents with Translations . . . published by command of His Majesty Frederick William IV King of Prussia* (London, 1883), p. 29.

[3] *Apologia pro Vita Sua*, Everyman edn (London, n.d.), pp. 139–47.

lasting effect in promoting Christian unity. Only two Prussians were ordained under the scheme. When they returned to their own country the Prussian Evangelical Church neither recognized their orders nor found pastoral employment for them.[4] After the death of the third bishop, in 1881, the bishopric was allowed to lapse, and the treaty between Prussia and England that enabled it was dissolved in 1886. P. J. Welch, in an article in the *Journal of Ecclesiastical History* in 1957, gave a detailed account of the political and constitutional events leading up to Alexander's consecration.[5] The present paper deals principally with earlier stages in his life, leading to his baptism. If it sometimes seems diffuse, that is because I have thought it worth while to tie up some ends, and to answer some questions of identity that are sometimes left begging.

The main English sources for Alexander's early years are his own appendix to the printed sermon preached at his baptism,[6] and a typed biography by Edith Wynne Willson and Michael Ransom, his descendants, in the archives of the Church Missionary Society at Partnership House, in London.[7] There is also a popular biography, *From Rabbi to Bishop* by Muriel W. Corey.[8]

Michael Solomon Alexander was born on 1 May 1799 at Schönlanke, a small town in the grand duchy of Posen, in Prussia, land lost to Poland in the second partition of 1793. He was the second son of a rabbi from England, but none the less was educated 'principally in the Talmud, and in the strictest principles of Judaism'.[9] The emancipation of the Jews in Prussia was not until 1869, and they lived as a race apart, Alexander knowing nothing of the New Testament in his early years, or even of its existence. At the age of sixteen he became a teacher of the Talmud, and of German language, but this study brought him growing dissatisfaction and unease. After his father's death, in 1817, his doubts led to a quarrel with his elder brother, and he decided to travel to England.

On arriving in London in 1819, Alexander introduced himself to Solomon Hirschel, who was the Chief Rabbi of the German and Polish Jews from 1802 to 1842. He hoped to find a position as a *shohet*, or ritual

[4] S. L. Ollard in Ollard, G. Crosse, and M. F. Bond, *A Dictionary of English Church History*, 3rd edn (London, 1948), p. 308.
[5] P. J. Welch, 'Anglican Churchmen and the Jerusalem Bishopric', *JEH*, 8 (1957), pp. 193–204.
[6] J. Hatchard, *The Predictions and Promises of God Respecting Israel* (Plymouth, 1825). Alexander's account occupies pp. 37–40 [hereafter *Appendix*].
[7] E. W. Willson and M. Ransom, *Life of Michael Solomon Alexander First Anglican Bishop of Jerusalem* [typescript] (n.d.).
[8] Muriel W. Corey, *From Rabbi to Bishop* (London, n.d.).
[9] *Appendix*, p. 38.

slaughterer, and he had prepared himself for this by special study before he came to England. As he was not at first successful, he was recommended to work as a tutor, and took a place at Colchester with a strict Jewish family.

One day he saw a poster advertising a meeting of the London Society for Promoting Christianity among the Jews. He asked his employer what it meant, and was warned that in England there were vigorous efforts to convert Jews to Christianity. The interdenominational LSPCJ had been formed in 1809 for that purpose—the first organized mission to Jews outside Germany. Alexander was told that he should read the New Testament 'in order thereby to be convinced the more fully of the errors of the followers of Jesus of Nazareth'—as the preacher at his baptism later recounted.[10] He did not know about the book, and could not read it in English, so he acquired a German translation. He was surprised that Christians should know about the Patriarchs, and he was much impressed by chapter 1 of the Gospel according to St Matthew. 'I was still more struck with the character of Christ, and the excellent morals that he taught; but having gone no further than merely to admire them, it produced no particular effect upon my mind though it considerably lessened my prejudices.'[11]

One of the keenest supporters of LSPCJ was William Marsh, 'Millennial Marsh' as he was later called when he was Rector of St Thomas's Birmingham. He was Rector of St Peter's Colchester from 1814 to 1829. He was a friend of Charles Simeon. They were both Reading men, and this connection with the town no doubt led to the gifts to Alexander in due course of a complete set of episcopal robes from the Mayor of Reading, Thomas Rickford, and a set of communion plate from the ladies of the town.[12] Simeon encouraged Marsh to be interested in the Jews, and in 1818 they went together to the Netherlands, to learn about their life in that country. In her biography of her father, Catherine Marsh states that he brought about the conversion of two young Jewish cousins and baptized them at St Peter's. One of them, after being disowned by his family, was assisted financially by Marsh, and after a distinguished career at Cambridge was ordained in Dublin, she wrote, but 'a bright career of usefulness . . . was suddenly brought to an end by an illness affecting his mental powers, from which he never recovered.'[13] The writer coyly

---

[10] Hatchard, *Predictions*, p. 23.
[11] *Appendix*, p. 38.
[12] Willson and Ransom, *Life*, p. 27.
[13] [Catherine Marsh], *The Life of the Rev.William Marsh, D.D.* (London, 1869), pp. 60–3.

refrained from naming the cousins, but they can be identified as John Michael Mayers, sometimes known as Michael John, and William Michael Mayers. Little seems to be known about them, but something can be pieced together, even though Catherine Marsh's account is not proved reliable. Their baptisms do not appear in the registers of St Peter's. William Michael was at St Catharine's, Cambridge, and took the Hulsean prize in 1826 and the Norrisian in 1827. He was ordained by the Bishop of Cloyne, deacon in 1827 and priest in 1828. The only office that I can find that he held was the prebend of Mulhuddart in St Patrick's, Dublin, from 1830 until his death in 1868. Perhaps that was given to him after his mental illness. John Michael was Vicar of Langham Bishops, in Norfolk, from 1845 to 1850, British chaplain at Marseilles from 1852 to 1864, and Rector of St Peter Chesil, Winchester, from 1865 until his death early in 1881. All this followed his ordination as a deacon by Archbishop Magee of Dublin on 10 June 1827; and at that same ceremony Alexander was also ordained. The Colchester connection was maintained. Marsh did meet Alexander during his months in Colchester, and he was one who encouraged him to study the New Testament.[14]

Alexander left Essex for another appointment, in Norwich, this time as a rabbi, with leisure to give lessons in Hebrew and German. His English was improving, and he met many Christians, and learnt more about their faith. As he read the New Testament, he saw how prophecies in the Scriptures that he knew so well were fulfilled. He grew more perplexed, 'but endeavoured to shrink and turn away from the divine light.'[15]

In 1823 Alexander was recommended by the Chief Rabbi in London to the Jewish congregation in Plymouth, and he was appointed prayer-reader and *shohet*. He went there, as he recalled, to make a new start, 'to regain my peace of mind, with a full determination to have no intercourse with Christians'.[16]

After the expulsion of the Jews from England in 1290, some quietly remained, and others returned, and there were some in Plymouth, working at seaport trades. After they were permitted to live openly in this country from 1655, settlement in the south-west was slow. Services were held in Exeter by 1734, where a synagogue was built in 1763,[17] and in

[14] Willson and Ransom, *Life*, p. 1.
[15] *Appendix*, p. 38.
[16] Ibid.
[17] The present Exeter synagogue dates from 1835.

Plymouth by 1745. The synagogue was built seventeen years later, and land for a cemetery was bought in 1811.[18]

There was no regular minister between 1815 and 1829. In 1822 a *shohet* was appointed by a general meeting of the congregation; presumably he was Alexander's predecessor. He was paid four guineas a month, with extra fees of ten shillings for each beast slaughtered, and a shilling for each birth registered. He probably received part of the guinea paid to the synagogue at the time of a wedding. With the *hazzan*, or reader, he taught children for two hours on Sunday, Monday, Tuesday, and Wednesday mornings.[19] We may imagine that Alexander's terms of employment were similar.

The synagogue records have no mention at all of M. S. Alexander. The present president of the Plymouth Hebrew congregation considers that the elders probably expunged all references to him from their books after his apostasy.[20]

Very soon after taking up his appointment in Plymouth, Alexander met Deborah Levy, the daughter of a widow at Stonehouse, and about three months later, in September, they were engaged to be married. Early in 1824 he was approached by the curate of Stonehouse, Benjamin Bass Golding, asking for Hebrew lessons. It did not take long for the pupil to become a 'spiritual preceptor', and when Alexander compared the Old Testament with the New, he 'came *almost* to the conviction that Jesus was the Messiah.'[21] He told Deborah Levy of the possibility of his becoming a Christian. She was astonished, but trusted him. Although the engagement was broken off five times by the influence of friends, the notice appeared in the *Plymouth and Devonport Weekly Journal* of 11 November 1824 that the wedding had taken place at the Crown Hotel Devonport of the Reverend M. S. Alexander and Miss Deborah Levy, late of Stonehouse. That was on 3 November. At that time Jewish weddings did not take place in synagogues, but where the family festivities were held. Before the Marriage Act of 1836, and the first civil registers of 1837, Jewish weddings were not registered. It has not been possible so far to identify which of Plymouth's Levy families Deborah belonged to.

The Jewish teacher's friendship with Christians, and his rising doubts

---

[18] Short accounts are given in Doris Black, *The Plymouth Synagogue 1761–1961 (5521–5721)*, (n.p., n.d.), and in B. Susser, *An Account of the Old Jewish Cemetery on Plymouth Hoe* (Plymouth, 1972).

[19] Black, *Plymouth Synagogue*, p. 9.

[20] P. R. Aloof to the author, 29 October 1990.

[21] *Appendix*, p. 39.

could not be kept secret. The elders of the Hebrew congregation came to hear of it, and consulted the Chief Rabbi, Solomon Hirschel, who ordered a temporary suspension from duty. Alexander was faced with the loss of his income, and with the pleas of his friends, but the attraction of the Gospel was too great. He could not return to his duties at the synagogue, and after more 'immediate connection with many Christian friends'[22] his mind was made up.

Alexander was baptized at St Andrew's parish church on Wednesday 22 June 1825. A new vicar had arrived at St Andrew's in August 1824, John Hatchard, the son of the founder of the publishing and bookselling firm. He was a strict Evangelical, and his memorial by H. H. Armstead in the south-east aisle displays his mutton-chop whiskers, and draws attention to his courage in the cholera epidemic of 1832, and to his part in founding new churches and the South Devon and East Cornwall Hospital. The baptism was not quiet or private. Alexander was well known, and St Andrew's is only fifty yards north of the synagogue. The *Plymouth and Devonport Weekly Journal* reported[23] that 'Mr Alexander, late Reader to the Jewish congregation in this town, and who has held other offices of character and respectability among the Jews, was baptized in the Christian Faith, by the Rev. Mr. Hatchard, in the presence of an immense congregation who appeared to take a great interest in the ceremony.' The prayers were read by Robert Lampen, the first perpetual curate of St Andrew's chapel, and the witnesses were Golding, Mrs Hatchard, and Captain Thicknesse, R.N. As well as administering the sacrament of baptism, Hatchard preached a substantial sermon on Hosea 3. 4–5:

> The children of Israel shall abide many days without a king, and without a prince, and without a sacrifice, and without an image, and without an ephod, and without teraphim. Afterward shall the children of Israel return, and seek the LORD their God, and David their king; and shall fear the LORD and his goodness in the latter days.

He dwelt at length on the persistent stubbornness of the Jews. 'The ox knoweth his owner, and the ass his master's crib: but Israel doth not know, my people doth not consider (Isaiah 1. 3).' He considered the prophecies of return, including those in Ezekiel 37, and continued:

[22] *Appendix*, p. 39.
[23] Ibid., p. 40.

If the conversion of a soul from the ways of sin to the ways of righteousness is a matter upon which there is joy among the angels in heaven, surely when the vail which remaineth upon the children of Israel is done away in Christ, it is a cause for *peculiar* thankfulness unto him ... Such an event, my Christian brethren, I have this day the delight to announce to you—A member of the house of Israel, will at this time 'Subscribe with his hand unto the Lord, and surname himself by the name of Israel [Isaiah 45. 5]'.

He encouraged any Jews who were present to follow Alexander's example. 'Let me entreat you not with wilful blindness and obduracy, to reject without due enquiry, the claims of him whom your forefathers have crucified and slain.' He begged Christians to pray for the conversion of Jews.

Is there anything in the formation of the Jewish mind, is there anything in the Jewish heart, which renders it impossible that God can have access there? Are there prejudices so deeply rooted, is the curse of God so irremediably upon them, that the voice of prayer, that the cry of faith cannot be heard, or will not be answered?—God forbid.

He urged the convert to pray for his 'brethren after the flesh'.[24] I have quoted Hatchard's rhetoric at length to illustrate the feelings of the time, and also the length of the step that Alexander took. In his own account Alexander promised to pray for his own people, and recorded his gratitude to his Jewish friends, 'though I am conscious of being an outcast from them.'[25]

The newspaper report continued, 'We ought perhaps to suffer Mr. Alexander to carry into private life the precepts and consolations of that religion which he has thus openly embraced, as it may not be grateful to his feelings to be dragged into notoriety.' Some had attempted to belittle his sacrifice, saying that he was of low rank, and the paper admitted that it had erred in this respect. Enquiry had revealed that Alexander had always been known as 'Rabbi', that he was a qualified reader, who deputized as reader, and 'also held the office of *Shochet*, or Inspector of Meat, which is an honourable office, and bestowed only on Priests of unblemished reputation.'

It would have been difficult for Alexander to remain in Plymouth, and

---

[24] Hatchard, *Predictions*, p. 34.
[25] *Appendix*, p. 40.

even more difficult for his wife. Another report of the baptism, in the *Western Flying Post and Yeovil Mercury*, stated, 'He is about to go abroad as a missionary.'[26] The day after the baptism, Alexander moved to Exeter, and there Deborah was baptized on 9 November at All Hallows Goldsmith Street. John Hatchard came from Plymouth to administer the baptism. In the register she appears as Deborah Mary, and seems to have taken the second name when she became a Christian.

This is not the place to describe Alexander's career in Ireland, where he was ordained; with the London Society for Promoting Christianity among the Jews, which sent him to Prussia, where he met members of his family amicably, and in London; or his episcopate, ending abruptly with his death on 23 November 1845, as he camped at Bilbeis on his way to Cairo. I will, however, attempt to shed a little light on some of the lines that led from the events in Plymouth that I have described.

The Hatchard connection was maintained and strengthened. The vicar of St Andrew's had a younger brother, Thomas, who was the partner of his father, and who was to inherit the publishing and bookselling business in 1849. His son, Thomas Goodwin Hatchard, was a clergyman. He visited the Alexanders in the Holy Land, and according to tradition proposed marriage to Fanny—the oldest surviving child, who had been born in Danzig in 1828—under Abraham's oak at Hebron. She was little more than a child at that time. They were married on 19 February 1846. The first ten years of their married life were spent at Havant Rectory, then in 1856 Hatchard became rector of Guildford St Nicolas'. His father died in 1858, and the family and friends built St Catherine's infants school at the end of the garden in his memory. The building, designed by Charles Henry Howell still stands, though it has not been a school since 1932. In 1857 they lost an 8-year-old daughter, Adelaide Charlotte, who was buried in the new municipal cemetery, just above the garden of the mansion that was then the rectory. On 24 February 1969 Hatchard was consecrated Bishop of Mauritius in Westminster Abbey. Fanny was a bishop's wife for less time even than her mother, for Hatchard died of fever on 28 February 1870, only a few months after reaching the island. Fanny returned to live in London, but died in December 1880 in the Hotel Beau Site in Cannes, where she was buried at Christ Church. She was only 52 years old. Her memorial in St Nicolas' is four very dull windows of the Evangelists by Clayton and Bell. The Bishop was already commemorated there by a sturdy pulpit, carved by Thomas Earp of Lambeth.

---

[26] 27 June 1825.

Another daughter of the Alexanders, Mary Ann, or Minnie, married William Wynne Willson, a fellow of St John's, Oxford, and Rector of Codford St Mary, in Wiltshire. Their son, St John Basil Wynne Willson, became Dean of Bristol, 1916–21, and Bishop of Bath and Wells, 1921–37, and as such was one of the supporters of King George VI at the coronation in 1937.

Deborah Mary Alexander lived at St Leonards-on-Sea, blind at the end, and died there on 13 May 1872, aged 68. She was buried at Churt, Surrey, where her son Alexander Benjamin Alexander was vicar. The grave, near the north-east corner of the chancel, is marked with a plain stone Latin cross, and the inscription ends, 'THINE EYES SHALL SEE THE KING IN HIS BEAUTY'.[27] The oldest of Benny's children who were born at Churt was Ronald Percy Goodwin Alexander. He studied at St Augustine's College, Canterbury, and then farmed in Ontario and Manitoba from 1888 to 1894. He then went as a lay SPG missionary to the diocese of Mashonaland, in British South Africa, where he was ordained deacon in 1899 and priest in 1901, serving as curate at St Augustine's, Penhalonga, and then Gwelo. He returned to England and lived with the Cowley Fathers in Oxford. It is not clear whether he sought to join the Society, as the novices' register has been lost, but he held a general licence in the diocese of Oxford, and also had some association with Holy Trinity, Winchester. In 1913 he was received into the Roman Catholic Church. In 1914 he entered the Benedictine abbey of Fort Augustus, in Inverness-shire, and was professed in 1915 as Dom Romuald, and ordained priest in 1920. He held pastoral positions in Scotland, England, and Wales. When he died, on 21 May 1948, it was recorded that he 'was something of a poet and wrote verses with facility; some of these he sang, accompanying them on an auto-harp; these were of a humorous kind and were sung for the entertainment of his brethren, parishioners and friends.'[28]

All this is a very long way from the rabbi's son in Schönlanke.

Guildford St Nicolas'

---

[27] Isaiah 33. 17.
[28] *Benedictine Almanack* (1949), p. 19.

ADVENTISTS DISCOVER THE SEVENTH-DAY SABBATH: HOW TO DEAL WITH THE 'JEWISH PROBLEM'

by KEITH A. FRANCIS

IN 1831 William Miller, a farmer from Low Hampton, New York, began to preach that the Second Advent would occur 'about the year 1843'.[1] From this rather inauspicious beginning the number of people who agreed with Miller's prediction grew, so that by 1844 they probably numbered more than 50,000 according to some estimates.[2] This phenomenon would be of little historical interest—except, perhaps, to historians studying nineteenth-century American religious history—had it not been for the fact that one legacy of Millerism is the Seventh-day Adventist Church, which has over six million members world-wide and can claim, for example, one of the largest educational systems run by a Protestant denomination.[3]

Nevertheless, very little of a historical nature has been written about the Seventh-day Adventist Church by non-Seventh-day Adventists;[4] this is rather surprising when one considers that this Church shares the doctrine of the seventh-day Sabbath with one of the major religions of the world, Judaism.[5] This study will investigate how and why a group of Millerites decided to adopt the seventh-day Sabbath as a doctrine of their

---

[1] William Miller, *Apology and Defense* (Boston, Mass., 1845), p. 12. The best collection of Millerite and early Adventist materials, such as pamphlets and periodicals, can be found in the Jenks Collection at Aurora University, Illinois, USA.

[2] See Francis D. Nichol, *The Midnight Cry: a Defense of William Miller and the Millerites* (Washington, DC, 1944), pp. 204–5; David L. Rowe, 'Millerites: a Shadow Portrait', in Ronald L. Numbers and Jonathan M. Butler, eds, *The Disappointed: Millerism and Millenarianism in the Nineteenth Century* (Indianapolis, Indiana, 1987), pp. 5–7. These estimates only apply to the United States; they do not include groups independent of the Millerites who made the same prediction, such as the Irvingites in England.

[3] Don F. Neufeld, *Seventh-Day Adventist Encyclopedia*, rev. edn (Washington DC, 1976), p. 1296, and General Conference of Seventh-day Adventists, *128th Annual Statistical Report—1990*, pp. 4 and 26.

[4] Most of the writing by non-Seventh-day Adventists on the Church has been of a polemical nature. A good example of this is Anthony A. Hoekema, *The Four Major Cults* (Grand Rapids, Michigan, 1963).

[5] There are a number of good histories of the Church written by Seventh-day Adventists which include summaries of the major doctrines. See, for example, Malcolm Bull and Keith Lockhart, *Seeking a Sanctuary: Seventh-day Adventism and the American Dream* (London, 1989), and R. Schwarz, *Light Bearers to the Remnant* (Boise, Idaho, 1979).

fledgeling Church and how they dealt with the fact that this doctrine was associated exclusively with Judaism.[6]

The story of how Adventists were introduced to the idea of seventh-day Sabbath keeping has been well documented by Seventh-day Adventist historians, so there is no need to restate it in great detail here.[7] A Seventh Day Baptist named Rachel Oakes had joined a congregation of Adventists in Washington, New Hampshire, in 1841. After numerous attempts to persuade her fellow church members that they should worship on Saturday instead of Sunday, she managed to convince her local minister, Frederick Wheeler, to change in 1844. About the same time another minister, Thomas Preble, published the first advocacy of the seventh-day Sabbath in print by an Adventist.[8] (It is not clear where Preble first heard about the doctrine; he may have been influenced by Wheeler and Oakes or by a tract written by Miller or may have learned about the doctrine by independent study.[9]) Preble's tract was read by another Adventist, Joseph Bates; and it was Bates's tract—*The Seventh Day Sabbath, a Perpetual Sign, from the Beginning, to the Entering into the Gates of the Holy City, According to the Commandment*'—which convinced future leaders of the Seventh-day Adventist Church, such as James White and Ellen Harmon, to accept the doctrine.

While the story of the acceptance of the doctrine of the seventh-day Sabbath by some Adventists is a fairly simple one to retell it does beg the question why they were willing to adopt this doctrine. Adventists had already been ridiculed for their predictions about the Second Advent,[10] and it would seem that this Sabbatarian group would only compound their problems by adopting a doctrine that could in no way be described as

---

[6] For the remainder of this paper the generic term 'Adventists' will be used. The people who believed the Second Advent would occur in 1843 did not think of themselves as 'followers' of William Miller and after 1844, when the movement began to splinter, each group called itself Adventist. See David Tallmadge Arthur, '"Come out of Babylon": A Study of Millerite Separatism and Denominationalism, 1840–1865' (University of Rochester Ph.D. thesis, 1970).

[7] See Goron O. Martinborough, 'The Beginning of a Theology of the Sabbath among American Sabbatarian Adventists, 1842–1850' (Loma Linda University, California, M.A. thesis, 1976); David M. Young, 'When Adventists became Sabbath-Keepers', *Adventist Heritage*, 2, 2 (1975), pp. 5–10; J. N. Andrews, *History of the Sabbath and First Day of the Week* (Battle Creek, Michigan, 1887); Schwarz, *Light Bearers*, pp. 59–61.

[8] Preble's arguments were published in an Adventist periodical called the *Hope of Israel*; this article was republished as *Tract Showing that the Seventh Day Should be Observed as the Sabbath, Instead of the First Day*; '*According to the Commandment*' (Nashua, New Hampshire, 1845).

[9] Young, 'When Adventists', pp. 7–10.

[10] There were numerous claims that Adventists engaged in odd and even subversive behaviour in the early 1840s; Clara Endicott Sears, *Days of Delusion: A Strange Bit of History* (Boston, 1924) contains a number of examples of these supposed incidents.

mainstream: rather, most Christians thought the doctrine 'Jewish'. In fact, the reason why the seventh-day Sabbath was adopted was quite the opposite: these Adventists believed that the doctrine solved rather than exacerbated their problems.

The problem facing Adventists in November 1844 was that their 'movement' was seen as a failure. The prediction that the Second Advent would occur in April 1844 had been changed after Adventists accepted the findings of Samuel Snow; Snow had calculated that the Second Advent would occur on 22 October 1844,[11] but in neither case had the prediction proved to be correct.[12] Sabbatarian Adventists[13] believed that the Miller–Snow chronology was correct but that they had predicted the wrong event. They argued that instead of returning to earth, Christ had begun a new phase of ministry in heaven. Part of this new ministry required a recovery of 'lost Christian doctrines' such as the seventh-day Sabbath by Christ's followers.[14] Thus Sabbatarian Adventists could affirm the importance of Adventism up to 1844 and infuse their own development with significance.[15]

This approach—the idea of recovery—was one of the ways that Sabbatarian Adventists refuted the charge that they were being 'Jewish'. In other words, they argued that the seventh-day Sabbath was not a peculiarly Jewish institution but one binding on all followers of God.[16]

Those Adventists who did not adopt the seventh-day Sabbath saw two 'Jewish problems' with the new doctrine. The first was that the necessity of keeping the seventh-day Sabbath had been removed by the death and Resurrection of Christ. The seventh-day Sabbath was as relevant to the Christian as Yom Kippur.[17] They argued that seventh-day Sabbath

---

[11] Snow published his conclusions on 22 August 1844 in a tract entitled *True Midnight Cry*. See also Nichol, *The Midnight Cry*, pp. 212–15.

[12] Adventists had changed the date predicted for the Second Advent three times previously, and 22 October 1844 was their last fall-back position; therefore this day was called 'the Great Disappointment' by Adventists for obvious reasons. See LeRoy Edwin Froom, *New World Recovery and Consummation of Prophetic Interpretation* = vol. 4 of *The Prophetic Faith of Our Fathers* (Washington DC, 1954), pp. 793–804, 810–14.

[13] The Seventh-day Adventist Church did not adopt an official name until 1860; I have chosen the term Sabbatarian Adventist as a designation because it states clearly their difference from other Adventists.

[14] See Andrew G. Mustard, *James White and SDA Organization: Historical Development, 1844–1881* (Michigan, USA, 1987), pp. 92–5; Jonathan M. Butler, 'Adventism and the American Experience', in Edwin S. Gaustad, ed., *The Rise of Adventism: Religion and Society in Mid-nineteenth-century America* (London, 1974), p. 178.

[15] Nichol, *The Midnight Cry*, pp. 460–1.

[16] Preble, *Tract*, pp. 4–5.

[17] *Proceedings of the Mutual Conference of Adventists, Held in the City of Albany, the 29th and 30th of April, and 1st of May, 1845* (New York, 1845), p. 20.

keeping was part of the old covenant God made with the nation of Israel, and so in the Christian era—or time of the New Covenant—such duties were unnecessary.[18] Second, these Adventists believed that the seventh-day Sabbath was the Jewish Sabbath and the first day of the week the Christian one.[19] In other words, the Christian Church kept the Sabbath but on the first day of the week as a commemoration of the Resurrection, of Christ.[20]

As said before, in reply to charges of 'pseudo-Judaism', Sabbatarian Adventists argued that the seventh-day Sabbath was not particular to the nation of Israel.

One argument used was that the seventh-day Sabbath was instituted at Creation: that is, long before a Jewish nation existed. Sabbatarian Adventists suggested that God had intended all mankind to keep the seventh-day Sabbath, and the function of the Jews was to enable other nations to see and desire the benefits of the provision.[21]

A second argument was that the seventh-day Sabbath was part of God's moral law, which is perpetual. Therefore, even if the Jewish feasts and festivals were irrelevant for the Christian, the moral law—which meant the Decalogue—was still binding; and, of course, the fourth commandment which enjoins the seventh-day Sabbath was part of the Decalogue.[22]

Lastly, Sabbatarian Adventists argued that the seventh-day Sabbath should be observed because it was the right thing to do. Quoting from texts such as 1 John 2. 2—'We . . . know that we know him, if we keep his commandments'—they asserted that a Christian could not ignore such injunctions, and these injunctions included the observance of the seventh-day Sabbath.[23]

Nevertheless, for all their efforts the Sabbatarian Adventists did not manage to avoid the contention that they had adopted a doctrine which really belonged to Judaism. Despite attempts to present the seventh-day Sabbath as non-Jewish, the charge was still made. Over a hundred years later a survey of the Seventh-day Adventist publications dealing with

---

[18] Enoch Jacobs, 'The Sabbath', *Day Star*, 11 Aug. 1845, pp. 3–7; 'The Lord's Day', *Midnight Cry*, 12 Sept. 1844, p. 77.

[19] Bates, *The Seventh Day Sabbath*, p. 12.

[20] Ibid., pp. 27–30.

[21] Ibid., pp. 3–5; Preble, *Tract*, p. 7.

[22] Bates, *The Seventh Day Sabbath*, pp. 24–6; Preble, *Tract*, pp. 8–9; J. N. Andrews, 'The Perpetuity of the Law of God', *Second Advent Review and Herald*, 1, 5 (Jan. 1851), pp. 33–6; ibid., 1, 6 (Feb. 1851), pp. 41–3.

[23] Bates, *The Seventh Day Sabbath*, pp. 22–3; Nichol, *The Midnight Cry*, pp. 460–1.

doctrinal beliefs reveals that the Church is still struggling with this 'problem'.[24] No doubt Sabbatarian Adventists and Seventh-day Adventists alike would understand well the sentiments expressed by a Seventh Day Baptist, Roswell Cottrell, in 1851:

When we present God's holy law,
And arguments from scripture draw;
Objectors say, to pick a flaw,
    'It's Jewish.'

Though at the first Jehovah blessed
And sanctified His day of rest;
The same belief is still expressed—
    'It's Jewish.'

Though with the world this rest began
And thence through all the scriptures ran,
And Jesus said 'twas *made for man*—
    'It's Jewish.'

Though not with Jewish rites, which passed
But with the moral law 'twas classed
Which must endure while time shall last—
    'It's Jewish.'

Though the disciples, Luke and Paul,
Continue still this rest to call
The 'Sabbath day,' this answers all—
    'It's Jewish.'

The gospel teachers' plain expression,
That 'Sin is of the law transgression,'
Seems not to make the least impression—
    'It's Jewish.'

---

[24] See Francis D. Nichol, *Answers to Objections: an Examination of the Major Objections Raised Against the Teachings of Seventh-day Adventists*, 3rd rev. edn (Washington DC, 1952), pp. 123–252; *Seventh-day Adventists Answer Questions on Doctrine: An Explanation of Certain Major Aspects of Seventh-day Adventist Belief* (Washington DC, 1957), pp. 149–76; *Seventh-day Adventists believe . . . An Exposition of 27 Fundamental Doctrines* (Hagerstown, Maryland, 1988), pp. 249–66.

They love the rest of man's invention,
But if Jehovah's day we mention,
This puts an end to all contention—
'It's Jewish.'[25]

Pacific Union College,
California

[25] Roswell F. Cottrell, 'It's Jewish', *Second Advent Review and Sabbath Herald*, 1, 6 (Feb. 1851),
front page. There is an ironic twist to the publication of this poem: Cottrell himself became a
Seventh-day Adventist soon after it was published, either in late 1851 or early 1852: see
Neufeld, *Seventh-day Adventist Encyclopedia*, p. 354.

POPERY, RABBINISM, AND REFORM: EVANGELICALS AND JEWS IN EARLY VICTORIAN ENGLAND

by DAVID FELDMAN

IN this brief paper I discuss the relation between Christianity and Jewish religious reform in early Victorian England. More specifically, I want to suggest that there was a close relation between the Evangelical critique of Judaism as a form of popery and the direction and meaning of religious reform within Anglo-Jewry. If, indeed, this was the case, then what follows has a significant bearing upon the way we interpret Jewish integration in nineteenth-century England.

There were roughly 50,000 Jews in England in 1850, two-thirds of whom lived in the capital. Synagogues, like other communal institutions, were dominated by a wealthy elite. Synagogue attendance was thin, and in 1851, on census Sabbath, only 10 per cent of London Jews were found in a metropolitan synagogue. Although nominally Orthodox, the general temper of religious observance within Anglo-Jewry was relaxed.[1]

One force driving the secessionists who established the West London Synagogue of British Jews in 1842—the first Reform synagogue in Britain—was a desire to halt the march of indifference. The synagogue's representatives claimed they had established their place of worship in response to gathering irreverence which they attributed to the 'antiquated mode of synagogue worship'. They dwelt on the need to improve the synagogue's devotional character and 'preserve proper decorum during the performance of Divine Worship'.[2] Most radical of all, the new synagogue challenged the authority of rabbis to legislate for Jewish religious practice. The members of the West London Synagogue celebrated festivals on a single day only instead of, as was customary, treating two days as a holiday. 'It is not the intention of the body of which we form a part', wrote the secessionists, 'to recognise as sacred, days which are evidently not ordained as such in scripture.'[3]

---

[1] V. D. Lipman, *Social History of the Jews in England, 1850–1950* (London, 1954), p. 36; S. Singer, 'Orthodox Judaism in early Victorian London' (Ph.D. dissertation, Yeshiva University, 1981), p. 217.

[2] *Jewish Chronicle*, 20 Feb. 1846, p. 80; C. Roth, ed., *Anglo-Jewish Letters* (London, 1938), pp. 281–6.

[3] Ibid.

379

The origins of the new congregation extended beyond its members' opinions on ritual, liturgy, and custom. There was, for example, a demographic aspect to its formation. The growing population of wealthy Jews living in the West End of London required a local synagogue, which the East End congregations refused to provide, fearing this would diminish their own membership, wealth, and status.[4] Moreover, for some of its members at least, the new congregation was intended to spearhead a vigorous campaign for political equality. In this light, its reforms, and, in particular, the decision to celebrate festivals on a single day, have been seen as part of a bid for political integration.[5]

Many Orthodox Jews also favoured measures of religious reform, even though they did not ally themselves with the West London Synagogue. The men who favoured change were also, with some notable exceptions, the men who dominated communal institutions.[6] And with the accession of a new Chief Rabbi, Nathan Adler, in 1845 the Orthodox reformers won a great deal of what they wanted. The Chief Rabbi's *Laws and regulations* placed great emphasis on decorum: infants below the age of four were to be excluded from services, loud responses by the congregation were discouraged, and the public sale of honours was discontinued.[7] The development of this broad reform movement within Anglo-Jewry was more than a programme of change dragged forward by the momentum of some Jews' political aspirations. In fact, programmes of synagogue Reform preceded the emergence of Jewish emancipation as a political question and had recurred from the 1820s.[8] Although the issue of religious Reform interacted with the cause of the Jews' political equality at many points, it went beyond this issue and reflected on the Jews' accommodation in English society in a wider sense.

Where did the ideas informing the direction and content of Reform come from? The prevailing interpretation is that Anglo-Jewry's concern with 'decorum' was a reflection of the desire of wealthy Jews to conform to 'English' or 'Anglican' norms of conduct and bibliocentric religion. In this view the reforming movement stemmed from a drive for *social*

[4] Lipman, *Social History*, p. 15.

[5] R. Liberles, 'The origins of the Jewish Reform Movement in England', *Association of Jewish Studies Review*, 1 (1976), pp. 121–50.

[6] On this see Singer, 'Orthodox Judaism', pp. 138, 207.

[7] Ibid., p. 148; T. Endelman, 'The Englishness of Jewish modernity in England', in J. Katz, ed., *Towards Modernity: the European Jewish model* (New Brunswick, NJ, 1987), p. 236; *Jewish Chronicle*, 26 June 1846, p. 161.

[8] C. Roth, *The Great Synagogue, 1690–1940* (London, 1950), pp. 250–1.

acceptance, which, moreover, was achieved with relative ease. This is a happy story, one which emphasizes choice rather than any pressure which privileged some options above others. It is a history of change which fits well with the accepted, benign view of Jewish integration in England, where Protestantism and, above all, the philo-Semitic strain within Evangelicalism, is seen to have generated a climate peculiarly favourable to the Jews and Judaism.[9]

But if we place Jewish Reform in the context of religious argument more widely and, in particular, in relation to a critique of Judaism, this interpretation appears less compelling. Christian critiques of Judaism were not novel, of course. But the desire of many Jews to take a full part, socially and, still more, politically, in British society was more recent, as was the prospect that this might be possible. Moreover, religion and political controversy drew close in early Victorian public life, as the divisions within the Established Church, as well as the political claims of Christians beyond it, became the stuff of politics. In these circumstances criticism of the Jewish religion possessed a powerful resonance for both Christians and Jews.[10]

The most productive source of Christian commentary on Judaism was the London Society for Promoting Christianity among the Jews. The Society was established in 1809 as an interdenominational mission, but in 1815 it narrowed to a purely Anglican basis. In the 1820s it attracted the energies of pre-millenarians in particular, whose Messianism and literal reading of prophecy in the Hebrew Bible led them to place special emphasis on the conversion of the Jews.[11] The Society's principal worker in London was Alexander McCaul; McCaul became Professor of Hebrew and Rabbinical Literature at King's College. He had spent most of the 1820s working among Jews in Poland and returned to work for the Society in London in 1831. Between 1832 and 1836 he delivered a series of addresses to Jews at Saturday-evening conferences, and these formed the basis for his weekly pamphlet *Old Paths*. In 1837 they were published as a single volume. Over 10,000 copies were distributed in the first year of

---

[9] For this interpretation see Endelman, 'The Englishness of Jewish modernity'.

[10] For example, G. I. T. Machin, *Politics and the Churches in Great Britain, 1832–68* (Oxford, 1977); R. Brent, *Liberal Anglican Politics: Whiggery, Religion and Reform, 1830–41* (Oxford, 1987); B. Hilton, *The Age of Atonement: the Influence of Evangelicalism on Social and Economic Thought, 1795–1865* (Oxford, 1988).

[11] M. Scult, *Millenial Expectations and Jewish Liberties: a Study of Efforts to Convert the Jews in Britain up to the mid-Nineteenth Century* (Leiden, 1978); D. W. Bebbington, *Evangelicalism in Modern Britain: a History from the 1730s to the 1980s* (London, 1989), pp. 76–7, 81–3, 88–9.

publication. In 1838 he followed *Old Paths* with *Sketches of Judaism and the Jews*, a collection of articles he had written for the *British Magazine* between 1834 and 1838.[12] McCaul's analysis was further repeated by others, with slight variations, in the political and literary reviews.

McCaul contrasted Judaism as he found it in the Bible with the religion he saw practised by the Jews. *Old Paths* was published with the informative subtitle '*or a comparison of the principles and doctrines of modern Judaism with the religion of Moses and the prophets*'. McCaul aimed to prove that Christianity was the faithful continuation of the writings of the Hebrew Bible, and Judaism 'a new and totally different system, devised by designing men and unworthy of the Jewish people'.[13] The Jewish religion had been corrupted by rabbis, and their instrument had been the oral law. Indeed 'Rabbinism' was a favoured term for Judaic practice. In the same vein, A. A. Cooper wrote in the *Quarterly Review*, 'Talmudical learning and the power of the Rabbis, the depositories of it, are the ultimate object of Jewish discipline.' As a result, Judaism was not a vital religion, it was a faith without engagement: 'The rabbinical Jew fulfills a commandment, and thinks he consequently lays up a portion of merit.'[14] Faced with a powerful class of priests who claimed to interpret the Bible for the people, and who had generated an elaborate ritual sustained by tradition, one for which there was no literal sanction in Scripture, these men found in 'Rabbinism' the same evils that evangelicals habitually found in 'Popery'. McCaul introduced his *Sketches of Jews and Judaism* by explaining that

> From the dispersion to the latter end of the last century, Rabbinism prevailed universally amongst the Jewish nation . . . If asked to give a concise yet adequate idea of this system, I should say it is Jewish Popery: just as Popery may be defined to [*sic*] by Gentile Rabbinism. Its distinguishing feature is that it asserts the transmission of an oral or traditional law of equal authority with the written law of God, at the same time, that, like Popery, it resolves tradition into the present opinions of the existing Church.[15]

[12] A. McCaul, *The Old Paths: or a comparison of the principles and doctrines of modern Judaism with the religion of Moses and the prophets*, 2nd edn (London, 1846), p. vii; W. T. Gidney, *The History of the London Society for Promoting Christianity among the Jews* (London, 1908), p. 217.

[13] McCaul, *Old Paths*, p. 645.

[14] A. A. Cooper, 'State and prospects of the Jews', *Quarterly Review*, Jan. 1839, p. 182. Cooper later became 7th Earl of Shaftesbury.

[15] A. McCaul, *Sketches of Jews and Judaism* (London, 1838), p. 2.

Anti-Popery was a more potent force than any hostility to Jews in mid-nineteenth-century Britain. Inevitably, for militant Protestants, Catholicism was a more significant opponent. However, this primary opposition did not deflect hostile attention away from Jews and Judaism. Instead, it could provide the terms within which the Jewish religion was understood.

Judaism, as it was understood by conversionists, was not wholly a negative force. Most obviously, as the precursor and foundation of Christianity it was not without value. Indeed, it was the double-sided and paradoxical aspect of the Jewish condition which held a special attraction for these evangelicals. The Jews were 'princes in degradation', 'sublime in misery', 'a people chastened but not wholly cast off.'[16] Both their decline and survival were confirmations of Christian truth.

In his *Sketches of Judaism*, McCaul did not doubt that in England 'the system' of Judaism was petrified. Yet he did acknowledge the existence of a dynamic element within Judaism. By 1846, when *Old Paths* entered its second edition, McCaul responded enthusiastically to the formation of the West London Synagogue. The new congregation had renounced much that he found objectionable and was testimony to the influence of his book.[17] At first sight, McCaul's claims to have influenced the development of Reform Judaism in England may seem far-fetched. Yet the parallels between the conversionists and the Jewish reformers are too striking to ignore, and if it is implausible to see reform as an embrace of McCaul and the London Society it was, in great measure, a response to them and the critique of Judaism they offered.

The *Jewish Chronicle*, for example, a newspaper which did support reform within the Orthodox community, was also bitter in its attacks on the conversionist system of 'fraud and imposition'. Naturally, it did Jewish reformers no good to be identified as the conversionists' parrots. This was particularly the case when some 'conversion-mongers', such as Sir Robert Inglis and Lord Ashley, were among the die-hard Conservatives who opposed Jewish emancipation—the admission of professing Jews to Parliament. But for Jews anxious for political equality, support for the London Society from a number of leading anti-emancipationists seemed only to render the need to refute its arguments all the more pressing.

The minister of the West London [Reform] synagogue, David Marks, explained his religious opinions, in part, as an attempt to preserve Judaism

---

[16] 'Present state and prospects of the Jews', *Frasers Magazine*, Sept. 1840, pp. 253–4; Cooper, 'State and prospects of the Jews', p. 191.
[17] McCaul, *Old Paths*, p. vii.

from external attack.[18] When he preached on the occasion of the synagogue's consecration Marks underlined the point: 'It is the spirit of the ritual to which we should have our attention directed, more than to any set form in which it is presented to our senses.'[19] Indeed, there is some evidence to suggest that Marks consulted with McCaul when making the innovations at the West London Synagogue.[20] In abolishing customs, such as the second day of holidays, and prayers, and references to angels and demons which had no scriptural basis, the innovations made at the West London Synagogue certainly appeared to answer Evangelical criticism.

At times the full weight of the Evangelical critique was adopted by the Jewish reformers in the course of their lengthy feud with the leaders of Orthodoxy. In 1854 Marks gave a course of four lectures, the title of which disclosed its anti-rabbinical message: *The Law is Light: A course of four lectures on the sufficiency of the Law of Moses as the guide of Israel.* In the first of these addresses Marks set out to remonstrate with 'a large class of our Jewish bretheren, who receive unconditionally, the rabbinical system as a whole.' More particularly he criticized the vindication of that system presented by Nathan Adler, the Chief Rabbi, in which Adler had defended the necessity for and the authority of rabbinical interpretation of the law.

> A doctrine like this, which is so boldly asserted in the sermon of the Reverend Rabbi, may well startle us, and induce us to question whether instead of listening here to the voice of Judaism, we are not having rehearsed to us the substance, though in a different phraseology, of the theology of Rome.[21]

The West London congregation had gone further than Orthodox reformers by questioning the status of rabbinical law. But in other respects its response to the conversionist assault was reproduced within the ranks of Anglo-Jewish Orthodoxy. The *Jewish Chronicle* campaigned in the 1840s for alterations in the synagogue service. The newspaper was the mouthpiece for familiar laments on the standard of decorum. In part this was seen as a question of manners and modernity. However, even this concern with modernity may be seen in the light of the incapacity for

[18] D. W. Marks, *Sermons preached on various occasions at the West London synagogue of British Jews* (London, 1851), p. 11.
[19] D. W. Marks, *The Law is light: A course of four lectures on the sufficiency of the Law of Moses as the guide of Israel* (London, 1854), p. 43.
[20] B.-Z. Lask Abrahams, 'Emanuel Deutsch of "The Talmud" fame', *TJHSE* (1969–73), p. 56.
[21] Marks, *The Law is light*, p. 8.

development ascribed to Judaism and the Jews; observance of the minutely-detailed rabbinical system had left Jews much as they had been centuries before. 'Rabbinism in our age is an incongruity', the *Jewish Chronicle* claimed.[22] The reasons for the turn to more decorous forms of worship went beyond a felt need to conform to modern manners. It encompassed a desire to find within Judaism a religion of the heart and a religion separate from the world, and in this it echoed clearly the Evangelical impulse. Consider, for example, this *Jewish Chronicle* editorial on devotion in the synagogue.

> Devotion in the general acceptation of the term signifies a condition of the mind, in which our senses and our feelings are absorbed in communication with the Supreme Being—a state of emotion produced by involuntary agency; a panting desire and an arduous longing to pour out our thoughts before our heavenly Creator, to whom we entirely *give up* ourselves, and to whose worship we resign for a time our powers and faculties.[23]

The service had to be purged of obstacles to this state of abandonment. We can highlight striking parallels elsewhere; above all in the emphases on 'unmysterious' forms of worship and a vital religion of the heart.

The doctrinal innovations of Reform Judaism in Britain were notably moderate in all but their decision to dispense with some customary holidays. Belief in the Jews' eventual restoration was not denied, as it was in Germany, and there was no suggestion that Hebrew should be replaced as the language of worship. In Britain, reformers wedded themselves to the word of the Bible. This limited their innovations, but it also led them to abolish the second day of festivals for which there was no scriptural authority; something beyond the agenda of European Reform. The Anglo-Jewish reformers reflected the force in Britain of a bibliocentric critique of Judaism. In Germany, Old Testament criticism was of a far more radical character than in Britain. Inevitably, in that context, a Reform movement which dealt with the Talmud only would have provided a less respectable basis for a revised Judaism. Whereas in Germany scholars 'adopted philosophically oriented views of religion and theology that led them to propose radical reconstructions of the history of Israelite religion based upon source criticism', in Britain they accepted 'the general reliability of the history and religion of Israel' presented in the

---

[22] *Jewish Chronicle*, 18 Aug. 1848, p. 641.
[23] *Jewish Chronicle*, 10 July 1846, p. 173.

Hebrew Bible.[24] The differences between the Jewish Reform movements in Britain and the German states were influenced strongly by the different paths of biblical criticism in the two contexts.

The drive for acceptability which Reform represented in England was both more defensive and intellectually more elaborate than has been acknowledged. Religious change in early Victorian England has been presented as one reflection of the desire of wealthy Jews for *social* acceptance.[25] But the drive for decorum signified more than a desire to render the Jews' devotional manners more delicate. The history of religious change has been divorced from the need to legitimize the persistence of Judaism in the face of a Christian state and society. Implausibly, it has been a history of change with its politics taken out. Religious Reform was a strategy designed to revise Judaism in the face of criticism which counterposed degenerate 'rabbinism' to a religion of the 'spirit'. The dominant answer to the charges of 'rabbinism' was to fall back on the Hebrew Bible and to cleanse the synagogue of those elements which contradicted not only the norms of Victorian decorousness, but which also offered the impression that Jews attended synagogue for any purpose other than prayer and spiritual elevation. The march of Reform reflected the force of a critique of traditional Judaism which received its most forceful expression, but not its only one, among Evangelical conversionists. English Protestantism and the philo-Semitic strain within it, have been widely thought of as an element which encouraged the Jews' integration in English society. At the very least, we must recognize that their impact was deeply ambivalent. Conversionists venerated Jews, but they also set the terms of a debate which set normative Jewish practice decisively on the defensive.

University of Bristol

---

[24] J. Rogerson, *Old Testament Criticism in the Nineteenth Century: England and Germany* (London, 1984), pp. 9, 219. On the influence of Protestant values in Germany see A. Altmann, 'The new style of preaching in nineteenth century Germany', in Altmann, ed., *Studies in Nineteenth Century Jewish Intellectual History* (Cambridge, Mass., 1964), pp. 65–116; M. Meyer, 'Christian influence in early German Reform Judaism', in C. Berlin, ed., *Studies in Jewish bibliography, History and Literature in Honour of I. Edward Kiev* (New York, 1971), pp. 289–303.

[25] Endelman, 'The Englishness of Jewish modernity', pp. 231–3.

THE BISHOPS AND THE JEWS, 1828–1858

by FRANCES KNIGHT

BETWEEN 1830 and 1858 fourteen separate attempts were made to remove the legal disabilities which prevented Jews from sitting in Parliament. The first bill was dismissed by the unreformed House of Commons, and the next twelve, from 1833 onwards, were rejected by the Lords after being passed by the Commons. It was only the fourteenth attempt, a carefully constructed compromise between leading members of both Houses, which finally was to prove acceptable.[1] The struggle for parliamentary representation became the longest and most bitter battle which the Anglo-Jewish community had to wage with the Christian Establishment during the nineteenth century. After the election of Lionel Nathan Rothschild as Member of Parliament for the City of London in 1847, the campaign became one of constitutional urgency, and not merely of hypothetical significance. Rothschild was re-elected with an increased majority in 1849, and returned again in 1852 and twice in 1857.[2] In 1851 he was joined in the shadows of Westminster by David Salomons, when Salomons won a seat at Greenwich.[3] The electorate, even in places such as Greenwich, which lacked a significant Jewish population, had apparently delivered its own verdict on the suitability of Jews being admitted to the legislature.

The protracted nature of the campaign for Jewish emancipation has a complex history, and must in part be attributed to divisions and conflict within the Jewish community itself.[4] The purpose of this paper, however, is not to highlight internal dissension amongst Jews themselves, but rather to investigate the attitudes of those Anglican bishops who used the debates in the House of Lords on the Jewish relief bills as a platform from which to articulate their own beliefs about the Jewish people and the Jewish faith.

---

[1] M. C. N. Salbstein, *The Emancipation of the Jews in Britain* (London and Toronto, 1982), p. 57.
[2] Ibid., p. 144.
[3] Ibid., p. 179.
[4] For the fullest account, see Salbstein, *Emancipation*, pp. 113–43. Shorter accounts are to be found in U. R. Q. Henriques, 'The Jewish emancipation controversy in nineteenth century Britain', *PaP*, 40 (1968), pp. 126–46; Israel Finestein, 'Anglo-Jewish opinion during the struggle for emancipation', *TJHSE*, 20 (1959–61); Polly Pinkser, 'English Opinion and Jewish Emancipation', *Jewish Social Studies*, 13–14 (1951–2), pp. 51–94; Geoffrey Alderman, *The Jewish Community in British Politics* (Oxford, 1983), pp. 14–30.

Prior to the repeal of the Test and Corporation Acts in 1828, and to Roman Catholic emancipation in 1829, the Jews were simply one among a plethora of non-Anglican groups, who were, in addition to other disabilities, denied access to Parliament. After 1828–9, however, the Jews found themselves almost uniquely disqualified from participation at Westminster, their position greatly weakened by an amendment introduced into the Test and Corporation Acts Repeal Bill by Edward Copleston, Bishop of Llandaff, which replaced the sacramental test with a requirement that those aspiring to corporate office or to a seat in Parliament swear an oath 'upon the true faith of a Christian'. Copleston's amendment was passed without a division, and it was not until the following week that he confessed to Lord Holland that he had been unaware of the implications of the amendment for the Jews.[5] He admitted that even had he been aware of its anti-Jewish construction, he would have had no hesitation in proposing the amendment, because it was an acknowledgement that Christianity constituted part of the law of the land. The incident is highly suggestive of the extent to which the Jews were an almost completely invisible minority in the 1820s, scarcely impinging at all upon the consciousness of a Parliament which considered itself not merely Christian, but wholly Anglican.

From the earliest debates, the bishops played a central role in determining the fate of Jewish relief measures. Michael Salbstein, Jewish emancipation's most recent historian, has argued that when the question was first discussed in the Lords, on 1 August 1833, the most important influence on the voting was episcopal opposition.[6] This hypothesis seems perfectly plausible; the debate was dominated by speeches from bishops and archbishops, and afterwards twenty of the Lords spiritual voted against the measure and only three in favour. The Bill fell by 104 votes to 54.

The spectrum of episcopal opinion on the question was, however, broad. Speaking in restrained opposition to the measure in 1833 and 1834 could be heard the voices of William Howley, the Archbishop of Canterbury, and C. J. Blomfield of London, High Churchmen whose thinking was shaped by the doctrine of the indissolubility of the relationship between Church and State. Both took pains to temper their hostility to the admission of Jews to Parliament by emphasizing the high esteem in

[5] Salbstein, *Emancipation*, p. 59; Hansard, ns, 18, 21 Apr. 1828, cols 1591–2, 1609; ns, 19, 28 Apr. 1828, col. 159; *Journal of the House of Lords*, 60, 25 Apr. 1828, p. 247.
[6] Salbstein, *Emancipation*, p. 71.

which they held the Jews themselves. Howley claimed that he looked upon the Jews with 'wonder mixed with admiration';[7] Blomfield described them as the 'most moral, liberal and loyal class of persons'.[8] The objections of these bishops were primarily constitutional and only secondarily theological. For Howley, the 'great principle of [the] State was, that the religion of the country should be Christian', and in the Jewish religion he found 'a positive contradiction of Christianity'.[9] Howley developed this thought further when he expressed a view shared by many opponents of emancipation, that if the legislature ceased to be Christian, divine displeasure might be unleashed on the nation.[10] For Blomfield, it was a matter of Christianity being 'part and parcel of the law of the land'; Jewish emancipation would give a clear signal that the legislature was indifferent to true religion.[11] Howley's speeches differed from Blomfield's in only one significant respect. The conversionism implicit in Howley's plea to the Jews to 'fall into the arms of the Saviour, who had all along considered them as erring children'[12] forms a marked contrast with Blomfield's cool observations on the Jews as essentially threatening to the Church.[13] Howley's remarks reveal that conversionism was not exclusively the prerogative of the Evangelicals.

By the time of the next debate on the Jewish question in 1848, Howley had been replaced at the helm of the Church of England by J. B. Sumner. Sumner, too, was implacably opposed to the admission of Jews, and in this respect differed from many of his fellow Evangelicals. Though a supporter of the campaigns of the Dissenters and Roman Catholics for admission to Parliament back in the 1820s, Sumner found no parallel in the case of the Jews. He informed their Lordships that 'the member of the Jewish faith must, if he acted up to his principles, be as diametrically hostile to the Christian Church as their Lordships would be to the promotion of Mahometanism.'[14] By contrast, Catholic and Nonconformist parliamentarians, though they might dislike Sumner's form of church government, would not, he alleged, wish to quarrel with his creed. 'We are not altogether a Church of England Legislature—we

---

[7] Hansard, ser. 3, 20, 1 Aug. 1833, col. 226.
[8] Ibid., col. 238.
[9] Ibid., col. 225.
[10] Hansard, ser. 3, 24, 23 June 1834, col. 725.
[11] Hansard, ser. 3, 20, 1 Aug. 1833, col. 237.
[12] Ibid., col. 226.
[13] Ibid., col. 238.
[14] Hansard, ser. 3, 98, 25 May 1848, col. 1350.

are not altogether a Protestant Legislature—but we are still a Christian Legislature.'[15] As it turned out, even this was only to be for another ten years. His remarks unwittingly capture the essence of the crisis which had befallen the Anglican establishment since 1828. It is sometimes the case that Hansard's accounts of the debates about Jewish relief prove to be as revealing about the bishops' understanding of the vestiges of Anglican hegemony as they do about attitudes to the Jews.

The effect of the political upheavals of 1848 was to make the Lords—naturally impervious to pressures from the electorate—even more reactionary than before.[16] Furthermore, during the 'papal aggression' of 1850, some began to doubt the wisdom of earlier emancipation measures. The hardening of attitudes characteristic of this period was reflected in Sumner's speech in the Parliamentary Oaths Bill debate of 1849. He depicted England, now standing alone in Europe as 'a monument and example of freedom and social order',[17] and the particular beneficiary of divine blessing. It was, Sumner suggested, the cohesion provided by 'our national and scriptural religion' which had permitted the country to stand securely against the prevailing tide of anarchy. He pointed to recent conquests in India, 'the victories which consolidated our Indian possessions',[18] as further evidence of divine favour. Sumner's reading of the recent past was unsophisticated, to put it charitably: 'England had not only been marked by peculiar privileges, but she had been the subject of many and peculiar blessings.'[19] It would be a dangerous folly to admit to the legislature a body of men from whom divine favour had been withdrawn because it had been forfeited. Samuel Wilberforce, Bishop of Oxford, pursued a similar line in the debate of 1848, when he asserted that it was only because the law of England was based on the law of God as revealed in Jesus Christ that Parliament was commissioned to make the laws which governed half the globe.[20] Increasingly intoxicated by foreign conquests which were founded on an explicitly formulated doctrine of Christian imperialism, by the late 1840s it was the English who had assumed the mantle of God's Chosen People.

Wilberforce stands out as the most hostile of the anti-emancipationist

[15] Hansard, ser. 3, 98, 25 May 1848, col. 1351.
[16] Salbstein, *Emancipation*, p. 161.
[17] Hansard, ser. 3, 106, 26 June 1849, col. 889. For Sumner's final speech on Jewish emancipation, see Hansard, ser. 3, 146, 10 July 1857, cols 1259–60.
[18] Hansard, ser. 3, 106, 26 June 1849, col. 890.
[19] Ibid., col. 889.
[20] Hansard, ser. 3, 98, 25 May 1848, col. 1378.

bishops. His speeches contain elements of anti-Semitism which are largely absent from the more circumspect opposition offered by Howley, Blomfield, and Sumner. An address given at a meeting of the Society for Promoting Christianity among the Jews, an Evangelical conversionist body which had been formed in 1808, was the occasion for a particularly controversial outburst. The *Jewish Chronicle* reported that Wilberforce had informed his audience that 'the Jews have no home for which to fight, no nation for which to feel, no literature by which to be lifted up, no hope and hardly a God.'[21] The *Jewish Chronicle* responded with two thundering editorials, both headed 'The Bishop of Oxford and the Jews':

> Take back your words, intolerant bishop, and learn that proud and firm in their ancient belief, Judaism rejects your God; while you, with all your arrogance, with all your persecution, yet must kneel before us, yet acknowledge Him, while with your poor lips in prayer, you, poor child of His mercy, would shut out from the portals of hope, those from whom you learnt thus to kneel, from whose sages you have been taught your precepts, and on whose creed are grounded the deeper principles of your own ... You, my Lord, as a minister of God, as a man to whom the world grants and acknowledges talent, you know that before you judge men you must know them; and yet without any knowledge of us, without any inquiry, you thus vilify us.[22]

In Parliament, Wilberforce was more restrained, though he did little to conceal his contempt for Judaism or his ignorance of Jewish theology. In the debate of 1849, he suggested that the Jews had no fixed dogmatic religious belief at all:

> For 1800 years they have been expecting and panting for the arrival of the Messiah, and they were now hovering between a miserable uncertainty whether the expectation of the Messiah was not altogether mistaken, which was only another form of direct infidelity, and the alternative, on the other hand, of joining the Christian faith, which they had so long reviled.[23]

In common with other opponents of emancipation, Wilberforce argued that the admission of Jews would sound the death-knell of Britain's

---

[21] Henriques, 'Jewish emancipation controversy', p. 137.
[22] *Jewish Chronicle*, 25 June 1847. See also 11 June 1847 and Henriques, 'Jewish emancipation controversy', p. 138.
[23] Hansard, ser. 3, 106, 26 June 1849, col. 914.

Christian nationhood and legislature, with the dire consequence of divine retribution. His major argument, however, advanced in the debates of 1848, 1849, and 1857 was that the right to sit in Parliament was conferred on one set of persons as a trust to be administered for the benefit of all, and not on any particular body for the representation of that specific group.[24] Wilberforce denounced the contrary opinion as being of the 'very essence of Chartism', and indeed, his was the sort of argument which would trip easily off the tongue of anyone suspicious of democracy. Wilberforce believed that the Jews were devoid of genuine religious feeling, and that their only guiding principle was the making of money. He gave the example of an English Jew, who, at the height of the Napoleonic war, had been prepared to contract a loan for Napoleon.[25] The Jews were, he claimed, 'a race immersed in the pursuit of gain'.[26] Pitching a volley in the direction of Rothschild, who had been elected two years previously, he declared that no Christian constituency would ever voluntarily return a Jewish member; if it did, it could only be the power of money which had secured the Jew's position. Wilberforce envisaged a future in which Jewish money would be used to corrupt large portions of the British electorate.[27] In addition to being money grabbing opportunists, Wilberforce depicted the Jews as essentially foreigners, a nation within a nation, a shipwrecked people without British loyalty, admitted on the understanding that they would receive shelter, but not political privileges.[28]

He alighted upon the works of Rabbi Joseph Crooll with particular relish. Crooll was a Hungarian *émigré* who had arrived in Cambridge in 1806 in order to teach Hebrew in the University. He became noted as an eccentric and rather outlandish figure, clothed in an incredible parchment-girdle, on which was inscribed passages from the Law and the Talmud.[29] An ultra-Orthodox millenarian, Crooll believed that the Jews constituted one nation living among many nations who would, if they adopted a rigorous and ascetical religious observance, in the near future be restored to Zion.[30] To maintain their identity as a separate nation, Crooll

[24] Hansard, ser. 3, 98, 25 May 1848, col. 1269. See also ibid. 106, 26 June 1849, col. 911, and 126, 10 July, col. 1269.
[25] Hansard, ser. 3, 98, 25 May 1848, col. 1374.
[26] Ibid., col. 1375. In fact, as Geoffrey Alderman has shown, it was Nathan Mayer Rothschild, the father of the first Jewish MP, who made available the bullion needed to enable the payment of Wellington's forces in Spain. See Alderman, *Jewish Community*, p. 10.
[27] Hansard, ser. 3, 106, 26 June 1849, cols 911–12.
[28] Hansard, ser. 3, 98, 25 May 1848, col. 1375.
[29] Salbstein, *Emancipation*, p. 78.
[30] For Crooll, see ibid., pp. 78–85.

believed that the Jews must be ever vigilant against sinking roots abroad, for the greater their attachment to the lands in which they were but temporary exiles, the correspondingly weaker must be their commitment to Judaism and the Promised Land. The ambition of British Jews to enter Parliament was not merely irrelevant to Crooll, it suggested a blasphemous lack of faith in God's promise to restore his people to Zion.[31] As early as 1812 Crooll had predicted that the restoration of Israel would take place in the Jewish year 5600 (1840), a date largely derived from calculations made from the Book of Ezekiel. So confident was he of the accuracy of this prediction that when he applied to the University Senate for a pension in 1832, he requested funding for only eight years, 'For in the end of the following eight years, we expect a great change to take place in the world.'[32]

When the Messiah failed to appear in 1840, Crooll became discredited as the spokesman of Orthodox Judaism. The publication of Lyell's work on geology made Crooll's dating appear improbable, thus undermining his method as well as his conclusion. Wilberforce, apparently ignorant of Crooll's relegation to the extreme fringes of Jewish opinion, was fond of citing him as representative of the 'pious' element in the community, even as late as 1848.[33] He studiously ignored those who could with credibility claim to speak for the Jews—among them Francis Goldsmid, Barnard van Oven, David Salomons, and Moses Montefiore.

It is difficult to discern what lay at the root of Wilberforce's vigorous anti-Semitism, and the standard biographies of the Bishop provide little in the way of illumination.[34] It is clearly insufficient to suggest that he merely shared the prejudices of his day, for Wilberforce's attitude to the Jews was markedly more hostile than that of his brother bishops. Neither may Wilberforce be dismissed as a man who lacked humanity. The son of the great advocate of slave emancipation, he consistently voted and spoke against the importation of slave-grown sugar from Cuba and Brazil, and he opposed public hangings and transportation.[35] The only plausible explanation of Wilberforce's attitude is that he regarded the Jews as the

---

[31] Between 1812 and 1829 Crooll wrote three books devoted to stating the ultra-Orthodox case against emancipation: *The Restoration of Israel*, *The Fifth Empire*, and *The Last Generation*: see Salbstein, *Emancipation*, pp. 80–1.

[32] CUL, C.U.R. 39.17.

[33] Hansard, ser. 3, 98, 25 May 1848, col. 1375.

[34] A. R. Ashwell and R. G. Wilberforce, *Life of Samuel Wilberforce D.D.* 3 vols (London, 1880); S. Meacham, *Lord Bishop: The Life of Samuel Wilberforce 1805–1873* (Cambridge, Mass., 1970).

[35] Meacham, *Lord Bishop*, pp. 271–2.

collective bearers of responsibility for the Crucifixion—a nation guilty of deicide.

Throughout the period during which Jewish relief was debated in the Lords a greater proportion of bishops voted against it than in favour, but the measures were never without some episcopal supporters, several of whom came frequently to their defence. One such was Richard Whately, the Archbishop of Dublin, who possessed one of the most able and original minds on the episcopal bench during the fourth, fifth, and sixth decades of the nineteenth century. In politics he became renowned for taking the unpopular side; in addition to advocating Jewish relief, he supported the Maynooth grant in 1845 and the legalizing of marriage with a deceased wife's sister. Whately felt an intense aversion to the swearing of oaths on secular occasions, believing that they resulted in a trivialization of the name of God. In 1837 he successfully petitioned the Queen to exempt him from administering oaths to those whom he installed to the Order of St Patrick.[36] Between 1833 and 1853 Whately delivered four speeches in the Lords in favour of removing the oaths which inhibited Jews from sitting in Parliament. It is a peculiar paradox that he was to become the leading episcopal critic of a measure which had been put in place by his former tutor and lifelong friend, Edward Copleston.[37]

Whately took a characteristically independent line when he offered the House his major argument in favour of Jewish emancipation. It was not, he declared, a matter of whether a Jew was the fittest person to sit in Parliament, but a question of whether Christian electors should be permitted a free hand in the selection of their representative.[38] In 1853 he suggested that the bill before the House be renamed as a measure for the relief of the electors, rather than for the relief of the Jews.[39] He regarded it as scandalous that the hands of a Christian electorate should be tied to preclude them from the election of Jews, as it seemed to infer that Christianity was 'so frail and brittle as not to bear touching'.[40] Whately supported this argument with the assertion, diametrically opposed to that made by Sumner, that the presence of Jews in Parliament was likely to

---

[36] E. J. Whately, *Life and Correspondence of Richard Whately D.D.*, 2 vols (London, 1866), 1, pp. 383–5, 405–7.

[37] Copleston had been Whately's tutor at Oriel College, Oxford, between 1805 and 1808. According to his biographer, the influence which the two men exercised on each other coloured the subsequent lives of both. See Whately, *Richard Whately*, 1, pp. 12–14 for an account of their friendship.

[38] Hansard, ser. 3, 106, 26 June 1849, col. 891.

[39] Hansard, ser. 3, 126, 29 Apr. 1853, col. 772.

[40] Hansard, ser. 3, 20, 1 Aug. 1833, col. 234.

prove considerably less of a threat to the Established Church than the presence of Nonconformists and Roman Catholics. Jews did not proselytize or attempt to mix Judaism into Christianity.[41] His speeches were peppered with historical allusions to the manner in which Christians had often interfered violently in each other's faith and worship. Whately took up a position which many bishops appeared to find unthinkable when he suggested that a Christian legislature did not necessarily afford religious or even personal security to a Christian; history revealed that the most merciless persecutions had been inflicted by Christians on each other.[42] He was scornful of Sumner's attitude to Britain's conquests abroad. How could victories in India be connected with the maintenance of civil disabilities on the Christian electors at home? Nine-tenths of the soldiers who had secured those victories were, in any case, 'Mahometans and Hindoos', and would have refused to take an oath 'on the true faith of a Christian'.[43] In a letter to his close friend and political ally Samuel Hinds, Bishop of Norwich, Whately described Sumner's views as 'mischievous'. It might as well have been argued that the potato-rot was a divine judgement on the continuance of Jewish disabilities.[44] Whately possessed considerably greater intellectual resources than the more simple-minded Sumner; on the Jewish question the two archbishops were diametrically opposed.

Towards the Jewish people themselves, Whately was cooler than might have been expected. In the debate of 1849 he declined to describe himself either as an advocate of the Jews or as one who wished to remove Jewish disabilities.[45] As has already been shown, he regarded the question as one of *Christian* disabilities. He believed the Jews to be a nation under divine judgement:

> I look on that nation as an extraordinary monument of the fulfilment of prophecies, and as paying the penalty of their rejection of the Messiah. But we must be very careful how we, without an express Commission, take upon ourselves to be the executioners of Divine judgment, lest we bring a portion of these judgments on ourselves.[46]

More ardent in his support for the Jewish people was Connop Thirlwall, the Bishop of St David's. He was a conversionist, but not an

---

[41] Ibid., col. 228.
[42] Ibid., col. 230.
[43] Hansard, ser. 3, 118, 17 July 1851, cols 880–1.
[44] Whately, *Richard Whately*, 2, pp. 148–51.
[45] Hansard, ser. 3, 106, 26 June 1849, col. 892.
[46] Hansard, ser. 3, 20, 1 Aug. 1833, col. 231.

Evangelical, and like Whately he had gained a reputation for taking the unpopular side. In 1834 he had been obliged to resign his fellowship at Trinity College, Cambridge, after he advocated the admission of Dissenters and the abandonment of compulsory attendance at chapel and collegiate lectures in divinity. In many respects he was the antithesis of Wilberforce; at St David's he was reclusive and scholarly, shunning the usual activities of a more conventionally pastoral bishop in favour of the solitude of his library. In 1848 he caused ripples of disquiet when he told the Lords that there was 'no adequate foundation' for the assertion, which had been implicitly or explicitly made by all the previous speakers, that it was of the essence of the Jewish religion to inspire feelings of abhorrence and aversion towards the person of Christ.[47] If some Jews were Christ-haters, this had more to do with the long ages of controversy, persecution, and oppression to which they had been subject, and was not intrinsic to the Jewish faith. Thirlwall saw little to separate a Jew from a Unitarian—both regarded Jesus as the human being who brought about the Christian religion.[48] Wilberforce was scandalized, and demanded that Thirlwall clarify his remarks, which Thirlwall refused to do.[49]

Thirlwall shared Whately's belief that the status quo unfairly restricted the electorate. He berated the Lords for depriving the constituents of the City of London of the MP of their choosing and for depriving the Commons of the Member whom they wished to see amongst them.[50] Like Whately, he felt that Dissenters posed a greater danger to the legislature than Jews, and he singled out Quakers in particular. It was foolish to entrust the legislature to 'persons who would feel it their duty, if they had the power, to disband our Army, to lay up our Navy, to melt down our ordnance, and to lay this country prostrate at the feet of the first invader who might assail our shores.'[51] As for the argument that the admission of the Jews to Parliament might provoke the wrath of God, Thirlwall believed that the only reason for supposing that divine vengeance might be impending was on account of the crimes of which the nation was guilty towards the ancestors of the Jewish people in times past. He considered that the Jews continued to be the objects of a 'very general, hereditary, unreasoning prejudice, aversion and contempt'.[52]

---

[47] Hansard, ser. 3, 98, 25 May 1848, col. 1360.
[48] Ibid., col. 1361.
[49] Ibid., cols 1379–80, 1384.
[50] Ibid., cols 1362–3.
[51] Hansard, ser. 3, 126, 29 Apr. 1853, col. 782.
[52] Hansard, ser. 3, 98, 25 May 1848, cols 1364, 1359.

The third important episcopal supporter of Jewish emancipation was A. C. Tait, who succeeded to the see of London after Blomfield's retirement in 1856. Tait's support was significant because it represented a reverse of the views of his predecessor, and also because some 20,000 of the 35,000 Jews resident in Britain at the beginning of the 1850s lived in his diocese.[53] A central figure in the mid-Victorian Broad Church Movement, Tait had been formed in a vastly different world from that which had shaped the Georgian Blomfield, with his belief that it was the duty of the Christian Parliament to function as the temporal dimension of the Christian State—Church and State tightly bound in an interdependent, reciprocal relationship. Tait was more of a pragmatist. The religious character of Parliament, he told the Lords in 1857, depended more upon the religious feeling in the country than upon the maintenance of oaths which excluded certain British citizens of the Jewish persuasion from the full enjoyment of their civil rights.[54] Tait argued that the Protestant character of the House of Lords had not been destroyed by the admission of the Roman Catholic peers in 1829, so it was unlikely to evaporate with the entry of one or two Jews. He suggested, with some justification, that both the country and the legislature appeared to be considerably more Christian than they had been at the time of Catholic emancipation.[55] Tait concluded that the matter of Jewish admission was one of justice: 'The Jew had a stake in the country . . . he was actuated by patriotic and loyal feelings; and surely, therefore, he was entitled to his full rights, unless it was made clear that his presence in Parliament would do real and obvious harm.'[56] Tait could see no danger in prospect.

What, then, is to be made of the episcopal contribution to the debates about Jewish admission to Parliament? The eventual success of the measure was, in Professor Machin's words, 'the most symbolic religious liberty measure of the 1850s'.[57] The British public were, however, largely unmoved by it, a phenomenon which Wilberforce interpreted as the 'crushed silence of great indignation and great apprehension',[58] and which Thirlwall perceived as an indication of the nation's utter indifference.[59]

[53] Salbstein, *Emancipation*, p. 38.
[54] Hansard, ser. 3, 146, 10 June 1857, col. 1257.
[55] Ibid., col. 1258.
[56] Ibid., col. 1259.
[57] G. I. T. Machin, *Politics and the Churches in Great Britain 1832 to 1868* (Oxford, 1977), p. 292.
[58] Hansard, ser. 3, 98, 25 May 1848, col. 1380.
[59] Hansard, ser. 3, 126, 29 Apr. 1853, col. 781.

Given that before the 1860s the Jewish population in Britain amounted to only 0.2 per cent of the total, public lack of interest in the question was hardly surprising. Most of those who lived outside the capital had probably never encountered a Jew in their lives. One wonders how many Jews some of the bishops had met. Certain conclusions emerge. The first is that the bishops, whether they supported or opposed the measure, did not regard the Jews as simply one among a number of non-Anglican dissenting groups. Those against Jewish emancipation regarded Jews as more dangerous than Christian Dissenters; those in favour believed them to be the least threatening of the religious minorities. The theological judgements of the bishops were generally crude; only Thirlwall hesitated to condemn the Jews explicitly for the death of Jesus.

The debate was in the hands of those who are generally regarded as the most active of the episcopal parliamentarians. Howley, Blomfield, Sumner, and Wilberforce were the main opponents; Whately, Thirlwall, and Tait the main supporters. Briefer contributions came from Edward Maltby of Chichester (who chose to remain silent on the issue after his elevation to Durham) and Samuel Hinds of Norwich—both in favour— and from Henry Phillpotts of Exeter, Edward Denison of Salisbury, and Robert Daly, Bishop of Cashel, who were against. The bishops were divided on the correct response to Jewish emancipation, and the divisions grew deeper as the years passed. In 1833 they almost produced a block vote, twenty against and three in favour. In 1857 the balance was different, sixteen against and seven in favour. But even those on the same side could argue from completely different premises, and conversionists were just as likely to oppose the measure as to favour it. The bishops who confronted each other on the Jewish question tended to oppose each other on other issues, too, as in the case of the Divorce and Matrimonial Causes Bill which was being debated at the same time as the Jewish relief question was being finally resolved. Amongst the diversity of episcopal opinion, Anglican unity seemed chimerical, the bishops acting more as spokesmen for themselves, and for their own party within the Church, than for the Church as a whole. It was but one sign of the lack of consensus in the leadership of the Church of England in the mid-nineteenth century.

Selwyn College,
Cambridge

'IN A PECULIAR RELATION TO CHRISTIANITY': ANGLICAN ATTITUDES TO JUDAISM IN THE ERA OF POLITICAL EMANCIPATION, 1830–1858

by SEAN GILL

ETWEEN 1830 and 1858 fourteen attempts were made to remove the words 'on the true faith of a Christian' from the oath required of new Members and thereby to allow Jews to gain admission to Parliament. After 1833, when a bill was passed in the Commons, all proposals for reform foundered on opposition in the Lords. Speaking against Jewish emancipation in the Upper House on 1 August 1833, the Archbishop of Canterbury, Dr Howley, made it clear that the issue was not one on which the Church of England could remain indifferent. In contrast to other religions, he argued, Judaism stood 'in a peculiar relation to Christianity', for its very existence was 'not simply a negative but a positive contradiction of Christianity'.[1]

The lengthy campaign for the admission of Jews to Parliament, and the opposition which it aroused, have provided the context for most discussions of Anglican attitudes to Judaism in the Victorian period.[2] In several important respects, however, concentration on this issue runs the risk of failing to grasp the variety and complexity of church responses to Judaism. An emphasis upon the opposition to reform of the House of Lords in general, and of the episcopal bench in particular, can easily obscure both the range of opinion expressed by the bishops, and the important part played by prominent laymen such as Robert Grant and Gladstone in bringing about change. Such an over-simplification was often made at the time. The emancipation debate was seen as just one of a series of clashes in which the forces of reaction—the landed aristocracy, the House of Lords, the Church of England, and the Conservative party—were pitted against the forces of enlightenment represented by the middle classes, Benthamism, and the coalition of Radicals, Whigs, and the Liberal party.[3]

---

[1] Hansard, ser. 3, 20, cols 225–6.

[2] For example, Ursula Henriques, 'The Jewish emancipation controversy in nineteenth-century Britain', *PaP*, 40 (1968), pp. 126–46; also M. Salbstein, *The Emancipation of the Jews in Britain* (London, 1982).

[3] G. Alderman, *The Jewish Community in British Politics* (Oxford, 1983), pp. 16–17.

As Dr Howley's attitude makes clear, this view was not groundless, but Anglican interest in the relationship between the two faiths began before the emancipation controversy. It was evident, for example, in the founding of the London Society for the Promotion of Christianity Amongst the Jews in 1809.[4] Moreover, the questions which taxed Anglicans when confronted by Judaism were wide-ranging and predominantly theological not political in nature. Unless these concerns are appreciated, it becomes difficult to understand the attitude of Evangelical Churchmen to emancipation. To suggest, for example, that 'the two broad ideological bases for support were Benthamism and evangelicalism' is misleading.[5] It was the conversion of the Jews, not their admission to Parliament, which galvanized the energies of the majority of Anglican Evangelicals. As Howley's speech suggests, Judaism raised not one but a number of acute problems for Anglican self-identity. These included arguments about the nature of a Christian society and the role of an established church within it, and the need both to come to terms with Christianity's past and present treatment of the Jews, as well as to explore the contemporary theological significance of Judaism—the last point being the subject of diverse but enthusiastic millenarian speculations about the restoration of Israel.

The first of these Anglican anxieties was repeatedly raised in the course of the emancipation debates both inside and outside Parliament. The issue was not primarily about the Jews, but about the maintenance of a Christian society and the denial of claims for religious pluralism. As Archbishop Sumner warned in the Lords debate of 25 May 1848, 'The same argument which is pleaded in favour of Jewish legislation would scarcely exclude a Mahometan or a Hindoo, or any idolater whatever.'[6] Sir Robert Inglis, the staunchest Tory opponent of emancipation, agreed: the real question was 'not between Christians and Jews; but between Christians and Non-Christians'.[7] Shaftesbury foresaw even worse possibilities. Having stood out for an exclusively Protestant Parliament in 1829 and been defeated, 'They would next have to stand out for a white Parliament; and perhaps they would have a final struggle for a male Parliament.'[8] For

---

[4] The Society became exclusively Anglican in 1815. For its early history see Roger H. Martin, *Evangelicals United: Ecumenical Stirrings in Pre-Victorian Britain, 1795–1830* (London, 1983), pp. 174–91.

[5] Polly Pinsker, 'English Opinion and Jewish Emancipation (1830–1860)', *Jewish Social Studies*, 14 (1952), p. 61.

[6] Hansard, ser. 3, 98, cols 1351–2.

[7] Ibid., 95, col. 1253.

[8] Ibid., col. 1278.

proponents of an organic theory of Church and State, religion could not be, as most supporters of emancipation claimed, a private matter. As T. R. Birks, a leading Evangelical clergyman put it, a creed could not be viewed 'as a private property, which each may claim to have protected, like property, by equal laws'; to do so, he warned in somewhat lurid tones, would be to bring about 'the Saturnalian triumph of infidelity, the reign of chaos restored in the moral world'.[9] It would also be to court divine disfavour, since the political stability and growing national power of Great Britain were held to be evidence of the Providential government of the world. As the Earl of Winchelsea argued, 'The Almighty had emphatically said that people who honoured Him He would honour, and that people who highly esteemed Him, by Him would be highly esteemed'—a truth strikingly evidenced by England's avoidance of revolution in 1848.[10] Nor was this kind of thinking necessarily the preserve of the politically and theologically conservative. Thomas Arnold's 1833 proposal for a comprehensive national church was not unlimited. As he explained to a friend in 1836, 'I would thank the Parliament for having done away with distinctions between Christian and Christian; I would pray that distinctions be kept up between Christians and non-Christians.' As for the Jews, they were 'strangers in England, and have no more claim to legislate for it than a lodger has to share with the landlords in the management of his house.'[11]

Not all churchmen, however, accepted this view of the matter. The first emancipation bill was introduced into the Commons in April 1830 by Robert Grant, an Evangelical supporter of the Philo-Judaean Society, which had broken away from the London Society for the Promotion of Christianity Amongst the Jews in 1826, and which viewed Jewish emancipation more favourably than the parent society. Grant was aware of the charge that the admission of Jews to Parliament would 'unchristianise the Legislature', but he drew a distinction between Judaism and other faiths on the grounds of its close relationship with Christianity:

> The very foundations of our religion were in the religious books of the Jews—in those books its principles were to be discovered, and the

---

[9] T. R. Birks, *The Christian State: Or the First Principles of National Religion* (London, 1847), pp. 24–5. Birks framed his argument to meet the objection that a confessional state was an oppressive imposition on 'the Deist or the Jew'.

[10] Hansard, ser. 3, 106, col. 902.

[11] A. P. Stanley, *The Life and Correspondence of Thomas Arnold*, 10th edn, 2 vols (London, 1877), 2, p. 28.

sincere professor of Christianity was deeply implicated in the past history, and in the future estimation of the Jewish people.[12]

This was not, of course, intended by Grant as an argument for a pluralist constitutional settlement, but the Archbishop of Dublin, Dr Whately, who had been a prominent Liberal at Oxford and tutor and friend of Newman, not only spoke in favour of emancipation in the Lords, but was fully aware of the implications of his advocacy of Jewish political rights. As he wrote to the Bishop of Norwich:

> I may perhaps have even damaged the immediate cause of Baron Rothschild, by advocating a principle (to the great dismay of one at least of the supporters of the bill), which would leave Parliament as open to a Mohametan or a Pagan as to a Jew, and by waiving altogether the question whether a Jew is a fitting person to sit in Parliament; but I must maintain my own principle, which is that a law giving to Christians generally as such, or to Christians of any particular church, a monopoly of any civil rights, is to make Christ's kingdom . . . a kingdom of this world and is a violation of the rule of 'rendering to Caesar the things that are Caesar's'.[13]

Whately's liberalism was, as he admitted, not typical of contemporary Anglican thought, and the most significant intervention in the debate on the issue of Church and State was made by Gladstone. In 1838 he had argued that the State 'had a conscience' which justified its exclusive support of the Established Church. This principle, he later recalled, proved to be an anachronism, and he found himself 'the last man on a sinking ship'.[14] From Gladstone's speech in favour of Jewish emancipation in the Commons in 1847 it is clear that he abandoned the ship reluctantly. The admission of a small number of non-Christians to Parliament would not, he argued, in substance 'unchristianise' the nation. The reason for Gladstone's cautious approach lay in High Church fears over the independence of the Church. Archdeacon Wilberforce had recently given him a clerical petition demanding the separation of Church and State if the Jews were admitted to Parliament.[15] As the prominent High Church lawyer James Hope-Scott told Gladstone, the Christianity of Parliament

[12] Hansard, ser. 2, 23, col. 1299.
[13] E. J. Whately, *The Life And Correspondence Of Richard Whately*, 2 vols (London, 1866), 2, pp. 149–51.
[14] W. E. Gladstone, *Gleanings of Past Years*, 7 vols (London, 1879), 7, pp. 104–15.
[15] Hansard, ser. 3, 95, cols 1282–1304.

had already become a sham, and Jewish emancipation would only make this clearer.[16]

Anglican fears over the Church's independence, which were fuelled by the repeal of the Test and Corporation Acts and by Catholic emancipation, undoubtedly sharpened resistance to the admission of Jews to Parliament, but the positions adopted by Grant and Gladstone were not without support. In the Lords division in 1848, five bishops voted in favour of emancipation and eighteen against. Rank and file clerical opinion is harder to judge, but in 1830 petitions were presented to Parliament in favour of the measure both from Christians of every denomination in Bristol, and from Liverpool. The latter included the signatures of several Anglican clergymen. Though he was in a small minority, emancipation was, as one clerical pamphleteer argued, 'a Christian duty'.[17]

So, too, was coming to terms with past and present Christian anti-Semitism. In introducing his Emancipation Bill in 1830 Robert Grant recited the history of anti-Jewish legislation in England, laws which he pointed out 'were enforced under circumstances of the most terrible and revolting cruelty'. Even until now, he went on, Jews 'had known Christianity only as the pretext for savage persecution'.[18] At the jubilee meeting of the London Society for Promoting Christianity Amongst the Jews in 1858, the Principal of Magdalen Hall, Oxford, John Macbride, reminded his audience that in the past Jews 'in every European state ... were frequently plundered, and even put to death on absurd rumours of sacrificing Christian children.'[19]

Condemning the past was one thing; overcoming contemporary prejudice was another. The image of the Jew as alien and materialistic was widespread in Victorian society and was shared by many Christians.[20] In opposing emancipation in the Commons in 1833, Cobbett's populist Toryism was extreme only in the vehemence of its invective. 'God knows,' he thundered, 'the Jews make free enough already, and certainly get more money together than any sect of Christians.' Another MP agreed, calling

---

[16] R. Ornsby, *Memoirs of James Robert Hope-Scott*, 2 vols (London, 1884), 2, p. 78. The Gorham Judgement proved the last straw, and he was received into the Roman Catholic Church with Manning in 1850.

[17] *Jewish Emancipation a Christian Duty. By a Country Vicar* (London, 1853), p. 4.

[18] Hansard, ser. 2, 23, col. 1289.

[19] *A Jubilee Memorial; Or Record of Proceedings of the London Society for Promoting Christianity Among the Jews* (London, 1867), p. 3.

[20] For one approach to this subject see A. A. Naman, *The Jew in the Victorian Novel* (New York, 1980).

on the house to 'rally round the cross'.[21] If admitted to Parliament, warned Sir Robert Inglis, Jews would promote 'their own selfish and unnational purposes'.[22] The slurs of being both foreign and grasping were combined by the Bishop of Oxford, Samuel Wilberforce, in the Lords in 1848, when he claimed that an English Jew had been ready to contract a loan with Napoleon—evidence that the Jews were 'a nation within a nation'.[23]

Such views did not, however, go unchallenged by both supporters and opponents of emancipation. As Grant argued in 1830, Jews 'lived usefully and peacefully under the Constitution'.[24] From the opposing camp, Shaftesbury rejected F. D. Maurice's charge that the Jews were a degenerate race, claiming that they could boast 'in proportion to their numbers, a far larger list of men of genius and learning than could be exhibited by any Gentile country.'[25]

Shaftesbury's real concern, however, was a theological one which preoccupied most churchmen who considered Judaism. Like many Christians, his view was decidedly two-edged. On the one hand, the Jews had been God's chosen people and were to be so again if biblical prophecy was to be believed; on the other hand, they had rejected Christ and had incurred divine punishment as a wandering people. The charge of deicide and its consequences were indeed sometimes invoked to justify resistance to emancipation. Inglis argued that 'this nation if true to themselves, and to their own prophetical destiny, can never be identified with us.' Their separation from other nations was 'for causes with which every man who reads his Bible must be well acquainted'.[26] In opposing emancipation in 1858, the Bishop of Cashel was more explicit. He could, he claimed, love the Jews, but could not accept in Parliament 'the degenerate children of Abraham' who 'in the day of the Saviour's humiliation, cried out, "Crucify him, crucify him!"'[27] An equally bitter view of the relationship between the two faiths was taken by the Bishop of Oxford. Judaism, Wilberforce told the Lords in 1848, 'rejected the Messiah, cast itself into utter darkness, and became an empty and unmeaning, but false and blasphemous faith'; and he concluded—in words which might be said to

---

[21] Hansard, ser. 3, 16, cols 11–17.

[22] Ibid., ser. 2, 23, col. 1305.

[23] Ibid., ser. 3, 98, col. 1374.

[24] Ibid., 23, col. 1292.

[25] Ibid., 95, col. 1282.

[26] Ibid., 25, col. 869.

[27] Quoted in Gerald Parsons, ed., *Religion in Victorian Britain*, 4 vols (Manchester, 1988), 3, p. 497. The choice of documents gives a somewhat unnuanced view of Anglican attitudes to Judaism.

encapsulate the darkest side of Christian anti-Semitism—'Between the Christian and the Jew there was a gulf as wide as eternity itself.'[28]

Speaking in the same debate, the Bishop of St David's, Connop Thirlwall, saw the relationship very differently. Thirlwall had studied law as a pupil of Disraeli's uncle Mr Basevi, and had later been forced to resign as assistant tutor at Trinity for his support of the admission of Dissenters to academic degrees.[29] Both personal experience and principle inclined him to liberalism, and he dealt crisply with the argument that Jewish emancipation would interfere with God's purposes in condemning them as a people:

> If there is any reason to dread that DIVINE vengeance may be impending over us, it would be rather on account of the crimes of which this nation was guilty towards the ancestors of this people in times past, than of any indulgence which we may show to them in the future.

Nor, he went on, was there any reason to doubt that 'Jews who strenuously uphold their own creed may nevertheless regard Christianity without bitterness and hatred.'[30]

Others also stressed not Wilberforce's gulf but the closeness of Judaism to Christianity. Disraeli's flamboyant conclusion that 'Jesus of Nazareth, the Incarnate Son of the Most High God, is the eternal glory of the Jewish race'[31] succeeded in angering all sides to the debate, but speaking in the Lords in 1833, the Bishop of Chichester described the Jews as 'the elder brothers of Christians, and … did not see much difference between them.' Sufficient difference remained for him to hope for their conversion, but he asked whether 'such a consummation was most likely to be accelerated or retarded by measures of peace and conciliation?'[32]

The consummation for which the Bishop hoped was the subject of much debate and speculation amongst Anglican Evangelicals. As the Revd Thomas Grimshawe told the London Society for Promoting Christianity Amongst the Jews at its annual meeting at Exeter Hall in 1838, the conversion of the Jews was of urgent concern to Christians for 'Until they are brought in, the diffusion of Divine truth will never be general and

---

[28] Hansard, ser. 3, 93, col. 1380.
[29] For Thirlwall's career see J. L. Perowne, ed., *Letters Literary and Theological of Connop Thirlwall Late Bishop of St. David's* (London, 1881).
[30] Hansard, ser. 3, 93, cols 1361–4.
[31] B. Disraeli, *Lord George Bentinck* (London, 1852), p. 507.
[32] Hansard, ser. 3, 20, col. 238.

universal.'[33] But how and when this was to occur provoked controversy. In its early years the London Society was post-millenarian in outlook and looked forward to the continued improvement of mankind. Included in this would be the gradual conversion of the Jews.[34] Increasingly, however, pre-millenarian views gained ground with an emphasis upon the imminent literal return of Christ.[35] In 1823 the committee of the London Society felt that these differences were threatening the work of the Society, and in response to criticisms from the Bishops of Gloucester and St David's they wrote that 'they decidedly disclaim all intention of promulgating any particular views of the nature of the Millennium.'[36] Nevertheless, pre-millenial views continued to feature in the annual sermons preached before the Society, and even those who did not share this perspective regarded the literal restoration of the Jews to the Holy Land as an important and neglected aspect of biblical teaching.[37] As the Revd W. Dalton told the Society in 1847:

> Whereas, in past years, the literal interpretation of prophecy, and by consequence, the national restoration of the Jews, were subjects either little thought of or greatly opposed, we now find a very general interest about God's ancient people, and a very general expectation that they will finally be converted to the faith of our glorious Shiloh, and restored to the possession of the land of promise.

This was on the basis of biblical prophecy, particularly in the Old Testament books of Daniel and Zechariah.[38]

In his study of Jewish emancipation, Salbstein is, in fact, wrong to suggest that Shaftesbury was an untypical Evangelical in his millenarianism.[39] In 1841 both Archbishops and fourteen Bishops became patrons of the London Society. It might be that Edward Bickersteth, a keen supporter of the Society, exaggerated the significance of this—a Derbyshire friend

[33] Jewish Intelligence, and Monthly Account of the Proceedings of the London Society for Promoting Christianity Among the Jews (London, 1838), 4, p. 38.
[34] W. T. Gidney, The History of the London Society for Promoting Christianity Amongst the Jews from 1808 to 1908 (London, 1908), p. 211.
[35] See D. W. Bebbington, Evangelicalism in Modern Britain (London, 1989), pp. 81–6; and W. H. Oliver, Prophets and Millenialists (Auckland, 1978), for a fuller treatment of this theme.
[36] Oxford, Bodleian Library, MS C.M.J. c.11, fols 60–1. I am grateful to the General Director of the Church's Ministry among the Jews for permission to quote from the Society's archives.
[37] See C.M.J. e.38, 44–5, for bound volumes of the annual sermons.
[38] W. Dalton, A Sermon Preached at the parish Church of the united parishes of Christ Church, Newgate Street, and St. Leonard, Foster Lane (London, 1847), p. 5.
[39] Salbstein, Emancipation, p. 147.

warned that 'it does not follow that all Derbyshire will rise up at a moment's notice, as if the Archbishop were an archangel'—but episcopal patronage and the founding of the Jerusalem bishopric in the same year increased the interest in the restoration of Israel in Anglican circles.[40]

Evangelicals were fired by millenarian enthusiasm for the conversion of the Jews, not with their claims to political emancipation. In this as on many other issues their perspective was not that of reforming Liberals with whom they sometimes found themselves in alliance. As Bickersteth warned in 1841, to grant emancipation to the Jews would be to 'renounce our own Christianity and seek to turn their hopes from their own inheritance'.[41]

Reviewing the range of opinion amongst churchmen towards Judaism in the first half of the nineteenth century, it is, in fact, clear from our vantage-point that there were definite boundaries within which they formulated their theology. The hope of converting the Jews to Christianity remained constant, and this was as true of Robert Grant and of Thirlwall as it was of Shaftesbury and Inglis. On this point, though for different reasons, the most liberal theology of the day agreed. In 1857 the Revd Baden Powell argued that 'Christianity was not the religion of Moses' since revelation was 'a progressive adaptation to the wants and capacities of different ages and nations'. He rejected the Conservative enthusiasm for the Old Testament as superstitious.[42] Yet in the twentieth century the issues raised by a religiously plural society and the problems of the relationship between the two faiths have become more not less pressing. Within the context of their age, churchmen like Grant, Gladstone, Thirlwall, and Whately deserve to be remembered for their contributions to these debates.

University of Bristol

---

[40] T. R. Birks, *Memoir of the Revd Edward Bickersteth*, 2 vols (London, 1852), 2, p. 173.
[41] E. Bickersteth, *The Restoration of the Jews to their own Land* (London, 1841), p. 90.
[42] Baden Powell, *Christianity without Judaism* (London, 1857), pp. 211–19. For similar developments in nineteenth-century German Liberal Protestantism, see U. Tal, *Christians and Jews in Germany* (London, 1975), pp. 160–222.

THE FACES OF JANUS: FREE-THINKERS, JEWS, AND CHRISTIANITY IN NINETEENTH-CENTURY BRITAIN

by EDWARD ROYLE

N INETEENTH-CENTURY Britain was a Christian country, in that its laws and institutions were based upon the Christian religion. Not to be a Christian was to be excluded from full citizenship, for Christianity was, in the eyes of the Common Law, 'parcel of the laws of England'.[1] Until the Catholic Relief Act of 1829 Christianity was still for some purposes equated with Protestantism and, after this date, Jews and other 'infidels' continued unable to sit in Parliament or swear an oath as witnesses in courts of law.[2] Conversely, those British Radicals of the nineteenth century who rejected the aristocratic politics of what they termed 'Old Corruption' frequently chose also to attack its religious base—Anglicanism or, in extreme cases, the entire Christian system under which they were required to live.

This anti-Christian political radicalism went back to the ideas of the European Enlightenment, but at a popular level in Britain it was very much identified with the writings of Thomas Paine, especially his *Age of Reason*, published in 1794–5. This tradition of militancy against the whole Establishment in Church and State was continued in the first half of the nineteenth century by radical publishers, such as Richard Carlile, James Watson, and Henry Hetherington, whose 'blasphemous and seditious press' was the scourge of governments in the years of social protest between 1815 and 1848. The theme was taken up also by the followers of the social Utopian Deist, Robert Owen, whose 'Rational Religion' of the 'New Moral World' was proclaimed in the 1840s by such social missionaries of unbelief as Charles Southwell, Robert Cooper, and

---

[1] *Rex* v. *Taylor*, King's Bench (1676). The full passage from which this important and oft-quoted phrase comes is: 'That such kind of wicked and blasphemous words were not only an offence to God and religion, but a crime against the laws, State, and Government, and therefore punishable in this Court; for to say "Religion is a cheat" is to dissolve all the obligations whereby civil societies are preserved, and Christianity is parcel of the laws of England, and, therefore, to reproach the Christian religion is to speak in subversion of the law'—quoted in W. H. Wickwar, *The Struggle for the Freedom of the Press* (London, 1928), p. 25.
[2] Those with a *religious* objection to the judicial oath (including Quakers) were permitted to affirm instead in 1855; those with an *irreligious* or *secular* objection had to wait until 1869; parliamentary affirmation was not permitted to free-thinkers until 1888.

George Jacob Holyoake—the latter founding a specifically anti-Christian republican movement known as Secularism in the early 1850s.[3] In mid- and late Victorian Britain this movement, organized largely through the National Secular Society founded by Charles Bradlaugh in 1866, achieved national notoriety. Bradlaugh's attempts to enter the House of Commons as a duly-elected atheist gripped political attention throughout the early 1880s; as did the blasphemously witty journalism of George William Foote, who was to succeed Bradlaugh as President of the National Secular Society in 1890.[4]

The aim of this communication is to see how some of these self-avowed anti-religionists handled the Jewish question, in which issues of race, religion, and culture were so delicately and dangerously entwined. Their propaganda could easily appear anti-Jewish, particularly as the word 'Jew' carried pejorative overtones which were useful in anti-Christian controversy. The fact that the Bible was largely about Jews, that Christianity was an outgrowth of Judaism, and that Jesus himself had been a Jew made it difficult for the Christian system to be attacked without anti-Jewish language being used. On the contrary, anti-Jewish language had the advantage of drawing on a customary language of abuse and associating with the attack on Christianity all the traditional antipathies held by many people towards the Jews. Thus the word 'Jew' was frequently used scornfully, and in what might seem to the modern reader an anti-Semitic way.

When the radical publisher Richard Carlile put the date at the heading of his free-thinking periodical, the *Republican*, he substituted for AD 1822, such phrases as '1822 of Jesus the Jew', an apparently gratuitous insult.[5] Similarly in 1841, in his paper the *Oracle of Reason*, Charles Southwell headed a blasphemous attack on the Bible 'The Jew Book'.[6] The sense of this article can be gained from its opening words:

> That revoltingly odious Jew production, called BIBLE, has been for ages the idol of all sorts of blockheads, the glory of knaves, and the disgust of wise men. It is a history of lust, wholesale slaughtering, and horrible depravity . . .

---

[3] For the early history of nineteenth-century British free-thought, see Edward Royle, *Victorian Infidels. The Origins of the British Secularist Movement, 1791–1866* (Manchester, 1974).

[4] The later period of free-thought is the subject of Edward Royle, *Radicals, Secularists and Republicans. Popular Freethought in Britain, 1866–1915* (Manchester, 1980). See also Walter L. Arnstein, *The Bradlaugh Case. Atheism, Sex and Politics among the Late Victorians*, 2nd edn (Columbia, 1983) [hereafter Arnstein].

[5] *Republican*, 6 (1822) [hereafter *R*]. Carlile was at this time in gaol for blasphemous libel.

[6] *Oracle of Reason; or, Philosophy Vindicated*, 27 Nov. 1841, pp. 25–7.

These words earned Southwell a year in gaol for blasphemous libel. A generation later, in 1881, George William Foote was similarly imprisoned for a year for blaspheming the Christian religion by attacking the Bible in his *Freethinker* newspaper. This paper had been started in 1881 with the intention of using impiety and bitter wit as tools against that Christianity which was denying Charles Bradlaugh the right to take his duly-elected seat for Northampton in the House of Commons. Undoubtedly in his anger Foote at times overstepped the mark. In particular, parts of his paper might at first glance look like anti-Jewish propaganda, for one highly popular device with which to make his point and to increase circulation was to reprint weekly comic Bible sketches. These were initially drawn from a French work, Leo Taxil's *La Bible amusante*, which represented Jehovah and other biblical characters in what appear to be crude, anti-Semitic stereotypes.[7]

A second line of attack on the Jews was developed in the 1870s by Radicals incensed by the politics of Disraeli. Here we can see an element of racism, for Disraeli's ancestry was, strictly speaking, irrelevant to his politics. But such was the intense hatred felt by some Radicals for Disraeli's policies in the later 1870s that racism could result. For example, George Jacob Holyoake, who since the 1840s had led the most mild and tolerant wing of the radical free-thought movement, gave a political speech in Leicester in 1878 entitled 'England under a Jewish Government',[8] in which he set about explaining Disraeli's pro-Turkish foreign policy in the Balkans in terms of an international conspiracy of Jewish financiers:

> Then who were their financiers? Why, the Jews. When efforts were made to rescue the subject races of Turkey from the oppression which bound them, the Jewish financiers prevented it, because Bulgaria was the hunting ground of interest on Turkish bonds. When England put £4,000,000 in the Suez Canal, for objects which no man could make out, the transaction was put into the hands of the Jews, who made hundreds of thousands of pounds by it.

One should note, however, that Disraeli himself had developed the conspiracy theory of ubiquitous Jewish influence in one of Sidonia's

---

[7] *Freethinker*, 4 Sept.1881, p. 38 [hereafter *F*]. The first of the cartoons appeared on 6 Nov. 1881. They caused great offence to some—see Malcolm Quin, *Memoirs of a Positivist* (London, 1924), pp. 68–70; Tom Barclay, *Memoirs and Medleys. The Autobiography of a Bottlewasher* (Leicester, 1934), p. 48—but they helped put up the circulation to an unprecedented 10,000 a week.
[8] *Secular Review*, 16 Nov. 1878, pp. 313–14 [hereafter *SR*].

heavily ironic speeches in *Coningsby*.[9] According to Holyoake, the Jews were behind British expansion in Cyprus, Egypt, and Afghanistan, stimulating jingoistic feelings in the public at large through the Jewish-controlled press—by which he appears to have meant the *Daily Telegraph*. This lecture stimulated a controversy in the local newspaper, the *Leicester Mercury*, with Israel Hart replying on behalf of the Jewish community that Jews occupied all kinds of positions in society. They were not just among the powerful and wealthy; but, if it did seem that some had enjoyed a disproportionate amount of worldly success, that was because their dietary laws had kept them away from strong drink! Hart was quite obviously a Liberal supporter and Holyoake at that time was seeking Liberal support. He protested that he had been misunderstood.[10] It is easy to see why.

The free-thinkers could certainly claim that they had grounds for mistrusting the Jews. Holyoake and others had, for example, been among the leading campaigners against the Christian monopoly of Parliament, which had been ended for Jews in 1858 with the suspension of the requirement that the parliamentary oath should be 'on the true faith of a Christian'. Yet when Charles Bradlaugh sought to enter the House of Commons in 1880 as a non-believer, he found himself opposed by Henry Drummond Wolff, the son of a German Jewish immigrant, and the Baron de Worms, another Jew. This produced a certain amount of anti-Jewish invective in both Bradlaugh's *National Reformer* and the *Freethinker* in the early 1880s.[11]

One face of radical free-thought was therefore hostile to the Jews. Nevertheless, first impressions of such language can be misleading. The proper historical question is not what do these sentiments mean to a late twentieth, post-Holocaust society, but what did they mean at the time, to those who spoke or wrote them and to those who heard them? The answer is more subtle than the obvious one, revealing a general impression in favour of the Jews—although one which was frequently couched in what might seem to a later generation to be ominously ambiguous language.

Richard Carlile dated his *Republican* in a disparaging manner, not because he was being particularly anti-Jewish, but because he was wanting to assert that Jesus was only a Jew, and he did not wish to accept the

[9] Benjamin Disraeli, *Coningsby or, the New Generation*, Everyman edn (London, 1911), ch. 25, pp. 208–9.
[10] *SR*, 23 Nov. 1878, pp. 328–9.
[11] Arnstein, pp. 57–8.

implied Christian chronology: Jesus was not *his* 'dominus'.[12] Charles Southwell similarly was concerned not so much to attack Jews as to condemn Christians. Despite the apparently anti-Jewish tone of the 'Jew Book' article, his meaning was simply that the Bible had been written not by the Christians' God, as some more extreme Evangelicals were apt to claim, but merely by some rather obscure, primitive, and frequently barbaric Jewish people.[13] The predominating influence of Southwell's anti-Christian sentiments becomes clear when one considers his second career, as an actor. Southwell was an extrovert performer, whether delivering atheistical lectures on the public platform or thundering out lines from his beloved Shakespeare on the stage of some south London hall. His favourite play was *The Merchant of Venice*, one of the most potent of anti-Jewish dramas. Yet Southwell loved it because he could exploit the inherent ambiguities in Shakespeare's plot to portray Shylock—played by himself—as the hero, the hapless victim of Christian greed and hypocrisy, thus reversing the stereotypes and re-enforcing his own anti-Christian message.[14]

Even Holyoake was genuinely trying not to attack all Jews, but only Disraeli and his financier friends, as a longer extract from his speech at Leicester makes clear.[15] He opened his argument in classic style:

> The Jews had a faculty for acquiring money which no other race possessed, and they had fewer scruples in getting money than any other race ever had . . .

Thus far he was expressing a traditional opposition to the stereotypical Jewish money-lender. But there immediately followed a recognition of why this was so:

> and what had always been a passion of theirs had been forced upon them as a policy by the persecution to which they had been subjected, which had left them often without the choice of any other profession.

---

[12] Among the other alternative dates used in the *Republican* in 1822 were: '1822, of the Carpenter's Wife's Son *alias* Ghost begotten God'; '1822 of the Christian Mythology'; 'Year 1822 of the Christian Delusion'; and 'Dec. 1, 1822, of Jehovah, jun.'

[13] Even this view was to change among some free-thinkers later in the century, as when F. J. Gould explained of the Bible in 1895, 'Through it the wondrous and profound emotions of the Jewish heart yet speak. From its pages there issue, not the accents of God, but the voices of a noble people': 'Who wrote *Genesis*?' *Watts's Literary Guide*, supplement, Jan. 1895, p. 4.

[14] *New Moral World*, 18 Feb. 1843, p. 276. Another anti-hero who attracted him was Iago in *Othello*—*Reasoner*, 18 April 1849, p. 256.

[15] *SR*, 16 Nov. 1878, pp. 313–14.

After examples of the exercise of this profession on the international financial stage, he admitted:

> His difficulty was so to speak of the operations of a Jewish government, and the influence and ways of that race, without expressing or inculcating a feeling of bitterness, or derision, or contempt of Jews personally.

Some might argue in the later twentieth century that to condemn the former in such racist language was to damn the latter also by implication if not intent. However, Holyoake's speech as a whole is clearly (in his own mind at least) directed not against the Jews but against Disraeli, the apostate Jew.

Bradlaugh was more judicious in his choice of words, and in his condemnation of de Worms he was careful to state that he was criticizing an individual Jew and not the Jews in general:

> The dust of the great ones of your grand old Hebrew race would almost be indignantly stirred in their graves by the bigot-breath of your maiden House of Commons speech, Baron H. de Worms; your place is not in a free assembly of true Britons . . .

and he dismissed Drummond Wolff with wit, as 'a hybrid rather than highbred'.[16] The conflict was one of party politics not race. Bradlaugh was well aware that, though Conservative Jews might oppose him, those Jews who supported the Liberal Party did not. As the *Jewish World* pointed out in 1883, the real cause being fought for in the Bradlaugh case was not atheism but religious liberty.[17]

Nevertheless, political controversy could easily appear to employ the language of racial and religious bigotry. German Jews, for example, were condemned by Bradlaugh's co-editor on the *National Reformer*, Annie Besant, in 1884 as 'wild refugees, alien to the national life, careless of the national welfare, and ignorant of the national traditions'. By this she meant—ironically in view of her own soon-to-be-changed political opinions—that the German Jews were Socialists.[18] Though her opinions were doubtless shared by some long-settled and prosperous capitalist members of the English Jewish community, the tone of the language was symptomatic of a change which entered the free-thought press towards

---

[16] Arnstein, p. 57.
[17] *National Reformer*, 13 May 1883, p. 364 [hereafter *NR*].
[18] *NR*, 11 May 1884, p. 324.

the close of the nineteenth century as Jewish refugees from Eastern Europe made the Jewish question now one of social as well as religious concern.

It is in this context that G. W. Foote's comic Bible sketches in the *Freethinker* need to be considered. On 30 April 1882 the front-page cartoon, entitled 'The First Religious Murder', dealt with the story of Cain and Abel. Jehovah has something of a Jewish appearance, although Cain has a positively English nose![19] However, the point is that the rest of the front page of that issue of the *Freethinker* carries a quite different message about the editor's attitude towards the Jews, for it is devoted to the pogroms in Russia, under the heading 'The Jew-Hunt'. There are three stages to Foote's argument in this article. The first is to condemn the pogroms as 'a disgrace to civilisation'. The second is to explore the social reasons for the pogroms, explaining why 'the Jews have to thank themselves for a good deal of their sufferings'. Unlike the Mohammedan subjects of Russia, the Jews

> act in a manner which too frequently makes them hated or loathed. They are in the country but not of it, and they usually regard the native inhabitants as Gentiles, to be spoiled even as their forefathers 'spoiled' the Egyptians.

After giving several examples of this, he concludes 'Men of alien race, religion, speech and social customs, cannot expect gentle treatment from the natives whom they systematically despoil.' In the third stage of the argument, Foote presents his solution. It is for the Jews either to integrate themselves into their host communities, as was being achieved in England and France, 'or they must make up their minds to a national reunion in Palestine or elsewhere.' Foote's preference was for integration to the benefit of both Jews and Gentiles.

These arguments are clearly recognizable as typical of their age in both their innocence and insidiousness. Yet as a free-thinker, Foote was not arguing from the same position as many others who put forward such views. He belonged to a tradition of advocacy which had long deplored the slaughter of the Amalekites, the merciless ferocity of the Psalms of David, and all the bloodthirsty crudities of Old Testament political history.[20] The continuance of such things in history since those days, and even into the rational modern age, he attributed to the powerful and

---

[19] *F*, 30 April 1882, p. 137.
[20] See G. W. Foote and W. P. Ball, *The Bible Handbook for Freethinkers and Inquiring Christians* (London, 1888).

dangerous effects of religion upon the human mind—any religion. His condemnation of the Jews was not for their Judaism but for their being religious in any sense. He condemned the lifestyle of the Russian Jews not because it was Jewish, but because it fell short of those enlightened, secularized, Western standards to which Foote himself adhered and with which he confidently believed the future lay once the baneful effects of all religions had been exorcized from civilization.[21]

In 1897, at the time of the Zionist Congress, Joseph Mazzini Wheeler, Foote's friend and sub-editor, took up this theme again in the *Freethinker*.[22] He, too, began by sympathizing with the Jews' plight, attributing it to Christian intolerance: 'The Jew everywhere is what centuries of Christian love have made him', he observed with heavy irony. In the relatively tolerant, modern countries of Western Europe, therefore, the cultured Jew was 'practically a Secularist', but in Russia persecution had begot Orthodoxy and bigotry. If Palestine—'which is as much holy to the Moslem as to the Jew'—were acquired by the Jews, only the backward Russian Jews would go there, thought Wheeler. A far better solution to the Jewish problem would come through enlightened toleration and absorption into a Western culture to which Judaism had much to contribute.

The argument here, as in Foote's earlier piece, is based on the assumption that religion is an aberration, fostered by persecution. The language used to describe the Russian Jews may resemble that of anti-Semitism, but it is not anti-Semitic. The Orthodox Jew is certainly seen as a 'problem' to be eliminated—and Wheeler cannot resist the gibe that while Messianic Jews are waiting for Jerusalem, they will continue to linger in Europe 'to find their account in trading among the Gentiles'—but the article is, in fact, a plea for religious toleration and should be interpreted in this light.

The supreme importance of religious toleration for the free-thinkers comes across at the end of the nineteenth century in their handling of the notorious Dreyfus case, in which the French army was only after many years brought to book for its persecution of a Jewish officer on a trumped-up charge of espionage. There was now no reference in the free-thought literature to comments on the toleration granted to liberal Jews in the civilized environment of Western Europe. The Dreyfus case plainly had a

---

[21] Foote referred with approval to the stand taken by the Society of Freethinkers of Antwerp against the growing anti-Semitic movement—'They object to religious prejudice being employed against any class or nation'—*F*, 16 Jan. 1887, p. 21.

[22] *F*, 5 Sept. 1897, pp. 561–2.

very unpleasant message for Western Liberals, and they were understandably reluctant to admit its implications for their rather cosy view of the position of Jews in the more civilized parts of Europe. Dreyfus was plainly a Jew who had not deserved his fate, and for that very reason his cause was taken up by Liberals and free-thinkers. Blame had for once to be placed elsewhere than on the isolated, foreign Jew from Poland or Russia, and the free-thinkers found their scapegoat without any difficulty:[23]

> The Catholic generals on the Staff have tried to get him out of the way more than once. Their consciences are easy, however, for the Church is always behind them, promising immunity on earth and felicity in heaven to her faithful sons, whatever sins they commit in furthering her interests. But, happily, this Jesuit plot is spoiled by exposure.

The heroes and champions of liberty were, on this occasion, Jews aided by Protestants as well as free-thinkers. The latter were proud to note how free-thinkers had taken a leading role in France with such men as Clemenceau, Brisson, Anatole France, Colonel Picquart, and Zola active among pro-Dreyfusards.[24]

These free-thinkers of nineteenth-century Britain provide the historian with a rehearsal of many of the arguments about and against the Jews which were being heard at the time in other quarters and which have become all too familiar since. There is nothing new in the free-thinkers' perception of the stereotypes of the rich financier or the poor, ignorant, bigoted refugee from Russia. What is different is that they provide a view from an unusual and revealing angle. Much of European anti-Jewish feeling had and has been generated from a Christian perspective. That of the British free-thinkers comes from an anti-Christian point of view, from people who prided themselves on their enlightenment, tolerance, and fearless outspokenness devoid of humbug. This meant that they were intellectually committed to being sympathetic towards the Jews as individuals, whilst being hostile to their religion and that cultural stereotype which they identified with that religion. On balance, intellect won over prejudice, at least so far as Western Jews were concerned. The strength of their persistent though reluctant prejudice against the Russian Jews, however, indicates the dangerous depths to which such anti-Jewish

---

[23] *F*, 20 Nov. 1898, p. 737.
[24] *F*, 22 July 1906, p. 449.

prejudice had penetrated, even amongst the most enlightened and even in late Victorian Britain.

One final point is worth a note. When G. W. Foote died, in 1915, his successor as President of the National Secular Society was an atheistic Jew from Leicester, by the name of Chapman Cohen.[25]

University of York

[25] Chapman Cohen, *Almost an Autobiography. The Confessions of a Freethinker* (London, 1940).

ORGANS AND ORGAN MUSIC IN VICTORIAN SYNAGOGUES: CHRISTIAN INTRUSIONS OR SYMBOLS OF CULTURAL ASSIMILATION?

by WALTER HILLSMAN

THE rise and decline of organs in British synagogues from about 1850 to the present day is intrinsically linked to social, political, and religious developments.[1] It therefore provides a fascinating focus for studying some of the complexities of change in Anglo-Jewry, the extent to which Victorian British Jews were affected by developments in Judaism elsewhere, and the adoption of, and reaction against, certain cultural phenomena perceived by Jews as Christian.

The importance of the organ controversy within nineteenth-century Judaism—that is, over whether organs should be used in synagogue worship on Sabbaths and festivals (like Rosh Hashanah and Yom Kippur)—should not be underestimated. The organ constituted, and still constitutes, one of the most important markers—many have said *the* most important—along the dividing-line between Orthodox and Reform Jewish services. In 1913 it was described by Ismar Elbogen as 'das Schibbolet der Parteien' (the shibboleth of the parties).[2]

As Orthodox objections to the use of organs in Reform services have sometimes focused on the instrument's connection with Christian worship, one must straight away consider the question of whether, in view of its history, the organ can be regarded as intrinsically Christian. If the ancient and early medieval worlds are taken as reference points, the answer must be 'no'. The ancient Greeks and Romans, for example, used organs on various indoor and outdoor occasions.[3] According to some Jewish writers, the *magrepha* of the Second Temple was a very loud, organ-like instrument. As other scholars have, however, translated that

---

[1] I am very much indebted to the following for help with the research for, and presentation of, this essay: Edward Cross, of the Hertsmere Progressive Synagogue in Elstree, Herts., Sydney Fixman, of the West London Synagogue, Ezra Kahn, of Jews' College, London, Alexander Knapp, of Cambridge, Michael Kramer-Mannion, of Stockport, Peter Ward Jones and Susan and Lionel Wollenberg, of Oxford.

[2] I. Elbogen, *Der jüdische Gottesdienst in seiner geschichtlichen Entwicklung* (Leipzig, 1913), p. 427.

[3] *New Grove Dictionary of Music* [hereafter *NG*], 'Organ', pp. 724–5.

Hebrew word as 'altar shovel',[4] one must be wary of the appeal of some nineteenth-century Reform Jews to ancient Temple precedent for introducing organs into synagogue services!

In any event, organs were never used in Christian liturgy until well into the Middle Ages, and then only in the West. Fathers of the Early Church condemned many musical instruments for their association with pagan rites and Jewish Temple worship.[5] Christian Byzantium, while allowing organs to be used for secular purposes, continued the Fathers' prohibition on musical instruments in Christian liturgy,[6] as Eastern Orthodox churches still do today.

The introduction of organs into Western European churches took place very gradually between about the years 900 and 1200. Initially they were probably used only for extra-liturgical purposes. Exactly *how* they came to be employed within the liturgy remains a mystery.[7] But by the late Middle Ages and Renaissance they were so frequently used there that they began to be associated by many Western Christians almost exclusively with Christianity, and to be categorized by some Jews as *chukkat haggoyim* (customs of the Gentiles),[8] an ancient Hebrew phrase meaning non-Jewish ritual or superstitious practices which Jews must avoid imitating. In subsequent centuries this latter view came to be more generally held by Jews. In the nineteenth, those adhering to it sometimes articulated their feelings with great emotion, or even bitterness, when condemning the use of organs in Reform synagogues. One Jewish writer called the organ 'das klingende Christenthum' (loosely, 'the resounding voice of Christendom'), and thought organs in synagogues about as appropriate as synagogues built in cruciform style![9]

Christian readers in our day may imagine from their knowledge of the Psalms that musical instruments were common features of worship in ancient Israel. It should be noted, however, that musical psalms concerned only worship at the one Temple in Jerusalem, and not services in the numerous synagogues of the Jewish world. Playing an instrument in the Temple on Sabbaths and festivals was allowed by special exemption from the law of the Sabbath. But in synagogues such playing was forbidden,

[4] B. L. Mosely, 'The magrepha', *Jewish Chronicle* (London) [hereafter *JC*] (25 Jan. 1878), p. 7.
[5] J. McKinnon, ed., *Music in Early Christian Literature* (Cambridge, 1987), pp. 1–4, 26, 97–8, 137; *NG*, 'Christian Church, music of the early', p. 368.
[6] *NG*, 'Organ', p. 727.
[7] Ibid., pp. 728–9.
[8] *EJ*, 'Organ', col. 1453.
[9] Dr Lehmann, *Die Orgel in der Synagoge* (Mainz, [1864]), p. 15.

since performance itself, or the possible repairing of an instrument during a service, counted as prohibited work.[10]

The destruction of the Second Temple in AD 70 did not cause Jews to transfer Temple exemptions to the synagogue and introduce instruments. It led, rather, to the notion that, out of mourning for the destruction of the Temple, synagogue worship should maintain an atmosphere of sobriety, and eschew any feature which might add joy or colour.[11] Instrumental music (apart from use of the *shofar* on high holy days) therefore remained non-existent in synagogue services up to the end of the eighteenth century.

In this and other respects, the contrast between Jewish and Western European Christian services grew gradually more glaring. Synagogues (with rare exceptions) had no choirs, practically no art music, usually just cantillations and modal prayer chanting by the *chazzan* (an adult male cantor), sometimes assisted by another adult male and one boy treble. The latter two—often musically illiterate—frequently just improvised (without rehearsal) harmony notes to the cantorial line in the course of services.[12] Synagogue worship maintained a type of Middle Eastern air which to Western European Christian observers seemed noisy, uncoordinated, and indecorous. There was a 'free and easy' atmosphere of spontaneity in prayer, and occasional disregard for the reader.[13] Synagogue liturgy had not been pruned since ancient times, but only added to, and synagogue services came to be regarded by acculturated eighteenth-century Western European Jews as dull and monotonous.[14]

Reaction in the early nineteenth century against the narrowly limited nature of synagogue music, and against the oriental atmosphere of synagogue worship, was just one manifestation of the dissatisfaction of a number of Jews with their cultural, social, and religious ethos. In these latter respects, Jews had often been forced to exist in ghettos by the Christian European society which disenfranchised them. However, with the effects of the Enlightenment and the French Revolution suddenly

[10] *Jüdisches Lexikon*, 'Orgelstreit', col. 602; *Protokolle und Aktenstücke der zweiten Rabbiner-Versammlung, abgehalten in Frankfurt am Main* (Frankfurt-on-Main, 1845), p. 147.

[11] D. W. Marks, *Sermons Preached on Various Occasions* (London, 1862), pp. 176–7.

[12] *EJ*, 'Music', col. 644; F. L. Cohen, 'The rise and development of synagogue music', in *Papers Read at the Anglo-Jewish Historical Exhibition, Royal Albert Hall, London* (London, 1888), pp. 129–30.

[13] M. Leigh, 'Reform Judaism in Britain 1840–1970', in D. Marmur, ed., *Essays on Reform Judaism in Britain* (London, 1973), p. 4.

[14] For dull and monotonous, see J. Katz, *The Social Background of Jewish Emancipation, 1770–1870* (Cambridge, Mass., 1973), p. 120.

causing political and economic barriers to Jews to recede and eventually fall, significant numbers of Jewish people wanted to bring themselves into closer cultural and educational conformity with Christian Europe, and thus to rise in the social scale.[15] Some of them went so far as to convert to Christianity. Others, wishing to stem the tide of conversions, established what became known as the Reform Movement in Judaism, which in its earliest stages allowed for the greatest possible cultural assimilation of its adherents to Christian European culture, while yet keeping them within—what to Reform leaders was still—the fold of Judaism.[16]

The most important principle setting Reform apart from Orthodox Judaism is the former's acknowledgement of the legitimacy of change.[17] In the realm of liturgy, Reform took the liberty of changing long-established traditions because it rejected post-biblical accretions as not of divine origin.[18]

Reform leaders also seized on Western European art music as a means of displacing cantorial music (which had by then fallen into the category of 'folk art'), of introducing an atmosphere of Western-style decorum into Sabbath and festival services, and thus of appealing to sophisticated contemporary Jews. Rehearsed four-part choir music and sometimes German-style hymns featured prominently in their earliest services, as did organ accompaniment to both.[19] Reform writers frequently praised organs as aids to devotion. Although some forward-looking Orthodox synagogues (for example, the Seitenstettengasse Synagogue, in Vienna, and the Great Synagogue, in Paris) also introduced choral art music,[20] they drew the line at Christian-type hymns and organs.

The nineteenth-century development of Reform took place in two stages, which at least one source describes as the 'aesthetic' and the 'scholarly and ideological'. The first manifested itself in changes in synagogue worship from 1810 in Westphalia, Berlin, and Hamburg, the second in the theological and intellectual debates among university-educated, progressive rabbis, which led up to the rabbinical conferences of 1844, 1845, and 1846 in Brunswick, Frankfurt, and Breslau.[21]

One of the leaders of the first stage was the layman Israel Jacobson,

[15] For ghettos/Enlightenment/French Revolution, see Leigh, 'Reform Judaism', pp. 3–6.
[16] Ibid., p. 6.
[17] EJ, 'Reform Judaism', col. 23.
[18] Jewish Encyclopedia [hereafter JE], 'Reform Judaism', pp. 349, 351.
[19] EJ, 'Music', cols 642–4.
[20] Ibid., cols 645–50.
[21] EJ, 'Reform Judaism', cols 23–4.

who in 1801 opened a non-sectarian boarding school in Seesen, near Hanover. Services in the school synagogue (dedicated 1810) included German prayers alongside Hebrew ones, congregational hymns in German, and organ and four-part choir music.[22] After moving in 1815 to Berlin, Jacobson quickly established Reform services with organ, first in his home, then in a newly-built Reform synagogue. Shortly after this, that synagogue was closed by imperial decree, after successful protests to the Kaiser from Orthodox Jews in Berlin.[23]

Seesen in its provinciality, and Berlin with its failure, were both eclipsed from 1818 by developments in Hamburg. The successful establishment in that major city of a Reform synagogue, also with an organ and vernacular prayers, and without traditional cantorial music, proved seminal in the history of Reform and of synagogue organs. Orthodox representations to the civil authorities, demanding closure of the synagogue, were rejected.[24] Significantly, the organ figured in the Hamburg Reformers' published justification of their innovations, the *Nogah ha-Zedek* ('Splendour of Justice') of 1818, and in the Orthodox reply to this, *Elleh Divrei ha-Berit* ('These are the Words of the Covenant') of 1819. These were the first of a veritable flood of publications in the nineteenth century and beyond, arguing at least in part about the use of organs in synagogues.[25]

The culmination of the second stage of Reform development, the rabbinical conferences, added further fuel to the fire. In their carefully recorded debates, rabbis justified organ use on the Sabbath by updating the interpretation of Sabbath law and other traditional attitudes. As contemporary organists were no longer expected to have to repair their instruments in the course of a service, as Reform synagogues (at least in Germany) had by that time almost entirely given up prayers for the return to Jerusalem and the restoration of the Temple's animal sacrifices (so that there was no longer any reason to distinguish between Temple and synagogue Sabbath regulations), and as organ playing should be seen as dignifying worship rather than breaking Sabbath law, the thinking of the conferences then ran heavily in favour of the instrument.[26]

---

[22] For Jacobson (1768–1828, wealthy banker and agent of King Jerome of Westphalia) and Seesen, see Leigh, 'Reform Judaism', pp. 6–7.

[23] M. Ydit, 'The controversy concerning the use of organ [*sic*] during the 19th century in Europe and in America' – Prize Essay, Hebrew Union College (Cincinnati, Ohio), 1962, p. 2.

[24] D. Philipson, *The Reform Movement in Judaism* (New York, 1907), pp. 42–9.

[25] See A. Sendrey, *Bibliography of Jewish Music* (New York, 1951), pp. 104–6.

[26] *Protokolle und Aktenstücke*, pp. 147–50.

Reform opinion on whether the organ contravened traditional mourning for the destruction of the Temple, and whether it represented a custom of the Gentiles which should be avoided, came from other quarters. On the former question, Professor David Woolf Marks (Senior Minister, 1851 to the early 1900s, of the West London Synagogue) was quite clear in his sermon at the 1859 dedication of West London's first organ. In view of the virtual command of the Psalms to use instrumental music in worship, and of Jewry's continuing emergence from the ghetto and its move toward political and economic emancipation, Jews should rejoice and adopt every means of elevating and enriching the aesthetic character of their worship, including organs. In denying that the organ should count as a custom of the Gentiles, Marks mistakenly gave the impression that Thomas Aquinas singled out organ use in church services as a Judaizing element.[27] Other Jewish Reformers, with greater accuracy, pointed out that organs were by no means essential to Christian worship. Eastern Orthodox Christians, for example, never used them.[28]

Orthodox rabbis refused to stop condemning organs in Reform Sabbath services. In asserting that playing the organ contravened Sabbath law and traditional mourning for the destruction of the Temple, the Orthodox could at least not be accused of hypocrisy. Although the Orthodox increasingly in the nineteenth century allowed relatively inexpensive, organ-like harmoniums to be used in their synagogues[29] for weddings and other special occasions, they steadfastly refused to allow their use on Sabbaths and festivals. Their shaky stance on the organ as a custom of the Gentiles, however, drew regular charges of hypocrisy from Reformers. The latter pointed out the glaring adoption of some Gentile customs by the Orthodox. In England, for example, the (Orthodox) Chief Rabbi had in several senses been assuming the function and trappings of a bishop (one Chief Rabbi wore a 'quasi-episcopal rosette in the ribbon of his top hat', and was at one time rumoured to have sported gaiters!).[30] The

---

[27] Marks, *Sermons*, pp. 176–9; for mistakenly, see Thomas Aquinas, *Summa Theologiae* (Rome, 1962), p. 1474. I am grateful to Dr Edward Yarnold of Campion Hall, Oxford, for confirming that Thomas was here using the word *organum* to mean musical instrument in the generic sense.

[28] L. Löw, *Gesammelte Schriften*, 2 vols (Szegedin, 1889, 1890), 2, p. 353.

[29] J. S. Curwen, *Studies in Worship Music, Chiefly as Regards Congregational Singing* (London, 1880), p. 190; *JC* (1880–1901), *passim*.

[30] S. Sharot, 'The social determinants in the religious practices and organization of English Jewry with special reference to the United Synagogue' (Oxford D.Phil. thesis, 1968), pp. 302–3, 351.

Orthodox also had clergy who often dressed like Anglican priests and called themselves 'Reverend' and 'Minister'.[31]

Reform synagogues spread widely in German and American cities in the nineteenth century. In England they made little headway. The only three to be founded there then were the West London Synagogue of British Jews (established 1840), the Manchester Synagogue of British Jews (1857), and the Bradford Synagogue (1873). Orthodox synagogues, on the other hand, were much more numerous. In 1903, for example, there were sixty-one of them in London alone. Synagogue attendance figures also made Reform seem insignificant. On the first day of Passover 1903, for instance, West London had 1,111 attendances, compared to total London Orthodox synagogue attendances of 25,501. That same year, the total Greater London Jewish population was 106,550, and the total British Isles Jewish population 188,000.[32] In Manchester, in the late 1870s, Reform synagogue membership was about 150, out of a total Manchester Jewish population of around 10,000. The relative failure of Reform in Victorian England has been attributed, among other factors, to the general conservatism and insularity of British Jewry, and to the then sometimes inward-looking and elitist predisposition of English Reform congregations. The wealth, importance, and influence of many Reform Jews then, however, must not be underestimated.[33]

Victorian conservatism and insularity is demonstrated in part by the late foundation of English Reform synagogues (1840–73) compared with that of many of their continental counterparts (early nineteenth century), and by their even greater delay in installing organs. The corresponding tardiness of English Orthodox Jewish objections to organs (which began in earnest only in the 1870s in the columns of the [London] *Jewish Chronicle*), the relatively refined tone of those objections compared with continental equivalents, and the near-refusal of English Reform to become embroiled in battle over the subject, also contributed to the impression that the organ controversy in England constituted only a delayed and muted echo of that on the Continent.

---

[31] For dress and titles, see Sharot, 'The social determinants', p. 310, and M. Kramer-Mannion, 'The growth and development of Reform Judaism in Manchester 1940–1985' (Manchester Ph.D. thesis, 1989), p. 470.

[32] S. Sharot, 'Reform and Liberal Judaism in London: 1840–1940', *Jewish Social Studies* (1979), p. 211; for 1903 see R. Mudie Smith, *The Religious Life of London* (London, 1904), pp. 15, 265, and *Jewish Year Book 1903–4*, pp. 219, 223.

[33] 'Our provincial congregations. Manchester.—VII.', *Jewish World* (9 Nov. 1877), p. 5, and 'The Jews in Manchester', *JC* (10 Oct. 1879), p. 7; Kramer-Mannion, 'Growth and development, p. ii.

*   *   *

The conservatism of the founders of the West London Synagogue was demonstrated in the reasons many of them had for establishing what was clearly a congregation of a new denomination. A majority had simply become frustrated with their original synagogue, the historic Sephardic Bevis Marks in the City of London, for its refusal to accede to their demands for increased decorum in services there, and to sanction the establishment of a branch synagogue in the fashionable part of the West End, where most of them lived.[34]

There is apparently no evidence to suggest that West London founders ever raised the question of an organ at Bevis Marks or in the early days of their independent existence. The first West London building, in Burton Street (off Euston Road), dedicated in 1842, was too small for an organ. In 1849 a new synagogue was dedicated in Margaret Street, off Cavendish Square.[35] Only in 1859, however, was the installation of an organ in that building approved—in order to increase the 'impressiveness' of the service[36]—and an organist engaged. The appointee, Charles Garland Verrinder, a Christian, was initially given only a six-month contract, whilst the Council advertised in the musical, secular, and Jewish press in Britain, France, and Germany. After receiving fifty or sixty applications from Christian organists, but only one or two (unsupported by satis-factory testimonials) from Jews—unsurprisingly, as organists are normally trained within Christian environments—the Council made Verrinder's contract permanent.[37] Soon Verrinder was entrusted with charge of the choir. He remained at West London after it moved in 1870 into its third (and still used) building in Upper Berkeley Street, near Marble Arch, and served there until shortly before his death in 1904.[38]

Details of the size of the 1859 organ are apparently not extant. But the 1870 instrument was a small, three-manual installation by Gray and Davidson (enlarged in 1908 by Harrison and Harrison).[39] Whether either

---

[34] Leigh, 'Reform Judaism', pp. 20–4.

[35] A. S. Diamond, '120th Anniversary: West London Synagogue', JC (7 June 1963), pp. 23, 26; 'The West London Synagogue of British Jews. A history of fifty years', JC (29 Jan. 1892), Sup-plement, p. 20.

[36] London, West London Synagogue, Safe, 'West London Synagogue British Jews 5602–1842 Minutes' [hereafter WLSM] (15 Dec. 1858), p. 374.

[37] On Verrinder (?–1904), see 'Obituary', Musical Times (1 Aug. 1904), p. 533; WLSM (12 Sept., 18 Dec. 1859), pp. 390, 396–8.

[38] WLSM (18 Dec. 1859), pp. 398–9; 'Consecration of the new West London Synagogue', JC (23 Sept. 1870), pp. 13–14; 'Obituary. Dr. Verrinder', JC (1 July 1904), p. 25.

[39] E. J. Hopkins and E. F. Rimbault, The Organ: its History and Construction, 3rd edn (London,

organ was intended to impress West London members, or Jewish or Gentile visitors, is not made clear by Council Minute Books. However, organs were spreading so widely at that time in Britain that West London members probably felt that they could no longer endanger their cultural status by being without one. After all, some wealthy homes, more and more town halls, and churches of every description were crowning their respectability with the largest organs they could afford or house. Even English Presbyterian synods around that time were ceasing their annual condemnations of organs![40]

As in all Reform Jewish services with organ, the instrument at West London was used to play only opening and closing voluntaries and accompaniments to singing within the service. It accompanied choir music and some monotoned clergy verses, but not congregational singing, as West London congregants then—unlike today's in Reform synagogues generally—did not sing.[41]

Verrinder apparently tried hard to play voluntaries which could count as Jewish. At weddings and other special occasions, for instance, he often played transcriptions of orchestral works by Jewish composers, like Meyerbeer's 'Schiller Festival March' and Mendelssohn's 'Wedding March'.[42] (Mendelssohn, incidentally, was invariably regarded by Jews as Jewish, despite his practice of Christianity from the age of seven.) Verrinder occasionally, however, stretched the definition of Jewish by playing works by non-Jewish composers based on Old Testament themes (for example, the 'Dead March' from Handel's oratorio *Saul*). After a special service in 1884 marking the hundredth birthday of Sir Moses Montefiore, Verrinder dropped all pretence of playing 'Jewish organ music' when he launched into Schumann's 'Birthday March'![43]

One aspect of organ performance practice within the liturgy at West London was borrowed directly from Victorian Anglican tradition. In the six volumes of music used at West London, printed in the late nineteenth century, in the accompaniment to the *Elohenu Shebashamayim* (Our God, who art in heaven), creeping chromatic chords on the organ provide

1877), repr. (Hilversum, 1965), p. 503; G. Benham, 'The Organ in the West London Synagogue, Upper Berkeley Street, W.', *The Organ*, 18 (1938–9), pp. 45–50.

[40] O. Chadwick, *The Victorian Church Part II*, 2nd edn (London, 1970), p. 327.

[41] Sharot, 'Reform and Liberal Judaism', p. 216.

[42] For Meyerbeer, see 'The Jubilee. The synagogues. Berkeley Street', *JC* (24 June 1887), p. 13; for Mendelssohn, 'Wedding at Berkeley Street Synagogue', *JC* (13 July 1883), p. 10.

[43] For Handel, see 'Berkeley Street', *JC* (8 July 1887), p. 14; for Schumann, 'Berkeley Street', *JC* (31 Oct. 1884), p. 2.

background to the minister's monotoned recitation of alternate verses, in much the same manner as they did in roughly equivalent parts of contemporary Anglican services (see Example One).[44] Such accompaniments were probably reckoned to increase the devotional impact of the words!

Organ accompaniments in the West London volumes to four-part choral, anthem-like music, are for the most part conservative compared with those of many late Victorian Anglican anthems and canticle settings, in that they frequently more or less double the voice parts and do not provide independent ingredients in the texture, like accompaniments in many of the anthems of Stanford and Stainer. On occasion, however, Verrinder does achieve quasi-orchestral effects (see Example Two).

*　　*　　*

In contrast to West London, the very establishment of the Manchester Synagogue of British Jews involved the organ question. The issue had temporarily split the Manchester Hebrew Congregation in the early 1840s, and played a part in the controversies which led in the mid-1850s to the organization of the independent Reform congregation.[45] As many of the founders of the latter were Anglicized and cultured North Germans,[46] and as organs were already widely used in North German Reform synagogues, the adoption of one in Manchester was in a sense only to be expected. From the 1858 consecration of the new building, an organ was used in weekly Sabbath services. It accompanied the regular choir (as at West London), and was supposed to encourage congregational singing.[47] *How* it accompanied the choir and congregation, and exactly *what* the congregation sang, are apparently not documented.

Whether Manchester organists (James P. Shepley, 1858–60; J. L. Goodwin, 1860–80; I. R. Buckton, 1880–1920)[48] were Christian or Jewish

---

[44] W. Hillsman, 'Trends and aims in Anglican church music 1870–1906 in relation to developments in churchmanship' (Oxford D.Phil. thesis, 1985), pp. 230–6.

[45] Manchester, Central Library, Local Studies Unit, M153/10, 'Correspondence of Mrs. Dorothy Quas-Cohen *re* origin of the [Manchester] Reformed [*sic*] Synagogue [1932–?]', 'Notes on the history and origin of the Reform Synagogue, and hence the origin of the Park Place Synagogue Choir' (1936) [hereafter MCL], p. 1.

[46] P. S. Goldberg, *Manchester Congregation of British Jews 1857–1957: A Short History* (Manchester, 1957), pp. 13, 34; V. D. Lipman, 'The Anglo-Jewish community in Victorian society', in D. Noy and I. Ben-Ami, eds, *Studies in the Cultural Life of the Jews in England = Folklore Research Center Studies*, no. 5 (Jerusalem, 1975), p. 161.

[47] Goldberg, *Manchester Congregation*, pp. 12–13, 26.

[48] MCL, p. 3.

Example One

ĔLO-HĔ-NU SHE-BA-SHA-MÁ-YIM.

MINISTER AND CHOIR ALTERNATE VERSES.
IN CHANT FORM.

HART.

1. Elo – | hēnu shebasha | – māyim shĕ – | māng kolēnu | vĕkabēl |tĕ-fil-la-tē-nu| bĕ ra – | tsōn

From *The Music Used in the Services of the West London Synagogue of British Jews, Principally Composed and Collected and Adapted by Charles Salaman. The Ancient Melodies harmonised and the whole Arranged with Obbligato Organ Accompaniments and Edited by C. G. Verrinder, Mus.Doc.*, 6 vols (London, [1892?]), 4, p. 23.

Example Two

"HALLĔLŪYAH."

C. G. Verrinder.

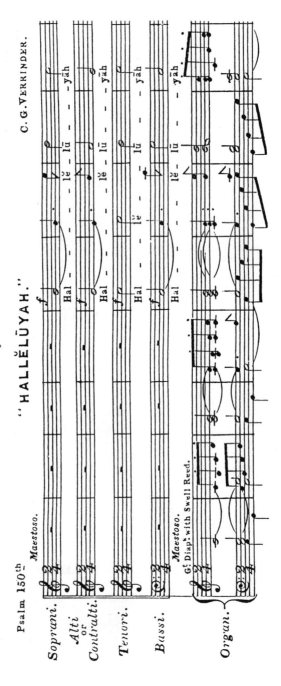

From *The Music Used in ... West London Synagogue ...*, 6 vols (London, [1892?]), 4, p. 111.

must probably remain a mystery. However, it seems unlikely that British Jews at that time would have had such names, and the West London experience of appointing an organist suggests that the Manchester ones were probably Christian.

Organ voluntaries in Manchester seem to have matched those of West London in character. The overture to Handel's *Samson* was played at the 1858 consecration, and the 'Dead March' from *Saul* at the 1901 memorial service for Queen Victoria.[49]

*   *   *

Bradford had a Jewish community of the Reform tradition, organized in 1873 as the Jewish Association of Bradford, and endowed from 1881 with its own synagogue.[50] As this community was heavily Germanic, highly cultured, and (by British standards) very assimilated, one would expect them to have had an organ and to have used it in Sabbath and festival services. Some descriptions of the 1881 consecration do, in fact, use the word 'organ', but one local press report says 'harmonium'.[51] I assume that the instrument from 1881 was actually a harmonium, in view of the latter press report, the opinion of the current Bradford Synagogue Choirmaster, Dr Rudi Leavor (whose family have been associated with that synagogue since 1937), and the apparent absence of any more detailed information, either written or oral.[52] Information on the service use of the harmonium or organ after the consecration is also lacking.

*   *   *

The spread of organs in British synagogues in the first half of the twentieth century was due to the establishment of English Liberal Judaism in 1902 and its subsequent growth (thirteen synagogues in 1950), to the

[49] For *Samson*, see 'Consecration of a synagogue', *Manchester Courier* (27 March 1858), p. 9; for *Saul*, London, University College, Jewish Studies Library, Mocatta Boxed Pamphlets, RP77, *Memorial Service . . . Park Place Synagogue . . . Manchester . . . Queen Victoria* (Cheetham, [1901]), p. 4.

[50] 'Bradford Hebrew Congregation', *JC* (25 March 1881), p. 12.

[51] Lipman, 'Anglo-Jewish community', p. 161; 'Notes of the week. Bradford Congregation', *JC* (16 April 1880), p. 4; 'Consecration of the Jewish Synagogue', *Bradford Daily Telegraph* (30 March 1881), p. 3; 'The new Bradford Synagogue. Consecration ceremony', *Bradford Observer* (30 March 1881), p. 3.

[52] Information from conversations with Rudi Leavor of Bradford (25 Nov. 1991) and Douglas Charing of Leeds (4 Sept. 1991).

growth of Reform Judaism in Britain (also thirteen in 1950), and to the increasing penchant of both Reform and Liberal Judaism for decorum in services and for cultural assimilation in general.[53] By the early 1950s, the Liberal Jewish Synagogue in St John's Wood (the most eminent in the denomination and therefore a model for many others) was including in its services choral music by Arthur Sullivan, Haydn, and Brahms, with organ accompaniment. West London, whose musical practice must have been noted by the newer Reform congregations, was still performing Victorian anthems by Anglican composers, also with organ accompaniment (*when* these anthems came in is apparently undocumented). In general, the use of hymns by Christian authors and composers had become common, for example, 'O God, our help in ages past', and the 'Old Hundredth' (the origins of this practice are also uncertain).[54] Organs were probably standard in all new Liberal and Reform synagogues, even if some of those synagogues could only afford the electronic variety.

Since the 1950s there has been a decline in the use of organs in some (but not all) Reform and Liberal synagogues; West London, Manchester Reform, and the Liberal Jewish Synagogue in St John's Wood still, however, maintain their organ traditions unchanged. Two factors in the decline have been musical. First, a large number of Reform and Liberal synagogues just after the Second World War began installing electronic organs which did not match the relative tonal success of some available today. Some congregants have not grown fonder of their 'early electronics'! Secondly, some congregations have come to feel that the use of an organ impedes their unison singing (*when* Reform congregations began to take their own singing seriously remains unclear).[55] A third, and perhaps even more important factor, has been the general inclination of Reform and Liberal Jews to revert to tradition.[56] As Edward Cross, Organist of the

---

[53] On 1902 and assimilation, see Sharot, 'Reform and Liberal Judaism', pp. 218–19, 222–3; on decorum, Kramer-Mannion, 'Growth and Development', p. 5. Much of the information from this point to the end of the essay is drawn from personal letters to the author from Ena Black of London, 22 Jan. 1992; Edward Cross of Radlett, Hertfordshire, 25 Nov. 1991, enclosing 'Music of the Service [that is, of the Rededication Service of the Liberal Jewish Synagogue, St John's Wood, London, 23 Sept. 1951]'; and Michael Kramer-Mannion of Stockport, 26 Nov. 1991. I am also indebted to the following for verbal information: Sydney Fixman of London, Alexander Knapp of Cambridge, and Michael Kramer-Mannion of Stockport.

[54] Kramer-Mannion, 'Growth and Development', p. 470.

[55] A. Knapp, 'Aspects of Jewish music in contemporary Britain', in A. Buckley *et al.*, eds, *Proceedings of the Second British–Swedish Conference on Musicology: Ethnomusicology, Cambridge, 5–10 August 1989* (Göteborg, 1991), p. 215.

[56] Kramer-Mannion, 'Growth and Development', p. ii.

Hertsmere Progressive Synagogue in Elstree, Hertfordshire, puts it: 'The more radical Victorian religious reformers treated Jewish tradition as guilty unless it could be vindicated intellectually, whereas current thought tends to regard tradition as right unless proved wrong.'[57] As already noted, synagogue tradition before 1800 did not include instrumental music in principal services. The decline of the Anglican and Christian establishment, and therefore the supposed desirability of aping its traditions, has gone hand in hand with the rise of the so-called 'multicultural society'. Jews feel more confident of, and less embarrassed about, their own traditions. The use of Hebrew, for instance, has been increasing in many Reform and Liberal services, and the singing of anthems and hymns by Christian composers has been declining. The parallel decline of organ use in Christian churches has, interestingly, taken place for quite different reasons—namely, the growing use of guitars and instrumental ensembles appropriate for accompanying folk music, and the decline of organists in number.

Although there has been a decline in organ use in some synagogues, the presence or absence of one in Sabbath and festival services still constitutes a very important marker dividing Reform and Liberal synagogues from Orthodox. But whether this will continue to be so must remain an open question.

Faculty of Music,
University of Oxford

---

[57] Cross, letter of 25 Nov. 1991.

IN THE SHADOW OF THE MILLENNIUM: AMERICAN FUNDAMENTALISTS AND THE JEWISH PEOPLE

by YAAKOV ARIEL

IN 1982 Menachem Begin, then Israel's Prime Minister, presented Jerry Falwell, an evangelist and leader of the fundamentalist group 'the Moral Majority', with a medal of the Jabotinsky Order, an organization associated with Begin's Likud Party. Observers both of American religion and Middle East politics could not help but notice the friendship that had developed between the Israeli government and conservative evangelical elements within American Protestantism. The special interest this segment of American Protestantism had in the fate of the Jewish people, and their support for a national Jewish home in the Land of Israel was evident from the early beginnings of the fundamentalist movement and was derived from their interpretation of biblical prophecy regarding the end of history—in which they see a prominent role for the Jewish people.

THE EARLY BEGINNINGS

The eschatological hope to which millions of American fundamentalists adhere is called dispensationalism, a school of Messianic belief which was crystallized in Britain in the 1830s, notably by John Darby, the leader of the Plymouth Brethren.[1] History, he and his followers asserted, is divided into a number of eras, for each of which God has a different plan for humanity. The present era is the penultimate one, to be followed by the millennium—the thousand-year reign of Jesus on earth. Dispensationalists hold that God's plans for the present and future dispensations are recorded in the Bible, and can be deduced from the Sacred Text.

In their understanding of the course of human history, God addresses

---

[1] On dispensationalism see Clarence B. Bass, *Background to Dispensationalism* (Grand Rapids, Michigan, 1960); Arnold D. Ehlert, *A Bibliographic History of Dispensationalism* (Grand Rapids, Michigan, 1965); Dave MacPherson, *The Incredible Cover Up: The True Story of the Pre-Trib Rapture* (Plainfield, New Jersey, 1975); Timothy P. Weber, *Living in the Shadow of the Second Coming* (Grand Rapids, Michigan, 1983). For details of this eschatological hope see, for example, Hal Lindsey's dispensationalist best seller *The Late Great Planet Earth* (Grand Rapids, Michigan, 1971).

three categories of human beings: the Jews, the Church, and the remainder of humanity. The Church refers only to those true believers who have undergone a conversion experience in which they accepted Jesus as their personal Saviour, and intend to live saintly Christian lives. They alone will be saved and spared the turmoils and destruction that will precede the arrival of the Messiah. A particular component of dispensational pre-millennialism is the belief in 'the secret, any-moment, rapture of the Church'. The arrival of Jesus, according to their scheme of history, will take place in two stages. In the first stage, the true believers (including those who have died prior to this time) will be 'raptured' from earth to meet Jesus in the air. They will remain with Jesus in the air for seven years, thus being spared the expected destruction in the end-times: natural disasters such as earthquakes and floods, famine, wars, and murderous dictatorial regimes. It is expected that two-thirds of humanity will perish in the tribulation before Jesus' actual reign on earth begins.

For the Jews, this period will be known as the 'time of Jacob's trouble'. The Jews will return to their ancient homeland 'in unbelief', without accepting Jesus as their Saviour, and will establish a commonwealth there. This would not be the millennial Davidic kingdom, but merely a necessary vehicle in the advancement of the Messianic timetable. The Jews, spiritually blind, will let themselves be ruled by anti-Christ, a Jewish imposter of the Messiah who will be worshipped as God. Anti-Christ is to inflict a reign of terror, during which many who have come to believe in Jesus will be martyred.

The arrival of Jesus and those who were raptured will end anti-Christ's rule and establish the millennial kingdom. Those Jews who survive 'the Great Tribulation' will by then accept Jesus as their Saviour. During the millennium, all nations will live in their lands; with the Jews inhabiting David's ancient kingdom, and Jerusalem will be the world's capital. The Jews will assist Jesus in administering the earth, as well as evangelizing the millennial kingdom, strengthening the knowledge of God among the nations.

Dispensationalism gained ground among American evangelicals following the Civil War (1861–5). Conservative members of major denominations that were shaped by nineteenth-century revivalism, such as Baptists, Presbyterians, Methodists, Congregationalists, and Disciples of Christ accepted the new Messianic hope. The pre-millennialist belief in the Second Coming of Christ in its dispensationalist form became a major component of the emerging fundamentalist movement towards the end of the nineteenth century. Fundamentalists objected to many of the developments that had taken place within American culture and religion. In particular, they opposed the rise of a new 'modernist' trend within American Protestantism, and especially what they regarded as dangerous and destructive teachings, such as higher criticism of the Bible.[2]

Major emphasis was placed on what they considered the fundamentals of their religious tradition: the insistence on the inerrancy and authority of the Bible, the need to undergo a personal conversion experience in order to be saved, and the expected millennium. Pre-millennialism formed the philosophy of history of this group, reflecting their interpretation of the world's situation as well as their understanding of their own position as the faithful remnant within an apostate culture. To this day, it has served to reassure them that they know the course of history and that whatever social, economic, political, or environmental developments take place, they will surely survive the turmoils of the end-times. From the end of the nineteenth century most American evangelists have adopted this stance and promoted it in their sermons.

Although this group stood in opposition to major trends in American culture and aroused at times suspicion and rejection in progressive circles, it should by no means be viewed as a marginal religious sect. By the 1970s to 1980s it had become one of the largest and most influential groups within American society, with direct influence on national leaders.

FUNDAMENTALIST ATTITUDES TOWARDS JEWS, JUDAISM, AND ZIONISM

Pre-millennialists recognize the Jews as the historical Israel, God's Chosen People, for whom he prophesied a restored Davidic kingdom in the Land of Israel, where they are destined for a glorious future in the millennial kingdom. Early pre-millennialists evinced great interest in the fate of the Jewish people, and in the prospect of their restoration to Palestine. They considered themselves friends of the Jews, and their support for the restoration to Palestine led them to refer to themselves as 'Christian Zionists'. One manifestation of their interest in Zionism was initiatives directed towards the restoration of the Jews to Palestine.

One such outstanding initative was that of William Blackstone, a lay Methodist who was converted to dispensationalism while a successful businessman in Chicago in the 1870s. He dedicated himself to evangelism and to the propagation of pre-millennialist belief. His first book, *Jesus is*

---

[2] George Marsden, *Fundamentalism and American Culture* (New York, 1982).

Coming, became a best seller; it was translated into forty-two languages and enjoyed a circulation of over a million and a half copies.[3] In this book, as in others, Blackstone emphasized the centrality of the Jewish people in the events of the End of Age and in the expected kingdom. In 1889 Blackstone visited Palestine, where he was deeply impressed by the developments that the first wave of Zionist immigration had brought about in a country he had considered to be desolate. Agricultural settlements, the new neighbourhoods of Jerusalem, and economic developments were 'signs of the times', he believed, indicating that the great events of the End of Age were to occur very soon.[4]

After returning from the Holy Land, Blackstone in 1891 organized a petition to the President of the United States, urging him to convene an international conference of the world powers that would decide to give Palestine back to the Jews. Four hundred and seventeen eminent Americans signed Blackstone's petition: congressmen, state governors, mayors, publishers and editors of leading newspapers, prominent clergymen, and notable businessmen. The petition reflected warm support among the American public for Jewish restoration to Palestine, but had little effect in causing the American government to take any meaningful action.[5]

Blackstone continued his efforts for many years. He devised a theory that has been a corner-stone of American pre-millennialist attitudes toward Zionism ever since: he asserted that the United States had, on account of its moral superiority, a special role in God's plans for humanity—that of a modern Cyrus—to help restore the Jews to Zion. America, he held, will be judged according to the way in which it carries out its God-given task. Thus American fundamentalists were able to combine their Messianic beliefs and understanding of the course of human history with their sense of American patriotism. Although they were far from happy with many of the developments that had taken place in American civilization, they were loyal citizens. This contrasted with other groups which hold intense Messianic beliefs, such as Jehovah's Witnesses, who became opponents of the American state.

Blackstone was able to bring major Church bodies, such as the Presbyterian Church, USA, to endorse his plan for another American initiative

[3] William E. Blackstone, *Jesus Is Coming*, 1st edn (Chicago, 1878), 2nd edn (Chicago, 1886), 3rd edn (Los Angeles, 1908).

[4] Blackstone, *Jesus Is Coming*, 3rd edn, pp. 211–13, 236–41.

[5] Yaakov Ariel, 'An American initiative for a Jewish State: William Blackstone and the petition of 1891', *Studies in Zionism*, 10 (1989), pp. 125–37.

to establish a Jewish state in Palestine. In 1916 a second petition was presented to the President of the United States. This time Blackstone also co-ordinated his efforts with those of American Zionist leaders such as Louis Brandeis, Steven Wise, and Jacob de Haas. They saw Blackstone's efforts as beneficial to the Zionist cause and maintained a warm relationship with him. Blackstone sent them his published works and expressed his pre-millennialist opinions in his correspondence with them. These Zionist leaders may have been unaware of the actual scope of Blackstone's involvement with attempts to evangelize the Jews. They were certainly unbothered by his prediction that great turmoils were awaiting the Jews in the end-times, or his belief that the Jews will accept Jesus as their Messiah when he arrives to crush anti-Christ and establish his kingdom. For them, what mattered was the support for Zionist aspirations.[6] Such an attitude was to characterize the Zionist, and later on, the Israeli, reaction to fundamentalist support.

The First World War, with its unprecedented killing and destruction, convinced American pre-millennialists that it was part of the events of the End of Age. The Balfour Declaration and the British take-over of Palestine were a further indication that the ground was being prepared for the arrival of the Lord. Their joy over these developments dominated the two 'prophetic conferences' that took place in Philadelphia and New York in 1918.[7]

The 1880s and 1890s saw the emergence of an aggressive evangelical movement in America to spread the Gospel among the Jews. 'Witnessing', from the fundamentalist point of view, derives from their essential good will and love for that people. Among other considerations, evangelicals wished to save some Jews from the turmoils awaiting them at the 'time of Jacob's trouble'. Such evangelism eventually led to 'Messianic Judaism', a movement of Jews who embraced Christianity but wished at the same time to retain their Jewish identity.

Pre-millennialists have voiced opposition to harassment of Jews, and sorrow at the unhappy record of Christian treatment of Jews throughout

[6] Yaakov Ariel, 'William Blackstone and the petition of 1916: a neglected chapter in the history of Christian Zionism in America', *Studies in Contemporary Jewry*, 7 (1991), pp. 68–85.

[7] Arno C. Gaebelein, 'The Capture of Jerusalem and the Great Future of that City', in *Christ and Glory: Addresses Delivered at the New York Prophetic Conferences, Carnegie Hall, November 25–28, 1918*, ed. Arno C. Gaebelein (New York, 1919); Albert E. Thompson, 'The Capture of Jerusalem', in *Light on Prophecy: a Coordinated, Constructive Teaching, Being the Proceedings and Addresses at the Philadelphia Prophetic Conference, May 28–30, 1918*, ed. William L. Pettingill, J. R. Schafter, and J. D. Adams (New York, 1918).

history. But these have not been the only feelings they have had toward Jews. Many have expressed frustration, even anger, at the Jews' refusal to accept Jesus as their Saviour. Traditional Orthodox Judaism is seen as a path of 'judicial blindness'. The Law, they hold, became completely futile after Jesus' sacrifice on the Cross and cannot bring observant Jews salvation. Nevertheless, as long as Jews keep to their old beliefs and ways, waiting for the Messiah, they will be able to fulfil their heroic role in the millennial age.[8] Reform or secular Jews, on the other hand, have turned their backs on their historical mission.[9]

It was because of Jewish refusal to recognize the Messiahship of Jesus, William Blackstone complained, that the kingdom of God on earth did not materialize when Jesus appeared for the first time.[10] Other fundamentalists have not abandoned common prejudices against Jews. One can find in the sermons and writings of many leading evangelists, for example, remarks about Jews that refer to them as shrewd businessmen.[11] Fundamentalists often shared the stereotype of secular Jews as active in various movements of social and political unrest, which in their eyes aimed to undermine Christian civilization.[12]

A sociological survey sponsored by the B'nai B'rith Anti-Defamation League in the early 1960s concluded that members of conservative evangelical churches were more likely to hold prejudices against Jews than members of main-line and liberal ones.[13] A similar survey done in the mid-1980s came out with more positive results.[14] The latter survey represents, no doubt, the intensified preaching on the positive role of Jews in history that American evangelicals have been exposed to since 1967, and the fact that they are now more knowledgeable about the Jews generally.

In all, we see a complex interplay between the expected role of Jews in the end-times, combined with what fundamentalists perceive as the most essential element of all: the acceptance of Jesus as God's Messiah, who alone can bring about God's kingdom on earth. Fundamentalists naturally

---

[8] Arno C. Gaebelein, *The Conflict of the Ages* (New York, 1933), p. 147.
[9] Ibid.
[10] Blackstone, *Jesus Is Coming*, p. 84.
[11] In one of his sermons Jerry Falwell exclaimed that, 'A few of you here today don't like the Jews. And I know why. He can make more money accidentally than you can on purpose': Flo Conway and Jim Siegelman, *Holy Terror* (New York, 1982), p. 168.
[12] For example, Arno C. Gaebelein, 'Aspects of Jewish Power in the United States', *Our Hope*, 29 (1922), p. 103.
[13] Charles Y. Glock and Rodney Stark, *Christian Beliefs and Anti-Semitism* (New York, 1966).
[14] L. Ianniello, 'Release for the Press', Anti-Defamation League, New York, 8 January 1986.

objected to the secular character of Zionism, even though they were enthusiastic about the development and resettlement of Palestine. The Zionists, they complained, were unaware of the true role and significance of their mission. Although Zionism was a blessed tool for carrying out God's plans, it was also, in terms of the perceptions and motivation of the participants, a vainglorious attempt on the part of the Jews to solve 'the Jewish problem' without accepting Christ. Such a secular attempt was, in their view, bound to fail. Jews would attain their physical and national security only when they were ready to recognize the Saviour.[15]

BETWEEN THE WARS

Blackstone's attempts actively to advance the Zionist cause were not pursued by his fellow believers for many years. American fundamentalists did maintain profound interest in the events that were taking place in the life of the Jewish people and in Palestine, interpreting these events in the light of their own distinct eschatological beliefs. Leading journals such as *Our Hope*, *The King's Business*, *The Moody Monthly*, and the Pentecostal *Evangel*, regularly published news on developments affecting the Jews, on the Zionist movement, and on the Jewish community in Palestine. Fundamentalists were encouraged by the new wave of Jewish immigration to Palestine in the early years of the British Mandate. The opening of the Hebrew University of Jerusalem in 1925, and of the new sea port of Haifa in 1932, were well publicized in their journals.[16] Although the dismay they felt for the secular nature of the Zionist movement was evident in their writings, some of their reports on developments in Palestine are reminiscent of those of American Jewish supporters of Zionism from that period. There was sympathy for Jews in their struggles with the British administration and with Arab antagonists. Fundamentalist journals criticized the British for restricting Jewish immigration and settlement, and the Arabs for their hostility toward the Zionist endeavour and for their violence against the Jews. Arab attempts to block the building of the Jewish commonwealth in Palestine were seen as equivalent to putting obstacles in the way of God's plans for the end-times. Such

---

[15] William E. Blackstone, *The Heart of the Jewish Problem* (Chicago, 1905).
[16] For example, George T. B. Davis, *Fulfilled Prophecies that Prove the Bible* (Philadelphia, 1931). Keith L. Brooks, *The Jews and the Passion for Palestine in Light of Prophecy* (Los Angeles, 1937).

attempts were futile, they asserted, and the Arabs would pay dearly for their 'rebellion against God'.[17]

Yet American fundamentalists expressed this protest only on the pages of their own journals. There was no organized effort on their part to combat the British policy on Palestine, no petitioning of the British government to open Palestine to wide-scale Jewish immigration, no appeals to the government of the United States to intervene with the British government to change its policy. One explanation for this passivity may have been that following the Scopes' Trial, in 1925, fundamentalists withdrew from the public arena to a great extent. Their leaders did not see themselves as influential national figures whose voices might be heard by the policy makers in Washington or as people who could advance a political agenda on national or international levels. Such a situation would come into being only in the 1970s.

In the 1930s and 1940s it was main-line and liberal Protestants who organized to help advance the Zionist cause. In 1932, for example, the 'Pro Palestine Federation' was founded, and in 1942 the 'Christian Council on Palestine'. Although liberal Protestantism in general could not be described as supportive in those years of the idea of a Jewish state,[18] thousands of Protestant clergymen did join these organizations, including some prominent liberal figures such as Reinhold Niebuhr and Paul Tillich. These organizations were active throughout the international debates that accompanied the establishment of the State of Israel in 1948. There was no fundamentalist, pro-Zionist organization of similar character at that time.

In another area the passive character of the fundamentalist attitude toward major world developments is exemplified by their reaction to the fate of the Jews under the Nazis. The fundamentalist journal *Our Hope* was among the first to alert its readers to the devastating scope of the destruction of European Jewry.[19] Arno C. Gaebelein, the journal's editor, expressed horror at the German regime's treatment of the Jews. The Nazis' position *vis-à-vis* Jews, he viewed as a rebellion against God, and he predicted the downfall of their regime. Gaebelein took particular offence at Nazi attempts to change basic Christian concepts, such as their 'Aryan-ization' of Jesus.[20] For biblical literalists like Gaebelein, the Nazis' innova-

---

[17] James Gray, 'Editorial', *Moody Bible Institute Monthly*, 31 (1931), p. 346.
[18] See Herzl Fishman, *American Protestantism and a Jewish State* (Detroit, 1973).
[19] David Rausch, 'Our Hope: An American Fundamentalist Journal and the Holocaust, 1937–1945', *Fides et Historia*, 12 (1980), pp. 89–103.
[20] For example *Our Hope*, 44 (1938), p. 686.

tions in Christian thinking and their secular, 'pagan' ideology indicated clearly that their regime was anti-Christian and diabolical. But for all their anger at the Nazis and their sympathy for the persecuted Jews, they did not organize to fight Nazi policy. In addition, many of the central leaders in the fundamentalist camp themselves had complicated reactions to anti-Semitism. Though such well-known figures as Arno C. Gaebelein, William B. Riley, and James Gray reaffirmed in their writings the centrality of the Jewish people in God's plans for humanity, at the same time they accepted the *Protocols of the Elders of Zion* as authentic.[21]

Most fundamentalist involvement with Jews in that period centred on proselytization. Only one organization was founded which dealt directly with the plight of Jewish refugees, aiding European Jews to resettle in America.

A rise in anti-Semitism occurred in America in the inter-war years, and some fundamentalist leaders denounced harassment of Jews, denying the blood-libel accusation and the 'conspiracy' outlined in the *Protocols of the Elders of Zion*. Others were outspoken in their anti-Jewish sentiments. Although no openly anti-Semitic movement arose within the ranks of pre-millennial fundamentalists, there were none the less a few activists who adopted a socially and politically white Protestant, exclusivist, 'nativist' stance. One well-known figure, Gerald L. K. Smith, laboured on the margins of fundamentalism.[22] Another, Gerald Winrod, founder and head of the 'Defenders of the Christian Faith', received more widespread recognition in fundamentalist circles.[23] Charles Fuller, a leading evangelist of the inter-war period, participated in the activities of Winrod's organization.[24]

THE BIRTH OF THE JEWISH STATE

The establishment of the State of Israel in 1948 received passive support from fundamentalists. Journals such as *Our Hope* had published sympathetic articles about the Zionist struggle for a Jewish state, and some individual American statesmen with conservative evangelical leanings

---

[21] Arno C. Gaebelein, 'Jewish Leadership in Russia', *Our Hope*, 27 (1921), pp. 734–5; James M. Gray, 'The Jewish Protocols', *Moody Bible Institute Monthly*, 22 (1921), p. 589; William B. Riley, *Wanted—A World Leader!* (privately published, n.p., n.d.), pp. 41–51, 71–2.

[22] On Gerald L. K. Smith and his activity, see Glen Jeansonne, *Gerald L. K. Smith: Minister of Hate* (New Haven, 1988).

[23] Ralph L. Roy, *Apostles of Discord* (Boston, 1953).

[24] George L. Marsden, *Reforming Fundamentalism* (Grand Rapids, 1988), p. 39.

supported it in the political and diplomatic arena,[25] but no lobby or organization was formed. In the late 1940s fundamentalism was beginning to recover its prestige in American public life. But this segment of American Protestantism was not yet nationally organized around its particular causes.

Unenthusiastic about the secular nature of the State of Israel, pre-millennialists still believed that developments there were cause for hope that the end-times were near.[26] The mass immigration of Jews to Israel in the 1950s from Asian, African, and Eastern European countries was seen as a clear demonstration of the ingathering of the exiles prophesied in the Bible.

Contrary to popular conceptions, fundamentalists did note and show concern for the fate of hundreds of thousands of Palestinian Arabs who lost their homes in 1948, becoming refugees in Arab lands. They had criticized Arab hostility to Israel and supported Israel in its struggles with its neighbours, yet they also held that the Land of Israel could maintain an Arab population alongside its Jewish one, and that Israel has an obligation to respect human rights and treat Arabs with fairness. John Walvoord, President of the Dallas Theological Seminary was one who expressed such ideas.[27] A few conservative evangelical churches, such as the Southern Baptists, the Christian and Missionary Alliance, the Assemblies of God, and the Plymouth Brethren have worked among Palestinian Arabs for years. In striving to reconcile pre-millennialist teachings with the hopes and fears of Arab congregants and potential converts, they strongly emphasized that the ingathering of the Jews in the Land of Israel and the eventual re-establishment of the Davidic kingdom does not necessitate the banishment of Arabs from that land.[28] Ironically, pre-millennialists accepted, in some ways, Martin Buber's concept of a 'land for two peoples'.

The fledgeling Israeli government was unaware of the special attitudes of the conservative evangelical elements within American Christianity

---

[25] Dwight Wilson, *Armageddon Now! The Premillenarian Response to Russia and Israel since 1917* (Grand Rapids, Michigan, 1977).

[26] Louis T. Talbot and William W. Orr, *The New Nation of Israel and the Word of God* (Los Angeles, 1948); M. R. DeHaan, *The Jew and Palestine in Prophecy* (Grand Rapids, 1950); William L. Hull, *The Fall and Rise of Israel* (Grand Rapids, 1954); Arthur Kac, *The Rebirth of the State of Israel: Is it of God or of Men?* (Chicago, 1958); George T. B. Davis, *God's Guiding Hand* (Philadelphia, 1962).

[27] John Walvoord, *Israel in Prophecy* (Grand Rapids, 1962), p. 19.

[28] Based on interviews with members of Arab evangelical pre-millennialist congregations in Israel and the West Bank.

towards the new state. Israeli officials could not tell the difference between liberal or main-line supporters of the country and conservative evangelical ones. They did not grasp the roots and motivations of 'Christian Zionists',[29] and were certainly unaware of the details of dispensationalist eschatological hopes. David Ben-Gurion, Israel's first Prime Minister, for example, was convinced that Christian supporters of Israel recognized in Israel the ultimate fulfilment of biblical prophecies. When addressing an international Pentecostal conference in Israel in 1961, Israeli officials present at the opening session were puzzled by the cool reaction of the Pentecostal participants to the Prime Minister's speech. It did not occur to them that 'Christian Zionists' saw in Israel only a step towards the realization of the millennial kingdom, rather than viewing the new society as the re-establishment of David's kingdom.[30] Certainly the Israeli government in those early days was unaware that Messianic hopes motivated not only support for Zionism and Israel, but also contributed to aggressive missionary activity among the Jews. When Oral Roberts visited Israel in 1959, Ben-Gurion met him, demonstrating a knowledge of Roberts's activity as an evangelist, but he may well have been unaware of his missionary work among the Jews.[31] At any rate, secular Israeli leaders did not take seriously the activities of Christian missionaries. Conversions to Christianity were thought to be motivated by socio-economic considerations, spiritual persuasion having little to do with it, and missionary efforts were considered to be futile for the most part, anyway.[32] The government of Israel tried to build good relations with Christian groups and thought it essential to assure them that their work would not be interfered with.

Evangelical missionaries were more than mere proselytizers of Jews, however: through their books, journal articles, broadcasting, and lecture tours, they presented Israel and its problems to evangelical circles world-wide.[33] Orthodox Jewish political parties and other activists protested against missionary work in Israel, and some Orthodox Jews occasionally

---

[29] A striking example is Michael Pragai's book *Faith and Fulfilment* (London, 1985). The author, who served as the head of the department for liaison with the Christian churches and organizations in the Israeli Foreign Office for many years, demonstrates a complete lack of knowledge of the nature of the fundamentalist support of Zionism and of the differences between fundamentalist and main-line or liberal churches.

[30] Yona Malachy, *American Fundamentalism and Israel* (Jerusalem, 1978), pp. 106–11.

[31] Oral Roberts, 'The Spell of Israel Over Me', *Abundant Life* (July 1959); David E. Harrel, *Oral Roberts: An American Life* (Bloomington, Indiana, 1985), p. 137.

[32] For example, David Eichhorn, *Evangelizing the American Jew* (New York, 1978).

[33] See, for example, Robert L. Lindsey, *Israel in Christendom* (Tel-Aviv, 1961).

harassed missions, but the government refused to change its policy, and the police were given the task of preventing interference with missionary work.[34]

THE SIX-DAY WAR AND BEYOND

The Six-day War probably affected American fundamentalist attitudes toward Israel and their perception of history more profoundly than had the birth of Israel in 1948. Since the French Revolution and the Napoleonic wars in the late eighteenth and early nineteenth centuries, there has probably not been a political–military event that has provided so much fuel for the engine of prophecy as this war between Israel and its neighbours in June 1967 which led to the reunification of Jerusalem. The unexpected Israeli victory, and the territorial gains it brought with it, strengthened the pre-millennialists' conviction that Israel was created for an important role in the process that would precede the arrival of the Messiah.[35]

After the war it became clear to those waiting for the Second Coming that Israel now held the territory on which the Temple could be rebuilt and the priestly sacrifices reinstated.[36] Indeed, many expected the imminent restoration of the Temple as part of the events of the end-times. One such believer, who decided to give God a hand, was Dennis Rohan, a young Australian who had joined the Church of God. After spending some time as a volunteer at an Israeli kibbutz, Rohan visited Jerusalem in July 1969. Convinced that God had designated him for the task, he set fire to the Al-Aksa Mosque, on the Temple Mount, in an attempt to secure the necessary ground for the building of the Temple.[37] The mosque was damaged, leading to Arab riots. Rohan was arrested, tried, and declared insane. He was returned to Australia to spend the rest of his life there in an asylum. It was an important lesson for Christians devoted to understanding biblical prophecy: an open promotion of the idea that the Jews should begin rebuilding the Temple would only serve to provoke Arab hostility, embarrass the State of Israel, and harm the fundamentalist image. Although many American fundamentalists were happy

---

[34] Per Osterlye, *The Church in Israel* (Lund, 1970).
[35] For example, L. Nelson Bell, 'Unfolding Destiny', *Christianity Today*, 9 (1967), pp. 1044–5.
[36] Raymond L. Cox, 'Time for the Temple?' *Eternity*, 19 (Jan. 1968), pp. 17–18; Malcolm Couch, 'When will the Jews rebuild the Temple?' *Moody Monthly*, 74 (Dec. 1973), pp. 34–5, 86.
[37] Jerusalem District Court Archive, Criminal File 69/173, pp. 503, 1206.

to discover that Jewish groups were preparing themselves for the time when the Temple ritual would be reinstated, few organizations openly advocated the rebuilding of the holy Jewish shrine. One organization with which many fundamentalists have had contact, however, is the Temple Mount Foundation, founded by Stanley Goldfoot. He was invited to lecture at Calvary Chapel, in Costa Mesa, California, the church of noted evangelist Chuck Smith, who secured financial support for exploration of the exact site of the Temple. One of the many researchers on this question has been Lambert Dolphin, a physicist from California with the group Science and Archaeology team. Using sophisticated technology, they concluded that the Temple's real location had been between the two major Muslim shrines, the Al-Aksa Mosque and the Dome of the Rock, thus the Temple could be rebuilt without destroying either of these—providing a 'peaceful solution' to the problem of building the Jewish Temple on a site holy to the Muslims.[38]

Continuing Arab hostility toward Israel and a perception that the Muslims were standing in the way of restoring the Temple were factors which helped enhance a more negative attitude towards Islam. Fundamentalists have not taken the liberal road of inter-faith dialogue, and Islam is often regarded as a superstitious, apostate faith.[39] A more recent change in their attitudes towards Muslims and Islamic countries stems from the radical social and political changes occurring in the Soviet Union and Eastern European countries in the last few years. As these countries allowed more freedom for the churches, fundamentalists were no longer certain that Russia represented the evil empire poised to initiate the final battle of Armageddon of which the prophecies spoke. In 1990–1, as events led up to the Gulf War, some fundamentalists believed that Saddam Hussein and Iraq were meant to fulfil that function.[40]

During the 1970s and 1980s Arab and pro-Arab antagonists of Israel have tried to counter fundamentalist support for Israel. They have warned against what they consider to be the potential dangers of the fundamentalist attitude; asserting that American fundamentalists could be expected to endorse giving to Israel any military and economic support it asked for, and that in case of a conflict between America and Israel, fundamentalists would stand by Israel.[41]

[38] Yisrayl Hawkins, *A Peaceful Solution to Building the Next Temple in Yerusalem* (Abilene, Texas, 1989).
[39] Peter A. Michas, *What is Islam* (Poway, California, n.d.).
[40] John Elson, 'Apocalypse Now?' *Time* (11 Feb. 1991), p. 64.
[41] For example, Davey M. Beegle, *Prophecy and Prediction* (Michigan, 1978); Hassan Haddad and

During the 1970s and 1980s fundamentalists were among Israel's strongest supporters in the American public arena.[42] They have involved themselves in Jewish issues such as the demand to facilitate Jewish emigration from the Soviet Union. Economic aid, arms, and diplomatic backing for Israel were seen as going hand in hand with American interests, for the most part. However, when support for Israel was seen to be contrary to American interests, they have been more reluctant to advance what Israel sees as its needs. A prominent example of this was the decision of the American government to sell sophisticated AWACS intelligence planes to Saudi Arabia in 1981. The Israeli lobby (AIPAC) in Washington attempted to block the deal. In this case, stalwart evangelical supporters of Israel accepted the American government's position: that the acquisition of the planes by Saudi Arabia would not undermine Israel's security, and that the sale was essential for maintaining good relations with Saudi Arabia.

The years following the 1967 Middle East War saw a dramatic increase in membership in fundamentalist churches, and a rising self-confidence. In the stormy 1960s many Americans had viewed fundamentalist churches as anachronistic, marginal, and irrelevant to general cultural trends. When Jimmy Carter was elected president in 1976, it surprised many to discover that evangelicalism was alive and well, that it had grown in influence as well as in numbers. Carter, however, proved a disappointment; he was not a pre-millennialist and did not promote specifically evangelical issues. He brought Israel and Egypt together to sign a peace treaty, but in doing so he was acting as an American statesman, not necessarily as an evangelical Christian. The Messianic hope of paving the way for the David kingdom was not his concern.

Was Ronald Reagan influenced in his Middle East policy by the pre-millennialist understanding of the course of history? Reagan did make a few remarks which made people speculate whether he held to fundamentalist Messianic convictions, but such remarks may well have been written into speeches by his advisers in an attempt to draw fundamentalist support.[43] Reagan's policy toward Israel could be summarized on the

---

Donald Wagner, eds, *All in the Name of the Bible — PHRC Special Report*, no. 5 (Chicago, 1985); Grace Halsell, *Prophecy and Politics: Militant Evangelicals on the Road to Nuclear War* (Westport, Connecticut, 1980).

[42] Cf. Peter L. Williams and Peter L. Benson, *Religion on Capital Hill: Myth and Realities* (New York, 1986); Allen D. Hertzke, *Representing God in Washington* (Knoxville, Tennessee, 1988); Mark Silk, *Spiritual Politics* (New York, 1989).

[43] For example, Martin Gardner, 'Giving God a Hand', *The New York Review of Books* (13 Aug. 1987), p. 22.

whole as having been extremely friendly, but he made no explicit remarks regarding Israel which had pre-millennialist overtones.

Dozens of pro-Israel fundamentalist organizations emerged in the United States in the 1970s and 1980s. They mustered political support for Israel among evangelicals, organized lectures, distributed information about Israel and its historical role, and organized tours to the Holy Land. One such was The Friends of Israel Gospel Ministry in Bellmaur, New Jersey, headed by Elwood McQuaid, a prolific writer on Jewish topics.[44] Another was the Washington-based American Christian Trust. Project Kibbutz, organized by Oral Roberts University, conducted field-study seminars and sent volunteers to work in Israel. Institutions of higher education were set up in Israel, such as the Holy Land Institute, established by Douglas Young, President of Trinity Divinity School, in Direfield, Illinois. And, of course, evangelization in Israel continued.

In 1981, when the Knesset, Israel's parliament, passed the Jerusalem Law making that city the political capital of the country, many states closed their consulates in Jerusalem. A group of European and American fundamentalists then established the International Christian Embassy there. This institution, composed of charismatic pre-millennialists, became the largest 'Christian Zionist' establishment. Besides holding lectures and distributing information about Israel and its role in history, the 'embassy' organizes groups of visitors to the country and collects money for various Israeli enterprises, such as the absorption of Russian immigrants.

The Israeli government took more notice of the evangelicals in America and their growing influence in the 1970s.[45] Prime Minister Menachem Begin appointed a special liaison for American evangelicals, Harry Horowitz. Israeli officials spoke at fundamentalist conferences, and evangelists met Israeli leaders as part of their touring schedules in Israel. Following the Israeli bombing of the Iraqi nuclear plant in 1981, Menachem Begin called Jerry Falwell, asking him to back Israel on this issue. He was scheduled to speak at Criswell's First Baptist Church in Dallas, Texas, but had to cancel his speech on account of his wife's death and return to Israel.

Despite these many contacts, the Israeli leadership has often shown ignorance of the real motivation and nature of fundamentalist friendship.

[44] For example, Elwood McQuaid, *It Is No Dream* (Bellmaur, New Jersey, 1978).
[45] 'Israel Looks on U.S. Evangelical Christians as Potent Allies', *Washington Post* (23 March 1981), A11.

On one occasion Begin exclaimed that 'the Christians in America supported Israel', and it was obvious from his words that he did not realize that pre-millennialist evangelicals were but one segment of American Christianity. This lack of understanding is illustrated in the government's reaction to evangelization. One of the Begin government's earliest acts of legislation was intended to restrict missionary activity by outlawing the 'buying' of converts through economic incentives. This legislation proved to be futile, for it was based on the Jewish myth that Christians 'buy' Jews' souls. Evangelicals were relieved to find that the law clearly would not affect their work. The Begin coalition had tried to terminate evangelization of Jews in Israel without realizing that this activity was carried out by the same elements in Christianity with whom it was also trying to establish friendly relations.

Intensive involvement and interest in the life of the Jewish people has continued for more than a century. Fundamentalists have continually interpreted events as 'signs of the times', indications that the End of Age is near, when Jesus will return in glory to establish God's kingdom. Their fascination with Zionism has, it seems, given them more than they have actually given the State of Israel. The Zionist self-perception has not been much influenced by fundamentalist interest, or by contacts with evangelicals. Most of the time, Jews have little noticed them. Fundamentalists would have had to rewrite almost their entire literature, theological and popular, if they had not seen in the history of Zionism so many 'signs' to point to as proofs that they had read the Scriptures correctly and that history is proceeding according to plan.

Will the American public continue to witness an intensive fundamentalist interest in Israel, its development seen as a preparation for the imminent events of the end-times? This naturally will depend upon both the centrality of the Messianic belief to the world view of this segment of Christianity, as well as on the continued secure existence of the Jewish state.

The Institute of Contemporary Jewry,
The Hebrew University of Jerusalem

JAMES PARKES, THE JEWS, AND CONVERSIONISM: A MODEL FOR MULTI-CULTURAL BRITAIN?

by TONY KUSHNER

B RITISH historians and others have been slow to recognize the tradition of immigration and ethnic, religious, and racial diversity that has marked the British experience in the modern era. The multi-cultural nature of British society today is harder to ignore, with black groups alone representing over 5 per cent of the total population.[1] Yet the implications of such diversity both in the past and in the present have not been properly acknowledged by academics, politicians, or society as a whole. Coloured immigration, following that of the Jews from Eastern and Central Europe, has tended to be viewed only in problematic terms—such newcomers are seen to bring with them the potential for racial strife. Immigration control—from the turn of the century to the present day—has been consistently justified by politicians, commentators, and agitators on the grounds that it will *improve* race relations in this country.[2] Of equal significance have been the limitations of those opposed to racism and the control of entry. Support of immigrants and minorities has been generally limited to attacks on racism. In the process, issues concerning pluralism and the need to accept diversity have been relatively ignored. Such tendencies within anti-racism reflect the domination of assimilationist assumptions with regard to minorities. This has been particularly the case with the left-liberal world which has been dominant in the campaign against racism in the twentieth century. It is thus not surprising that the Rushdie affair caused enormous shock in Britain amongst those who assumed that religion no longer mattered in this country. It was, in the words of Fay Weldon, 'like a tidal wave' removing what was left of liberal illusions concerning race relations.[3]

The Rushdie affair illustrated most clearly that, in our supposed secular society, anger could still be generated on all sides by the expression

---

[1] See C. Holmes, *John Bull's Island: Immigration and British Society, 1871–1971* (London, 1988) for the first major attempt to synthesize minority studies into British history.

[2] P. Foot, *Immigration and Race in British Politics* (Harmondsworth, 1965).

[3] For the limitations of anti-racism see P. Gilroy, *There Ain't No Black in the Union Jack: the Cultural Politics of Race and Nation* (London, 1987); F. Weldon, *Sacred Cows* (London, 1989), p. 4.

and persistence of faith—a fact that Rabbi Jonathan Sacks so brilliantly emphasized in the Reith Lectures.[4] The various Muslim groups did not demonstrate against *The Satanic Verses* simply for religious reasons—their anger was also part of a general alienation from a society which promised conditional acceptance but in reality offered rejection in the form of violence and discrimination. Similarly, those who have attacked the Muslim campaigners (whether in print or on the streets) have not just been animated by anti-Islamic sentiment. Nevertheless, at the heart of the Rushdie affair was religion and the place of faith in modern British society. In particular, the affair exposed the limitations of those who had formerly portrayed themselves as allies of 'black' groups in Britain. As Tariq Modood suggests, 'No minority in the context of British race relations has been as friendless as Muslims in spring 1989.' Muslims as an under-class or as victims of racism may have appealed to Socialists and Liberals. Yet when it came to Muslims as aggressive campaigners for equality under the blasphemy laws and other issues which concerned culture and religion rather than race and class, their former supporters were either silent or to be found in the opposition.[5] No one revealed the tensions more clearly than the individualist Fay Weldon, who post-Rushdie commented that 'Our attempt at multi-culturalism has failed.' Weldon, as an alternative, wrote in support of what she naïvely labels 'the uni-culturalist policy of the United States ... welding its new peoples, from every race, every nation, every belief, into a whole'. Weldon's solution in the light of the Rushdie affair was simple—to follow America, where 'in the school the one flag is saluted, the one God worshipped, the one nation acknowledged.' Weldon the Liberal was, in fact, echoing what the Conservative Home Secretary had already told Muslims in this country in blunter terms; 'Be British ... respect *our* laws and customs.' All this, of course, predicted Norman Tebbit's comments with regard to the cricket test and minorities.[6]

The idea, then, in late twentieth-century Britain, that Muslims should have equality of treatment with Christianity in law; that they should have an equal right to state funding of their schools as do Christians and Jews, and that they can have the right to protest about the protection of their religion (in a manner which itself had a long British tradition), has been

---

[4] Jonathan Sacks, *The Persistence of Faith* (London, 1991).

[5] T. Madood, 'British Asian Muslims and the Rushdie Affair', *Political Quarterly*, 61 (April–June 1990), p. 143; M. Ruthven, *A Satanic Affair* (London, 1990) for a general overview.

[6] Weldon, *Sacred Cows*, p. 32; Douglas Hurd quoted by the *Daily Mail*, 24 Feb. 1989; for Tebbit see M. Ignatieff, 'Britain's Dracula Draws Blood', *Observer*, 16 Sept. 1990.

proved to be unacceptable to the vast majority of British society. The Rushdie affair showed that the rejection of cultural and religious equality was not just a problem for conservative elements in Britain, but was also difficult for liberals and radicals to accept—groups which had previously supported anti-racist and multi-cultural initiatives. The relative failure of British society in the late 1980s and early 1990s to adjust to the sensitivities of its religious minorities makes the achievements of James Parkes *half a century earlier* all the more remarkable. Who was James Parkes, and how does his career relate to contemporary issues such as the Rushdie affair?

The Revd Dr James Parkes was born in Guernsey in 1896 and died in England in 1981. Writing in 1969, towards the end of Parkes's active career, Alan Davies described him as 'a dedicated and courageous foe of anti-semitism ... before, as well as after Auschwitz—and, in some respects, close to a lonely crusader in the Christian world.'[7] Parkes survived the trenches of the First World War, yet retained a faith in radical liberalism both in politics and religion. From Oxford University he worked for the Student Christian Movement and came under the influence and encouragement of the Bishop of Manchester, William Temple, who was developing the idea of Christian social ethics. In the 1920s Temple helped Parkes achieve his ordination as an Anglican clergyman, but also supported Parkes in his researches and work in Christian–Jewish relations. In 1928 Parkes moved to Geneva to run the International Student Service, and from then on his life was totally dominated by the study and solution of the problem of anti-Semitism.[8]

Parkes soon discovered that racism and rampant nationalism were creating immense problems for Jewish students on European campuses. In the late 1920s and early 1930s he spent much time on a practical level helping individual Jews to leave the Continent. He also started his researches into the roots of anti-Semitism, which Parkes soon decided rested with the Christian Church in the medieval period. To connect Christianity with the existence and causes of medieval anti-Semitism today is unremarkable. Scholars dispute how far religious anti-Judaism has influenced modern forms of hostility towards Jews, but that the Church was, in Bob Moore's terminology, the basis of a 'persecuting

[7] A. Davies, *Anti-Semitism and the Christian Mind* (New York, 1969), p. 142.
[8] J. Parkes, *Voyage of Discoveries* (London, 1969), chs 1–6; see also R. Everett, 'James Parkes: Historian and Theologian of Jewish–Christian Relations' (Columbia Ph.D. thesis, 1983). For Temple see A. Suggate, *William Temple and Christian Social Ethics Today* (Edinburgh, 1987).

society' in the medieval period is now scholarly orthodoxy.[9] This was not the case, it must be stressed, in the early 1930s, when Parkes's work was first published in the United Kingdom and the United States. A few scholars, such as George Foot Moore and Travers Hertford, had examined the historical roots of the relationships between Jews and Christians. Their work had only a limited impact, however, and essentially the Christian view of anti-Semitism in the 1930s remained that it was due to Jewish behaviour or was a punishment for the rejection and killing of Jesus. Such an interpretation was dominant even in the United Kingdom—a country with a theology which, as Alan Wilkinson has argued, was dominated by liberalism in the inter-war period. As Parkes soon found out, to suggest that anti-Semitism was 'a problem for the Gentiles', and 'To evolve a new attitude to Jewish–Christian relations was to [embark upon] a lonely job.'[10]

With the Nazi rise to power and the escalating persecution of the Jews, Parkes's work was to grow in importance and urgency and he became less isolated in Britain in his battle against anti-Semitism. In other areas, how-ever, and particularly in his work on Jewish–Christian relations, Parkes remained as isolated in 1945 as he was in 1933. It is only by considering together the two aspects of James Parkes's work—that of helping the Jews of Europe, but also in reaching for a new understanding from Christians towards Jews—that the radicalism and forward-looking nature of his position in the Nazi era can be properly assessed.

Analysing a cross-section of the Christian press on a local and national level in the 1930s, Alan Wilkinson has concluded that 'Anti-semitic attitudes were among the stock responses of many Christians, as among the general population in Britain.' Richard Gutteridge has provided an alternative analysis, pointing to the 'by and large . . . good record of the Churches in England during the Hitler period' with regard to the persecu-tion of the Jews. The two interpretations are not necessarily incompatible. Wilkinson himself refers to Christians in Britain who disliked Jews, but 'when it came to the crunch . . . condemn[ed] the Nazi persecution of the

---

[9] Parkes, *Voyage of Discoveries*, ch. 6; R. Moore, *The Formation of a Persecuting Society: Power and Deviance in Western Europe, 950–1250* (Oxford, 1987).

[10] For Moore and Hertford see J. Parkes, *The Way Forward* (Southampton, 1969), p. 5; A. Wilkinson, *Dissent or Conform? War, Peace and the English Churches 1900–1945* (London, 1986); J. Parkes, *A Problem for the Gentiles* (London, 1945) and *Voyage of Discoveries*, p. 117. His early publications included *The Jew and His Neighbour* (London, 1930) and *The Conflict of the Church and the Synagogue* (London, 1934).

Jews.'[11] Nevertheless, there is a great deal of evidence concerning Christians in Britain who continued to blame Jews for the existence of anti-Semitism throughout the 1930s and even during the War itself. In 1939 Mass-Observation, a British social survey organization, carried out a detailed investigation into anti-Semitism. In terms of anti-Semitism, Mass-Observation discovered widespread belief in the idea that 'The Jews really bring it all on themelves', or, as one Christian bluntly stated: 'The Jews crucified Christ. They are now suffering for their actions.'[12]

Extremist anti-Semitism in Britain certainly owed much to religious antipathy towards Jews. Nevertheless, what is of greater significance is how major church figures, such as Arthur Headlam, Bishop of Gloucester and Chairman of the Church of England Council on Foreign Relations throughout the Nazi era, crudely blamed Jewish behaviour for the existence of Nazi anti-Semitism. 'They are not', he wrote in 1933, 'altogether a pleasant element in German ... life.' Headlam focused particularly on Communist and Socialist Jews, whom he blamed for Europe's post-war problems—an anti-Semitic argument he shared with many mainstream Catholic papers at that time.[13] The obsession with the alleged Jewish Socialist peril led many Christian pacifist and Catholic groups in Britain to fail to recognize the full implications of what was happening to the Jews. Claims that atrocity stories were part of a left-wing Jewish plot were an unpleasant (but persistent) aspect of the Christian response in Britain, especially during the War.[14]

It would be misleading, however, to indicate that this was the only Christian response from 1933 to 1945. A series of important church leaders, including William Temple (who had progressed to the Archbishopric of York and then became the Archbishop of Canterbury in 1942) made public protests about the treatment of the Jews. Similarly, Hensley Henson, Bishop of Durham, was appalled by Nazi brutality towards Jews and disgusted by the forms of Nazi apologia offered by

---

[11] Wilkinson, *Dissent or Conform?* pp. 143, 98; R. Gutteridge, 'The Churches and the Jews in England, 1933–1945', in O. Kulka and P. Mendes-Flohr, eds, *Judaism and Christianity under the Impact of National Socialism, 1919–1945* (Jerusalem, 1987), p. 353.

[12] T. Kushner, 'Ambivalence or Antisemitism?: Christian attitudes and responses in Britain to the crisis of European Jewry during the Second World War', *Holocaust and Genocide Studies*, 5 (1990), pp. 175–89; Brighton, University of Sussex, Mass-Observation Archive DR 1182, June 1939, and FR A12.

[13] Headlam, 1933, quoted by Wilkinson, *Dissent or Conform?* p. 148. Papers such as the *Catholic Herald* followed a similar line.

[14] Kushner, 'Ambivalence or Antisemitism?' pp. 178–9.

Arthur Headlam. Bishop Bell of Chichester and the Catholic Archbishop of Westminster, Cardinal Hinsley, amongst others, were all vocal and unambiguous in their attacks on the persecution of the Jews.[15] Moreover, the anti-religious and persecuting aspects of Nazism provided a forum through which Jews and Christians in Britain could unite in common protest. The refugee movement, in particular, provided an ideal forum for Jews and Christians to work together in pursuit of a single, unifying cause. The work of Bishop Bell in rescuing non-Aryan Christian refugees provided a particularly close linkage. In this sense, Parkes became a less eccentric and isolated figure in the 1930s.[16] Nevertheless, despite the progress made through refugee work, Jews still largely remained outside the growing ecumenical movement of the 1930s. An informal group exploring Christian–Jewish relations—consisting of Parkes and his close ally W. W. Simpson, and the Archbishops of Canterbury, York, and Westminster—had been created by 1939, but attempts to transform this network into a formal group failed at the start of the War. Parkes wished for a powerful joint organization which could act as a strong protest group on behalf of the persecuted Jews. Yet Simpson, summarizing the Christian response as late as July 1941, could write to Parkes that 'When one thinks of Hitler's anti-Jewish acts . . . the sum total of all that everybody has tried to do in this country so far seems very small indeed.'[17]

By 1942 the evidence of atrocities committed by the Nazis provided the final stimulus needed for the group Parkes had been demanding, and the Council of Christians and Jews (CCJ) came into being. It is significant, however, that the common experience of both religions in facing persecution was stressed by the new organization. Thus in its second meeting, the CCJ 'place[d] on record its increasing concern at the Nazi treatment of the Christian Church and the Jewish community in Germany and German-occupied territories'.[18] The prominent Christians involved in the CCJ had little difficulty in condemning Nazi anti-Semitism, but they were still

[15] F. Iremonger, *William Temple* (Oxford, 1948), pp. 565–7; H. Henson, *Retrospect of an Unimportant Life*, 1 1920–1939 (Oxford, 1943), pp. 376, 413–14; R. Jasper, *George Bell* (London, 1967), pp. 136–7, 145, 156–9; T. Moloney, *Westminster, Whitehall and the Vatican: the Role of Cardinal Hinsley, 1935–43* (Tunbridge Wells, 1985), ch. 11.

[16] R. Gutteridge, 'Some Christian Responses in Britain to the Jewish Catastrophe, 1933–1945', in Y. Bauer *et al.*, eds, *Remembering for the Future: Jews and Christians During and After the Holocaust*, 1 (Oxford, 1989), pp. 352–62.

[17] London, Board of Deputies of British Jews Archive, B5/4/3 Dean of St Paul's, proposal on Jewish–Christian co-operation; Southampton, University Archive, Parkes papers 16/715, Simpson to Parkes, 15 July 1941.

[18] Southampton, University Archive, CCJ papers, Executive minutes, 13 April 1942.

reluctant to accept the clear message of James Parkes—that Christianity was also responsible for the Jewish catastrophe. Ultimately, the CCJ spent little time in protesting about the *specifically* Jewish tragedy in the War. Its universalist leanings led to a reluctance to deal with the particular problems faced by the Jews. Indeed, its historian has recently suggested that William Temple, who was the CCJ chairman until his untimely death in 1944, 'was anxious to avoid specific mention of antisemitism. He saw it and the war itself as symptomatic of an even deeper evil and crisis.' Parkes was similarly concerned about larger issues and wrote about them through his pseudonym, John Hadham.[19] Yet he was also aware that something unique was occurring during the War—the destruction of a whole people and their culture and history. To Parkes the Jews were not just a persecuted group following an outmoded creed; they were practitioners of a valid and living religion. Yet if Parkes's views on the origins and implications of anti-Semitism set him off from most other church figures in Britain, then his views on how the Jews should be regarded by Christians placed him firmly in a category on his own.

Just before the outbreak of war Parkes, in a sermon at Oxford University, had stated:

> We have failed to convert the Jews, and we shall always fail, because it is not the will of God that they shall become Gentile Christians; antisemitism has failed to destroy the Jews, because it is not the will of God that essential parts of His Revelation should perish. Our immediate duty to the Jew is to do all in our power to make the world safe for him to be a Jew.[20]

Parkes was aware of the deep hurt caused to Jews by Christians who assisted Jews in the growing anti-Semitic atmosphere of Europe, yet ultimately sought to convert the people they were 'helping'. Organizations such as the International Missionary Council's Christian Approach to the Jew and, in Britain, the Church of England's Church Mission to Jews (later the Church Ministry Among the Jews) were, in Parkes's view, a major obstacle in the way of any dialogue based on equality. They created on the Jewish side justified suspicion of any Christian interest. Parkes also believed that missions intensified the Christian

---

[19] See M. Braybrooke, *Children of One God: a History of the Council of Christians and Jews* (London, 1991), p. 11; John Hadham, *Good God* (Harmondsworth, 1940).
[20] Southampton, University Archive, Parkes papers, 17/10/1.

tendency to dismiss the Jewish religion as lacking any validity.[21] In 1942 Parkes believed that the election of William Temple as Archbishop of Canterbury provided an opportunity for a new approach to develop. Parkes, as we have seen, had always enjoyed Temple's support in his work on Christian–Jewish relations. He thus wrote to the Archbishop Elect pointing out that due to

> the natural consequence of your new office . . . you will be asked to be Patron of the Church Mission to Jews, and I wonder whether it is possible for you to take a stand about the adoption of an official missionary attitude to Judaism by refusing our patronage? . . . I believe that the time is ripe for a 'show down', and it might have invaluable repercussions at this juncture.

Temple wrote back to Parkes in clear terms:

> I do not think I could interpret my interest in promoting Christian–Jewish friendship as in any way precluding an equal interest in attempting to convert Jews, because that does appear to me to be a Christian obligation; and if I had to choose it would take precedence of the other. On the other hand I have no doubt that the methods of our approach to Jews are very often extremely gauche, and there is obviously need in that case . . . of even greater tact than is called for in other efforts to convert—and one must try to do something in that direction.

Shortly after Temple sent a message to the Church Mission to Jews—supporting friendship and help to the Jews but ultimately praising their missionary work.[22]

By the time of the formation of the CCJ only limited progress had been made in achieving Parkes's objectives of treating the Jews as equals. William Paton, the leading force in the International Christian Council on the Approach to the Jews, was excluded from membership so as not to alienate the Jewish representatives. This had been essential as the Chief Rabbi had already resigned from the CCJ as he feared it could become a 'Society for Spiritual Inter-Marriage between Christians and Jews'. Temple's diplomacy had been required to get the Chief Rabbi and then

[21] Parkes, *Voyage of Discoveries*, pp. 116–17 and 'A Christian looks at the Christian Mission to the Jews', *Theology*, 292 (Oct. 1944), pp. 218–21.
[22] Southampton, University Archive, Parkes papers, 17/10/2, Parkes to Temple, 16 April 1942, and Temple to Parkes, 19 April 1942; Temple in *English Churchman*, 15 Oct. 1942.

the Catholic representatives to rejoin. Nevertheless, even the liberal-minded Temple stopped well short of the mutual recognition between Christianity and Judaism demanded by Parkes and Simpson.[23]

After the War the Christian response to the new situation was slow. Marcus Braybrooke has suggested that

> Whilst many continental European and American theologians are grappling with Holocaust theology, its impact seems to have been far less on British theologians. This gives the impression that there is a reluctance both to take seriously enough the pervasive anti-Jewishness of Christian teaching and to face the deep questions to faith posed by the Shoah.

Braybrooke has also commented that, even within the CCJ, in the first decades after Auschwitz there was a reluctance to confront the Holocaust.[24] Within its growing (although still limited) membership, however, the Simpson–Parkes view became more dominant. Yet the official Church of England policy on the Jews remained that of the Church Mission. In 1947, in response to a genuine Jewish–Christian dialogue service, *Jewish Missionary News* commented that such an event had given the dangerous 'impression that Judaism and Christianity are equally valid and effective ways of communion with God'. The paper of the Church Mission to the Jews concluded that Christians had to avoid giving the impression that 'Judaism is good enough for the Jews.'[25]

From the 1960s slow progress was made in acknowledging the Church's role in the creation of anti-Jewish prejudice and also in accepting Judaism as a living religion. This culminated, in terms of the Church of England, in the 1988 Lambeth Conference which called for genuine dialogue between Jews and Christians—one which 'demands that each partner brings to it the fullness of themselves and the tradition in which they stand.' The document which came out of the conference also acknowledged that Church anti-Judaism had allowed 'the evil weed of Nazism . . . to take root and spread its poison.'[26]

Has, then, the position of James Parkes now been accepted, albeit a half century later? In many ways the Lambeth document owes much to

---

[23] E. Jackson, *Red Tape and the Gospel: a Study of William Paton (1886–1943)* (Birmingham, 1980), pp. 283–4; London, Greater London Record Office, papers of the Chief Rabbinate 2805/124, Hertz to Temple, 7 July 1942, and Braybooke, *Children of One God*, pp. 15–17.

[24] M. Braybrooke, *Time to Meet* (London, 1990), p. 114, and *Children of One God*, p. 52.

[25] *Jewish Missionary News*, 38 (Sept. 1947), p. 12.

[26] See Braybrooke, *Time to Meet*, pp. 29–32 for the Lambeth document.

Parkes's influence, yet it is, as Braybrooke suggests, a watered-down version of the original draft. On conversionism 'aggressive and manipulative' approaches are rejected, but this echoes the approach of Temple in 1942. It is significant that at the time of the Lambeth Conference, the Archbishop of Canterbury, Robert Runcie, refused to resign as patron of the Church Ministry Among the Jews, which itself has supported aggressive conversionist groups such as 'Jews for Jesus'.[27] George Carey, as successor to Runcie, has asked how 'may we, with our deep attachment to Jesus Christ, share him with others, particularly the Jewish community?' Carey has revealed his dislike of 'the "targeting" of Jews for conversion' and of conversionism which involves pressure or manipulation. At first Carey remained as the patron of the Church Ministry, but he has recently (1992) resigned from it—a belated tribute to the efforts of Parkes and those who have followed him.[28]

For over a century and a half Christian missionary groups have actively sought to convert Jews, who through reasons of poverty or personal psychology, have been marginalized in society. Those in grief or personal despair have been particularly vulnerable to such approaches. The success rate in terms of individual conversions has so far not been remarkable compared to the energy and resources committed. Nevertheless, the activities of such missions have reinforced the sense of unease and marginality faced by Jews living in a Christian society; Jews who still see their acceptance as being totally conditional on behaving in a conformist manner.[29] As Parkes realized, Jews could never feel confident in Christian company and dialogue if the integrity of their faith was questioned. A decade after Parkes's death the director of the Church Ministry Among the Jews claimed that his organization did not seek to target the Jews! If the churches in Britain wish to convince the Jews of their good intentions, such a response, especially in the light of the *Shoah*, is clearly unacceptable.[30]

In June 1942 (when the 'Final Solution' had already been implemented for six months) the Chief Rabbi, Joseph Hertz, wrote to the Archbishop of Canterbury stating that 'There are things that I fear far more than pogroms.'[31] Hertz was concerned about the CCJ becoming a missionizing

[27] Braybrooke, *Time to Meet*, pp. 31–2; Runcie, quoted in the *Jewish Chronicle*, 21 Oct. 1988.

[28] George Carey, 'A good result for both sides', *Jewish Chronicle*, 14 June 1991.

[29] For the impact of missionary work see *Jewish Chronicle*, 16 Aug. 1985, 14 Oct. 1988, 7 July 1989. The sense of marginality amongst the Jews in Britain was stressed in Paul Morrison's film 'Exile', Channel 4, 7 July 1991.

[30] The Revd John Fieldsend in 'King of the Jews?' *Heart of the Matter*, BBC 1, 31 March 1991.

[31] London, Greater London Record Office, papers of the Chief Rabbinate 2805/124, Hertz to Temple, 23 June 1943.

organization. Given the context, this was a remarkable statement. At that stage in history there was a distinct possibility that *all* Jews would be physically destroyed. Yet Hertz was more concerned for the spiritual welfare of those Jews who would survive. James Parkes spent most of the 1930s and the Second World War in trying to rescue Jews, but he also shared Hertz's view when he stated on the eve of the conflict that 'Our immediate duty to the Jew is to do all in our power to make the world safe for him to be a Jew.' In conclusion, it is here that Parkes offers such an important model for modern Britain. In recent years James Parkes has been rediscovered as a figure of historical significance. Yet, if the Rushdie affair acts as an indication, Parkes's philosophy has enormous relevance for practical issues today. The Rushdie affair has shown that Muslims in Britain have only been supported if they have been poor or because they are seen as 'black'. Parkes realized that racism should be fought not just because it was immoral but because it made it impossible for groups like Jews to develop freely. He wanted Jews and Christians to enter dialogue to see what they had in common, but also to acknowledge and accept their *differences*. Tariq Modood had written with regard to Britain's largest non-Christian group today, the Muslims, that 'Hopefully we can begin to think through an ethnic pluralism which has to balance the demands of a common core of values and rights with giving respect to ethnic minorities on their own terms.'[32] James Parkes wrote before the term ethnicity came in to vogue and at a time when the Jews and not the Muslims were the subject of British public scrutiny. He nevertheless provided, in his positive, pluralistic approach, a philosophy of multi-culturalism based on common respect. In Parkes's vision minorities would be free from attack not just in the form of bricks and baseball bats but also from an intolerance based on an assimilationist liberal belief in Anglo-Saxon, Christian superiority. The work and life of James Parkes reveals that the pursuit of genuinely multi-cultural policies will be challenging and difficult; it will require scarce resources, time, and, ultimately, compromise. After Auschwitz, however, this challenge must be met; there is no longer any excuse.

University of Southampton

---

[32] See Nicholas de Lange, 'James Parkes', in Robert Blake and C. S. Nicholls, eds, *The Dictionary of National Biography 1981–1985* (Oxford, 1990), pp. 307–8; T. Madood, 'Religious anger and minority rights', *Political Quarterly*, 60 (July 1989), p. 284.

THE ROMAN CATHOLIC CHURCH AND GENOCIDE IN CROATIA, 1941–1945*

by JONATHAN STEINBERG

JUST before I sat down to write this paper, I heard the editor of the Serbian newspaper in Knin giving an interview to the BBC. 'Remember', he said over the crackling telephone line, 'we Serbs had our Auschwitz too; it was called Jasenovac.' Jasenovac can legitimately be compared with Auschwitz in the annals of human horror. Nobody knows how many Serbs, Jews, and Gypsies were hacked to pieces with butcher knives, beaten to death with clubs and rifle butts, worked to death on detachments, or died of fright, illness, and starvation in the Croatian death camp. A Serb friend of mine recalls being pulled by his mother from the rails of a ferry on the river Sava, near Jasenovac, in 1941 as he stared at the bits of human anatomy bobbing in the current. In the archives of the Italian Foreign Ministry in Rome there is a file of photographs of the butcher knives and mallets used in the camp and elsewhere by the Ustaše in their pogroms, as well as pictures of the mutilated victims. Those pictures have been indelibly burned on to the retina of my memory. Vladko Maček, the leader of the Croatian Peasants Party, was arrested and sent to Jasenovac on 15 October 1941, six months after the foundation of

---

* The primary and secondary sources on which this paper rests are listed below in the notes. About half the references have been drawn from German and Italian military, political, and personal archives. For the student of Croatia during the war, and especially of the relations between the German military and political authorities and the Independent State of Croatia, the personal correspondence of General Edmund Glaise von Horstenau is essential. It can be found in folders 1–13 of the file RH 31 III 'Bevollmächtigter deutscher General in Agram', housed in the West German Federal Military Archive in Koblenz. Glaise von Horstenau had a rank as *SS Brigadeführer*, equivalent to his *Wehrmacht* rank of *Generalleutnant*. Hence some of his personal correspondence is housed in the SS files in the Berlin Document Centre. Peter Broucek is the author of a three-volume edition of the papers of Glaise von Horstenau in which much of the material can be found, *Ein General im Zwielicht. De Lebenserinnerungen Edmund Glaises von Horstenau*, 3 vols (Vienna, 1980, 1983, 1989). The Italian military and diplomatic archives are unusually rich because the Independent State of Croatia was nominally an Italian protectorate. In order to make reference to these primary sources less tedious, I refer to the page and note number in my recent book, *All or Nothing: the Axis and the Holocaust 1941–1943* (London and New York, 1990) as follows: 'Steinberg, p. 274, n. 134'. The other primary source used in this paper is the diplomatic documents published by the Vatican itself in the series *Actes et Documents du Saint Siège Relatifs à la seconde guerre mondiale*, 4, 5, and 8 (Vatican City, 1975) [hereafter StS]. Other references are drawn from secondary sources. I do not, alas, read Croatian.

the *Nezavisna Država Hrvatska*, the Independent State of Croatia. He described it in his memoirs:

> The camp had previously been a brick-yard and was situated on the embankment of the Sava river. In the middle of the camp stood a two-storey house, originally erected for the offices of the enterprise ... The screams and wails of despair and extreme suffering, the tortured outcries of the victims, broken by intermittent shooting, accompanied all my waking hours and followed me into sleep at night.[1]

Maček was too important to be hacked to death, but he was too dangerous to be left. One of those who guarded him night and day was an Ustaša officer who used to make the sign of the Cross each night before going to sleep. Maček pointed out

> the monstrosity of his actions. I asked if he were not afraid of the punishment of God. 'Don't talk to me about that,' he said, 'for I am perfectly aware of what is in store for me. For my past, present and future deeds I shall burn in hell but at least I shall burn for Croatia.'[2]

This combination of Catholic piety, Croatian nationalism, and human bestiality raises uncomfortable questions about what happened fifty years ago in Europe, and why. The standard image of Fascism has been sketched for us by secular historians and sociologists. For most of them, religion is an opiate of the elderly, a childhood complaint, or, perhaps, the source of an occasional pang of guilt. As a result, recent explanatory approaches to the Holocaust and genocide in the Second World War—with the notable exception of Arno Mayer's *Why did the heavens not darken?*—confront the questions with resolutely secular assumptions. At best Nazism and Fascism have been seen as surrogate religions, taking the place of traditional Christianity in a world in which God had long since died and been interred.

Yet Croatia was by no means the only avowedly Catholic state in Hitler's new order. Father Tiso's Slovakia bore the Cross as prominently and deported its Jews as thoroughly as did Ante Pavelić's Croatia. Much of the legitimacy of Pétain's Vichy regime came from those traditions of reactionary Catholicism which had never accepted the Republic, the separation of Church and State, civil marriage and divorce, and Jewish

---

[1] Vladko Maček, *In the Struggle for Freedom* (University Park, Pennsylvania, 1957), p. 234.
[2] Ibid., p. 245.

emancipation. The story of German Protestantism's enthusiastic reception of the Nazi renewal of morality has been traced by a small industry of scholars, and was recognized by the Church itself in a collective act of expiation in 1945.[3]

In all these studies, religion and churches react; they do not act. Even those who criticize the silence of Pius XII never suggest that the Vatican caused the massacres; the issue is whether the Pope and the clergy did enough to stop them. The Croatian case will not fit such comfortable secular categories. Croatian Fascism, the *Ustaša* movement (the word means 'to stand up' or 'rebel'), combined Catholic piety, Croatian nationalism, and extreme violence. The terrible evidence of those years and the terrible revenge claimed in ours reminds us of the religious wars of the sixteenth century. The Croats were Catholic the way that the people of South Armagh are Catholic; religion, nation, and self merged into an explosive, unstable mixture.

This essay begins with the moral obligation of every historian to remember what happened, not to let the suffering and cries of those years simply die away. We cannot understand the tragedy of Yugoslavia in the 1990s unless we remember the tragedy of the 1940s. It may also serve to remind us that the professional historian belongs to an untypical group of people: well fed (on the whole), literate (more or less), dispassionate, objective, and remote from daily life. This is not a description which fits the majority of mankind. Historians need to remind themselves at all times and in all places of the horror, violence, cruelty, unreason, indifference, exhaustion, ignorance, halucination, greed, cynicism, generosity, kindness, bravery, good humour, loyalty, honesty, self-sacrifice, and charity which make their subject, their fellow human beings, so hard to define and even harder to explain.

* * *

The establishment of a Catholic Croatia and its immediate resort to genocide confronted the Roman Catholic hierarchy in Croatia and the Vatican in Rome with a terrible dilemma. The Nuncio to the Italian Government, Monsignor Francesco Borgoncini Duca, a man who made two trips to darkest Calabria to bring the Holy Father's greetings to the

---

[3] John S. Conway, 'How shall the nations repent? The Stuttgart Declaration of Guilt, October, 1945', *JEH*, 38 (1987), pp. 596–622.

Jews interned at Ferramonti Tarsia,[4] rebuked Stiepo Perić, the Croatian Minister to the Kingdom of Italy 'about the well-known atrocities of the Croatians against the Orthodox Serbs and Muslims and the violence perpetrated against them'. As he reported to the cardinal Secretary of State, Cardinal Luigi Maglione,

> I added that the Catholic church cannot and will not make propaganda by violence. Jesus said 'go and preach' not 'go and take the people by gun shots'. He replied that 350,000 orthodox had 'converted'. I replied that these conversions did not persuade me very much because for a conversion sentiment was necessary . . . He said, 'sentiment will come later.'[5]

On the other hand, the Independent State of Croatia, the NDH, enshrined in its constitution and laws the aims that the Church had designed for decades and had despaired of achieving. First, the conversion of the schismatics, as the youthful Archbishop Alojzije Stepinac said to the Regent Prince Paul in 1940:

> The most ideal thing would be for the Serbs to return to the faith of their fathers, that is, to bow the head before Christ's representative, the Holy Father. Then we could at last breathe in this part of Europe, for Byzantinism has played a frightful role in the history of this part of the world.[6]

As for the Jews, the semi-official diocesan weekly *Katolički List* had condemned them frequently during the 1930s as the source of Communism, Freemasonry, abortion, and irreverence. Jews were aliens and could not be true Croatians.[7] Nor were any tears shed for the destruction of the unitary kingdom of Yugoslavia. The Yugoslav government had, according to Father Ivo Guberina, Reader in the University of Zagreb, undermined Catholicism in every way. It built 'splendid orthodox churches' in towns historically and actually Catholic:

> The government of Belgrade helped both morally and materially the foundation in Croatia of the so-called 'Old Catholics', which was intended as a means to make catholics go into schism . . . Going over

---

[4] Steinberg, p. 80 and p. 280, notes 117–19.
[5] Borgoncini Duca to Cardinal Maglione, 22 Sept. 1941, StS, 5, no. 95, pp. 244–5.
[6] Stella Alexander, *The Triple Myth. A Life of Archbishop Alojzije Stepinac — East European Monographs Boulder*, no. 227 (New York, 1987), p. 26.
[7] Ibid., p. 52.

to Orthodoxy was more or less openly favoured . . . Mixed marriages at the expense of the Catholic Church were skilfully encouraged . . . Catholic areas were systematically colonized . . .[8]

Now at last, as *Katolički List* wrote on 21 April 1941, not quite two weeks after the establishment of the new *Ustaša* State, the dark days of humiliation were over.

> The NDH is thus a fact established by Almighty Providence on the 1300th anniversary of Croatia's first links with the Holy See. The Catholic Church which has been the spiritual leader of the Croatian people for 1300 years in all its difficult, painful and joyful days now accompanies the Croatian people with joy in these days of the establishment and renewal of its independent state.[9]

The Serbs, observed the new Minister of Education, Mile Budak,

> are not Serbs but people brought here from the East by the Turks . . . as the plunderers and refuse of the Balkans . . . God is one, and the people that govern is also one: and this is the Croatian people . . . it would be as well for them to know our motto: 'either submit or get out'.[10]

The new state was not, however, the result of a heroic rising by the people of God but of outside intervention. At 5.15 a.m. on 6 April 1941, the *Wehrmacht* crossed the frontiers of Yugoslavia and Greece from the north and the east. Zagreb fell on 10 April, Belgrade on the 12th, and six days later Yugoslavia capitulated. On 27 April German troops after unexpectedly fierce resistance from the Greek and British forces finally entered Athens.

The Germans and their allies redrew the Balkan map. Yugoslavia ceased to exist. On 10 April 1941 the Independent State of Croatia was proclaimed with its capital in Zagreb, its frontiers from the Drau and Danube in the north-east to those parts of the Dalmatian coast left it by the Italians in the south. A line running north-west to south-east divided the new state into German and Italian spheres of influence. Slovenia was split on the same basis, with the southern part, including the capital Ljubljana, annexed to Italy, the northern part to Germany. Hungary

---

[8] Carlo Falconi, *The Silence of Pius XII*, tr. Bernard Wall (London, 1970), pp. 267–8.
[9] Alexander, *Triple Myth*, p. 90.
[10] Falconi, *Pius XII*, p. 277.

annexed outright Bačka and Baranja and the region Medjimurje. Bulgaria 'redeemed' what it had always regarded as its ancient provinces of Macedonia and Thrace. Serbia was put under direct German military rule, and Serbs and their officers were, according to OKW (High Command of the *Wehrmacht*) instructions, 'to be treated exceptionally badly'.[11] As Mark Wheeler has put it, 'This was no simple military defeat. It was the fracture and destruction of an entire ruling order and of the political and national conception that underlay it.'[12]

The new Croatian state lacked everything. It scarcely had enough autos to drive its cabinet officers about, but it soon developed legislation to please Hitler. Within three weeks of its establishment it passed legislation defining Jews in racial terms. In the months of May and June 1941 it rapidly passed the laws that the Nazis had taken years to work out, prohibiting inter-marriage, employment of Aryan female servants by Jews, marking of Jewish stores and persons, registration of property, removal from the bureaucracy and professions, and the 'Aryanization' of Jewish capital. As early as May 1941 some of the Jews of Zagreb were rounded up and sent to the Danica camp and later in the summer to Jasenovac.[13]

The real enemy was the Serbs. As Mark Wheeler writes, the NDH came to power with 'a threefold scheme to rid Croatia of its "oriental minority—by expelling a third to rump Serbia, forcibly converting a second third to Roman Catholicism and slaughtering the remainder".'[14] The numbers involved were impressive. While the new Croatian state had doubled the territory which the former Yugoslav state had allotted to it as an autonomous region, much of it had inconveniently large settlements of non-Croats. Of the 6,700,000 citizens of the new state, only 3,300,000 were Croats. There were 2,200,000 Serbs, 750,000 Muslims, 80,000 Jews, 70,000 Protestants and other minorities.[15]

Hitler left the Independent State of Croatia to the Italians as part of their sphere of influence in the Balkans, but negotiations between Italy and the new Croatian state produced no easy agreement. Ante Pavelić, its leader or *Poglavnik*, modelled himself and his *Ustaša* movement on Mussolini and Fascism. He owed his and its survival to Fascist protection

[11] Steinberg, p. 271, n. 43.
[12] Mark Wheeler, 'Pariahs to Partisans to Power: the Communist Party of Yugoslavia', in Tony Judt, ed., *Resistance and Revolution in Mediterranean Europe* (London, 1989), p. 124.
[13] Raul Hilberg, *The Destruction of European Jews*, rev. and definitive edn, 3 vols (New York and London, 1985), 2, pp. 710–11.
[14] Wheeler, 'Pariahs', p. 129.
[15] Falconi, *Pius XII*, p. 274.

and support during the 1930s, when Pavelić and his followers were in exile in Italy. In spite of his debt to Italy and to Mussolini, he was appalled when the Italians annexed historic Croatian lands on the Dalmatian coast. Most of the coast with its beaches, the Dalmatian islands, the cities of Zara, Dubrovnik, Split, and the city and bay of Kotor either became provinces of metropolitan Italy or were subsequently occupied by the Italian Second Army. Hitler refused to intervene, and Pavelić had no choice but to sign a state treaty on 18 May 1941 in Rome.[16]

By the time that Pavelić arrived in Rome, the character of the new regime was already clear. Hundreds of Serbs had already been killed within the first three weeks by methods later perfected by the SS *Einsatzgruppen*. Serb men, women, and children were forced to dig ditches into which their mutilated bodies were then hurled, often still alive. At Otočac, early in May 1941, the usual slaughter was made worse by holding back the Greek Orthodox priest and his son to the end. The boy was cut to pieces under the eyes of his father, who was then forced to recite prayers for the dying. At Glina, on 14 May, the Serbs were invited to hear a *Te Deum*. Once inside the church, the *Ustaša* officer asked whether any present had certificates of conversion. Two did. The rest were hacked to death inside the sanctuary.[17]

The distinguished Austrian military historian Edmund Glaise von Horstenau had persuaded the German High Command that it needed an expert to handle German–Croatian relations and secured an appointment as 'plenipotentiary German General in Agram [Zagreb]',[18] one of the first of many Austrian officers to serve in the Balkans. A week before the state treaty was signed, Glaise summed up his first impressions in a report from Zagreb dated 12 May 1941:

> The Croatian revolution is largely the revolution of old men and former imperial Austrian officers ... A heavy burden, alongside the Italian mortgage, is the deep conflict with the Serbians, a consequence to a considerable extent of the unholy policies of the Magyars in the last years of the Danube Monarchy ...[19]

By early June the *carabinieri* in Split were reporting streams of Serbian and Jewish refugees crossing into Italian territory with tales of atrocities

---

[16] Steinberg, pp. 24ff. for the negotiations that led to the partitioning of the Balkan territories, which all qualified observers considered absurd.

[17] Falconi, *Pius XII*, p. 271.

[18] Steinberg, p. 271, n. 48.

[19] Ibid., no. 53.

and massacres carried out by the *Ustaše*.[20] Glaise von Horstenau reported that 'according to reliable reports from countless German military and civil observers during the last few weeks in country and town the *Ustaše* have gone raging mad.'[21] He reported that Serbian and Jewish men, women, and children were literally hacked to death, while villages were razed to the ground and the people driven into barns to which the *Ustaše* set flame. At one point the *Ustaše* had thrown so many corpses into the river Neretva, near Metkovic, that the government began to pay peasants 100 *kune* for each body hauled out, lest they float downstream into the Italian zone.[22] Neighbours murdered neighbours, as Menachem Shelach points out, people whose families had lived side by side for generations.[23] The Croatian militia were often egged on by local priests. When an Italian junior officer asked a Croatian priest for his authorization, the priest replied, 'I have one authorization and only one: to kill the Serb sons of bitches.'[24] Early the following year Cardinal Tisserant confronted the Croatian emissary to the Vatican, Dr Nikola Rusinović, with the appalling behaviour of Croatian Franciscans.

> I know for a fact that it is the Franciscans themselves, as for example Fr Simić of Knin, who have taken part in attacks against the Orthodox populations so as to destroy the Orthodox Church (in the way you destroyed the Orthodox Church in Banja Luka). I know for sure that the Franciscans in Bosnia and Herzegovina have acted abominably, and this pains me. Such acts cannot be committed by educated, cultivated people, let alone by priests.[25]

Observers within the German army also disapproved of uncontrolled violence. Early in July 1941 Glaise reported with dismay that the Croatians had expelled all Serbian intellectuals from Zagreb. When he went to see the *Poglavnik*, Pavelić promised humane treatment for them. The fact that they were only allowed 30 kg. of luggage made Glaise suspicious.[26] He had good reasons. On 10 July he reported the 'utterly inhuman treatment of the Serbs living in Croatia', the embarrassment of the Germans, who 'with

---

[20] Steinberg, p. 271, n. 56.
[21] Ibid., n. 57.
[22] Ibid., p. 272, n. 59.
[23] Menachem Shelach, *Heshbon Damim. Hatzlat Yehudi Croatiah al yiday haitalikim 1941–43* [Blood Reckoning. The Rescue of Croatian Jews by the Italians] (Tel-Aviv, 1986), p. 30.
[24] Ibid., p. 31n.
[25] Falconi, *Pius XII*, p. 308.
[26] Steinberg, p. 272, n. 63.

six battalions of foot soldiers' could do nothing and who had to watch the 'blind, bloody fury of the *Ustaše*'.[27] On 19 July he wrote: 'Even among the Croatians nobody can feel safe in this land any more ... The Croatian revolution is by far the harshest and most brutal of all the different revolutions that I have been through at more or less close hand since 1918.'[28]

The Italian representative in Zagreb, Casertano, reported with equal dismay that 'persecutions of Jews are continuing. Foreign influence [that is, German] is clearly visible in the recent decree prohibiting Jews from circulating in the city before ten in the morning and at any hour in markets or banks.'[29]

Small communities were not spared. The adjutant major of the 32nd Infantry Regiment stationed in Bileca recorded in the unit's war diary on 16 June that 'searches and arrests are continuing day and night. Numerous murders have taken place. Jews and Serbs are being robbed of all their goods by the *Ustaše* who are profiting from that in their greed for personal enrichment.'[30]

Meanwhile, in Zagreb, the NDH had set about reconquering the country for the true faith. In June 1941 all primary and infant schools belonging to the Serbian Church were closed, and the 10 per cent tax levied by the State for the Orthodox Church abolished. In July the use of the phrase 'Serbo-Orthodox religion' was forbidden and replaced by the term 'Greco-Oriental'. On 14 July 1941 the Ministry of Justice and Religion issued a decree to the bishops within the territory of the NDH in which it announced that Orthodox converts were forbidden to join the Greco-Catholic Church, that is, the Greek-rite churches in communion with Rome, and added, 'The Croatian government does not intend to accept within the Catholic church either priests or school-masters or, in a word, any of the intelligentsia—including rich Orthodox tradesmen and artisans ... Reception of the common Orthodox people and the poor is allowed after instruction in the truths of Catholicism.'[31]

In a speech to the *Sabor* (parliament) in February 1942 Pavelić explained that he had nothing against Orthodoxy as such, but the Serbian Orthodox Church could not be allowed to exist within the NDH because Orthodox

[27] Ibid., n. 64.
[28] Ibid., n. 65.
[29] Ibid., n. 66.
[30] Ibid., n. 67.
[31] Falconi, *Pius XII*, p. 276.

churches were always national. It had been the state religion of the old Yugoslav Kingdom; its bishops and priests were all Serbs and hence inadmissible in Croatia.[32]

The Catholic hierarchy within Croatia watched the unfolding events with complicated and conflicting feelings. Archbishop Stepinac, who was a man of deep personal piety and puritan tastes, could not fail to welcome some aspects of them.[33] He said in a sermon at a penitential rally of 200,000 people at Marija Bistrica in June 1943:

> ... we are all deeply convinced that this dreadful war with all its evil consequences is a justified punishment of God for so many sins ... sins of impurity, adultery, disorderly marriages, abortion, contraception, drunkenness, thieving and cheating, lying and swearing, indifference to holy days, to Sunday mass and the holy sacraments; they all cry to heaven for vengeance.[34]

While the NDH enforced a puritanism which he welcomed, it assumed an authority in matters of faith and doctrine which he could not. The Minister of Justice and Religion bombarded the bishops in the new state with decrees like the one just cited. Wholesale deportations of Jews and Serbs worried him, not least because the NDH apparently made no distinction between those converted to Catholicism and those who were not. The Archbishop began discreetly to protest. On 16 July he wrote to the Minister of Justice and Religion to complain that 'it would be against the spirit and duty of the Catholic Church to refuse to receive the whole intelligentsia on principle. Christ came into the world to save all men.'[35] A week later he wrote directly to the *Poglavnik* himself:

> I am convinced that these things have been happening without your knowledge and that others may not dare to tell you about them; so I am all the more obliged to do so myself. I hear from many sides that there are instances of inhumane and brutal treatment of non-Aryans during the deportations and at the camps, and even worse that neither children, old people nor the sick are spared. I know that among recent deportees there have been converts to catholicism, so that it is even more my duty to concern myself with them. Allow me to make a general observation; the measures which have been under-

---

[32] Alexander, *Triple Myth*, p. 68.
[33] Ibid., p. 90.
[34] Ibid., p. 105.
[35] Falconi, *Pius XII*, p. 281.

taken would have their full effect if they were carried out in a more humane and considerate way, seeing in human beings the image of God; human and Christian consideration should be shown especially to weak, old people, young and innocent children and the sick.[36]

The Archbishop had, in effect, condoned the end but condemned the means. He must surely have known, as General Glaise knew, that the NDH intended to carry out its own 'final solution' of the Serb question. A state agency, the *Državno Ravnateljstvo za Ponovu* (State Directorate of Renewal), had been charged with its execution. A day after the Archbishop's letter, the Minister of Education, Mile Budak, speaking in Gospic, made clear that one-third of the two million Serbs would be deported, one-third converted to Catholicism, and one-third killed.[37]

While Budak was announcing that genocide was now official in Croatia, the *Poglavnik*'s ally, Adolf Hitler, began his greatest enterprise. At 3.15 on the morning of 22 June 1941 'Operation Barbarossa' went into effect, and German troops crossed the frontiers of the Soviet Union. The Communist parties of all the Balkan states now joined the anti-Fascist front and in time came to dominate those movements. Yugoslav Communists were free to attack the Croatian Fascists directly and took to the hills.

Non-Communist Serbs had not been sitting idly waiting for extermination. In rump Serbia, bands of irregulars, known as *četniks*, had gathered around the Serb General Staff Officer, Draza Mihailović, who was loyal in his way to the exiled King and the Allies. The Serbs of Montenegro and Croatia, especially those behind the coastal strip in towns such as Knin and Gračac, took up arms. Incidents like the following became common. Two lorries of Italian Fascist militiamen, fifty-five black shirts, two officers, and a doctor set out from Bileca, in the hills behind Dubrovnik, for Gacko, in the mountains of Herzegovina. Thirty-five km. from Bileca the transport was caught in a storm of automatic fire and explosions. The militiamen threw themselves to the ground crying, 'Siamo italiani! siamo italiani! (we are Italians!)', at which point the firing suddenly stopped, and a group of sheepish Serbs emerged from the undergrowth to apologize for mistaking the Fascists for *Ustaše*. They also reported that in the next village they had found 200 Serb corpses.[38]

---

[36] Alexander, *Triple Myth*, pp. 71–2.
[37] Ibid., p. 71n.
[38] Steinberg, p. 272, n. 68.

The situation was rapidly becoming intolerable for the Italian occupation forces. As the Serbs took to the hills and fired back, the Italian army got caught in the cross-fire. In the meantime they had to watch as the 'friendly and allied independent state of Croatia' committed atrocities in front of their barracks. On 24 June the Governor of Dalmatia, Giuseppe Bastianini, wrote a strong letter to Rome. Italian troops were

> constrained to stand-by inactive in the face of such acts carried out under their very eyes ... I cannot guarantee that in reaction to some act of violence carried out in our presence there will not be an energetic intervention which could collide with the sensibilities and sentiments of the local 'lords and masters'.[39]

The Vatican, too, had problems with the new state which pressed its claims by every means available. The British Minister, for example, demanded that the Holy See condemn 'the brutal and unjustified attack on Yugoslavia', as did the exiled government of the Kingdom of Yugoslavia, still accredited to the Holy See.[40] The Croatians pressed hard for full recognition as a Catholic state. When Pavelić came to Rome to sign the state treaty with Italy, the Pope refused to receive him as a head of state, but conceded 'an audience without exteriority, as to a private person, as to a simple catholic'.[41]

In the long run the Vatican could not leave the new state without any direct diplomatic channels, and in late July 1941 Cardinal Maglione informed Archbishop Stepinac that His Holiness intended to send an Apostolic Visitor to the bishops, not a Nuncio to the state. The Pope named a Benedictine father, Monsignor Ramiro Marcone, for this delicate mission.[42] Although Monsignor Marcone spoke no Croatian, his secretary, Father Masucci, soon learned it, and for the greater part of the War the two Benedictines passed on vital information from and to the Holy See. By August 1941 the Vatican understood only too well what was happening in Croatia. The Roman Catholic Archbishop of Belgrade begged the Pope to intervene to prevent 'the violent persecutions being carried out in the kingdom of Croatia against the Orthodox Serbs ...

---

[39] Steinberg, p. 272, n. 69.

[40] Osborne to Cardinal Maglione, 7 April 1941, StS, 4, no. 313, p. 447; Legation of Yugoslavia to Cardinal Maglione, 17 May 1941, ibid., no. 355, p. 498.

[41] Note de Mgr Montini, 16 May 1941, ibid., no. 348, pp. 491–2; Note de Mgr Tardini, 17 May 1941, no. 352, p. 495; Note de Mgr Montini, 18 May 1941, no. 358, p. 500.

[42] Cardinal Maglione to Archbishop Stepinac, 25 July 1941, ibid., 5, no. 21, p. 106.

an outrage to good sense and civil law … not to mention Christian charity'.[43]

In November 1941, Bishop Mišić of Mostar wrote to Archbishop Stepinac:

> A reign of terror has come to pass … men are captured like animals. They are slaughtered, murdered; living men are thrown off cliffs. The under-prefect of Mostar, Bajič, a Moslem has said—he should keep silent and not utter such things—that at Ljubinje in a single day 700 schismatics were thrown into their graves. From Mostar and Capljina a train took six carloads of mothers, young girls and children ten years old to the station at Surmanci … they were led up the mountains and mothers together with their children were thrown alive off the precipices …[44]

The Archbishop wrote another letter to the *Poglavnik* and protested. The episcopal conference met and sent in a protest, but at the state opening of Parliament in February 1942, the Archbishop blessed its proceedings and the *Poglavnik*.[45] On the first anniversary of the establishment of the NDH, *Katolički List* wrote enthusiastically that

> under the former government freemasons, Jews, communists and such people had a big say and abortion was widely practised … One year of freedom and independence and what a rich harvest for the Croatian people. The NDH is a renewal of Zvonimir's Croatia and the Poglavnik follows in his footsteps.

A solemn *Te Deum* was celebrated, and the Archbishop preached a sermon.[46]

Private protests and interventions continued. The Germans, well informed as always, regarded Stepinac as *judenfreundlich*,[47] and even the Yugoslav government in exile grudgingly admitted, in July 1942, that 'according to reports from Serbs in Zagreb Stepinac is behaving well.'[48] Yet he never spoke out nor openly criticized Pavelić and his regime. Nor did he imitate his colleague in Slovakia who had a pastoral letter read out,

---

[43] Archbishop Joseph Ujcic to Cardinal Maglione, 24 July 1941, ibid., 5, no. 20, pp. 104–5.
[44] Alexander, *Triple Myth*, p. 80.
[45] Ibid., pp. 84–5.
[46] Ibid., p. 90.
[47] Steinberg, p. 80, and p. 280, n. 115.
[48] Alexander, *Triple Myth*, p. 101.

signed by the entire Slovak episcopate, condemning the deportation of the Jews.[49]

The silence of Archbishop Stepinac recalls the greater silence of Pius XII and the Holy See. In October 1942 d'Arcy Godolphin Osborne, British Ambassador to the Holy See, wrote a furious letter to Monsignor Tardini, Vatican Under-Secretary of State, complaining that if His Holiness granted an audience to Pavelić, it would create a very bad impression in England: 'The Croatian regime over which he presides and his Ustaschi [*sic!*] have been responsible for the murder of some 600,000 Serbs and at the present moment his troops are destroying Serbian villages in Bosnia and exterminating the Serbian population.'

Monsignor Tardini noted that in conversation with the Ambassador he had responded that Osborne, who had not been instructed by his government to make such a protest, had exceeded his competence. In the margin he observed, 'Il Ministro è, da qualche tempo, un po' eccitato.'[50] Whatever passion or cries of outrage the Vatican Archives reveal always comes from the outside; for Maglione and his staff the whole world appeared to be 'un po' eccitato'. Harold Macmillan caught the special atmosphere when he had an audience with the Pope in 1944:

> A sense of timelessness—time means nothing here, centuries come and go, but this is like living in a sort of fourth dimension. And at the centre of it all, past the papal guards, and the monsignori, and the bishops, and the cardinals, and all the show of ages—sits the little saintly man, rather worried, obviously quite selfless and holy—at once a pathetic and tremendous figure.[51]

Archbishop Stepinac shared with the Pope the selflessness, the austerity, and, from reports of those close to him, the holiness as well. But his world was not timeless. He lived amidst the terrors and dangers of the greatest charnel-house in human history. Moreover, as the scanty evidence presented so far makes clear, there can be no question that he did not know what was going on. He was not an old man—he had been consecrated when not yet forty and was in his mid-forties during the Second World War. He showed great personal courage and dignity both during his trial by the Communist regime in 1946 as a war criminal and in

---

[49] Steinberg, p. 119, and p. 286, n. 132.
[50] Osborne to Tardini, 3 Oct. 1942, StS, 5, no. 498, pp. 736–7.
[51] Owen Chadwick, *Britain and the Vatican during the Second World War* (Cambridge, 1986), pp. 302–3.

the long years of imprisonment which he had to undergo. Some commentators have argued that Pius XII was simply weak. Nobody has ever suggested such a thing about Archbishop Alojzije Stepinac. Why, then, did he keep silent?

Part of the answer can be read in a circular he published after the bombing of Zagreb, on 22 February 1944:

> I raise my voice in bitter protest and justified condemnation against those who do not flinch from any measures . . . and are destroying the living organism of the Croatian people . . . Croats have fought over the centuries to defend the ideals of real human freedom and Christian culture . . . Because of which the Pope, the greatest defender of real culture and freedom of mankind, gave them the honourable title of '*Antemurale Christianitatis*'.

A few days later he declared in a letter to d'Arcy Osborne that 'without exaggeration one can assert that no people during this war has been so cruelly stricken as the unhappy Croatian people.'[52] Not a view which would have been shared by Jews, Poles, Great Russians, Ukrainians, White Russians, Serbs, or Gypsies. Stepinac failed to see that because in the end Croatians were the only people who mattered to him, and with the exception of those Italians he had known as a seminarian, the only people he had ever known. Archbishop Stepinac saw himself as the pastor to his people; he was both archbishop and nationalist. Indeed, as we have seen, nationalism in the Balkans was hardly a secular category; to be Croatian was to be Catholic. In this respect the charges made at his trial in 1946 were correct. He had welcomed the foundation of the NDH; he had repeatedly said prayers and offered thanksgiving for it; he had celebrated with ecclesiastical pomp and splendour its official holidays and its leader's birthday. He had half-condoned atrocities because they were committed by 'our' people and not 'theirs'. The Croatian Emissary to the Holy See, Rusinović, noted with satisfaction during the Archbishop's visit to Rome in 1942 that Stepinac was 'really belligerent about the potential enemies of our country . . . In his attack on the Serbs, the Cetniks and the Communists as the cause of all the evil that has befallen Croatia he produced arguments that not even I knew.'[53]

On a visit to Rome in late May of 1943, the Archbishop told Prince

---

[52] Alexander, *Triple Myth*, pp. 104–5.
[53] Falconi, *Pius XII*, p. 314.

Lobkowicz, who had replaced Rusinović as Emissary of the Independent State of Croatia to the Holy See, that

> he had kept quiet about some things with which he is not at all in agreement in order to be able to show Croatia in the best possible light. He mentioned our laws on abortion, a point very well received in the Vatican. Basing his arguments on these laws, the Archbishop justified in part the methods used against the Jews, who in our country are the greatest defenders of crimes of this kind and the most frequent perpetrators of them.[54]

Such behaviour may be reprehensible, but it is all too common. How many Jews excuse Israeli violations of civil rights, illegal deportations, and police brutality 'to be able to show Israel in the best possible light'? After all, if given the chance, 'they' would destroy 'us'. Strong and secure national states can afford tolerance and legality; 'we' have to use every means available. 'We' are threatened with extermination.

It may help to place Archbishop Stepinac's equivocations in more familiar context if I compare him with another prelate, the late Cardinal Tomas O'Fiaich, Archbishop of Armagh and Primate of all Ireland, who died on 8 May 1990. The Times in its obituary wrote of him:

> His sense of identity with the Catholic people of South Armagh from whom he sprang and whose spiritual leader he became could be doubted by none who knew him ... The very attributes which endeared him to the local people made him appear narrow-minded and one-sided on the broader stage.

What were these attributes? 'Simple habits of speech, behaviour and leisure interests'; for example, he would regularly turn out to support the local Gaelic football team in his home town of Crosmaglen. He was a passionate Irish linguistic nationalist and changed his name from 'Fee' to its Gaelic form. He taught Irish medieval history, founded, and in due course presided over, the association of Irish-speaking priests. He had a brilliant record of firsts and *summa cum laudes* and became lecturer and then professor at Maynooth. In 1974 he became its President. In short, he was for the non-Catholic world the very embodiment of the 'impossible Irishman', loved and revered by his people; as The Times put it, 'the right man at the right place at tragically the wrong time.'[55]

---

[54] Falconi, *Pius XII*, pp. 315–16.
[55] *The Times*, obituary, 10 May 1990.

In Crosmaglen the time is never right. Since the seventeenth century South Armagh has been a frontier zone, the border between one ethno-religious community and another. Crosmaglen was the site of a famous atrocity in 1791 and of bomb outrages in 1991.[56] Out of Crosmaglen, son of the local primary school teacher, Cardinal Tomas O'Fiaich, a warm, pious, and saintly man, rose to be Primate, while remaining not merely the spokesman but the embodiment of Crosmaglen and South Armagh.

The people of Croatia are border people. As Archbishop Stepinac reminded his congregation in 1944, the Pope had consecrated them by giving them 'the honourable title of *antemurale Christianitatis*' or, as Father Ivo Guberina put it, 'the bulwark and stronghold of Catholicism and Christianity in its most critical moments'.[57] Like Archbishop O'Fiaich, Archbishop Stepinac came from the heart of his people. He was born on 8 July 1898 in Krašić, south-west of Zagreb, into a large, prosperous peasant family. He always saw his pastoral mission as service to those peasant communities from which he, a man of the people, had sprung.

Like the Jews of Israel, the Protestants of Northern Ireland, and the Afrikaners in South Africa, the Croatians are surrounded by peoples more numerous than they. They count and re-count their numbers. Contraception, known in Croatian Catholic writing as 'the white plague' (*bijela kuga*), offended God's laws and betrayed the Croatian people. Religion and nation demanded the same behaviour. How could a Croatian priest, a man concerned for the future of his people, condemn a state which had not only outlawed abortion but introduced the death penalty for those daring to practise it?

Like almost all European nationalisms, Croatian nationality itself had only been defined and then, as it happens, wrongly in the nineteenth century. The father of modern Croatian nationalism, Ljudevit Gaj, confronted a situation common to almost all Eastern European national movements in their early stages. There were in Croatia three spoken variants and no literary language when in 1825 Gaj began his crusade to create an 'Illyrian' nationality.[58] This was no different from the dilemmas

[56] J. Smyth, *'The Men of No Property': Irish Radicals and Popular Politics in the Late Eighteenth Century* (London, 1992), pp. 49–50. See also pp. 40–1 for South Armagh as a trouble-spot and pp. 46–7 for the frontier as an ethnic and cultural divide. I am grateful to Dr Jim Smyth, my colleague at Trinity Hall, for helping me to understand the world of nationalism in Ireland. He is, of course, not responsible for the conclusions I draw from his lessons.

[57] Falconi, *Pius XII*, p. 265.

[58] Elizabeth Murray Despalatović, *Ljudevit Gaj and the Illyrian Movement — East European Monographs Boulder*, no. 12 (New York, 1975), pp. 18ff.

of the Slovaks, whose language was divided between a Protestant, old Czech variant and numerous unwritten variants spoken by the Catholic communities, or that of the Daco-Romans in Wallachia and Moldavia. Whatever national identity is, it is not self-evidently 'out there' like the system of tillage or the character of the geology. Nationalism, like religion, rests on an act of faith, an act of self-definition; it provides an answer to the question 'Who am I?' by saying, 'You are one of us.'

These considerations help to explain how and why Archbishop Stepinac and the higher clergy in Croatia were guilty, in the words of *The Times* obituary of Cardinal O'Fiaich, of 'half-condonation of violence', but they do not excuse them. A massacre is a massacre, whether by 'our' people or 'their' people. Internment without trial, beatings, deportations, and forced confessions are crimes against humanity whether 'our' people do it or 'theirs'. Archbishop Stepinac had a duty to condemn the murder of Serbs, no matter how deep his Croatian feelings. Had he done so, the editor of the Serb paper in Knin might be covering local news instead of giving interviews to the BBC.

Trinity Hall,
Cambridge

JEWISH AND CHRISTIAN CONCEPTS OF TIME AND MODERN ANTI-JUDAISM: OUSTING THE GOD OF TIME

by MARGARET F. BREARLEY

O NE of the major factors which distinguish Judaism and Christianity from virtually all non-monotheistic religions is the concept of time. The Jews were alone among ancient peoples in worshipping the God of Time. In most ancient religions the pagan gods of space, embodied in sacred places and things, were worshipped. Nature was perceived pantheistically, as sacred, inhabited by spirits and devas. Gods of space were visualized in images: 'Where there is no image, there is no god',[1] their worship necessarily involving idolatry. Generally anthropomorphic and often personifying man's own instincts, such gods could inspire no clear moral code. Separation from them could be bridged only by physical means—by Dionysiac frenzy, by re-enactment of myths about them. Thus Cretans tore apart a living bull to re-enact Hera's murder of Dionysos Zagreus; worshippers of Attis in Phrygia engaged in self-castration. Shamanistic trances, eating sacrifices, and temple prostitution were among other means of temporarily embodying the spatial gods.

Although in Zoroastrianism and elsewhere time was an independent deity, in general, time was subordinated to space; stone circles were often designed so that the sun penetrated the centre at the summer solstice—the ritual mating of sun and earth. Pagans viewed time as an amorphous flow, differentiated only by movements of sun or moon, the rhythmic cycle of nature. C. S. Lewis wrote: 'To the Greeks . . . the historical process was a meaningless flux or cyclic reiteration.'[2] The sacred times of paganism—equinoxes, midsummer and midwinter, full moons—celebrated nature's fertility and man's sexuality—the life-force manifest in space. Distinctions between mythological and historical time were blurred. Time, viewed pessimistically as continual decline from a past golden age or as a

---

[1] A. J. Heschel, 'The Sabbath', in *The Earth is the Lord's*, Harper Torchbook edn (New York and London, 1966).

[2] C. S. Lewis, *The Discarded Image* (Cambridge, 1967), p. 174. For an excellent general survey of concepts of time, cf. Murad D. Akhundov, *Conceptions of Space and Time: Sources, Evolution, Directions*, tr. C. Rougle (Cambridge, Mass. and London, 1986); Elliott Jaques, *The Form of Time* (New York and London, 1982); J. B. Priestley, *Man and Time* (London, 1964); P. Ricoeur, ed., *Cultures and Time* (Paris, 1976).

grim wheel of circular history, had no intrinsic meaning and inspired little belief in progress or reform. The spiritual ideal was withdrawal from time rather than active eradication of evil—itself, like time, an illusion. Mircea Eliade wrote that 'In the traditional societies men endeavoured, consciously and voluntarily, to abolish time.... The myth takes man out of his own time.... The myth implies a break away from Time and the surrounding world; it opens up a way into the sacred Great Time ... he rediscovers the cosmic rhythms.' In Hinduism, too, the 'escape from Time' served as the 'royal road to deliverance.... Even to make oneself conscious of the ontological unreality of Time, and to realise the rhythms of cosmic Great Time, is enough to free oneself from illusion.'[3]

The Jews were called not to worship the pagan gods of space nor to escape from time into forgetfulness and myth. Israel was to worship the real, holy God of Time, manifest in historical events rather than in space. Even the Holy of Holies was empty of images. Not images but words—of Torah, Tenach (Bible), and later Talmud—were paramount. God was encountered by experiencing his direct intervention and word in history. Hence time is pre-eminent in Judaism. 'Judaism is a religion of time aiming at the sanctification of time.... Judaism teaches us to be attached to holiness in time ... to sacred events.'[4] Because in the beginning God created, in Judaism time comes before space, event before matter, word before object. Jewish time is historical, not mythological. Because God rested on the seventh day, Judaism distinguishes times—above all, the holy time of Shabbat. Instead of worshipping anthropomorphic gods, Jews were to become deomorphic—to imitate God's holy characteristics and acts in time. At Sinai a radical society based on humane ethics and absolute moral commands was created. Uniquely, there were to be no human sacrifices, no temple prostitution, no caste system, no euthanasia, infanticide, torture, or bribery. The nomadic Levites and Prophets embodied, in the words of Andre Neher, 'a permanent and concrete expression of the rejection of space.'[5]

The God of Time is not primarily encountered in space. There are no saints' relics, no holy water, images, or shrines. Judaism has no places of

[3] Mircea Eliade, *Images and Symbols. Studies in Religious Symbolism*, tr. P. Mairet (London, 1961), pp. 58, 36; ibid., p. 91. Cf. M. Eliade, *Cosmos and History: the Myth of the Eternal Return*, tr. W. R. Trask (New York, 1959).
[4] Heschel, 'Sabbath', p. 8.
[5] Andre Neher, 'The View of Time and History in Jewish Culture', in Ricoeur, *Cultures and Time*, pp. 149–68, at p. 152.

awe—but Days of Awe. Rabbi Heschel wrote: 'Our Holy of Holies is a shrine that neither the Romans nor the Germans were able to burn . . . the Day of Atonement.'[6] The God of Israel is encountered in time—in daily prayer, on festivals, above all, on Sabbaths, called by Heschel 'our great cathedrals'. Jewish time is deeply rational. It does not subordinate human time to nature's times. Equinoxes, midwinter, and midsummer were ignored, and superstitious belief in astrology treated with suspicion, even condemned as prolonging the exile and denying Providence.[7] Nature's rhythms were subordinated to festivals celebrating God's acts in time— Passover, the Exodus, Shavuot, the giving of the Law at Sinai, Succoth, the tabernacles in the wilderness: 'To Israel the unique events of historic time were more significant than the repetitive processes in the cycle of nature.'[8] Rabbi Greenberg wrote that the Exodus

> teaches us that history is not an eternal recurrence . . . but a time stream with direction. History is not a meaningless cycle but the path along which the Divine-human partnership is operating to perfect the world. Time is linear, not circular; all humans are walking toward the end time when the final peace and dignity for humankind will be accomplished.[9]

Judaism thus taught optimistic belief in reform, progress, a future just kingdom of God, and the need to fight against the reality of evil.

Christianity inherited from Judaism its conception of historical, linear time: 'The governing principle of Christianity is to be found within history and along the axis of time.'[10] It shared with Judaism an optimistic vision of a future kingdom of God and a belief in the intrinsic meaning of events: 'Every temporal event is filled with extra-temporal significance. The Scriptures were proof that every man's life had meaning and that history . . . was really the fulfilment of God's design.'[11] Yet the historical development of Christianity resulted in marked divergences from Jewish concepts of time. At least from the fourth century the Church specifically divorced itself from Jewish times, substituting Sunday as a day of rest and commemoration for the Jewish Sabbath, and deliberately linking Easter

---

[6] Heschel, *Sabbath*, p. 8.

[7] Lionel Kochan, *Jews, Idols, Messiahs. The Challenge from History* (Oxford, 1990), p. 173.

[8] Heschel, *Sabbath*, p. 8.

[9] Irving Greenberg, *The Jewish Way: Living the Holidays* (London, 1990), p. 38.

[10] Germano Pattero, 'The Christian Conception of Time', in Ricoeur, *Cultures and Time*, pp. 169–95, at p. 170.

[11] Gabriel Josipovici, *The World and the Book* (St Alban's, 1973), p. 48.

with the spring equinox rather than with the Jewish Passover.[12] The placing of the memorial of Christ's birth at the time of the midwinter celebration of the Mithraic Sol Invictus was one of a number of conscious adaptations of pagan times, designed to suppress them but, in effect, often resulting in assimilation of pre-Christian rhythms of nature, later to be rejected by Calvin and Puritan Reformers.[13]

Confronted as it was by the cyclical time of Greek philosophy and the thought of Heraclitus and Parmenides, by the solar pantheism of Late Antiquity, with its astrological determinism, and by the radical dualism of Gnostic heresies,[14] Christianity developed a profound philosophy of time, particularly from St Augustine's *Confessions* onwards; 'In some ways the problem of time constitutes the core element in Christianity's conception of itself.'[15] Christianity generally infused time with meaning, attributing 'the maximum potentiality to time. It conceives of time as liberation. . . . Events give time its significance and its orientation.' It understood Jesus Christ, God incarnate in time, as the beginning and end of history, the 'lord of all times'.[16] For most Christians his death and Resurrection marked the end of the Jewish dispensation of the 'Old' Testament and inaugurated the new historical age of grace, which would last until the Second Coming and eternal age of glory.

As in Judaism, time was patterned in weekly and annual cycles, but according to events in Christ's life rather than in the history of Israel. Time was viewed optimistically, by and large. Monastic orders patterned even the hours of the day meaningfully, while church bells throughout the Middle Ages gave sacred significance to the passage of time. Medieval Christian historiographers opposed the cultural pessimism of Gnostic Cathars and Albigensians by infusing historical chronicles with religious and ethical teaching.[17] Rather than what Brandon termed the 'Ritual Perpetuation of the Past' typical of pagan myth, Christianity commemorated in the present, through the Eucharist and the annual liturgical cycle, the past of Christ's birth, death, and Resurrection, and anticipated his future return. Christian evaluation of time has remained: 'One of the most thorough and comprehensive attempts on the part of man to assign a

[12] Pattero, 'Conception of Time', pp. 182–6.
[13] Ninian Smart, *The Phenomenon of Christianity* (London, 1969), pp. 188–93.
[14] Rudolf Bultmann, *Primitive Christianity in its Contemporary Setting* Eng. tr. (London, 1983), pp. 135–71.
[15] Pattero, 'Conception of Time', p. 169.
[16] Ibid., pp. 172f.
[17] Cf. Friedrich Heer, *The Medieval World: Europe from 1100–1350* (London, 1974), pp. 274–87.

definitive significance to time both in terms of the destiny of the individual and of mankind as a whole, and even of the physical universe'.[18]

The contrast between worship of the God of time and spatially-conceived gods, resulting in historical, linear time rather than mythical, cyclical time, is thus one of the most distinctive traits of Judaism and Christianity. It is, incidentally, also fundamental to the phenomenon of anti-Semitism. Historian Will Herberg suggested that anti-Judaism and anti-Semitism are 'the other side of the election and vocation of Israel . . . the revolt of the pagan against the God of Israel and his absolute demand . . . one of the ways—the typical, symbolic way—in which the pagan "gods of space" revenge themselves on the people of the "Lord of time"'.[19]

In the nineteenth century there arose deeply anti-Judaic thinkers, who wished not only systematically to destroy Judaeo-Christian monotheism, but also to replace it with world-views which had a radically different concept of time. Schopenhauer, who was described by Nietzsche as 'the first avowed and unyielding atheist that we Germans have ever had',[20] argued in *The World as Will and Representation* that 'The innermost core and spirit of Christianity is identical with that of Brahminism and Buddhism.'[21] Christianity derived from these and not from Judaism, which he described as 'the crudest and worst of all religions'.[22] He adopted an explicitly Buddhist vision of 'the misery of life . . . This truth . . . soon overcame the Jewish dogmas with which I had been imbued.'[23] 'The sole purpose of man's existence is to recognise that it would be better never to have existed.'[24]

Schopenhauer believed that the world was created not by a benevolent God, 'the old Jew in Cloud-cuckooland',[25] but by a huge, diabolic,

---

[18] S. G. Brandon, 'Time and the Destiny of Man', in J. T. Fraser, ed., *The Voices of Time: a Co-operative Survey of Man's Views on Time as Expressed by the Sciences and by the Humanities* (London, 1968), pp. 140–57.

[19] Will Herberg, *Judaism and Modern Man* (New York, 1951), pp. 273–4: cited by A. Roy Eckardt, *Elder and Younger Brothers. The Encounter of Jews and Christians* (New York, 1967), p. 20.

[20] Karl Schlechta, *Friedrich Nietzsche. Werke in Drei Banden*, 3rd edn (Munich, 1976), 2, p. 227; *Die fröhliche Wissenschaft*, 5, p. 357.

[21] S. Friedlaender, ed., *Arthur Schopenhauer. Auswahl aus seinen Schriften* (Munich, 1962), p. 217.

[22] *Parerga and Paralipomena*, tr. E. F. J. Payne (Oxford, 1974), 1, p. 126.

[23] A. Hubscher, ed., *Arthur Schopenhauer. Welt und Mensch. Eine Auswahl aus dem Gesamtwerk* (Stuttgart, 1960) [hereafter Hubscher], p. 213.

[24] Ibid., p. 163.

[25] Cited by J. P. Stern, *Reinterpretations. Seven Studies in Nineteenth Century German Literature* (London, 1964), p. 191.

impersonal force, the Universal Will to Life. '"The Will to Life, as it shows itself in man, is also the Will to Reproduction". Schopenhauer's emphasis upon the importance of sex was quite new and astonishing.'[26] This Universal Will alone is undivided and real; it alone is noumenon, true subject. It is space and time, which Schopenhauer called the *principium individuationis*, which cause all outward individuations of the single Will to Life. It is these which cause conflict and inevitable suffering; they are ultimately unreal, are simply object. Space and time are no more than devices in the mind to give an appearance of reality to the total nullity of existence of objects and ourselves. They create the illusion of separateness, of individual identity. Schopenhauer shared with Kant the view that space and time pertain only to the world of phenomena and sense-experience, to matter, 'the union of space and time'.[27] He firmly rejected, however, any notion of Newtonian linear time. Instead, he compared time to 'an endlessly turning circle';[28] 'Life is a journey on a circular track of glowing coals.'[29] Time itself is an illusion; only the present is real. Bryan Magee argued that, for Schopenhauer, 'Wherever there is a time it always *is* now . . . there is a continuous present, and this is the only time that ever actually exists.'[30] Schopenhauer declared: 'The world . . . is wholly present. There is no past and no future. . . . But for this individuation to which we owe our distinct existences—the "veil of Maya"—we would see the whole in its timeless meaningless stability.'[31] Even the apparent evenness of time's passage in individual minds is a major proof 'that we are all sunk into the same dream, indeed that it is *one single being, which dreams the dream*.'[32]

Detached from time, the world is seen for what it is—as a mistake, a penal institution, even demonic; in it only pain and suffering have meaning. But precisely by detachment from both notions of objective reality and the will itself, there can be escape from suffering into timeless nirvana:

> With the surrender of the will, 'all those phenomena are also abolished . . . the multifarious forms succeeding each other in grada-

[26] V. J. McGill, *Schopenhauer. Pessimist and Pagan*, 1st edn, 1931, repr (New York, 1971), p. 25.
[27] Patrick Gardiner, *Schopenhauer* (London, 1963), p. 100.
[28] Hubscher, p. 55.
[29] Stern, *Reinterpretations*, p. 169.
[30] Bryan Magee, *The Philosophy of Schopenhauer* (Oxford, 1983), p. 213. Cf. also Chr. Janaway, *Self and World in Schopenhauer's Philosophy* (Oxford, 1989), pp. 37–52.
[31] Stern, *Reinterpretations*, pp. 181–2.
[32] Hubscher, p. 56.

tion; the whole manifestation of the will; and, finally, also the universal forms of this manifestation, time and space, and also its last fundamental form, subject and object; all are abolished. No will; no idea, no world. Before us there is certainly only nothingness.'[33]

Schopenhauer believed that these Buddhist truths would replace the 'fables of Christianity', increasingly rejected in his day. 'Hence men will have to turn to my philosophy',[34] in which objective reality disappears in the light of subjective perception and the abolition of time.

Richard Wagner wrote to Liszt in 1853 of his encounter with Schopenhauer's work: 'It has come to me in my loneliness like a gift from heaven', claiming that through it he had come to understand fully his own *Ring*.[35] Of Schopenhauer he later wrote: 'It was reserved for this mastermind to light this more than thousand-years' confusion into which the Jewish God-idea had plunged the whole of Christendom.'[36] Wagner shared his deep loathing of Judaism: 'I hold the Jewish race to be the born enemy of pure humanity and everything noble in it.'[37] He believed that first Judaism and then its agent, Christianity, had destroyed the 'joyful paganism' of the idyllic ancient world and with it man's true understanding of himself. Man had been deflected away from worshipping himself and nature as divine by worship of the 'absolute and superhuman God', whom Wagner hated. Natural instincts, including cruelty and lust, had been wrongly repressed. Man had learned to feel guilty, had lost his primal heroism and true contact with nature and art.

Wagner longed to restore paganism to Europe through the 'artwork of the future' and 'a new religion'—first embodying Dionysiac ecstasy, then ultimately based on Schopenhauerian pessimism and renunciation. He wished to free Aryans from enslavement to Jewish ethics, the Jewish God, and linear time.[38] Initially he tried to do this by reminding the Aryan Germans of their descent from pagan gods, primarily from Woden (Wotan). In the *Ring*, Wagner reasserted the power of instinct—strength,

[33] Bertrand Russell, *History of Western Philosophy*, 10th impr. (London, 1967), p. 726.

[34] Hubscher, p. 222.

[35] McGill, *Schopenhauer*, p. 23.

[36] *Religion and Art* in *Richard Wagner's Prose Works*, tr. W. Ashton Ellis (London, 1973), 6, pp. 256–7.

[37] Letter to King Ludwig II of Bavaria, 22 Nov. 1881, cited in Jacob Katz, *The Darker Side of Genius. Richard Wagner's Anti-Semitism* (Waltham, Mass., Hanover, and London, 1986), p. 115.

[38] Cf. Margaret Brearley, 'Hitler and Wagner: the Leader, the Master and the Jews', *Patterns of Prejudice*, 22, 2 (1988), pp. 5–28.

lust, cruelty, and heroism. Earth becomes a green goddess again and man (Siegfried) is reunited with nature, with his own instincts, and with sexuality. Morality is overthrown, as Siegfried, the 'fair young form of Man', is created out of incest by Wotan. The settings are timeless and mythical; the action is circular—its end is its beginning, in the river Rhine. Despite its nineteen hours' duration, in the *Ring* it is space that matters—a clearly pagan space, with sacrificial stones to the gods on stage in *Götterdämmerung*. Three characters—Mime, Alberich, and Hagen—represent power-hungry, evil Jews; they alone in the *Ring* use ethical vocabulary, they alone are strongly aware of past and future time. They are eliminated, two by murder and one by self-drowning.

The first performances of the *Ring* in 1876 were a failure, attributed by Wagner to the Germans' wish to see not heathen gods and heroes but something Christian. Consequently his last opera, *Parsifal* (1882) was his 'holiest' opera, 'this most Christian of all art works'[39]—and his most anti-Jewish. For he had adopted a radically de-Judaized Christianity based on Schopenhauerian renunciation, Aryan racism, and rejection of Judaeo-Christian ethics. The biblical God was dismissed as a 'tribal god', Jesus Christ—emphatically not Jewish—reinterpreted as stemming from the pre-Judaic Aryan 'god who dwells in us', namely, Siegfried. In *Parsifal* time is completely blurred; each character represents several historical periods and people rolled into one. At a critical moment, Gurnemanz says to Parsifal: 'Time is turned here into space.'[40] But even space is blurred; one scene is transformed into the next, the onlooker almost unconscious of the change. Objective reality melts into subjective perception.

Wagner's artwork of the future is Schopenhauer's philosophy on stage; he described *Parsifal* as 'an exhortation of the world's inmost soul, prophesying redemption . . . the image of a prophetic dream.'[41] As in the *Ring*, the representatives of Judaism, Kundry—a mythical, seductive wandering Jewess—and malevolent Klingsor—are eliminated from time and space. Gentiles were to be cleansed of all racial and spiritual contamination by Jews—this is the meaning of the Grail's cleansing blood. Jews as Jews were to be eradicated; in his anti-Semitic essay *Judaism in Music* (1850) Wagner demanded their 'self-annulment':

---

[39] Cited by Robert Gutman, *Richard Wagner: the Man, his Mind and his Music* (New York, 1968), p. 407. Cf. 'Parsifal at Bayreuth', in *Prose Works*, 6, pp. 303–4.

[40] R. Wagner, *Parsifal. Ein Buhnenweihfstspiel in Drei Aufzugen* (Stuttgart, 1982), p. 24.

[41] Cited by Gutman, *Richard Wagner*, p. 426.

To become Man at once with us means firstly for the Jew . . . ceasing to be a Jew. Without once looking back, take your part in this regenerative work of deliverance through self-annulment . . . Only one thing can redeem you from the burden of your curse: the redemption of Ahasuerus—Destruction![42]

The destruction of the Jews meant for Wagner nothing other than the destruction of the Jewish and Christian God. He, too, must disappear from time and space. 'Only when the fiend [the Jewish God] . . . can no more find a where or when to lurk among us, will there also be no longer—any Jews.'[43]

Friedrich Nietzsche was antipathetic to Wagner's anti-Semitism and his late apparent conversion to Christianity. Yet as his disciple, friend, and finally antagonist, Nietzsche held much in common with Wagner. He described Schopenhauer as 'the last German worthy of consideration'.[44] He shared Wagner's vision of a Greek world enslaved by Judaeo-Christian resentment[45] and slave morality of weakness, compassion, envy, pity—ethics of the herd. He, too, spoke of a 'return'—or rather an 'ascent'—to nature.[46] While Nietzsche admired certain aspects of 'the ancient Jewish God' and the Old Testament, his vision of the world as 'Chaos . . . foolish, blind, mad' was Schopenhauerean—and he was deeply antipathetic to Christianity: 'The God on the cross is a curse on life';[47] 'The practice of the church is hostile to life.'[48] Its morality, dependent on its God, should be abandoned now that God was dead.[49] It was hostile to life, to sexuality, to the Dionysian orgiastic frenzy at the heart of all art and creativity and power. Nietzsche argued for sexuality, 'the most profound instinct of life', to be understood as 'the holy way',[50] and named Zarathustra as 'the concept of Dionysus . . . a God'.[51]

Nietzsche replaced the now defunct Christianity with Zarathustra's teaching of 'higher men', paradoxically—like Richard Wagner—embracing the concept of evolution. Similarly he replaced the traditional

---

[42] 'Judaism in Music', in *Prose Works*, 3, p. 100.
[43] 'Know Thyself', in *Prose Works*, 6, p. 274.
[44] *Gotzendammerung* in Friedrick Nietzsche, *Werke*, ed. K. Schlechta (Munich, 1954–65), 2, p. 1002.
[45] *Zur Genealogie der Moral* in *Werke*, 2, p. 782.
[46] *Gotzendammerung*, p. 1023.
[47] From 'Notes (1888)', in *The Portable Nietzsche*, ed. W. Kaufmann (New York, 1954), p. 459.
[48] *Gotzendammerung*, p. 965.
[49] *Die frohliche Wissenschaft* III.108 and 125, in *Werke*, 2, pp. 115, 127.
[50] *Gotzendammerung*, p. 1032.
[51] *Ecce Homo* in *Werke*, 2, p. 1138.

Christian symbolism of time. In *Also Sprach Zarathustra* winter is preferred to summer, cold to warmth, and 'old deep, deep midnight' is preferred to noon. Just as Zarathustra's journey is circular and without goal, so, too, Nietzsche replaces Judaeo-Christian linear time with cyclical time. He strongly attacked the concepts of linear and continuous time as reflecting only the structure of the intellect and man's organic needs; historically they had been imposed by dominant members of social groupings and did not reflect reality.[52] He believed that perceptions of change could therefore evolve, and he promoted instead of continuous linear time a conception of time as discontinuous moments,[53] reflecting his belief that the world comprises essentially forces in flux: 'There is no overarching universal time in Nietzsche's cosmology. There are only moments of local force-systems.'[54]

Historical consciousness is replaced by 'the myth-orientated consciousness', in which 'each new event is experienced as a re-enactment of some archetypal mythical event.' Since 'every moment of time partakes in this eternal sameness',[55] eternity can be found in embracing single moments worthy of 'eternal recurrence'. This cyclical concept of time results in a loss of all value systems, for in perpetual flux each event is simply a manifestation of timeless forces, no more good or evil than any other event. Similarly the past and future no longer have any meaning:

> The past is no longer anything.... The future is seen as so extensive that it scarcely touches contemporary man... 'A few millenniums do not matter!' The present is conceived as encompassing mankind in its entirety... In Nietzsche's view, Providence no longer guides human destiny; God is dead, and man can place no trust in any power beyond himself. Hence he himself must take his entire destiny in hand.[56]

Wager and Nietzsche were not alone in their opposition to Judaeo-Christian monotheism, ethics, and linear time. Their radical approach to time was shared by many later thinkers including Ouspensky, Rudolf Steiner, and Arnold Toynbee, and writers including W. B. Yeats, James Joyce, and the Expressionists. (From the 1880s onwards, literature, art, and

---

[52] Cf. Alistair Moles, *Nietzsche's Philosophy of Nature and Cosmology* — American University Studies, ser. 5, 80 (New York, 1990), pp. 223–46.

[53] Ibid., p. 393, n. 35.

[54] Ibid., p. 233.

[55] Ibid., p. 238.

[56] K. Jaspers, *Nietzsche. An Introduction to the Understanding of his Philosophical Activity*, tr. C. F. Wallraff and F. J. Schmitz (New York and London, 1965), p. 276.

music were increasingly permeated by concepts of multiple time and space; results included 'stream of consciousness' novels, experimentation with simultaneity in music, and fragmentation of space in art, and ideas of ubiquity in time and blurring of normal spatial and temporal boundaries.[57] Bergson, furthermore, pioneered the psychological and psychic understanding of time.) Both Wagner and Nietzsche influenced Hitler, who created Nazi festivals based on nature's cycles,[58] and whose Holocaust intended the final elimination of Jews and Judaism from space and time. After the Second World War, theosophist Alice Bailey, the major occult thinker behind the current New Age movement, continued the pattern. Like her nineteenth-century predecessor Helena Petrovna Blavatsky, she regarded their God as 'the tribal Jehovah, as the soul (the rather unpleasant soul) of a nation'.[59] She described the Jews as full of hatred, aggression, and separativeness, in league with the dark forces, the anti-Christ governing humanity.[60] Judaism presents 'a basic evil'; it is 'so ancient that its teachings are obsolete'.[61] Jews are condemned for 'their ancient sin of non-response to the evolutionary process',[62] representing a defunct form of humanity, being incarnations of the previous solar system.[63] She wished to found a world religion combining Eastern, esoteric, and pagan spirituality based on full-moon festivals and nature's rhythms, led by 'highly-evolved men and women'.[64] All traces of Judaism would be removed and Christian symbols would be reinterpreted: 'The Cross is strictly the symbol of Aryan unfoldment.'[65] Hence she called in 1946 for 'the gradual dissolution of Orthodox Judaism, with its obsolete teaching, its separative emphasis'[66] as a major priority. Regarding time, Bailey described it as cyclic in nature and 'entirely a brain event',[67] but denied any reality to time. She wrote of 'the non-existence of time in relation to reality'[68] and stressed the need 'to transcend time'.[69] 'There is no

---

[57] Cf. Stephen Kern, *The Culture of Time and Space: 1880–1918* (London, 1983).
[58] Cf. R. Grunberger, *A Social History of the Third Reich* (Harmondsworth, 1971), pp. 101–3, 560–1.
[59] Alice Bailey, *The Reappearance of the Christ* (New York, 1984), p. 145.
[60] A. Bailey, *The Rays and the Initiations* (New York, 1988), pp. 429–30, 635, 681, 705.
[61] A. Bailey, *The Externalisation of the Hierarchy* (New York, 1982), p. 551.
[62] Bailey, *Rays*, p. 534.
[63] Ibid., p. 243.
[64] A. Bailey, *Serving Humanity* (New York and London, 1982), p. 33.
[65] Bailey, *Rays*, p. 561.
[66] Bailey, *Externalisation*, pp. 544, 551.
[67] A. Bailey, *The Destiny of the Nations* (New York and London, 1982), p. 32.
[68] Ibid., p. 42.
[69] Bailey, *Externalisation*, p. 509.

such thing as time on the inner planes'; and an evolved spiritual Master 'is free from the limitations of time, though not of space, because space is an eternal Entity.'[70] Space alone truly exists: 'Space is an entity. The glory of man lies in the fact that he is aware of space, and can imagine this space as the field of divine living activity, full of active intelligent forms.'[71]

Arnold Toynbee argued that the most important event in the twentieth century would be the coming together of Christianity and Buddhism, and John Cobb, who wrote *Towards a Mutual Transformation of Buddhism and Christianity*, argued that this would involve 'the abolition of time and history'.[72] The New Age 'Perennial Philosophy' described by Aldous Huxley depends for its power on creating a sense of timelessness and of blurred space. Michael Tippett's latest opera, *New Year*, explicitly abolishes historical time and resurrects mythical timelessness. Its final act is set in the Sacred Place, a pagan stone circle with phallic tree, magical foundation of fertility, and ritual meanings. Similarly the recent opera by Harrison Birtwhistle, *Gawain*, explicitly rejects linear time as Western and dissolves time into timeless myth. For in Buddhism, 'when this illusoriness of time is experientially realized, time is existentially dissolved.'[73]

There is currently a growing ideology which blames Judaeo-Christian monotheism for ecological catastrophe, for having divorced man from nature. Gore Vidal has on this basis recently argued that '[the] single god—Judaic, Islamic—is one of immaculate evil . . . It is time for us in the West to look to more subtle religions and ethical systems, particularly those of China and India . . . Let us give thanks to the Protean Green God!'[74] Aldous Huxley was deeply attracted to the Buddhist 'deliverance out of time into eternal Suchness or Buddhahood'. He wrote: 'Unfortunately . . . Christianity has remained a religion . . . overlaid . . . by an idolatrous preoccupation with events and things in time . . . regarded . . . as . . . intrinsically sacred and indeed divine . . . There are no chosen people in Nature, no holy lands, no unique historical revelations. Elementary ecology leads straight to elementary Buddhism.'[75] The Jewish philosopher Emil Fackenheim recently wrote: 'It is perhaps the essence of paganism to

[70] A. Bailey, *Ponder on This* (New York and London, 1987), p. 415.
[71] Ibid., p. 381.
[72] John B. Cobb, *Beyond Dialogue. Toward a Mutual Transformation of Christianity and Buddhism* (Philadelphia, 1982), pp. 90–5.
[73] Ibid., p. 94.
[74] Gore Vidal in *The Observer*, 27 Aug. 1989.
[75] A. Huxley, *The Perennial Philosophy* (London, 1946), p. 63: cited by Matthew Fox, *The Coming of the Cosmic Christ* (San Francisco, 1988), p. 232.

deny all uniqueness—the uniqueness of crimes and the uniqueness of anguish, as well as that of holiness and moments of joy—and to assert that the rhythm of nature covers it all.'[76]

Within Christianity itself, Teilhard de Chardin, who adopted Julian Huxley's concept that 'man discovers that he is nothing else than evolution become conscious of itself',[77] foresaw 'the end of a "thinking species"; not disintegration and death, but a new breakthrough and a rebirth, this time outside Time and Space'.[78] Matthew Fox, the contemporary influential Dominican writer on creation spirituality, now goes further. He demands rejection of the Jewish God and biblical morality, and recognition of ecstasy and sexuality as dominant values. The erect phallus should be celebrated as sacred, 'the symbol of the god',[79] and ourselves and nature's rhythms recognized as divine.[80] The times of full moon are sacred. The historical Jesus should be abandoned in favour of the (theosophist) cosmic Christ in nature and the subconscious: 'Jesus is time; Christ is space.'[81] The historical Cross is replaced by Mother Earth crucified, yet rising daily. Time becomes irrelevant: 'The past and the future are not what exist; it is the now moment that exists most richly.'[82] Fox argues: 'Space takes over, spacefulness ... The resurrection was nothing if not a conquest of time and place ... by space ... the inner, psychic space of mysticism ... the Cosmic Christ says, "Listen to your inner space for the divine.... And love space as yourself." '[83] Emil Fackenheim wrote: 'Christians, like Jews, know about uniqueness ... they will ... refuse refuge in a paganism that denies all uniqueness and lets the grass of nature cover it all.'[84] One wonders for how long that will remain true.

Centre for the Study of Judaism and Jewish–Christian Relations,
Selly Oak Colleges,
Birmingham

---

[76] Emil Fackenheim, *The Jewish Return into History. Reflections in the Age of Auschwitz and a New Jerusalem* (New York, 1978), p. 132.

[77] Teilhard de Chardin, *The Phenomenon of Man* (London and New York, 1959), p. 221.

[78] Teilhard de Chardin, *The Future of Man*, tr. N. Denny (London, 1969), p. 302.

[79] Fox, *Coming of the Cosmic Christ*, pp. 176–7, 69. Cf. M. F. Brearley, 'Matthew Fox: Creation Spirituality for the Aquarian Age', *Christian Jewish Relations*, 22, no. 2 (1989), pp. 37–49.

[80] Fox, *Coming of the Cosmic Christ*, p. 221.

[81] Ibid., p. 143. Cf. M. F. Brearley, 'Matthew Fox and the Cosmic Christ', *Anvil* (forthcoming, spring 1992).

[82] Ibid., p. 155.

[83] Ibid., pp. 141–2.

[84] Fackenheim, *Jewish Return*, p. 133.